D1093249

nall

-9-2002

Microsoft®

Microsoft® Windows® 2000 TCP/IP Protocols and Services Technical Reference

**Thomas Lee and
Joseph Davies**

PUBLISHED BY
Microsoft Press
A Division of Microsoft Corporation
One Microsoft Way
Redmond, Washington 98052-6399

Copyright © 2000 by Thomas Lee and Joseph Davies

All rights reserved. No part of the contents of this book may be reproduced or transmitted in any form or by any means without the written permission of the publisher.

Library of Congress Cataloging-in-Publication Data
Lee, Thomas.
    Microsoft Windows 2000 TCP/IP Protocols and Services Technical Reference / Thomas
Lee, Joseph Davies.
        p. cm.
    Includes index.
    ISBN 0-7356-0556-4
    1. TCP/IP (Computer network protocol) 2. Microsoft Windows (Computer file) 3.
Operating systems (Computers) I. Lee, Thomas. II. Title.
TK5105.585 D38   1999
004.6'2--dc21   99-056120

Printed and bound in the United States of America.

1 2 3 4 5 6 7 8 9   WCWC   5 4 3 2 1 0

Distributed in Canada by Penguin Books Canada Limited.

A CIP catalogue record for this book is available from the British Library.

Microsoft Press books are available through booksellers and distributors worldwide. For further information about international editions, contact your local Microsoft Corporation office or contact Microsoft Press International directly at fax (425) 936-7329. Visit our Web site at mspress.microsoft.com.

Microsoft, Microsoft Press, Windows, and Windows NT are either registered trademarks or trademarks of Microsoft Corporation in the United States and/or other countries.

The example companies, organizations, products, people and events depicted herein are fictitious. No association with any real company, organization, product, person or event is intended or should be inferred.

Any RFC excerpts are subject to the following statement:

Copyright © The Internet Society (1999). All Rights Reserved. This document and translations of it may be copied and furnished to others, and derivative works that comment on or otherwise explain it or assist in its implementation may be prepared, copied, published and distributed, in whole or in part, without restriction of any kind, provided that the above copyright notice and this paragraph are included on all such copies and derivative works. However, this document itself may not be modified in any way, such as by removing the copyright notice or references to the Internet Society or other Internet organizations, except as needed for the purpose of developing Internet standards in which case the procedures for copyrights defined in the Internet Standards process must be followed, or as required to translate it into languages other than English. The limited permissions granted above are perpetual and will not be revoked by the Internet Society or its successors or assigns. This document and the information contained herein is provided on an "AS IS" basis and THE INTERNET SOCIETY AND THE INTERNET ENGINEERING TASK FORCE DISCLAIMS ALL WARRANTIES, EXPRESS OR IMPLIED, INCLUDING BUT NOT LIMITED TO ANY WARRANTY THAT THE USE OF THE INFORMATION HEREIN WILL NOT INFRINGE ANY RIGHTS OR ANY IMPLIED WARRANTIES OF MER-CHANTABILITY OR FITNESS FOR A PARTICULAR PURPOSE.

Acquisitions Editor: David Clark
Project Editor: Michael Bolinger

Contents

5 Internet Protocol (IP) Addressing 107

PART III Transport Layer Protocols

Tables

Preface

I can still remember picking up my first TCP/IP book in early 1994. Up to that point, I'd had several years of networking experience with Windows for Workgroups, Novell NetWare, and Windows NT 3.1, but knew little of UNIX or of TCP/IP. I had finally broken down and decided to get onto the Internet, but all the instructions my ISP gave me were totally foreign.

So I went out and bought a book—actually, I bought several. At first the concepts were foreign and seemed so contrary to what I knew. Reading W. Richard Steven's books really brought the subject to light, and gradually, like peeling an onion, I worked through the layers and discovered the wonderful world of TCP/IP.

Why We Wrote This Book

I started thinking about writing this book many years ago. Most of the good TCP/IP books available then were either aimed at the UNIX market or were completely generic. As I did more and more with Microsoft's TCP/IP offerings and watched the Windows 2000 product slowly evolve, it was obvious a book focusing on TCP/IP with a Windows 2000 focus would be very useful.

Joe and I worked together several years ago as part of a team that was rolling out advanced TCP/IP training to Microsoft product support engineers. Joe was the course author and I was one of the many trainers who delivered this material to a very tough audience. It took time, and a lot of convincing by those nice people at Microsoft Press, but here we are.

We wrote this book as an in-depth reference to the TCP/IP protocol suite and the related network services. We explain how this suite of protocols and related services work and how they function in Windows 2000.

We have aimed this book at several different audiences:

- **General technical staff** Anyone interested in learning the details of TCP/IP, as implemented in Windows 2000.
- **TCP/IP administrators** This book contains details of the protocols and services administrators need to do problem solving and TCP/IP infrastructure planning.

- **MCSE candidates** Those studying for their Windows 2000 exams would find this book a useful reference text.
- **Microsoft certified trainers** They can use this book to learn the protocols and as to recommend to their students.

–Thomas Lee

Acknowledgments

During the writing of this book, I found that W. Richard Stevens had passed away. Rich was a friend who shared a love for TCP/IP. He motivated us both to write this book. I'm only sorry I wasn't able to send him a copy.

While writing a book can look easy, there are a lot of people behind this effort. Both Joe and I would like to thank all the great people at Microsoft Press, including Anne Hamilton (who chased Thomas across two publishers before finally getting him nailed down), David Clark, and Michael Bolinger (two great managers). After we finished writing, it was up to Sarah Hains and her editing team at nSight, Inc., including Tony Northrup, our technical editor, to make the text make sense to you, the reader.

This book was written as the Windows 2000 operating system was being built. As the product changed, so did the book. We'd like to thank our partners, the Windows 2000 networking team, including Jawad Kakhi, Bernard Abbobo, Ken Crocker, William Dixon, Dave Eitlebach, Peter Ford, Art Shelest, and Glen Zorn.

I would like to give thanks to my wonderful wife, Susan Lee-Tanner, for her patience during the many months it took to get this project out the door, and to my darling daughter, Rebecca, who was a constant companion in my office during the days (and some of the nights) that I worked on the book.

I would also like to express my deep appreciation to the engineers in the Windows 2000 beta support team, notably John Gray, for getting the CDs to me when I needed them. Thanks also to all the engineers for reading the many bug reports and patiently answering them, providing workarounds when I really needed them, and keeping a continual sense of humor. Also a big thank you to all the folks in BEDM Training, including Dean Murray, Keith Cotton, Angie Fultz, Susan Greenberg, Paul Howard, Rodney Miller, Ken Rosen, Paul Adare, Kathleen Cole, Robert Deupree, Brian Komar, Doug Steen, and Joern Wettern. You guys taught me a lot—thanks.

Joe would like to say thanks to his wonderful wife, Kara, and beautiful daughter, Katherine Rose, for their support, sacrifice, and patience while Joe worked early mornings, late evenings, and weekends to complete the chapters in this book.

And finally, special thanks to Laura Robinson, who was drafted in at the last minute to write additional content for this book. She was working under a tremendous amount of pressure and her efforts were very much appreciated. I hope we can work together again in the future.

Introduction

The Transmission Control Protocol/Internet Protocol (TCP/IP) protocol suite is the foundation of today's Internet, as well as the foundation of many private computer networks. The TCP/IP protocol suite, which comprises more than just TCP and IP, enables computers within a network to communicate with each other.

TCP/IP was originally developed to enable ARPANET sites to communicate. ARPANET sites used different computers manufactured by different vendors and running different operating systems. The only common element between them was that they ran a common protocol.

As the ARPANET grew to become the Internet, many companies began to utilize TCP/IP. With Windows 2000, the Active Directory (AD) service requires the use of TCP/IP in the Internet.

This introduction provides a brief introduction to the TCP/IP protocol suite, including:

- A potted history of the TCP/IP protocol suite
- A look at the Open Systems Interconnection (OSI) model and a comparison to the model that TCP/IP uses
- An overview of the Windows 2000 network architecture illustrating how TCP/IP is implemented

This introduction also serves as a foundation for this book.

Brief History of TCP/IP

In the mid-to-late 1960s the U.S. Department of Defense's Advanced Research and Projects Administration (ARPA, or DARPA, as it later became known) began researching the creation of a network that would link up various ARPA contractors. They issued a contract to build the first Interface Message Processors (IMP) to Bolt, Baranek, and Newman (BBN), a consulting firm in Cambridge, Mass. The IMP, which today probably would be called a router, was based on a Honeywell 516 minicomputer and was a system the size of a large refrigerator.

In the days of the first IMPs, there were no protocols to purchase—everything had to be designed from scratch. The concept of packet switching-based networks wasn't new, but there were no significant implementations that ARPA or BBN could go out and buy.

The first IMP was delivered toward the end of the summer of 1969 at UCLA; the second IMP was delivered to Stanford Research Institute a month later. Additional IMPs were added over the coming months and years, and the ARPANET slowly became a reality.

During the 1970s, the number of sites connected to the ARPANET grew, initially, at a linear rate (one per month or so), but toward the end of the 1970s, the growth became exponential.

The initial protocols and addressing schemes that were used within the ARPANET were adequate to connect the first IMPs, and to prove that the concept of a heterogeneous packet-switching network was valid, but they didn't scale. Something better was needed, and in the late 1970s the development of what we now know as TCP/IP began to see the light of day. RFC 760, which described the Internet Protocol, was published on January 1, 1980. It was subsequently replaced by RFC 791, which was published in September 1981, along with an RFC describing TCP (RFC 793). RFC 768, describing User Datagram Protocol (UDP), had been issued the year before.

These RFCs define the core of the TCP/IP protocol suite and are in use today. While some of the details have changed, and some additional functionality has been added, such as flow control with TCP, these protocols have withstood the test of time and continue to serve their purpose. IP's addressing scheme, based on a 32-bit IP address, has proven inadequate for today's Internet, but no one in the 1970s could have foreseen what the Internet has become.

Perhaps the biggest boost to the adoption of TCP/IP was the publication of the BSD 4.2 version of UNIX in 1983, which incorporated a TCP/IP suite. UNIX, which Bell Laboratories developed, had been viewed as a possible ARPA mini-host, as noted in RFC 681. It was attractive for many reasons, not the least of which was that Bell licensed the operating system for a nominal fee, $150.00 for colleges and universities (although for "non-university" institutions the license fee was $20,000.00). With the release of BSD 4.2, many universities could now afford additional mini-computers and the software to run on them. The result was an explosive growth in the use of the ARPANET and in the development of many of the tools and facilities we now take for granted, such as the Domain Name Server (DNS) system.

The International Organization for Standardization (ISO) Open Systems Interconnection (OSI) Model

The development of the ARPANET was undertaken in an academic setting. At that time, it didn't capture much commercial interest. During the 1970s, the need for more open networking was a hot topic of conversation in the computer industry. Because networking was largely homogenous, computers from different manufacturers generally couldn't communicate.

In 1977, the ISO began the development of a detailed reference model for OSI. The idea behind the OSI model was to enable the development of software that would allow an open system; one that's open to others for the purpose of information exchange with another. The assumption was that an open system would use the applicable standards and therefore be able to interoperate.

The OSI model is a very loose standard in which the definitions and much of the terminology are vague. This was deliberate to ensure that the model didn't attempt to constrain an implementer to use existing techniques or terminology. Rather, it was intended to promote the development of protocols that could provide heterogeneous systems to interoperate. The OSI model also functions as a reference model, to enable other standards and protocols to be compared.

The OSI model starts from the premise that communication between two computers is sufficiently complex enough that it couldn't be considered as a single entity. Instead, the functions that make up the communications process should be broken up into a series of separate layers, with each successive layer built on top of a lower layer, and using the functions assigned to each layer. What the precise internal workings of the layers would be, however, was a detail left to developers—the key was to standardize the functions contained in each of the layers and the interfaces between them.

The ISO OSI model is made up of seven levels, as shown in Figure I-1.

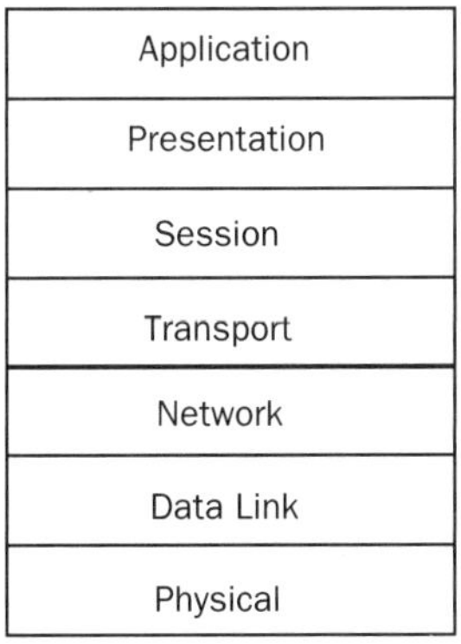

| Application |
| Presentation |
| Session |
| Transport |
| Network |
| Data Link |
| Physical |

Figure I-1. *The seven layers of the ISO OSI model.*

In this model, the application and the users are at the top, while at the bottom are some physical communications media. The functions of the layers, in ascending order, are as follows:

- **Physical** Puts a stream of bits on the physical media, the *wire*, and pulls them back off. This layer is typically implemented in hardware.

- **Data Link** Defines the concept of a packet (a frame) and enables a computer to send a frame to another computer connected to the same wire. This layer is typically implemented in a mixture of hardware and system software.

- **Network** Enables two end systems to send packets of data across an internetwork based on the lower levels. This layer, implemented in software, is inherently unreliable because a frame being sent out across a network might get lost, be badly routed, or become corrupted. The higher layers are responsible for reliability.

- **Transport** Enables the reliable transmission of data across the network provided. It utilizes the end-to-end communication provided by the network layer and adds reliability.

- **Session** Adds in the concept of sessions between two systems where the computers in the session will save information about the state of the session and later use that state information as the basis for future processing.

- **Presentation** Meant for the translation of data between different formats as needed (e.g., between ASCII and EBCIDC), thus separating the wire formats from the view of data seen by an application.

- **Application** Where the applications and users reside. These applications use the other six layers to implement a business function based on the underlying network.

The designers of the OSI model had hoped that vendors would build protocols that mapped directly to this model. But with seven layers, this model added a considerable overhead. Functions at each level needed to make procedure calls to lower levels, which involved a higher level layer packing up parameters and making a procedure call to the lower level which would then need to validate those parameters. A few implementations were developed, but these implementations didn't achieve a significant commercial success.

The DARPA Model

The designers of the TCP/IP suite of protocols chose a simpler model with fewer layers to improve performance and ease of implementation. This model, known as the Defense Advanced Research and Projects Authority (DARPA) model, is simpler than the ISO model, having only four layers. The DARPA model is shown in Figure I-2, which also shows the correspondence between the two models.

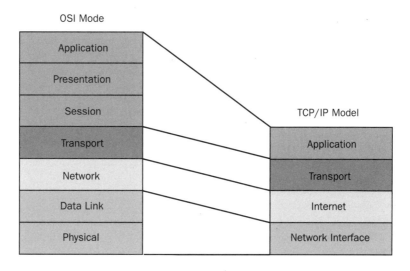

Figure I-2. *Comparing the DARPA model to the ISO model.*

The four layers of the DARPA model are broadly compatible with the ISO model, although the mapping is not perfectly clean. The ISO session layer, for example, doesn't perfectly map onto the DARPA model. Additionally, some protocols break the model. Asynchronous Transfer Mode (ATM), for example, is a connection-oriented protocol effectively implemented in the hardware. Nevertheless, these models are still very useful because they enable the complex tasks involved with computer networking to be broken down into pieces that are more manageable.

Note In this book, we use both the OSI and DARPA models when discussing the TCP/IP protocol suite and associated services.

Windows 2000 Network Architecture Overview

One of the unique features of Microsoft Windows NT 3.1, when it was first released, was that it was supplied with a full suite of networking protocols. These came "in the box" and there was no need to buy and add extra software to enable a Windows NT system to interoperate with other Windows computers on a corporate network. These networking protocols have matured and been improved as Windows NT evolved to become Windows 2000, but the basic design has remained broadly the same.

A key characteristic of Windows 2000 networking is that it provides administrators with the ability to fully integrate third-party components. Additionally, the designers built the networking components to enable the user to view and work with remote and local files in similar ways. Figure I-3 shows a high-level overview of the Windows 2000 networking architecture.

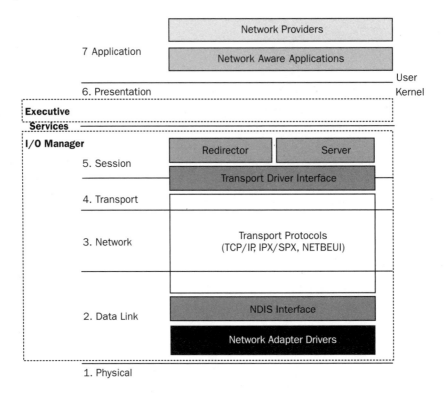

Figure I-3. *Windows 2000 network architecture.*

As with all the other components of Windows 2000, the networking architecture is layered, which allows third-party vendors to add in different components. Microsoft builds the Transport Driver Interface (TDI) and Network Device Interface Specification (NDIS) layers, which third-party vendors can utilize to provide new network card drivers, new transport protocols, and new network providers, redirectors, and servers.

At the bottom of the network architecture diagram reside the Network Devices and Device Drivers. This includes both connectionless adapter types, such as Ethernet and Token Ring; wide area network (WAN) drivers for support of WAN Protocols, such as Frame Relay and X.25; and connection-oriented adapters, such as ATM.

The NDIS interface serves as a dividing line between the transport protocols and the network hardware and drivers. This interface enables the transport protocols to use virtually any network device driver seamlessly.

The transport protocols include the core of the TCP/IP protocol suite as well as NWLink (Microsoft's implementation of Internetwork Packet Exchange/Sequenced Packet Exchange (IPX/SPX)), NetBIOS Enhanced User Interface (NetBEUI), and the Data Link Control protocol (DLC). In addition, this layer also holds the Virtual Private Network (VPN) protocols (PPTP, L2TP), and some of the Internet Protocol Security (IPSec) driver.

The TDI, which sits above the transport protocols, provides an interface into the transport protocols for kernel mode components, such as the redirectors and servers.

At the top of this model, you will find the network services DHCP, DNS, WINS, and IIS that are network-aware applications.

What's in This Book

This chapter has provided the background to and an overview of the TCP/IP protocol suite as implemented in Windows 2000. The remainder of this book describes the TCP/IP protocols and the related Windows 2000 networking services in more detail. We have divided the book into four parts:

- **The Network Interface Layer** This part contains two chapters describing the local area network (LAN) and WAN technologies supported within Windows 2000 and, in particular, how they carry IP datagrams. This section also includes a chapter on hardware address resolution.

- **Internet Layer Protocols** This part includes chapters describing IP, Internet Control Message Protocol (ICMP), and Internet Group Management Protocol (IGMP). We've also included a chapter on IP version 6 (IPv6), although this isn't included in Windows 2000.

- **Transport Layer Protocols**   This part contains chapters describing UDP and TCP.
- **Application Layer Protocols and Services**   This part contains chapters describing the key TCP/IP related services, including DHCP, DNS, WINS, and IIS. This section also includes chapters on Windows 2000 File and Print sharing, IPSec, and VPNs.

Network Monitor Traces

Throughout this book, we have illustrated the theory with packet captures. These show the actual behavior of a protocol or service "on the wire." To improve the value of this book to you, we have included all of the traces referenced in this book on the companion CD-ROM.

The traces taken in the book, and included on the CD-ROM, were captured using Microsoft Network Monitor, Version 2.0, which is a component of Systems Management Server V2.0. Windows 2000 Server Standard Edition, Windows 2000 Advanced Server, and Windows 2000 Datacenter Server ship with Microsoft Network Monitor Lite version 2.0, which should enable you to view almost all of the traces. However, a few of the traces are only fully readable with the full version.

To assist readers who do not have the full version of Network Monitor, we also include a full text dump of each trace.

Companion CD-ROM

We also include a companion CD-ROM with the following contents:

- **Full set of Request for Comment (RFC) documents**
- **Full set of Internet drafts**   Those documents which may one day become RFCs.
- **White papers**   Key TCP/IP related white papers.
- **Network Monitor traces**

The RFCs and Internet Drafts were the full set of obtainable drafts as of mid-September 1999. And as is the way with such book projects, this list most likely will have changed by the time you buy this book—although the RFCs that have been implemented will be included on the companion CD-ROM.

Errors and All That

We both hope this book has no errors, and that everything here is perfect. But sometimes errors do, sadly, creep in. If you find any, we apologize. But please let Thomas know, by sending email to *tfl@kapoho.com*. Any errors that we do find, plus any updates, will be found at *http://www.kapoho.com/tcpip/default.htm*.

Microsoft Press provides corrections for books through the World Wide Web at the following address:

http://mspress.microsoft.com/support/

Please note that product support is not offered through the above mail addresses. For further information regarding Microsoft software support options, please connect to *http://www.microsoft.com/support/* or call Microsoft Professional Support Sales at 800-936-3500.

For information about ordering the full version of any Microsoft software, please call Microsoft Sales at 800-426-9400 or visit *www.microsoft.com*.

Part I
The Network Interface Layer

Chapter 1
Local Area Network (LAN) Technologies

To successfully troubleshoot TCP/IP problems on a local area network (LAN), it is important to understand how IP datagrams and ARP messages are encapsulated when sent by a Microsoft Windows 2000 computer on a LAN technology link such as Ethernet, Token Ring, or Fiber Distributed Data Interface (FDDI). For example, IP datagrams sent over an Ethernet network segment can be encapsulated two different ways. If two hosts are not using the same encapsulation, communication cannot occur. It is also important to understand LAN technology encapsulations to correctly interpret the Ethernet, Token Ring, and FDDI portions of the frame when using Microsoft Network Monitor.

LAN Encapsulations

Because Internet Protocol (IP) datagrams are an Open Systems Interconnection (OSI) Network Layer entity, IP datagrams must be encapsulated with a Data Link Layer header and trailer before being sent on the physical medium. The Data Link Layer header and trailer provide the following services:

- **Delimitation** Frames at the Data Link Layer must be distinguished from each other. For each frame, the start and end of the frame are indicated and the frame's payload is distinguished from the Data Link Layer header and trailer.

- **Protocol identification** Because many organizations use multiple protocol suites such as TCP/IP, Internetwork Packet Exchange (IPX), or AppleTalk, the protocols must be distinguished from each other.

- **Addressing** For shared access LAN technologies such as Ethernet, the source node and destination node must be identified.

- **Bit-level integrity check** To detect bit-level errors in the entire frame received by the hardware, a bit-level integrity check in the form of a checksum is needed. The checksum is computed by the source node and included in the frame header or trailer. The destination recalculates the checksum and checks it against the included checksum. If the checksums match, the frame is considered free of bit-level errors. If the checksums don't match, the frame is silently discarded. This frame checksum is in addition to the checksums provided by upper layer protocols such as IP or TCP.

The particular way a network type (such as Ethernet or Token Ring) encapsulates data to be transmitted is called a frame format. The frame format corresponds to the information placed on the frame at the Logical Link Control (LLC) and Media Access Control (MAC) sublayers of the OSI Data Link Layer, and the frame format manifests itself as a header and trailer. If multiple frame formats exist for a given network type (such as Ethernet), the frame formats represent different header and trailer structures and are therefore incompatible with each other. In other words, all the nodes on the same network segment (bounded by routers) must use the same frame format in order to communicate.

This chapter is a discussion of Ethernet, Token Ring, and FDDI LAN technologies and their frame formats for IP datagrams and Address Resolution Protocol (ARP) messages. ARCnet is not discussed as it is not a widely used networking technology.

Ethernet

Ethernet evolved from a 9.6 Kbps radio transmission system developed at the University of Hawaii called ALOHA. A key feature of ALOHA was that all transmitters shared the same channel and contended for access to the channel in order to transmit. This became the basis for the contention-based Ethernet that we know today.

In 1972, the Xerox Corporation created a 2.94 Mbps network, based on the principles of the ALOHA system. This new network, called Ethernet, featured carrier sense, where the transmitter listens before attempting to transmit. In 1979, Digital, Intel, and Xerox (DIX) created an industry standard 10 Mbps Ethernet known as Ethernet II. In 1981, the Institute of Electrical and Electronics Engineers (IEEE) Project 802 formed the 802.3 subcommittee to make 10 Mbps Ethernet an international standard. In 1995, the IEEE approved a 100 Mbps version of Ethernet called Fast Ethernet.

Ethernet existed before the IEEE 802.3 specification and, because there are multiple Ethernet standards, there are multiple ways of encapsulating data to be transmitted on an Ethernet network. This can be very confusing when two hosts on an Ethernet network segment cannot communicate, even though they are using the correct communication protocol (such as TCP/IP) and Application Layer protocol (such as File Transfer Protocol [FTP]).

More Info   IP datagrams and ARP messages sent on an Ethernet network segment use either Ethernet II encapsulation (described in RFC 894) or IEEE 802.3 Sub-Network Access Protocol (SNAP) encapsulation (described in RFC 1042). These RFCs are included in the \RFC folder on the companion CD-ROM.

Ethernet II

The Ethernet II frame format was defined by the Ethernet specification created by Digital, Intel, and Xerox before the IEEE 802.3 specification. The Ethernet II frame format is also known as the Digital Intel Xerox (DIX) frame format. Figure 1-1 shows Ethernet II encapsulation for an IP datagram.

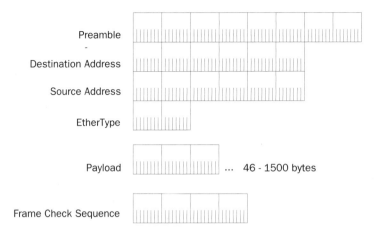

Figure 1-1. *Ethernet II encapsulation showing the fields in the Ethernet II header and trailer.*

Ethernet II Header and Trailer

The fields in the Ethernet II header and trailer are defined as follows:

Preamble

The Preamble field is 8 bytes long and consists of 7 bytes of alternating 1s and 0s (each byte is the bit sequence 10101010) to synchronize a receiving station and a 1-byte 10101011 sequence that indicates the start of a frame. The Preamble provides receiver synchronization and frame delimitation services.

Note   The Preamble field isn't visible with Network Monitor.

Destination Address

The Destination Address field is 6 bytes long and indicates the destination's address. The destination can be a unicast, a multicast, or the Ethernet broadcast address. The unicast address is also known as an individual, physical, hardware, or MAC address. For the Ethernet broadcast address, all 48 bits are set to 1 to create the address 0xFF-FF-FF-FF-FF-FF.

Source Address

The Source Address field is 6 bytes long and indicates the sending node's unicast address.

EtherType

The EtherType field is 2 bytes long and indicates the upper layer protocol contained within the Ethernet frame. After the network adapter passes the frame to the host's network operating system, the EtherType field's value is used to pass the Ethernet payload to the appropriate upper layer protocol. If no upper layer protocols have registered interest in receiving payload at the frame's EtherType field value, the payload is silently discarded.

The EtherType field acts as the protocol identifier for the Ethernet II frame format. For an IP datagram, the field is set to 0x0800. For an ARP message, the EtherType field is set to 0x0806. The current list of defined EtherType field values can be found at *http:// www.isi.edu/in-notes/iana/assignments/ethernet-numbers/*.

Payload

The Payload field for an Ethernet II frame consists of a protocol data unit (PDU) of an upper layer protocol. Ethernet II can send a maximum-sized payload of 1500 bytes. Because of Ethernet's collision detection facility, Ethernet II frames must send a minimum payload size of 46 bytes. If an upper layer PDU is less than 46 bytes long, it must be padded so that it is at least 46 bytes long. The Ethernet minimum frame size is discussed in greater detail in the "Ethernet Minimum Frame Size" section of this chapter.

Frame Check Sequence

The Frame Check Sequence (FCS) field is 4 bytes long and provides bit-level integrity verification on the bits in the Ethernet II frame. The FCS is also called a cyclical redundancy check (CRC). The source node calculates the FCS and places the result in this field. When the destination receives the FCS, it runs the same CRC algorithm and compares its own value with the one placed in the FCS field by the source node. If the two values match, the frame is considered valid and the destination node processes it. If the two values don't match, the frame is silently discarded.

The FCS calculation consists of dividing a 33-bit prime number into the number consisting of the bits in the frame (not including the Preamble and FCS fields). The result of the division is a quotient and a remainder. The 4-byte FCS field is set to the remainder—always a 32-bit value. The FCS can detect 100 percent of all single-bit errors. While it's mathematically possible to selectively change bits in the frame without invalidating the value of the FCS field, it's highly improbable that the type of random noise and damage that occurs on networks will result in a frame whose bits are changed, but retains a valid FCS.

The FCS calculation provides only a bit-level integrity service; not a data integrity or authentication service. A valid FCS doesn't imply that only the node with the unicast address stored in the Source Address field could have sent it and that it wasn't modified in transit. The FCS calculation is well known and an intermediate node could easily intercept the frame, alter its contents, perform the FCS calculation, and place the new value in the FCS field before forwarding the frame. The receiver of the frame couldn't detect that the frame contents were altered using just the FCS field. For data integrity and authentication services, use IP Security (IPSec). For more information on IPSec, see Chapter 20, "Securing IP Communications with IP Security (IPSec)."

The FCS field provides only bit-level error detection; not error recovery. When the receiver-calculated FCS value doesn't match the value of the FCS stored in the frame, the only conclusion that can be reached is that, somewhere in the frame, a bit or bits were changed. The FCS calculation doesn't produce any information on where the error occurred or how to correct it. However, other types of CRC calculations provide information on where the error occurred and how to correct it. An example of such a CRC calculation is the 1-byte Header Checksum field in the Asynchronous Transfer Mode (ATM) cell header, which provides error detection and limited-error recovery services for the bits in the ATM header.

Note   The FCS field isn't visible with Network Monitor.

The following Network Monitor trace (Capture 01-01, included in the \Captures folder on the companion CD-ROM) shows the Ethernet II frame format for an IP datagram:

```
+ Frame: Base frame properties
  ETHERNET: ETYPE = 0x0800 : Protocol = IP:  DOD Internet Protocol
    + ETHERNET: Destination address : 001054CAE140
    + ETHERNET: Source address : 00600852F9D8
      ETHERNET: Frame Length : 74 (0x004A)
      ETHERNET: Ethernet Type : 0x0800 (IP:  DOD Internet Protocol)
      ETHERNET: Ethernet Data: Number of data bytes remaining = 60 (0x003C)
+ IP: ID = 0xAE09; Proto = ICMP; Len: 60
+ ICMP: Echo: From 192.168.160.186 To 192.168.160.01
```

Note   The ETHERNET: Frame Length and ETHERNET: Ethernet Data fields are Network Monitor informational fields, and don't correspond to fields that are physically present in the Ethernet header.

The Ethernet Interframe Gap

Unlike Token Ring and FDDI, Ethernet frame formats don't have a way to explicitly indicate the end of the frame. Rather, Ethernet frames use an implied postamble by leaving a gap between each Ethernet frame. This gap, known as the Ethernet interframe gap, is used to space Ethernet frames apart. The Ethernet interframe gap is a specific measure of the time required to send 96 bits of data (9.6 µs on a 10 Mbps Ethernet network segment).

The Ethernet interframe gap is used as a postamble; after receiving bits of a frame, if the wire falls silent for 96 bit times, the last bit in the received frame occurred 96 bit times ago.

Ethernet Minimum Frame Size

All Ethernet frames must carry a minimum payload of 46 bytes. The Ethernet minimum frame size is a result of the Ethernet collision detection scheme applied to a maximum extent Ethernet network. To detect a collision, Ethernet nodes must be transmitting long enough for the signal indicating the collision to be propagated back to the sending node. The maximum extent Ethernet network consists of Ethernet segments configured using 10Base5 cabling and the IEEE 802.3 Baseband 5-4-3 rule.

The IEEE 802.3 Baseband 5-4-3 rule states that there can be a maximum of five physical segments between any two nodes, with four repeaters between the nodes. However, only three of these physical segments can have connected nodes (populated physical segments). The other two physical segments can be used only to link physical segments to extend the network length. Repeaters count as a node on the physical segment. When using 10Base5 cabling, each physical segment can be up to 500 meters long. Therefore, an Ethernet network's maximum linear length is 2500 meters.

Figure 1-2 shows Ethernet node A and Ethernet node B at the farthest ends of a 5-4-3 network using 10Base5 cabling.

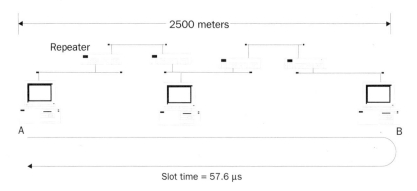

Figure 1-2. *The maximum extent Ethernet network and the slot time.*

When node A begins transmitting, the signal must propagate the network length. In the worst-case collision scenario, node B begins to transmit just before the signal for node A's frame reaches it. The collision signal of node A and node B's frame must travel back to node A in order for node A to detect that a collision has occurred.

The time it takes for a signal to propagate from one end of the network to the other is known as the propagation delay. In this worst-case collision scenario, the time that it takes for A to detect that its frame has been collided with is twice the propagation delay. Node A's frame must travel all the way to node B, and then the collision signal must travel all the way from node B back to node A. This time is known as the slot time. An Ethernet node must be transmitting a frame for the slot time in order for a collision with that frame to be detected. This is the reason for the minimum Ethernet frame size.

The propagation delay for this maximum extent Ethernet network is 28.8 μs. Therefore, the slot time is 57.6 μs. To transmit for 57.6 μs with a 10 Mbps bit rate, an Ethernet node must transmit 576 bits. Therefore, the entire Ethernet frame, including the Preamble field, must be a minimum size of 576 bits, or 72 bytes long. Subtracting the Preamble (8 bytes), Source Address (6 bytes), Destination Address (6 bytes), EtherType (2 bytes), and the FCS (4 bytes) fields, the minimum Ethernet payload size is 46 bytes long.

Upper layer PDUs that are under 46 bytes are padded to 46 bytes, ensuring the minimum Ethernet frame size. This padding isn't part of the IP datagram or the ARP message, and isn't included in any length indicator fields within the IP datagram or ARP message. For example, this padding isn't included in the IP header's Total Length field. The IP header's Total Length field indicates only the size of the IP datagram, and is used to discard the padding bytes.

IEEE 802.3

The IEEE 802.3 frame format is the result of the IEEE 802.2 and 802.3 specifications, and consists of an IEEE 802.3 header and trailer and an IEEE 802.2 LLC header. Figure 1-3 shows the IEEE 802.3 frame format.

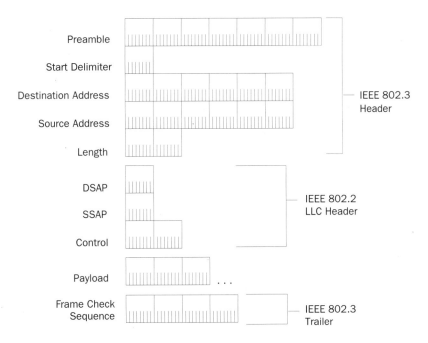

Figure 1-3. *The IEEE 802.3 frame format, showing the IEEE 802.3 header and trailer and the IEEE 802.2 header.*

IEEE 802.3 Header and Trailer

The fields in the IEEE 802.3 header and trailer are defined as follows:

Preamble

The Preamble field is 7 bytes long and consists of alternating 1s and 0s that synchronize a receiving station. Each byte is the bit sequence 10101010.

Note The Preamble field isn't visible with Network Monitor.

Start Delimiter

The Start Delimiter field is 1 byte long consisting of the bit sequence 10101011 that indicates the start of a frame. The combination of the IEEE 802.3 Preamble and Start Delimiter fields is the exact same bit sequence as the Ethernet II Preamble field.

Note The Start Delimiter field isn't visible with Network Monitor.

Destination Address

The Destination Address field is the same as the Ethernet II Destination Address field except that IEEE 802.3 allows both 6-byte and 2-byte addresses. IEEE 802.3 2-byte addresses aren't commonly used.

Source Address

The Source Address field is the same as the Ethernet II Source Address field except that IEEE 802.3 allows both 6-byte and 2-byte addresses.

Length

The Length field is 2 bytes long and indicates the number of bytes from the LLC header's first byte to the payload's last byte. The Length field doesn't include the IEEE 802.3 header or the FCS field. This field's minimum value is 46 (0x002E), and its maximum value is 1500 (0x05DC).

Frame Check Sequence

The Frame Check Sequence (FCS) field is 4 bytes long and is identical to the Ethernet II FCS field.

IEEE 802.2 LLC Header

The fields in the IEEE 802.2 LLC header and trailer are defined as follows:

DSAP

The Destination Service Access Point (DSAP) field is 1 byte long and indicates the destination upper layer protocol for the frame.

SSAP

The Source Service Access Point (SSAP) field is 1 byte long and indicates the source upper layer protocol for the frame.

The DSAP and SSAP fields act as protocol identifiers for the IEEE 802.3 frame format. The defined value for the DSAP and SSAP fields for IP is 0x06. However, it's not used in the industry. Instead, the SNAP header is used to encapsulate IP datagrams with an IEEE 802.3 header. The SNAP header is discussed in greater detail in the "IEEE 802.3 SNAP" section of this chapter. The current list of defined DSAP and SSAP values can be found at http://www.isi.edu/in-notes/iana/assignments/ieee-802-numbers.

Control

The Control field can be 1 or 2 bytes long depending on whether the LLC-encapsulated data is an LLC datagram, known as a Type 1 LLC operation, or part of an LLC session, known as a Type 2 LLC operation.

- A Type 1 LLC operation (a 1-byte Control field) is a connectionless, unreliable LLC datagram. With an LLC datagram, LLC isn't providing reliable delivery service on behalf of the upper layer protocol. A Type 1 LLC datagram is known as an Unnumbered Information (UI) frame and is indicated by setting the Control field to the value 0x03.

- A Type 2 LLC operation (a 2-byte Control field) is a connection-oriented, reliable LLC session. Type 2 LLC frames are used when LLC is providing reliable delivery service for the upper layer protocol.

For IP datagrams and ARP messages, reliable LLC services are never used. Therefore, IP datagrams and ARP messages are always sent as a Type 1 LLC datagram with the Control field set to 0x03 to indicate a UI frame.

Differentiating an Ethernet II Frame from an IEEE 802.3 Frame

It's common for a network operating system to support multiple frame formats simultaneously. Microsoft Windows 2000 supports both Ethernet II and IEEE 802.3 frame formats for IP datagrams and ARP messages. There are many similarities between the Ethernet II and IEEE 802.3 frame formats, such as the following:

- The Ethernet II Preamble field is identical to the IEEE 802.3 Preamble and Start Delimiter fields.
- With the exception of the 2-byte address allowed by IEEE 802.3, the Source Address and Destination Address fields are identical.
- The FCS is identical.

The ability to differentiate between the Ethernet II and the IEEE 802.3 frame formats lies in the first 2 bytes past the Source Address field. For the Ethernet II frame format, these 2 bytes are the EtherType field. For the IEEE 802.3 frame format, these 2 bytes are the Length field. The following algorithm is used to determine whether these 2 bytes are an EtherType field or a Length field:

- If the value of these 2 bytes is greater than 1500 (0x05DC), it is an EtherType field and an Ethernet II frame format.
- If the value of these 2 bytes is less than or equal to 1500 (0x05DC), it is a Length field and an IEEE 802.3 frame.

This comparison can be made because there are no defined EtherType values less than 0x05DC. The lowest EtherType value is 0x0600, used to indicate the Xerox Network Systems (XNS) protocol.

IEEE 802.3 SNAP

While there is a defined value of 0x06 for the Service Access Point (SAP) for IP, it's not used in the industry. RFC 1042 states that IP datagrams and ARP frames sent over IEEE 802.3, 802.4, and 802.5 networks must use the Sub-Network Access Protocol (SNAP) encapsulation.

The IEEE 802.3 SNAP was created as an extension to the IEEE 802.3 specification to allow protocols that were designed to operate with an Ethernet II header to be used in an IEEE 802.3 compliant environment. Figure 1-4 shows the IEEE 802.3 SNAP frame format.

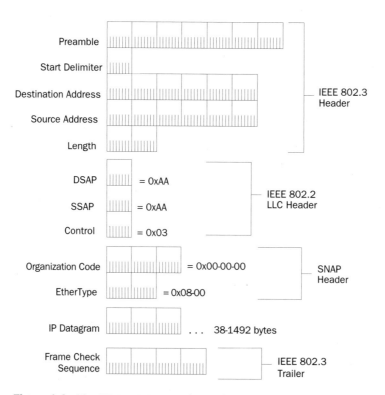

Figure 1-4. *The IEEE 802.3 SNAP frame format showing the SNAP header and an IP datagram.*

To denote a SNAP frame, the DSAP and SSAP fields are set to the SNAP-defined value of 0xAA within the LLC header. Because all SNAP-encapsulated payloads aren't using reliable LLC services, every SNAP frame is an LLC datagram. Therefore, the Control field is set to 0x03 to indicate a UI frame.

The SNAP header consists of the following two fields:

- The Organization Code field is 3 bytes long and is used to indicate the organization that maintains the meaning of the 2 bytes that follow. For IP datagrams and ARP messages, the Organization Code field is set to 0x00-00-00.

- For the Organization Code field set to 0x00-00-00, the next 2 bytes of the SNAP header are the 2-byte EtherType field. The same values for IP (0x0800) and ARP (0x0806) are used.

Because of the increased overhead of the LLC header (3 bytes total) and the SNAP header (5 bytes), the payload for an IEEE 802.3 SNAP frame can have a maximum size of 1492 bytes and a minimum size of 38 bytes. Padding is added when needed to ensure that the payload is a minimum length of 38 bytes.

The following Network Monitor trace (Capture 01-02, included in the \Captures folder on the companion CD-ROM) shows the IEEE 802.3 SNAP frame format for an ARP Request frame:

```
+ Frame: Base frame properties
  ETHERNET: 802.3 Length = 50
    + ETHERNET: Destination address : FFFFFFFFFFFF
    + ETHERNET: Source address : 00AA004BB147
      ETHERNET: Frame Length : 50 (0x0032)
      ETHERNET: Data Length : 0x0024 (36)
      ETHERNET: Ethernet Data: Number of data bytes remaining = 36 (0x0024)
  LLC: UI DSAP=0xAA SSAP=0xAA C
      LLC: DSAP = 0xAA : INDIVIDUAL : Sub-Network Access Protocol (SNAP)
      LLC: SSAP = 0xAA: COMMAND : Sub-Network Access Protocol (SNAP)
      LLC: Frame Category: Unnumbered Frame
      LLC: Command = UI
      LLC: LLC Data: Number of data bytes remaining = 33 (0x0021)
  SNAP: ETYPE = 0x0806|
      SNAP: Snap Organization code = 00 00 00
      SNAP: Snap etype : 0x0806
      SNAP: Snap Data: Number of data bytes remaining = 28 (0x001C)
+ ARP_RARP: ARP: Request, Target IP: 192.168.50.2
```

> **Note**   The ETHERNET: Data Length, ETHERNET: Ethernet Data, LLC: Frame Category, LLC: LLC Data, and SNAP: Snap Data fields are Network Monitor informational fields and don't correspond to fields that are physically present in the Ethernet header.

By default, Windows 2000 uses the Ethernet II encapsulation when sending and receiving frames on an Ethernet network. Windows 2000 will receive both types of frame formats but, by default, will only respond with Ethernet II-encapsulated frames. To send IEEE 802.3 SNAP-encapsulated IP and ARP messages, add the ArpUseEtherSNAP registry setting.

ArpUseEtherSNAP

```
Location: HKEY_LOCAL_MACHINE\SYSTEM\CurrentControlSet\Services\
Tcpip\Parameters
Data type: REG_DWORD
Valid range: 0-1
Default value: 0
Present by default: No
```

ArpUseEtherSNAP either enables (=1) or disables (=0) the use of the IEEE 802.3 SNAP frame format when sending IP and ARP frames. ArpUseEtherSNAP is disabled by default, meaning that IP and ARP frames are sent with Ethernet II encapsulation. Regardless of the ArpUseEtherSNAP setting, both types of frame formats are received.

With ArpUseEtherSNAP disabled, Windows 2000 TCP/IP will recognize a SNAP-encapsulated ARP Request message and respond with an Ethernet II-encapsulated ARP Reply frame. The assumption is that the node sending the ARP Request message will recognize the Ethernet II encapsulation on the ARP Reply and use Ethernet II encapsulation for subsequent communications. If the node sending the ARP Request doesn't switch, IP communication between the node sending the ARP Request and the Windows 2000 node sending the ARP Reply is impossible.

With ArpUseEtherSNAP enabled, Windows 2000 TCP/IP will switch to Ethernet II encapsulation if one of the following two scenarios occurs: a SNAP-encapsulated ARP Request frame is responded to with an Ethernet II-encapsulated ARP Reply frame, or an Ethernet II-encapsulated ARP Request is received.

Special Bits on Ethernet MAC Addresses

Within the Source Address and Destination Address fields of the Ethernet II and IEEE 802.3 frame formats, special bits are defined, as Figure 1-5 shows.

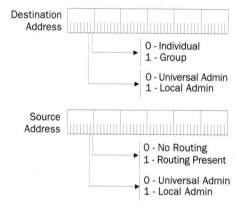

Figure 1-5. *The special bits defined for Ethernet source and destination MAC addresses.*

The Individual/Group Bit

The Individual/Group (I/G) bit is used to indicate whether the address is a unicast (individual) or multicast (group) address. For a unicast address, the I/G bit is set to 0. For a multicast address, the I/G bit is set to 1. The broadcast address is a special case of multicast and its I/G bit is set to 1. The I/G bit is also known as the multicast bit.

The Universal/Locally Administered Bit

The Universal/Locally (U/L) Administered bit is used to indicate whether the IEEE allocated the address. For a universal address allocated by the IEEE, the U/L bit is set to 0. Universal addresses are guaranteed to be universally unique because network adapter manufacturers obtain universally unique vendor identifiers from the IEEE and assign unique 3-byte serial numbers to each network adapter. The 6-byte physical address of a network adapter, as programmed into the adapter during the manufacturing process, is a universally administered address.

For a locally administered address, the U/L bit is set to 1. Some network adapters allow you to override the network adapter's physical address and specify a new physical address. In this case, the new address must have the U/L bit set to 1 to indicate that it is locally administered.

The U/L bit is significant only for unicast addresses (the I/G bit is set to 0). When the I/G bit is set to 1, this bit doesn't imply a locally or universally administered address. The U/L bit is relevant for both the Source Address and Destination Address.

Routing Information Indicator Bit

The Routing Information Indicator bit indicates whether MAC-level routing information is present. This bit is meaningful only for Token Ring addresses. Token Ring has a MAC-level routing mechanism known as Token Ring source routing. Even though this bit is meaningless for Ethernet addresses, it's still reserved and set to 0 to prevent problems when employing a translating bridge or Layer 2 switch between an Ethernet segment and a Token Ring.

For example, suppose the Routing Information Indicator bit isn't reserved at the value of 0 for Ethernet addresses, and this bit is set to 1 through a universal or locally administered address. When the address is translated to a Token Ring address, the Routing Information Indicator bit is set to 1 when there is no source routing information present. This can cause the Token Ring node to drop the frame.

The following Network Monitor trace (Capture 01-03, included in the \Captures folder on the companion CD-ROM) shows the special bits for Ethernet MAC addresses:

```
+ Frame: Base frame properties
  ETHERNET: ETYPE = 0x0800 : Protocol = IP:  DOD Internet Protocol
      ETHERNET: Destination address : 01005E400009
          ETHERNET: .......1 = Group address
          ETHERNET: ......0. = Universally administered address
      ETHERNET: Source address : 00E034C0A060
          ETHERNET: .......0 = No routing information present
          ETHERNET: ......0. = Universally administered address
      ETHERNET: Frame Length : 591 (0x024F)
      ETHERNET: Ethernet Type : 0x0800 (IP:  DOD Internet Protocol)
      ETHERNET: Ethernet Data: Number of data bytes remaining = 577 (0x0241)
+ IP: ID = 0xDBD2; Proto = UDP; Len: 577
+ UDP: IP Multicast: Src Port: Unknown, (3985); Dst Port: Unknown (20441);
Length = 557 (0x22D)
```

Token Ring

Token Ring is a ring access network technology originally proposed by Olaf Soderblum in 1969. IBM purchased the rights to the original design and created and released its Token Ring product in 1984. Key elements of the original IBM design were the use of proprietary connectors, twisted pair cable out to the network node, and structured wiring systems using centralized active hubs.

In 1985, the IEEE 802 project created the 802.5 subcommittee and Token Ring became an international standard. IBM created Token Ring to replace Ethernet as the most popular LAN technology. Although Token Ring is in many ways a superior technology to Ethernet, a combination of cost issues and marketing has made Token Ring less popular than Ethernet.

The original specification was for a 4 Mbps transmission rate, but was followed by an additional specification at 16 Mbps. On the same ring, all nodes must operate at the same speed. Common implementations use 4 Mbps rings connected together, using 16 Mbps rings as a high-speed backbone.

More Info IP and ARP encapsulation over Token Ring networks are described in RFC 1042, which can be found in the \RFC folder on the companion CD-ROM.

IEEE 802.5

The IEEE 802.5 frame format is the result of the IEEE 802.2 and 802.5 specifications, and consists of an IEEE 802.5 header and trailer and an IEEE 802.2 LLC header. The IEEE 802.5 frame format is shown in Figure 1-6.

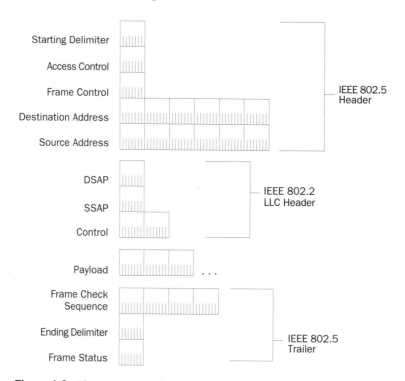

Figure 1-6. *The IEEE 802.5 frame format showing the IEEE 802.5 header and trailer and the IEEE 802.2 header.*

IEEE 802.5 Header and Trailer

The fields in the IEEE 802.5 header and trailer are defined as follows:

Start Delimiter

The Start Delimiter field is 1 byte long and identifies the start of the frame. The Start Delimiter field contains nondata symbols known as J and K symbols that are deliberate violations of the Token Ring signal encoding scheme. The J symbol is an encoding violation of a 1 and the K symbol is an encoding violation of a 0. The Start Delimiter field provides a very explicit preamble. Unlike Ethernet, Token Ring frames don't have an interframe gap to separate frames on the wire. The Start Delimiter field also provides synchronization for the receiver.

Note The Start Delimiter field isn't visible with Network Monitor.

Access Control

The Access Control field is 1 byte long and contains bits for:

- Setting the current priority of the token (3 bits). An interesting facility of Token Ring is its ability to prioritize access to the token and, therefore, the right to transmit data based on seven priority levels.

- Setting the token reservation level (3 bits). The token reservation bits set the priority of the token once the station that is currently transmitting releases it.

- Indicating whether the frame has passed the ring monitor station (1 bit). As the frame passes the ring monitor station, the Monitor bit is set to 1. If the ring monitor station sees a frame with the Monitor bit set to 1, the frame has already been sent on the ring. The ring monitor station removes the frame from the ring and then purges the ring.

- Indicating whether the frame that follows is a token or a frame (1 bit). If set to 0, what follows is a token. If set to 1, what follows is a frame.

Frame Control

The Frame Control field is 1 byte long and contains bits for:

- Indicating whether the frame that follows is a Token Ring MAC management frame or an LLC frame (2 bits).

- Indicating the type of Token Ring MAC management frame such as Purge, Claim Token, Beacon, and so forth (4 bits).

Two bits within the Frame Control field are reserved.

Destination Address

The Destination Address field is 6 bytes long and indicates the address of the destination. For Token Ring, the Destination Address field can be:

- A universal or locally administered unicast address.

- The universal broadcast address (0xFF-FF-FF-FF-FF-FF).

- The Token Ring broadcast address (0xC0-00-FF-FF-FF-FF). A frame using the Token Ring broadcast address is designed to remain on a single ring and isn't forwarded by Token Ring source-route bridges.
- A multicast address.
- A Token Ring functional address. A functional address is a type of multicast address that's specific to Token Ring and is typically used by Token Ring MAC management frames.

Source Address

The Source Address field is 6 bytes long and indicates the sending node's unicast address.

Payload

The Payload field for a Token Ring frame consists of a PDU of an upper layer protocol. Unlike Ethernet, there is no minimum frame size and the maximum transmission unit for Token Ring isn't a defined number, but dependent on factors such as the bit rate and the token holding time. Token ring MTUs are further complicated by the presence of Token Ring source-routing bridges. More information on Token Ring MTUs for IP datagrams can be found in the "IEEE 802.5 SNAP" section of this chapter.

Frame Check Sequence

The Frame Check Sequence field is a 4-byte CRC that uses the same algorithm as Ethernet to provide a bit-level integrity check of all fields in the Token Ring frame, from the Frame Control field to the Payload field. The FCS doesn't provide bit-level integrity for the Access Control or Frame Status field. This allows bits in these fields, such as the Monitor bit, to be set without forcing a recalculation of the FCS.

The FCS is checked as it passes each node on the ring. If the FCS fails at any node, the Error bit in the End Delimiter field is set to 1 and the receiving node doesn't copy the frame.

Note The Frame Check Sequence field isn't visible with Network Monitor.

End Delimiter

The End Delimiter is a 1-byte field that identifies the end of the frame. Like the Start Delimiter, the End Delimiter contains J and K non-data symbols to provide an explicit postamble. The End Delimiter field also contains:

- An Intermediate Frame indicator (1 bit), used to indicate whether this frame is the last frame in the sequence (set to 0) or more frames are to follow (set to 1).
- An Error Detected indicator (1 bit), used to indicate whether this frame has failed the FCS.

Because there is no Length field in the IEEE 802.5 frame, the End Delimiter is used to locate the end of the payload and the position of the Frame Check Sequence and Frame Status fields.

Note The End Delimiter field isn't visible with Network Monitor.

Frame Status

The Frame Status field is a 1-byte field that contains:

- Two copies of the Address Recognized indicator. The destination node sets the Address Recognized indicator to indicate that the address in the Destination Address field was recognized.

- Two copies of the Frame Copied indicator. The Destination node sets the Frame Copied indicator to indicate that the frame was successfully copied into a buffer on the network adapter.

Two copies of each indicator are needed because the Frame Status field isn't protected by the Frame Check Sequence field.

The Address Recognized and Frame Copied indicators aren't used as acknowledgments for reliable data delivery. The sending Token Ring network adapter uses these indicators to retransmit the frame, if necessary.

Note The Frame Status field isn't visible with Network Monitor.

IEEE 802.2 LLC Header

The fields in the IEEE 802.2 LLC header are defined and used in the same way as the IEEE 802.2 LLC header for the IEEE 802.3 frame format, as discussed in the "IEEE 802.3" section of this chapter.

IEEE 802.5 SNAP

As described earlier in this chapter, the value of 0x06 is defined as the SAP for IP. However, it's not defined for use in RFC 1042 and not used in the industry. Therefore, similar to the case of IEEE 802.3 frames, to send an IP datagram over an IEEE 802.5 network, the IP datagram must be encapsulated using SNAP, as Figure 1-7 shows.

The following Network Monitor trace (Capture 01-04, included in the \Captures folder on the companion CD-ROM) shows the IEEE 802.5 SNAP frame format for an IP datagram:

```
+ Frame: Base frame properties
  TOKENRING: Length =  66, Priority Normal (No token) LLC Frame
     TOKENRING: Access control = 16 (0x10) Original, Frame, Priority: Normal
(No token)
         TOKENRING: .....000   Reservation bits: Reservation = Normal, No
token needed.
         TOKENRING: ....0...  Monitor bit = Original (non-repeated)
         TOKENRING: ...1....  Token bit = Frame
         TOKENRING: 000.....  Priority bits: Priority = Normal, No token needed.
     TOKENRING: Frame control = 64 (0x40), LLC Frame
         TOKENRING: ....0000   Control bits = Normal Buffered
         TOKENRING: 01......  Frame type = LLC Frame
   + TOKENRING: Destination address : 400030370AF4
   + TOKENRING: Source address      : 10007038213A
```

```
       TOKENRING: Frame length : 66 (0x0042)
       TOKENRING: Tokenring data: Number of data bytes remaining = 52 (0x0034)
  LLC: UI DSAP=0xAA SSAP=0xAA C
       LLC: DSAP = 0xAA : INDIVIDUAL : Sub-Network Access Protocol (SNAP)
       LLC: SSAP = 0xAA: COMMAND : Sub-Network Access Protocol (SNAP)
       LLC: Frame Category: Unnumbered Frame
       LLC: Command = UI
       LLC: LLC Data: Number of data bytes remaining = 49 (0x0031)
  SNAP: ETYPE = 0x0800
       SNAP: Snap Organization code = 00 00 00
       SNAP: Snap etype : 0x0800
       SNAP: Snap Data: Number of data bytes remaining = 44 (0x002C)
+ IP: ID = 0xCA3D; Proto = TCP; Len: 44
+ TCP: ....S., len: 0, seq:364446-364446, ack: 0, win: 16384, src:50982  dst: 21
```

Note The TOKENRING: Frame length, TOKENRING: Tokenring data, LLC: Frame Category, LLC: LLC Data, and SNAP: Snap Data fields are Network Monitor informational fields and don't correspond to fields that are physically present in the Token Ring header.

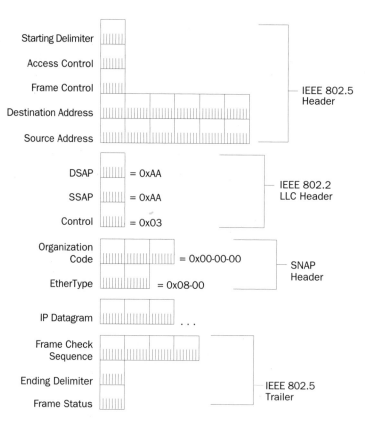

Figure 1-7. *The IEEE 802.5 SNAP frame format showing the SNAP header and an IP datagram.*

For a 10-millisecond (ms) token-holding time, the maximum sizes for IP datagrams are 4464 bytes for 4 Mbps Token Ring network adapters, and 17,914 bytes for 16 Mbps Token Ring network adapters. If Token Ring source-routing bridges are present, the maximum size of IP datagrams can be 508, 1020, 2044, 4092, and 8188 bytes.

More Info   For more information on Token Ring MTUs, see RFC 1042 in the \RFC folder of the companion CD-ROM.

Special Bits on Token Ring MAC Addresses

Within the Source Address and Destination Address fields of the IEEE 802.5 frame format, special bits are defined, as shown in Figure 1-8.

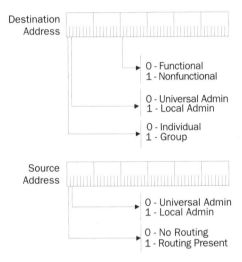

Figure 1-8. *The special bits defined on Token Ring source and destination MAC addresses.*

The Individual/Group Bit

Identical to Ethernet, the I/G bit for Token Ring addresses is used to indicate whether the address is a unicast (individual) or multicast (group) address. For unicast addresses, the I/G bit is set to 0. For multicast addresses, the I/G bit is set to 1.

The Universal/Locally Administered Bit

Identical to Ethernet, the U/L Administered bit for Token Ring addresses is used to indicate whether the IEEE has allocated the address. For universal addresses allocated by the IEEE, the U/L bit is set to 0. For locally administered addresses, the U/L bit is set to 1. The U/L bit is relevant for both the Source Address and Destination Address fields.

Functional Address Bit

The Functional Address bit indicates whether the address is a functional address (set to 0) or a nonfunctional address (set to 1). Token Ring defines the following two types of multicast addresses:

- **Functional addresses** Multicast addresses that are specific to Token Ring. There are specific functional addresses for identifying the ring monitor, the ring-parameter server, and a source-routing bridge.
- **Nonfunctional addresses** General multicast addresses that aren't Token Ring-specific.

The Functional Address bit is significant only if the I/G bit is set to 1.

Routing Information Indicator Bit

The Routing Information Indicator bit indicates whether MAC-level routing information is present. In the case of Token Ring, the Routing Information Indicator bit indicates the presence of a source-routing header between the IEEE 802.5 header and the IEEE 802.2 LLC header. Token Ring source routing isn't OSI Network Layer routing, but rather a MAC sublayer routing scheme that allows a sending node to discover and specify a route through a defined series of rings and bridges within a Token Ring network segment.

The following Network Monitor trace (Capture 01-04, included in the \Captures folder on the companion CD-ROM) shows the special bits for Token Ring addresses:

```
+ Frame: Base frame properties
  TOKENRING: Length =  66, Priority Normal (No token) LLC Frame
    + TOKENRING: Access control = 16 (0x10) Original, Frame, Priority: Normal
(No token)
    + TOKENRING: Frame control = 64 (0x40), LLC Frame
     TOKENRING: Destination address : 400030370AF4
        TOKENRING: Destination Address I/G Bit    = Individual address
        TOKENRING: Destination Address U/L bit    = Locally administered
address
        TOKENRING: Destination Address Functional bit = Functional address
     TOKENRING: Source address      : 10007038213A
        TOKENRING: Source Address Routing bit = No routing information
present
        TOKENRING: Source Address U/L bit     = Universally administered
address
     TOKENRING: Frame length : 66 (0x0042)
     TOKENRING: Tokenring data: Number of data bytes remaining = 52 (0x0034)
+ LLC: UI DSAP=0xAA SSAP=0xAA C
+ SNAP: ETYPE = 0x0800
+ IP: ID = 0x21E0; Proto = TCP; Len: 44
+ TCP: ....S., len:    0, seq:1891988225-1891988225, ack:        0, win:
8192, src:50982  dst: 3180
```

FDDI

Fiber Distributed Data Interface (FDDI) is a network technology that the American National Standards Institute (ANSI) developed. FDDI is an optical fiber-based token passing ring with a bit rate of 100 Mbps. It was designed to span long distances and, in most implementations, it acts as a campus-wide high-speed backbone. FDDI offers advanced features beyond Token Ring, such as the ability to self-heal a break in the ring, and the use of guaranteed bandwidth.

Although not developed by the IEEE as part of the 802.x standards, the FDDI specification is quite similar to the IEEE 802.3 and 802.5 specifications; it defines the MAC sublayer of the OSI Data Link Layer and the Physical Layer, and it uses the IEEE 802.2 LLC sublayer. Copper Data Distributed Interface (CDDI) is a version of FDDI that operates over twisted pair copper wire.

More Info   RFC 1188 describes IP encapsulation over FDDI networks. You can find RFC 1188 in the \RFC folder on the companion CD-ROM.

FDDI Frame Format

The FDDI frame format is the result of the IEEE 802.2 and ANSI FDDI specifications, and consists of a FDDI header and trailer and an IEEE 802.2 LLC header. Figure 1-9 shows the FDDI frame format.

FDDI Header and Trailer

The fields in the FDDI header and trailer are defined as follows:

Preamble

The Preamble field is 2 bytes long and provides receiver synchronization.

Note   The Preamble field isn't visible with Network Monitor.

Start Delimiter

The Start Delimiter field is 1 byte long and identifies the start of the frame. Like Token Ring, the Start Delimiter field contains non-data symbols known as J and K symbols that are deliberate violations of the FDDI signal encoding scheme. The J symbol is an encoding violation of a 1 and the K symbol is an encoding violation of a 0.

Note   The Start Delimiter field isn't visible with Network Monitor.

Frame Control

The Frame Control field is 1 byte long and contains bits for the following:

- Setting the class of the frame (1 bit). FDDI frames can be sent as synchronous or asynchronous frames. Synchronous frames are used for guaranteed bandwidth and response time. Asynchronous frames are used for dynamic bandwidth sharing. The Class bit is set to 1 for synchronous frames and 0 for asynchronous frames.

- Setting the length of the Destination Address and the Source Address fields (1 bit). Like IEEE 802.3, FDDI supports 2-byte and 6-byte addresses. The Address bit is set to 1 for 6-byte addresses and 0 for 2-byte addresses.

- Indicating that what follows is a token (either non-restricted or restricted), a station management frame, a MAC frame, and LLC frame, or an LLC frame with a specific priority (6 bits).

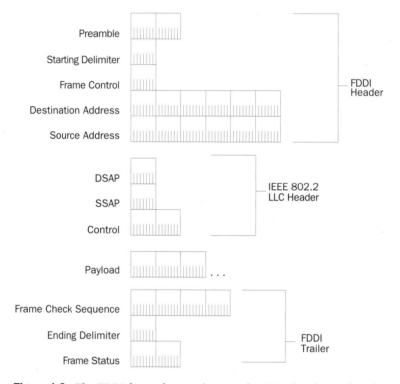

Figure 1-9. *The FDDI frame format showing the FDDI header and trailer and IEEE 802.2 header.*

Destination Address

The Destination Address field is either 2 bytes or 6 bytes long and indicates the address of the destination (2-byte addresses are seldom used). For 6-byte addresses, FDDI Destination Address fields are defined the same as Ethernet Destination Address fields to provide easy interoperability between bridged or Layer 2-switched Ethernet and FDDI segments. The destination address is a unicast, multicast, or broadcast address.

Source Address

The Source Address field is either 2 bytes or 6 bytes long and indicates the unicast address of the sending node (2-byte addresses are seldom used).

Frame Check Sequence

The FCS field is a 4-byte CRC that uses the same algorithm as Ethernet to provide a bit-level integrity check of all fields in the FDDI frame, from the Frame Control field to the Payload field. The FCS is checked as it passes each node on the ring. If the FCS fails at any node, the Error bit in the Frame Status field is set to 1 and the receiving node doesn't copy the frame.

Note   The Frame Check Sequence field isn't visible with Network Monitor.

End Delimiter

The End Delimiter field is 1 byte long and identifies the end of the frame. Like the Start Delimiter field, the End Delimiter field contains J and K non-data symbols to provide an explicit postamble. Because there is no Length field in the FDDI frame, the End Delimiter field is used also to locate the end of the payload, and the position of the Frame Check Sequence and Frame Status fields.

Note   The End Delimiter field isn't visible with Network Monitor.

Frame Status

The Frame Status field is typically 2 bytes long and contains bits for the following:

- **The Address Recognized indicator**   The destination node sets the Address Recognized indicator to show that the address in the Destination Address field was recognized.

- **The Frame Copied indicator**   The destination node sets the Frame Copied indicator to show that the frame was successfully copied into a buffer on the network adapter.

- **The Error indicator**   Any FDDI station sets the Error indicator to 1 when the Frame Check Sequence field is invalid.

Similar to Token Ring, the Address Recognized and Frame Copied indicators aren't used as acknowledgments for reliable data delivery. Rather, the sending FDDI network adapter uses these indicators to retransmit the frame if necessary.

Note   The Frame Status field isn't visible with Network Monitor.

IEEE 802.2 LLC Header

The fields in the IEEE 802.2 LLC header are defined and used in the same way as the IEEE 802.2 LLC header for the IEEE 802.3 and IEEE 802.5 frame format discussed earlier in this chapter.

Payload

The payload for an FDDI frame consists of a PDU of an upper layer protocol. The entire FDDI frame from the Preamble field to the Frame Status field can be a maximum size of 4500 bytes. Once you subtract the FDDI and IEEE 802.2 LLC headers, the maximum payload size is 4474 bytes with a 3-byte LLC header, and 4473 bytes with a 4-byte LLC header.

FDDI SNAP

As described earlier in this chapter, the value of 0x06 is defined as the SAP for IP. However, it's not defined for use in RFC 1188 and not used in the industry. Therefore, similar to the case of IEEE 802.3 frames and IEEE 802.5 frames, to send an IP datagram over an FDDI network, the IP datagram must be encapsulated using the SNAP, as shown in Figure 1-10.

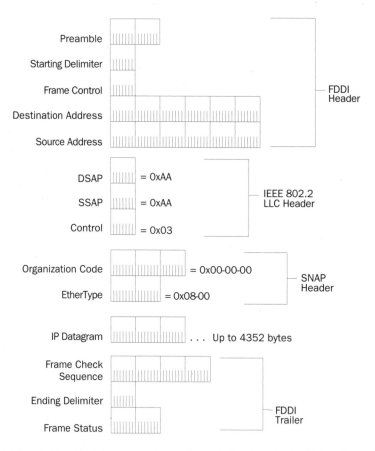

Figure 1-10. *The FDDI SNAP frame format showing the SNAP header and an IP datagram.*

The following Network Monitor trace (Capture 01-05, included in the \Captures folder on the companion CD-ROM) shows the FDDI SNAP frame format for an IP datagram:

```
+ Frame: Base frame properties
  FDDI: Length = 81, type = 0x57 (LLC).
      FDDI: Frame control bits = 87 (0x57)
           FDDI: ..01.... = LLC frame
           FDDI: 0....... = Asynchronous frame
           FDDI: .1...... = 48-bit addresses
    + FDDI: Destination address : 00608C14AF25
    + FDDI: Source address : 00608C13182A
      FDDI: Frame Length : 81 (0x0051)
      FDDI: Fddi Data: Number of data bytes remaining = 68 (0x0044)
  LLC: UI DSAP=0xAA SSAP=0xAA C
      LLC: DSAP = 0xAA : INDIVIDUAL : Sub-Network Access Protocol (SNAP)
      LLC: SSAP = 0xAA: COMMAND : Sub-Network Access Protocol (SNAP)
      LLC: Frame Category: Unnumbered Frame
      LLC: Command = UI
      LLC: LLC Data: Number of data bytes remaining = 65 (0x0041)
  SNAP: ETYPE = 0x0800
      SNAP: Snap Organization code = 00 00 00
      SNAP: Snap etype : 0x0800
      SNAP: Snap Data: Number of data bytes remaining = 60 (0x003C)
+ IP: ID = 0xA665; Proto = ICMP; Len: 60
+ ICMP: Echo: From 192.168.44.01 To 192.168.44.254
```

Note   The FDDI: Frame Length, FDDI: FddiData, LLC: Frame Category, LLC: LLC Data, and SNAP: Snap Data fields are Network Monitor informational fields and don't correspond to fields that are physically present in the FDDI header.

The maximum-sized IP datagram that can be sent on an FDDI network is 4352 bytes. The 4352 bytes is the result of taking the maximum FDDI frame size of 4500 bytes and subtracting the FDDI header and trailer (22 bytes), the LLC header (3 bytes), the SNAP header (5 bytes), and reserving 117 bytes for future purposes.

IP datagrams and ARP messages sent over FDDI networks also have the following constraints:

- Only 6-byte FDDI source and destination addresses can be used.
- All IP and ARP frames are transmitted as asynchronous class LLC frames using unrestricted tokens.

RFC 1188 doesn't define how frame priorities are used or how the FDDI node deals with the values of the Address Recognized and Frame Copied indicators.

FDDI nodes send ARP Requests using the Ethernet ARP Hardware Type value of 0x00-01, but can receive ARP Requests using the ARP Hardware Types of 0x00-01 and 0x00-06 (IEEE networks). The use of the Ethernet ARP Hardware Type value is designed to allow FDDI hosts and Ethernet hosts in a bridged or Layer 2-switched environment to send and receive ARP messages.

Special Bits on FDDI MAC Addresses

Because FDDI MAC addresses are defined in the same way as Ethernet MAC addresses, the special bits on FDDI MAC addresses are the same as those defined for Ethernet MAC addresses.

Network Monitor trace 1-5 (Capture 01-05, included in the \Captures folder on the companion CD-ROM) shows the special bits in the FDDI header.

Summary

LAN technology encapsulations provide delimitation, addressing, protocol identification, and bit-level integrity services. IP datagrams and ARP messages sent over Ethernet links are encapsulated using either the Ethernet II or IEEE 802.3 SNAP frame formats. IP datagrams and ARP messages sent over Token Ring links are encapsulated using the IEEE 802.5 SNAP frame format. IP datagrams and ARP messages sent over FDDI links are encapsulated using the FDDI SNAP frame format.

Chapter 2
Wide Area Network (WAN) Technologies

To successfully troubleshoot TCP/IP problems on a wide area network (WAN), it is important to understand how IP datagrams and Address Resolution Protocol (ARP) messages are encapsulated by a Microsoft Windows 2000 computer that uses a WAN technology such as T-carrier, an analog phone line, Integrated Services Digital Network (ISDN), X.25, Frame Relay, or Asynchronous Transfer Mode (ATM). It is also important to understand WAN technology encapsulations to understand the WAN encapsulation portions of the frame when using Microsoft Network Monitor or other types of WAN frame capture programs or facilities.

WAN Encapsulations

As discussed in Chapter 1, "Local Area Network (LAN) Technologies," Internet Protocol (IP) datagrams are an Open Systems Interconnection (OSI) Network Layer entity that require a Data Link Layer encapsulation before being sent on a physical medium. For WAN technologies, the Data Link Layer encapsulation provides the following services:

- **Delimitation**   Frames at the Data Link Layer must be distinguished from each other, and the frame's payload must be distinguished from the Data Link Layer header and trailer.

- **Protocol identification**   On a multiprotocol WAN link, protocols such as TCP/IP, Internetwork Packet Exchange (IPX), or AppleTalk must be distinguished from each other.

- **Addressing**   For WAN technologies that support multiple possible destinations using the same physical link, the destination must be identified.

- **Bit-level integrity check**   A checksum provides a bit-level integrity check between either the source and destination, or between forwarding nodes on a packet-switching network.

This chapter discusses WAN technologies and their encapsulations for IP datagrams and ARP messages. WAN encapsulations are divided into two categories based on the types of IP networks of the WAN link:

- Point-to-point links support an IP network segment with a maximum of two nodes. These links include analog phone lines, Integrated Services Digital Network (ISDN) circuits, Digital Subscriber Lines (DSL), and T-carrier links such as T-1, T-3, Fractional T-1, E-1, and E-3. Point-to-point links do not require Data Link Layer addressing.

- Non-broadcast multiple access (NBMA) links support an IP network segment with more than two nodes; however, there's no facility to broadcast a single IP datagram to multiple locations. NBMA links include packet-switching WAN technologies such as X.25, Frame Relay, and Asynchronous Transfer Mode (ATM). NBMA links require Data Link Layer addressing.

Point-to-Point Encapsulation

The two most prominent industry standard encapsulations for sending IP datagrams over a point-to-point link are Serial Line Internet Protocol (SLIP) and Point-to-Point Protocol (PPP).

SLIP

As RFC 1055 describes, SLIP is a very simple packet-framing protocol that offers only frame delimitation services. SLIP does not provide protocol identification, or bit-level integrity verification services. SLIP was designed to be easy to implement for links that didn't require these types of services.

More Info SLIP is described in RFC 1055, which can be found in the \RFC folder on the companion CD-ROM.

To delimit IP datagrams, SLIP uses a special character called the END character. The END character (0xC0) is placed at the beginning and end of each IP datagram. Successive IP datagrams have two END characters between them: one to mark the end of one datagram and one to mark the beginning of another.

The END character presents a problem; if the END character occurs within the IP datagram and is sent unmodified, the receiving node will interpret the END character as the marker for the end of the IP datagram. If this happens, the originally sent IP datagram is truncated and will eventually be discarded because of failed checksums in the IP header and upper layer protocol headers. Figure 2-1 shows a SLIP-encapsulated IP datagram.

To prevent the occurrence of the END character within the IP datagram, SLIP uses a technique called *character stuffing*. The END character is escaped, or replaced, with a

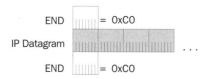

Figure 2-1. *SLIP encapsulation, showing the simple frame delimitation services for an IP datagram.*

sequence beginning with another special character called the ESC (0xDB) character. The SLIP ESC character has no relation to the American Standard Code for Information Interchange (ASCII) ESC character.

If the END character occurs within the original IP datagram, it's replaced with the sequence 0xDB-DC. To prevent the misinterpretation of the ESC character by the receiving node, if the ESC (0xDB) character occurs within the original IP datagram, it's replaced with the sequence 0xDB-DD. Therefore:

- END characters can occur only at the beginning and end of the SLIP frame and SLIP places them on the point-to-point link medium.

- SLIP replaces the END character within the IP datagram with the sequence 0xDB-DC. On the receiving node, the 0xDB-DC sequence is translated back to 0xC0.

- SLIP replaces the ESC character within the IP datagram with the sequence 0xDB-DD. On the receiving node, the 0xDB-DD sequence is translated back to 0xDB. If the IP datagram contains the sequence 0xDB-DC, the escaping of the ESC character turns this sequence into 0xDB-DD-DC to prevent the receiver from misinterpreting the 0xDB-DC sequence to 0xC0.

Figure 2-2 shows SLIP character stuffing.

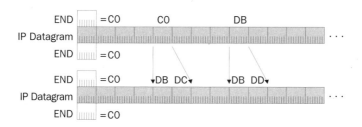

Figure 2-2. *SLIP character stuffing, showing the escaping of the END and ESC characters within an IP datagram.*

As RFC 1055 describes, the maximum size of an IP datagram over a SLIP connection is 1006 bytes—the size imposed by Berkeley UNIX drivers that existed when the RFC was written. Most systems adhere to the industry standard maximum size of 1006 bytes. However, some systems, such as Windows 2000, allow a maximum packet size of 1500 bytes over a SLIP connection to prevent fragmentation of IP datagrams when SLIP links are used in conjunction with Ethernet network segments.

While SLIP doesn't provide for the negotiation of compression methods during the connection setup, SLIP does support a compression scheme known as Compressed SLIP or C-SLIP.

More Info RFC 1144 describes C-SLIP and how it's used to compress IP and TCP headers to a 3-5-byte header on the SLIP link. This RFC can be found in the \RFC folder on the companion CD-ROM.

Windows 2000 Network and Dial-Up Connections use SLIP and C-SLIP to create SLIP remote access connections to a network access server. The Windows 2000 Routing and Remote Access service doesn't support SLIP or C-SLIP.

PPP

PPP is a standardized point-to-point network encapsulation method that addresses the shortcomings of SLIP and provides Data Link Layer functionality comparable to local area network (LAN) encapsulations. PPP provides frame delimitation, protocol identification, and bit-level integrity services.

More Info PPP is described in RFC 1661, which can be found in the \RFC folder on the companion CD-ROM.

RFC 1661 describes PPP as a suite of protocols that provide the following:

- A Data Link Layer encapsulation method that supports multiple protocols simultaneously on the same link.
- A protocol for negotiating the Data Link Layer characteristics of the point-to-point connection called the Link Control Protocol (LCP).
- A series of protocols for negotiating the Network Layer properties of Network Layer protocols over the point-to-point connection called Network Control Protocols (NCPs). For example, RFCs 1332 and 1877 describe the NCP for IP called Internet Protocol Control Protocol (IPCP). IPCP is used to negotiate an IP address, the addresses of name servers, and the use of the Van Jacobsen TCP compression protocol.

This chapter discusses only the Data Link Layer encapsulation.

PPP encapsulation and framing is based on the International Organization for Standardization (ISO) High-Level Data Link Control (HDLC) protocol. HDLC was derived from the Synchronous Data Link Control (SDLC) protocol developed by IBM for the Systems Network Architecture (SNA) protocol suite. HDLC encapsulation for PPP frames is shown in Figure 2-3.

More Info HDLC encapsulation for PPP frames is described in RFC 1662, which can be found in the \RFC folder on the companion CD-ROM.

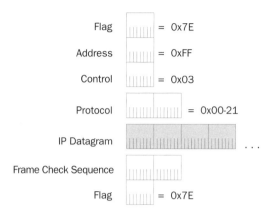

Figure 2-3. *PPP encapsulation using HDLC framing for an IP datagram, showing the PPP header and trailer.*

The fields in the PPP header and trailer are defined as follows:

- **Flag** A 1-byte field set to 0x7E (bit sequence 01111110) that indicates the start and end of a PPP frame. Unlike SLIP, a single FLAG character is used between back-to-back PPP frames.

- **Address** A 1-byte field that is a by-product of HDLC. In HDLC environments, the Address field is used as a destination address on a multi-point network. PPP links, however, are point-to-point, and the destination node is always the other node on the point-to-point link. Therefore, the Address field for PPP en-capsulation is set to 0xFF—the broadcast address.

- **Control** A 1-byte field that is also an HDLC by-product. In HDLC environ-ments, the Control field is used to implement sequencing and acknowledgments to provide Data Link Layer reliability services. For session-based traffic, the Con-trol field is multiple bytes long. For datagram traffic, the Control field is 1-byte long and set to 0x03 to indicate an unnumbered information (UI) frame. Because PPP doesn't provide reliable Data Link Layer services, PPP frames are always UI frames. Therefore, PPP frames always use a 1-byte Control field set to 0x03.

- **Protocol** A 2-byte field used to identify the upper layer protocol of the PPP payload. For example, 0x00-21 indicates an IP datagram, 0x00-29 indicates an AppleTalk datagram, and 0x00-2B indicates an IPX datagram.

More Info For a complete list of defined PPP protocol numbers, see RFC 1661, in the \RFC folder on the companion CD-ROM.

- **Frame Check Sequence (FCS)** A 2-byte field used to provide bit-level integrity services for the PPP frame. The sender calculates the FCS, which is then placed in the FCS field. The receiver performs the same FCS calculation and compares its result with the result stored in this field. If the two FCS values match, the PPP frame is considered valid and is processed further. If the two FCS values don't match, the PPP frame is silently discarded.

Figure 2-4 shows a typical PPP framing for an IP datagram.

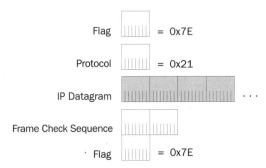

Figure 2-4. *Typical PPP encapsulation for an IP datagram when using address, control, and protocol compression.*

This abbreviated form of PPP framing is a result of the following:

- Because the Address field is irrelevant for point-to-point links, in most cases the PPP peers agree to not include the Address field during LCP negotiation. This is done through the Address and Control Field Compression LCP option.

- Because the Control is always set to 0x03 and provides no other service, in most cases the PPP peers agree to not include the Control field during the LCP negotiation. This, too, is done through the Address and Control Field Compression LCP option.

- Because the high-order byte of Network Layer protocols such as IP, AppleTalk, and IPX are always set to 0x00, in most cases the PPP peers agree to use a 1-byte Control field during the LCP negotiation. This is done through the Protocol Compression LCP option.

Note PPP frames captured with Windows 2000 Network Monitor will not display the HDLC structure, as shown in Figures 2-3 and 2-4. PPP control frames contain simulated source and destination MAC addresses and only the PPP Protocol field. PPP data frames contain a simulated Ethernet II header.

PPP on Asynchronous Links

As in SLIP, PPP on asynchronous links such as analog phone lines uses character stuffing to prevent the occurrence of the FLAG character within the PPP payload. The FLAG character is escaped, or replaced, with a sequence beginning with another special character called the ESC (0x7D) character. The PPP ESC character has no relation to the ASCII ESC character.

If the FLAG character occurs within the original IP datagram, it's replaced with the sequence 0x7D-5E. To prevent the misinterpretation of the ESC character by the receiving node, if the ESC (0x7D) character occurs within the original IP datagram, it's replaced with the sequence 0x7D-5E. Therefore:

- FLAG characters can occur only at the beginning and end of the PPP frame, and PPP places them on the point-to-point link medium.

- PPP replaces the FLAG character within the IP datagram with the sequence 0x7D-5E. On the receiving node, the 0x7D-5E sequence is translated back to 0x7E.

- PPP replaces the ESC character within the PPP frame with the sequence 0x7D-5D. On the receiving node, the 0x7D-5E sequence is translated back to 0x7D. If the IP datagram contains the sequence 0x7D-5E, the escaping of the ESC character turns this sequence into 0x7D-5D-5E to prevent the receiver from misinterpreting the 0x7D-5E sequence to 0x7E.

Additionally, character stuffing is used to stuff characters with values less than 0x20 (32 in decimal) to prevent these characters from being misinterpreted as control characters when software flow control is used over asynchronous links. The escape sequence for these characters is 0x7D—(original character with the fifth bit set to 1). The fifth bit is defined as the third bit from the high-order bit using the bit position designation of 7-6-5-4-3-2-1-0. Therefore, the character 0x11 (bit sequence 0-0-0-1-0-0-0-1) would be escaped to the sequence 0x7D-31 (bit sequence 0-0-1-1-0-0-0-1).

The use of character stuffing for characters less than 0x20 is negotiated using the Asynchronous Control Character Map (ACCM) LCP option. This LCP option uses a 32-bit bitmap to indicate exactly which character values need to be escaped.

More Info   For more information on the ACCM LCP option, see RFCs 1661 and 1662. These can be found in the \RFC folder on the companion CD-ROM.

PPP on Synchronous Links

Character stuffing is an inefficient method of escaping the FLAG character. If the PPP payload consists of a stream of 0x7E characters, character stuffing roughly doubles the size of the PPP frame as it's sent on the medium. For asynchronous, byte-boundary media such as analog phone lines, character stuffing is the only alternative.

On synchronous links such as T-carrier, ISDN, and Synchronous Optical Network (SONET), a technique called *bit stuffing* is used to mark the location of the FLAG character. Recall that the FLAG character is 0x7E, or the bit sequence 01111110. With bit stuffing, the only time six 1 bits in a row are allowed is for the FLAG character as it's used to mark the start and end of a PPP frame. Throughout the rest of the PPP frame, if there are five 1 bits in a row, a 0 bit is inserted into the bit stream by the synchronous link hardware. Therefore, the bit sequence 111110 is stuffed to produce 1111100 and the bit sequence 111111 is stuffed to become 1111101. Therefore, six 1 bits in a row can't occur except for the FLAG character when it's used to mark the start and end of a PPP frame. If the FLAG character does occur within the PPP frame, it's bit stuffed to produce the bit sequence 011111010. Bit stuffing is much more efficient than character stuffing. If stuffed, a single byte becomes 9 bits, not 16 bits, as is the case with character stuffing. With synchronous links and bit stuffing, data sent no longer falls along bit boundaries. A single byte sent can be encoded as either 8 or 9 bits, depending on the presence of a 11111 sequence within the byte.

PPP MTU

The maximum-sized PPP frame, the maximum transmission unit (MTU) for a PPP link, is known as the Maximum Receive Unit (MRU). The default value for the PPP MRU is 1500 bytes. The MRU for a PPP connection can be negotiated to a lower or higher value using the Maximum Receive Unit LCP option. If an MRU is negotiated to a value lower than 1500 bytes, a 1500-byte MRU must still be supported in case the link has to be resynchronized.

PPP Multilink Protocol

The PPP Multilink Protocol (MP) is an extension to PPP that allows you to bundle or aggregate the bandwidth of multiple physical connections. It is supported by Windows 2000 Network and Dial-Up Connections and the Routing and Remote Access Service. MP takes multiple physical connections and makes them appear as a single logical link. For example, two analog phone lines operating at 28.8 Kbps appear as a single connection operating as 57.6 Kbps using MP. Another example is the aggregation of multiple channels of an ISDN Basic Rate Interface (BRI) or Primary Rate Interface (PRI) line. In the case of a PRI line, MP makes the two 64-Kbps PRI B-channels appear as a single connection operating at 128 Kbps.

More Info Multiple Protocol is described in \RFC 1991, which can be found in the \RFC folder on the companion CD-ROM.

MP is an extra layer of encapsulation that operates within a PPP payload. To identify an MP packet, the PPP Protocol field is set to 0x00-3D. The payload of an MP packet is a PPP frame or the fragment of a PPP frame. If the size of the PPP payload that would be sent on a single-link PPP connection, plus the additional MP header, is greater than the MRU for the specific physical link over which the MP packet is sent, MP will fragment the PPP payload.

MP fragmentation divides the PPP payload along boundaries that will fit within the link's MRU. The fragments are sent in sequence using an incrementing sequence number, and flags are used to indicate the first and last fragments of an original PPP payload. A lost MP fragment will cause the entire original PPP payload to be silently discarded.

MP encapsulation has two different forms: the long sequence number format (as Figure 2-5 shows) and the short sequence number format. The long sequence number format adds 4 bytes of overhead to the PPP payload.

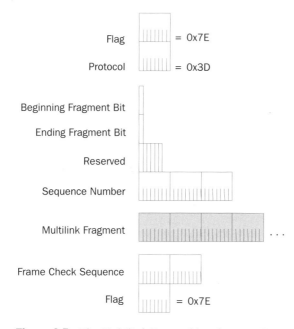

Figure 2-5. *The Multilink Protocol header as a PPP payload, using the long sequence number format.*

The fields in the MP long sequence number format header are defined as follows:

- **Beginning Fragment Bit**   Set to 1 on the first fragment of a PPP payload and to 0 on all other PPP payload fragments.

- **Ending Fragment Bit**   Set to 1 on the last fragment of a PPP payload and to 0 on all other PPP payload fragments. If a PPP payload isn't fragmented, both the Beginning Fragment Bit and Ending Fragment Bit are set to 1.

- **Reserved** Set to 0.
- **Sequence Number** Set to an incrementally increasing number for each MP payload sent. For the long sequence number format, the Sequence Number field is 3 bytes long. The Sequence Number field is used to number successive PPP payloads that would normally be sent over a single link PPP connection, and is used by MP to preserve the packet sequence as sent by the PPP peer. Additionally, the Sequence Number field is used to number individual fragments of a PPP payload so that the receiving node can detect a fragment loss.

Figure 2-6 shows the short sequence number format. The short sequence number format adds 2 bytes of overhead to the PPP payload.

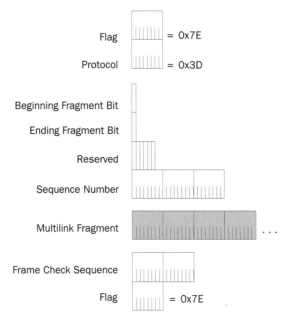

Figure 2-6. *The Multilink Protocol header as a PPP payload, using the short sequence number format.*

The short sequence format has only 2 reserved bits, and its Sequence Number field is only 12 bits long. The long sequence number format is used by default unless the Short Sequence Number Header Format LCP option is used during the LCP negotiation.

X.25

In the 1970s, a standard set of protocols known as X.25 was created to provide users with a standard way to send packetized data across a packet-switched public data network (PSPDN). Until X.25, PSPDNs and their interfaces were proprietary and completely incompatible. Changing PSPDN vendors meant purchasing new Public Data Network (PDN) interfacing equipment. X.25 is an international standard, as specified by the International Telecommunications Union-Telecommunication sector (ITU-T).

X.25 was developed during a time when the telecommunication infrastructure was largely based on noisy copper cabling. A typical use for PSPDNs at that time was the communication of a dumb terminal with a mainframe computer. Errors in transmission because of noisy cabling couldn't be recovered by dumb terminal equipment. Therefore, X.25 was designed to provide a reliable data transfer service—an unusual feature for a Data Link Layer protocol. All data sent to the PSPDN using X.25 was reliably received and reliably forwarded to the desired endpoint. The reliable service of X.25 typically isn't needed for the communication of more intelligent endpoints using protocol suites such as TCP/IP. However, X.25 is still used as a WAN technology over which to send TCP/IP data because of its international availability.

As Figure 2-7 shows, X.25 defines the interface between data terminal equipment (DTE) and data circuit-terminating equipment (DCE). A DTE can be a terminal that doesn't implement the complete X.25 functionality; as such, it is known as a non-packet mode DTE. A non-packet mode DTE is connected to a DCE through a translation device called a packet assembler/disassembler (PAD). X.25 doesn't attempt to define the nature of the DIE to DCE communication within the PSPDN. These details are left to the X.25 vendor.

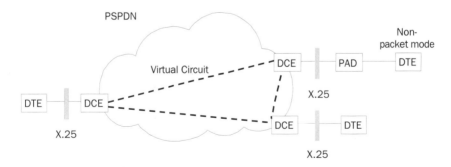

Figure 2-7. *The X.25 WAN service, showing DTE, DCE, PAD, and the X.25 interface to the PSPDN.*

End-to-end communication between DTEs is accomplished through a bi-directional and full-duplex logical connection called a virtual circuit. Virtual circuits permit communication between DTEs without the use of dedicated circuits. Data is sent as it's produced, using the bandwidth of the PDN infrastructure more efficiently. X.25 can support permanent virtual circuits (PVCs) or switched virtual circuits (SVCs). A PVC is a path through a packet-switching network that is statically programmed into the switches. An SVC is a path through a packet-switching network that is negotiated using a signaling protocol each time a connection is initiated.

Once a virtual circuit is established, a DTE sends a packet to the other end of a virtual circuit by using an X.25 virtual-circuit identifier called the Logical Channel Number (LCN). The DCE uses the LCN to forward the packet within the PDN to the appropriate destination DCE.

X.25 encompasses the Physical, Data Link, and Network Layers of the OSI model.

- **Physical Layer** X.25 can use a variety of interface standards such as X.21*bis* (roughly equivalent to EIA/TIA232C [formerly RS-232-C]) or V.35.
- **Data Link Layer** X.25 at the Data Link Layer uses a framing called Link Access Procedure-Balanced (LAPB), another variant of the HDLC protocol.
- **Network Layer** X.25 at the Network Layer uses a framing called Packet Layer Protocol (PLP). For X.25 SVCs, X.25 call setup packets contain a connection establishment address known as an X.121 address, also referred to as an International Data Number (IDN). X.121 addresses have a variable length (up to 14 decimal digits). Once the SVC is created, the LCN is used for data transfer. User data transfer is performed reliably between endpoints using flow control, sequencing, and acknowledgments.

While X.25 is defined at the Physical, Data Link, and Network Layers of the OSI model, relative to sending IP datagrams, X.25 is a Data Link and Physical Layer technology.

Typical packet sizes for X.25 PSPDNs are 128, 256, or 512 bytes. User information, such as IP datagrams that are beyond the packet size of the X.25 PSPDN, are segmented by X.25 and reliably reassembled.

X.25 Encapsulation

X.25 encapsulation can take two different forms:

- If IP datagrams are the only type of data being sent across the virtual circuit, IP traffic is identified by setting the 1-byte Network Layer Protocol Identifier (NLPID) to 0xCC in the first octet in the Call User Data (CUD) field of the X.25 Call Request packet. IP datagrams are encapsulated with the X.25 PLP and LAPB headers.
- If IP datagrams are one of many types of data being sent across the virtual circuit (a multiprotocol link), the NLPID in the CUD field of the X.25 Call Request packet is set to 0x00 to indicate null encapsulation. IP datagrams are encapsulated with the NLPID header set to 0xCC and the X.25 PLP and LAPB headers.

More Info   X.25 encapsulation of IP datagrams is described in RFC 1356, which can be found in the \RFC folder on the companion CD-ROM.

Figure 2-8 shows the X.25 encapsulation for IP datagrams on a multiprotocol link.

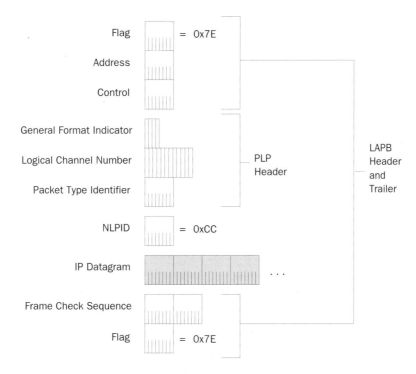

Figure 2-8. *X.25 encapsulation for IP datagrams, when sent on a multiprotocol link.*

NLPID

For multiprotocol virtual circuits, the 1-byte NLPID field is present and set to 0xCC to indicate an IP datagram. For a single protocol virtual circuit, the NLPID field isn't present. If the IP datagram is fragmented, the NLPID is fragmented along with the IP datagram.

PLP Header

The fields in the X.25 PLP header are defined as follows:

- **General Format Indicator (GFI)**   A 4-bit field that identifies the PLP payload as a user data or an X.25 message, the packet numbering scheme (modulo 8 or modulo 128), and whether delivery confirmation with the endpoint is required.

- **Logical Channel Number (LCN)**   A 12-bit field that identifies the virtual circuit over which the X.25 packet is to travel. The LCN is only locally significant between the DTE and DCE. When an X.25 connection is negotiated, an X.25

LCN is assigned so that the originating node can multiplex data to the proper destination. Up to 4095 virtual circuits can be identified (LCN = 0 is used for X.25 signaling). The first 4 bits of the LCN were originally defined for use as a Logical Group Number (LGN). The LGN was intended for use as a method of bundling multiple logical X.25 channels together for X.25 virtual circuit routing, but it was never used. However, the concept of having a two-level hierarchy for virtual circuit identification is used for ATM.

- **Packet Type Identifier** For X.25 protocol messages, the 1-byte Packet Type Identifier field identifies the type of X.25 message. When user data is being sent, the Packet Type Identifier field is used to provide sequencing, acknowledgments, and X.25 fragmentation.

RFC 1356 sets the IP MTU for X.25 networks at 1600 bytes. However, most X.25 networks support only X.25 packet sizes of 128, 256, or 512 bytes. To accommodate the sending of a 1600-byte IP datagram over an X.25 network, X.25 fragments the IP datagram along boundaries that will fit on the X.25 network. A bit within the PTI field called the M-bit is used for fragment delimitation. Similar to the More Fragments flag in the IP header, the M-bit in the X.25 PLP header is set to 1 if more fragments follow, and set to 0 for the last fragment. Unlike IP fragmentation, X.25 fragmentation recovers from lost fragments.

LAPB Header and Trailer

The following fields are in the LAPB header and trailer:

- **Flag** As in PPP frames, the 1-byte Flag field is set to 0x7E to mark the beginning and end of the X.25 frame. Bit stuffing is used on synchronous links, and character stuffing is used on asynchronous links to prevent the occurrence of the FLAG character within the X.25 frame.
- **Address** A 1-byte field used to specify X.25 commands and responses.
- **Control** A 1-byte field that provides further qualifications of command and response frames, and also indicates the frame format and function. For X.25 protocol messages, the Control field provides send and receive sequence numbers.
- **Frame Check Sequence** (FCS) A 2-byte CRC used to check for errors in the LAPB frame.

Frame Relay

When packet-switching networks were first introduced, they were based on existing analog copper lines that experienced a high number of errors. X.25 was designed to compensate for these errors and provide connection-oriented reliable data transfer. In these days of high-grade digital fiber-optic lines, there is no need for the overhead associated with X.25. Frame Relay is a packet-switched technology similar to X.25, but without the added framing and processing overhead to provide guaranteed data transfer.

Unlike X.25, Frame Relay doesn't provide link-to-link reliability. If a frame in the Frame Relay network is corrupted in any way, it's silently discarded. Upper layer communication protocols such as TCP must detect and recover discarded frames.

A key advantage Frame Relay has over private-line facilities, such as T-Carrier, is that Frame Relay customers can be charged based on the amount of data transferred, instead of the distance between the endpoints. It is common, however, for the Frame Relay vendor to charge a fixed monthly cost. In either case Frame Relay is distance-insensitive. A local connection, such as a T-1 line, to the Frame Relay vendor's network is required. Frame Relay allows widely separated sites to exchange data without incurring long-haul telecommunications costs.

Frame Relay is a packet-switching technology defined in terms of a standardized interface between user devices (typically routers) and the switching equipment in the vendor's network (Frame Relay switches).

Frame Relay is similar to X.25 in the following ways:

- A packet-switching technology designed to send variable-sized packets.
- Designed for the transfer of LAN traffic (computer communication protocols such as TCP/IP).
- Provides a mechanism for multiplexing multiple logical connections (virtual circuits) over a single physical link.

However, Frame Relay differs from X.25 in the following ways:

- Frame Relay is an unreliable data transfer service. Frame Relay switches silently discard frames lost as a result of congestion or corruption.
- Frame Relay provides no flow control. However, Frame Relay does provide for basic congestion notification that can be used to notify upper-layer protocols to implement their own flow control.

Typical Frame Relay service providers currently only offer PVCs. The Frame Relay service provider establishes the PVC when the service is ordered. New specifications for an SVC version of Frame Relay use the ISDN signaling protocol as the mechanism for establishing the virtual circuit. This standard isn't widely used in production networks.

Frame Relay speeds range from 56 Kbps to 1.544 Mbps. The required throughput for a given link will determine the committed information rate (CIR). The CIR is the throughput guaranteed by the Frame Relay service provider. Most Frame Relay service providers allow a customer to transmit bursts above the CIR for short periods of time. Depending on congestion, the bursted traffic can be delivered by the Frame Relay network. However, traffic that exceeds the CIR is delivered on a best-effort basis only. This flexibility allows for network traffic spikes without having to drop frames.

Frame Relay Encapsulation

Frame Relay encapsulation of IP datagrams is based on HDLC, as RFC 2427 describes. Unlike X.25, Frame Relay encapsulation assumes that multiple protocols are sent over each Frame Relay virtual circuit. IP datagrams are encapsulated with the NLPID header set to 0xCC and a Frame Relay header and trailer. Figure 2-9 shows the Frame Relay encapsulation for IP datagrams.

> **More Info** HDLC, as the basis for Frame Relay encapsulation of IP datagrams, is described in RFC 2427, which can be found in the \RFC folder on the companion CD-ROM.

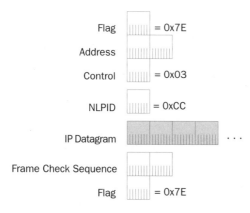

Figure 2-9. *Frame Relay encapsulation for IP datagrams, showing the Frame Relay header and trailer.*

The fields in the Frame Relay header and trailer are defined as follows:

- **Flag** As in PPP and X.25 frames, the Flag field is 1 byte long and is set to 0x7E to mark the beginning and end of the Frame Relay frame. Bit stuffing is used on synchronous links to prevent the occurrence of the FLAG character within the Frame Relay frame.

- **Address** The Address field is multiple bytes long, typically 2 bytes long, and contains the Frame Relay virtual circuit identifier called the Data Link Connection Identifier (DLCI) and congestion indicators. The Address field's structure is discussed in the "Frame Relay Address Field" section of this chapter.

- **Control** A 1-byte field set to 0x03 to indicate an Unnumbered Information (UI) frame.

- **NLPID** A 1-byte field set to 0xCC to indicate an IP datagram.

- **Frame Check Sequence** A 2-byte CRC used for bit-level integrity verification in the Frame Relay frame. If a Frame Relay frame fails integrity verification, it's silently discarded.

Frame Relay Address Field

The Frame Relay Address field can be 1, 2, 3, or 4 bytes long. Typical Frame Relay implementations use a 2-byte Address field, as shown in Figure 2-10.

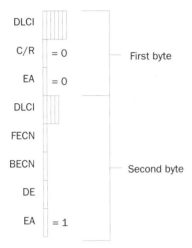

Figure 2-10. *A 2-byte Frame Relay Address field.*

The fields within the 2-byte Address field are defined as follows:

- **DLCI**   The first 6 bits of the first byte and the first 4 bits of the second byte comprise the 10-bit DLCI. The DLCI is used to identify the Frame Relay virtual circuit over which the Frame Relay frame is traveling. Like the X.25 LCN, the DLCI is only locally significant. Each Frame Relay switch changes the DLCI value as it forwards the Frame Relay frame. The devices at each end of a virtual circuit use a different DLCI value to identify the same virtual circuit. Table 2-1 lists the defined values for the DLCI.

Table 2-1. Defined Values for the Frame Relay DLCI

DLCI Value	Use
0	In-channel signaling
1-15	Reserved
16-991	Assigned to user connections
992-1022	Reserved
1023	In-channel signaling

- **Extended Address (EA)**   The last bit in each byte of the Address field is the EA bit. If this bit is set to 1, the current byte is the last byte in the Address field. For the 2-byte Address field, the value of the EA bit in the first byte of the Address field is 0, and the value of the EA bit in the second byte of the Address field is 1.

- **Command/Response (C/R)** The seventh bit in the first byte of the Address field is the C/R bit. It currently isn't used for Frame Relay operations, and is set to 0.

- **Forward Explicit Congestion Notification (FECN)** The fifth bit in the second byte of the Address field is the FECN bit. It is used to inform the destination Frame Relay node that congestion exists in the path from the source to the destination. The FECN bit is set to 0 by the source Frame Relay node, and set to 1 by a Frame Relay switch if it's experiencing congestion in the forward path. If the destination Frame Relay node receives a Frame Relay frame with the FECN bit set, the node can indicate the congestion condition to upper layer protocols that can implement receiver-side flow control. The interpretation of the FECN bit for IP traffic isn't defined.

- **Backward Explicit Congestion Notification (BECN)** The sixth bit in the second byte of the Address field is the BECN bit. The BECN bit is used to inform the destination Frame Relay node that congestion exists in the path from the destination to the source (in the opposite direction in which the frame was traveling). The BECN bit is set to 0 by the source Frame Relay node, and set to 1 by a Frame Relay switch if it's experiencing congestion in the reverse path. If the destination Frame Relay node receives a Frame Relay frame with the BECN bit set, the node can indicate the congestion condition to upper layer protocols that can implement sender-side flow control. The interpretation of the BECN bit for IP traffic isn't defined.

- **Discard Eligibility (DE)** The seventh bit in the second byte of the Address field is the DE bit. Frame Relay switches use the DE bit to decide which frames to discard during a period of congestion. Frame Relay switches consider the frames with the DE bit lower priority frames and discard them first. The initial Frame Relay switch sets the DE bit to 1 on a frame when a customer has exceeded the CIR for the virtual circuit.

The maximum-sized frame that can be sent across a Frame Relay network varies according to the Frame Relay provider. RFC 2427 requires all Frame Relay networks to support a minimum frame size of 262 bytes, and a maximum of 1600 bytes for IP datagrams, although maximum frame sizes of up to 4500 bytes are common.

ATM

ATM, or cell relay, is the latest innovation in broadband networking and is destined to eventually replace most existing WAN technologies. As with Frame Relay, ATM provides a connection-oriented, unreliable delivery service. ATM allows for the establishment of a connection between sites, but reliable communication is the responsibility of an upper layer protocol such as TCP.

ATM improves on the performance of Frame Relay. Instead of using variable-length frames, ATM takes a LAN traffic protocol data unit (PDU) such as an IP datagram and segments it into 48-byte segments. A 5-byte ATM header is added to each segment. The 53-byte ATM frames consisting of the segments of the IP datagram are sent over the ATM network, which the destination then reassembles. The fixed-length 53-byte ATM frame, known as an ATM cell, allows the performance of the ATM-switching network to be optimized.

ATM is available today as a PVC or an SVC through an ATM-switched network. ATM has been demonstrated at data rates up to 9.6 Gbps using Synchronous Optical Network (SONET), an international specification for fiber-optic communication. ATM is a scalable solution for data, voice, audio, fax, and video, and can accommodate all of these information types simultaneously. ATM combines the benefits of circuit switching (fixed-transit delay and guaranteed bandwidth) with the benefits of packet switching (efficiency for bursty traffic).

The ATM Cell

The ATM cell consists of a 5-byte ATM header and a 48-byte payload. The following are two types of ATM headers:

- **User network interface (UNI) header**   The ATM header that exists within a private network or between a customer site and a public ATM service provider.
- **Network-to-network interface (NNI) header**   The ATM header that exists within a public ATM service provider's network.

Figure 2-11 shows the ATM cell header's format at either a public or private UNI.

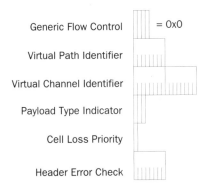

Generic Flow Control	= 0x0
Virtual Path Identifier	
Virtual Channel Identifier	
Payload Type Indicator	
Cell Loss Priority	
Header Error Check	

Figure 2-11. *The ATM header format that exists at the ATM UNI.*

The fields in the ATM header are defined as follows:

- **Generic Flow Control (GFC)**   A 4-bit field that was originally added to support the connection of ATM networks to shared access networks such as a Distributed Queue Dual Bus (DQDB) ring. The GFC field was designed to give the UNI 4 bits in which to negotiate multiplexing and flow control among cells of a single ATM virtual circuit. However, the use and exact values of the GFC field have not been standardized, so the value is always set to 0x0.

- **Virtual Path Identifier (VPI)** The identifier of the virtual path for this particular cell. VPIs for a particular ATM virtual circuit are discovered during the virtual-circuit setup process for SVCs, and are manually configured for PVCs. At the UNI, the VPI is 8 bits, allowing up to 256 different virtual paths. VPI 0 exists by default on all ATM equipment and is used for administrative purposes, such as signaling to create and delete dynamic ATM connections.

- **Virtual Channel Identifier (VCI)** The identifier of the virtual channel within the specified virtual path. Like VPIs, VCIs are dynamically allocated for SVC connections and manually configured for PVC connections. The VCI is 16 bits, allowing up to 65,536 different virtual channels for each virtual path. For each VPI, the ITU reserves VCIs 0–15, and the ATM Forum reserves VCIs 16–32. The reserved VCIs are used for signaling, operation and maintenance, and resource management.

The combination of VPI and VCI identifies the virtual circuit for a given ATM cell. The VPI/VCI combination is the ATM routing information that is used by ATM switches to forward the cell to its destination. The VPI/VCI combination acts as a local virtual-circuit identifier in the same way as an LCN in X.25 and the DLCI in Frame Relay.

- **Payload Type Indicator (PTI)** A 3-bit field consisting of the following fields:

  - **ATM Cell Type** The first bit of the PTI field is used as an indicator of the type of ATM cell. Set to 0 to indicate user data, and set to 1 to indicate operations, administration, and management (OA&M) data.

  - **Explicit Forward Congestion Indication (EFCI)** The second bit of the PTI field is used as an indicator of whether the cell experienced congestion in its journey from the source to the destination. The source sets the EFCI bit to 0. If an interim switch is experiencing congestion during the forwarding of the cell, the switch sets the bit to 1. Once set to 1, all other switches in the path leave this bit set at 1. Destination ATM endpoints can use the EFCI bit to implement receiver-side flow control mechanisms until cells with an EFCI bit set to 0 are received. The EFCI bit is similar in function to the FECN bit used in Frame Relay.

  - **AAL5 Segmentation Flag** Used in user ATM cells to indicate the last cell in a block for ATM Adaptation Layer 5 (AAL5). For non-user ATM cells, the third bit is used for OA&M functions. AAL5 is described in detail in the "AAL5" section of this chapter.

- **Cell Loss Priority (CLP)**   A 1-bit field that is used as a cell priority indicator. If set to 0, the cell is high priority and interim switches must make every effort to forward the cell successfully. If the CLP bit is set to 1, the interim switches can elect to discard the cell in congestion situations. The CLP bit is similar to the DE bit in Frame Relay. Setting the CLP bit to 1 can be done by the ATM endpoint upon creation, as a way to indicate a lower-priority cell, or at the ATM switch, if the cell is beyond the negotiated parameters of the virtual circuit (similar to bursting above the CIR in Frame Relay).

- **Header Error Check (HEC)**   A 1-byte field that allows an ATM switch or ATM Endpoint to correct a single-bit error, or to detect multi-bit errors in the first 4 bytes of the ATM header. Multi-bit errored cells are silently discarded. Note that the HEC checks only the ATM header and not the ATM payload. Checking the payload for errors is the responsibility of upper layer protocols.

Figure 2-12 shows the ATM cell header format at the public NNI.

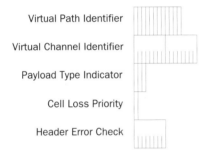

Virtual Path Identifier

Virtual Channel Identifier

Payload Type Indicator

Cell Loss Priority

Header Error Check

Figure 2-12. *The ATM header format that exists at the ATM NNI.*

The only differences between the UNI and NNI headers are as follows:

- **No GFC field**   ATM switches in an ATM service provider don't need a way to negotiate the multiplexing from various types of shared-access user connections.

- **VPI is now 12 bits long**   This allows up to 4096 virtual paths per transmission path. With an extended VPI, ATM service providers have more flexibility to perform virtual path switching and to create a backbone architecture to support trunk lines in the voice telephone system.

ATM Architecture

The ATM architectural model (known as the B-ISDN/ATM Model) has three main layers, as shown in Figure 2-13.

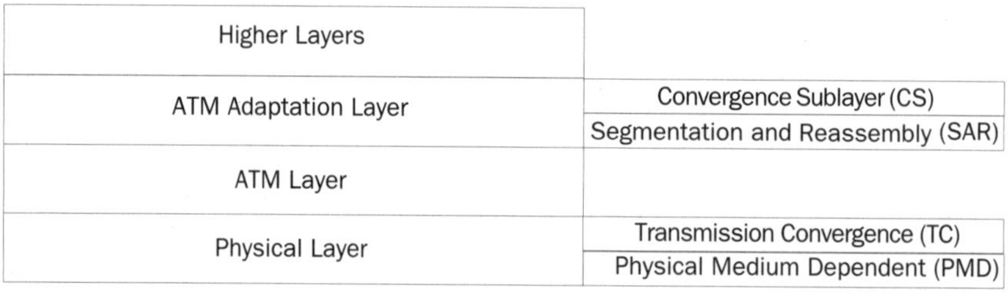

Higher Layers	
ATM Adaptation Layer	Convergence Sublayer (CS)
	Segmentation and Reassembly (SAR)
ATM Layer	
Physical Layer	Transmission Convergence (TC)
	Physical Medium Dependent (PMD)

Figure 2-13. *The ATM architectural model, showing the three main layers and their sublayers.*

Physical Layer

The Physical Layer provides for the transmission and reception of ATM cells across a physical medium between two ATM devices. The Physical Layer is subdivided into a Physical Medium Dependent (PMD) sublayer and Transmission Convergence (TC) sublayer.

The PMD sublayer is responsible for the transmission and reception of individual bits on a physical medium. These responsibilities encompass bit-timing, signal-encoding, interfacing with the physical medium, and the physical medium itself. ATM doesn't rely on any specific bit rate, encoding scheme, or medium. Various specifications for ATM exist for coaxial cable, shielded and unshielded twisted pair wire, and optical fiber at speeds ranging from 64 Kbps through 9.6 Gbps.

The TC sublayer acts as a converter between the bit stream at the PMD sublayer and ATM cells. When transmitting, the TC sublayer maps ATM cells onto the format of the PMD sublayer (such as DS-3 or SONET frames). Because a continuous stream of bytes is required, idle cells occupy portions in the ATM cell stream that are not used. The receiver silently discards idle cells. Idle cells are never passed to the ATM layer for processing. The TC sublayer also is responsible for generation and verification of the HEC field for each cell, and for determining ATM cell delineation (where the ATM cells begin and end).

ATM Layer

The ATM Layer provides cell multiplexing, demultiplexing, and VPI/VCI routing functions. In addition, the ATM Layer is responsible for supervising the cell flow to ensure that all connections remain within their negotiated cell throughput limits. The ATM Layer can take corrective action so that those connections operating outside their negotiated parameters don't affect those connections that are obeying their negotiated connection parameters. Additionally, the ATM Layer ensures that the cell sequence from any source is maintained.

The ATM Layer multiplexes/demultiplexes, routes ATM cells, and ensures their sequence from end to end. However, if a switch drops a cell because of congestion or corruption, it's not the ATM Layer's responsibility to correct the dropped cell through retransmission or to notify other layers of the dropped cell. Layers above the ATM Layer must sense the lost cell and decide whether to correct for its loss.

ATM Adaptation Layer

The ATM Adaptation Layer (AAL) is responsible for the creation and reception of 48-byte payloads via the ATM Layer on behalf of different types of applications. The AAL Layer is subdivided between the Convergence sublayer (CS) and the Segmentation and Reassembly (SAR) sublayer. ATM adaptation is necessary to interface the cell-based technology at the ATM Layer, to the bit-stream technology of digital devices (such as telephones and video cameras), and the packet-stream technology of modern data networks (such as Frame Relay or LAN protocols including TCP/IP).

Convergence Sublayer

The CS is the last place that an application block of data (also known as a PDU) has its original form before being handed to the SAR sublayer for division into 48-byte ATM payloads. The CS is responsible for an encapsulation that allows the application data block to be distinguished and handed to the destination application. The CS is further subdivided into two sublayers: the Common Part CS (CPCS), which must be implemented, and the Service Specific CS (SSCS), which might be implemented depending on the actual service. If the SSCS is not implemented, it won't add headers to the data being sent.

SAR Sublayer

On the sending side, the SAR sublayer takes the block of data from the CS (hereafter known as the CPCS PDU), and divides it into 48-byte segments. Each segment is then handed to the ATM Layer for final ATM encapsulation. On the receiving side, the SAR sublayer receives each ATM cell and reassembles the CPCS PDU. The completed CPCS PDU is then handed up to the CS for processing.

To provide a standard mechanism for the CPCS and SAR sublayers, the ITU-T has created a series of ATM Adaptation Layers:

- **AAL1**   Designed for isochronous (time-dependent), constant bit rate, connection-oriented applications, and is used to provide circuit emulation.
- **AAL2**   Designed for isochronous, variable bit rate, connection-oriented applications, and is used for compressed voice or video.
- **AAL3/4**   Designed for non-isochronous, variable bit rate, connection-oriented or connectionless applications, and is used for X.25 or LAN traffic.
- **AAL5**   Designed for non-isochronous, variable bit rate, connection-oriented or connectionless applications. It's typically used for LAN traffic such as IP datagrams because its overhead is lower than that of AAL 3/4.

AAL5

AAL5 provides a way for non-isochronous, variable bit rate, connectionless applications to send and receive data. The data communications industry developed AAL5 as a straight-forward framing at the CPCS that tends to behave like existing LAN technologies such as Ethernet. AAL5 is the AAL of choice when sending connection-oriented (Frame Relay) or connectionless (IP or IPX) LAN protocol traffic over an ATM network.

AAL5 Framing

Figure 2-14 shows the framing that occurs at AAL5.

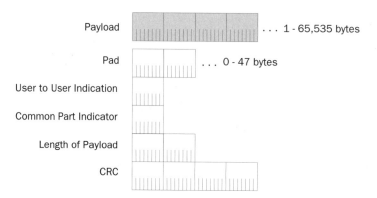

Figure 2-14. *AAL5 framing, showing the payload and the AAL5 trailer.*

The fields in the AAL5 frame are defined as follows:

- **Payload**   The block of data that an application sends. The size can vary from 1 byte to 65,535 bytes.

- **Pad**   Of variable length (0–47 bytes). The Pad field is present to make the entire CPCS PDU an integral number of 48-byte units.

- **User To User Indication**   A 1-byte field that is used to transfer information between AAL users. The exact use of this byte isn't defined and is left to the implementation.

- **Common Part Indicator**   A 1-byte field that is currently used only for alignment processes so that the non-padded portion of the AAL5 trailer is on a 64-bit boundary.

- **Length Of Payload**   A 2-byte field used to indicate the length in bytes of the Payload field so that the Pad field can be discarded by the receiver.

- **CRC**   A 4-byte CRC that provides bit-level integrity services on the entire CPCS PDU. The AAL5 CRC uses the same checksum algorithm as 802.x network technologies such as Ethernet and Token Ring.

The SAR sublayer for AAL5 segments the CPCS PDU along 48-byte boundaries and passes the segments to the ATM Layer for encapsulation with an ATM header. On the receiving side, the SAR sublayer reassembles the incoming 48-byte ATM payloads and passes the result to the CPCS. The SAR uses the AAL5 Segmentation Flag field, the third bit in the Payload Type Indicator (PTI) field, to indicate when the last 48-byte unit in a CPCS PDU is sent. On the receiving side, when the ATM cell is received with the AAL5 Segmentation Flag field set, the ATM Layer indicates this to AAL5 so that analysis of the full CPCS PDU can begin.

Sending an IP Datagram Over an ATM Network

The method of sending IP datagrams over an ATM network using AAL5 is known as classical IP over ATM, and is described in RFCs 1577 and 1626. To ensure compatibility with IP datagrams sent over a Switched Multimegabit Data Service (SMDS) network, another cell-based WAN technology, IP datagrams have a maximum size of 9180 bytes. Figure 2-15 shows IP datagram encapsulation using AAL5.

More Info   RFCs 1577 and 1626 describe classical IP over ATM. These can be found in the \RFC folder on the companion CD-ROM.

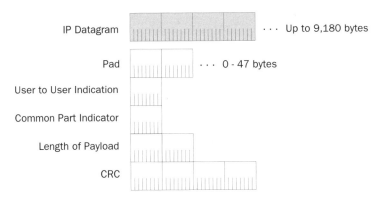

Figure 2-15. *IP Datagram encapsulation, using AAL5.*

At the SAR sublayer, the CPCS PDU is segmented into 48-byte units that become the ATM payloads for a stream of ATM cells. When the last cell in the CPCS PDU is sent, the AAL5 Segmentation Flag field is set to 1. When the last cell is received, the receiver uses the CRC to check the validity of the bits in the CPCS PDU. If the CRC is valid, the Length field is used to discard the Pad field. The AAL trailer is stripped, and the end result is the originally transmitted IP datagram that is then passed to the IP layer for processing.

For a given ATM virtual circuit, IP datagrams must be sent one at a time. The cells of multiple IP datagrams can't be mixed on the same virtual circuit. The ATM header contains no information to signify which cells belong to which CPCS PDU. ATM segmentation differs from IP fragmentation in this regard. With IP fragmentation, the Identification field serves to group all the fragments of the original IP datagram together. An IP router can send the fragments of different IP packets alternately without a reconstruction issue on the receiving side. With ATM segmentation, there is no fragment ID field or equivalent that can be used to differentiate CPCS PDUs.

Example of Sending an IP Datagram

Figure 2-16 shows an example of sending a 128-byte IP datagram across an ATM network using AAL5.

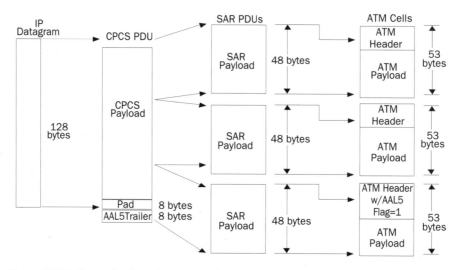

Figure 2-16. *Example of sending an IP datagram over ATM, using AAL5 encapsulation.*

The AAL5 trailer with an 8-byte Pad field is added to the IP datagram. The 8 bytes of the Pad field make the entire AAL5 CPCS PDU 144 bytes, an integral multiple of 48. The resulting AAL5 CPCS PDU is then segmented into three 48-byte segments. Each 48-byte segment becomes the payload of an ATM cell sent in sequence to the destination ATM endpoint on the virtual circuit. When the last segment is sent, the AAL5 Segmentation Flag field is set to 1.

Note   ATM traffic captured with Windows 2000 Network Monitor will not display the individual ATM cells or the ATM header. The ATM header displayed with Network Monitor contains a simulated source and destination MAC address and the VPI and VCI fields for the virtual circuit.

Multiprotocol Encapsulation with AAL5

When multiple protocols are sent over the same ATM virtual circuit, a protocol identifier is needed to differentiate the various Network Layer protocols.

More Info   Multiprotocol encapsulation over ATM is described in RFC 1483, which can be found in the \RFC folder on the companion CD-ROM.

To add a protocol identifier to the CPCS PDU, the Sub-Network Access Protocol (SNAP) method used by IEEE 802.x networks is used. Figure 2-17 shows multiprotocol encapsulation over AAL5.

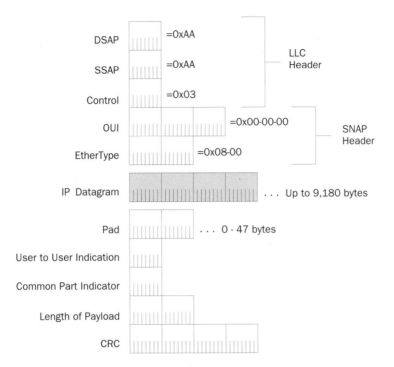

Figure 2-17. *Multiprotocol encapsulation for AAL5, using the LLC and SNAP headers.*

As described in Chapter 1, "Local Area Network (LAN) Technologies," the SNAP header consists of a Logical Link Control (LLC) header and a SNAP header. Within the LLC header, the Destination Service Access Point (DSAP) is set to 0xAA, the Source Service Access Point (SSAP) is set to 0xAA, and the Control field is set to 0x03. Within the SNAP header, the Organization Unique Identifier (OUI) is set to 00-00-00 and the EtherType field is set to 0x08-00 for IP.

When the ATM virtual circuit is created, both ATM endpoints negotiate the use of either single protocol or multiprotocol AAL5 encapsulation.

Summary

Typical WAN technology encapsulations used by Windows 2000 provide delimitation, addressing, protocol identification, and bit-level integrity services. IP datagrams and ARP messages sent over point-to-point WAN links can be encapsulated using SLIP, PPP, or MP. IP datagrams and ARP messages sent over NBMA links such as X.25, Frame Relay, or ATM use the appropriate single or multiprotocol encapsulation.

Chapter 3
Address Resolution Protocol (ARP)

To successfully troubleshoot problems forwarding IP datagrams on a local area network (LAN) link, it is important to understand how ARP is used to resolve a node's IP address to its corresponding Network Interface Layer address. Microsoft Windows 2000 TCP/IP supports ARP for address resolution and duplicate IP address detection. The Windows 2000 Routing and Remote service uses a variation of ARP called proxy ARP to forward IP datagrams between remote access clients and the network attached to the remote access server.

Overview of ARP

ARP is the protocol used by shared access, broadcast-based networking technologies such as Ethernet and Token Ring. This protocol is used to resolve the forwarding IP address of a node to its corresponding media access control (MAC) address. The MAC address also is known as the physical, hardware, or network adapter address. The resolved MAC address becomes the destination MAC address in the Ethernet or Token Ring header to which an IP datagram is addressed when it's sent on the medium. ARP resolves an Internet Layer address (an Internet Protocol (IP) address) to a Network Interface Layer address (MAC address).

> **More Info** ARP is described in RFC 826, which can be found in the \RFC folder on the companion CD-ROM.

The forwarding IP address isn't necessarily the same as the destination IP address of the IP datagram. As is discussed in detail in Chapter 6, "Internet Protocol (IP) Routing," the result of the route determination process for every outgoing IP datagram is an interface and a forwarding IP address. For direct deliveries to destinations on the same subnet, the forwarding IP address is the datagram's destination IP address. For indirect deliveries to remote destinations, the forwarding IP address is the IP address of a router on the same subnet as the forwarding host.

IP was designed to be independent of any specific Network Interface Layer technology. Therefore, there's no way to determine the destination Network Interface Layer address from the forwarding IP address. For example, Ethernet and Token Ring MAC addresses are 6 bytes long, and IP addresses are 4 bytes long. During the manufacturing process, the MAC address is assigned to the adapter. A network administrator assigns the IP address. Because there's no correlation between the assignment of these two addresses for a given IP node, it's impossible to derive one address from the other. ARP is a broadcast-based, request-reply protocol that provides a dynamic-resolution facility to map forwarding IP addresses to their corresponding MAC addresses.

ARP consists of the following two messages:

- The forwarding node uses the ARP Request message to request the MAC address for a specific forwarding IP address. The ARP Request is a MAC-level broadcast frame intended to reach all the nodes on the physical network segment to which the interface sending the ARP Request is attached. The node sending the ARP Request is known as the ARP requester.

- The ARP Reply message is used to reply to the ARP requester. The node whose IP address matches the requested IP address in the ARP Request message sends the ARP Reply. The ARP Reply is a unicast MAC frame sent to the destination MAC address of the ARP requester. The node sending the ARP Reply is known as the ARP responder.

Because the ARP Request is a MAC-level broadcast packet, all forwarding IP addresses to be resolved must be directly reachable (on the same subnet) from the interface used to send the ARP Request. For proper routing table entries, this is always the case. If a routing table entry contains an invalid forwarding IP address where that address isn't directly reachable for the interface, ARP will fail to resolve the forwarding IP address.

All nodes within the same broadcast domain receive the ARP Request. A broadcast domain is a portion of a network over which a broadcast frame is propagated. Hubs, bridges, and, more recently, Layer 2 switches propagate the ARP Request. However, IP routers or Layer 3 switches don't propagate ARP frames.

The ARP Cache

As is common in many TCP/IP implementations, Windows 2000 TCP/IP maintains a RAM-based table of IP and MAC address mappings known as the ARP cache. When an ARP exchange is complete (both the ARP Request and the ARP Reply are sent and received), both the ARP requester and the ARP responder have each other's IP address to MAC address mappings in their ARP caches. Subsequent packets forwarded to the previously resolved IP addresses use the ARP cache entry's MAC address. The ARP cache is always checked before an ARP Request is sent. There is a separate ARP cache for each IP interface.

After the MAC address for a forwarding IP address is determined using an ARP Request-ARP Reply exchange, the resolved MAC address is used as the destination MAC address for subsequent packets. If the node whose IP address has been resolved fails, the ARP requester node will continue to use its ARP cache entry and send packets on the medium to the resolved MAC address. Because the resolved MAC address corresponds to a network adapter that's no longer present on the network, all of the network segment's nodes ignore the frame. Because the forwarding IP address was mapped to a MAC address with the ARP cache entry, and the frame was sent on the medium, IP and ARP on the sending node consider the IP datagram to be successfully delivered.

This condition is known as a network black hole; packets sent on the network are dropped and the sender or forwarder is unaware of the condition. The user at the ARP requester computer won't notice this condition until TCP connections or other types of session-oriented traffic begin to time out. This particular type of network black hole will persist as long as the entry for the mapping remains in the ARP cache. After the entry is removed, an ARP Request-ARP Reply exchange is attempted again. Because the failed node won't respond to the ARP Request, the lack of an ARP Reply can be used to indicate an unsuccessful delivery of IP packets using the forwarding IP address.

By default, ARP cache entries in Windows 2000 persist for only 2 minutes. If the ARP cache entry is used within 2 minutes, it's given additional time in 2-minute increments, up to a maximum lifetime of 10 minutes. After a maximum time of 10 minutes, the ARP cache entry is removed and must be resolved through another ARP Request-ARP Reply exchange. The time-out of ARP cache entries is configurable with the ArpCacheLife and ArpCacheMinReferencedLife registry settings.

ArpCacheLife

```
Location: HKEY_LOCAL_MACHINE\SYSTEM\CurrentControlSet\Services\Tcpip\Parameters
Data type: REG_DWORD
Valid range: 0-0xFFFFFFFF
Default value: 120
Present by default: No
```

ArpCacheLife sets the number of seconds that an unused ARP cache entry is kept in the ARP cache. The default value of ArpCacheLife is 120 seconds (2 minutes).

ArpCacheMinReferencedLife

```
Location: HKEY_LOCAL_MACHINE\SYSTEM\CurrentControlSet\Services\Tcpip\Parameters
Data type: REG_DWORD
Valid range: 0-0xFFFFFFFF
Default value: 600
Present by default: No
```

ArpCacheMinReferencedLife sets the number of seconds that a used ARP cache entry persists in the ARP cache. The default value of ArpCacheMinReferencedLife is 600 seconds (10 minutes). The ArpCacheMinReferencedLife and ArpCacheLife registry settings are used in the following ways:

- If ArpCacheLife is greater than or equal to ArpCacheMinReferencedLife, both used and unused ARP cache entries persist for ArpCacheLife seconds.

- If ArpCacheLife is less than ArpCacheMinReferencedLife, unused ARP cache entries expire in ArpCacheLife seconds, and used entries expire in ArpCacheMinReferencedLife seconds.

In addition, Microsoft Windows 2000 TCP/IP allows the use of static ARP cache entries. Static ARP cache entries can be added through the use of the ARP utility using the "-s" command-line option. Static ARP cache entries don't time out of the ARP cache. However, static ARP cache entries are stored in RAM and must be added each time TCP/IP is initialized.

While a forwarding IP address is being resolved with ARP, Microsoft Windows 2000 ARP will store only one IP datagram for that forwarding IP address. If multiple datagrams are sent to the same forwarding IP address without pause, it's possible that some datagrams might be dropped before the ARP exchange completes. This isn't a problem for TCP connection data, but User Datagram Protocol (UDP) messages might experience packet loss because of this behavior. In this case, use the *SendArp()* function to create the ARP cache entry prior to sending packets.

Updating the MAC Address

The default behavior of Windows 2000 TCP/IP is to update the ARP cache entry with additional time, in 2-minute increments, while it's in use. Another way of updating the ARP cache entry is through the receipt of an ARP Request sent by the node with the ARP cache entry's IP address. When an ARP Request that was sent by an IP node corresponding to an existing entry in the ARP cache is received, update the ARP cache entry with the received ARP Request's MAC address.

When a network black hole is caused by a failed interface, and when the interface is replaced, the first ARP Request frame sent on that interface will contain the interface's new MAC address. Upon receipt of that ARP Request, all of the network segment's nodes that have an ARP cache entry for that node's IP address will update the ARP cache entry with the new MAC address. The network black hole is removed by the resetting of ARP cache entries when the ARP Request is sent.

Windows 2000 ARP Registry Settings

By default, Windows 2000 uses the Ethernet II encapsulation described in Chapter 1, "Local Area Network (LAN) Technologies," when sending both IP and ARP frames. Windows 2000 will receive both Ethernet II and IEEE 802.3 SubNetwork Access Protocol (SNAP)-encapsulated frames, but, by default, it will respond only with Ethernet II-encapsulated frames. To send IEEE 802.3 SNAP-encapsulated IP and ARP frames, use the ArpUseEther-SNAP registry setting.

ArpUseEtherSNAP

```
Location: HKEY_LOCAL_MACHINE\SYSTEM\CurrentControlSet\Services\Tcpip\Parameters
Data type: REG_DWORD
Valid range: 0-1
Default value: 0
Present by default: No
```

ArpUseEtherSNAP either enables (=1) or disables (=0) the use of the IEEE 802.3 SNAP frame format when sending IP and ARP frames. ArpUseEtherSNAP is disabled by default, meaning that IP and ARP frames are sent with Ethernet II encapsulation. Regardless of the ArpUseEtherSNAP setting, both types of frame formats are received.

For Token Ring, the ArpTRSingleRoute and ArpAlwaysSourceRoute provide control over broadcast ARP Requests in a Token Ring source-routed environment.

ArpTRSingleRoute

```
Location: HKEY_LOCAL_MACHINE\SYSTEM\CurrentControlSet\Services\Tcpip\Parameters
Data type: REG_DWORD
Valid range: 0-1
Default value: 0
Present by default: No
```

ArpTRSingleRoute either disables (=0) or enables (=1) the sending of ARP Requests as single-route broadcasts. When disabled, the default ARP Requests are sent as all-routes broadcasts.

A Token Ring source-routed environment is a series of rings connected by source-routing bridges. The rings can be connected so that there are multiple paths to any given node. While this creates fault tolerance for the source-routing bridges, it also causes a problem for all-routes broadcast frames. An all-routes broadcast frame travels all possible paths. If there are five different paths between a node sending an all-routes broadcast frame and a ring, five copies of that all-routes broadcast frame appear on that ring.

To prevent this problem, nodes are configured to send single-route broadcast frames, and source-routing bridges are configured to either propagate single-route or all-routes broadcast frames. With proper design, a network administrator can define a single path over which single-route broadcast traffic travels even though multiple paths exist for all-routes broadcast traffic. Using single-route broadcasts, a Token Ring environment can maintain its fault tolerance while avoiding the duplication of broadcast traffic.

ArpAlwaysSourceRoute

```
Location: HKEY_LOCAL_MACHINE\SYSTEM\CurrentControlSet\Services\Tcpip\Parameters
Data type: REG_DWORD
Valid range: 0-1 or not present
Default value: Not present
Present by default: No
```

ArpAlwaysSourceRoute either disables (=0) or enables (=1) the use of source routing on broadcast ARP Requests. When the ArpAlwaysSourceRoute setting isn't present in the registry, the default setting causes the ARP to send the ARP Request without source-routing first. If no reply is received, ARP sends the ARP Request with source routing.

ARP Frame Structure

ARP frames use the EtherType of 0x08-06. ARP isn't a client protocol of IP, and ARP frames don't contain an IP header. Thus, ARP is useful only for resolving MAC addresses for IP addresses that are on the same physical network segment, the boundaries of which are defined by IP routers. IP routers will never forward an ARP Request or ARP Reply frame.

As RFC 826 describes, an ARP frame's structure suggests that ARP could be used for MAC address resolution for protocols other than IP. However, in practice, IP is the only protocol that uses the ARP frame format. Figure 3-1 shows the structure of the ARP frame.

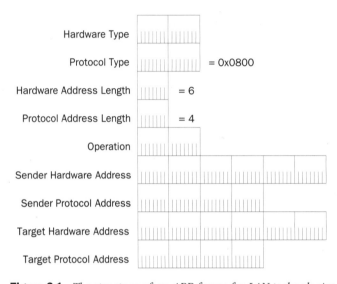

Figure 3-1. *The structure of an ARP frame for LAN technologies.*

More Info ARP as a potential MAC address resolution for non-IP protocols is discussed in RFC 826, which can be found in the \RFC folder on the companion CD-ROM.

The fields in the ARP header are defined as follows:

- **Hardware Type** A 2-byte field that indicates the type of hardware being used at the Data Link Layer. Table 3-1 lists some commonly used ARP Hardware Type values. Upon receipt of an ARP frame, an IP node verifies that the Hardware Type of the ARP frame matches the Hardware Type of the interface on which the ARP frame was received. If it doesn't match, the frame is silently discarded. For a complete list of ARP Hardware Type values, see *http://www.isi.edu/in-notes/iana/assignments/arp-parameters*.

Table 3-1. ARP Hardware Type Values

Hardware Type Value	Data Link Layer Technology
1 (0x00-01)	Ethernet (10 Mbps)
6 (0x00-06)	IEEE 802 Networks (Token Ring)
15 (0x00-0F)	Frame Relay
16 (0x00-10)	Asynchronous Transfer Mode

- **Protocol Type**   A 2-byte field that indicates the protocol for which ARP is providing address resolution. The ARP Protocol Type field uses the same values as the Ethernet II EtherType field. For IP address resolution, the Protocol Type field is set to the EtherType for IP, 0x0800. Upon receipt of an ARP frame, an IP node verifies that the ARP Protocol Type is set to 0x0800. If it's not set to 0x0800, the frame is silently discarded.

- **Hardware Address Length**   A 1-byte field that indicates the length in bytes of the hardware address in the Sender Hardware Address and Target Hardware Address fields. For Ethernet and Token Ring, the Hardware Address Length field is set to 6. For Frame Relay, the Hardware Address Length typically is set to 2 (for the commonly used 2-byte Frame Relay Address field).

- **Protocol Address Length**   A 1-byte field that indicates the length in bytes of the protocol address in the Sender Protocol Address and Target Protocol Address fields. For the IP protocol, the length of IP addresses is 4 bytes.

- **Operation (Opcode)**   A 2-byte field that indicates the type of ARP frame. Table 3-2 lists the commonly used ARP Operation values. For a complete list of ARP Operation values, see *http://www.isi.edu/in-notes/iana/assignments/arp-parameters*.

Table 3-2. ARP Operation Values

Operation Value	Type of ARP Frame
1	ARP Request
2	ARP Reply
8	Inverse ARP Request
9	Inverse ARP Reply

- **Sender Hardware Address (SHA)**   A field that is the length of the value of the Hardware Address Length field and contains the hardware or Data Link Layer address of the ARP frame's sender. For Ethernet and Token Ring, the SHA field contains the MAC address of the node sending the ARP frame.

- **Sender Protocol Address (SPA)**   A field that is the length of the value of the Protocol Address Length field and contains the protocol address of the ARP frame's sender. For IP, the SPA field contains the IP address of the node sending the ARP frame.

- **Target Hardware Address (THA)** A field that is the length of the value of the Hardware Address Length field and contains the hardware or Data Link Layer address of the ARP frame's target (destination). For Ethernet and Token Ring, the THA field is set to 0x00-00-00-00-00-00 for ARP Request frames, and it's set to the MAC address of the ARP requester for ARP Reply frames.
- **Target Protocol Address (TPA)** A field that is the length of the value of the Protocol Address Length field and contains the protocol address of the ARP frame's target (destination). For IP, the TPA field is set to the IP address being resolved in the ARP Request frame, and it's set to the IP address of the ARP requester in the ARP Reply frame.

ARP Request and ARP Reply Example

The ARP Request and ARP Reply exchange contains all the information for the ARP requester to determine the IP address and MAC address of the ARP responder, and for the ARP responder to determine the IP address and MAC address of the ARP requester. Figure 3-2 shows an ARP Request and ARP Reply exchange.

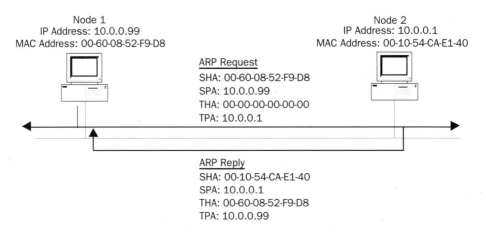

Figure 3-2. *The resolution of Node 2's MAC address by Node 1, using an exchange of ARP Request and ARP Reply frames.*

Node 1, with the IP address of 10.0.0.99 and the MAC address of 0x00-60-08-52-F9-D8, needs to forward an IP datagram to Node 2 at the IP address of 10.0.0.1. Based on information in Node 1's routing table, the forwarding IP address to reach Node 2 is 10.0.0.1, using the Ethernet interface. Node 1 constructs an ARP Request frame and sends it as a MAC-level broadcast using the Ethernet interface.

The following Network Monitor trace (Capture 03-01 in the \Captures folder on the companion CD-ROM) is for the ARP Request frame sent by Node 1.

```
+ Frame: Base frame properties
  ETHERNET: ETYPE = 0x0806 : Protocol = ARP:  Address Resolution Protocol
    + ETHERNET: Destination address : FFFFFFFFFFFF
    + ETHERNET: Source address : 00600852F9D8
      ETHERNET: Frame Length : 42 (0x002A)
      ETHERNET: Ethernet Type : 0x0806 (ARP:  Address Resolution Protocol)
      ETHERNET: Ethernet Data: Number of data bytes remaining = 28 (0x001C)
  ARP_RARP: ARP: Request, Target IP: 10.0.0.1
      ARP_RARP: Hardware Type = Ethernet (10Mb)
      ARP_RARP: Protocol Type = 2048 (0x800)
      ARP_RARP: Hardware Address Length = 6 (0x6)
      ARP_RARP: Protocol Address Length = 4 (0x4)
      ARP_RARP: Opcode = Request
      ARP_RARP: Sender's Hardware Address = 00600852F9D8
      ARP_RARP: Sender's Protocol Address = 10.0.0.99
      ARP_RARP: Target's Hardware Address = 000000000000
      ARP_RARP: Target's Protocol Address = 10.0.0.1
```

The known quantity—the IP address of 10.0.01—is set to the Target Protocol Address field. The unknown quantity—the hardware address of 10.0.0.1—is the Target Hardware Address field in the ARP Request frame, which is set to 000000000000. Included in the ARP Request are the IP and MAC addresses of Node 1 so that Node 2 can add an entry for Node 1 to its own ARP cache.

Upon receipt of the ARP Request frame at Node 2, the node checks the values of the ARP Hardware Type and Protocol Type fields. Node 2 then examines its own ARP cache for an entry matching the SPA. If an entry exists, Node 2 updates the MAC address of the ARP cache entry with the value stored in the SHA. For our example purposes, no entry for 10.0.0.99 exists.

Node 2 then examines the value of the TPA. Because the TPA is the same as Node 2's IP address, Node 2 adds an ARP cache entry consisting of [SPA, SHA] to its ARP cache. It then checks the ARP Operation field. Because the received ARP frame is an ARP Request, Node 2 constructs an ARP Reply to send back to Node 1.

The following Network Monitor trace (Capture 03-01 in the \Captures folder on the companion CD-ROM) is for the ARP Reply frame sent by Node 2.

```
+ Frame: Base frame properties
  ETHERNET: ETYPE = 0x0806 : Protocol = ARP:  Address Resolution Protocol
    + ETHERNET: Destination address : 00600852F9D8
    + ETHERNET: Source address : 001054CAE140
      ETHERNET: Frame Length : 60 (0x003C)
      ETHERNET: Ethernet Type : 0x0806 (ARP:  Address Resolution Protocol)
      ETHERNET: Ethernet Data: Number of data bytes remaining = 46 (0x002E)
  ARP_RARP: ARP: Reply, Target IP: 10.0.0.99 Target Hdwr Addr: 00600852F9D8
```

```
ARP_RARP: Hardware Type = Ethernet (10Mb)
ARP_RARP: Protocol Type = 2048 (0x800)
ARP_RARP: Hardware Address Length = 6 (0x6)
ARP_RARP: Protocol Address Length = 4 (0x4)
ARP_RARP: Opcode = Reply
ARP_RARP: Sender's Hardware Address = 001054CAE140
ARP_RARP: Sender's Protocol Address = 10.0.0.1
ARP_RARP: Target's Hardware Address = 00600852F9D8
ARP_RARP: Target's Protocol Address = 10.0.0.99
ARP_RARP: Frame Padding
```

In the ARP Reply, all quantities are known and the frame is addressed at the MAC level using Node 1's unicast MAC address. The quantity that Node 1 needs—Node 2's MAC address—is the SHA field's value.

Upon receipt of the ARP Reply frame, Node 1 checks the values of the ARP Hardware Type and Protocol Type fields. Node 1 then examines its own ARP cache for an entry matching the SPA. No entry exists; otherwise, an ARP Request would not have been sent. Node 1 then examines the TPA's value. Because the TPA is the same as Node 1's IP address, Node 1 adds an ARP cache entry consisting of [SPA, SHA] to its ARP cache. Node 1 then checks the ARP Operation field. Because the received ARP frame is an ARP Reply, the ARP frame is discarded.

Frame Padding and Ethernet

Notice that the ARP frames of Network Monitor trace contain a Frame Padding field. This Frame Padding field isn't an ARP field, but the consequence of sending an ARP frame on an Ethernet network. As discussed in Chapter 1, "Local Area Network (LAN) Technologies," Ethernet payloads using the Ethernet II encapsulation must be a minimum length of 46 bytes to adhere to the minimum Ethernet frame size. The ARP frame is only 28 bytes long. Therefore, to send the ARP frame on an Ethernet network, the ARP frame must be padded with 18 padding bytes.

Tip When using Network Monitor, you might notice that sometimes the Frame Padding field doesn't appear on either the ARP Request or the ARP Reply frames. Does this mean that the ARP frame was sent as a runt—an Ethernet frame with a length below the minimum frame size? No. The answer to the mystery lies in the implementation of Network Monitor within Windows 2000. Network Monitor receives frames by acting as a Network Driver Interface Specification (NDIS) protocol. When any frame is sent or received, Network Monitor receives a copy. However, when frames are sent, Network Monitor receives a copy of the frame before the frame padding is added. When the frame is received, Network Monitor receives a full copy of the frame. Therefore, you won't see a Frame Padding field on an ARP frame if it was captured on the node sending the ARP frame. The example Network Monitor trace given in this chapter was taken on Node 1. Therefore, the frame padding is only seen on the ARP Reply frame.

Gratuitous ARP and Duplicate IP Address Detection

ARP also is used to provide duplicate IP address detection through the transmission of ARP Requests known as gratuitous ARPs. A gratuitous ARP is an ARP Request for a node's own IP address. In the gratuitous ARP, the SPA and the TPA are set to the same IP address.

If a node sends an ARP Request for its own IP address and no ARP Reply frames are received, the node can assume that its assigned IP address isn't being used by other nodes. If a node sends an ARP Request for its own IP address and an ARP Reply frame is received, the node can determine that its assigned IP address is already being used by another node.

The ArpRetryCount registry setting controls the number of gratuitous ARPs that are sent.

ArpRetryCount

```
Location: HKEY_LOCAL_MACHINE\SYSTEM\CurrentControlSet\Services\Tcpip\Parameters
Data type: REG_DWORD
Valid range: 1-3
Default value: 3
Present by default: No
```

ArpRetryCount sets the number of times that a gratuitous ARP is sent when initializing IP for a specific IP address. If no ARP Reply is received after sending ArpRetryCount gratuitous ARPs, IP assumes the IP address is unique on the network segment.

Note   The gratuitous ARP attempts to detect the use of a duplicate IP address by a node on the same network segment. Because ARP frames aren't propagated by routers, a gratuitous ARP won't detect an IP address conflict between two nodes that are located on different network segments.

IP Address Conflict Detection

In an IP address conflict, the node that is already successfully configured with the IP address is known as the defending node. The node that is sending the gratuitous ARP is known as the offending node. Based on the ARP Reply, the offending node can determine the defending node's MAC address.

On the Offending Node

If the offending node is a Windows 2000 computer manually configured with a conflicting IP address, the receipt of the ARP Reply to the gratuitous ARP will prevent TCP/IP from initializing using the conflicting address. An error message is displayed and an event is logged in the System Event log.

If the offending node is a Windows 2000 computer using Dynamic Host Configuration Protocol (DHCP), gratuitous ARPs are sent for the IP address received in the DHCPOFFER message. If an ARP Reply is received in response to the gratuitous ARPs, the DHCP client sends a DHCPDECLINE message to the DHCP server. If the DHCP server is a Windows 2000 DHCP server, the IP address sent in the DHCPOFFER is flagged as a bad IP address and isn't allocated to any other DHCP clients. The DHCP client starts the DHCP lease allocation process by sending a new DHCPDISCOVER message. For more information on Windows 2000 DHCP, see Chapter 15, "Dynamic Host Configuration Protocol (DHCP) Service."

On the Defending Node

The defending node detects an address conflict whenever the SPA of the incoming ARP Request is the same as an IP address configured on the defending node. For gratuitous ARPs from an offending node, both the SPA and TPA are set to the conflicting address. However, gratuitous ARPs aren't the only ARP Requests that can have the SPA set to the conflicting address.

For example, if a node using a conflicting address is started without being connected to its network segment, no replies to the gratuitous ARPs are received and the node will initialize TCP/IP using the conflicting address. If the node is then placed on the same network segment as the defending node, no additional gratuitous ARPs are sent. However, each time either node using the conflicting address sends an ARP Request, the SPA is set to the conflicting address. In this case, an error message is displayed and an event is logged in the System Event log. Both nodes continue to use the conflicting IP address, but display an error message and log an event every time the other node sends an ARP Request.

The Gratuitous ARP and Address Conflict Exchange

The gratuitous ARP and address conflict detection for Windows 2000 is an exchange of three frames. The first two frames, as noted below, are the ARP Request-ARP Reply for the conflicting address.

1.   The offending node attempting to detect another node on the same network segment using the same IP address sends the gratuitous ARP Request.
2.   The defending node sends the ARP Reply to the offending node.

When the gratuitous ARP is sent, the SPA is set to a conflicting IP address and the SHA is set to the offending node's MAC address. Nodes on the network segment that have an ARP cache entry for [conflicting IP address, defending node's MAC address] will have their ARP cache entries updated to [conflicting IP address, offending node's MAC address]. The gratuitous ARP sent by the offending node updates all the ARP cache entries for the nodes communicating with the defending node; this causes future IP datagrams to be sent to the offending node's MAC address. A worst-case scenario is when the defending node is the default gateway for the network segment. Sending the gratuitous ARP Request causes all nodes on that network segment, with an entry in their ARP cache for the default gateway IP address, to forward all traffic off the subnet to the offending node's MAC address.

When the ARP Reply is sent, it's sent to the defending node's MAC address. The unicast ARP Reply doesn't correct the improper ARP cache entries. Therefore, to reset the ARP cache entries that were improperly updated by the offending nodes' sending of the gratuitous ARP Request, the defending node sends another broadcast ARP Request. The defending node's ARP Request is a gratuitous ARP as if the defending node were doing its own conflict detection. The defending node's ARP Request contains the SHA set to the offending node's MAC address. Network segment nodes that have had their ARP cache entries improperly set to [conflicting IP address, offending node's MAC address] are reset to the proper mapping of [conflicting IP address, defending node's MAC address].

Network Monitor trace 3-2 (Capture 03-02 in the \Captures folder on the companion CD-ROM) shows the gratuitous ARP and address conflict exchange. Frame 1 is the offending node's gratuitous ARP. Frame 2 is the defending node's ARP Reply. Frame 3 is the defending node's gratuitous ARP. At the end of frame 3, all network segment nodes that have the IP address 192.168.0.1 in their ARP caches have been reset to the proper MAC address of 0x00-60-97-02-6D-3D.

Inverse ARP (InARP)

For Non-Broadcast Multiple Access (NBMA)-based WAN technologies such as X.25, Frame Relay, and ATM, the Network Interface Layer address isn't a MAC address but a virtual-circuit identifier. For example, for Frame Relay, the virtual-circuit identifier is the Frame Relay Data Link Connection Identifier (DLCI). To address frames for a given destination, the Frame Relay header's DLCI is set to the value that corresponds to the virtual circuit over which the frame is traveling. With NMBA technologies, the virtual-circuit identifier is known but the IP address of the interface on the other end of the virtual-circuit isn't.

InARP is used to resolve the IP address on the other end of a virtual circuit based on a known Frame Relay DLCI. As RFC 2390 describes, InARP was designed specifically for Frame Relay virtual circuits. Frame Relay link management protocols such as Local Management Interface (LMI) determine which virtual circuits are in use over the physical connection to the Frame Relay service provider. Once the DLCIs are determined, InARP is used to query each virtual circuit to determine the IP address of the interface on the other end. The response to the InARP is used to build a table of entries consisting of [DLCI, forwarding IP address].

> **More Info**   InARP, as designed for Frame Relay virtual circuits, is described in RFC 2390, which can be found in the \RFC folder on the companion CD-ROM.

Because the DLCI values are only locally significant, the SHA and THA are irrelevant. In both the InARP Request and InARP Reply, the SHA field is typically set to 0 and the TPA field is set to the local DLCI value. The relevant information is the value of the SPA field in the InARP Request and the InARP Reply. The InARP responder uses the InARP Request's SPA to add an entry to its table consisting of [local DLCI, SPA of InARP Request]. The InARP requester uses the InARP Reply's SPA to add an entry to its table consisting of [local DLCI, SPA of InARP Reply].

The InARP Request and Reply have the same structure as the ARP Request and Reply, except 2-byte hardware adresses are used. The ARP Operation field is set to 0x0008 for an InARP Request and 0x0009 for an InARP Reply.

Proxy ARP

Proxy ARP is the answering of ARP Requests on behalf of another node. As RFC 925 describes, Proxy ARP is used in situations where a subnet is divided without the use of a router. A proxy ARP device is placed between nodes on the same subnet. The proxy ARP device is aware of what nodes are available on which segment. The proxy ARP device also answers ARP Requests and facilitates the forwarding of unicast IP packets for communication between nodes on separate segments. The existence of the proxy ARP device is transparent to the nodes on the subnet. A proxy ARP device is often physically a router device; however, it is not acting as an IP router, forwarding IP datagrams between two IP subnets. Figure 3-3 shows an example of a proxy ARP configuration.

 More Info   Use of Proxy ARP in divided subnet situations is described in RFC 925, which can be found in the \RFC folder on the companion CD-ROM.

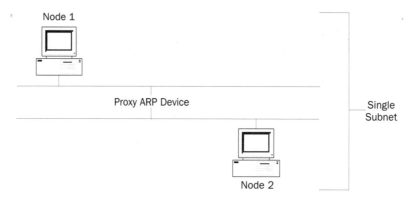

Figure 3-3. *A single subnet configuration, using a Proxy ARP device.*

When Node 1 wants to send an IP datagram to Node 2 on the other side of the proxy ARP device, because Node 1 and Node 2 are on the same logical IP subnet, Node 1 sends an ARP Request with Node 2's IP address as the TPA. The proxy ARP device receives the ARP Request and, even though the TPA isn't its own address, the proxy ARP device sends an ARP Reply to Node 1 with the proxy ARP device's MAC address as the SHA. Node 1 then sends the IP datagram to the proxy ARP device's MAC address. As far as Node 1 is concerned, it has resolved Node 2's MAC address and delivered the IP datagram to Node 2. The proxy ARP device next delivers the IP datagram to Node 2, using ARP if necessary to resolve Node 2's MAC address.

The Windows 2000 Routing and Remote Access service uses proxy ARP to facilitate communications between remote access clients and nodes on the network segment to which the remote access server is attached. When IP-based remote access clients connect, the remote access server assigns them an IP address. The IP address assigned can either be from the address range of a subnet to which the remote access server is attached, an on-subnet address, or from the address range of a separate subnet, an off-subnet address. Proxy ARP is used when the remote access server assigns an on-subnet address. An on-subnet address range is used when either the Routing and Remote Access service is configured to use DHCP to obtain addresses, or a range of addresses from a directly attached subnet is manually configured. Figure 3-4 shows an example of a remote access server manually configured with an on-subnet address range.

The subnet to which the remote access server is attached is 10.1.1.0/24, implying a range of usable addresses from 10.1.1.1 through 10.1.1.254. In this case, the network administrator is using the high end of the range (10.1.1.200 through 10.1.1.254) for assignment to remote access clients.

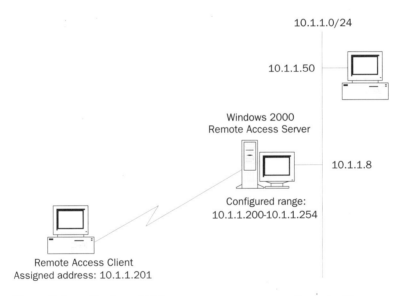

Figure 3-4. *A Windows 2000 remote access server, configured with an on-subnet address range using proxy ARP.*

When an IP-based remote access client successfully connects and is assigned an IP address, the Routing and Remote Access service tracks the assigned address in a connection table. When a host on the network to which the remote access server is attached sends an ARP Request for the remote access client's assigned on-subnet IP address, the remote access server answers with an ARP Reply and receives the forwarded IP datagram. The Routing and Remote Access service then forwards the IP datagram addressed to the remote access client over the appropriate remote access connection.

If the remote access server is manually configured with a range of addresses that represents a different subnet (an off-subnet address range), the remote access server acts as an IP router forwarding IP datagrams between separate subnets.

Summary

ARP is used as a translation layer between Internet Layer addresses and Network Interface Layer addresses. ARP on LAN links is used to resolve the forwarding IP address of a node to its corresponding MAC address and to detect IP address conflicts. InARP on NBMA links is used to map a DLCI value to the IP address of the node on the other end of the virtual circuit. Proxy ARP is used to subdivide an IP subnet and provide transparent communication without using a IP router.

Part II
Internet Layer Protocols

Chapter 4
Internet Protocol (IP) Basics

To fully grasp TCP/IP, users need to completely understand one of its most important protocols: Internet Protocol (IP). IP is the internetworking building block of all the other protocols at the Internet Layer and above.

Introduction to IP

IP embodies the Internet Layer of the DARPA model and provides the internetworking functionality that makes possible large-scale internetworks such as the Internet. IP has lasted since it was formalized in 1981, and will continue to be used on the Internet for years to come. Only relatively recently have IP's shortcomings been addressed in a new version known as IP version 6 (IPv6). For more information on IPv6, see Chapter 9, "Internet Protocol Version 6 (IPv6)." IP's amazing longevity is a tribute to its original design.

More Info   RFC 791, "Internet Protocol," documents IP. This RFC can be found in the \RFC folder on the companion CD-ROM.

Note   This chapter uses IP to refer to version 4 of IP that is in widespread use today. IP version 6 will be denoted as IPv6.

IP Services

IP offers the following services to upper layer protocols:

- **Internetworking protocol**   IP is an internetworking protocol, also known as a routable protocol. The IP header contains information necessary for routing the packet, including source and destination IP addresses. An IP address is composed of two components: a network address and a node address. Internetwork delivery, or routing, is possible because of the existence of a destination network address. IP allows the creation of an IP internetwork, which is two or more networks interconnected by IP router(s).

  The IP header also contains a link count, which is used to limit the number of links on which the packet can travel before being discarded.

- **Multiple client protocols** IP is an internetwork carrier for upper layer protocols. IP can carry several different upper layer protocols, but each IP packet can contain data from only one upper layer protocol at a time. Because each packet can carry one of several protocols, there must be a way to indicate which upper layer protocol a packet contains so that the data can be forwarded to the appropriate upper layer protocol at the destination. Both the client and the server always use the same protocol for a given exchange of data. Therefore, the packet does not need to indicate separate source and destination protocols.

  Examples of upper layer protocols include other Internet Layer protocols such Internet Control Message Protocol (ICMP) and Internet Group Management Protocol (IGMP). Further examples include Transport Layer protocols such as Transmission Control Protocol (TCP) and User Datagram Protocol (UDP).

- **Datagram delivery** IP is a datagram protocol that provides a connectionless, unreliable delivery service for upper layer protocols. Connectionless means that no handshaking occurs between IP nodes prior to sending data, and that no logical connection is created or maintained at the Internet Layer. Unreliable means that IP sends a packet without sequencing and without an acknowledgment that the destination was reached. IP makes a best effort to deliver packets to the next hop or the final destination. End-to-end reliability is the responsibility of upper layer protocols such as TCP.

- **Independence from Network Interface Layer** At the Internet Layer, IP is designed to be independent of the network technology present at the Network Interface Layer. IP is independent of OSI Physical Layer attributes such as cabling, signaling, and bit rate. It also is independent of OSI Data Link Layer attributes such as media access control scheme, addressing, and maximum frame size. IP uses a 32-bit address that is independent of the addressing scheme used at the Network Interface Layer.

- **Fragmentation and reassembly** To support the maximum frame sizes of different Network Interface Layer technologies, IP allows for the fragmentation of a payload when forwarding onto a link that has a lower MTU than the IP datagram size. Routers or sending hosts fragment an IP payload, and fragmentation can occur multiple times. The destination host then reassembles the fragments into the originally sent IP payload. More information on fragmentation and reassembly are provided in the "Fragmentation" section of this chapter.

- **Extensible through IP options** When features are required that are not available using the standard IP header, IP options can be used. IP options are appended to the standard IP header and provide custom functionality, such as the ability to specify a path that an IP datagram will follow through the IP internetwork.

- **Datagram packet-switching technology** IP is an example of a datagram packet-switching technology: each packet is a datagram, an unacknowledged and non-sequenced message, that is forwarded by the switches of the switching network using a globally significant address. In the case of IP, each switch in the switching network is an IP router, and the globally significant address is the destination IP address. This address is examined at each router. The router makes an independent routing decision and forwards the packet. Because each router decides independently where to forward a packet, a packet's path from Node 1 to Node 2 is not necessarily the packet's path from Node 2 to Node 1. Additionally, because each packet is separately switched, each can take a different path between the source and destination; and, because of various transit delays, each packet can arrive in a different order from which it was sent.

Note   The term *switch* used here is for a generalized forwarding device and is not meant to imply a Layer 2 or Layer 3 switch. A Layer 2 switch is typically used in Ethernet environments to segment traffic. A Layer 3 switch is equivalent to a router.

IP MTU

Each Network Interface Layer technology imposes a maximum-sized frame that can be sent. The maximum-sized frame consists of the framing header and trailer, and a payload. The maximum size of a frame for a given Network Interface Layer technology is called the maximum transmission unit (MTU). For an IP packet, the Network Interface Layer payload is an IP datagram. Therefore, the maximum-sized payload becomes the maximum-sized IP datagram. This is known as the IP MTU.

Table 4-1 lists the IP MTUs for the various Network Interface Layer technologies that Chapters 1 and 2 discuss.

Table 4-1. IP MTUs for Common Network Interface Layer Technologies

Network Interface Layer Technology	IP MTU
Ethernet (Ethernet II encapsulation)	1500
Ethernet (IEEE 802.3 SNAP encapsulation)	1492
Token Ring (4 and 16 Mbps)	varies based on token holding time
FDDI	4352
X.25	1600
Frame Relay	1600
ATM (Classical IP over ATM)	9180
Minimum MTU	576

In an environment with mixed Network Interface Layer Protocols, fragmentation can occur when crossing a router from a link with a higher IP MTU to a link with a lower IP MTU. IP fragmentation is discussed in more detail in the "Fragmentation" section of this chapter.

Microsoft Windows 2000 Registry Setting for IP MTU

In Windows 2000 it is possible to override the MTU as normally reported to the Network Driver Interface Specification (NDIS) by the NDIS Media Access Control (MAC) driver. When TCP/IP initializes, it queries its bound NDIS network adapter driver and receives the MTU. The MTU registry setting is used to set an MTU that is lower than the default MTU, as reported by the NDIS driver, and greater than the minimum value of 68. Values in the MTU registry setting that are greater than the default MTU are ignored; if the MTU registry setting is set to a value less than 68, 68 is used.

It is useful to change the default MTU size for testing or for solving MTU issues in translational bridge environments.

MTU

```
Key: HKEY_LOCAL_MACHINE\SYSTEM\CurrentControlSet\Services\<Adapter
Name>\Parameters\Tcpip
Data type: REG_DWORD
Valid range: 68 - <the MTU reported by the network adapter>
Default: 0xFFFFFFFF (the MTU reported by the network adapter)
Present by default: No
```

The IP Datagram

An IP datagram consists of an IP header and an IP payload, as Figure 4-1 illustrates.

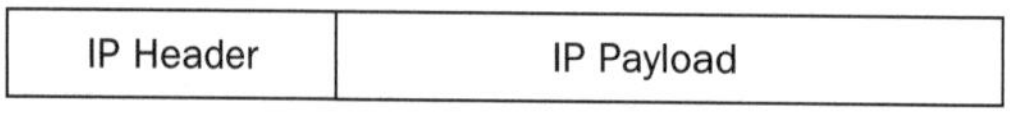

IP Header	IP Payload

Figure 4-1. *The IP datagram consists of an IP header and an IP payload.*

- **IP header**   The IP header is of variable size, between 20 and 60 bytes, in 4-byte increments. It provides routing support, payload identification, IP header and datagram size indication, fragmentation support, and options.

- **IP payload**   The IP payload is of variable size, ranging from 8 bytes (a 68-byte IP datagram with a 60-byte IP header) to 65,515 bytes (a 65,535-byte IP datagram with a 20-byte header).

The IP Header

Figure 4-2 displays the IP header's structure. The following sections discuss the fields of the IP (version 4) header.

Version

The Version field is 4 bits long and is used to indicate the IP header version. A 4-bit field can have values from 0 through 15. The standard IP version used today on corporate networks and the Internet is version 4, or IPv4. The next version of IP is version 6, or IPv6. All other values for the version field are either undefined or not in use. For the latest list of the defined values of the IP Version field, see http://www.isi.edu/in-notes/iana/assignments/version-numbers.

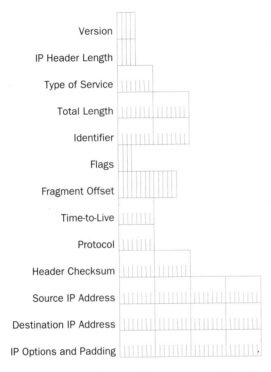

Figure 4-2. *The format of the IP version 4 header.*

Header Length

The Header Length field is 4 bits long and is used to indicate the IP header size. The maximum number that can be represented with 4 bits is 15. Therefore, the Header Length field cannot possibly be a byte counter. Rather, the Header Length field indicates the number of 32-bit words (4-byte blocks) in the IP header. The typical IP header does not contain any options and is 20 bytes long. The smallest possible header length is 5 (0x5). With the maximum amount of IP options, the largest IP header can be 60 bytes long, indicated with a header length of 15 (0xF).

Using a 4-byte block counter to indicate the IP header size means that the IP header size must always be a multiple of 4. If IP options extend the IP header, they must do so in 4-byte increments. If an IP option is not 4 bytes long, option padding must be used so that the IP header is always along 4-byte boundaries.

Type Of Service

The Type Of Service (TOS) field is 8 bits long and is used to indicate the quality of service with which this datagram is to be delivered by the internetwork routers. The TOS field contains sub-fields and flags to indicate desired precedence, delay, throughput, reliability, and cost characteristics.

Within the 8 bits of the TOS field are five fields that indicate a different quality of the datagram delivery, as Figure 4-3 illustrates. The TOS field is set by the sending host and is not modified by routers. All IP datagram fragments contain the same TOS setting as the original IP datagram.

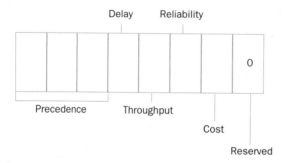

Figure 4-3. *The format of the IP Type Of Service field.*

Normally, a sending host sends an IP datagram with the TOS field set to the value of 0x00: routine precedence, normal delay, normal throughput, normal reliability, and normal cost. Routers normally ignore the values in TOS field and forward all datagrams as if the fields are not set. This is known as TOS0 routing. However, modern routing protocols such as OSPF and Integrated IS-IS now support the calculation of routes for each value of the TOS field.

The routers and the routing protocol determine how the various values in the TOS field are interpreted. In a properly configured network, packets with specific TOS values are forwarded over different paths. This can improve routing and delivery efficiency in a multi-path IP internetwork. For example, an IP internetwork could have one path for general traffic, one for low-delay traffic, and another path for high reliability traffic. When sending hosts set various combinations of TOS values, routers can choose between those paths.

The TOS field is used for quality of service (QoS) in IP internetworks.

Precedence

The Precedence field is 3 bits long and is used to indicate the importance of the datagram. Table 4-2 lists the defined values of the Precedence field.

Table 4-2. Values of the IP Precedence Field

Precedence Value	Precedence
000	Routine
001	Priority
010	Immediate
011	Flash
100	Flash Override
101	CRITIC/ECP
110	Internetwork Control
111	Network Control

The Precedence field is set to 000 (Routine) by default.

Delay

The Delay field is a flag indicating either Normal Delay (=0) or Low Delay (=1). If Delay is set to 1, the IP router forwards the IP datagram along the path that has the lowest delay characteristics. An application can request the low delay path when sending either time-sensitive data, such as digitized voice or video, or interactive traffic, such as Telnet sessions. Based on the Delay flag, the router might choose the lower delay terrestrial WAN link over the higher delay satellite link, even if the satellite link has a higher bandwidth.

Throughput

The Throughput field is a flag indicating either Normal Throughput (=0) or High Throughput (=1). If the Throughput field is set to 1, the IP router forwards the IP datagram along the path that has the highest throughput characteristics. An application can request the high throughput path when sending bulk data. Based on the Throughput flag, the router can choose the higher throughput satellite link over the lower throughput terrestrial WAN link, even if the terrestrial link has a lower delay.

Reliability

The Reliability field is a flag indicating either Normal Reliability (=0) or High Reliability (=1). During periods of congestion at an IP router, the Reliability field is used to decide which IP datagrams to discard first. If the Reliability field is set to 1, the IP router discards these datagrams last. An application can request the high reliability path when sending time-sensitive data, so that it cannot be discarded. For example, with some methods of sending digital video, the digitized video is sent as two types of packets: the primary type is used to reconstruct the basic video image, and a secondary type is used to provide a higher resolution image. In this case, the primary packets are sent with the Reliability field set to 1 and the secondary packets are sent with the Reliability field set to 0. If congestion occurs at the router, the router discards the secondary packets first.

Cost

The Cost field is a flag indicating either Normal Cost (=0) or Low Cost (=1), where cost indicates monetary cost. If the Cost field is set to 1, the IP router forwards the IP datagram along the path that has the lowest cost characteristics. An application can request the low cost path when sending non-critical data. Based on the Cost flag, the router can choose a lower cost terrestrial link over a higher cost satellite link, even if the terrestrial link has a lower bandwidth.

Reserved

The Reserved field is the last bit and must be set to 0. Routers ignore this field when forwarding IP datagrams.

Microsoft Windows 2000 Registry Setting for Default TOS

DefaultTOS

In Windows 2000, it is possible to set the default value for the TOS field for packets that a host sent. Microsoft Windows Sockets applications can override this default value. By default, the DefaultTOS value is set to 0.

Changing the value of DefaultTOS is necessary only for testing, when all traffic from a host can be characterized in terms of a specific TOS, and TOS routing is supported by your routing infrastructure.

```
Key: HKEY_LOCAL_MACHINE\SYSTEM\CurrentControlSet\Services\Tcpip\Parameters
Value type: REG_DWORD
Valid range: 0 - 255
Default: 0
Present by default: No
```

For example, to set all traffic from a host for routine precedence, minimum delay, and maximum reliability, set DefaultTOS to 20 (20 = 00010100).

Setting the TOS with PING.EXE

The Microsoft Windows 2000 PING utility with the "-v" option can be used to set the TOS value in ICMP Echo Request messages. The syntax is as follows:

```
PING -v [TOS value] [IP address or host name]
```

The TOS value is expressed in decimal. For example, to ping 10.0.0.1 with a TOS field that is normal precedence, minimum delay, and minimum monetary cost, use the following command:

```
PING -v 18 10.0.0.1
```

Total Length

The Total Length field is 2 bytes long and is used to indicate the size of the IP datagram (IP header and IP payload) in bytes. With 16 bits, the maximum total length that can be indicated is 65,535 bytes. For maximum-sized IP datagrams, the total length is the same as the IP MTU for that Network Interface Layer technology.

Between the header length and the total length, the IP payload length can be determined:

IP payload length (bytes) = total length (bytes) - 4*header length (32-bit words)

Identification

The Identification field is 2 bytes long and is used to identify a specific IP packet sent between a source and destination node. The sending host sets the Identification field's value, and the field is incremented for successive IP datagrams. The Identification field is used to identify the fragments of an original IP datagram.

Flags

The Flags field is 3 bits long and contains two flags for fragmentation. One flag is used to indicate whether the IP datagram is eligible for fragmentation, and the other indicates whether or not there are more fragments to follow for this fragmented IP datagram.

More information on these flags and their uses can be found in the "Fragmentation" section in this chapter.

Fragment Offset

The Fragment Offset field is 13 bits long and is used to indicate the offset of where this fragment begins relative to the original IP payload.

More information on the Fragment Offset field can be found in the "Fragmentation" section in this chapter.

Time To Live

The Time To Live field is 1 byte long and is used to indicate on how many links this IP datagram can travel before an IP router discards it. The Time To Live field (TTL) was originally intended to be used as a time counter, to indicate the number of seconds that the IP datagram could exist on the Internet. An IP router was intended to keep track of the time that it received the IP datagram and the time that it forwarded the IP datagram. The TTL was then decreased by the number of seconds that the packet resided at the router.

However, the latest modern standard (RFC 1812) specifies that IP routers decrement the TTL by one when forwarding an IP datagram. Therefore, the TTL is an inverse link count. The sending host sets the initial TTL, which acts as a maximum link count. The maximum value limits the number of links on which the datagram can travel and prevents a datagram from indefinitely looping.

Some additional aspects of the TTL field include:

- Routers decrement the TTL in received packets to be routed before consulting the routing table. If the TTL is 0, the packet is discarded and an ICMP Time Expired-TTL Expired In Transit message is sent back to the sending host.

- Destination hosts do not check the TTL field.

- Sending hosts must send IP datagrams with a TTL greater than 0. The exact value of the TTL for sent IP datagrams is either an operating system default or is specified by the application. The maximum value of the TTL is 255.

- A recommended value of the TTL is twice the diameter of your internetwork. The diameter is the number of links between the farthest two nodes on the IP internetwork.

- The TTL is independent of routing protocol metrics such as the Routing Information Protocol (RIP) hop count and the Open Shortest Path First (OSPF) cost.

Note The TTL can be mistakenly referred to as a hop count when in fact it is a link count. The difference is subtle but important. Hop count is the number of routers to cross to reach a given destination. Link count is the number of Network Interface Layer links to cross to reach a given destination. The difference between hop count and link count is 1. For example, if host A and host B are separated by five routers, the hop count is 5, but the link count is 6. An IP datagram sent from host A to host B with a TTL of 5 will be discarded by the fifth router. An IP datagram sent from host A to host B with a TTL of 6 will arrive at host B.

Microsoft Windows 2000 Registry Setting for Default TTL

DefaultTTL

In Windows 2000 it is possible to set the default value for the TTL field for packets sent by a host. Windows Sockets applications can override this default value.

Changing the value of Default TTL is necessary only when the diameter of your network changes.

```
Key: HKEY_LOCAL_MACHINE\SYSTEM\CurrentControlSet\Services\Tcpip\Parameters
Value type: REG_DWORD
Valid range: 1 - 255
Default: 128
Present by default: No
```

The default value of DefaultTTL is set to 128 so that IP packets sent by a Windows 2000 computer can reach locations on the Internet that might need to traverse many links.

Setting the TTL with PING

The Windows 2000 PING utility with the "-i" option can be used to set the TTL value in ICMP Echo messages. The syntax is:

```
PING -i [TTL value] [IP address or host name]
```

The TTL value is expressed in decimal. For example, to ping 10.0.0.1 with a TTL field that is set to 7, use the following command:

```
PING -i 7 10.0.0.1
```

The default TTL for ICMP Echo messages sent by PING is 32.

Protocol

The Protocol field is 1 byte long and is used to indicate the upper layer protocol contained within the IP payload. The Protocol field is an explicit indication of the client protocol. Some common values of the IP protocol field are 1 for ICMP, 6 for TCP, and 17 (0x11) for UDP. The Protocol field acts as a multiplex identifier so that the payload can be passed to the proper upper layer protocol upon receipt at the destination node.

Windows Sockets applications can refer to protocols by name. Protocol names are resolved to protocol numbers through the PROTOCOL file stored in the \SystemRoot\ system32\drivers\etc directory.

Table 4-3 lists some of the values of the IP Protocol field for protocols that Windows 2000 supports.

Table 4-3. Values of the IP Protocol Field

Value	Protocol
0	Reserved
1	Internet Control Message Protocol (ICMP)
2	Internet Group Management Protocol (IGMP)
4	IP in IP encapsulation
6	Transmission Control Protocol (TCP)
8	Exterior Gateway Protocol (EGP)
17	User Datagram Protocol (UDP)
46	Resource Reservation Protocol (RSVP)
47	Generic Routing Protocol (GRE)
50	IP Security Encapsulating Security Payload (ESP)
51	IP Security Authentication Header (AH)
89	Open Shortest Path First (OSPF)

For a complete list of IP Protocol field values, see *http://www.isi.edu/in-notes/iana/ assignments/protocol-numbers*.

Header Checksum

The Header Checksum field is 2 bytes long and performs a bit-level integrity check on the IP header only. The IP payload is not included. IP payloads must include their own checksums to check for bit-level integrity. The sending host performs an initial checksum in the sent IP datagram. Each router in the path between the source and destination verifies the Header Checksum field before processing the packet. If the verification fails, the router silently discards the IP datagram.

Because each router in the path between the source and destination decrements the TTL, the header checksum changes at each router.

To compute the header checksum, each 16-bit quantity in the IP header is one's complemented; bits within the 16-bit quantity that are set to 0 are changed to 1, bits within the 16-bit quantity that are set to 1 are changed to 0. The one's complemented 16-bit quantities are added together and the sum is one's complemented. The result is placed in the Header Checksum field.

For the purposes of computing the header checksum over all the fields in the IP header, the value of the Header Checksum field is set to 0.

Source Address

The Source Address field is 4 bytes long and contains the IP address of the source host, unless a network address translator (NAT) is translating the IP datagram. A NAT is used to translate between public and private addresses when connecting to the Internet.

More Info For more information on NAT, see RFC 1631 in the \RFC folder on the companion CD-ROM.

Destination Address

The Destination Address field is 4 bytes long and contains the IP address of the destination host, unless the IP datagram is being translated by a network address translator or being loose or strict source routed. More information on IP source routing can be found in the "IP Options" section of this chapter.

Options and Padding

Options and padding can be added to the IP header, but must be done so in 4-byte increments so that the size of the IP header can be indicated using the Header Length field.

The following Network Monitor trace (Capture 04-01 in the \Captures folder on the companion CD-ROM) shows the structure of the IP header:

```
+ Frame: Base frame properties
+ ETHERNET: ETYPE = 0x0800 : Protocol = IP:   DOD Internet Protocol
  IP: ID = 0x34CD; Proto = ICMP; Len: 60
```

```
   IP: Version = 4 (0x4)
   IP: Header Length = 20 (0x14)
   IP: Precedence = Routine
   IP: Type of Service = Normal Service
   IP: Total Length = 60 (0x3C)
   IP: Identification = 13517 (0x34CD)
   IP: Flags Summary = 0 (0x0)
       IP: .......0 = Last fragment in datagram
       IP: ......0. = May fragment datagram if necessary
   IP: Fragment Offset = 0 (0x0) bytes
   IP: Time to Live = 128 (0x80)
   IP: Protocol = ICMP - Internet Control Message
   IP: Checksum = 0xB869
   IP: Source Address = 157.59.8.1
   IP: Destination Address = 157.59.8.1
   IP: Data: Number of data bytes remaining = 40 (0x0028)
 + ICMP: Echo: From 157.59.11.19 To 157.54.08.01
```

Fragmentation

When a source host or a router must transmit an IP datagram on a link and the MTU of the link is less than the IP datagram's size, the IP datagram must be fragmented. When IP fragmentation occurs, the IP payload is segmented and each segment is sent with its IP header.

The IP header contains information required to reassemble the original IP payload at the destination host. Because IP is a datagram packet-switching technology and the fragments can arrive in a different order from which they were sent, the fragments must be grouped (using the Identification field), sequenced (using the Fragment Offset field), and delimited (using the More Fragments flag).

Virtual circuit packet-switching technologies such as X.25 and ATM require only fragment/segment delimitation. For example, with ATM Adaptation Layer 5, an IP datagram is segmented into 48-byte segments that become the payloads for ATM cells. ATM sends the stream of cells that comprise the IP datagram and uses the third bit of the Payload Type field in the ATM header to indicate the end of the stream of cells for an IP datagram.

Fragmentation Fields

Figure 4-4 shows the fragmentation fields in the IP header.

Identification

The IP Identification field is used to group all the fragments of an original IP datagram together. The sending host sets the Identification field, and the field is preserved during the fragmentation process. The Identification field is set even when fragmentation of the IP payload is not allowed by setting the Don't Fragment flag.

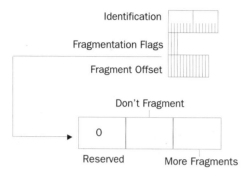

Figure 4-4. *The fields in the IP header used for fragmentation.*

Don't Fragment Flag

The Don't Fragment (DF) flag is set to 0 to allow fragmentation and set to 1 to prohibit fragmentation. Therefore, fragmentation will occur only if the DF flag is set to 0. If fragmentation is needed to forward the IP datagram and the DF flag is set to 1, the router discards the IP datagram and sends back an ICMP Destination Unreachable-Fragmentation Needed And DF Set message back to the source host.

Fragmentation is an expensive process at the routers and the destination host. The DF flag and the ICMP Destination Unreachable-Fragmentation Needed And DF Set message are the mechanisms by which a sending host discovers the MTU of the path between the source and the destination, or Path MTU Discovery. For more information, see Chapter 7, "Internet Control Message Protocol (ICMP)."

More Fragments Flag

The More Fragments (MF) flag is set to 0 if there are no more fragments that follow this fragment (this is the last fragment), and set to 1 if there are more fragments that follow this fragment (this is not the last fragment).

Fragment Offset

The Fragment Offset field is set to indicate the position of the fragment relative to the original IP payload. The Fragment Offset is an offset used for sequencing during reassembly, putting the incoming fragments in proper order to reconstruct the original payload. The Fragment Offset field is 13 bits long. With a maximum IP payload size of 65,515 bytes (the maximum IP MTU of 65,535 less a minimum-sized IP header of 20 bytes), the Fragment Offset field cannot possibly indicate a byte offset. At 13 bits, the maximum value is 8191. The fragment offset must be 16 bits long to be a byte offset.

Because 16 bits are required to indicate a maximum-sized IP payload and only 13 bits are available in the Fragment Offset field, each value of the fragment offset must represent 3 bits. Therefore, the Fragment Offset field is defined in terms of 8-byte blocks, called *fragment blocks*.

During fragmentation, the payload is fragmented along 8-byte boundaries and the maximum number of 8-byte fragment blocks is placed in each fragment. The Fragment Offset field is set to indicate the starting fragment block for the fragment relative to the original IP payload.

For each fragment being fragmented by a router, the original IP header is copied and the following fields are changed:

- **Header Length**   Might or might not change depending on whether IP options are present and whether the options are copied to all fragments or just the first fragment. IP options are discussed in the "IP Options" section in this chapter.
- **TTL**   Decremented by 1.
- **Total Length**   Changed to reflect the new IP header and IP payload size.
- **MF**   Set to 1 for first or middle fragments. Set to 0 for the last fragment.
- **Fragment Offset**   Set to indicate the position of the fragment in fragment blocks relative to the original payload.
- **Header Checksum**   Recalculated based on the changed fields in the IP header.

The Identification field does not change for each fragment.

Fragmentation Example

As an example of the fragmentation process, a node on a Token Ring network wants to send a fragmentable IP datagram with the IP Identification field set to 9999 to a node on an Ethernet network.

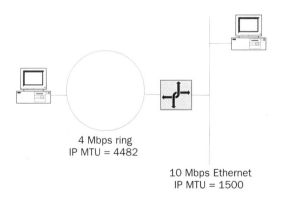

4 Mbps ring
IP MTU = 4482

10 Mbps Ethernet
IP MTU = 1500

Assuming a 9-millisecond token holding time, a 4-Mbps ring, and no Token Ring source routing header, the IP MTU for the Token Ring network is 4482 bytes. The Ethernet IP

MTU is 1500 bytes using Ethernet II encapsulation. Table 4-4 shows the fields relevant to fragmentation in the IP header and their values for the original IP datagram.

Table 4-4. Original IP Datagram

IP Header Field	Value
Total Length	4482
Identification	9999
DF	0
MF	0
Fragment Offset	0

The IP router connecting the two networks receives the IP datagram, checks its routing table, and notes that the interface on which to forward the datagram has a lower IP MTU than the datagram's size. The router then checks the Don't Fragment flag. If set to 1, the router discards the IP datagram and sends an ICMP Destination Unreachable-Fragmentation Needed And DF Set message back to the source host. If set to 0, the IP router fragments the 4462 byte IP payload (assuming no IP options are present) into four fragments, each of which can be sent on the 1500-byte Ethernet network.

IP payloads on an Ethernet network can be 1480 bytes long, assuming no IP options are present. Each 1480-byte payload is 185 fragment blocks (185*8 = 1480). Therefore, the four fragments are three fragments each with payloads of 1480 bytes and the last fragment with 22 bytes (4462 = 1480 + 1480 + 1480 + 22). Figure 4-5 shows the fragmentation process.

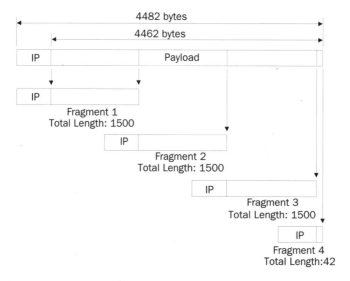

Figure 4-5. *The IP fragmentation process when fragmenting from a 4482-byte IP MTU link to a 1500-byte IP MTU link.*

Table 4-5 shows the fields relevant to fragmentation in the IP header of the four fragments.

Table 4-5. Fragments of the Original IP Datagram

IP Header Field	Value
Fragment 1	
Total Length	1500
Identification	9999
DF	0
MF	1
Fragment Offset	0
Fragment 2	
Total Length	1500
Identification	9999
DF	0
MF	1
Fragment Offset	185
Fragment 3	
Total Length	1500
Identification	9999
DF	0
MF	1
Fragment Offset	370
Fragment 4	
Total Length	42
Identification	9999
DF	0
MF	0
Fragment Offset	555

Reassembly Example

The fragments are forwarded by the intermediate IP router(s) to the destination host. Because IP is a datagram-based packet-switching technology, the fragments can take different paths to the destination and arrive in a different order from which the fragmenting router forwarded them. IP uses the Identification and Source IP Address fields to group the arriving fragments together.

Upon receiving a fragment (not necessarily the first fragment of the original IP payload), IP allocates reassembly resources comprised of:

- A data buffer to contain the IP payload (65,515 bytes)

- A header buffer to contain the IP header (60 bytes)
- A fragment block bit table (1024 bytes or 8192 bits)
- A total length data variable
- A timer

IP knows that a fragment arrived because either the MF flag or the Fragment Offset field has a non-zero value. An unfragmented IP datagram has MF flag = 0 and Fragment Offset = 0. When the first fragment arrives (the Fragment Offset field is 0), its IP header is placed in the header buffer. When the last fragment arrives (the MF flag is 0), the total data length is computed.

For each fragment arriving, the IP payload is placed in the data buffer according to the values of the Fragment Offset and Total Length fields; the bits corresponding to the arriving fragment blocks are set in the fragment block bit table. When the final fragment arrives (which may not be the last fragment), all the bits in the fragment block bit table are set and reassembly of the original IP datagram is complete. IP delivers the IP payload to the appropriate upper layer protocol based on the Protocol field's value.

The reassembly timer is used to abandon the reassembly process within a certain amount of time. If all the fragments do not arrive before the reassembly timer expires, the IP datagram is discarded and the destination host can send an ICMP Time Exceeded-Fragmentation Time Expired message to the source host. RFC 791 recommends a default reassembly timer of 15 seconds; as fragments arrive, the reassembly timer is set to the maximum of the current value and the value of the arriving fragment's TTL field.

Figure 4-6 shows the reassembly process for our example fragmentation.

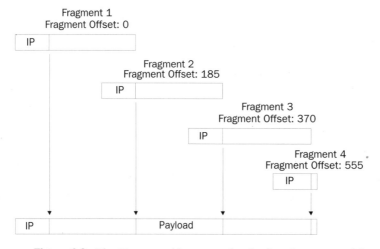

Figure 4-6. *The IP reassembly process for the four fragments of the original IP datagram.*

Fragmenting a Fragment

It is possible for fragments to become further fragmented. In this case, each fragment is fragmented to fit the MTU of the link onto which it is being forwarded. The process of fragmenting a fragment is slightly different from fragmenting an original IP datagram. The difference is in how the MF flag is set.

When fragmenting a fragment, the MF flag is always set to 1, except when the fragment of the fragment is the last fragment of the last fragment.

- If an IP router fragments a previously fragmented first or middle fragment, all of the fragments will have the MF flag set to 1.
- If an IP router fragments a previously fragmented last fragment, all of the fragments except the last fragment will have the MF flag set to 1.

Therefore, regardless of how many times the IP datagram is fragmented, only one fragment will have the MF flag set to 0, indicating the last fragment of the original IP datagram.

Avoiding Fragmentation

As seen from the preceding discussion, while fragmentation allows IP nodes to connect regardless of differing MTUs in intermediate network segments and without user intervention, IP fragmentation and reassembly is a relatively expensive process—both at the routers (or sending hosts) and at the destination host. On the modern Internet, fragmentation is highly discouraged; Internet routers are busy enough with the forwarding of IP traffic.

Fragmentation can be avoided by taking the following measures:

- Set the DF flag to 1 on all IP datagrams sent.
- Discover the IP MTU that is supported by all of the links in the path between the source and the destination (the path MTU).

For more information on the path MTU discovery process, see Chapter 7, "Internet Control Message Protocol (ICMP)."

Setting the DF with PING

The Windows 2000 PING utility with the "-f" option can be used to set the DF flag to 1 in ICMP Echo messages. The syntax is:

```
PING -f [IP address or host name]
```

For example, to ping 10.0.0.1 and set the DF to 1:

```
PING -f 10.0.0.1
```

The default DF flag ICMP Echo messages sent by PING is 0 (fragmentation allowed).

Setting the Payload Size with PING

The Windows 2000 PING utility with the "-l" option can be used to set the size of the ICMP payload in ICMP Echo messages. The syntax is:

```
PING -1 [payload size] [IP address or host name]
```

The payload value is expressed in decimal.

For example, to ping 10.0.0.1 with an ICMP payload size of 5000:

```
PING -1 5000 10.0.0.1
```

The default ICMP payload size PING is 32.

The ICMP payload size is not the same as the IP payload size because ICMP Echo messages include an ICMP header 8 bytes long. Therefore, to calculate the IP payload's size, add 8 to the size of the ICMP payload. To calculate the IP datagram's size, add 20 to the IP payload's size. To ping with an Echo at the maximum size allowed by the Network Interface technology, subtract 28 from the IP MTU. For example, to ping with a maximum-sized Echo on an Ethernet network (with an IP MTU of 1500), the PING command becomes:

```
PING -1 1472 10.0.0.1
```

Using PING to Create Source-Fragmented Packets

The Windows 2000 PING utility with the "-l" option can be used to produce source-fragmented packets. Pinging with an ICMP payload size that is greater than [IP MTU - 28] bytes produces source-fragmented packets. For example, pinging from an Ethernet node with an ICMP payload size of 1472 or less will not produce fragmented packets. Pinging from an Ethernet node with an ICMP payload size greater than 1472 will produce fragmented packets.

Fragmentation and Translational Bridging Environments

Translational bridging is the interconnection of two different Network Interface Layer technologies on the same network by a Layer 2 device such as a bridge or switch. A common use for translational bridges is to connect an Ethernet segment to a Token Ring segment. In modern networks, translational bridging is done by switches to connect 10-Mbps or 100-Mbps Ethernet nodes to servers on high-speed ports. Common high-speed port technologies include FDDI, gigabit Ethernet, and ATM.

The most serious obstacle to translational bridging is the difference in MTU between various Network Interface Layer technologies. Because there is no router involved, we cannot rely on either fragmentation or Path MTU Discovery processes to account for the differing MTUs. A translational bridge does not have the capability to fragment. Frames larger than the MTU of the link onto which they are to be forwarded are silently discarded by the bridge.

As discussed in Chapter 11, "Transmission Control Protocol (TCP) Basics," when a TCP connection is established, both nodes communicate MTU information in the form of the TCP Maximum Segment Size (MSS) option. After receiving each other's TCP MSS, both nodes agree to send TCP segments at the lowest MSS of the two nodes. However, despite this MTU negotiation, proper communication between all nodes in a translational bridging environment might require the modification of the IP MTU of specific nodes.

For example, as Figure 4-7 shows, two Ethernet switches are connected together on an Ethernet backbone. On each Ethernet switch is the same FDDI port connected to an FDDI ring containing application servers. When the servers on the same FDDI ring communicate with each other, they can send packets with the FDDI MTU of 4352 bytes. When an Ethernet node on one of the switches uses TCP to connect to an application server on either FDDI ring, the TCP MSS option lowers the MTU of TCP-based IP datagrams to 1500.

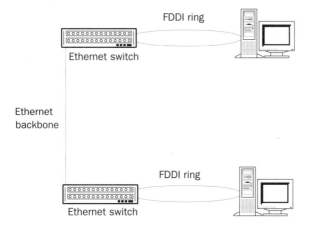

Figure 4-7. *An MTU problem in a translational bridging environment, caused by two FDDI hosts connected to two Ethernet switches.*

However, consider the communication between application servers on different FDDI rings. In creating the TCP connection, each server will negotiate an FDDI-based TCP MSS. Therefore, Ethernet switches will silently discard TCP-based IP datagrams sent between servers on different rings that have an IP total length greater than 1500.

The solution to this problem is to manually configure the application servers' IP MTU for the smallest IP MTU of all the links within the translational-bridged network.

Using our example, the IP MTU of the application servers on the FDDI rings are set to 1500. Now translational bridges can forward IP datagrams between FDDI rings. Changing the application servers' MTU means that when sending packets to application servers on the same ring, the packets will be sent at the lower MTU of 1500, a lower efficiency than when sent at the default FDDI MTU of 4352. However, it is better to have lower efficiency between servers on the same ring than zero efficiency between servers on different rings.

For Windows 2000 nodes, use the MTU registry setting to override the default MTU setting reported by NDIS.

IP Options

IP options are additional fields appended to the standard 20-byte IP header. While IP options are not required on each IP header, the ability to process IP option fields is required. IP options are used infrequently for network testing purposes.

The IP options portion size of the IP header will vary in length based on the IP options that are being used. The individual IP options vary in length also, from a single octet to multiple 4-octet quantities. Recall that the maximum-sized IP header that can be indicated with the Header Length field is 60 bytes. With a standard IP header size of 20 bytes, 40 bytes are left for IP options.

The first byte of each IP option has the format shown in Figure 4-8.

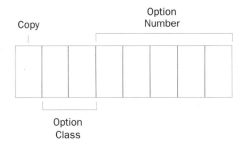

Figure 4-8. *The format of the IP option octet.*

Copy

The Copy field is 1 bit long and is used when a router or a sending host must fragment the IP datagram. When the Copy field is set to 0, the IP option should be copied only into the first fragment. When the Copy field is set to 1, the IP option should be copied into all fragments.

Option Class

The Option Class field is 2 bits long and is used to indicate the general class of the option. Table 4-6 lists the defined option classes.

Table 4-6. Option Classes

Option Class	Description
0	Network control
1	Reserved for future use
2	Debugging and measurement
3	Reserved for future use

Option Number

The Option Number field is 5 bits long and is used to indicate a specific option within the option class. Each option class can have up to 32 different option numbers.

Table 4-7 lists the defined option classes and numbers for non-military computing.

Table 4-7. Option Classes and Numbers

Option Class	Option Number	Description
0	0	**End Of Option List** A 1-octet option used to indicate the end of an option list.
0	1	**No Operation** A 1-octet option used to align octets in a list of options.
0	3	**Loose Source Routing** A variable length option used to route a datagram through a specified path where alternate routes can be taken.
0	7	**Record Route** A variable length option used to trace a route through an IP internetwork.
0	9	**Strict Source Routing** A variable length option used to route a datagram through a specified path where alternate routes cannot be taken.
0	20	**IP Router Alert** A fixed length option used to inform the router that additional processing of the datagram is required.
2	4	**Internet Timestamp** A variable length option used to record a series of timestamps at each hop.

End Of Option List

Option Code | 0 | 0 | 0 | 0 | 0 | 0 | 0 | 0 |

The End Of Option List option is always a single octet in length and is used at the end of the IP options when the IP options do not fall on a 4-byte boundary. The End Of Option List option is used only at the end of the IP options, not at the end of each option.

No Operation

Option Code `0 0 0 0 0 0 0 1`

The No Operation option is always a single octet in length and is used between IP options when an IP option does not fall on a 4-byte boundary.

Record Route

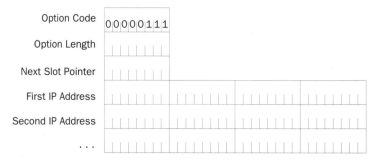

The Record Route option is a variable size option and is used to record the IP addresses of the far side interfaces of IP routers as it traverses the IP internetwork. The far side interface is the interface on the router on which the IP datagram is forwarded. The far side interface is presumed to be farthest from the sending host.

As the IP datagram is forwarded from router to router, each router adds its IP address to the list; each router also modifies the Next Slot Pointer field. The route from the source host to the destination host is recorded. To get the complete route, there must be enough room in the Record Route option header. Unlike Token Ring source routing, the number of IP address slots is specified by the sending host and is fixed in the IP header.

The Record Route option contains the following fields:

- **Option Code** Set to 7 (Copy Bit=0, Option Class=0, Option Number=7).
- **Option Length** Set by the sending host to the number of octets in the Record Route option.
- **Next Slot Pointer** Set to the octet offset (starting at 1) within the Record Route option of the next available IP address. The minimum value of the Next Slot Pointer field is 4.
- **First IP Address, Second IP Address** Set to the IP address of the far side interface by routers. With a maximum of 40 bytes in the IP options portion of the IP header, there is enough room for a maximum of nine IP addresses.

Record Route Processing

An IP router receiving an IP datagram with the Record Route option compares the Option Length and Next Slot Pointer fields. If the Next Slot Pointer field is less than the Option Length field, there are open IP address fields. The router records the IP address of the interface that is forwarding the datagram in the next available IP address field; the router also updates the Next Slot Pointer field by adding 4. If the value of the Next Slot Pointer field is greater than the Option Length field, all of the available IP address fields have been used by previous routers. The router then forwards the IP datagram without modifying the Record Route option.

Both hosts must agree that the information in the Record Route option will be processed in IP datagrams sent between them. If one host does not agree, the information in the Record Route option is ignored upon receipt and return IP datagrams are not sent with the Record Route option.

Because the Record Route option size is not a multiple of 4 bytes, either an End Of Options option (if there are no more options) or a No Operation option (if there are more options) must be added to ensure that the IP header is an integral multiple of 4 bytes.

Setting the Record Route Option with PING

The Windows 2000 PING utility with the "-r" option can be used to add the Record Route option and set the number of IP address slots in the Record Route option within an ICMP Echo message. The syntax is:

```
PING -r [IP address slots] [IP address or host name]
```

where the IP address slots value is expressed in decimal.

For example, to ping 10.0.0.1 with seven IP address slots, use the following command:

```
PING -r 7 10.0.0.1
```

When both hosts are Windows 2000 computers, the Record Route option records the IP addresses of the far side interfaces of forwarding routers in the ICMP Echo. When the Echo is received, the IP addresses recorded are maintained and the Echo Reply is sent with the same Record Route option. The Echo Reply contains the recorded route for the Echo and the recorded route for the Echo Reply.

Therefore, with the PING -r option, it is possible to record the far side router interfaces for the Echo (the path from host A to host B) and the far side router interfaces for the Echo Reply (the path from host B to host A). However, because there is only room for nine IP address slots, this is possible only if there are no more than four routers between hosts.

Note   The TRACERT utility does not use the PING -r option.

Strict and Loose Source Routing

The IP routing process at IP routers is performed through a comparison of the destination IP address with entries in a local routing table. Each router makes a forwarding decision. However, it is sometimes necessary to specify a path that an IP datagram is to take regardless of the router's routing table entries. The path is specified before the source host sends the datagram; this is known as source routing.

For example, in a multi-path IP internetwork (where there is more than one path between IP networks), routers choose the best path based on a lowest cost metric. Once a router determines all of the best paths, the higher cost paths are not used unless the topology of the internetwork changes. To check that higher cost paths contain valid links, you must do source routing.

Source routing in IP is done by specifying the IP address(es) of the near side interfaces of the desired routers between the source and its destination. At each leg of the journey, the destination IP address in the IP header is set to the IP address of the next near side router interface. IP supports both loose and strict source routing. In loose source routing, the next router's IP address does not have to be a neighboring router; it can be multiple hops away. In strict source routing, the next router's IP address must be a neighboring router (a single hop away).

IP source routing also records the path taken in the same way as the Record Route option. For each leg of the journey, the IP address of the interface on the router that forwarded the IP datagram is recorded.

Note To use IP source routing, source routing must be enabled on all the routers in the path between the source and destination hosts. It is a common practice to disable source routing on routers, especially those connected to the Internet.

Strict Source Route Option

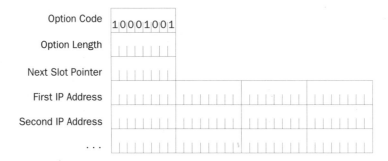

The Strict Source Route option contains the following fields:

- **Option Code**   Set to 137 (Copy Bit=1, Option Class=0, Option Number=9).
- **Option Length**   Set by the sending host to the number of octets in the Strict Source Route option.
- **Next Slot Pointer**   Set to the octet offset (starting at 1) within the next router's Strict Source Route option. The Next Slot Pointer field's minimum value is 4. The Next Slot Pointer field is used also in the same manner as the Record Route option to determine the location of the next IP address slot for recording the route.
- **First IP Address, Second IP Address**   Set by the sending host for the series of IP addresses for successive router destinations in the strict source route; set also by IP routers to the IP address of the forwarding interface. With a maximum of 40 bytes in the IP options portion of the IP header, there is enough room for only a maximum of nine IP addresses.

When a sending host sends an IP datagram with the Strict Source Route option, the sending host:

1. Sets the Next Slot Pointer field's value to 4.
2. Places the first IP address in the strict source route in the IP header's Destination IP Address field.

When an IP router receives an IP datagram with the Strict Source Route option, it compares the Option Length and Next Slot Pointer fields. If the Next Slot Pointer field is less than the Option Length field, the router:

1. Adds 4 to the Next Slot Pointer field's value.
2. Replaces the IP header's destination IP address with the IP address that is recorded in the next slot (based on the Next Slot Pointer field's new value).
3. Records the IP address of the forwarding interface in the previous slot.

If the next destination IP address is not reachable using a directly attached network (the IP address of a neighboring router or host), the IP datagram is discarded and an ICMP Destination Unreachable-Source Route Failed message is sent back to the source host.

If the Next Slot Pointer field's value is greater than the Option Length field's value, the IP datagram has reached its final destination.

Because the size of the Strict Source Route option is not a multiple of 4 bytes, either an End Of Options option (if there are no more options) or a No Operation option (if there are more options after the Strict Source Route option) must be added to ensure that the IP header is an integral multiple of 4 bytes. Windows 2000 TCP/IP places the Strict Source Route option as the last option in the list and uses an End Of Options option to specify the end of the list of options.

Setting the Strict Source Route Option with PING

The Windows 2000 PING utility with the "-k" option can be used to add the Strict Source Route option. The PING utility also can be used to set the IP addresses of successive routers and the final destination in ICMP Echo messages. The syntax is:

```
PING -k [IP address of first hop] [IP address of second hop] …[destination IP
address]
```

For example, to ping 10.0.0.1 through neighboring router interfaces 192.168.1.1 and 192.168.2.1, use the following command:

```
PING -k 192.168.1.1 192.168.2.1 10.0.0.1
```

Loose Source Route Option

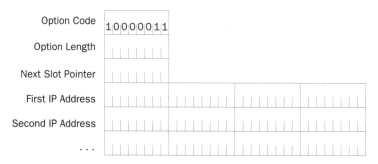

The Strict Source Route option contains the following fields:

- **Option Code**   Set to 131 (Copy Bit=1, Option Class=0, Option Number=3).
- **Option Length**   Set by the sending host to the number of octets in the Loose Source Route option.
- **Next Slot Pointer**   Set to the octet offset (starting at 1) within the next router's Loose Source Route option. The Next Slot Pointer field's minimum value is 4. The Next Slot Pointer field also is used in the same manner as the Record Route option to determine the location of the next IP address slot for recording the route.
- **First IP Address, Second IP Address**   Set by the sending host for the series of IP addresses for successive router destinations in the strict source route, and set by IP routers to the forwarding interface's IP address. With a maximum of 40 bytes in the IP options portion of the IP header, there is enough room for only a maximum of nine IP addresses.

When a sending host sends an IP datagram with the Loose Source Route option, the sending host:

1. Sets the Next Slot Pointer field's value to 4.

2. Places the first IP address in the loose source route in the IP header's Destination IP Address field.

When an IP router receives an IP datagram with the Loose Source Route option, it compares the Option Length and Next Slot Pointer fields. If the Next Slot Pointer field's value is less than the Option Length field's value, the router:

1. Adds 4 to the Next Slot Pointer field's value.

2. Replaces the IP header's destination IP address with the IP address that is recorded in the next slot (based on the Next Slot Pointer field's new value).

3. Records the IP address of the forwarding interface in the previous slot.

If the Next Slot Pointer field's value is greater than the Option Length field's value, the IP datagram has reached its final destination.

Because the size of the Loose Source Route option is not a multiple of 4 bytes, either an End Of Options option (if there are no more options) or a No Operation option (if there are more options) must be added to ensure that the IP header is an integral multiple of 4 bytes.

Setting the Loose Source Route Option with PING

The Windows 2000 PING utility with the "-j" option can be used to add the Loose Source Route option. Additionally, it is used to set the IP addresses of successive routers and the final destination in ICMP Echo messages. The syntax is

```
PING -j [IP address of first hop] [IP address of second hop] …[destination IP address]
```

For example, to ping 10.0.0.1 through neighboring router interfaces 192.168.1.1 and 192.168.2.1, use the following command:

```
PING -j 192.168.1.1 192.168.2.1 10.0.0.1
```

IP Router Alert

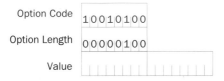

The IP Router Alert option is used to indicate to IP routers that additional processing of the IP datagram is required even when the IP datagram is not addressed to the router. The IP Router Alert option is used for the Resource Reservation Protocol (RSVP) and Internet Group Management Protocol (IGMP) version 2. For example, when a router receives an IP datagram with the IP Router Alert Option, it looks at the IP Protocol field to see if the IP payload requires additional processing before making a forwarding decision. RFC 2113 describes the IP Router Alert Option.

The IP Router Alert option contains the following fields:

- **Option Code**   Set to 148 (Copy Bit=1, Option Class=0, Option Number=20).
- **Option Length**   Set to the fixed length of 4.
- **Value**   A 2-byte field set to 0. All other values are reserved. The value of 0 indicates that the router must examine the packet.

Internet Timestamp

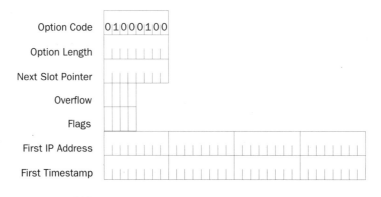

The Internet Timestamp option is used to record the time that an IP datagram arrived at each IP router in the path between the source and destination host. The Internet Timestamp option is similar to the Record Route option in that the sending node creates blank entries in the IP header that routers fill out as the packet travels through the IP internetwork. Each entry consists of the router's IP address and a 32-bit integer timestamp that indicates the number of milliseconds since midnight, Universal Time. If Universal Time is not being used, the high-order bit of the timestamp field is set to 1.

Note To use Internet timestamps, Internet timestamping must be enabled on all the routers in the path between the source and destination hosts. It is common for routers to either not support Internet timestamping or have it disabled.

The Internet Timestamp option contains the following fields:

- **Option Code**   Set to 68 (Copy Bit=0, Option Class=2, Option Number=4).
- **Option Length**   Set by the sending host to the number of octets in the Internet Timestamp option.

- **Next Slot Pointer**   Set to the octet offset (starting at 1) within the Internet Timestamp option of the next slot for the recording of the IP address and timestamp. The Next Slot Pointer field's minimum value is 5.

- **Overflow**   Set by routers to indicate the number of routers that were unable to record their IP address and timestamp.

- **Flags**   Set by the sending host to indicate the format of the IP Address/Timestamp slots. When Flags = 0, the IP address is omitted. This allows up to nine timestamps to be recorded. When Flags = 1, the IP address is recorded, allowing up to four IP address/timestamp pairs to be recorded. The Internet Timestamp option format shown assumes Flags = 1. When Flags = 3, the sending node specifies the IP addresses of successive routers: a timestamp is recorded only if the IP address in the slot matches the router's IP address.

- **First IP Address/First Timestamp**   Set by routers to record the IP address and timestamp of the routers encountered (Flags = 1) or specified (Flags = 3).

When a sending host sends an IP datagram with the Internet Timestamp option, the sending host:

1. Sets the Next Slot Pointer field's value to 5.

2. For a specified route (Flags = 3), places the series of IP addresses in the Internet Timestamp option.

When an IP router receives an IP datagram with the Internet Timestamp option, it compares the Option Length and Next Slot Pointer fields. If the Next Slot Pointer field's value is less than the Option Length field's value:

- If Flags = 3, the router replaces the IP header's destination IP address with the IP address that is recorded in the next slot (based on the Next Slot Pointer field).

- If Flags = 1 or Flags = 3, the router records the IP address of the interface on which the IP datagram was received in the same slot.

- If Flags = 0, the router records the timestamp and adds 4 to the Next Slot Pointer field. If Flags = 1, the router records the timestamp after the IP address and adds 8 to the Next Slot Pointer field. If Flags = 3, the router replaces the IP address and adds 4 to the Next Slot Pointer field.

If the Next Slot Pointer field's value is greater than the Option Length field's value, the router increments the Overflow field. If the Overflow field is 15 before incrementing, an ICMP Parameter Problem is sent back to the source host.

Setting the Internet Timestamp Option with PING

The Windows 2000 PING command and the "-s" option can be used to send ICMP Echo messages with the Internet timestamp. The syntax is:

```
PING -s [slots] [IP Address of destination]
```

For example, to ping the IP address of 10.9.1.1 using Internet timestamps with three slots, use the following command:

```
PING -s 3 10.9.1.1
```

Summary

The Internet Protocol (IP) provides the internetworking building block for all other Internet Layer and above protocols in the TCP/IP suite. IP provides a best-effort, unreliable, connectionless datagram delivery service between networks of an IP internetwork. The IP header provides addressing, type of delivery, maximum link count, fragmentation, and checksum services. IP fragmentation provides a way for IP datagrams to travel over links with a lower IP MTU than the original IP datagram. The basic services of the IP header are extended through IP options, the most common of which provide source routing, path recording, router alert, and timestamping functions.

Chapter 5
Internet Protocol (IP) Addressing

To successfully administer and troubleshoot IP internetworks, it is important to understand all aspects of IP addressing. One of the most important aspects of TCP/IP network administration is the assignment of unique and proper IP addresses to all the nodes of an IP internetwork. While the concept of IP address assignment is simple, the actual mechanics of efficient allocation of IP addresses using subnetting techniques are somewhat complicated. Additionally, it is important to understand the role of IP broadcast and multicast traffic and how these addresses map to Network Interface Layer addresses such as Ethernet and Token Ring media access control (MAC) addresses.

Types of IP Addresses

An IP address is a 32-bit logical address and can be one of the following types:

- **Unicast** A unicast IP address is assigned to a single network interface attached to an IP internetwork. Unicast IP addresses are used in one-to-one communications.
- **Broadcast** A broadcast IP address is designed to be processed by every IP node on the same network segment. Broadcast IP addresses are used in one-to-everyone communications.
- **Multicast** An IP multicast address is an address on which one or multiple nodes can be listening on the same or different network segments. IP multicast addresses are used in one-to-many communications.

Expressing IP Addresses

The IP address is a 32-bit quantity that computers are adept at manipulating. Humans, however, do not think in binary mode, 32 bits at a time. Because most humans are trained in the use of decimal (base 10 numbering system) rather than binary (base 2 numbering system), it is common to express the IP address in a decimal form.

The 32-bit IP address is divided from the high-order bit to the low-order bit into four 8-bit quantities called octets. IP addresses are normally written as four separate decimal octets and are delimited by a period (a dot). This is known as dotted decimal notation.

For example, the IP address:

00001010000000011111000101000011

is subdivided into four octets:

00001010 00000001 11110001 01000011

Each octet is converted to a base 10 number and separated by periods:

10.1.241.67

A generalized IP address is indicated with *w.x.y.z,* as Figure 5-1 shows.

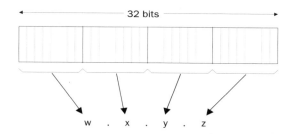

Figure 5-1. *The generalized IP address consisting of 32 bits expressed in dotted decimal notation.*

Converting from Binary to Decimal

To convert a binary number to its decimal equivalent, add the numbers represented by the bit positions that are set to 1. Figure 5-2 shows an 8-bit number and the decimal value of each position.

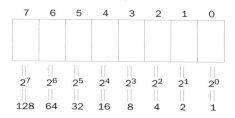

Figure 5-2. *An 8-bit number showing bit positions and their decimal equivalents.*

For example, the 8-bit binary number 01000011 is 67 (= 64 + 2 + 1). The maximum number that can be expressed with an 8-bit number (11111111) is 255 (= 128 + 64 + 32 + 16 + 8 + 4 + 2 + 1).

Converting from Decimal to Binary

To convert from decimal to binary, the decimal number is analyzed to see if it contains the quantities represented by the bit positions from the high-order bit to the low-order bit. Starting from the high-order bit quantity (128), if each quantity is present, the bit in that bit position is set to 1. For example, the decimal number 211 contains 128, 64, 16, 2, and 1. Therefore, 211 is 11010011 in binary.

IP Addresses in the IP Header

IP addresses are used in the IP header's Source Address and Destination Address fields.

- The IP header's Source Address field is always either a unicast address or the special address 0.0.0.0. The unspecified IP address, 0.0.0.0, is used only when the IP node is not configured with an IP address and the node is attempting to obtain an address through a configuration protocol such as Dynamic Host Configuration Protocol (DHCP).

- The IP header's Destination Address field is always a unicast address, multicast address, or a broadcast address.

Unicast IP Addresses

Each network interface on which TCP/IP is active must be identified by a unique, logical, unicast IP address. The unicast IP address is a logical address because it is an Internet Layer address that has no direct relation to the address being used at the Network Interface Layer. For example, the unicast IP address assigned to a host on an Ethernet network has no relation to the 48-bit MAC address used by the Ethernet network adapter.

The unicast IP address is an internetwork address for IP nodes that contains a network ID and a host ID:

- The network ID, or network address, identifies the nodes that are located on the same logical network. In most cases, a logical network is the same as a physical network segment whose boundaries are defined by IP routers. In some cases, multiple logical networks exist on the same physical network using a practice called multinetting. All nodes on the same logical network share the same network ID. If all nodes on the same logical network aren't configured with the same network ID, routing or delivery problems will occur. The network ID must be unique to the internetwork.

- The host ID, or host address, identifies a node within a network. A node is a router or host (a nonrouter interface such as a workstation, server, or other TCP/IP-based system). The host ID must be unique within each network segment.

Note   The term *network ID* applies to class-based network IDs, subnetted network IDs, and classless network IDs.

Figure 5-3 is an example of a unicast IP address and its network ID and host ID portions:

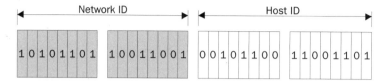

Figure 5-3. *The structure of an example IP address showing the network ID and host ID.*

A History Lesson: IP Address Classes

This section is titled "A History Lesson" because modern-day networks are not based on the Internet address classes. Because of the Internet's recent rapid expansion, the Internet authorities saw clearly that the originally designed class-based structure did not scale well to the size of a global internetwork. For example, if the Internet authorities were still handing out class-based addresses, there would be hundreds of thousands of routes in the routing tables of Internet backbone routers. To prevent this scaling problem, addressing on the modern Internet is classless. However, the understanding of Internet address classes is an important element of understanding IP addressing.

RFC 791 defined the unicast IP address in terms of address classes to create well-defined networks of various sizes. The design goal was to create:

- A small number of large networks (networks with a large amount of nodes)
- A moderate number of moderate-sized networks
- A large number of small networks

The result was the creation of address classes, subdivisions of the 32-bit IP address space defined by setting high-order bits and dividing the remaining bits into network ID and host ID.

Address Class A

Class A addresses are designed for networks with a large amount of hosts. The high-order bit is set to 0. The first 8 bits (the first octet) are defined as the network ID; the last 24 bits (the last three octets) are defined as the host ID. Figure 5-4 illustrates the class A address.

Figure 5-4. *The class A address showing the network ID and the host ID.*

Class B

Class B addresses are designed for moderate-sized networks with a moderate amount of hosts. The 2 high-order bits are set to 10. The first 16 bits (the first 2 octets) are defined as the network ID; the last 16 bits (the last 2 octets) are defined as the host ID. Figure 5-5 illustrates the class B address.

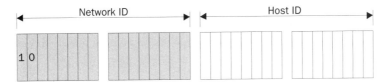

Figure 5-5. *The class B address showing the network ID and the host ID.*

Class C

Class C addresses are designed for small networks with a small amount of hosts. The 3 high-order bits are set to 110. The first 24 bits (the first 3 octets) are defined as the network ID; the last 8 bits (the last 3 octets) are defined as the host ID. Figure 5-6 illustrates the class C address.

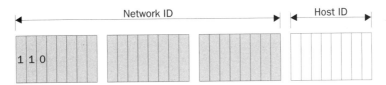

Figure 5-6. *The class C address showing the network ID and the host ID.*

Additional Address Classes

Class D and E addresses are defined, in addition to unicast address classes A, B, and C.

Class D

Class D addresses are for IP multicast addresses. The 4 high-order bits are set to binary 1110. The next 28 bits are used for individual IP multicast addresses. For more information on IP multicast addresses, see the "IP Multicast Addresses" section of this chapter. Microsoft Windows 2000 supports class D addresses for IP multicast traffic.

Class E

Class E addresses are experimental addresses, reserved for future use. The 5 high-order bits in a class E address are set to 11110. Windows 2000 does not support the use of class E addresses.

Rules for Enumerating Network IDs

In enumerating IP network IDs, the following rules apply:

- **The network ID cannot begin with 127 as the first octet.** All 127.*x.y.z* addresses are reserved as loopback addresses.
- **All the bits in the network ID cannot be set to 1.** Network IDs set to all 1s are reserved for broadcast addresses.
- **All the bits in the network ID cannot be set to 0.** Network IDs set to all 0s are reserved for indicating a host on the local network.
- **The network ID must be unique to the IP internetwork.**

Table 5-1 lists the ranges of network IDs based on the IP address classes. Network IDs are expressed by setting all host bits to 0 and expressing the result in dotted decimal notation.

Table 5-1. Address Class Ranges of Network IDs

Address Class	First Network ID	Last Network ID	Number of Networks
Class A	1.0.0.0	126.0.0.0	126
Class B	128.0.0.0	191.255.0.0	16,384
Class C	192.0.0.0	223.255.255.0	2,097,152

Note IP network IDs, even though expressed in dotted decimal notation, are not IP addresses assigned to network interfaces. The IP network ID is the network address that is common for all network interfaces attached to the same logical network.

Rules for Enumerating Host IDs

In enumerating IP host IDs, the following rules apply:

- **All bits in the host ID cannot be set to 1.** Host IDs set to all 1s are reserved for broadcast addresses.
- **All the bits in the host ID cannot be set to 0.** Host IDs set to all 0s are reserved for the expression of IP network IDs.
- **The host ID must be unique to the network.**

Table 5-2 lists the ranges of host IDs based on the IP address classes.

Table 5-2. Address Class Ranges of Host IDs

Address Class	First Host ID	Last Host ID	Number of Hosts
Class A	*w*.0.0.1	*w*.255.255.254	16,777,214
Class B	*w.x*.0.1	*w.x*.255.254	65,534
Class C	*w.x.y*.1	*w.x.y*.254	254

Subnets and the Subnet Mask

Subnetting is designed to make more efficient use of a fixed address space. A fixed address space is an IP network ID. The network bits are fixed and the host bits are variable. Originally, the host bits were designed to indicate host IDs within an IP network ID. With subnetting, host ID bits can be used to express a combination of a subnetwork ID and a subnetwork host ID, thereby better utilizing the host bits.

Consider a class B network that has 65,534 possible hosts. A network segment of 65,534 hosts is technically possible but impractical because of the accumulation of broadcast traffic. All nodes on the same physical network segment belong to the same broadcast domain and share the same broadcast traffic. Because 65,534 hosts all sharing the same broadcast traffic don't make a practical configuration, most of the host IDs are not usable.

To create smaller broadcast domains and make better use of the host bits, RFC 950 defines a method of subdividing a network ID into subnetworks—subsets of the original class-based network—by using bits in the host ID portion of the original IP network ID. Each subnetwork, or subnet, is assigned a new subnetted network ID. Hosts on subnets are assigned host IDs from the remaining host bits in the subnetted network ID.

While RFC 950 discusses subnetting in terms of class-based network IDs, subnetting is a general technique that can be used on classless network IDs or used recursively on subnetted network IDs. This is described in the "Variable-Length Subnetting" section of this chapter.

The proper subnetting of a network ID is transparent to the rest of the IP internetwork. For example, consider the class B network ID of 131.107.0.0, shown in Figure 5-7, that is connected to the Internet. The class-based network ID was obtained from the InterNIC and is a fixed address space. Because this class B network ID represents an impractical broadcast domain, it is subnetted. However, in subnetting 131.107.0.0, we should not require any reconfiguration of the Internet routers.

Figure 5-7. *The class B network 131.107.0.0 before subnetting.*

From an analysis of broadcast traffic, it is determined that there should be no more than 250 nodes on each broadcast domain. Therefore, network ID 131.107.0.0 is subnetted to look like a class C address by using the first 8 high-order host bits (the third octet represented by *y*) for the subnetted network ID. Note that before the subnetting, only the first 2 octets are considered the network ID. After the subnetting, the first 3 octets are considered the network ID. The new network IDs are 131.107.1.0, 131.107.2.0, and 131.107.3.0, as Figure 5-8 shows.

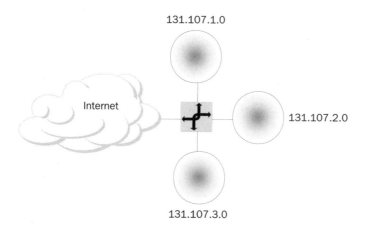

Figure 5-8. *The class B network 131.107.0.0 after subnetting.*

The IP router connected to the Internet has an interface on each of the subnets and is aware of the new subnetting scheme. The IP router forwards IP datagrams from the Internet to the host on the appropriate subnet. The Internet routers are completely unaware of the subnetting of 131.107.0.0. They still consider all IP addresses in the range of 131.107.0.0 through 131.107.255.255 to be reachable through the IP router's Internet interface.

The Subnet Mask

With subnetting, a host or router can no longer assume the network ID and host ID designations of the IP address classes. The node needs additional configuration to distinguish the network ID and host ID portions of an IP address, whether the network ID is class-based, classless, or a subnetted network ID.

RFC 950 defines the use of a bit mask to identify which bits in the IP address belong to the network ID and which belong to the host ID. This bit mask, called a subnet mask or address mask, is defined by the following:

- If the bit position corresponds to a bit in the network ID, it is set to 1.
- If the bit position corresponds to a bit in the host ID, it is set to 0.

Since the publication of RFC 950, TCP/IP nodes require a subnet mask to be configured for each IP address, even when class-based addressing is being used. A default subnet mask corresponds to a class-based network ID. A custom subnet mask corresponds to either a classless network ID or a subnetted network ID. The subnet mask is the definitive piece of configuration information that allows the node to determine its own network ID.

Subnet Masks in Dotted Decimal Representation

Frequently, the subnet mask is expressed in dotted decimal notation. Although expressed in the same form as an IP address, the subnet mask is not an IP address. As an example of subnet masks in dotted decimal notation, default subnet masks are based on the IP address classes. Table 5-3 lists the default subnet masks for class A, B, and C network IDs in dotted decimal notation.

Table 5-3. Dotted Decimal Notation for Default Subnet Masks

Address Class	Bits for Subnet Mask	Subnet Mask
Class A	11111111 00000000 00000000 00000000	255.0.0.0
Class B	11111111 11111111 00000000 00000000	255.255.0.0
Class C	11111111 11111111 11111111 00000000	255.255.255.0

A custom subnet mask is used whenever you perform non-classful addressing. In our previous example, the classful network ID 131.107.0.0 is subnetted by using the third octet for subnets. The subnetted network ID 131.107.1.0 no longer uses the default subnet mask 255.255.0.0. To express the third octet as part of the network ID, the custom subnet mask 255.255.255.0 is used.

The subnetted network ID and its corresponding subnet mask are expressed in dotted decimal notation as 131.107.1.0, 255.255.255.0.

Network Prefix Length Representation of Subnet Masks

While it is technically possible to subnet IP network IDs by choosing host bits in a non-contiguous fashion, it is impractical and mathematically challenging to enumerate the subnetted network IDs and the host IDs per subnet. For this reason, subnetting must be done by choosing host bits in a contiguous fashion from the high-order host bit.

Because the network ID bits are always contiguous starting from the highest order bit, an easier and more compact way of expressing the subnet mask is to indicate the number of network ID bits using network prefix notation, or Classless Inter-Domain Routing (CIDR) notation. Network prefix notation views the IP address in terms of the prefix (the network ID) and the suffix (the host ID). Network prefix notation is:

/# of bits in the network ID

Network prefix notation is commonly used with TCP/IP implementations other than Windows 2000, and it is an important notation to understand looking forward to IP version 6 (IPv6).

Table 5-4 lists the equivalent subnet mask in network prefix notation for the IP address classes.

Table 5-4. Network Prefix Notation for Default Subnet Masks

Address Class	Bits for Subnet Mask	Network Prefix
Class A	11111111 00000000 00000000 00000000	/8
Class B	11111111 11111111 00000000 00000000	/16
Class C	11111111 11111111 11111111 00000000	/24

In our previous example, the classful network ID 131.107.0.0, with the subnet mask of 255.255.0.0, is expressed in network prefix notation as 131.107.0.0/16. If 131.107.0.0 were subnetted by using the third octet to express subnets, a total of 24 contiguous bits would be used for the subnetted network ID. The subnetted network ID 131.107.1.0 and its corresponding subnet mask are expressed in network prefix notation as 131.107.1.0/24.

Expressing Network IDs

A network ID is defined by the fixed network ID bits and the subnet mask. Therefore, network IDs must always be expressed by the combination of the network ID and a subnet mask. Expressing a network ID without its subnet mask is ambiguous. For example, for the network ID 10.16.0.0, which bits are used for the network ID? The first 16? The first 24? The first 12?

The following are examples of properly expressed network IDs:

- 192.168.45.0, 255.255.255.0
- 10.99.0.0/16

All hosts on the same logical network must be using the same network ID bits and the same subnet mask. For example, 131.107.0.0/16 is not the same as 131.107.0.0/24. For the network ID 131.107.0.0/16, the usable IP addresses range from 131.107.0.1 through 131.107.255.254. For the network ID 131.107.0.0/24, the usable IP addresses range from 131.107.0.1 through 131.107.0.254. Clearly, 131.107.0.0/16 and 131.107.0.0/24 do not represent the same group of hosts.

Determining the Network ID

In earlier examples, classful network IDs and subnetted network IDs all fell along octet boundaries where it was easy to determine the network ID and host ID portion of the IP address. However, real world subnetting is not always done along octet boundaries. For example, some network administrators might determine that, for their situation, they need only three host bits for subnetting.

Because subnetting can occur along non-octet boundaries, there must be a method of determining the network ID from an IP address with an arbitrary subnet mask. IP uses a method called a *bit-wise logical AND* to extract the network ID.

Recall how the subnet mask is defined: a 1 is used to indicate a network ID bit and a 0 is used to indicate a host ID bit. In a logical AND comparison, the result is 1 when the value of the two bits being compared is 1. Otherwise, the result is 0. This comparison is done for all 32 bits of the IP address and subnet mask. The result of the bit-wise logical AND of the IP address and the subnet mask is the network ID.

For example, what is the network ID of the IP node 131.107.164.26 with a subnet mask of 255.255.240.0? To obtain the result in binary, convert both the IP address and subnet mask to binary. Then perform the logical AND comparison for each bit.

IP address	10000011 01101011 10100100 00011010
Subnet mask	11111111 11111111 11110000 00000000
Network ID	10000011 01101011 10100000 00000000

The result of the bit-wise logical AND of the 32 bits of the IP address and the subnet mask is the network ID 131.107.160.0 with the subnet mask of 255.255.240.0.

Notice that:

- The bits in the network ID portion of the IP address are copied directly to the result. A value of 1 in the network ID portion of the IP address becomes a 1 in the result. A value of 0 in the network ID portion of the IP address becomes a 0 in the result.
- All bits in the host ID portion of the IP address are set to 0. Because the subnet mask uses a 0 for host ID bit positions, the logical AND comparison always yields a 0.

Therefore, the bits in the network ID are copied and the bits in the host ID are set to 0. The result must be the network ID.

How to Subnet

The act of subnetting a network ID is a relatively complex procedure; although there are numerous subnet calculators available, the ability to subnet is a vital skill for any TCP/IP network administrator.

Subnetting is done in two basic steps:

1. Based on your design requirements, decide how many host bits you need for the proper balance between number of subnets and number of hosts per subnet.

2. Based on the number of host bits chosen, enumerate the subnetted network IDs, including the ranges of usable IP addresses for each subnetted network ID. The actual mechanics of defining the subnetted network IDs can be done in binary or decimal.

There are two methods for the second step of subnetting, the enumeration of the subnetted network IDs:

1. The binary method, where the individual bits of the subnetted network IDs are manipulated and converted to dotted decimal notation, can be used to subnet, but the method does not scale well to large numbers of subnets. It is described here primarily to illustrate the subnetting process in its most fundamental form.

2. The decimal method, where subnetted network IDs are derived from calculations on decimal numbers, scales well to large numbers of subnets and lends itself well to spreadsheets and programming code.

Step 1: Determining the Number of Host Bits

To determine the number of host bits required for subnetting, perform an analysis of your internetwork. You should determine the following:

- **The number of subnets needed both now and in the future**   Be sure to plan for expansion. Subnetting an existing network requires reassigning IP addresses to IP interfaces. While DHCP can ease this burden, routers and other fixed-address types of hosts might need to be manually reconfigured. Subnetting is not something you want to do often.

- **The maximum number of hosts needed on each subnet**   This number will depend on how many hosts you want sharing the same broadcast traffic. In most cases, when choosing between more subnets and more hosts per subnet, the practical choice is to choose more subnets.

There is an inverse relationship between the number of subnets and the number of hosts per subnet that can be supported by a given subnetting scheme. As Figure 5-9 illustrates, when you choose more host bits, the number of subnets goes up, but the number of hosts per subnet goes down by approximately a factor of 2.

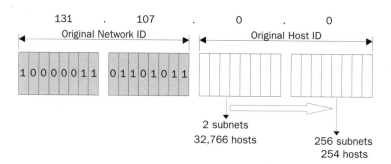

Figure 5-9. *The relationship between the number of subnets and hosts per subnet when subnetting the class B network ID 131.107.0.0.*

If we choose one host bit when subnetting the class B network ID 131.107.0.0, two subnets can be expressed, with 32,766 hosts per subnet. If we choose 8 host bits, 256 subnets can be expressed with 254 hosts per subnet.

Determine how many subnets you need now, and plan for growth by estimating how many you'll need in the next five years. Each physical network segment is a subnet. Point-to-point wide area network (WAN) connections such as leased lines might need subnetted network IDs, unless your routers support unnumbered connections. Non-broadcast multiple access WAN technologies such as Frame Relay need subnetted network IDs. Use additional host bits if the remaining host bits can express more hosts per subnet than you'll need.

Subnetting always starts with a fixed address space in the form of a network ID. The network ID to be subnetted can be a classful network ID, a classless network ID (as allocated using CIDR), or a previously subnetted classful or classless network ID. The fixed address space contains a sequence of bits that are fixed (the network ID bits) and a sequence of bits that are variable (the host ID bits).

Based on your analysis of the desired number of subnets and number of hosts per subnet, a specific number of high-order host bits is converted from host bits into subnet bits. The combination of the original network ID bits and the converted host bits becomes the new subnetted network ID.

As you determine how many host bits you need, you determine the new subnet mask for your subnetted network IDs.

Tables 5-5, 5-6, and 5-7 list the subnetting of classful network IDs according to the requirement of a specific number of subnets. These tables can be useful when determining a subnetting scheme for a class-based network ID based on a required number of subnets and a desired number of hosts per subnet.

Table 5-5. Subnetting of a Class A Network ID

Required Number of Subnets	Number of Host Bits	Subnet Mask	Number of Hosts per Subnet
1-2	1	255.128.0.0 or /9	8,388,606
3-4	2	255.192.0.0 or /10	4,194,302
5-8	3	255.224.0.0 or /11	2,097,150
9-16	4	255.240.0.0 or /12	1,048,574
17-32	5	255.248.0.0 or /13	524,286
33-64	6	255.252.0.0 or /14	262,142
65-128	7	255.254.0.0 or /15	131,070
129-256	8	255.255.0.0 or /16	65,534
257-512	9	255.255.128.0 or /17	32,766
513-1024	10	255.255.192.0 or /18	16,382
1025-2048	11	255.255.224.0 or /19	8190
2049-4096	12	255.255.240.0 or /20	4094
4097-8192	13	255.255.248.0 or /21	2046
8193-16,384	14	255.255.252.0 or /22	1022
16,385-32,768	15	255.255.254.0 or /23	510
32,769-65,536	16	255.255.255.0 or /24	254
65,537-131,072	17	255.255.255.128 or /25	126
131,073-262,144	18	255.255.255.192 or /26	62
262,145-524,288	19	255.255.255.224 or /27	30
524,289-1,048,576	20	255.255.255.240 or /28	14
1,048,577-2,097,152	21	255.255.255.248 or /29	6
2,097,153-4,194,304	22	255.255.255.252 or /30	2

Table 5-6. Subnetting of a Class B Network ID

Required Number of Subnets	Number of Host Bits	Subnet Mask	Number of Hosts per Subnet
1-2	1	255.255.128.0 or /17	32,766
3-4	2	255.255.192.0 or /18	16,382
5-8	3	255.255.224.0 or /19	8190
9-16	4	255.255.240.0 or /20	4094
17-32	5	255.255.248.0 or /21	2046
33-64	6	255.255.252.0 or /22	1022
65-128	7	255.255.254.0 or /23	510
129-256	8	255.255.255.0 or /24	254
257-512	9	255.255.255.128 or /25	126
513-1024	10	255.255.255.192 or /26	62
1025-2048	11	255.255.255.224 or /27	30
2049-4096	12	255.255.255.240 or /28	14
4097-8192	13	255.255.255.248 or /29	6
8193-16,384	14	255.255.255.252 or /30	2

Table 5-7. Subnetting of a Class C Network ID

Required Number of Subnets	Number of Host Bits	Subnet Mask	Number of Hosts per Subnet
1-2	1	255.255.255.128 or /25	126
3-4	2	255.255.255.192 or /26	62
5-8	3	255.255.255.224 or /27	30
9-16	4	255.255.255.240 or /28	14
17-32	5	255.255.255.248 or /29	6
33-64	6	255.255.255.252 or /30	2

Step 2: Defining the Subnetted Network IDs (Binary Method)

The following technique describes how to subnet an arbitrary network ID into subnets that yield both subnetted network IDs, and their corresponding range of valid IP addresses, using binary analysis. While there are other techniques that might seem easier, they are typically limited in scope. This technique will work for any subnetting situation.

Step 2a: Enumerating the Subnetted Network IDs (Binary)

Create a three-column table with 2^n rows where n is the number of host bits chosen for the subnetting. Column one is used for the subnet number. Column two is for the binary representation of the subnetted network ID. Column three is for the dotted decimal representation of the subnetted network ID.

For the binary representation for each entry in the table, the original network ID bits are fixed at their original values. The host bits chosen for subnetting, hereafter known as the subnet bits, are allowed to vary over all of their possible values, and the remaining host bits are set to 0.

The table's first entry is the subnet, defined by setting all the subnet bits to 0 (also called the all-zeros subnet). The result is converted to dotted decimal notation. This subnetted network ID does not appear to be different from the original network ID; but remember that a network ID is a combination of the dotted decimal notation and a subnet mask. With the new subnet mask, the subnetted network ID is clearly different from the original network ID.

In the following entries, treat the subnet bits as though they were distinct binary numbers. Increment the value within the subnet bits and convert the result of the entire 32-bit subnettted network ID to dotted decimal notation.

As an example of this technique, subnet the class B network ID 131.107.0.0 by using three bits of the classful host ID. The new subnet mask for the subnetted network IDs is 255.255.224.0, or /19. Based on using three host bits, create a table with eight entries (8 = 2^3). The first entry is the all-zeros subnet. The additional entries are increments of the binary number represented by the subnet bits (underlined). Table 5-8 lists the subnetted network IDs.

Table 5-8. 3-Bit Subnetting of 131.107.0.0 (Binary)

Subnet	Binary Representation	Subnetted Network ID
1	10000011.01101011.00000000.00000000	131.107.0.0/19
2	10000011.01101011.00100000.00000000	131.107.32.0/19
3	10000011.01101011.01000000.00000000	131.107.64.0/19
4	10000011.01101011.01100000.00000000	131.107.96.0/19
5	10000011.01101011.10000000.00000000	131.107.128.0/19
6	10000011.01101011.10100000.00000000	131.107.160.0/19
7	10000011.01101011.11000000.00000000	131.107.192.0/19
8	10000011.01101011.11100000.00000000	131.107.224.0/19

Step 2b: Enumerating IP Address Ranges for Each Subnetted Network ID (Binary)
For each subnetted network ID, the range of valid IP addresses must be determined.

1. Create a three-column table with 2^n entries where n is the number of host bits chosen for the subnetting. Column one is used for the subnet number. Column two is for the binary representation of the first and last IP address in the range. Column three is for the dotted decimal representation of the first and last IP address in the range. Alternately, you can extend the table created for enumerating the subnetted network IDs by adding two columns.

2. Express the first and last IP address in the range in binary. The first IP address is defined by setting the remaining host bits to 0, except for the last host bit. The last IP address is defined by setting the remaining host bits to 1, except for the last host bit.

3. Convert the binary representation of the first and last IP address to dotted decimal notation.

4. Repeat steps 2–3 until the table is complete.

To continue our example, Table 5-9 lists the enumeration of the range of valid IP addresses for the 3-bit subnetting of 131.107.0.0. The host bits are underlined.

Table 5-9. Enumeration of IP Addresses for the 3-Bit Subnetting of 131.107.0.0 (Binary)

Subnet	Binary Representation	Range of IP Addresses
1	10000011.01101011.000<u>00000.00000000</u> - 10000011.01101011.000<u>11111.11111110</u>	131.107.0.1 - 131.107.31.254
2	10000011.01101011.001<u>00000.00000001</u> - 10000011.01101011.001<u>11111.11111110</u>	131.107.32.1 - 131.107.63.254
3	10000011.01101011.010<u>00000.00000001</u> - 10000011.01101011.010<u>11111.11111110</u>	131.107.64.1 - 131.107.95.254
4	10000011.01101011.011<u>00000.00000001</u> - 10000011.01101011.011<u>11111.11111110</u>	131.107.96.1 - 131.107.127.254
5	10000011.01101011.100<u>00000.00000001</u> - 10000011.01101011.100<u>11111.11111110</u>	131.107.128.1 - 131.107.159.254
6	10000011.01101011.101<u>00000.00000001</u> - 10000011.01101011.101<u>11111.11111110</u>	131.107.160.1 - 131.107.191.254
7	10000011.01101011.110<u>00000.00000001</u> - 10000011.01101011.110<u>11111.11111110</u>	131.107.192.1 - 131.107.223.254
8	10000011.01101011.111<u>00000.00000001</u> - 10000011.01101011.111<u>11111.11111110</u>	131.107.224.1 - 131.107.255.254

Step 2: Defining the Subnetted Network IDs (Decimal Method)

The previous technique describes a subnetting technique using binary. While this method will work for any valid subnetting scheme, it does not scale well. For example, if you were performing a 10-bit subnetting, you would have 1024 entries in the table. While programmers are adept at binary manipulation and could create programs to automate this process, non-programmers find it easier to work with decimal numbers. Therefore, the following technique treats the 32-bit network ID and IP address as a single decimal number to enumerate the subnetted network ID and its corresponding range of IP addresses. Either technique—binary or decimal—yields the same result.

Step 2a: Enumerating the Subnetted Network IDs (Decimal)

1. Create a three-column table with 2^n entries where n is the number of host bits chosen for the subnetting. Column one is used for the subnet number. Column two is for the decimal representation of the subnetted network ID. Column three is for the dotted decimal representation of the subnetted network ID.

2. Convert the original network ID from dotted decimal notation ($w.x.y.z$) to N, its decimal representation.

$$N = w*16777216 + x*65536 + y*256 + z$$

3. Compute I, the increment value, based on h, the number of host bits remaining.

    $$I = 2^h$$

4. For the first table entry, the all-zeros subnet, the decimal representation of the subnetted network ID is N, and the subnetted network ID is $w.x.y.z$, with its new subnet mask.

5. For the decimal representation of the next table entry, add the increment I to the previous entry.

6. Convert the decimal representation of the subnetted network ID to dotted decimal notation (W.X.Y.Z) using the following formula (where s is the decimal representation of the subnetted network ID):

    $$W = INT (s/16777216)$$

    $$X = INT ((s \bmod 16777216)/65536)$$

    $$Y = INT ((s \bmod 65536)/256)$$

    $$Z = s \bmod 256$$

    INT () denotes integer division and yields the integer multiple. Mod () denotes the modulus operator and yields the remainder upon division.

7. Repeat steps 5–6 until the table is complete.

To compare the two techniques and verify that they will both yield the same result, let's perform a decimal 3-bit subnetting of 131.107.0.0.

Based on $n = 3$, we create a table with eight entries. The entry for subnet 1 is the all-zeros subnet. N, the decimal representation of 131.107.0.0, is 2204827648 (131*16777216 + 107*65536). Because there are 13 remaining host bits, the increment value I is 2^{13}, or 8192. Entries for subnets 2–8 are incremented by 8192.

Table 5-10 lists the subnetted network IDs of 131.107.0.0.

Table 5-10. 3-Bit Subnetting of 131.107.0.0 (Decimal)

Subnet	Decimal Representation	Subnetted Network ID
1	2204827648	131.107.0.0/19
2	2204835840	131.107.32.0/19
3	2204844032	131.107.64.0/19
4	2204852224	131.107.96.0/19
5	2204860416	131.107.128.0/19
6	2204868608	131.107.160.0/19
7	2204876800	131.107.192.0/19
8	2204884992	131.107.224.0/19

Step 2b: Enumerating IP Address Ranges for Each Subnetted Network ID (Decimal)

For each subnetted network ID, the range of valid IP addresses must be determined.

1. Create a three-column table with 2^n entries where n is the number of host bits chosen for the subnetting. Column one is used for the subnet number. Column two is for the decimal representation of the first and last IP address in the range. Column three is for the dotted decimal representation of the first and last IP address in the range. Alternately, you can extend the table created for enumerating the subnetted network IDs by adding two columns.

2. Compute the increment value J based on h, the number of host bits remaining.

   $J = 2^h - 2$

3. The decimal representation of the first IP address is $N + 1$ where N is the decimal representation of the subnetted network ID. The decimal representation of the last IP address is $N + J$.

4. Convert the decimal representation of the first and last IP address to dotted decimal notation (W.X.Y.Z) using the following formula (where s is the decimal representation of the first or last IP address):

   W = INT (s/16777216)

   X = INT ((s mod 16777216)/65536)

   Y = INT ((s mod 65536)/256)

   Z = s mod 256

   INT () denotes integer division and yields the integer multiple. Mod () denotes the modulus operator and yields the remainder upon division.

5. Repeat steps 3–4 until the table is complete.

To continue with our example, we will enumerate the range of valid IP addresses for the 3-bit subnetting of 131.107.0.0. Compute the increment value $J = 2^{13} - 2 = 8190$. Table 5-11 lists the ranges of IP addresses for the eight subnetted network IDs.

Table 5-11. Enumeration of IP Addresses for the 3-Bit Subnetting of 131.107.0.0 (Decimal)

Subnet	Binary Representation	Range of IP Addresses
1	2204827649 - 2204835838	131.107.0.1 - 131.107.31.254
2	2204835841 - 2204844030	131.107.32.1 - 131.107.63.254
3	2204844033 - 2204852222	131.107.64.1 - 131.107.95.254
4	2204852225 - 2204860414	131.107.96.1 - 131.107.127.254
5	2204860417 - 2204868606	131.107.128.1 - 131.107.159.254
6	2204868609 - 2204876798	131.107.160.1 - 131.107.131.107
7	2204876801 - 2204884990	131.107.192.1 - 131.107.223.254
8	2204884993 - 2204893182	131.107.224.1 - 131.107.255.254

All-Zeros and All-Ones Subnets

In the previous discussion's examples, we used the subnet where all the host bits were set to 0 (the all-zeros subnet), and the subnet where all the host bits were set to 1 (the all-ones subnet). The use of these subnets is somewhat controversial.

Originally, RFC 950 forbade the use of these subnets as valid subnets because:

- The all-zeros subnet caused problems for early routing protocols that did not use a subnet mask to distinguish a network ID. Therefore, 131.107.0.0/16 was the same network to the router as 131.107.0.0/19.

- The subnet broadcast address for the all-ones subnet uses the same address as a special broadcast address, called the all-subnets-directed broadcast address. An IP datagram for the all-subnets-directed broadcast was designed to be forwarded by routers to all classful network ID subnets. For more information on the all-subnets-directed broadcast address, see the "IP Broadcast Addresses" section of this chapter.

The restriction on the use of the all-zeros and all-ones subnets is part of the legacy of classful networks. The result of this restriction is that substantial portions of a fixed address space are unusable and wasted. For example, when performing a 3-bit subnetting of 131.107.0.0 and excluding the all-zeros and all-ones subnets, only six subnets are available. The range of IP addresses, 131.107.0.1 through 131.107.31.254 for the all-zeros subnet, and the range, 131.107.224.1 through 131.107.255.254 for the all-ones subnet, are unusable.

RFC 1812 now allows the use of all-zeros and all-ones subnets for classless environments.

- Classless environments use routing protocols that advertise the subnet mask with the network ID. Therefore, 131.107.0.0/16 is distinguishable from 131.107.0.0/19.

- The all-subnets-directed broadcast has no meaning in a classless environment.

Even though RFC 1812 now allows the use of these special subnets, there is no guarantee that all of your routers and hosts support them. For routers, it is a common default configuration that they do not support one or the other special subnet and must be instructed to do so. Verify that your routers and hosts support the all-zeros and all-ones subnets before using them. Microsoft Windows 2000 hosts and routers support the use of the all-zeros and all-ones subnets without additional configuration.

Variable-Length Subnetting

The preceding discussion illustrates how a fixed network ID can be subdivided into equally sized subnets. The 3-bit subnetting of the classful network ID 131.107.0.0/16 produced eight equally sized subnets, each containing 8190 possible IP addresses. However, in the real world, network segments are not equal sizes. Some network segments require more IP addresses than others. For example, a network segment containing hosts requires more IP addresses than a backbone network segment containing just a few routers. And point-to-point WAN connections require only two IP addresses.

If equally sized subnetting were done, the subnetting would have to be done based on the network segment that required the largest amount of hosts. All other network segments would have the same amount of IP addresses, some of which are unassigned or unusable.

To maximize the use of the fixed address space, the technique of subnetting is applied recursively to produce subnets of different sizes all derived from the same original network ID. This is known as variable-length subnetting. Differently sized subnets use different subnet masks, or variable-length subnet masks (VLSM).

Because all of the subnets are derived from the same network ID, if the subnets are contiguous, the routes for all the subnets can be summarized by advertising the original network ID. Contiguous subnets are subnets of the same network ID that are connected to each other.

When performing variable-length subnetting, care must be taken so that each subnet is unique, and with its subnet mask, can be distinguished from all other subnets of the original network ID. Variable-length subnetting requires a careful analysis of your network segments to determine how many of each sized network you require. Then, starting from your network ID, subnetting is performed as many times as needed to express as many subnets as desired with the proper sizes.

With variable-length subnetting, the subnetting technique is applied recursively: you subnet a previously subnetted network ID. When subnetting a previously subnetted network ID, the subnetted network ID bits are fixed and an appropriate number of remaining host bits is chosen for subnetting.

Example of Variable-Length Subnetting

To expand on our earlier example, let's continue subnetting the classful network ID of 131.107.0.0/16. After the 3-bit subnetting has been performed, the remaining addresses must be divided such that:

- Half of the addresses are reserved for future use
- Three subnets are allocated with up to 8190 IP addresses
- 31 subnets are allocated with up to 254 IP addresses
- 64 subnets are allocated with only 2 IP addresses

Recall that the 3-bit subnetting of 131.107.0.0/16 produced the following eight subnets as Table 5-12 lists.

Table 5-12. The Eight Subnets for the 3-Bit Subnetting of 131.107.0.0/16

Subnet	Subnetted Network ID
1	131.107.0.0/19
2	131.107.32.0/19

(continued)

Table 5-12. *(continued)*

Subnet	Subnetted Network ID
3	131.107.64.0/19
4	131.107.96.0/19
5	131.107.128.0/19
6	131.107.160.0/19
7	131.107.192.0/19
8	131.107.224.0/19

Reserve Half of the IP Addresses for Future Use

To reserve half of the addresses for future use, set aside the first four subnets (131.107.0.0/19, 131.107.32.0/19, 131.107.64.0/19, 131.107.96.0/19).

Obtain Three Subnets with up to 8190 IP Addresses

To obtain three subnets with up to 8190 IP addresses per subnet, choose the next 3 subnets (131.107.128.0/19, 131.107.160.0/19, 131.107.192.0/19). Each subnet has 13 host bits for a total of 8190 IP addresses per subnet.

Obtain 31 Subnets with up to 254 IP Addresses

To obtain 31 subnets, each with up to 254 IP addresses, perform a 5-bit subnetting of 131.107.224.0/19. The result is 32 subnets (131.107.224.0/24, 131.107.225.0/24, 131.107.226.0/24 . . .131.107.253.0/24, 131.107.254.0/24, 131.107.255.0/24). To fulfill the requirement, choose the first 31 subnets (131.107.224.0/24 to 131.107.254.0/24).

Obtain 64 Subnets with only 2 IP Addresses

To obtain 64 subnets with only 2 usable IP addresses, perform a 6-bit subnetting of 131.107.255.0/24. The result is 64 subnets (131.107.255.4/30, 131.107.255.8/30, 131.107.255.12/30 . . .131.107.255.244/30, 131.107.255.248/30, 131.107.255.252/30).

Figure 5-10 shows the variable-length subnetting of 131.107.0.0/16.

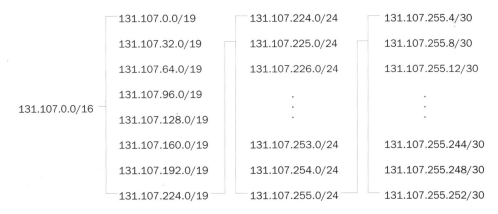

Figure 5-10. *The variable-length subnetting of 131.107.0.0/16 into differently sized subnets.*

Variable-Length Subnetting and Routing

Variable-length subnetting requires routing protocols to advertise the subnet mask with the network ID. Routing Information Protocol (RIP) version 2, Open Shortest Path First (OSPF), and Border Gateway Protocol version 4 (BGPv4) support variable-length subnetting environments. RIP version 1 does not support variable-length subnetting environments.

Supernetting and Classless Inter-Domain Routing (CIDR)

As the Internet grew suddenly from a collection of educational institutions and government agencies to a business-oriented, pervasive, global internetwork, great stress was placed on the IP address space. Assigning classful network IDs to organizations meant a quick and wasteful depletion of the Internet address space.

For example, a large number of organizations worldwide require more than 254 IP addresses. Therefore, a single class C network ID is insufficient. A single class B network ID, however, provides sufficient IP addresses and enough host bits to implement subnetting within the organization's internal network. While this is good for the organization, it is bad for the Internet IP address space. Consider the smaller organization that needs only 4000 IP addresses. Assigning a class B network with 65,534 possible IP addresses means that 61,534 IP addresses are unassigned and wasted.

Now, instead of an entire class B network ID, the InterNIC assigns a range of class C network IDs. For example, InterNIC assigns 16 class C network IDs to an organization needing 4000 IP addresses. Each class C network ID allows for 254 IP addresses. Therefore, 16 class C network IDs allow for 4064 IP addresses.

This technique minimizes the wasting of Internet IP addresses. However, it produces a new problem. If a single class B network ID is assigned, that single class B network ID becomes a single route in the routing tables of the Internet backbone routers. If 16 class C network IDs are assigned, 16 class C network IDs become 16 routes in the routing tables of the Internet backbone routers.

Extending this example to its ultimate limits, there are over two million class C network IDs. After assigning them all, it is possible to have over two million routes in the routing tables of the Internet backbone routers. Even with today's technology, it is difficult to build an IP router that can have a routing table with millions of entries, and forward IP datagrams at megabit or gigabit per second speeds.

To prevent this scaling problem from overwhelming Internet routers, a route aggregation technique is used to express a range of class C network IDs as a single route. This technique is called CIDR, which is the method of address allocation that the modern Internet uses. CIDR solves the scaling problem by minimizing the total number of routes that must be stored in the routing tables of Internet routers.

CIDR uses a supernetted subnet mask to express the range of class C network IDs. A supernetted subnet mask is less specific or contains less network ID bits than a classful subnet mask. In contrast, a subnetted subnet mask is more specific, or contains more network ID bits, than a classful subnet mask.

Views on CIDR Allocation

The CIDR method of address allocation can be viewed in two different ways:

1. A range of class C network IDs

2. An address space in which multiple classful networks are combined into a single classless network

The latter perspective is more appropriate for today's Internet and for looking forward to IP version 6 (IPv6).

A Range of Class C Network IDs

Viewed as a range of class C network IDs, our requirement is based on the number of class C network segments needed in our organization. The following are requirements for a range of class C network IDs to be expressible as a single route using a network ID and a subnet mask:

- The class C network IDs must be sequential.

- The number of allocated class C network IDs must be expressed as a power of 2.

For example, Table 5-13 lists the range (or block) of eight class C network IDs, starting with network ID 223.1.184.0.

Table 5-13. A Block of Eight Class C Network IDs Starting with 223.1.184.0

Starting Network ID	223.1.184.0	<u>11011111 00000001 10111</u>000 00000000
Ending Network ID	223.1.191.0	<u>11011111 00000001 10111</u>111 00000000

Notice that the first 21 bits (underlined) of the range of class C network IDs are the same. The last three bits of the third octet vary over all possible values from 000 through 111. This range of class C network IDs can be aggregated with the following network ID and subnet mask, as listed in Table 5-14.

Table 5-14. The Aggregated Block of Class C Network IDs

Network ID	223.1.184.0
Subnet Mask (binary)	1111111111 11111111 11111000 00000000
Subnet Mask	255.255.248.0
Network Prefix	/21

A block of class-based network IDs, as allocated in this example, is known as a CIDR block.

Table 5-15 lists the number of class C network IDs and the supernetted subnet mask for a required number of hosts.

Table 5-15. Supernetting and Class C Addresses

Required Hosts	Number of Class C Network IDs	Supernetted Subnet Mask
2-254	1	255.255.255.0 or /24
255-508	2	255.255.254.0 or /23
509-1016	4	255.255.252.0 or /22
1017-2032	8	255.255.248.0 or /21
2033-4064	16	255.255.240.0 or /20
4065-8128	32	255.255.224.0 or /19
8129-16,256	64	255.255.192.0 or /18
16,257-32,512	128	255.255.128.0 or /17
32,513-65,024	256	255.255.0.0 or /16

An Address Space

From the perspective of an address space, CIDR blocks are no longer viewed as a range of class C network IDs. Even though the CIDR block is obtained from the class-defined range of class C network IDs, it does not necessarily represent a range of class C network IDs. Viewing the CIDR block as a range of class C network IDs implies that we will assign each class C network ID within the block to each of our networks.

In reality, we typically want to assign network IDs of various sizes to the networks of our intranet in a variable-length subnetting scheme. Now our requirement is based on the number of IP addresses required, rather than the number of class C networks in our organization.

For example, to assign 4000 IP addresses to an organization, determine the number of bits required to express 4000 IP addresses. Using powers of 2, 12 bits are needed to express 4094 IP addresses. Therefore, 12 bits are used for the host ID portion, and 20 bits for the network ID portion. The subnet mask indicates 20 bits of network ID. Starting from an unassigned portion of the IP address space, the InterNIC allocates the 223.1.176.0 network with the subnet mask of 255.255.240.0 (or 223.1.176.0/20) address space to the organization.

The allocated address space allows the assignment of the range of IP addresses from 223.1.176.1 through 223.1.191.254. However, it is unlikely that the organization will use all 4094 IP addresses on the same network segment. Rather, the organization can use variable-length subnetting and the 12 host bits to create a series of subnets containing the appropriate number of appropriately sized subnets.

With CIDR, IP network IDs lose their classful heritage and become address spaces where certain bits are fixed (the network ID bits), and certain bits are variable (the host ID bits). Using variable-length subnetting techniques, the organization's needs can determine how to best utilize the host bits.

CIDR and Routing

CIDR, like variable-length subnetting, requires routing protocols to advertise the subnet mask with the network ID. RIP version 2, OSPF, and BGPv4 support CIDR environments. RIP version 1 does not support CIDR environments.

Public and Private Addresses

When deploying an IP addressing scheme in your organization, the main consideration is whether your intranet is connected to the Internet.

- If your organization is not connected to the Internet, it is technically possible to choose any IP network IDs—classful or classless—without regard to using overlapping addresses that are being used on the Internet. However, it is highly recommended that you choose a private address range.

- If your organization is connected to the Internet, it can be connected one of two ways. If your organization uses a direct-routed connection using a router or firewall, you must use InterNIC-compliant addresses as allocated by the InterNIC or an ISP. If your organization uses an indirect connection using a proxy server or a network address translator, you must use addresses that do not overlap with addresses that do, or might, exist on the Internet.

For organizations connected to the Internet, the organizations must choose between the use of public or private addresses.

Public Addresses

The InterNIC assigns public addresses that are within the public address space consisting of all of the possible unicast addresses on the worldwide Internet. Historically, the InterNIC assigned classful network IDs to organizations connecting to the Internet without regard to geographical location. Today, the InterNIC assigns CIDR blocks to ISPs based on geographical location; the ISPs then subdivide their assigned CIDR blocks to customers. The subdivision of the remaining class C address space based on geographical location was done to provide hierarchical routing. Its purpose was also to minimize the number of routes in the Internet backbone routers. Public addresses are guaranteed to be globally unique.

When an organization or an ISP is assigned a block of addresses in the public address space, a route exists in the Internet routers' routing tables so that the assigned public addresses are reachable through the ISP. Historically, a classful network ID was added to all the Internet routers. Today, a route consisting of the range of assigned addresses is added to the routing tables of regional and ISP Internet routers.

The range of public IP addresses assigned to an organization are summarized by one or more (network ID, mask) pairs. These pairs become the routes in the ISP and Internet routers so that the IP addresses of the organization can be reached.

Illegal or Overlapping Addresses

Organizations that are not connected to the Internet either directly or indirectly are free to choose any addressing scheme without regard to whether the addresses have been assigned to another ISP or organization. However, if that organization later decides to connect to the Internet, implementing a new addressing scheme might be required.

The addresses assigned when the organization was not connected to the Internet might include public addresses that have been assigned to other organizations or ISPs by the InterNIC. If that is the case, these addresses are duplicates, and in conflict with assigned addresses. This is known as illegal, or overlapping, addressing. Internet traffic from hosts using illegal addresses is forwarded to the routers of the organization who were originally assigned those addresses. Therefore, organizations using illegal addressing are not reachable on the Internet.

For example, an organization that is not connected to the Internet decides to use the address space 207.46.130.0/24 for its intranet. As long as the organization does not connect to the Internet, the use of 207.46.130.0/24 is not an issue. If the organization then connects to the Internet using a direct routed connection, the use of 207.46.130.0/24 is illegal and no responses from hosts on the 207.46.130.0/24 network segment are received.

In this configuration, when a host sends traffic to an Internet location, it sends the traffic with the source IP address within the address space of 207.46.130.0/24. When the Internet host sends a response, it sends the response to the destination IP address within the address space of 207.46.130.0/24. InterNIC assigned the Microsoft Corporation the address space 207.46.130.0/24, and a route exists in Internet routers to forward traffic with the destination IP address in this range to the Microsoft Corporation's routers. Therefore, the responses to traffic sent by the hosts on the illegal address space 207.46.130.0/24 are forwarded to the Microsoft Corporation's routers, and not to the routers of the organization using the illegal addresses.

Note It is common practice among Internet service providers to discard IP packets sent from a customer site when the source IP address field is not set to a valid public address assigned to the customer. This prevents the sending of traffic from hosts using illegal addresses and address spoofing. Address spoofing is the sending of IP traffic from a source IP address that is not assigned to a host.

Private Addresses

As the Internet experienced exponential growth, the demand for public IP addresses increased commensurately. Because each node on an organization's intranet required a globally unique public IP address, organizations requested from the InterNIC enough IP addresses to assign unique IP addresses to all of the nodes within their organizations.

However, when an analysis of IP addressing within organizations was done, the Internet authorities noticed that most organizations actually needed very few public addresses. The only hosts that required public IP addresses were those that communicated directly with systems on the Internet. Examples are Web servers, FTP servers, e-mail servers, proxy servers, and firewalls. Most of the hosts within an organization's intranet obtained access to Internet resources through Application Layer gateways such as proxy servers and e-mail servers.

For the hosts within the organization's intranet that do not require direct access to the Internet, a legal IP address space needs to be used. For this purpose, the Internet authorities created the private address space, a subset of the Internet IP address space that can be used without conflict within an organization, for hosts that do not require a direct connection to the Internet.

The private and public address spaces are separate and do not overlap. The InterNIC never assigns private addresses—IP addresses within the private address space—to an organization or ISP. This also means that private IP addresses are not reachable on the Internet.

Because private addresses are not reachable on the Internet, hosts on an intranet with private addressing cannot be directly connected to the Internet. Rather, hosts on an intranet with private addressing must be indirectly connected to the Internet using a network address translator or an Application Layer gateway such as a proxy server.

A network address translator is a router that translates between private addresses and public addresses for Internet traffic. The proxy server receives a request from a host on the intranet for Internet resources. The proxy server then sends the request to the Internet resource and the response traffic is forwarded back to the requesting host. When the proxy server sends the request to the Internet resource, it uses public addressing. Both proxy servers and network address translators have private addresses on their intranet interface and public addresses on their Internet interface.

More Info   For more information on network address translation, see RFC 1631, which can be found in the \RFC folder on the companion CD-ROM.

The private address space is defined by the following three address blocks:

- **10.0.0.0/8**   The 10.0.0.0/8 private network is an address space with 24 host bits that can be used for any subnetting scheme within the private organization.

- **172.16.0.0/12**   The 172.16.0.0/12 private network is an address space with 20 host bits that can be used for any subnetting scheme within the private organization. From a classful perspective, the 172.16.0.0/12 private network ID is the range of 16 class B network IDs from 172.16.0.0/16 through 172.31.0.0/16.

- **192.168.0.0/16**   The 192.168.0.0/16 private network is an address space with 16 host bits that can be used for any subnetting scheme within the private organization. From a classful perspective, the 192.168.0.0/16 private network ID is the range of 256 class C network IDs from 192.168.0.0/24 through 192.168.255.0/24.

More Info   For more information on the public address space, see RFC 1918, which can be found in the \RFC folder on the companion CD-ROM.

Microsoft Windows 2000 Automatic Private IP Addressing

When you configure a Windows 2000 computer to use Dynamic Host Configuration Protocol (DHCP) to obtain its IP address automatically and a DHCP server does not respond to the DHCPREQUEST and DHCPDISCOVER messages, TCP/IP for Windows 2000 configures itself using the Automatic Private IP Address (APIPA) feature. Using APIPA, TCP/IP for Windows 2000 randomly picks an IP address in the address space of 169.254.0.0/16. This address space has been reserved by the Internet Assigned Numbers Authority (IANA) and is not reachable on the Internet.

After choosing an IP address, TCP/IP for Windows 2000 sends a gratuitous Address Resolution Protocol (ARP) to check for IP address uniqueness. After receiving no response to the gratuitous ARP, TCP/IP for Windows 2000 is configured for the randomly chosen IP address and the subnet mask of 255.255.0.0. If a response to the gratuitous ARP is received, TCP/IP for Windows 2000 randomly chooses a new address in the 169.254.0.0/16 address space. After APIPA configuration, TCP/IP for Windows 2000 continues to send DHCP-DISCOVER messages every five minutes. If a DHCP server responds, TCP/IP for Windows 2000 abandons the APIPA configuration and the DHCP-allocated address takes effect. For more information on gratuitous ARP, see Chapter 3, "Address Resolution Protocol (ARP)."

APIPA was designed to simplify the configuration of a single subnet small office/home office (SOHO) network that is not connected to the Internet or any other IP internetwork. With APIPA, all the computers on a single subnet SOHO network configure themselves and are able to communicate without manually configuring TCP/IP or setting up a DHCP server.

APIPA does not provide automatic configuration of a default gateway, the IP address of a Domain Name Server (DNS) server, a DNS domain name, the IP address of a Windows Internet Name Service (WINS) server, or NetBIOS node type. A single subnet SOHO network does not need a default gateway, and broadcast NetBIOS name queries resolve names for communication between computers.

IP Broadcast Addresses

IP broadcast addresses are used for single packet one-to-everyone delivery. A sending host addresses the IP packet using a broadcast address and every node on the sending node's network segment receives and processes the packet. IP broadcast addresses can be used only as the destination IP address.

There are four different types of IP broadcast addresses. For each type, the broadcast IP packet is addressed at the Network Interface Layer using the network technology's broadcast address. For example, for Ethernet and Token Ring networks, all IP broadcasts are sent using the Ethernet and Token Ring broadcast address of 0xFF-FF-FF-FF-FF-FF.

Network Broadcast

The IP network broadcast address is the address formed by setting all the host bits to 1 for a classful address. An example of a network broadcast address for the classful network ID 131.107.0.0/16 is 131.107.255.255. Network broadcasts are used to send packets to all hosts of a classful network. All hosts of a classful network listen for and process packets addressed to the network broadcast address. IP routers do not forward network broadcast packets.

Subnet Broadcast

The IP subnet broadcast address is the address formed by setting all the host bits to 1 for a non-classful address. An example of a network broadcast address for the non-classful network ID 131.107.26.0/24 is 131.107.26.255. Subnet broadcasts are used to send packets to all hosts of a subnetted, supernetted, or otherwise non-classful network. All hosts of a non-classful network listen for and process packets addressed to the subnet broadcast address. IP routers do not forward subnet broadcast packets.

For a classful network, there is no subnet broadcast address, only a network broadcast address. For a non-classful network, there is no network broadcast, only a subnet broadcast address.

All-Subnets-Directed Broadcast

The IP all-subnets-directed broadcast address is the address formed by setting all the original classful network ID host bits to 1 for a non-classful network. A packet addressed to the all-subnets-directed broadcast is intended to reach all hosts on all of the subnets of a subnetted class-based network ID. An example of an all-subnets-directed broadcast address for the subnetted network ID 131.107.26.0/24 is 131.107.255.255. The all-subnets-directed broadcast is the network broadcast address of the original classful network ID.

All hosts of a non-classful network listen for and process packets addressed to the all-subnets-directed broadcast address. RFC 922 required IP routers to forward all-subnets-directed broadcast packets to all subnets of the original classful network ID implied in the address. However, this forwarding was not widely implemented.

With the advent of classless network IDs, the all-subnets-directed broadcast address is no longer relevant. According to RFC 1812, the use of the all-subnets-directed broadcast has been deprecated.

Notice how the all-subnets-directed address is the same as the subnet broadcast for the all-ones subnet. For example, the 8-bit subnetting of the class B network ID 157.54.0.0 produces the subnets {157.54.0.0/24, 157.54.1.0/24 . . . 157.54.254.0/24, 157.54.255.0/24}. For the last subnet, 157.54.255.0/24, the subnet broadcast is 157.54.255.255, which is the same as the all-subnets-directed broadcast address of 157.54.255.255. This address conflict is not an issue for routers that do not forward all-subnets-directed broadcast traffic.

Limited Broadcast

The limited broadcast address is the address formed by setting all 32 bits of the IP address to 1 (255.255.255.255). The limited broadcast address is used when an IP node must perform a one-to-everyone delivery on the local network but the network ID is unknown.

The limited broadcast address is typically used only by nodes during an automated configuration process such as BOOTP or DHCP. For example, with DHCP, a DHCP client must use the limited broadcast address for all traffic sent until the IP address lease is acknowledged by the DHCP server.

All hosts, classful or non-classful, listen for and process packets addressed to the limited broadcast address. While it appears that the limited broadcast address is addressed to all nodes on all networks, it appears only on the local network and is never forwarded by routers. The limited broadcast packet is limited to the local network segment.

IP Multicast Addresses

IP multicast addresses are used for single packet one-to-many delivery. A sending host addresses the IP packet using an IP multicast address; every node on the sending node's internetwork that is listening for the multicast traffic receives and processes the packet. Unlike broadcast packets, routers forward IP multicast packets and only the hosts listening for the IP multicast traffic are disturbed. IP multicast addresses can be used only as the destination IP address.

As RFC 1112 describes, the set of hosts listening for the traffic of a specific IP multicast address is called a host group. Host group members can be located anywhere on the IP internetwork. They also can join and leave the host group at any time. In order for routers to forward IP multicast traffic to host group members, the routers must be aware of where the members of a multicast group are located. For more information on how hosts and routers facilitate the forwarding of IP multicast traffic, see Chapter 8, "Internet Group Management Protocol (IGMP)."

Multicast IP addresses are in the class D range. Multicast IP addresses range from 224.0.0.0 through 239.255.255.255. Multicast IP addresses in the range 224.0.0.0 through 224.0.0.255 are reserved for local subnet traffic. Table 5-16 lists some of the reserved IP addresses in this range used by Windows 2000. For a complete list, see *http://www.isi.edu/in-notes/iana/assignments/multicast-addresses*.

Table 5-16. Reserved Local Subnet IP Multicast Addresses

Multicast IP Address	Purpose
224.0.0.1	The all-hosts multicast address. Designed to reach all hosts on a subnet.
224.0.0.2	The all-routers multicast address. Designed to reach all routers on a subnet.
224.0.0.5	The AllOSPFRouters address. Designed to reach all OSPF routers on a subnet.
224.0.0.5	The DRRouters address. Designed to reach all OSPF designated routers on a subnet.
224.0.0.9	The RIPv2 multicast address. Designed to reach all RIPv2 routers on a subnet.

Mapping IP Multicast Addresses to MAC Addresses

To fulfill the promise of IP multicast traffic—where a single IP datagram is processed only by the host group members—IP multicast traffic must be mapped to a corresponding MAC-level multicast address. The corresponding MAC-level multicast becomes an interesting address to the network interface card (NIC), and all traffic addressed to that interesting address with a valid frame check sequence is passed up through a hardware interrupt to the operating system.

Ethernet and FDDI

To denote a MAC-level multicast address, Ethernet and FDDI NICs set the Individual/Group (I/G) bit, the low-order bit of the first byte of the destination MAC address, to 1. For IP multicast addressing, the range of multicast MAC addresses is 0x01-00-5E-00-00-00 to 0x01-00-5E-7F-FF-FF. The high-order 25 bits are set to 0000001 00000000 01011110 0. The low-order 23 bits are available for use by IP multicast addresses.

To map an IP multicast address to an Ethernet or FDDI MAC-level multicast address, the low-order 23 bits of the IP multicast address are copied to the low-order 23 bits in the Ethernet multicast address as Figure 5-11 shows.

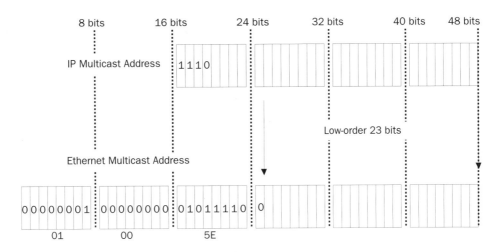

Figure 5-11. *The mapping of IP multicast addresses to Ethernet and FDDI MAC addresses.*

In the high-order nine bits of the IP multicast address, the first four bits are set to 1110; the next five bits are variable. These five bits do not map to the corresponding Ethernet and FDDI multicast address. Therefore, up to 32 different IP multicast addresses can map to the same Ethernet and FDDI MAC-level multicast address. IP multicast packets received that do not correspond to a multicast address registered by an application or another protocol are silently discarded.

A node registers interest in a specific multicast group by informing the NIC to listen for another interesting destination address for incoming frames. In Windows 2000, this is done through the *NDISRequest()* function. For example, by default Windows 2000 TCP/IP listens for all multicast traffic sent to the all-host multicast address 224.0.0.1. Therefore, TCP/IP informs the NIC through NDIS to pass up frames with the destination MAC address of 0x01-00-5E-00-00-01.

Token Ring

As RFC 1469 describes, Token Ring can support the same type of multicast IP address to MAC mapping as Ethernet and FDDI. However, because of the hardware limitations of most Token Ring network adapters, all IP multicast addresses are mapped to the single Token Ring functional address of 0xC0-00-00-04-00-00.

Summary

IP addresses can be unicast, broadcast, or multicast. For unicast addresses, subnetting techniques allow a network ID to be allocated, in an efficient manner, to the subnets of an IP internetwork. The Internet authorities have defined public addresses that are reachable on the Internet, and private addresses that are designed to be used on private intranets not directly connected to the Internet. IP broadcast addresses are used to send IP datagrams to all the nodes on a physical or logical subnet. IP multicast addresses are used to send IP datagrams to all members of a multicast host group.

Chapter 6
Internet Protocol (IP) Routing

In order to troubleshoot TCP/IP connectivity problems, it is important to understand how packets are forwarded from a source to a destination node on an IP internetwork. In order for data to be exchanged between any two nodes, each node must be reachable from the other. For universal reachability, a forwarding path between any two nodes must exist in both directions. The forwarding paths are determined by the contents of local IP routing tables and the nature of the IP routing infrastructure.

Introduction to IP Routing

IP routing is the process of forwarding unicast IP traffic to its destination in an IP internetwork with an arbitrary topology. Specifically, IP routing is the process of forwarding packets from the sending host and through a series of intermediate routers. To facilitate the forwarding process, the sending host and each router make a forwarding decision based on the contents of their local IP routing table. For Microsoft Windows 2000 hosts and routers, the IP routing table entries are created based on the TCP/IP configuration, static routing table entries, ICMP Redirect, or routing protocols.

For discussion in this chapter, a *node* is a network device running the TCP/IP protocol; a *host* is a TCP/IP node that does not have routing capability; and a *router* (or gateway) is a TCP/IP node that does have routing capability. Both hosts and routers are considered nodes.

Direct and Indirect Deliveries

When forwarding an IP datagram, the sending host performs either a direct or indirect delivery to the destination. If the destination is directly reachable—on a directly attached network segment—the forwarding node performs a direct delivery by resolving the destination node's Media Access Control (MAC) address and sending the frame to the destination. If the destination is not directly reachable—not on a directly attached network segment—the host uses its IP routing table to determine an intermediate router's forwarding IP address. The forwarding node performs an indirect delivery by resolving the intermediate router's MAC address and sending the frame to the intermediate router.

The IP routing process is a series of direct and indirect deliveries, as shown in Figure 6-1. For Host A and Host B, on the same network segment, Host A performs a direct delivery when sending packets to Host B. For Host A and Host C, on different network segments separated by a single IP router, Host A performs an indirect delivery to the router. The router then performs a direct delivery to Host C.

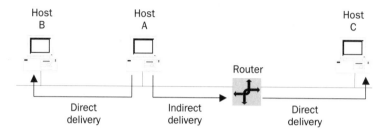

Figure 6-1. *IP forwarding showing direct and indirect delivery.*

For more details on the behavior of the Address Resolution Protocol (ARP) during direct and indirect deliveries, see Chapter 3, "Address Resolution Protocol (ARP)."

Types of Links

The IP forwarding process and IP routing table entries vary depending on the type of link over which the packet is being forwarded. The following are the three types of links:

- Broadcast
- Point-to-point
- Non-broadcast multiple access

Broadcast

The broadcast link type is characterized by its ability to have more than two nodes on the same network segment, and each frame sent is received at the Network Interface Layer by all of the network segment's nodes. Ethernet, Token Ring, and FDDI are examples of broadcast links. In each case, one of possible multiple nodes on the network segment must be distinguished using a Network Interface Layer address. For Ethernet, Token Ring, and FDDI, the Network Interface Layer address is the destination MAC address. ARP is used to resolve the destination MAC address for a given forwarding IP address.

The broadcast link type supports the ability to multicast to a group of hosts on the network segment, or to broadcast to all hosts on the segment. Routing protocols such as Routing Information Protocol (RIP) or Open Shortest Path First (OSPF) use the ability to multicast to propagate routing information. RIP routers can use either subnet broadcasts or the 224.0.0.9 multicast address. OSPF routers use the multicast addresses of 224.0.0.5 and 224.0.0.6. Figure 6-2 shows Ethernet, an example of a broadcast link.

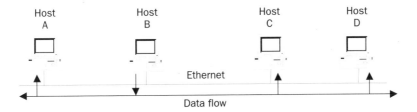

Figure 6-2. *A broadcast link such as Ethernet where a single packet is received by multiple nodes.*

To forward an IP datagram on a broadcast network, knowledge of the forwarding IP address is required.

Point-to-Point

The point-to-point link type is characterized by its ability to support only two IP nodes. Examples of point-to-point links are typical leased-line and circuit-switched wide area network (WAN) links such as analog phone lines, T-Carrier (including T1/E1 and T3/E3), and ISDN. For point-to-point links, there is only one possible node that receives the forwarded IP datagram. Therefore, ARP is not used to resolve a Network Interface Layer address and the forwarding IP address is irrelevant.

Routing protocols such as RIP and OSPF will work over point-to-point links without modification. For broadcast RIP announcements, the two routers' IP addresses on the point-to-point link network segment must be from the same IP network ID. If the IP addresses of the two routers' interfaces on the point-to-point link are from different network IDs, the receiving router will not process broadcast RIP requests or announcements. If this is the case, use RIP version 2 and multicast announcements.

For OSPF, the router interfaces are configured for the OSPF point-to-point network type. In this configuration, OSPF routers always use the multicast address of 224.0.0.5. Figure 6-3 shows a leased-line connection between two routers using T1, an example of a point-to-point link.

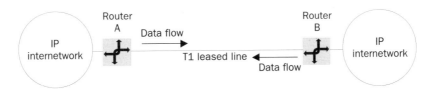

Figure 6-3. *A point-to-point link such as a T1 leased line contains a maximum of two nodes.*

Non-Broadcast Multiple Access

The non-broadcast multiple access (NBMA) link type is characterized by its ability to support more than two IP nodes; however, this link type cannot multicast or broadcast. Examples of NBMA links are packet-switched WAN technologies such as X.25, Frame Relay, and ATM. In each of these technologies, a single WAN adapter can support multiple virtual circuits. However, with the exception of recent developments in Frame Relay, NBMA links have no capability of sending a single packet that is copied to all the configured virtual circuits.

For X.25, Frame Relay, and ATM adapters operating in NBMA mode, the forwarding IP address is relevant. However, because there is no multicast or broadcast facility, ARP is not used. Inverse ARP can be used to discover the IP addresses of the routers on the other end of the virtual circuit. The forwarding IP address from the route in the routing table is mapped to the appropriate virtual-circuit identifier using a table maintained by the adapter.

For RIP and OSPF operation over an NBMA network, instead of broadcasting or multicasting, RIP or OSPF neighbors are configured. Each neighbor is a unicast location to which RIP or OSPF traffic is sent. Figure 6-4 shows a Frame Relay spoke and hub configuration, an example of an NBMA link.

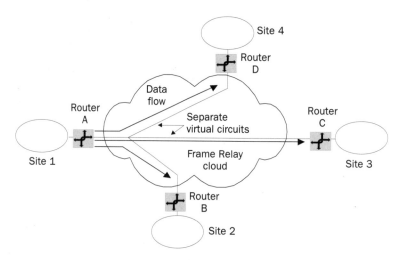

Figure 6-4. *An NBMA link such as Frame Relay, where a single interface supports multiple virtual circuits without a broadcast facility.*

For X.25, Frame Relay, and ATM adapters operating in multi- or sub-interface mode, each virtual circuit is represented as a separate logical adapter. Each logical adapter is the equivalent of a point-to-point adapter. RIP and OSPF are configured the same way as a point-to-point link.

The IP Routing Table

The IP routing table is a database of routes present in memory on all IP nodes. Each entry, or route, in the routing table contains forwarding information for a range of destination IP addresses. The level of detail for destination IP addresses—the number of routes in the routing table—depends on whether the IP node is a host or a router. Typically, IP hosts have few entries and IP routers have many.

It is common on IP internetworks to configure IP hosts with a "default gateway." The default gateway configuration creates a default route that effectively summarizes all destinations. For IP routers, it is common for the routing table to contain an entry for every reachable network on the IP internetwork, although route summarization and default routing are also commonly used.

In each case, the IP routing table's purpose is to yield two values for the destination IP address of each packet being forwarded:

- **The interface**   The interface is the representation of a physical or logical device over which the IP datagram is forwarded.
- **The forwarding IP address**   The forwarding IP address is the node's IP address to which the IP datagram is forwarded. For direct deliveries, the forwarding IP address is the destination IP address of the IP datagram being forwarded. For indirect deliveries, the forwarding IP address is the IP address of a directly reachable intermediate router to which the IP datagram is being forwarded.

Structure

A route in the IP routing table contains enough information to identify the destination, identify the interface and forwarding IP address, and distinguish the best route to use when multiple routes to the destination are found.

Typical IP routing tables contain the following fields for each route:

- **Destination**   Used in conjunction with the Network Mask, this field is a representation of a range of IP addresses that is reachable with this route. The Destination field can be an IP network ID (classful, subnet, supernet) or an IP address.
- **Network Mask**   The bit mask that is used to determine the significant bits in the Destination field. A 1 bit in the Network Mask field identifies a bit that must match the Destination field for this route. A 0 bit in the Network Mask field is a bit that does not have to match the Destination field. The Network Mask field must consist of a series of contiguous 1 bits followed by a series of contiguous 0 bits. The Destination and the Network Mask fields define a range of IP addresses. An IP datagram with a destination IP address within the range will match the route.

  To determine whether the destination IP address of an IP datagram being forwarded matches a route, the destination IP address is bit-wise logically ANDed with the Network Mask. The result is compared with the value of the

Destination field for the route. If they match, the route matches the destination IP address for the packet and the corresponding forwarding IP address will be used.

Due to the ANDing process used between the Network Mask field and the Destination field, the Destination field cannot be more specific than the Network Mask field. In binary terms, the Destination field cannot have bits set to 1 in bit positions where the Network Mask field has bits set to 0. Because the logical ANDing of a 1 and a 0 is always a 0, the ANDing of the Network Mask field with any IP address never results in a match to the Destination field. This is a useless route because it never matches any destination. Windows 2000 will not allow such a route to be added to the IP routing table. To test whether a destination and network-mask combination is invalid, perform a bit-wise logical AND of the destination and the network mask. If the result is not the destination, the combination is invalid.

- **Forwarding IP Address**   Indicates the IP address to which the IP datagram is to be forwarded if it matches this route. The Forwarding IP Address field's value is relevant for broadcast or NBMA links, and irrelevant for point-to-point links. For routes of directly attached network segments, the Forwarding IP Address field can be set to the IP address of that network segment's interface. This is the behavior of the Windows 2000 IP routing table.

- **Interface**   This is the designation of the logical or physical interface used when forwarding IP datagrams using this route. The Interface field's value can be a logical name or the IP address assigned to the interface. The Windows 2000 IP routing table uses the IP address assigned to the interface.

- **Metric**   Indicates the route's cost and is used by the route determination process to choose among multiple routes with the same destination and network mask. When there are multiple routes that match the same destination and network mask, the route with the lowest metric is used. The Metric field is commonly used to reflect the hop count—the number of routers to the destination—although routing protocols such as OSPF use customizable link costs that take into account the bandwidth, delay, and physical link costs when calculating the metric.

Types of Routes

A route in the IP routing table is one of the following types (in order of most to least specific):

- **Host Route**   A route to a specific IP address; therefore, the network mask is 255.255.255.255 (/32). Host routes allow you to customize IP routing on a per IP address basis. Host routes are commonly used to specify a more optimal route to specific hosts on a remote subnet.

- **Network ID Route**   A route for classful, classless, subnet, and supernetted destinations. The network mask for a network ID route is somewhere between 128.0.0.0 (/1) and 255.255.255.254 (/31).

Each Network ID route can be either a directly attached network ID route or a remote network ID route. A directly attached network ID route is a route for a network segment on which the router has an interface. Routes for directly attached network IDs might not have a value for the forwarding IP address. A remote network ID is a network ID that is available across another router. For remote network ID routes, the forwarding IP address is an intermediate router's IP address. The forwarding IP address must be directly reachable using the interface in the Interface field.

- **Default Route**   A route to all destinations, used when no other host route or network ID route matching the destination is found. The default route has a destination of 0.0.0.0 and a network mask of 0.0.0.0 (/0) and is sometimes expressed as 0/0. Notice that the default route is a matching route for any destination IP address (any IP address AND 0.0.0.0 is 0.0.0.0). A default route is used to summarize all possible destinations. The *default gateway* configured on an IP host creates a default route in the IP routing table. For routers, a default route is used to summarize all destinations, and is typically used for static routing and summarizing all the destinations of a large IP internetwork such as the Internet.

Route Determination Process

For any IP datagram being forwarded, a single route in the routing table must be chosen to determine the interface and the forwarding IP address for the forwarding process. To determine the single best route for forwarding, IP uses the following process:

1. For each route in the IP routing table, determine which routes match the destination IP address in the IP datagram by performing a bit-wise logical AND between the destination IP address and the network mask, and comparing the result to the value of the Destination field. If they match, mark the route as a matching route.

2. From the routes that matched the destination, determine which route(s) have the largest number of 1 bits in the Network Mask field. The route(s) with the largest number of 1 bits are the route(s) that most closely matched the destination IP address. This is known as the longest match or closest match paradigm. The longest match is the most specific route to the destination node. Note that for the default route, there are no 1 bits in the Network Mask field; however, it is a matching route.

3. From the list of longest matching routes, determine which of the longest matching routes has the lowest metric.

4. From the list of longest matching routes with the lowest metric, the router is free to choose from the remaining routes.

The end result of the route determination process is the choice of a single route that is the most specific route to the destination with the lowest metric. The single route chosen yields the forwarding IP address and the interface over which to forward the IP datagram.

If no matching route is found, IP indicates a routing error. For a sending host, an internal IP routing error informs the upper layer protocol. For a router, the IP datagram is discarded and an Internet Control Message Protocol (ICMP) Destination Unreachable-Host Unreachable message is sent back to the sending host.

The closest matching route process favors routes matching the destination in the following order:

1. **Host Route**   For a host route, all 32 bits match the destination IP address.

2. **Subnet Route**   For a route representing a subnetted network ID, all the class-based network bits and all the subnet bits match the destination IP address.

3. **Class-Based Network Route**   For a route representing a class-based network ID, all class-based network bits match the destination IP address.

4. **Supernet or Summarized Route**   For a route representing a supernetted (Classless Inter-Domain Routing [CIDR]) or summarized route, all the bits in the summarized network ID match the destination IP address.

5. **Default Route**   For the default route, none of the bits matches the destination IP address. ˜

The Microsoft Windows 2000 IP Routing Table

The Windows 2000 IP routing table for a single interface host with the IP address 172.16.1.99, subnet mask 255.255.255.0, and default gateway 172.16.1.1 as displayed by typing **route print** at a command prompt is shown below:

```
D:\>route   print

Interface   List
0x1 ..........................MS  TCP  Loopback  interface
0x2 ...00  60  08  3e  4f  1a ......3Com  3C90x  Ethernet  Adapter
```

Active   Routes:

Network Destination	Netmask	Gateway	Interface	Metric
0.0.0.0	0.0.0.0	172.16.1.1	172.16.1.99	1
127.0.0.0	255.0.0.0	127.0.0.1	127.0.0.1	1
172.16.1.0	255.255.255.0	172.16.1.99	172.16.1.99	1
172.16.1.99	255.255.255.255	127.0.0.1	127.0.0.1	1
172.16.255.255	255.255.255.255	172.16.1.99	172.16.1.99	1
224.0.0.0	224.0.0.0	172.16.1.19	172.16.1.19	1
255.255.255.255	255.255.255.255	172.16.1.99	172.16.1.99	1

```
Default  Gateway:          172.16.1.1
```

```
Persistent   Routes:
  None
```

This example of a Windows 2000 IP routing table consists of the following routes:

- **Default Route (0.0.0.0 with 0.0.0.0 or 0/0)**   The closest matching route when there are no other matches. If the default route is chosen, the packet is forwarded to the default gateway's IP address (172.16.1.1) using the interface assigned to the IP address 172.16.1.99.

- **Loopback Network Route (127.0.0.0 with 255.0.0.0 or 127.0.0.0/8)**   Matches any IP address in the range 127.0.0.0 through 127.255.255.255. All IP addresses beginning with 127 are reserved for loopback. All IP datagrams addressed in this range are forwarded to the reserved loopback address 127.0.0.1 using the loopback interface.

- **Directly Attached Network Route (172.16.1.0 with 255.255.255.0 or 172.16.1.0/24)**   A route to the locally attached subnet. When this route is chosen, the IP datagram is forwarded to the destination IP address using the interface assigned the IP address 172.16.1.99.

- **Local Host Route (172.16.1.99 with 255.255.255.255 or 172.16.1.99/32)**   A host route for the assigned IP address. All traffic addressed to the local host IP address is forwarded to the reserved loopback address 127.0.0.1 using the loopback interface.

- **All-Subnets Directed Broadcast Route (172.16.255.255 with 255.255.255.255 or 172.16.255.255/32)**   A host route for the all-subnets directed broadcast address for the class B network ID 172.16.0.0/16. Packets addressed to the all-subnets directed broadcast address are sent as MAC-level broadcasts, using the interface assigned the IP address of 172.16.1.99. An all-subnets directed broadcast route is present only if the locally attached network segment is subnetted. For more information on the all-subnets directed broadcast, see Chapter 5, "Internet Protocol (IP) Addressing."

- **Multicast Addresses Route (224.0.0.0 with 224.0.0.0 or 224.0.0.0/3)**   Used to match all Class D addresses reserved for IP multicast traffic. IP multicast packets are sent as MAC-level multicasts, using the interface assigned the IP address of 172.16.1.99.

- **Limited Broadcast Route (255.255.255.255 with 255.255.255.255 or 255.255.255.255/32)**   A host route for the limited broadcast address. Datagrams addressed to the limited broadcast address are sent as MAC-level broadcasts using the interface assigned the IP address 172.16.1.99.

These are the routes in the IP routing table created based on the common configuration of an IP address, a subnet mask, and a default gateway. Additional routes can be added through static routes, the receipt of ICMP Redirect messages, or a routing protocol.

Multihomed Nodes

For multihomed nodes—nodes with more than one IP address—additional entries for the local host route, the directly attached network ID route, the multicast route, and the limited broadcast address are present for each IP address added. An example is shown below:

```
D:\>route  print
```

```
Interface  List
0x1 .......................... MS  TCP  Loopback  interface
0x2 ...00 60 08 3e 4f 1a ..... 3Com  3C90x  Ethernet  Adapter
0x3 ...00 60 97 01 54 d3 ..... ELNK3  Ethernet  Adapter
```

Active   Routes:

Network Destination	Netmask	Gateway	Interface	Metric
0.0.0.0	0.0.0.0	172.16.1.1	172.16.1.99	1
127.0.0.0	255.0.0.0	127.0.0.1	127.0.0.1	1
172.16.1.0	255.255.255.0	172.16.1.99	172.16.1.99	1
172.16.1.99	255.255.255.255	127.0.0.1	127.0.0.1	1
172.16.255.255	255.255.255.255	172.16.1.99	172.16.1.99	1
169.254.0.0	255.255.0.0	169.254.155.89	169.254.155.89	1
169.254.155.89	255.255.255.255	127.0.0.1	127.0.0.1	1
224.0.0.0	224.0.0.0	157.59.11.19	157.59.11.19	1
224.0.0.0	224.0.0.0	169.254.155.89	169.254.155.89	1
255.255.255.255	255.255.255.255	172.16.1.99	172.16.1.99	1
255.255.255.255	255.255.255.255	169.254.155.89	169.254.155.89	1

Default Gateway: 172.16.1.1

```
Persistent   Routes:
   None
```

In the above example, the 3Com 3C90x Ethernet Adapter is configured with the IP address 172.16.1.99, the subnet mask 255.255.255.0, and the default gateway of 172.16.1.1. The ELNK3 Ethernet Adapter is configured through the Windows 2000 Automatic Private IP Addressing (APIPA) feature with the IP address 169.254.155.89 and the subnet mask 255.255.0.0.

Maintaining the Microsoft Windows 2000 IP Routing Table

You maintain the Windows 2000 IP routing table with the ROUTE command-line utility. With ROUTE, you can view the routing table, add routes, change routes, and delete routes. The IP routing table is stored in RAM and is not preserved when the computer is restarted. It will rebuild a default routing table based on the TCP/IP configuration when TCP/IP is initialized.

To make additional static routes persistent so that they are always added when TCP/IP is initialized, add the routes using the ROUTE ADD command with the "-p" option. Routes added with the "-p" option are stored in the Windows 2000 registry under:

```
HKEY_LOCAL_MACHINE\SYSTEM\CurrentControlSet\Services\TCPIP\
Parameters\PersistentRoutes
```

For a Windows 2000 Server computer running the Routing and Remote Access service, the IP routing table also can be maintained from the Routing and Remote Access administrative tool. Use context menu options available from the IP Routing\Static Routes object to view the IP routing table and add static routes. Figure 6-5 shows the IP routing table as it appears in the Routing and Remote Access administrative tool.

RRAS-ROUTER1 - IP Routing Table

Destination	Network mask	Gateway	Interface	Metric	Protocol
0.0.0.0	0.0.0.0	172.16.1.1	Local Area Connection 2	1	Network ...
127.0.0.0	255.0.0.0	127.0.0.1	Loopback	1	Local
127.0.0.1	255.255.255.255	127.0.0.1	Loopback	1	Local
169.254.0.0	255.255.0.0	169.254.155.89	Local Area Connection	1	Local
169.254.155.89	255.255.255.255	127.0.0.1	Loopback	1	Local
172.16.1.0	255.255.255.0	172.16.1.99	Local Area Connection 2	1	Local
172.16.1.99	255.255.255.255	127.0.0.1	Loopback	1	Local
172.16.255.255	255.255.255.255	172.16.1.99	Local Area Connection 2	1	Local
224.0.0.0	240.0.0.0	172.16.1.99	Local Area Connection 2	1	Local
224.0.0.0	240.0.0.0	169.254.155.89	Local Area Connection	1	Local
255.255.255.255	255.255.255.255	172.16.1.99	Local Area Connection 2	1	Local
255.255.255.255	255.255.255.255	169.254.155.89	Local Area Connection	1	Local

Figure 6-5. *The IP routing table as viewed from the Routing and Remote Access administrative tool.*

The Windows 2000 IP Routing Process

The Windows 2000 IP routing process is as follows:

1. Perform the route determination process previously described to choose a single route that is the closest match to the destination and has the lowest metric.

2. From the chosen route, examine the gateway and interface IP addresses.

3. If the gateway IP address is the same as the interface IP address, set the forwarding IP address to the destination IP address in the IP datagram being forwarded.

4. If the gateway IP address is not the same as the interface IP address, set the forwarding IP address to the gateway IP address.

The result of the Windows 2000 IP routing process is the IP address of the interface over which the packet is to be forwarded (the Interface field's IP address) and the forwarding IP address (either the IP datagram's destination IP address or the Gateway field's value). This result is then passed to the ARP module to determine:

- For unicast IP traffic sent over broadcast links, the unicast MAC address of the node using the forwarding IP address

- For multicast IP traffic sent over broadcast links, the multicast MAC address corresponding to the multicast IP address

- For broadcast IP traffic sent over broadcast links, the MAC-level broadcast address

For more details on how ARP resolves the unicast MAC address of the node to which the datagram is being forwarded, see Chapter 3, "Address Resolution Protocol (ARP)."

Examples of Windows 2000 Route Determination

A Windows 2000 host has the following Windows 2000 IP routing table:

```
D:\>route  print

Interface  List
0x1 ...........................MS  TCP  Loopback  interface
0x2 ...00 60 08 3e 4f 1a ......3Com  3C90x  Ethernet  Adapter

Active   Routes:
Network   Destination          Netmask          Gateway      Interface  Metric
           0.0.0.0             0.0.0.0        172.16.1.1   172.16.1.99      1
         127.0.0.0           255.0.0.0        127.0.0.1    127.0.0.1       1
        172.16.1.0       255.255.255.0      172.16.1.99   172.16.1.99      1
       172.16.1.99     255.255.255.255      127.0.0.1    127.0.0.1       1
     172.16.255.255    255.255.255.255     172.16.1.99   172.16.1.99      1
         224.0.0.0           224.0.0.0      172.16.1.19   172.16.1.19      1
   255.255.255.255     255.255.255.255     172.16.1.99   172.16.1.99      1
Default Gateway:         172.16.1.1

Persistent   Routes:
  None
```

When sending traffic to the destination IP address 172.16.1.47 (local subnet traffic), the matching routes are the default route (0.0.0.0 with 0.0.0.0) and the local subnet route (172.16.1.0 with 255.255.255.0). Because the local subnet route is a closer match to the destination IP address (24 bits in the network mask matched rather than 0 bits for the default route), the directly attached network ID route is chosen. Because the Gateway and Interface fields are set to the same value, the forwarding IP address for the datagram is set to 172.16.1.47. The IP datagram, the forwarding IP address (172.16.1.47), and the interface (172.16.1.99) are passed to ARP to perform a direct delivery.

When sending traffic to the destination IP address 10.1.1.100 (remote traffic), the only matching route is the default route (0.0.0.0 with 0.0.0.0). Because the Gateway and Interface fields are different, the forwarding IP address for the datagram is set to 172.16.1.1. The IP datagram, the forwarding IP address (172.16.1.1), and the interface (172.16.1.99) are passed to ARP to perform an indirect delivery.

IP Routing from Sending Host to Destination

To fully understand IP routing, we must examine the series of forwarding processes that occur at the sending host, the intermediate routers, and the destination host. The following processes assume an IP header without Loose Route, Strict Route, or Record Route IP options.

Sending Host Forwarding Process

When the sending host (a Windows 2000 computer) forwards an IP datagram, IP performs the following:

1. The Time-to-Live (TTL) is set to either the default value or the value specified by an upper layer protocol.

2. The destination IP address is passed to the Windows 2000 IP routing process, which determines the interface and the forwarding IP address. If no route is chosen, IP indicates a routing error to the upper layer protocol.

3. IP passes the IP datagram, the forwarding IP address, and the interface to ARP.

4. ARP resolves the forwarding IP address to a unicast MAC address for the indicated interface. For a direct delivery, ARP resolves the destination's MAC address. For an indirect delivery, ARP resolves the intermediate router's MAC address. Once ARP determines the MAC address for the forwarding IP address, it calls *NDISSend()* to send the frame using the appropriate network adapter.

IP Router Forwarding Process

When an IP datagram is received by a Windows 2000 computer, acting as an IP router, IP performs the following:

1. IP verifies the IP header checksum. It runs the checksum calculation and compares the result with the value stored in the IP datagram's Header Checksum field. If the result does not match the value of the Header Checksum field, IP silently discards the IP datagram.

2. IP checks the IP version field. If the IP version does not equal 4, IP silently discards the IP datagram.

3. IP checks the destination IP address in the IP datagram.

4. If the destination address in the datagram is an IP multicast address and multicast forwarding is enabled, IP forwards the datagram appropriately. For more information on this process, see Chapter 8, "Internet Group Management Protocol (IGMP)."

5. If the destination address corresponds to local host traffic (it is an IP address of a router interface or a broadcast address of a locally attached network), IP processes the datagram as the destination host.

6. If the destination IP address in the datagram is a unicast address that is not a local host IP address, IP decrements the TTL value in the IP header.

7. If the TTL is 0 (or less), IP submits the IP header and the first 8 bytes of the IP payload to ICMP with an error indication. IP then discards the IP datagram. ICMP includes the IP header and first 8 bytes of the IP payload as the payload of an ICMP Time Expired-TTL Expired message that is sent back to the sending host.

8. If the TTL is 1 or greater after decrementing, IP updates the TTL field with its new value, recalculates the IP header checksum, and updates the Header Checksum field's value.

9. IP passes the value of the destination IP address in the IP datagram to the IP route determination process. If no route is found, IP submits the IP header and the IP payload's first 8 bytes to ICMP with an error indication. IP then discards the IP datagram. ICMP includes the IP header and first 8 bytes of the IP payload as the payload of an ICMP Destination Unreachable-Host Unreachable message that is sent back to the sending host.

10. If a route is found, IP passes the modified IP datagram, the interface, and the forwarding IP address to ARP.

11. ARP resolves the forwarding IP address to a unicast MAC address for the indicated interface. For a direct delivery, ARP resolves the destination's MAC address. For an indirect delivery, ARP resolves the intermediate router's MAC address. Once the MAC address for the forwarding IP address is determined, ARP calls *NDISSend()* to send the frame using the appropriate network adapter.

This forwarding process is repeated at each intermediate router in the path between the sending host and the destination host.

Destination Host Receiving Process

When the final intermediate router performs a direct delivery to the destination host, IP on the destination host performs the following:

1. IP verifies the IP header checksum. It runs the checksum calculation and compares the result with value stored in the IP datagram's Header Checksum field. If the result does not match the Header Checksum field's value, IP silently discards the datagram.

2. IP checks the IP version field. If the IP version does not equal 4, IP silently discards the datagram.

3. IP checks the destination IP address in the datagram.

4. If the destination address in the datagram is a unicast address that is not a local host IP address, IP silently discards the datagram.

5. If the destination IP address corresponds to local host traffic (it is an IP address of a host interface or a broadcast address of a locally attached network) or an IP multicast address, IP checks the Protocol field.

6. If the Protocol field's value corresponds to an upper layer protocol that is being used on the host, IP passes the IP payload to the appropriate upper layer protocol.

7. If the Protocol field's value does not correspond to an upper layer protocol that is being used on the host, IP forwards the IP header and the first 8 bytes of the IP payload to ICMP with an error indication. IP then discards the IP datagram. ICMP includes the IP header and first 8 bytes of the IP payload as the payload of an ICMP Destination Unreachable-Protocol Unreachable message that is sent back to the sending host.

8. If the IP payload is a TCP segment, IP hands the TCP segment to TCP. After TCP verifies the TCP checksum, it checks the destination port in the TCP header. If the value of the Destination Port field corresponds to an application running on the host, the TCP segment is processed further. If the value of the Destination Port field does not correspond to an application running on the host, a TCP Connection Reset segment is sent back to the sending host. For more information on TCP connections, see Chapter 12, "Transmission Control Protocol (TCP) Connections."

9. If the IP payload is a User Datagram Protocol (UDP) message, IP hands the UDP message to UDP. After UDP verifies the UDP checksum, it checks the Destination Port field in the UDP header. If the value of the Destination Port field corresponds to an application running on the host, the UDP message is processed further. If the value of the Destination Port field does not correspond to an application running on the host, UDP submits the IP header and the first 8 bytes of the IP payload to ICMP with an error indication. UDP then discards the UDP message. ICMP includes the IP header and first 8 bytes of the IP payload as the payload of an ICMP Destination Unreachable-Port Unreachable message that is sent back to the sending host.

IP Routing Infrastructure Overview

For the successful delivery of IP datagrams to an arbitrary location in an IP internetwork, you must employ an IP routing infrastructure. Hosts and routers must have the supporting routes in their routing table to forward unicast traffic to any reachable location. Typically for hosts, all destinations are either directly reachable or reachable through a default route pointing to their default gateway. Routers, however, have either explicit routes for each network segment in the IP internetwork, summarized or aggregated routes, or a default route. The combination of the host's routing table entries and the routers comprise the IP routing infrastructure.

The type of IP routing infrastructure that you deploy can have the following characteristics:

- Single-path vs. multi-path
- Class-based vs. classless
- Flat vs. hierarchical

- Static vs. dynamic
- Single vs. multiple autonomous systems

Single-Path vs. Multi-Path

For a single-path routing infrastructure, IP traffic can only travel a single path between any source and any destination. Single-path infrastructures are simple but are intolerant of network faults. A downed link or a downed router creates physically separate portions of the internetwork that are unreachable for the duration of the fault.

For a multi-path routing infrastructure, IP traffic can travel different paths between any source and destination. Typically, a multi-path environment forwards IP traffic along a single path until the network topology changes. When coupled with dynamic routing, multi-path routing infrastructures can be fault-tolerant. Multi-path infrastructures are more complex to plan and implement and there exists a possibility that, either because of misconfiguration or during a period when the internetwork topology is changing, a routing loop can form. A routing loop is a path through the routing infrastructure that loops back on itself. It occurs when routers forward traffic in a loop that does not include the network segment of the destination. Traffic caught in a routing loop is forwarded between the routers of the loop until the TTL in the IP header becomes 0. Figure 6-6 shows a routing loop created by misconfiguration of the default route (0/0) between three routers (Router B, Router C, and Router D).

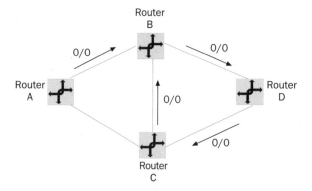

Figure 6-6. *A default routing loop between Router B, Router D, and Router C.*

One way to detect routing loops in your internetwork is to use the PING command-line utility with the "-i" option set to 255. The "-i" option sets the TTL in the ICMP Echo message. If the PING utility displays "TTL Expired In Transit," there is a good chance you have a routing loop. To ensure that you do have a routing loop, use the TRACERT command-line utility to trace the route to the destination. In the TRACERT display, look for a set of router IP addresses or names that repeat themselves.

Class-Based vs. Classless

Your routing infrastructure can be either class-based or classless. While originally a class-based routing infrastructure, address allocation and routing on the modern Internet is classless.

Class-Based Routing

Class-based routing is the determination of the network ID based on the IP address classes. Class-based routing protocols such as Routing Information Protocol (RIP) version 1 do not advertise a subnet mask when advertising routes. You can subnet with class-based routing protocols; however, there are limitations to the types of addresses and configurations that are permitted.

For example, when subnetting a class-based network ID, all of the subnets of the class-based network ID must be contiguous. Class-based routing protocols do not advertise the subnets of a class-based network ID on network segments that are not a subnet of the class-based network ID. Rather, on network segments that are not a subnet of the class-based network ID, they advertise the summarized class-based network ID. Class-based IP routers summarize the subnets of a class-based network ID by advertising the class-based network ID. Because of this behavior, all subnets must be contiguous. Two different subnets of the same class-based network ID in different parts of the IP internetwork (discontiguous subnets) will both separately advertise the summarized class-based network ID. With two routes to the same class-based network ID, routers will use the route with the lowest metric. Regardless of which route is chosen, because of proximity to the advertising router, incorrect routing will occur. The locations on both subnets are not reachable by all hosts on the IP internetwork. Because routes learned from neighboring routers are received without a network mask, the class-based router must assume the subnet mask based on the following:

- If the route fits the class (there are no 1 bits in the host ID portion of the class-based network ID), the class-based default subnet mask is assumed. For example, if the route 195.241.4.0 is received, the network mask of 255.255.255.0 is assumed. This assumption will assign the incorrect mask for CIDR blocks and other uses of aggregated routes. For example, for the CIDR block 195.241.8.0/21, the route assumed by the class-based router is 195.241.8.0/24.

- If the route does not fit the class (there are more host bits than the class-based network ID), but fits the subnet mask of the interface on which it was received, the subnet mask of the interface on which it was received is assumed. This assumption can assign the incorrect mask for subnetting situations where the advertised route just happens to fit the subnet mask of the interface on which it was received but not be the correct network mask for the route.

- If the route does not fit the class or the subnet mask of the interface on which it was received, it is assumed to be a host route with a network mask of 255.255.255.255. This assumption can assign the incorrect mask for many subnetting situations where the network segment's mask is more specific than the class or the mask of the interface on which it was received. For example, when you subnet 128.1.0.0/16 using variable-length subnetting and the network ID of a network segment is 128.1.64.0/18, the route for the subnetted network ID 128.1.176.0/20 is incorrectly assumed to be 128.1.176.0/32. All locations on the 128.1.176.0/20 network segment are unreachable from the router receiving the advertisement.

Classless Routing

With classless routing, routers never assume that the network mask is based on address classes. Classless routing protocols such as RIP version 2 and Open Shortest Path First (OSPF) advertise the network mask with the network ID. Because no mask assumptions are made, classless routing allows discontiguous subnets of a network ID, variable-length subnetting, CIDR blocks, and route aggregation. In today's classless world, IP internetworks should be using classless routing with an appropriate routing protocol. Class-based routing should be used only in networks that require compatibility with legacy routing protocols such as RIP version 1.

Flat vs. Hierarchical

For a flat routing infrastructure, each separate network segment is represented as a single route in the IP routers' routing table (assuming no use of default routing). The entire internetwork is a collection of IP network segments having no structure. While a flat routing infrastructure can work well for small- to medium-sized internetworks, flat routing, when scaled to large networks, produces a large number of routes in routing tables. Consider the example of the Internet. The Internet Network Information Center (InterNIC) at one time allocated class-based network IDs to organizations upon request, creating a flat routing infrastructure on the Internet. As the number of allocated network IDs grew, so did the number of routes in the routing tables of the Internet backbone routers. Today, Internet backbone routers have more than 45,000 routes in their routing tables.

For a hierarchical routing infrastructure, ranges of network IDs are collapsed to a single network ID and, therefore, a single route through the use of route aggregation techniques. Also, in a hierarchical routing infrastructure, IP network segments that share a common network ID prefix are grouped together and have a network/subnetwork/sub-subnetwork structure. With a hierarchical routing infrastructure, routers at the border of a region of network segments sharing the same set of network ID prefixes advertise a single route that summarizes or aggregates all of the network IDs of the region. In this way, routing information propagated outside the region is highly simplified. Very few routes exist on the backbone of a properly configured hierarchical internetwork.

There are many advantages to a hierarchical routing infrastructure. However, hierarchical infrastructure requires proper planning and an addressing scheme that allows groups of network IDs to be grouped together. Figure 6-7 shows an example of a hierarchical routing infrastructure based on the private network ID 10.0.0.0/8. The arrows and routes represent the summarized route that is advertised outside the region by the router(s) at the region's border.

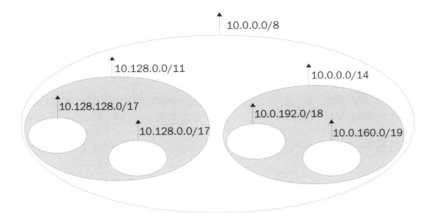

Figure 6-7. *A hierarchical addressing and routing scheme showing routing regions and route summarization at region borders.*

For a variety of reasons having to do with the impracticality of renumbering the IP internetwork, some IP internetworks have a combination of flat and hierarchical routing infrastructure. Before the development of CIDR, the Internet had a flat routing infrastructure. Post-CIDR, IP addresses are allocated using a hierarchical global addressing scheme. However, because of the difficulty of reallocating public network IDs to existing organizations, today's Internet remains a mixed flat and hierarchical routing infrastructure.

Static vs. Dynamic

The ongoing maintenance of routing tables can be done either manually through static routing or automatically using dynamic routing.

Static Routing

Static routing relies on manually configured routes. It supports classless routing because each route must be added with a network mask, making the destination unambiguous. Static routing can work well for small internetworks but it does not scale well because of the manual administration involved. Static routing can also work well in branch office scenarios where, rather than using a routing protocol across the WAN link to the branch office, static routes are added to the branch office and hub office routers to make the locations on each other's network segments reachable.

Ideally, an IP router has explicit knowledge of each network ID in the internetwork, either through an explicit or aggregated route. Default routing is used when connecting a smaller set of network segments to a much larger set of network segments and the creation of explicit or aggregated routes is not practical or possible. Static routes are often used to connect to the Internet. It is impractical to add the Internet's 45,000 routes to the routing table of the static router; therefore, add a single default route pointing to the downstream Internet service provider (ISP) router.

Static routing is not fault-tolerant. A static router cannot sense that a neighboring router is no longer available (if the link to the neighboring router remains operational) or that a remote network segment is no longer reachable and make adjustments to its routing table.

Microsoft Windows 2000 as a Static IP Router

A Windows 2000 computer can act as a static IP router by installing multiple network adapters, creating a multihomed computer. A separate IP address and subnet mask is configured for each network adapter, defining routes for the directly attached networks. It is natural to want to configure a default gateway. However, the configuration of a default gateway creates a default route, and a default route on a static router is based on a de-sign decision of your static routing environment.

If you use default routing, it is also natural for you to configure a default gateway for each network adapter. However, you must configure a default gateway for a single network adapter corresponding to the network adapter attached to the network segment of the router you want to use for your default route. If you configure a default gateway for more than one network adapter, a default route with a metric of 1 is added for each default gateway. This leads to multiple default routes in the routing table with the same metric. In this situation, TCP/IP for Windows 2000 picks a default route based on the first net-work adapter binding. This can lead to undesired behavior if TCP/IP for Windows 2000 chooses a less-than-optimal default route.

Once the network adapters are configured, enable IP routing for Windows 2000 Server com-puters by configuring and enabling the Routing and Remote Access service. For Windows 2000 professional computers, set the following Windows 2000 registry setting to 1:

```
HKEY_LOCAL_MACHINE\System\CurrentControlSet\Services\Tcpip\
Parameters\IpEnableRouter
```

Unlike previous versions of Microsoft Windows NT, there is no option in the properties of TCP/IP for Windows 2000 that allows you to enable routing.

Once you enable IP routing, add the appropriate specific or aggregated routes of your internetwork using either the Routing and Remote Access administrative tool or the ROUTE ADD command at a Windows 2000 command prompt.

Dynamic Routing

Dynamic routers rely on routing protocols—protocols used by routers to communicate routing information—to maintain IP routing tables. Routes for remote network IDs are learned through routing protocol traffic and added or removed from IP routing tables. When all of the IP internetwork routers have received all the information needed to create routes that reflect the internetwork's current topology, the internetwork has converged.

Dynamic routing in a multi-path routing infrastructure can provide fault tolerance. When a route becomes unreachable, it is removed from the routing table and its unreachability is conveyed to neighboring routers. When a link or router goes down, routes are adjusted for a new path to the network segments affected by the network fault. Routing protocols can be either class-based or classless depending on how the route is advertised.

The two most common IP routing protocols for private IP internetworks are RIP and OSPF, both of which Windows 2000 Server computers support.

RIP

RIP is a distance vector routing protocol. Distance vector routing protocols propagate routing information in the form of a network ID and its "distance" or hop count. RIP has a maximum distance of 15 hops. Locations 16 or greater hops away are considered unreachable. The original version of RIP, known as RIP version 1, described in RFC 1058, is a class-based routing protocol. The network ID is announced without its network mask. Therefore, the restrictions of class-based routing apply. A newer version of RIP called RIP version 2, described in RFC 1723, is a classless routing protocol. The RIP v2 announcement includes a network ID and a subnet mask.

More Info   RFCs 1058 and 1723 describe RIP versions 1 and 2. These RFCs can be found in the \RFC folder on the companion CD-ROM.

RIP is a simple routing protocol with a periodic route-advertising mechanism designed for use in small- to medium-sized IP internetworks. RIP doesn't scale well to the large or very large IP internetwork.

RIP v1 and v2 Operation

When a RIP router is initialized, it announces the appropriate routes in its routing table on all interfaces. The RIP router also sends a RIP General Request message on all interfaces. All neighboring routers—routers on the same network segments as the router sending the request—send the contents of their routing tables in response; those responses build the initial routing table. Learned routes are given a 3-minute lifetime (by default) before being removed by RIP from the IP routing table.

After initialization, the RIP router periodically announces (every 30 seconds, by default) the appropriate routes in its routing table for each interface. The exact set of routes being announced depends on whether the RIP router is implementing split horizon (where routes are not announced over the interfaces on which they were learned) or split horizon with poison reverse (where routes learned on interfaces are announced as unreachable).

Fault tolerance for RIP internetworks is based on the timeout of RIP-learned routes. If a change occurs in the internetwork topology, RIP routers can send a triggered update—a routing update, sent immediately—rather than waiting for a scheduled announcement.

OSPF

OSPF is a link state routing protocol. Link state routing protocols propagate routing information in the form of link state advertisements (LSAs) that contain the connected networks and their cost. The cost of each router interface is a unitless number that the network administrator assigns, and it can include delay, bandwidth, and monetary cost factors. The accumulated cost between network segments in an OSPF internetwork must be less than 65,535. OSPF is a classless routing protocol; OSPF LSAs contain the network ID and subnet mask for routes.

OSPF Operation

Each router has an LSA that describes its current state. The LSA of each OSPF router is efficiently propagated throughout the OSPF internetwork through logical relationships between neighboring routers called adjacencies. When the propagation of all current router LSAs is complete, the OSPF internetwork has converged.

Based on the collection of OSPF LSAs—known as the link state database—OSPF calculates the lowest-cost path to each route, and those paths become OSPF routes in the IP routing table. To keep the size of the link state database down, OSPF allows the creation of areas. An OSPF area is a grouping of contiguous networks. In all OSPF networks, there is at least one area called the backbone area. OSPF areas allow the summarization or aggregation of routing information at the boundaries of an OSPF area. A router at the boundary of an OSPF area is known as an area border router (ABR).

Figure 6-8 shows an example of a multiple-area OSPF internetwork. Area 1 consists of a series of variable-length subnetted network segments from the address space 10.47.0.0/16. By default, the ABR for Area 1 will propagate routing information in the form of LSAs for each separate network segment within Area 1. Using route summarization, the ABR is configured to propagate only the single route 10.47.0.0/16. All of the destinations within Area 1 are reachable outside of that area using this route. Areas and route summarization allow OSPF internetworks to scale to large organizational IP internetworks.

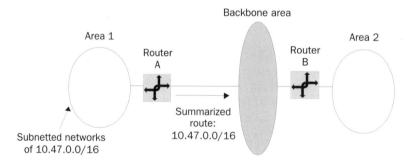

Figure 6-8. *A multiple-area OSPF internetwork showing the route summarization of Area 1.*

Microsoft Windows 2000 as a Dynamic Router

A Windows 2000 Server computer can act as a dynamic router supporting RIP and OSPF by installing multiple network adapters and enabling the Routing and Remote Access service. A separate IP address and subnet mask is configured for each network adapter, defining the directly attached network ID routes. In the case of dynamic routing, default routes are less typically used so a default gateway need not be configured for any network adapter.

Once the Routing and Remote Access service is enabled, static IP routing is enabled. Using the Routing and Remote Access administrative tool, add the RIP for IP or OSPF routing protocols and then enable them on your installed network adapters by adding your network adapters to the appropriate routing protocol. The detailed configuration of RIP and OSPF options is beyond the scope of this book. For more information, see Windows 2000 Server Help and the *Microsoft Windows 2000 Server Resource Kit Internetworking Guide*.

A Windows 2000 Professional computer can use the RIP protocol to listen to RIP traffic using the RIP Listener—a service installed as a separate networking component. A computer using the RIP Listener service is known as a silent RIP host. The RIP Listener service listens for all RIP v1 broadcast traffic on the local network segment and maintains routes in the IP routing table.

Single vs. Multiple Autonomous Systems

Very large IP internetworks such as the Internet are divided into regions called autonomous systems. An autonomous system (AS) is a contiguous region of the internetwork under the same administrative control. Administrative control is typically defined by an organization such as an institution or corporation. Within an AS, one or more Interior Gateway Protocols (IGPs) are used. Examples of IGPs include RIP and OSPF. Between autonomous systems, Exterior Gateway Protocols (EGPs) are used. An example of an EGP is the Border Gateway Protocol (BGP), version 4. EGPs used between autonomous systems are independent of the IGPs used within the AS.

For most organizations, a single AS is often sufficient. The Internet, however, is a multiple AS environment, composed of a somewhat hierarchical organization of autonomous systems using BGPv4 as the EGP. As seen with OSPF, each AS can be subdivided into areas or domains (if you are using multiple IGPs) to define a hierarchical structure within the AS. If you are an ISP, you may need to implement BGPv4 to communicate routing information to other Internet autonomous systems. Windows 2000 does not provide support for BGPv4.

Routing Utilities

Windows 2000 provides the following command-line utilities for maintaining and testing routing functionality:

- **ROUTE**   Used to view the IP routing table, add temporary and persistent routes, change existing routes, and remove routes from the IP routing table.

- **PING**   Used to verify reachability by sending ICMP Echo messages to intended destinations. It also supports the use of IP strict and loose source route options.

- **TRACERT**   Sends ICMP Echo messages with incrementally higher values of the TTL field to discover the path between a node and a destination. In list form, TRACERT displays the series of near-side router interfaces encountered by the ICMP Echo message as it traverses the internetwork toward the destination. For more information on how TRACERT works, see Chapter 7, "Internet Control Message Protocol (ICMP)."

- **PATHPING**   Used to discover the path between a host and a destination, and also to identify high-loss links or routers. For more information on how PATHPING works, see Chapter 7, "Internet Control Message Protocol (ICMP)."

Summary

IP routing is a combination of direct and indirect delivery processes that forward an IP datagram from the source node to the destination node. At each hop, a local IP routing table is consulted to determine how the datagram is delivered to the next hop or to the final destination. The route determination process results in a forwarding interface and a forwarding IP address. The routing infrastructure of an IP internetwork provides reachability between any source and destination node and can be class-based or classless, flat or hierarchical, static or dynamic, and consist of a single system or multiple autonomous systems. Windows 2000 supports static routing and dynamic routing using RIP v1, RIP v2, and OSPF.

Chapter 7
Internet Control Message Protocol (ICMP)

Internet Protocol (IP) provides end-to-end datagram delivery capabilities for IP datagrams. However, IP doesn't provide any facilities for reporting routing or delivery errors encountered by an IP datagram in its journey from the source to the destination. ICMP reports error and control conditions on behalf of IP.

When a protocol encounters an error that can't be recovered in the processing of a packet, it has one of the two following choices:

1. Discard the offending packet without sending an error notification to the sending host. This is known as a *silent discard*. For example, an Ethernet network adapter checks each Ethernet frame for bit-level errors by performing a checksum and comparing its own result with the Frame Check Sequence value stored in the frame. If the two checksums do not match, the adapter considers the frame invalid and silently discards it.

2. Discard the offending packet and send an error notification to the sending host. This is known as an *informed discard*. ICMP provides an informed discard service for specific types of IP routing and delivery errors.

ICMP is an extensible protocol that also provides functions to check IP connectivity and aid in the automatic configuration of hosts.

ICMP doesn't make IP reliable. There are no facilities within IP or ICMP to provide sequencing or retransmission of IP datagrams that encounter errors. ICMP messages are unreliably sent as IP datagrams; and while ICMP will report an error, there are no requirements for how the sending host will treat the error. It's up to the TCP/IP implementation to interpret the error and adjust its behavior accordingly.

ICMP messages are sent only for the first fragment of an IP datagram. ICMP messages are not sent for problems encountered by ICMP error messages or for problems encountered by broadcast or multicast datagrams.

More Info   ICMP is documented in RFCs 792, 950, 1812, 1122, 1191, and 1256. These RFCs can be found in the \RFC folder on the companion CD-ROM.

ICMP Message Structure

ICMP messages are sent as IP datagrams. Therefore, an ICMP message consisting of an ICMP header and ICMP message data is encapsulated with an IP header using IP Protocol number 1. The resulting IP datagram is then encapsulated with the appropriate Network Interface Layer header and trailer. Figure 7-1 shows the resulting frame.

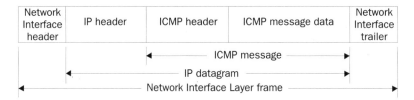

Figure 7-1. *ICMP message encapsulation showing the IP header and Network Interface Layer header and trailer.*

In the IP header of ICMP messages, the Source IP Address field is set to the router or host interface that sent the ICMP message. The Destination IP Address field is set to the sending host of the offending packet (in the case of ICMP error messages), a specific host, an IP broadcast, or IP multicast address. Every ICMP message has the same structure, as Figure 7-2 shows.

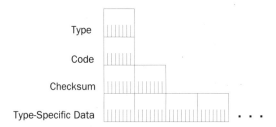

Figure 7-2. *The structure of an ICMP message showing the fields that are common to all types of ICMP messages.*

The common fields in the ICMP message are defined as follows:

- **Type**   A 1-byte field that indicates the type of ICMP message (Echo vs. Echo Reply, etc.). Table 7-1 lists the defined ICMP types.
- **Code**   A 1-byte field that indicates a specific ICMP message within an ICMP message type. If there is only one ICMP message within an ICMP type, the Code field is set to 0. The combination of ICMP Type and Code determines a specific ICMP message.
- **Checksum**   A 2-byte field for a 16-bit checksum covering the ICMP message. ICMP uses the same checksum algorithm as IP for the IP header checksum.
- **Type-Specific Data**   Optional data for each ICMP type.

ICMP Messages

Table 7-1 lists the most commonly used ICMP types.

Table 7-1. Common ICMP Types

ICMP Type	Description
0	Echo Reply
3	Destination Unreachable
4	Source Quench
5	Redirect
8	Echo (also known as an Echo Request)
9	Router Advertisement
10	Router Selection
11	Time Exceeded
12	Parameter Problem

More Info   For a complete list of ICMP types, see http://www.isi.edu/in-notes/iana/assignments/icmp-parameters.

The following sections discuss the ICMP messages supported by TCP/IP for Microsoft Windows 2000.

ICMP Echo/Echo Reply

One of the most heavily used ICMP facilities is the ability to send a simple message to an IP node and have the message echoed back to the sender. This facility is useful for network troubleshooting and debugging. The simple message sent is an ICMP Echo, and the message echoed back to the sender is an ICMP Echo Reply. Windows 2000 Packet InterNet Groper (PING) and Trace Route (TRACERT) utilities use Echo/Echo Reply to provide information about reachability and the path taken to reach a destination node. Figure 7-3 displays the ICMP Echo message structure.

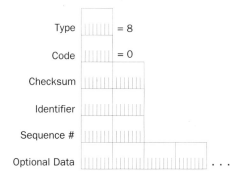

Figure 7-3. *The structure of the ICMP Echo message.*

The fields in the ICMP Echo message are defined as follows:

- **Type** Set to 8.
- **Code** Set to 0.
- **Identifier** A 2-byte field that stores a number generated by the sender that is used to match the ICMP Echo with its corresponding Echo Reply.
- **Sequence Number** A 2-byte field that stores an additional number that is used to match the ICMP Echo with its corresponding Echo Reply. The combination of the values of the Identifier and Sequence Number fields identifies a specific Echo.
- **Optional Data** Optionally, data can be added at the end of the ICMP packet.

For information on how Windows 2000 determines Identifier, Sequence Number, and Optional Data fields, see the "PING Utility" and "TRACERT Utility" sections later in this chapter.

The Network Monitor trace Capture 07-01, in the \Captures folder on the companion CD-ROM, shows the structure of an ICMP Echo message.

Figure 7-4 shows the ICMP Echo Reply message structure.

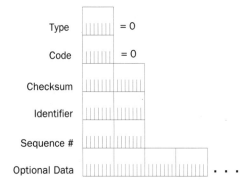

Figure 7-4. *The structure of the ICMP Echo Reply message.*

The fields in the ICMP Echo Reply message are defined as follows:

- **Type** Set to 0.
- **Code** Set to 0.
- **Identifier** Set to the value of the Identifier field of the Echo message being echoed.
- **Sequence Number** Set to the value of the Sequence Number field of the Echo message being echoed.
- **Optional Data** Set to the value of the Optional Data field of the Echo message being echoed.

Echoed in the Echo Reply are the Identifier, Sequence Number, and Optional Data fields. The host that sent the original Echo verifies these fields upon receipt. If the fields are not correctly echoed, the Echo Reply is ignored.

The Network Monitor trace Capture 07-01, in the \Captures folder on the companion CD-ROM, shows the structure of an ICMP Echo Reply message sent in reply to an Echo message.

Sending ICMP Echo packets and receiving ICMP Echo Replies checks for the following:

- The host sending the Echo can forward the Echo to either the destination (direct delivery) or to a router (indirect delivery).
- The routing infrastructure between the host sending the Echo and the destination can forward the Echo to the destination.
- The host sending the Echo Reply can forward the Echo Reply to either the destination (the sender of the Echo) or to a router.
- The routing infrastructure between the host sending the Echo Reply and the destination can forward the Echo Reply to the destination.

ICMP Destination Unreachable

IP attempts a best-effort delivery of datagrams to their destination. Routing or delivery errors can occur along the path or at the destination. When a routing or delivery error occurs, a router or the destination will discard the offending datagram and attempt to report the error by sending an ICMP Destination Unreachable message to the source IP address of the offending packet. Figure 7-5 shows the ICMP Destination Unreachable message structure.

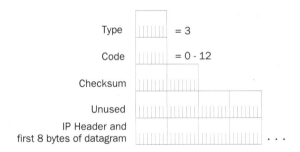

Figure 7-5. *The structure of the ICMP Destination Unreachable message.*

The fields in the ICMP Destination Unreachable message are defined as follows:

- **Type**   Set to 3.
- **Code**   Set to a value from 0 to 12. Table 7-2 lists and discusses the different ICMP Destination Unreachable Code values.
- **IP Header + First 8 Bytes Of Offending Datagram**   To provide meaningful information to the sender of the offending datagram, the ICMP Destination Un-

reachable message contains the IP header and the first 8 bytes of the discarded datagram. The IP header contains the IP Identification field. For Transmission Control Protocol (TCP) segments, the first 8 bytes of IP payload contain the source and destination port numbers and the sequence number. For User Datagram Protocol (UDP) messages, the first 8 bytes contain the entire UDP header including the source and destination port numbers.

Table 7-2. Code Values for ICMP Destination Unreachable Messages

Code Value	Meaning
0 - Network Unreachable	Sent by an IP router when a route for the destination IP address can't be found in the routing table. The source IP address of this message identifies the router that could not find a route. This message is largely obsolete in today's classless Internet due to the inability of the router to determine the network ID of the destination.
1 - Host Unreachable	Sent by an IP router when a route to the destination was not found in the routing table. In today's classless Internet, this is the more appropriate message to send when a router cannot determine the next hop for an IP datagram. This message's source IP address identifies the router that could not deliver the datagram to the destination host.
2 - Protocol Unreachable	Sent by the destination host when the Protocol field in the datagram's IP header doesn't match a client protocol of IP that is being used by the destination. For example, if a host is sent an Open Shortest Path First (OSPF) packet (IP protocol 89), it will send a Protocol Unreachable message back to the sender.
3 - Port Unreachable	Sent by the destination host when the destination port in the UDP or TCP header doesn't match an application running on the destination. In practice, however, when TCP ports can't be found, TCP sends a Connection Reset segment. Therefore, Port Unreachable messages are sent only for UDP messages.
4 - Fragmentation Needed and DF Set	Sent by an IP router when fragmentation is needed in order to forward the IP datagram but the Don't Fragment (DF) flag is set in the IP header. The Fragmentation Needed and DF Set message is an important part of the Path Maximum Transmission Unit (PMTU) Discovery process discussed in the "Path MTU Discovery" section of this chapter. This message's source IP address identifies the router that could not fragment the IP datagram.
5 - Source Route Failed	Sent by an IP router when it can't forward an IP datagram using information stored in the Source Route option in the IP header. For example, this ICMP Destination Unreachable message is sent if the sending host is using a strict source route and the next router is not directly reachable. The Source Route Failed message contains source route options of the same type as the offending datagram and includes the path back to the sending host. This message's source IP address identifies the router that could not forward the source-routed IP datagram. For more information on IP source routing, see Chapter 4, "Internet Protocol (IP) Basics."

(continued)

Table 7-2. *(continued)*

Code Value	Meaning
6 - Destination Network Unknown	Sent by an IP router when the destination network for the destination IP address is indicated in the routing table as an unknown network. In practice, the Destination Network Unknown message is obsolete; IP routers send a Host Unreachable message instead.
7 - Destination Host Unknown	Sent by an IP router when the destination host doesn't exist as detected through Network Interface Layer mechanisms. In practice, the Destination Host Unknown message is sent only when the router can't deliver to a host that is connected to the router by a point-to-point link. This message's source IP address identifies the router that could not deliver the IP datagram.
8 - Source Host Isolated	An obsolete message sent by an IP router when it can detect that the source host is isolated from the rest of the network.
9 - Communication with Destination Network Administratively Prohibited	Sent by an IP router when a route to the destination IP address was found but the router can't forward the IP datagram because of a prohibitive network policy. This message's source IP address identifies the router that could not forward the IP datagram.
10 - Communication with Destination Host Administratively Prohibited	Sent by an IP router when it can't deliver to the destination host because of a prohibitive network policy. This message's source IP address identifies the router that could not deliver the IP datagram.
11 - Network Unreachable for Type of Service	Sent by an IP router when a route to the destination IP address for the Type Of Service (TOS) indicated in the IP header of the IP datagram was not found. This message is sent only by routers that use the TOS field when forwarding IP datagrams. This message's source IP address identifies the router that could not forward the IP datagram.
12 - Host Unreachable for Type of Service	Sent by an IP router when it can't deliver to the destination host for the TOS indicated in the IP header of the IP datagram. This message is sent only by routers that use the TOS field when forwarding IP datagrams. This message's source IP address identifies the router that could not forward the IP datagram.
13 - Communication Administratively Prohibited Because of Firewalls	Sent by an IP router when it can't forward or deliver the IP datagram because of administratively configured packet filters on the router. This message's source IP address identifies the router that could not deliver the IP datagram.

Network Monitor Example

To illustrate a Destination Unreachable message, examine the following Network Monitor trace (Capture 07-02 in the \Captures folder on the companion CD-ROM). Frame 1 is an Echo sent to a private address while on the Internet. Because private addresses are not reachable on the Internet, Frame 2 is the ICMP Destination Unreachable-Host Unreachable message sent by an Internet router.

Frame 1: The ICMP Echo message

```
+ FRAME: Base frame properties
+ ETHERNET: ETYPE = 0x0800 : Protocol = IP:  DOD Internet Protocol
```

```
IP: ID = 0x8A03; Proto = ICMP; Len: 60
    IP: Version = 4 (0x4)
    IP: Header Length = 20 (0x14)
    IP: Precedence = Routine
    IP: Type of Service = Normal Service
    IP: Total Length = 60 (0x3C)
    IP: Identification = 35331 (0x8A03)
 +  IP: Flags Summary = 0 (0x0)
    IP: Fragment Offset = 0 (0x0) bytes
    IP: Time to Live = 32 (0x20)
    IP: Protocol = ICMP - Internet Control Message
    IP: Checksum = 0x26AA
    IP: Source Address = 134.39.89.236
    IP: Destination Address = 10.0.0.1
    IP: Data: Number of data bytes remaining = 40 (0x0028)
ICMP: Echo: From 134.39.89.236 To 10.00.00.01
    ICMP: Packet Type = Echo
    ICMP: Echo Code = 0(0x0)
    ICMP: Checksum = 0x1B5C
    ICMP: Identifier = 256 (0x100)
    ICMP: Sequence Number = 12544 (0x3100)
    ICMP: Data: Number of data bytes remaining = 32 (0x0020)
```

Frame 2: The ICMP Destination Unreachable-Host Unreachable message

```
+ FRAME: Base frame properties
+ ETHERNET: ETYPE = 0x0800 : Protocol = IP:  DOD Internet Protocol
  IP: ID = 0x7AA9; Proto = ICMP; Len: 56
    IP: Version = 4 (0x4)
    IP: Header Length = 20 (0x14)
    IP: Precedence = Routine
    IP: Type of Service = Normal Service
    IP: Total Length = 56 (0x38)
    IP: Identification = 31401 (0x7AA9)
  + IP: Flags Summary = 0 (0x0)
    IP: Fragment Offset = 0 (0x0) bytes
    IP: Time to Live = 252 (0xFC)
    IP: Protocol = ICMP - Internet Control Message
    IP: Checksum = 0xBA4A
    IP: Source Address = 168.156.1.33
    IP: Destination Address = 134.39.89.236
    IP: Data: Number of data bytes remaining = 36 (0x0024)
  ICMP: Destination Unreachable: 10.0.0.1    (See frame 1)
    ICMP: Packet Type = Destination Unreachable
    ICMP: Unreachable Code = Host Unreachable
```

```
ICMP: Checksum = 0xA7A2
ICMP: Unused Bytes = 0 (0x0)
ICMP: Data: Number of data bytes remaining = 28 (0x001C)
    ICMP: Description of original IP frame
    ICMP: (IP) Version = 4 (0x4)
    ICMP: (IP) Header Length = 20 (0x14)
  + ICMP: (IP) Service Type = 0 (0x0)
    ICMP: (IP) Total Length = 60 (0x3C)
    ICMP: (IP) Identification = 35331 (0x8A03)
  + ICMP: (IP) Flags Summary = 0 (0x0)
    ICMP: (IP) Fragment Offset = 0 (0x0) bytes
    ICMP: (IP) Time to Live = 28 (0x1C)
    ICMP: (IP) Protocol = ICMP - Internet Control Message
    ICMP: (IP) Checksum = 0x2AAA
    ICMP: (IP) Source Address = 134.39.89.236
    ICMP: (IP) Destination Address = 10.0.0.1
    ICMP: (IP) Data: Number of data bytes remaining = 8 (0x0008)
    ICMP: Description of original ICMP frame
        ICMP: Checksum = 0x1B5C
        ICMP: Identifier = 256 (0x100)
        ICMP: Sequence Number = 12544 (0x3100)
```

Notice that the ICMP Destination Unreachable-Host Unreachable contains the IP header and the first 8 bytes (the ICMP header) of Frame 1.

Path MTU Discovery

As discussed in Chapter 4, "Internet Protocol (IP) Basics," IP fragmentation is an expensive process for both routers and the destination host and should be avoided. An early solution to avoiding fragmentation was the use of a 576-byte IP MTU to send data to a location on another network. RFC 791 requires Network Interface Layer technologies to support an IP MTU size of 576 bytes. However, this solution is inefficient; two Ethernet nodes separated by routers send each other 576-byte IP datagrams rather than 1500-byte IP datagrams.

The current solution to avoiding fragmentation is known as Path MTU Discovery (PMTU Discovery) and is documented in RFC 1191. With PMTU Discovery, hosts send all IP datagrams with the DF flag set to 1. If a router can't forward an IP datagram onto a link because the datagram's size exceeds the link's MTU, it sends an ICMP Destination Unreachable-Fragmentation Needed and DF Set message (ICMP Type 3, Code 4) back to the sender. While this has been the behavior since the inception of IP and ICMP, PMTU Discovery support on the router modifies the ICMP message to include the IP MTU of the network onto which it needs to forward the IP datagram.

Figure 7-6 shows the modified ICMP Destination Unreachable message. The previous 32-bit Unused field is now a 16-bit Unused field and a 16-bit Next Hop MTU field. The router sets the Next Hop MTU field to the next hop network segment's IP MTU. Upon receiving this message, the sending host adjusts the size of the IP datagram to the Next Hop MTU size and retransmits the IP datagram. Sending hosts and all the IP routers in your internetwork must support PMTU.

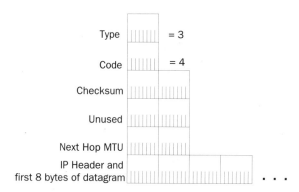

Figure 7-6. *A PMTU-compliant ICMP Destination Unreachable-Fragmentation Needed And DF Set message showing the Next Hop MTU field.*

To discover the initial PMTU, a sending host that supports PMTU sets the initial PMTU to the IP MTU of the directly attached network. The host then sends an IP datagram with the DF flag set to 1 at the PMTU size.

Upon receipt of an ICMP Destination Unreachable-Fragmentation Needed and DF Set with the Next Hop MTU indicated, the sending host sets the PMTU to the value of the Next Hop MTU and resends the adjusted IP datagram.

The PMTU is determined when no more ICMP Destination Unreachable-Fragmentation Needed and DF Set messages are received.

In the Network Monitor trace Capture 07-03, in the \Captures folder on the companion CD-ROM, Frame 1 shows an ICMP Echo with the DF set to 1 and a 1000 byte Optional Data field. This packet is being forwarded across a router interface that supports only a 576-byte IP MTU. Frame 2 is an ICMP Destination Unreachable-Fragmentation Needed And DF Set message indicating the Next Hop MTU of 576.

Adjusting the PMTU

In a single-path internetwork, the PMTU remains the same once discovered. In a multi-path internetwork, the PMTU can change based on the paths that the IP datagrams travel because of changing conditions in the routing infrastructure. The PMTU can change to be either higher or lower than the currently known PMTU.

- For a lower PMTU, the sending host is immediately informed through a Destination Unreachable message.
- For a higher PMTU, because there's no mechanism on the routers to inform the sending host that larger datagrams can now be sent, it's up to the host to redis-

cover the new larger PMTU. If the Windows 2000 host's PMTU is smaller than the IP MTU of the locally attached network, the sending host attempts to send larger IP datagrams 5 minutes after receiving the last ICMP Destination Unreachable-Fragmentation Needed and DF Set messages, and at 1-minute intervals thereafter.

Routers that Do Not Support PMTU

PMTU Discovery relies on PMTU support on the sending host and all of the internetwork's routers. TCP/IP for Windows 2000 supports PMTU Discovery for both hosts and routers. However, what happens when an intermediate router doesn't support PMTU Discovery?

The lack of support for PMTU Discovery on IP routers can occur on the following two levels:

1. The router sends back ICMP Destination Unreachable-Fragmentation Needed and DF Set messages without the Next Hop MTU field.

2. The router doesn't send back ICMP Destination Unreachable-Fragmentation Needed and DF Set messages.

In the first case, the router is not RFC 1191-compliant and according to the sending host, the Destination Unreachable-Fragmentation Needed and DF Set message contains a 0 Next Hop MTU. The sending host assumes that PMTU Discovery is not possible and will either use the minimum PMTU of 576 bytes or use a series of plateau values for the PMTU until Destination Unreachable-Fragmentation Needed and DF Set messages are no longer received. Table 7-3 lists the plateau values, which correspond to the IP MTUs of common Network Interface Layer technologies. Windows 2000 nodes do not use this behavior. PMTU behavior for TCP/IP for Windows 2000 is described in the "Windows 2000 Registry Settings for PMTU" section of this chapter.

Table 7-3. Plateau Values for PMTU

Plateau Value	Representing
65,535	Maximum IP MTU
32,000	Just in case
17,914	16 Mbps IBM Token Ring
8166	IEEE 802.4
4352	IEEE 802.5 (4 Mbps) and FDDI
2002	Wideband Network and IEEE 802.5 (4 Mbps)
1492	Ethernet/IEEE 802.3 (SNAP)
1006	SLIP
508	X.25 and ARCnet
296	Point-to-Point (low delay)
68	Minimum IP MTU

When a router doesn't send back Destination Unreachable-Fragmentation Needed and DF Set messages, it's called a PMTU Black Hole Router. PMTU Black Hole Routers perform silent discards for datagrams that can't be fragmented. Because IP is unreliable, it's the responsibility of an upper layer protocol to recover from the discarded packet. For example, TCP segments will be retransmitted when their retransmission timer expires.

To successfully detect a PMTU Black Hole Router, discarded packets with the DF flag set to 1 are retransmitted with the DF flag set to 0. If an acknowledgment is received, the TCP Maximum Segment Size (MSS) is lowered to the next lowest plateau value and the DF flag for subsequent IP datagrams is set to 1. This process repeats until the PMTU is found.

Windows 2000 Registry Settings for PMTU

The following Windows 2000 registry settings allow modification of the PMTU behavior for TCP/IP.

EnablePMTUBHDetect

```
Location: HKEY_LOCAL_MACHINE\SYSTEM\CurrentControlSet\Services\Tcpip\Parameters
Data type: REG_DWORD
Valid range: 0-1
Default: 0
Present by default: No
```

EnablePMTUBHDetect enables (=1) or disables (=0) the detection of Black Hole PMTU routers. By default, detection of PMTU Black Hole Routers is disabled. TCP sends segments with the DF flag set to 1. If no acknowledgments are received after the maximum number of TCP retransmissions, the TCP connection is terminated. If enabled, the PMTU is set at 576 bytes after no acknowledgment is received for a large segment after several retransmissions.

EnablePMTUDiscovery

```
Location: HKEY_LOCAL_MACHINE\SYSTEM\CurrentControlSet\Services\Tcpip\Parameters
Data type: REG_DWORD
Valid range: 0-1
Default: 1
Present by default: No
```

Enable PMTUDiscovery enables (=1) or disables (=0) the PMTUDiscovery for TCP connection data. By default, PMTU Discovery is enabled. TCP will attempt to discover the PMTU by initially transmitting segments at the largest segment size and then adjusting the segment size when Destination Unreachable-Fragmentation Needed and DF Set messages are received.

If disabled, PMTU Discovery is not performed and an IP MTU of 576 bytes is assumed for traffic not destined to a host on a locally attached network.

ICMP Source Quench

When a router becomes congested because of either a sudden increase in traffic, a slow link, or inadequate processor and memory resources, the router begins to discard incoming IP datagrams. When a router discards an IP datagram because of congestion, it might send an ICMP Source Quench message back to the sending host. The Source IP Address field of the ICMP Source Quench message identifies the congested router. ICMP Source Quench messages can be sent also by the destination host when IP datagrams are arriving too quickly to be buffered.

RFC 792 doesn't document the specific implementation details of when a router or destination host sends ICMP Source Quench messages. A router can begin sending Source Quench messages when its memory buffers for storing incoming packets is approaching its maximum capacity, rather than waiting for the buffer to fill. A router doesn't have to send a Source Quench message for every packet discarded. In fact, RFC 1812 states that routers should not send ICMP Source Quench messages. Creating more traffic on a congested internetwork creates more congestion.

The ICMP Source Quench message is an Internet Layer notification. However, the Internet Layer has no mechanism for flow control. IP is unaware of when to increase or decrease its transmission rate. Similarly, UDP has no mechanism for flow control.

TCP is an upper layer protocol that has flow control mechanisms to lower the transmission rate. Therefore, upon receipt of the ICMP Source Quench message for a discarded TCP segment, a notification is made to TCP. TCP treats the receipt of the ICMP Source Quench message for a specific TCP segment as a lost TCP segment that needs to be retransmitted. TCP then adjusts its transmission rate for the connection according to the slow start and congestion avoidance algorithms. The sending host gradually increases its transmission rate, giving time for the routers to clear their buffers. For more information, see Chapter 13, "Transmission Control Protocol (TCP) Data Flow." Figure 7-7 shows the ICMP Source Quench message structure.

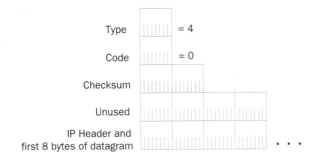

Figure 7-7. *The structure of the ICMP Source Quench message.*

The fields in the ICMP Source Quench message are defined as follows:

- **Type**   Set to 4.
- **Code**   Set to 0.
- **IP Header + First 8 Bytes Of Discarded Datagram**   The ICMP Source Quench message contains the IP header and the first 8 bytes of that discarded datagram.

TCP/IP for Windows 2000 properly implements TCP flow control if an ICMP Source Quench message is received and contains the IP header and TCP header (only the first 8 bytes) for an active TCP connection. As a router, TCP/IP for Windows 2000 doesn't send ICMP Source Quench messages when the router buffers fill and packets are discarded.

ICMP Redirect

It's common practice for hosts to have minimal routing tables. A typical host has a route to the locally attached network and a default route corresponding to the host's configured default gateway. The routers keep all other knowledge of the internetwork's topology—the entire list of network IDs and the best forwarding IP addresses to reach them. For network segments containing a single router and hosts configured with the IP address of the single router as their default gateway, all routing from hosts to remote networks occurs through the optimal path—the single router.

However, if there are multiple routers on a network with hosts configured with a default gateway of a single router, the possibility exists for non-optimal routing. Consider the IP internetwork in Figure 7-8.

Host A, 10.0.0.99/24, is configured with the default gateway of 10.0.0.1. Host A sends an IP datagram to Host B at 192.168.1.99. Router 1 is attached to network 10.0.0.0/24 and the rest of the IP internetwork. Router 2 is attached to network 10.0.0.0/24 and 192.168.1.0/24. According to the default route in Host A's IP routing table, to reach 192.168.1.99, forward the IP datagram to 10.0.0.1. This is not the optimal path, however. For the optimal path, the datagram must be forwarded to 10.0.0.2.

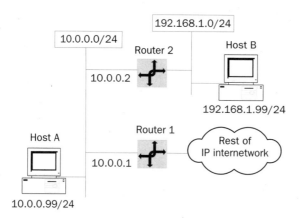

Figure 7-8. *An ICMP Redirect scenario where a host with a configured default gateway must forward an IP datagram using another router.*

To inform Host A of the more optimal route for traffic to Host B at 192.168.1.99, Router 1 uses an ICMP Redirect message. Host A uses the contents of the ICMP Redirect message to create a host route in its routing table so that subsequent IP datagrams to Host B take the more optimal route through Router 2 at 10.0.0.2.

The ICMP Redirect process in detail is as follows:

1. Host A forwards the IP datagram destined for Host B to its default gateway, Router 1, at the IP address of 10.0.0.1.

2. Router 1 receives the IP datagram. Because the IP datagram is not destined for an IP address assigned to Router 1, Router 1 checks the contents of its routing table for a route to Host B. A route is found for 192.168.1.0/24 at the forwarding IP address of 10.0.0.2.

3. Before forwarding the IP datagram to Router 2 at 10.0.0.2, Router 1 notices that the sending host's IP address, the IP address of the interface on which the IP datagram was received, and the forwarding IP address are all on the same network, 10.0.0.0/24.

4. Router 1 forwards the IP datagram to Router 2.

5. Router 1 sends an ICMP Redirect message to Host A. The Redirect message contains the forwarding IP address for Router 2, 10.0.0.2, and the IP header of the originally sent IP datagram.

6. Based on the contents of the Redirect message, Host A creates a host route for the IP address of Host B, 192.168.1.99, at the forwarding IP address of 10.0.0.2.

7. Subsequent packets from Host A to Host B are forwarded to Router 2 at the IP address of 10.0.0.2.

ICMP Redirect messages are never sent for IP datagrams using source route options. The presence of source route options means that a specific path must be followed without regard to whether it's optimal. Source route options are sometimes used to test connectivity along non-optimal paths.

When a TCP/IP for Windows 2000 host receives an ICMP Redirect message, it first checks the source IP address to ensure that it was sent from the router indicated by the gateway column for the route to the destination in the IP routing table. TCP/IP for Windows 2000 also ensures that the source IP address of the ICMP Redirect is directly reachable. If the ICMP Redirect didn't come from the directly reachable indicated router, the ICMP Redirect is ignored. Host routes created through ICMP Redirect messages persist in the routing table for 10 minutes. After 10 minutes, the redirect process occurs again. Figure 7-9 shows the ICMP Redirect message structure.

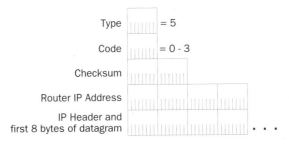

Figure 7-9. *The structure of the ICMP Redirect message.*

The fields in the ICMP Redirect message are defined as follows:

- **Type** Set to 5.
- **Code** Set to 0–3 (see Table 7-4).
- **Router IP Address** A 4-byte field set to the forwarding IP address for the more optimal route to the destination of the offending IP datagram. This IP address becomes the address in the Gateway column of the host route created in the Windows 2000 IP routing table.
- **IP Header + First 8 Bytes Of Forwarded Datagram** To identify the forwarded IP datagram, the IP header and first 8 bytes of the IP payload are encapsulated and sent back to the sending host. Included in the encapsulated IP header is the destination IP address that becomes the value in the Destination Network column for the host route created in the Windows 2000 IP routing table. The Network Mask for the host route is set to 255.255.255.255.

Table 7-4. Values of the Code Field in an ICMP Redirect

Code Value	Meaning
0	Redirected datagrams for the network (obsolete)
1	Redirected datagrams for the host
2	Redirected datagrams for the TOS and the network
3	Redirected datagrams for the TOS and the host

Note ICMP Redirect messages are sent only when the sending host forwards an IP datagram using a non-optimal route. ICMP Redirect messages are never sent when routers forward IP datagrams using non-optimal routes.

The Network Monitor trace Capture 07-04, in the \Captures folder on the companion CD-ROM, shows an ICMP Echo and the ICMP Redirect for the example previously discussed.

ICMP Router Discovery

ICMP Router Discovery is a set of ICMP messages documented in RFC 1256 that are used by both routers to advertise their presence and by hosts to discover their network segment's routers, and choose which router will be the host's default gateway. ICMP Router Discovery provides a fault-tolerance mechanism for downed routers. Hosts eventually realize that their current default gateway has become unavailable and switch their default gateway to the next most preferred router.

ICMP Router Discovery uses the following two different ICMP messages:

- **ICMP Router Advertisement** The ICMP Router Advertisement message is sent pseudo-periodically by a router to advertise its continued existence, a preference level, and a time after which it can be considered unavailable.

- **ICMP Router Solicitation**   Hosts send an ICMP Router Solicitation message whenever they need to discover the most preferred router to use as their default gateway. ICMP Router Discovery-capable hosts that have not been configured with a default gateway will send an ICMP Router Solicitation message upon startup. Additionally, hosts send an ICMP Router Solicitation message when the availability time of their current default gateway (discovered through ICMP Router Discovery) expires.

ICMP Router Discovery is not a routing protocol; it provides information only on a preferred default gateway for hosts on a network segment. ICMP Router Discovery doesn't provide any information on network IDs or optimal paths.

ICMP Router Advertisement

Routers send the ICMP Router Advertisement message to either the all-hosts multicast IP address (224.0.0.1), the subnet (or network) broadcast address, or the limited broadcast address. ICMP Router Advertisements are sent pseudo-periodically (at a random interval between a minimum and maximum value) and in response to an ICMP Router Solicitation. The default interval for ICMP Router Advertisements is between 7 and 10 minutes. The Windows 2000 Routing and Remote Access service implementation of ICMP Router Discovery sends ICMP Router Advertisements to the all-hosts multicast IP address. Figure 7-10 shows the ICMP Router Advertisement message structure.

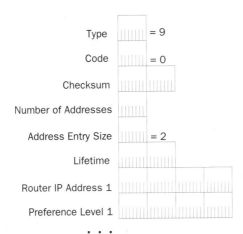

Figure 7-10. *The structure of the ICMP Router Advertisement message.*

The fields in the ICMP Router Advertisement message are defined as follows:

- **Type**   Set to 9.
- **Code**   Set to 0.

- **Number Of Addresses** A 1-byte field that indicates how many IP addresses are being advertised. Normally, only a single IP address is advertised. For a router with multiple interfaces on the same network segment, multiple IP addresses are advertised.

- **Address Entry Size** A 1-byte field that indicates how many 32-bit words (4-byte quantities) are contained in a Router Advertisement entry. A Router Advertisement entry consists of an IP address (32 bits) and a preference level (32 bits). Therefore, the Address Entry Size field is always set to 2.

- **Lifetime** A 2-byte field that indicates the time in seconds after the last received Router Advertisement that the router can be considered down. This is equivalent to the Dead Interval for the OSPF routing protocol. The Lifetime field has a default value of 3600 (30 minutes).

- **Router Address** A 4-byte field that indicates the IP address of the network segment's router interface on which the advertisement was sent.

- **Preference Level** A 4-byte field that indicates the level of preference for using the Router Address as the IP address of your default gateway. The router advertising the highest preference level is the most preferred router. If there are two or more routers with the same preference level, the router with the numerically smallest router address becomes the default gateway.

Router Advertisement behavior for the Windows 2000 Routing and Remote Access service is configured per interface through the properties of an interface in the IP Routing\General node in the Routing and Remote Access administrative tool.

ICMP Router Solicitation

Hosts send the ICMP Router Solicitation message to either the all-routers multicast IP address (224.0.0.2), the subnet (or network) broadcast address, or the limited broadcast address.

TCP/IP for Windows 2000 listens for ICMP Router Advertisements that are sent to the all-hosts multicast address of 224.0.0.1 and sends up to three ICMP Solicitation messages spaced 600 milliseconds apart to the all-routers multicast IP address. Figure 7-11 shows the ICMP Router Solicitation message structure.

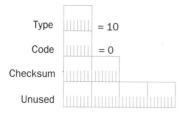

Figure 7-11. *The structure of the ICMP Router Solicitation message.*

The fields in the ICMP Router Solicitation message are defined as follows:

- **Type**   Set to 10.
- **Code**   Set to 0.
- **Reserved**   A 4-byte field that is set to all 0's.

Windows 2000 Registry Settings for Host Router Discovery

Host Router Discovery behavior for TCP/IP for Windows 2000 can be modified through the following registry settings:

PerformRouterDiscovery

```
Location:  HKEY_LOCAL_MACHINE\SYSTEM\CurrentControlSet\Services\
Tcpip\Parameters\Interfaces\<interface>
Data type: REG_DWORD
Valid range: 0-1
Default: 1
Present by default: Yes
```

PerformRouterDiscovery enables (=1) and disables (=0) ICMP Router Discovery for each interface. The default is enabled.

SolicitationAddressBCast

```
Location:  HKEY_LOCAL_MACHINE\SYSTEM\CurrentControlSet\Services\
Tcpip\Parameters\Interfaces\<interface>
Data type: REG_DWORD
Valid range: 0-1
Default: 0 (disabled)
Present by default: No
```

SolicitationAddressBCast enables (=1) or disables (=0) the use of the subnet (or network) broadcast address as the destination IP address of ICMP Router Solicitation messages. When disabled (the default), TCP/IP for Windows 2000 uses the all-routers IP multicast address (224.0.0.2).

ICMP Time Exceeded

The ICMP Time Exceeded message is sent in the following instances:

- When a router decrements the IP header's Time-to-Live (TTL) field to 0
- When the reassembly timer for a fragmented IP datagram expires

When the TTL goes to 0 for an IP datagram, it can mean one of two things:

- The IP datagram was sent with an inadequate TTL that doesn't reflect the current number of links between the source and destination nodes. In this case, the TTL should be increased.

- A routing loop exists in the internetwork. As discussed in Chapter 6, "Internet Protocol (IP) Routing," a routing loop occurs when IP routers have incorrect routing information and forward an IP datagram in a loop that never reaches the destination. To test for a routing loop, send an IP datagram with a TTL of 255, the maximum value. If an ICMP Time Exceeded message is still received, a routing loop exists in your internetwork.

Destination hosts receiving a fragmented IP datagram use a reassembly timer as a maximum time to wait before discarding the incomplete IP datagram. If all of an IP datagram's fragments arrive within the time allotted in the reassembly timer, the IP datagram is successfully reassembled. If the reassembly timer expires before all of an IP datagram's fragments have been received, the destination host discards the incomplete payload and can send an ICMP Time Exceeded message back to the source. Figure 7-12 shows the ICMP Time Exceeded message structure.

The fields in the ICMP Time Exceeded message are defined as follows:

- **Type** Set to 11.
- **Code** Set to 0 or 1. Set to 0 by a router to indicate a TTL expiration. Set to 1 by a destination host to indicate a reassembly expiration.
- **IP Header + First 8 Bytes Of Discarded Datagram** To identify the discarded IP datagram, the ICMP Time Exceeded message contains the IP header and the first 8 bytes of the IP payload.

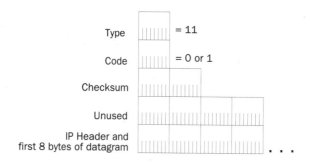

Figure 7-12. *The structure of the ICMP Time Exceeded message.*

The Network Monitor trace Capture 07-05, in the \Captures folder on the companion CD-ROM, shows an ICMP Echo from an Internet host sent to an Internet Web site with an insufficient TTL.

ICMP Parameter Problem

A router or a destination host sends an ICMP Parameter Problem message when an error occurs in the processing of the IP header causing the IP datagram to be discarded, and there are no other ICMP messages that can be used to indicate the error. ICMP Parameter Problem messages can be sent because of errors in TCP/IP implementations causing incorrect formatting of IP header fields. Typically, ICMP Parameter Problem messages are sent because of incorrect arguments in IP option fields. Figure 7-13 shows the ICMP Parameter Problem message structure.

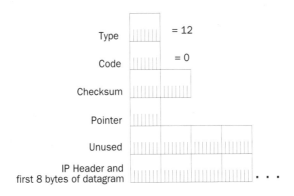

Figure 7-13. *The structure of the ICMP Parameter Problem message.*

The fields in the ICMP Parameter Problem message are defined as follows:

- **Type**   Set to 12.
- **Code**   Set to 0–2. See Table 7-5.
- **Pointer**   A 1-byte field set to the byte offset (starting at 0) in the encapsulated IP header where the error was detected for Parameter Problem messages with the Code field set to 0.
- **IP Header + First 8 Bytes Of Discarded Datagram**   To identify the discarded IP datagram, the ICMP Parameter Problem message contains the IP header and the first 8 bytes of the IP payload.

Table 7-5. ICMP Parameter Problem Code Values

Code Value	Meaning
0	Pointer indicates error
1	Missing a required option
2	Bad length

Note   ICMP Parameter Problem messages are never sent for IP datagrams with an invalid checksum. IP datagrams that fail the checksum are silently discarded.

PING Utility

The PING command-line utility for Windows 2000 is the primary network troubleshooting tool. The PING utility tests reachability, name resolution, source routing, network latency, and other issues. PING sends an ICMP Echo to a specified destination and records the round-trip time, the number of bytes sent, and the corresponding Echo Reply's TTL. When PING finishes sending ICMP Echoes, it displays statistics on the average number of replies and round-trip time.

When you ping a destination IP address, the default behavior is to send four fragmentable, non-source routed ICMP Echoes with an optional data field of 32 bytes and wait one second for the corresponding ICMP Echo Reply. When you ping a name, normal Windows 2000 name resolution mechanisms resolve the name to an IP address before the Echoes are sent. If Windows 2000 is unable to resolve the name to an IP address, the PING utility displays the message Unknown Host. If a corresponding Echo Reply is not received within one second, PING displays the error message Request Timed Out.

In the ICMP header of Windows 2000 PING-generated ICMP Echoes:

- The Identifier field is set to 256 (0x100).
- The Sequence Number field for the first Echo is chosen as a multiple of 256 (0x100) and the Sequence Number for subsequent Echoes is incremented by 256 (0x100).
- The Optional Data field is 32 bytes (by default), consisting of the string "abcdefghijklmnopqrstuvwabcdefghi."

PING Options

Table 7-6 lists the use and default values of PING utility options.

Table 7-6. PING Utility Options

Option	Use	Default
-t	Sends Echoes until interrupted.	Not used
-a	Performs a Domain Name System (DNS) reverse query to resolve the DNS host name of the specified IP address.	Not used
-n *count*	The number of Echoes to send.	4
-l *size*	The size of the Optional Data field up to a maximum of 65,500.	32
-f	Sets the Don't Fragment (DF) flag to 1.	Not used
-i *TTL*	Sets the value of the TTL field in the IP header.	32
-v *TOS*	Sets the value of the Type Of Service field in the IP header. The TOS value is in decimal.	0
-r *count*	Sends the ICMP Echoes using the IP Record Route option and sets the value of the number of slots. Count has a maximum value of 9.	Not used

(continued)

Table 7-6. *(continued)*

Option	Use	Default
-s *count*	Sends the ICMP Echoes using the IP Internet Timestamp option and sets the value of the number of slots. Count has a maximum value of 4. Windows 2000 PING uses the Internet Timestamp FLAG set to 1 (records both the IP addresses of each hop and the timestamp).	Not used
-j *host-list*	Sends the ICMP Echoes using the Loose Source Route option and sets the next hop addresses to the IP addresses in the host list. The host list is made up of IP addresses separated by spaces corresponding to the loose source route. There can be up to nine IP addresses in the host list.	Not used
-k *host-list*	Sends the ICMP Echoes using the Strict Source Route option and sets the next hop addresses to the IP addresses in the host list. The host list is made of IP addresses separated by spaces corresponding to the loose source route. There can be up to 9 IP addresses in the host list.	Not used
-w *timeout*	Waits the specified amount of time, in milliseconds, for the corresponding Echo Reply before displaying a Request Timed Out message.	1000

Network Monitor Example

The following Network Monitor trace (Capture 07-01 in the \Captures folder on the companion CD-ROM) illustrates a summary of a typical use of the PING utility to ping a destination IP address. Four Echoes are sent and four Echo Replies are received. The summarized frames have been indented for readability.

```
Frame  Time   Src MAC Addr   Dst MAC Addr   Protocol  Description
1      0.271  0060083E4607   00502AB9A440   ICMP      Echo, From 157.59.11.19
                                                       To    157.59.08.01
2      0.271  00502AB9A440   0060083E4607   ICMP      Echo Reply, To
                                                       157.59.11.19 From
                                                       157.59.08.01
3      1.271  0060083E4607   00502AB9A440   ICMP      Echo, From 157.59.11.19
                                                       To 157.59.08.01
4      1.271  00502AB9A440   0060083E4607   ICMP      Echo Reply, To
                                                       157.59.11.19 From
                                                       157.59.08.01
5      2.273  0060083E4607   00502AB9A440   ICMP      Echo, From 157.59.11.19
                                                       To 157.59.08.01
6      2.273  00502AB9A440   0060083E4607   ICMP      Echo Reply, To
                                                       157.59.11.19 From
                                                       157.59.08.01
7      3.275  0060083E4607   00502AB9A440   ICMP      Echo, From 157.59.11.19
                                                       To    157.59.08.01
8      3.275  00502AB9A440   0060083E4607   ICMP      Echo Reply, To
                                                       157.59.11.19 From
                                                       157.59.08.01
```

TRACERT Utility

The TRACERT utility uses ICMP Echo messages to determine the path—the series of rout-ers—that unicast traffic takes from a source host to a destination host. TRACERT tests reachability, name resolution, network latency, routing loops, and other issues.

When you tracert a destination IP address, the default behavior is to trace the route and report the round-trip time, the near-side router IP address, and the DNS name correspond-ing to the near-side router IP address. When you tracert a name, normal Windows 2000 name resolution techniques resolve the name to an IP address before the Echo messages are sent. If Windows 2000 is unable to resolve the name to an IP address, the TRACERT utility displays the message Unknown Host.

TRACERT works in the following manner:

1. An ICMP Echo is sent to the destination with the TTL in the IP header set to 1. If the destination is on a directly attached network, the destination responds with a corresponding Echo Reply and TRACERT is done.

2. If the destination is not in a directly attached network, the Echo is forwarded to an IP router.

3. The IP router determines that the IP datagram is transit traffic (not destined for the router) and decrements the TTL. Because the TTL is now 0, the IP router discards the IP datagram and sends back an ICMP Time Exceeded-TTL Expired In Transit message to the sending host with the source IP address set to the IP address of the interface on which the ICMP Echo was received. The interface on which the Echo was received is the near-side interface, the interface that is the smallest number of hops from the sending host.

4. Upon receipt of the ICMP Time Exceeded-TTL Expired In Transit message, the TRACERT utility records the round-trip time and the source IP address.

5. TRACERT sends two more ICMP Echo messages and records their round-trip time.

6. An ICMP Echo is sent to the destination with the IP header's TTL set to 2. The Echo is forwarded to an IP router.

7. The IP router determines that the IP datagram is transit traffic, decrements the TTL to 1, and forwards it to the next hop or the final destination.

8. If the destination is on a directly attached network, the destination responds with a corresponding Echo Reply and TRACERT is done.

9. If the destination is not on a directly attached network, the IP router determines that the IP datagram is transit traffic and decrements the TTL. Because the TTL is now 0, the IP router discards the IP datagram and sends back an ICMP Time Exceeded-TTL Expired In Transit message to the sending host with the source IP address set to the IP address of the interface on which the ICMP Echo was received. The interface on which the Echo was received is the near-side inter-face, the interface that is smallest number of hops from the sending host.

10. Upon receipt of the ICMP Time Exceeded-TTL Expired In Transit message, the TRACERT utility records the round-trip time and the source IP address.

11. TRACERT sends two more ICMP Echo messages and records their round-trip time.

This process continues until the destination is reached and replies with ICMP Echo Reply messages.

The TRACERT utility records the series of near-side router interfaces in the path from the sending host to a destination. By default, TRACERT also performs a DNS reverse query on each near-side router interface and displays the host name corresponding to the IP address.

> **Note**   If a router silently discards packets with an expired TTL, TRACERT shows a series of "*" characters for that hop. If ICMP packet filtering is occurring on a near-side router interface, that router and all subsequent routers will show the "*" character until 30 hops are attempted (the default).

Network Monitor Example

The following frames from a Network Monitor trace (Capture 07-06 in the \Captures folder on the companion CD-ROM) summarize a typical use of the TRACERT utility to trace the route to a destination IP address. In this case, TRACERT is used to trace the path across two routers, and the -d option is used to simplify the process and the display. The summarized frames have been indented for readability.

Frame	Time	Src MAC Addr	Dst MAC Addr	Protocol	Description
1	1.241	0060083E4607	00502AB9A440	ICMP	Echo, From 157.59.11.19 To 157.59.224.33
2	1.241	00502AB9A440	0060083E4607	ICMP	Time Exceeded while trying to deliver to 157.59.224.33 See frame 1
3	1.242	0060083E4607	00502AB9A440	ICMP	Echo, From 157.59.11.19 To 157.59.224.33
4	1.242	00502AB9A440	0060083E4607	ICMP	Time Exceeded while trying to deliver to 157.59.224.33 See frame 3
5	1.260	0060083E4607	00502AB9A440	ICMP	Echo, From 157.59.11.19 To 157.59.224.33
6	1.260	00502AB9A440	0060083E4607	ICMP	Time Exceeded while trying to deliver to 157.59.224.33 See frame 5
7	2.263	0060083E4607	00502AB9A440	ICMP	Echo, From 157.59.11.19 To 157.59.224.33
8	2.263	00502AB9A440	0060083E4607	ICMP	Time Exceeded while trying to deliver to 157.59.224.33 See frame 7

9	2.264	0060083E4607	00502AB9A440	ICMP	Echo, From 157.59.11.19 To 157.59.224.33
10	2.265	00502AB9A440	0060083E4607	ICMP	Time Exceeded while trying to deliver to 157.59.224.33 See frame 9
11	2.265	0060083E4607	00502AB9A440	ICMP	Echo, From 157.59.11.19 To 157.59.224.33
12	2.266	00502AB9A440	0060083E4607	ICMP	Time Exceeded while trying to deliver to 157.59.224.33 See frame 11
13	3.264	0060083E4607	00502AB9A440	ICMP	Echo, From 157.59.11.19 To 157.59.224.33
14	3.265	00502AB9A440	0060083E4607	ICMP	Echo Reply, To 157.59.11.19 From 157.59.224.33
15	3.266	0060083E4607	00502AB9A440	ICMP	Echo, From 157.59.11.19 To 157.59.224.33
16	3.267	00502AB9A440	0060083E4607	ICMP	Echo Reply, To 157.59.11.19 From 157.59.224.33
17	3.268	0060083E4607	00502AB9A440	ICMP	Echo, From 157.59.11.19 To 157.59.224.33
18	3.268	00502AB9A440	0060083E4607	ICMP	Echo Reply, To 157.59.11.19 From 157.59.224.33

Frames 1-6 are the first hop. In frames 1, 3, and 5, the IP header's TTL is set to 1. The local router decrements the TTL to 0 and sends back ICMP Time Exceeded-TTL Expired In Transit messages (frames 2, 4, and 6).

Frames 7-12 are the second hop. In frames 7, 9, and 11, the IP header's TTL is set to 2. The second router in the path decrements the TTL to 0 and sends back the ICMP Time Exceeded-TTL Expired In Transit messages (frames 8, 10, and 12).

Frames 13-18 reach the destination. In frames 13, 15, and 17, the IP header's TTL is set to 3, which is an adequate TTL to reach a destination two routers away. The destination sends back the appropriate Echo Reply messages (frames 14, 16, and 18).

Tip The round-trip times reflected in the TRACERT display are not necessarily the same round-trip times for normal traffic. Most routers process ICMP errors and messages at a lower priority. Therefore, the round-trip times reflected in the TRACERT display may be larger than the round-trip times for normal traffic. Additionally, it is possible for network conditions and the path to change during the route-tracing process, giving misleading results.

TRACERT Options

Table 7-7 lists the use and default values of TRACERT utility options.

Table 7-7. TRACERT Utility Options

Option	Use	Default
-d	Instructs TRACERT to not perform a DNS reverse query on every router IP address. If the host name of each router is unimportant, the -d option accelerates the TRACERT display of the path.	Performs DNS reverse queries on each router IP address
-h *max_hops*	Instructs TRACERT to increment the TTL up to *max_hops*.	30
-j *host-list*	Sends the ICMP Echo messages using the loose source route specified in the *host-list*. The host list is up to nine IP addresses separated by spaces corresponding to the loose-source route to the destination.	Not used
-w *timeout*	Waits the specified amount of time in milliseconds for the response before displaying a "*".	1000

PATHPING Utility

The PATHPING command-line utility for Windows 2000 is used to test router and link latency and packet losses. PATHPING works by sending successive ICMP Echo messages to each point in the path and recording the following: the average round-trip time, the packet loss when sending ICMP Echo messages to the router, and the packet loss when sending ICMP Echo messages across a router.

The following is an example of the display of the PATHPING utility:

```
D:\>pathping -n 10.0.224.33
Tracing route to 10.0.224.33 over a maximum of 30 hops
  0   10.1.11.19
  1   10.1.8.1
  2   10.0.231.130
  3   10.0.224.33
Computing statistics for 75 seconds...
            Source to Here   This Node/Link
Hop  RTT    Lost/Sent = Pct  Lost/Sent = Pct  Address
  0                                            10.1.11.19
                                0/ 100 =  0%   |
  1   0ms    0/ 100 =   0%     0/ 100 =  0%   10.1.8.1
                                0/ 100 =  0%   |
  2   0ms    0/ 100 =   0%     0/ 100 =  0%   10.0.231.130
                                0/ 100 =  0%   |
  3   0ms    0/ 100 =   0%     0/ 100 =  0%   10.0.224.33
Trace complete.
```

In the preceding example, PATHPING is sending ICMP Echo messages from a host (10.1.11.19) to a destination host (10.0.224.33) across two routers (10.1.8.1 and 10.0.231.130). PATHPING first resolves the path using the same mechanism as TRACERT. Then, PATHPING sends two series of ICMP Echo messages to each hop in the path; one series to determine the packet loss to each destination (the Source To Here column), and another series to determine the packet loss of each link (the This Node/Link column).

PATHPING Options

Table 7-8 lists the use and default values of PATHPING utility options.

Table 7-8. PATHPING Utility Options

Option	Use	Default
-n	Instructs PATHPING to not perform a DNS reverse query on every router IP address. If the host name of each router is unimportant, the -n option accelerates the PATHPING display of the path.	Performs DNS reverse queries on each router IP address
-h *max_hops*	Instructs PATHPING to increment the TTL up to *max_hops*.	30
-g *host-list*	Sends the ICMP Echoes using the loose-source route specified in the *host-list*. The host list is up to nine IP addresses separated by spaces corresponding to the loose-source route to the destination.	Not used
-p *period*	Waits the specified amount of time in milliseconds between successive Echoes.	250
-q *num_queries*	Sends the *num_queries* number of queries for each hop.	100
-w *timeout*	Waits the specified amount of time in milliseconds for the response.	3000
-T	Adds a layer-2 priority tag to the ICMP Echoes to test for Quality of Service (QoS) functionality.	Not used
-R	Uses the Resource Reservation Protocol (RSVP) to test QoS functionality.	Not used

Summary

ICMP is a set of messages that provides services that are not part of IP. ICMP includes the following services: diagnostic (Echo and Echo Reply messages), delivery error reporting (Destination Unreachable, Time Exceeded, Source Quench, and Redirect messages), router discovery (Router Advertisement and Router Solicitation messages), and IP header problems (Parameter Problem message). The ICMP Destination Unreachable-Fragmentation Needed And DF Set message is used for PTMU discovery. The Windows 2000 PING, TRACERT, and PATHPING utilities make use of ICMP messages to provide diagnostic functionality.

Chapter 8
Internet Group Management Protocol (IGMP)

Historically, data transfer services used one-to-one delivery, using unicast addressing and routing across an IP internetwork. The utility of one-to-many delivery across an IP internetwork has recently become an interesting and cost-effective way to deliver audio, video, and other types of content to multiple destinations. One-to-many delivery service requires hosts to inform local routers of their interest in receiving the traffic so that routers can forward the traffic to the network segments of the listening hosts.

Introduction to IP Multicast and IGMP

IP multicast provides an efficient one-to-many delivery service. To achieve one-to-many delivery using IP unicast traffic, each datagram needs to be sent multiple times. To achieve one-to-many delivery using IP broadcast traffic, a single datagram is sent, but it is processed by all nodes, even those nodes that aren't interested. Broadcast delivery service is unsuitable for internetworks, as routers are designed to prevent the spread of broadcast traffic. With IP multicast, a single datagram is sent and forwarded across routers only to nodes who are interested in receiving it.

Historically, Internet Protocol (IP) multicast traffic has been little utilized. However, recent developments in audio and video teleconferencing, distance learning, and data transfer to a large number of hosts have made IP multicast traffic more important.

> **More Info** RFCs 1112 and 2236 describe IP multicast and IGMP. These RFCs can be found in the \RFC folder on the companion CD-ROM.

IP Multicasting Overview

The essential details of IP multicast operation are the following:

- All multicast traffic is sent to a class D address in the range 224.0.0.0 through 239.255.255.255 (224.0.0.0/4). All traffic in the range 224.0.0.0 through 224.0.0.255 (224.0.0.0/24) is for the local subnet and is not forwarded by routers. Multicast-enabled routers forward multicast traffic in the range 224.0.1.0 through 239.255.255.255 with an appropriate TTL.

- A specific multicast address is called a *group address*.
- The set of hosts that listen for multicast traffic at a specific group address is called a *multicast group* or *host group*. Multicast group members can receive traffic to their unicast address and the group address. Multicast groups can be permanent or transient. A *permanent group* is assigned a well-known group address. An example of a permanent group is the all-hosts multicast group, listening for traffic on the well-known multicast address of 224.0.0.1. The membership of a permanent group is transient; only the group address is permanent.
- There are no limits on a multicast group's size.
- A host can send multicast traffic to the group address without belonging to the multicast group.
- There are no limits to how many multicast groups a host can belong to.
- There are no limits on when members of a multicast group can join and leave a multicast group.
- There are no limits on the location of multicast group members.

IP multicast must be supported on hosts and routers.

Host Support

To support IP multicast, hosts must be able to send and receive IP multicast traffic. RFC 1112 defines three levels of IP multicast support for hosts as follows:

- Level 0: No support for sending or receiving IP multicast traffic
- Level 1: Support for sending IP multicast traffic
- Level 2: Support for sending and receiving IP multicast traffic

By default, Microsoft Windows 2000 TCP/IP supports level 2 IP multicasting.

Microsoft Windows 2000 Registry Setting for the Level of IP Multicasting

The following Windows 2000 registry setting allows modification of the IP multicast support level:

IGMPLevel

```
Location:HKEY_LOCAL_MACHINE\SYSTEM\CurrentControlSet\Services\Tcpip\Parameters
Value Type: REG_DWORD
Valid Range: 0-2
Default: 2
Present by Default: No
```

Sending IP Multicast Traffic

A host sending an IP multicast packet must first determine the IP multicast address. The IP multicast address is determined by either the application or protocol (a well-known or reserved IP multicast address), or obtained from a server allocating unique IP multicast addresses. Multicast Address Dynamic Client Allocation Protocol (MADCAP) is an extension to the DHCP standard that is used to obtain an internetwork's unique IP multicast address. Multicast scopes configured on the DHCP server define ranges of IP multicast addresses. Similar to allocating unicast IP addresses, unique IP multicast addresses are allocated to a single DHCP client. If multiple hosts use the same IP multicast address for different applications, forwarding of the wrong traffic to host group members could occur. For more information on multicast support by the Windows 2000 DHCP service, see Chapter 15, "Dynamic Host Configuration Protocol (DHCP) Service."

After determining the destination IP multicast address, the sending host must construct the IP datagram with its own IP address as the source IP address, the intended IP multicast address as the Destination IP Address, and an appropriate Time-to-Live (TTL) value. For local subnet IP multicast traffic destined for addresses in the range 224.0.0.0 through 224.0.0.255, the TTL is set to 1. Routers won't forward IP multicast traffic in this range even if the TTL is greater than 1. For non-local subnet traffic, the TTL should be set to a value that's high enough to reach all host group members. Table 8-1 lists the recommended values of the TTL for IP multicast traffic and their scope.

Table 8-1. Recommended Values of the TTL for IP Multicast Traffic

TTL Value	Description
0	Restricted to the same host
1	Restricted to the same subnet
15	Restricted to the same site
63	Restricted to the same region
127	Worldwide
191	Worldwide; limited bandwidth
255	Unrestricted

Once the sending host constructs the IP multicast datagram, the IP packet is passed through the IP forwarding process. The multicast entry in the IP routing table (the route(s) with the destination of 224.0.0.0 and the network mask of 240.0.0.0) informs IP that the datagram must be forwarded to the destination IP address, using the local network interface. The IP datagram, the forwarding IP address, and the interface are submitted to ARP.

The ARP module checks the forwarding IP address. Because the forwarding IP address is in the range 224.0.0.0 through 239.255.255.255 (224.0.0.0/4), ARP bypasses the process of checking the ARP cache and sending a broadcast ARP Request frame. For Ethernet and Fiber Distributed Data Interface (FDDI) hosts, the destination IP address is mapped to the destination MAC address using the process described in Chapter 5, "Internet Protocol (IP) Addressing." For Token Ring hosts, all IP multicast traffic is addressed to the Token Ring functional address of 0xC0-00-00-04-00-00.

Receiving IP Multicast Traffic

To receive IP multicast traffic, a host informs the IP layer to process traffic for a specific group address. To facilitate the request, the IP module:

- Informs the Network Interface Layer technology to add the MAC-level multicast address that corresponds to the group address to the list of interesting destination MAC addresses. In Windows 2000, the IP module within the TCP/IP protocol uses the *NDISRequest()* function.

- If the group address isn't in the range 224.0.0.1 through 224.0.0.255 (224.0.0.0/24), an IGMP Host Membership Report message is sent to inform local routers to forward the host group traffic to the network segment of the listening host.

If there are multiple applications on the host using the same group address, IP tracks application group membership and passes a copy of the received IP multicast datagram to each listening application. For a multihomed host, IP tracks group membership for each network segment.

Router Support

To support IP multicast forwarding and routing, a router must be able to do the following:

- Listen for IGMP Host Membership Report messages sent from hosts on local network segments.

- Track and maintain group membership for hosts on local network segments. Routers maintain host group membership through the receipt of IGMP Host Membership Report messages and the sending of IGMP Host Membership Query messages.

- In a multicast-enabled intranet with more than two routers, a router must be able to communicate host group membership information to neighboring routers. This is done using a multicast routing protocol such as Distance Vector Multicast Routing Protocol (DVMRP), Multicast Extensions To Open Shortest Path First (MOSPF), or Protocol Independent Multicast (PIM).

- Listen for all IP multicast traffic on all attached network segments. To do this, the router must put the network interface into either promiscuous listening mode or multicast promiscuous listening mode. In promiscuous mode, all incoming frames are considered interesting and passed to Windows 2000 for processing. Promiscuous mode is a processor and interrupt-intensive listening mode, and is typically used only for protocol analysis or network sniffing.

  Multicast promiscuous mode is a special listening mode where all packets with the Individual/Group (I/G) bit, also known as the multicast bit, in the destination MAC address that are set to 1, are considered interesting. For Ethernet frames, the multicast bit is the last bit of the first byte in the destination MAC address. In multicast promiscuous mode, all frames with the multicast bit set and a valid Frame Check Sequence (FCS) are passed up to the operating system for processing. See Chapter 1, "Local Area Network (LAN) Technologies," for more information on the multicast bit. In multicast promiscuous mode, an IP multicast router receives a copy of every IP multicast packet for processing or forwarding.

Not all network adapters support multicast promiscuous mode. A network adapter that supports promiscuous mode might not support multicast promiscuous mode.

- Forward IP multicast traffic with a valid TTL on appropriate network segments where there are host group members or where there are downstream routers that have host group members. The IP multicast forwarding capability is provided by the TCP/IP protocol. Similar to unicast forwarding, when IP multicast forwarding is enabled, the TTL of the packet being forwarded is decremented, and is then forwarded over the appropriate interfaces based on the entries in a local multicast forwarding table. IP silently discards multicast traffic with a TTL of 0.

IP multicast traffic is forwarded to network segments that have either a listening host, or a router that has informed the router forwarding the IP multicast traffic that there are host group members downstream. The entries in the IP multicast forwarding table don't indicate which hosts are listening or how many group members there are on a network segment—only that at least one host member is present on the network segment (or a downstream network segment).

The Multicast-Enabled IP Internetwork

Figure 8-1 shows a multicast-enabled intranet. To support the forwarding of IP multicast traffic from any host to any group member, hosts and routers must support the following:

- Any host receiving IP multicast traffic joins the multicast group by sending IGMP Host Membership Report messages on the local network segment.

- Any host sending IP multicast traffic forms the IP multicast frame and sends it on the local network segment.

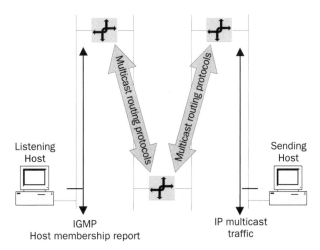

Figure 8-1. *A multicast-enabled intranet showing multicast-enabled hosts and routers.*

- IP multicast routers forward the IP multicast traffic from the originating network segment to all segments where there are group members. IGMP Host Membership Report messages inform the routers about group members on locally attached network segments. For downstream host members, IP multicast routers communicate downstream host member information using multicast routing protocols. In both cases, IGMP and multicast routing protocols update the router's local TCP/IP multicast forwarding tables.

The Internet's Multicast-Enabled Backbone

The portion of the Internet that is IP-multicast-enabled is known as the Multicast Backbone or MBONE. The MBONE was created originally to multicast the audio for Internet Engineering Task Force (IETF) meetings for IETF members who couldn't attend. Today, the MBONE is used for the audio and video of IETF meetings, the launches of the National Aeronautic and Space Administration (NASA) space shuttle, and teleconferences of all kinds. The MBONE is also the testbed for the development of IP multicast technology such as applications, tools, and routing protocols.

The MBONE is a logical IP multicast topology overlaid on the Internet's physical unicast topology. Not all Internet portions and Internet service providers (ISPs) support the forwarding of IP multicast traffic. To connect two portions of the Internet that do support IP multicast traffic, IP multicast traffic is tunneled or wrapped with another IP header addressed from one router to another router. The typical tunneling is called IP-in-IP tunneling, and is described in RFC 1853. The MBONE is a series of multicast-enabled islands connected together with IP-in-IP tunnels.

More Info IP-in-IP tunneling is described in RFC 1853, which can be found in the \RFC folder on the companion CD-ROM.

IGMP Message Structure

The protocol used to maintain local subnet host group membership is IGMP, which is required for hosts that support level 2 IP multicasting. IGMP messages are sent as IP datagrams with the IP Protocol field set to 2. Therefore, an IGMP message is encapsulated with an IP header. The resulting IP datagram is then encapsulated with the appropriate Network Interface Layer header and trailer. Figure 8-2 shows the resulting frame.

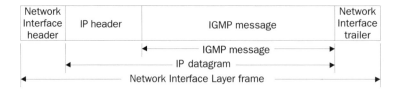

Figure 8-2. *IGMP message encapsulation showing the IP header and Network Interface Layer header and trailer.*

In the IP header of IGMP messages, the Source IP Address field is set to the router or host interface that sent the IGMP message; the Destination IP Address field depends on the type of IGMP message.

IGMP Version 1 (IGMPv1)

IGMPv1, described in Appendix I of RFC 1112, defines two types of IGMP messages:

1. The Host Membership Report
2. The Host Membership Query

More Info   IGMPv1 is described in Appendix I of RFC 1112, which can be found in the \RFC folder on the companion CD-ROM.

Host Membership Report

A host sends a Host Membership Report message to inform local routers that the host wants to receive IP multicast traffic at a specified group address. A host also sends a Host Membership Report in response to a Host Membership Query message sent by a router. Host Membership Report messages are sent, with a Time-To-Live (TTL) of 1, to the destination IP address of the multicast group.

Host Membership Query

A router sends a Host Membership Query message to poll a network segment and verify that there are hosts still listening for IP multicast traffic. Host Membership Query messages are sent, with a TTL of 1, to the destination IP address of the all-hosts IP multicast address (224.0.0.1). An IGMPv1 Host Membership Query is a general query, attempting to identify all multicast groups being listened to by hosts on a network segment.

Hosts that receive the Host Membership Query message send a Host Membership Report for all the host groups for which the host is a member. To prevent an avalanche of response traffic, host group members choose a random report delay time for each host group and wait to hear from other host group members on the network segment. If a Host Membership Report message is sent by another host group member, the waiting host doesn't send a reply.

This behavior is consistent with the information kept by multicast routers. A multicast router doesn't track which hosts on a network segment are members of a host group, only that there is at least one host group member.

If no hosts respond with a Host Membership Report to a group address that the multicast router is tracking for the network segment, the multicast router can remove that entry from the multicast forwarding table and inform other multicast routers through multicast routing protocols. Multicast traffic to the removed group address will no longer be forwarded to the network segment.

IGMPv1 Message Structure

Figure 8-3 shows the structure of the IGMPv1 message.

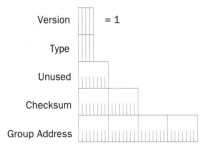

Figure 8-3. *The structure of the IGMPv1 message.*

The fields in the IGMPv1 header are defined as follows:

- **Version** A 4-bit field set to 1 to indicate IGMPv1.
- **Type** A 4-bit field that indicates the type of IGMP message. Set to 1 for a Host Membership Query. Set to 2 for a Host Membership Report.
- **Unused** A 1-byte field zeroed by the sender and ignored by the receiver.
- **Checksum** A 2-byte field that stores the 16-bit checksum on the 8-byte IGMP header.
- **Group Address** A 4-byte field that for a Host Membership Report stores the multicast group address being joined by the listening host. In a Host Membership Query, the Group Address field is 0.0.0.0.

Table 8-2 summarizes the addresses used in IGMPv1 Host Membership Report and Host Membership Query messages.

Table 8-2. Addresses Used in IGMPv1 Messages

	Host Membership Report	Host Membership Query
Source IP Address (IP header)	Host IP Address	Router IP Address
Destination IP Address (IP header)	Group IP Address	224.0.0.1
Group Address	Group IP Address	0.0.0.0

Network Monitor Examples

The following Network Monitor trace (Capture 08-01 in the \Captures folder on the companion CD-ROM) is an IGMPv1 Host Membership Report message for a host joining the host group 224.0.1.41:

```
+ FRAME: Base frame properties
  ETHERNET: ETYPE = 0x0800 : Protocol = IP:  DOD Internet Protocol
```

```
    ETHERNET: Destination address : 01005E000129
        ETHERNET: .......1 = Group address
        ETHERNET: ......0. = Universally administered address
  + ETHERNET: Source address : 00C04FD7BAEC
    ETHERNET: Frame Length : 60 (0x003C)
    ETHERNET: Ethernet Type : 0x0800 (IP:  DOD Internet Protocol)
    ETHERNET: Ethernet Data: Number of data bytes remaining = 46 (0x002E)
 IP: ID = 0xB201; Proto = IGMP; Len: 28
    IP: Version = 4 (0x4)
    IP: Header Length = 20 (0x14)
    IP: Precedence = Routine
    IP: Type of Service = Normal Service
    IP: Total Length = 28 (0x1C)
    IP: Identification = 45569 (0xB201)
  + IP: Flags Summary = 0 (0x0)
    IP: Fragment Offset = 0 (0x0) bytes
    IP: Time to Live = 1 (0x1)
    IP: Protocol = IGMP - Internet Group Management
    IP: Checksum = 0x118E
    IP: Source Address = 10.0.11.40
    IP: Destination Address = 224.0.1.41
    IP: Data: Number of data bytes remaining = 8 (0x0008)
 IGMP: IGMP Group Report,    From 10.00.11.40 To    224.00.01.41
    IGMP: Version = 1 (0x1)
    IGMP: Type = IGMP Group Report
    IGMP: Unused = 0 (0x0)
    IGMP: Checksum = 0x0CD6
    IGMP: Group Address = 224.0.1.41
```

Note that the group address of 224.0.1.41 is being mapped to the Ethernet destination address of 01-00-5E-00-01-29 (41 in hexadecimal is 0x29). Also note that IGMP messages must be padded with 18 padding bytes on Ethernet networks to adhere to the Ethernet minimum payload size of 46 bytes (padding bytes not shown).

The following Network Monitor trace (Capture 08-02 in the \Captures folder on the companion CD-ROM) is an IGMPv1 Host Membership Query:

```
+ FRAME: Base frame properties
  ETHERNET: ETYPE = 0x0800 : Protocol = IP:  DOD Internet Protocol
    ETHERNET: Destination address : 01005E000001
        ETHERNET: .......1 = Group address
        ETHERNET: ......0. = Universally administered address
  + ETHERNET: Source address : 00E034C0A060
    ETHERNET: Frame Length : 60 (0x003C)
    ETHERNET: Ethernet Type : 0x0800 (IP:  DOD Internet Protocol)
```

```
      ETHERNET: Ethernet Data: Number of data bytes remaining = 46 (0x002E)
  IP: ID = 0x0; Proto = IGMP; Len: 28
      IP: Version = 4 (0x4)
      IP: Header Length = 20 (0x14)
      IP: Precedence = Internetwork Control
      IP: Type of Service = Normal Service
      IP: Total Length = 28 (0x1C)
      IP: Identification = 0 (0x0)
    + IP: Flags Summary = 0 (0x0)
      IP: Fragment Offset = 0 (0x0) bytes
      IP: Time to Live = 1 (0x1)
      IP: Protocol = IGMP - Internet Group Management
      IP: Checksum = 0xC71E
      IP: Source Address = 10.0.8.1
      IP: Destination Address = 224.0.0.1
      IP: Data: Number of data bytes remaining = 8 (0x0008)
  IGMP: IGMP Group Query,    From 10.00.08.01 To   224.00.00.01
      IGMP: Version = 1 (0x1)
      IGMP: Type = IGMP Group Query
      IGMP: Unused = 100 (0x64)
      IGMP: Checksum = 0xEE9B
      IGMP: Group Address = 0.0.0.0
```

Notice that for both traces, the IP header's TTL field is set to 1.

IGMP Version 2 (IGMPv2)

IGMPv2, described in RFC 2236, provides additional capabilities to help multicast routers converge a multicast group to the set of hosts listening for traffic. IGMPv2 is backward compatible with IGMPv1.

The additional capabilities of IGMPv2 are:

- The Leave Group message
- The Group-Specific Query message
- The election of a multicast querier
- The IGMPv2 Host Membership Report message

More Info IGMPv2 is described in RFC 2236, which can be found in the \RFC folder on the companion CD-ROM.

The Leave Group Message

With IGMPv1, if a host leaves a specific multicast group and it's the last member of the multicast group for that subnet, the local router isn't explicitly informed. The router maintains the entry in its multicast forwarding table and continues to forward multicast traffic to the host's subnet. Only after the router sends a Host Membership Query message and receives no response for the multicast group does the router recognize that there are no more hosts on that network segment for that group address. The router then updates its multicast forwarding table, discontinues forwarding IP multicast traffic to the network segment, and informs neighboring routers of the new state. This can lead to long-leave latency times. During the leave latency time, multicast traffic is forwarded to network segments that don't contain group members.

During the periodic polling process, when a host responds to a Membership Query, it assumes that it's potentially the last member in the group for that subnet because no other hosts responded before it. If that host leaves the group, it sends an IGMP Leave Group message to the all-routers IP multicast address. To ensure that the host leaving is truly the last host in the group for the subnet, the multicast router sends a series of group-specific Membership Queries. If the multicast router receives a response from another host for that group, the router maintains the group membership state for that group on that subnet. If the multicast router doesn't receive any responses, it can prevent the forwarding of traffic to that group to the subnet. If there are host members on downstream subnets available across subnet routers, multicast traffic for the group is still forwarded to the subnet.

The Group-Specific Query Message

In the case of IGMPv2, two different types of Host Membership Query messages are defined: the General Query and the Group-Specific Query. The General Query is the same as the IGMPv1 Host Membership Query. The Group-Specific Query is designed to check for host membership in a specific group. In the Group-Specific Query, the IP header's destination IP address and the IGMP header's group address are set to the group address being queried.

The Multicast Querier

IGMPv2 supports the election of a multicast querier, a single router per network segment that sends Host Membership Query messages. With IGMPv1, the designation of a single multicast router to perform queries is a function of the multicast routing protocol. Because all IGMP traffic is sent to multicast addresses, every multicast router on a network segment receives all IGMP messages. Therefore, only a single router is needed to send queries.

The IGMPv2 multicast querier election is simple: a router assumes that it's the multicast querier until it receives a Host Membership Query (either General or Group-Specific) from another router with a numerically lower IP address. If it is the only router on a subnet and it doesn't receive a query from another router in an interval called the Other Querier Present Interval (by default set for 255 seconds), the router becomes the querier for that network.

IGMPv2 Message Structure

Figure 8-4 shows the structure of the IGMPv2 message.

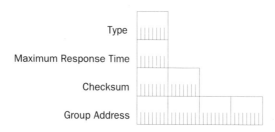

Figure 8-4. *The structure of the IGMPv2 message.*

The IGMPv2 header contains the following fields:

- **Type** IGMPv2 combines the IGMPv1 4-bit Version field and IGMPv1 4-bit Type field into a single 8-bit Type field. Table 8-3 lists the Type field values.

Table 8-3. Values of the IGMPv2 Type Field

Type	Message
17 (0x11)	**Host Membership Query** The previous Version 0x1 and Type 0x1 are combined to form 0x11, or 17.
18 (0x12)	**IGMPv1 Host Membership Report** The previous Version 0x1 and Type 0x2 are combined to form 0x12, or 18.
22 (0x16)	**IGMPv2 Host Membership Report** The IGMPv2 Host Membership Report has the same function as the IGMPv1 Host Membership Report and is intended to be received by only IGMPv2-capable multicast routers.
23 (0x17)	**Leave Group Message**

- **Maximum Response Time** The IGMPv1 Unused field is used in IGMPv2 Membership Query messages (either General or Group-Specific) to store a maximum time in 1/10th of a second within which a host must respond to the query. The maximum response time becomes the maximum value of the report delay timer for subnet host members.

- **Checksum** A 2-byte field that stores a 16-bit checksum on the 8-byte IGMP header.

- **Group Address** Set to 0.0.0.0 for the general Host Membership Query and set to the specific group address for all other IGMPv2 message types.

Table 8-4 summarizes the addresses used in IGMPv2 Group-Specific Host Membership Query and Group Leave messages.

Table 8-4. Addresses Used in IGMPv2 Messages

	Group-Specific Query	Group Leave
Source IP Address (IP header)	Router IP Address	Host IP Address
Destination IP Address (IP header)	Group IP Address	224.0.0.2
Group Address	Group IP Address	Group IP Address

Network Monitor Example

The following Network Monitor trace (Capture 08-03 in the \Captures folder on the companion CD-ROM) shows an IGMPv2 Host Membership Report for a host registering the group address 239.255.255.252:

```
+ Frame: Base frame properties
  ETHERNET: ETYPE = 0x0800 : Protocol = IP:  DOD Internet Protocol
      ETHERNET: Destination address : 01005E7FFFFC
          ETHERNET: .......1 = Group address
          ETHERNET: ......0. = Universally administered address
    + ETHERNET: Source address : 0060083E4607
      ETHERNET: Frame Length : 46 (0x002E)
      ETHERNET: Ethernet Type : 0x0800 (IP:  DOD Internet Protocol)
      ETHERNET: Ethernet Data: Number of data bytes remaining = 32 (0x0020)
    IP: ID = 0x1A26; Proto = IGMP; Len: 32
      IP: Version = 4 (0x4)
      IP: Header Length = 24 (0x18)
      IP: Precedence = Routine
      IP: Type of Service = Normal Service
      IP: Total Length = 32 (0x20)
      IP: Identification = 6694 (0x1A26)
      IP: Flags Summary = 0 (0x0)
          IP: .......0 = Last fragment in datagram
          IP: ......0. = May fragment datagram if necessary
      IP: Fragment Offset = 0 (0x0) bytes
      IP: Time to Live = 1 (0x1)
      IP: Protocol = IGMP - Internet Group Management
      IP: Checksum = 0x07ED
      IP: Source Address = 10.1.8.200
      IP: Destination Address = 239.255.255.252
      IP: Option Fields
          IP: Unrecognized Option
              IP: Option Type = 0x94
              IP: Option Length = 4 (0x4)
              IP: Option data: Number of data bytes remaining = 2 (0x0002)
      IP: Data: Number of data bytes remaining = 8 (0x0008)
    IGMP: Version 2 Membership Report
      IGMP: Type = Version 2 Membership Report
      IGMP: Unused = 0 (0x0)
      IGMP: Checksum = 0xFA02
      IGMP: Group Address = 239.255.255.252
```

Notice the existence of the IP Router Alert option (Option Type 0x94) that is used to inform the router that further processing of the IP header is required. For more information on the IP Router Alert option, see Chapter 4, "Internet Protocol (IP) Basics."

Microsoft Windows 2000 and IGMP

Windows 2000 supports IP multicast sending, receiving, and forwarding through the TCP/IP protocol and the Routing and Remote Access service.

TCP/IP Protocol

TCP/IP for Windows 2000 supports IP multicast traffic in the following ways:

- To support host reception of IP multicast traffic, TCP/IP for Windows 2000 is an RFC 2236-compliant IGMPv2 host.

- To support host transmission and reception of IP multicast traffic, TCP/IP for Windows 2000 supports the mapping of IP multicast addresses to MAC addresses for Ethernet and FDDI network adapters as described in RFC 1112. For Token Ring network adapters, all IP multicast traffic is mapped to the Token Ring functional address of 0x-C0-00-00-04-00-00.

- To support the forwarding of IP multicast traffic, TCP/IP for Windows 2000 supports multicast forwarding based on the entries in the TCP/IP multicast forwarding table and the setting of the EnableMulticastForwarding registry setting. You can view the contents of the TCP/IP multicast forwarding table from the Routing and Remote Access administrative tool.

EnableMulticastForwarding

```
Location: HKEY_LOCAL_MACHINE\SYSTEM\CurrentControlSet\Services\Tcpip\Parameters
Data Type: REG_DWORD
Valid Range: 0-1
Default: 0
Present by Default: No
```

EnableMulticastForwarding enables (=1) or disables (=0) the forwarding of IP multicast traffic. The EnableMulticastForwarding registry setting is set to 1 (enabled) when the Routing and Remote Access service is enabled and configured.

The Routing and Remote Access Service

The Windows 2000 Server Routing and Remote Access service functions as a limited multicast router using IGMPv1 or v2 to track local group membership. Because IGMP isn't a true multicast routing protocol, Windows 2000 routers can support only limited multicast configurations. For more information on recommended configurations, see Windows 2000 Server Help or the *Microsoft Windows 2000 Server Resource Kit Internetworking Guide*.

In the Routing and Remote Access service, IGMP is implemented as a routing protocol added and configured through the Routing and Remote Access administrative tool. After adding the IGMP routing protocol, add individual routing interfaces to the IGMP routing protocol and configure them for either IGMP router mode or IGMP proxy mode.

Interfaces in IGMP Router Mode

An interface in IGMP router mode acts as an IGMP-capable IP multicast router and performs the following:

- **Places network adapter in multicast promiscuous mode**   If the network interface is a broadcast network type such as Ethernet or FDDI, the network adapter is placed in multicast promiscuous mode. If the network adapter doesn't support multicast promiscuous mode, an event is logged in the system event log.

- **Manages local subnet multicast group membership**   The routing interface uses IGMP to listen for IGMP Host Membership Report and Leave Group messages, to elect an IGMP querier, and to send General and Group-Specific Host Membership Query messages.

- **Updates the TCP/IP multicast forwarding table**   Based on ongoing group membership for the interface, IGMP in conjunction with other components of the Routing and Remote Access service maintains the TCP/IP multicast forwarding table.

Interfaces in IGMP Proxy Mode

An interface in IGMP proxy mode acts as an IGMP-capable IP multicast proxy host for hosts on IGMP router mode interfaces and performs the following:

- **Forwards IGMP Host Membership Reports**   IGMP Host Membership Report messages received on IGMP Router mode interfaces are forwarded on the IGMP proxy mode interface. The forwarded Host Membership Report messages have a TTL of 1. The received Host Membership Reports aren't forwarded using the entries in the TCP/IP multicast forwarding table.

- **Adds multicast MAC addresses to network adapter table**   For each group address registered by proxy, the corresponding multicast MAC address is added to the table of interesting MAC addresses on the network adapter (for LAN technologies such as Ethernet and FDDI). The network adapter won't be placed in promiscuous mode unless the network card can't support listening to all required multicast MAC addresses. Non-local IP multicast traffic received on the IGMP proxy mode interface is passed to the TCP/IP protocol for multicast forwarding.

- **Updates the TCP/IP multicast forwarding table**   To facilitate the forwarding of multicast traffic from a multicast source on an IGMP router mode interface to a group member downstream from the IGMP proxy mode interface, the IGMP routing protocol adds entries to the TCP/IP multicast forwarding table so that all non-local IP multicast traffic received on IGMP router mode interfaces is forwarded over the IGMP proxy mode interface. The IGMP proxy mode interface forwards all non-local multicast traffic received from IGMP router mode interfaces regardless of whether or not there are group members present downstream from the IGMP proxy mode interface.

IGMP proxy mode is designed to connect a Windows 2000 router to a fully capable IP multicast internetwork, as Figure 8-5 shows. A good example of this is the connection of a single router intranet to the MBONE. IGMP proxy mode is enabled on a single interface connected to the multicast-enabled internetwork.

The combination of IGMP router mode interfaces and the IGMP proxy mode interface allows the sending and receiving of IP multicast traffic for hosts on a Windows 2000 router network segment.

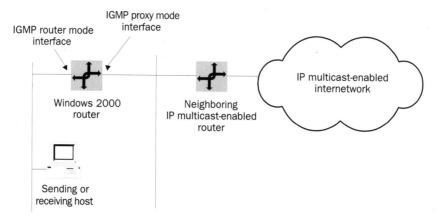

Figure 8-5. *The use of IGMP router mode and proxy mode to connect a single router intranet to an IP multicast-enabled internetwork.*

Multicast Group Members on IGMP Router Mode Interfaces

Host members on IGMP router mode interfaces receive host group traffic through the following process:

1. A host sends an IGMP Host Membership Report message on the local subnet.

2. The Windows 2000 router updates its multicast forwarding table with the appropriate entry.

3. The IGMP routing protocol uses the *NDISRequest()* function to add the multicast MAC address corresponding to the IP multicast address to the table of interesting MAC addresses on the network adapter on which IGMP proxy mode is enabled.

4. The Windows 2000 router forwards the IGMP Host Membership Report on the IGMP proxy mode interface.

5. The neighboring IP multicast-enabled router receives the IGMP Host Membership Report, makes the appropriate changes to its multicast forwarding table, and informs downstream IP multicast-enabled routers using multicast routing protocols that a host member exists on the IGMP proxy mode interface network segment.

Routers of the IP multicast-enabled internetwork forward IP multicast traffic sent to the host group to the neighboring IP multicast-enabled router, which forwards the traffic on the IGMP proxy mode interface network segment. The IGMP proxy mode interface receives the multicast traffic and submits it to the TCP/IP multicast forwarding process. Based on the entries in the multicast forwarding table, the IP multicast traffic is forwarded on the IGMP router mode interface to the network segment containing the host member.

Multicast Sources on IGMP Router Mode Interfaces

The multicast traffic of multicast sources on IGMP router mode interfaces are forwarded through the following process:

1. A multicast source host sends non-local IP multicast traffic to a specific group address.

2. The IGMP router mode interface receives the multicast traffic.

3. For the first multicast packet, the IGMP routing protocol adds an entry to the TCP/IP multicast forwarding table, indicating that there are host members present on the IGMP proxy mode interface.

4. The multicast traffic is passed to the multicast forwarding process. Based on the entries in the multicast forwarding table, the multicast traffic is forwarded on the IGMP proxy mode interface.

5. The neighboring IP multicast-enabled router receives the IP multicast traffic and passes it to the multicast forwarding process. Based on the entries in the multicast forwarding table of the IP multicast-enabled router, the multicast packet is either forwarded to host members (local or downstream) or silently discarded.

Summary

IGMP provides a mechanism for hosts to register their interest in receiving IP multicast traffic sent to a specific group address (the Host Membership Report message), for hosts to indicate that they are no longer interested in receiving IP multicast traffic sent to a specific group address (the Leave Group message), and for routers to query the membership of all host groups (the general Host Membership Query) or a single host group (the group-specific Host Membership Query). TCP/IP for Windows 2000 supports IGMPv2 and IP multicast forwarding. The Windows 2000 Server Routing and Remote Access service uses IGMP to maintain the IP multicast forwarding table and provide multicast routing in limited configurations.

Chapter 9
Internet Protocol Version 6 (IPv6)

Over the course of the evolution of the current IP version, version 4 (IPv4), the inevitable exhaustion of the address space has become increasingly apparent. While mechanisms such as Classless Inter-Domain Routing (CIDR) and the use of proxies have served to increase the longevity of IPv4, development of a larger, more flexible version of IP, version 6 (IPv6), is well underway.

In its original inception, the Internet (then ARPANET) was designed primarily to facilitate communication between research entities and military organizations. However, the extraordinary longevity and functionality of the TCP/IP protocol suite has allowed the Internet to become a communications mechanism of an enormity that couldn't have been foreseen in its early stages.

Now there are even newer arenas that require the addressing and routing capabilities that IP provides. Cellular phones, pagers, and personal digital assistants (PDAs) have become ubiquitous accessories whose nature dictates that mechanisms be available for secure, portable communication. Entertainment media such as digital television and real-time audio require similar connectivity, with the imperative of guaranteed delivery rates. Additionally, the still largely untapped area of power and device management will demand the same capabilities. The once fantastic "home of the future," with electronically controlled temperature, lighting, and gadgetry is fast approaching reality.

If these markets are to utilize IP rather than be forced into developing proprietary solutions, mechanisms will be required that aren't easily provided in IPv4. Rather than investigate methods to extend an already strapped address space with limited future potential, research has been heavily dedicated to devising a new version of IP—IPv6. To successfully meet current and future needs, the following are several key capabilities that must be addressed by this new IP version:

- First and foremost, any new IP version must be capable of coexistence and interoperability with current IP specifications. Attempts to make a sweeping conversion from one version to the next would be both unrealistic and chaotic. Therefore, IPv6 must have inherent mechanisms for communicating with both IPv4 and IPv6 hosts.

- IPv6 must support an exponentially larger address space than IPv4.

- IPv6 packets must be as lightweight as possible to facilitate transmission of IPv6 over diverse media.

- Quality of Service (QoS), or the ability to prioritize traffic and allocate bandwidth, must be built into IPv6 to accommodate functionality required by low-latency applications.

- IPv6 routing capabilities must be designed so that intermediate nodes on a path can be specified in the packets themselves, similar to IPv4's Record Route and Loose Source routing options.

- Mechanisms for secure transmission of data must be inherent in IPv6's structure.

With both an eye turned toward future needs and an awareness of past and current issues, the IETF IPv6 working group continues to work to develop a solution.

Chapter Contents

This chapter looks at the current specifications for IPv6. Related RFCs are included on the companion CD-ROM.

Microsoft Research IPv6

The most current version of the Microsoft Research IPv6 stack may be downloaded at *http://www.research.microsoft.com/msripv6*. This implementation runs as a separate protocol stack on both Microsoft Windows NT 4.0 and Microsoft Windows 2000. There are no plans to implement IPv6 for the Microsoft Windows 95 or Windows 98 operating systems at this time.

The stack currently supports the following: basic IPv6 header processing; hop-by-hop options; destination options; fragmentation and routing headers; neighbor discovery; stateless address autoconfiguration; Internet Control Message Protocol version 6 (ICMPv6); Ethernet and FDDI media; automatic and configured tunnels; IPv6 over IPv4; IPv6 to IPv4 tunneling; UDP and TCP over IPv6; correspondent node mobility; host and router functionality; and IP Security (IPSec) authentication. Version 1.3 doesn't yet support full mobility and encryption.

Also available for download at the research site are several IPv6 applications, including the following: ping6; tracert6; Test TCP 6 (ttcp6) (over both User Datagram Protocol [UDP] and TCP); File Transmission Protocol v6/File Transmission Protocol Daemon v6 (ftp6/ftpd6); wininet.dll, which adds IPv6 functionality to Microsoft Internet Explorer; multicast conferencing applications; an IPv6 FTP client; an IPv6/v4 translator; and a protocol parser for Network Monitor that allows the capture and display of IPv6 packets.

A mailing list is also available to help users keep abreast of developments in the implementation. To subscribe, send mail to *listserv@list.research.microsoft.com*. In the body of the mail, include the following:

subscribe msripv6-users *yourfirstname yourlastname*

This chapter contains the following sections:

- **Introduction to IPv6**   A description of IPv6 and its intended function, as well as an introduction to terminology in IPv6
- **IPv6 Addressing**   An overview of addressing in IPv6
- **IPv6 Header Format**   A look at header formats in IPv6
- **Transition Mechanisms**   A brief description of the intended methodology for integration of IPv6 with current formats

This chapter doesn't cover every detail of IPv6, nor does it attempt to fully describe its integration with Windows 2000 services.

Introduction to IPv6

As RFC 2460 describes, IPv6 is the intended replacement for IPv4. It increases the size of IP addresses from 32 to 128 bits, allowing for 2^{96} (2^{128-32}) times the number of addresses in IPv4. This gives a total of 340,282,366,920,938,463,463,374,607,431,768,211,456 addresses, a seemingly endless supply. This increase in the address space not only provides for more hosts, but also for an expanded addressing hierarchy.

> **More Info**   IPv6 specifications are defined in RFC 2460, which can be found in the \RFC folder on the companion CD-ROM.

Packet headers have been improved by dropping some IPv4 header fields, making others optional, and utilizing extension headers. Extension headers are separate headers that, with one exception, aren't examined by any hosts on a path between the source and destination, helping to improve routing efficiency. Additionally, they allow for more flexibility in options encoding and expansion capabilities for future options.

Flow labeling is introduced in IPv6, which allows packets to be designated as belonging to a specific "flow" of traffic, thus allowing for QoS handling and bandwidth management without having to parse TCP and UDP headers. Extensions also have been introduced that allow for authentication, data integrity assurance, and optional packet encryption.

Before looking at IPv6 in detail, it's important to understand some of the basic terminology used in the protocol specifications.

Nodes, Routers, Hosts, and Interfaces

A node is any device that implements IPv6. It can be a router, which is a device that forwards packets that aren't directed specifically to it, or a host, which is a node that doesn't forward packets. An interface is the connection to a transmission medium through which IPv6 packets are sent. While a distinction is made between routers and hosts, it's possible, albeit unlikely, for a single node to have multiple interfaces, and potentially be forwarding packets addressed to other nodes on only a subset of its interfaces. Thus, this device would be acting both as a host (on its non-forwarding interfaces) and as a router (on its forwarding interfaces).

Links, Neighbors, Link MTUs, and Link Layer Addresses

A link is the medim over which IPv6 is carried. Neighbors are nodes that are connected to the same link. A link maximum transmission unit (MTU) is the maximum packet size that can be carried over a given link medium, and is expressed in octets. A Link Layer address is the "physical" address of an interface, such as media access control (MAC) addresses for Ethernet links.

Unicast, Multicast, and Anycast Addresses

In IPv6, all addressing is directed to interfaces rather than to nodes. A unicast address specifies that a packet be sent to a particular interface. A multicast address is sent to a set of interfaces, typically encompassing multiple nodes. An anycast address, while identifying multiple interfaces (and typically multiple nodes), is sent only to the interface that's determined to be "nearest" to the sender. Each of these types of addressing will be discussed in more detail later in this chapter.

Note Unless otherwise specified, terms used in this chapter refer to IPv6.

Addressing

Text Representation of IPv6 Addresses

Perhaps the most obvious difference between IPv4 and IPv6 is the increase in the number of bits used for addressing. Instead of using 32-bit dotted-decimal notation, IPv6 uses 128-bit addressing expressed in hexadecimal format. Text depiction of these addresses might vary, with the following three acceptable representations:

- In the preferred text representation, addresses are listed as eight 16-bit hexadecimal sections, separated by colons. For example, an IPv6 address for an interface would look like:

  `ABCD:EF12:3456:7890:ABCD:EF12:3456:7890`

  Any field containing leading zeros doesn't need to display the leading zeros, although no field can be left blank. For example:

  `1234:0:0:0:ABCD:123:45:6`

- Because of the mechanisms for address allocation in IPv6, long strings of zero bits will be common. Consequently, an alternate form of address representation allows "::" to be used to represent a portion of the address containing zero bits. The "::" placeholder can be used to represent more than one section of zero bits, but may not be used more than once in an address.

For example:

```
1234:0:0:0:ABCD:0:0:123
```

could be represented as:

```
1234::ABCD:0:0:123
```

or

```
1234:0:0:0:ABCD::123
```

but not

```
1234::ABCD::123
```

- The third method of textually displaying addresses is used in environments with a mixture of IPv4 and IPv6 nodes. In this notation, the six high-order (leftmost) 16-bit sections are displayed in hexadecimal, but the remaining bits are displayed in the familiar dotted-decimal notation.

  For example, an address might appear in any of these formats:

  ```
  0:0:0:0:0:0:131.107.6.100     or
  ```

  ```
  ::131.107.6.100   (compressed format)
  ```

  ```
  0:0:0:0:0:FFFF:131.107.4.99     or
  ```

  ```
  ::FFFF:131.107.4.99   (compressed format)
  ```

  ```
  ABCD:EF:12:34:0:0:131.107.2.98     or
  ```

  ```
  ABCD:EF:12:34::131.107.2.98   (compressed format)
  ```

More Info   IPv6 addressing architecture is described in detail in RFC 2373, which can be found in the \RFC folder on the companion CD-ROM.

Unicast Addresses

A variable-length field of leading bits, referred to as the Format Prefix (FP), identifies the type of address in IPv6. An FP value of 11111111 (FF) identifies an address as a multicast address. Any other value in the high-order bits identifies the address as a unicast address. Anycast addresses are taken from the unicast space, and will be discussed in the "Anycast Addresses" section of this chapter. Unicast addresses refer to a single node on the link; however, a single unicast address can be assigned to multiple interfaces on that node, provided that the interfaces are presented to upper layer protocols as a single entity. Unicast addresses can be of several types, including Aggregatable Global unicast addresses, link local unicast addresses, site local unicast addresses, and IPv6 Addresses with Embedded IPv4 Addresses.

Reserved Unicast Addresses

Currently, RFC 2373 defines two specialized reserved unicast addresses. The first is called the unspecified address. The unspecified address, 0:0:0:0:0:0:0:0, or :: in compressed format, can't be assigned to any node, nor can it be used as the source address in IPv6 packets or routing headers. Typically, it's used while nodes are initializing IPv6, and indicates that they haven't yet "learned" their own addresses. The second reserved unicast address, 0:0:0:0:0:0:0:1, or ::1 in compressed format, is the loopback address, which is used by a node to send a packet to itself—much like the loopback address of 127.0.0.1 in IPv4.

Aggregatable Global Unicast Addresses

In IPv4, under Classless Inter-Domain Routing (CIDR), ISPs (Internet Service Providers) allocate addresses in "pools." Aggregatable Global unicast addresses in IPv6 function in a similar manner, and will be used for global communication on the IPv6-enabled portion of the Internet. The format of an Aggregatable Global unicast address is shown in Figure 9-1.

More Info The format of an Aggregatable Global unicast address is defined in RFC 2374, which can be found in the RFC folder on the companion CD-ROM.

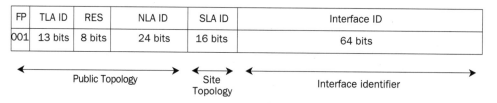

Figure 9-1. *An Aggregatable Global unicast address format.*

Before looking at the internal structure of an Aggregatable Global unicast address, it's important to understand the overall structure of these addresses. Aggregatable addresses will be organized into a three-tiered hierarchical structure. The top level of this hierarchy will be the Public Topology, or the portion of the address space that will be managed by entities that provide public Internet services. The Public Topology will provide a mechanism for what are referred to as long-haul transit providers and public exchanges to provide aggregates, or collections, of addresses. These providers will be responsible for providing routing that occurs outside an organization's internal corporate structure.

Because organizations maintain internal routing topologies, a portion of an aggregatable address is devoted to allowing for internal routing. This is the Site Topology portion of the address, and represents the bits that will identify internal routing paths. One of the chief advantages to this three-tiered approach to address allocation is that if a company changes long-haul transit providers, or uses multiple providers, that company won't need to obtain reassigned Site Topology addresses.

The interface identifier of an aggregatable address is the portion that identifies individual interfaces on the organization's physical links. Similar to how IPv4 addresses use network IDs and host IDs, IPv6 addresses will use Site and Interface identifiers. Table 9-1 summarizes the structure of an Aggregatable Global unicast address.

Table 9-1. Aggregatable Global Unicast Address Fields

Abbreviation	Field	Length	Description
FP	Format Prefix	3 bits	"001" indicates that this is an Aggregatable Global unicast address.
TLA ID	Top-Level Aggregation Identifier	13 bits	TLAs will be responsible for maintaining the upper levels of the public routing hierarchy. The use of 13 bits for these IDs allows for 8192 TLAs.
RES	Reserved	8 bits	Reserving these bits allows for the expansion of TLA and NLA fields, should future needs dictate.
NLA ID	Next-Level Aggregation Identifier	24 bits	NLAs will be used by organizations that are assigned a TLA to create an internal addressing hierarchy, and to allow transit providers to identify sites that they service. The use of 24 bits for this identifier will allow each TLA to service approximately 16 million sites if used in a flat fashion, or roughly the equivalent of the entire IPv4 address space if used hierarchically.
SLA ID	Site-Level Aggregation Identifier	16 bits	SLAs allow organizations to create an internal routing structure independent of the external public routing topologies. Approximately 65,536 internal subnets will be supported by the use of 16 bits for SLAs.
Interface ID	Interface Identifier	64 bits	Interface IDs must be unique to the link, might often match the Link Layer address, and actually might be assigned to multiple interfaces on a single node, thus allowing for load balancing over multiple interfaces.

Local-Use Unicast Addresses

Link-local unicast addresses, shown in Figure 9-2, are used for communication within a single link. They are used on links where no routers are present, or for purposes such as address autoconfiguration (the process by which nodes obtain an IPv6 address) and neighbor discovery (a method used for finding other nodes on a link).

10 bits	54 bits	64 bits
1111111010	0	Interface ID

Figure 9-2. *Link-local unicast address format.*

Site-local unicast addresses, shown in Figure 9-3, are the equivalent of IPv4 private addresses and are used for addressing and communication within a single private organization. Routers must not forward these packets outside the site where they're used.

10 bits	38 bits	16 bits	64 bits
1111111011	0	Subnet ID	Interface ID

Figure 9-3. *Site-local unicast address format.*

IPv6 Addresses with Embedded IPv4 Addresses

To successfully facilitate the transition from IPv4 to IPv6, mechanisms have been developed for tunneling IPv6 packets over IPv4 infrastructures. One mechanism for encoding packets allows nodes to carry an IPv4 address in the low-order bits of the IPv6 packet, which uses a specialized unicast address. This type of packet is referred to as an IPv4-compatible IPv6 address, as seen in Figure 9-4, and zeros out all fields in the interface identifier except for the 32 low-order IPv4 bits. A second type of transition packet exists to allow nodes to specify addresses for nodes that don't use IPv6 in any form, and precedes the 32 bits of the IPv4 address with "FFFF" to indicate that this is what is termed an "IPv4-mapped IPv6 address."

80 bits	16 bits	32 bits
0000..........................0000	0000 or FFFF	IPv4 address

Figure 9-4. *IPv6 with embedded IPv4 address format.*

Anycast Addresses

Anycast addresses are structurally identical to other unicast addresses, and are pulled from the pool of available unicast addresses in a given organization. However, rather than being assigned to a single node, as with unicast addresses, the anycast address is assigned to a group of nodes, typically routers on the site. Each of the routers is assigned the same address, and configured to use it as an anycast address.

When a source node wishes to send a packet to this address, it uses a discovery mechanism to find the nearest node that owns the address. Thus, the source node doesn't need to have knowledge that the address is an anycast address, as subsequent communication occurs only between the source node and the nearest router configured to use the anycast address.

As RFCs 2373 and 2526 state, anycast addresses are currently subject to certain limitations as research progresses. At this time, anycast addresses can't be used as the source address in any IPv6 packet, and can be used only by routers, not by hosts. Additionally, routers are required to support the anycast addresses for each subnet to which they are connected, to ensure that a local router will receive the packet sent to an anycast address on that subnet.

Multicast Addresses

As defined in RFCs 2373 and 2375, multicast addresses are used for IPv6 multicast traffic and replace broadcast addresses in IPv6. A multicast address is assigned to a group of nodes, but unlike an anycast address, all nodes configured with the multicast address will receive packets sent to that address. A node can belong to more than one multicast group; however, no node can use a multicast address as a source address in any packet; nor can a multicast address be used in routing headers. Figure 9-5 shows the format of an IPv6 multicast address.

> **More Info**   Read about multicast addresses and IPv6 traffic in RFCs 2373 and 2375, which can be found in the \RFC folder on the companion CD-ROM.

8 bits	4 bits	4 bits	112 bits
11111111	flgs	scop	Group ID

Figure 9-5. *IPv6 multicast address format.*

Table 9-2 describes each of the fields in a multicast address.

Table 9-2. Multicast Address Fields

Abbreviation	Field	Length	Description
FP	Format Prefix	8 bits	"11111111" indicates that this is a multicast address.
Flgs	Flags	4 bits	The first 3 bits of the Flags field are reserved, and must be zeroed out. If the fourth flag is "0," this indicates a permanently assigned multicast address; if it's "1," the multicast address is "transient," or not assigned by the Internet Assigned Numbers Authority (IANA).
Scop	Scope	4 bits	Scope values limit the scope of the multicast group. Values of "0" or "F" are reserved; "1" indicates a node-local scope; "2" indicates a link-local scope; "5" indicates a site-local scope; "8" indicates an organization-local scope; "E" indicates a global scope; and all other values are currently unassigned.
Group ID	Group Identifier	112 bits	This is a unique identifier for the multicast group that will accept packets sent to this address.

For example, the following multicast addresses are used to address packets to groups of routers:

```
FF01:0:0:0:0:0:0:2 Node-local; all routers.
```

This address identifies all routing interfaces on a single node.

```
FF02:0:0:0:0:0:0:2 Link-local; all routers.
```

This address identifies all routers on a link.

```
FF05:0:0:0:0:0:0:2 Site-local; all routers.
```

This address identifies all routers in a site.

Neighbor Discovery

"Discovery" can be a misleading term, as nodes use discovery mechanisms to both advertise their presence to other nodes on the network and to determine parameters such as node location, router availability, link MTU, and address configuration. Some discovery methods are specific to the physical link type, although RFC 2461 defines general discovery mechanisms. Discovery mechanisms are often implemented as multicasts, and replace IPv4 functionality such as ARP, ICMP router discovery, Internet Group Management Protocol (IGMP), and ICMP redirect.

Router Discovery Mechanisms

Routers use discovery for a multitude of purposes. Both at regular intervals and in response to router solicitation requests, routers issue router advertisements. These advertisements can include information that informs nodes of Link Layer router addresses, link prefixes (the approximate equivalent to the IPv4 netmask), suggested hop limits, and link MTU.

By advertising its own physical address, each router enables other nodes on the network to ascertain the router's existence. Router advertising of link prefixes allows nodes to determine to which subnet they're attached, and thus to build their internal routing tables. In IPv6, packets are now decremented by hop, rather than by Time-to-Live (TTL) values. By sending suggested hop limits, a router aids nodes in determining whether a destination is reachable by a given path. Additionally, for multicasting to function correctly on a link, all nodes must use the same MTU. Router advertisements enable nodes to configure their packets correctly for the link MTU.

Using Router Advertisement, routers also can be configured for inbound load balancing. A router can have multiple interfaces to a given link. However, these interfaces can be presented as a single interface with multiple bound addresses, and the router can omit the source address in its router advertisement packets. Consequently, hosts wanting to send packets to the router would use a neighbor solicitation request to obtain a router interface's address. The router can then provide different addresses in response to requests from different hosts. All hosts will believe that they're sending packets to a single interface with multiple addresses when, in reality, the router might divide incoming traffic over all connected interfaces.

Host Discovery

Hosts use discovery mechanisms primarily as an investigative tool, although they'll also respond to requests for information regarding their own configuration. Upon initializing, a host might use discovery to query a router as to whether it should configure its address via "stateless" or "stateful" configuration. Stateful autoconfiguration is used to issue host address parameters via Dynamic Host Configuration Protocol (DHCP). As defined in RFC 2462, stateless autoconfiguration enables the host to assign itself an address, issue a discovery packet to determine if the address is being used by any other node on the link, and configure remaining link and site parameters based on the information the host received in the router advertisement packet.

More Info Stateless autoconfiguration is defined in RFC 2462, which can be found in the \RFC folder on the companion CD-ROM.

When a node wants to communicate with another node, it issues a neighbor solicitation to the solicited node multicast address of the target node requesting its Link Layer address. The source node includes its own Link Layer address in the solicitation packet so that the target node can cache the results and thus doesn't need to issue its own solicitation. In response, the target node issues a neighbor advertisement listing its own Link Layer address.

When communication between two nodes is actively occurring, each node relies on upper layer protocols to provide confirmation that packets are successfully being sent and received. If this confirmation isn't forthcoming, a node uses neighbor unreachability detection to determine if the other node is still functional by sending a unicast neighbor solicitation directly to its partner. If two-way connectivity isn't confirmed, the node will stop sending packets to the target.

> **More Info**   RFC 2463 discusses how ICMP addresses error handling in IPv6. This RFC can be found in the \RFC folder on the companion CD-ROM.

Should a node's Link Layer address change, it will issue an unsolicited multicast neighbor advertisement to announce the change to other nodes on the network. By issuing the announcement immediately, other nodes can purge cached Link Layer addresses for that node, and thus decrease the likelihood that they will attempt communication with an unreachable node.

IPv6 Header Format and Routing Mechanisms

Address information in IPv6 comprises only a portion of each packet header. The remainder of an IPv6 header contains information necessary for nodes to effectively evaluate and process each packet. Figure 9-6 shows the general format of an IPv6 header.

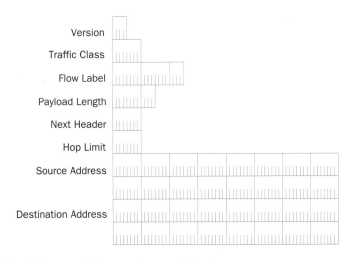

Fig 9-6. *General format of an IPv6 header.*

Table 9-3 discusses the fields in an IPv6 header.

Table 9-3. IPv6 Header Fields

Field	Length	Description
Version	4 bits	"0110" indicates version 6.
Traffic Class	8 bits	Used to identify traffic "class," or priority, so that packets can be forwarded at different priorities to ensure QoS.
Flow Label	20 bits	Packets that belong to a specific traffic class stream are labeled to identify to which "flow" they belong.
Payload Length	16 bits	Length, in octets, of the remainder of the packet, including extension headers.
Next Header	8 bits	Identifies the type of header immediately following the IPv6 header, and uses the same values as the IPv4 protocol field (RFC 1700).
Hop Limit	8 bits	Number of links on which the packet can travel before being discarded. Each forwarder decrements this field by 1.
Source Address	128 bits	Sending node's address.
Destination Address	128 bits	Target node's address, which can be the final destination, or an intermediate node.

Following the IPv6 header there can be one or more extension headers, which are used to provide additional information about the packet, such as routing information, whether the packet has been fragmented, and the next hop on the path specified by the sender. With the exception of a header called the Hop-by-Hop Options header, no node along the routing path processes these headers. Only the destination node specified in the packet (whether this is the final destination or an intermediate destination node) must evaluate and process all extension headers. Each extension header is a multiple of 8 octets long to preserve packet alignment and to allow nodes that don't need to process the extension headers to pass over them. Figure 9-7 shows the structure of an IPv6 packet containing extension headers.

IPv6 header	Hop-by-Hop Options header	Desti-nation Options header	Routing header	Fragment header	Authenti-cation header	Encap-sulating Security Payload header	Desti-nation Options header (2)	TCP header and data
Next header: Hop-by-Hop Options	Next header: Desti-nation Options	Next header: Routing	Next header: Fragment	Next header: Authenti-cation	Next header: Encap-sulating Security Payload	Next header: Destination Options	Next header: TCP	

Figure 9-7. *IPv6 extension headers.*

Packets can include all, some, or none of the extension headers in IPv6, but should always implement them in the order shown in Figure 9-7. Each extension header shouldn't occur more than once in a packet, with the exception of the Destination Options header, which can be used once to specify IP options, and used a second time to specify upper layer options. Extension headers of all types use a next-header field, which is 8 bits in length and specifies the type of header following this header. If this field contains the value "59," this indicates that there are no subsequent headers.

Hop-by-Hop Options Header

Each node along the delivery path must examine the Hop-by-Hop Options header, shown in Figure 9-8. Multiple options can be encoded in the header, must be processed in order, and define actions that occur at intermediate hops along the routing path. The 8-bit next-header field identifies the header that follows this one, as mentioned above. The header extension length field specifies the length of this extension header in octets. The option type 8-bit identifier specifies what action a node takes if the options in the packet aren't recognized by that node. As instructed by this identifier, the node can discard the packet, skip the option, and continue through the rest of the header, or send an ICMP Unrecognized Option Type message to the source address.

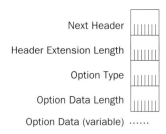

Figure 9-8. *Hop-by-Hop Options header.*

Destination Options Header

The Destination Options header is nearly identical to the Hop-by-Hop Options header, except that it's examined only by the packet's destination node and not by intermediate nodes on the path. A next-header value of 60 in the preceding header indicates the presence of the Destination Options header. Hop-by-Hop and Destination Options are identical.

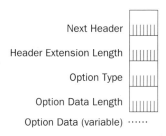

Figure 9-9. *Destination Options header.*

Routing Header

In IPv6, a source node can list one or more *stops* along the packet's path. The Routing header, shown in Figure 9-10, isn't examined until the packet reaches the destination listed in the IPv6 header. This destination then examines the Routing header, processes it according to the algorithm specified in the Routing Type field, and uses the results to send the packet to the next destination address specified in the packet. The 8-bit Segments Left field specifies the number of addresses remaining to be *visited*, and the 32-bit Reserved field is zeroed and ignored on transmission. As the packet is sent to each node specified in the Routing header, the visited addresses are stripped from the packet and the hop count is decremented, eventually resulting in the packet reaching its final destination.

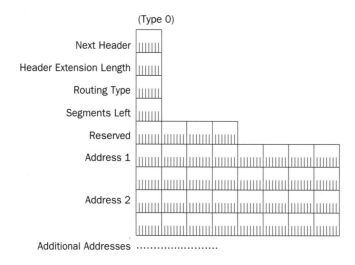

Figure 9-10. *Routing header.*

Fragment Header

Figure 9-11 shows the structure of an IPv6 Fragment header. IPv6 requires a minimum link MTU of 1280 octets; any links that don't support this specification must provide link-specific mechanisms for fragmentation and reassembly below the IPv6 layer. If the link MTU is at least 1280 octets, but the packet being sent is too large for this MTU, IPv6 provides its own fragmentation mechanisms. In IPv6, the source node performs the fragmentation rather than the routers. The presence of a Routing header, however, can require intermediate nodes to fragment the packet as a result of different MTUs along the path. Because each of these hops becomes the source node as it sends the packet to the next address, the node need be only concerned with the MTU of the link between itself and the destination, rather than *know* the MTU of all the network links. The Fragment Offset field determines packet reassembly order at the target node, and each fragmented packet is assigned a unique value in the Identification field to facilitate retransmission of lost packets. An M flag value of "0" indicates that this is the last of the fragments, and a value of "1" indicates that more fragments are to follow.

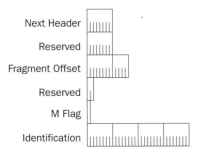

Figure 9-11. *Fragment header.*

Authentication Header

Authentication headers can be used alone or in conjunction with Encapsulating Security Payload (ESP) headers, and provide verification of data source and integrity. However, Authentication headers don't provide data encryption; in IPv6, this is ESP's responsibility. Authentication and ESP header formats are outlined in RFCs 2402 and 2406, and IP security is discussed in Chapter 20, "Securing IP Communications with IP Security (IPSec)." The 8-bit Payload Length field in an Authentication header specifies the length of that header in 32-bit words. The 16-bit Reserved field isn't currently used, and must be set to "0." The Security Paremeters Index (SPI) field is an arbitrary 32-bit value. In conjunction with the destination node address and security protocol negotiated between two nodes, this value uniquely identifies the packet's security association. The 32-bit Sequence Number field is incremented by 1 for each packet, and this counter isn't allowed to "roll over" without the sending and receiving nodes first establishing a new security association. The authentication data length can vary, but it must be a multiple of 32 bits and is padded when necessary to meet this requirement.

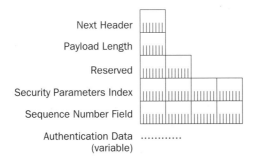

Figure 9-12. *Authentication header.*

Transition Mechanisms

Mechanisms for transitioning from IPv4 to IPv6 are defined in RFC 1933, and are continuing to be developed at this time. The primary goal in the transition process is a successful co-existence of the two protocol versions until such time as IPv4 can be retired if, indeed, it's ever completely decommissioned. Transition plans fall into two primary categories: dual-stack implementation, and IPv6 over IPv4 tunneling.

> **More Info** Mechanisms for transitioning from IPv4 to IPv6 are defined in RFC 1933, which can be found in the \RFC folder on the companion CD-ROM.

Dual-Stack Implementation

The simplest method for providing IPv6 functionality allows the two IP versions to be implemented as a dual stack on each node. Nodes using the dual stack can communicate via either stack. While dual-stack nodes can use IPv6 and IPv4 addresses that are related to each other, this isn't a requirement of the implementation, so the two addresses can be totally disparate. These nodes also can perform tunneling of IPv6 over IPv4. Because each stack is fully functional, the nodes can configure their IPv6 addresses via stateless autoconfiguration or DHCP for IPv6, while configuring their IPv4 addresses via any of the current configuration methods.

IPv6 Over IPv4 Tunneling

The second method for implementing IPv6 in an IPv4 environment is by tunneling IPv6 packets within IPv4 packets. These nodes can *map* an IPv4 address into an IPv4-compatible IPv6 address, preceding the IPv4 address with a 96-bit "0:0:0:0:0:0" prefix. Routers on a network don't need to immediately be IPv6-enabled if this approach is used, but Domain Name System (DNS) servers on a mixed-version network must be capable of supporting both versions of the protocol. To help achieve this goal, a new record type, "AAAA," has been defined for IPv6 addresses. Because Windows 2000 DNS servers implement this record type as well as the IPv4 "A" record, IPv6 can be easily implemented in a Windows 2000 environment. For more information on DNS in Windows 2000, see Chapter 16, "Domain Name Service (DNS)."

Summary

While IPv4 will undoubtedly continue to be implemented for years to come, IPv6 provides extensibility and configuration capabilities that will provide IP functionality far beyond what is currently possible. IPv6 development continues as of this writing, but the protocol is fast approaching a completed state. When it is finally deployed on a wide scale, IPv6 will give an estimated 1500-plus unique addresses for every square meter on the planet, and may well serve to provide networking options that have previously been considered science fiction.

Part III
Transport
Layer Protocols

Chapter 10
User Datagram Protocol (UDP)

At the Transport Layer there are two protocols that Application Layer protocols typically use for transporting data: Transmission Control Protocol (TCP) and UDP. UDP is the Transport Layer protocol that offers a minimum of services, but also has the minimum overhead for Application Layer protocols that do not require an end-to-end reliable delivery service.

Introduction to User Datagram Protocol

UDP is a minimal Transport Layer protocol that is a direct reflection of IP's datagram services, except that UDP provides a method to pass the message portion of the UDP message to the Application Layer protocol. UDP has the following characteristics:

- **Connectionless** UDP messages are sent without a UDP-based connection establishment negotiation.

- **Unreliable** UDP messages are sent as datagrams without sequencing or acknowledgment. The Application Layer protocol must recover lost messages. Typical UDP-based Application Layer protocols provide either their own reliable service, or retransmit UDP messages periodically or after a defined time-out value.

- **Provides identification of Application Layer protocols** UDP provides a mechanism to send messages to a specific Application Layer protocol or process on an internetwork host. The UDP header provides both source and destination process identification.

- **Provides checksum of UDP message** The UDP header provides a 16-bit checksum on the entire UDP message.

UDP does not provide the following services for end-to-end delivery:

- **Buffering** UDP doesn't provide any buffering of incoming or outgoing data. The Application Layer protocol must provide all buffering.

- **Segmentation** UDP doesn't provide any segmentation of large blocks of data. Therefore, the application must send data in small enough blocks so that the IP datagrams for the UDP messages are no larger than the MTU of the Network Interface Layer technology on which they are sent.

- **Flow control** UDP doesn't provide any sender-side or receiver-side flow control. UDP message senders can react to the receipt of an ICMP Source Quench message, but it isn't required.

Uses for UDP

Because UDP doesn't provide any services beyond Application Layer protocol identification and a checksum, it's hard to imagine why UDP is needed at all. However, the following are specific uses for sending data using UDP:

- **Lightweight protocol** To conserve memory and processor resources, some Application Layer protocols require the use of a lightweight protocol that performs a specific function using a simple exchange of messages. A good example of a lightweight protocol is Domain Name System (DNS) name queries. Typically, a DNS client sends a DNS Name Query message to a DNS server. The DNS server responds with a DNS Name Response message. If the DNS server doesn't respond, the DNS client retransmits the DNS Name Query.

    Imagine the resources required at the DNS server if all the DNS clients used TCP rather than UDP. All DNS interactions would be sent reliably, but the DNS server would have to support hundreds or, on the Internet, thousands of TCP connections. The low overhead solution of using UDP is the best choice for simple request-reply-based Application Layer protocols.

- **Reliability provided by the Application Layer protocol** If the Application Layer protocol provides its own reliable data transfer service, there's no need for the reliable services of TCP. Examples of reliable Application Layer protocols are Trivial File Transfer Protocol (TFTP) and Network File System (NFS).

- **Reliability not required due to periodic advertisement process** If the Application Layer protocol periodically advertises information, reliable delivery is not required. If an advertisement is lost, it is announced again at the period interval. An example of an Application Layer protocol that uses periodic advertisements is the Routing Information Protocol (RIP).

- **One-to-many delivery** UDP is used as the Transport Layer protocol whenever Application Layer data must be sent to multiple destinations using an IP multicast or broadcast address. TCP can be used only for one-to-one delivery. For example, Microsoft NetShow sends multicast traffic using UDP.

The UDP Message

UDP messages are sent as IP datagrams. A UDP message consisting of a UDP header and a message is encapsulated with an IP header using IP Protocol number 17 (0x11). The message can be a maximum size of 65,507 bytes: 65,535 less the minimum-size IP header (20 bytes) and the UDP header (8 bytes). The resulting IP datagram is then encapsulated with the appropriate Network Interface Layer header and trailer. Figure 10-1 shows the resulting frame. UDP is described in RFC 768.

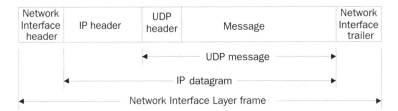

Figure 10-1. *UDP message encapsulation showing the IP header and Network Interface Layer header and trailer.*

In the IP header of UDP messages, the Source IP Address field is set to the host interface that sent the UDP message. The Destination IP Address field is set to the unicast address of a specific host, an IP broadcast address, or an IP multicast address.

The UDP Header

The UDP header is a fixed-length size of 8 bytes consisting of four fixed-length fields, as Figure 10-2 shows.

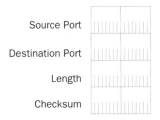

Figure 10-2. *The structure of the UDP header.*

The fields in the UDP header are defined as follows:

- **Source Port**   A 2-byte field used to identify the source Application Layer protocol sending the UDP message. The use of a source port is optional and, when not used, is set to 0x00-00. IP multicast traffic, such as videocasts sent using UDP, could use 0x00-00 because no reply to the video traffic is assumed. Typical Application Layer protocols use the source port of the incoming UDP message as the destination port for replies.

- **Destination Port**   A 2-byte field used to identify the destination Application Layer protocol. The combination of the IP header's destination IP address and the UDP header's destination port provides a unique, globally significant address for the process to which the message is sent.

- **Length**   A 2-byte field used to indicate the length in bytes of the UDP message (UDP header and message). The minimum length is 8 bytes (the UDP header's size), and the maximum is 65,515 bytes (maximum-sized IP datagram of 65,535 bytes less minimum-sized IP header of 20 bytes). The actual maximum length is confined by the MTU of the link on which the UDP message is sent. The Length field is a redundant field. The UDP length can always be calculated from the Total Length and the IP Header Length fields in the IP header (UDP length = payload length = total length − 4*IP header length [in 32-bit words]).

- **Checksum**   A 2-byte field that provides a bit-level integrity check for the UDP message (UDP header and message). The UDP checksum calculation uses the same method as the IP header checksum over the UDP pseudo header, the UDP header, the message, and, if needed, a padding byte of 0x00. The padding byte is used only if the message's length is an odd number of bytes. The use of the UDP Checksum field is optional. If not used, the UDP Checksum field is set to 0x00-00. For details on the checksum calculation, see Chapter 4, "Internet Protocol (IP) Basics."

Note   TCP/IP for Windows 2000 always calculates a value for the UDP checksum.

The following Network Monitor trace (Capture 10-01 in the \Captures folder on the companion CD-ROM) shows the structure of the UDP header for a DNS Name Query:

```
+ ETHERNET: ETYPE = 0x0800 : Protocol = IP:   DOD Internet Protocol
+ IP: ID = 0x4001; Proto = UDP; Len: 58
  UDP: Src Port: DNS, (53); Dst Port: DNS (53); Length = 38 (0x26)
        UDP: Source Port = DNS
        UDP: Destination Port = DNS
        UDP: Total length = 38 (0x26) bytes
        UDP: UDP Checksum = 0x6AA1
        UDP: Data: Number of data bytes remaining = 30 (0x001E)
+ DNS: 0x2:Std Qry for www.acme.com. of type Host Addr on class INET addr.
```

Note   The last item in the Network Monitor display of the UDP header (UDP: Data: Number of data bytes remaining) is a Network Monitor information field and doesn't correspond to a field in the UDP header.

The UDP Pseudo Header

The UDP pseudo header is used to associate the UDP message with the IP header. The UDP pseudo header is added to the beginning of the UDP message only for the checksum calculation, and isn't sent as part of the UDP message. The UDP pseudo header assures that a routing or fragmentation process didn't improperly modify the IP header's key fields.

The UDP pseudo header consists of the Source IP Address field, the Destination IP Address field, the Protocol field for UDP (17 or 0x11), an Unused field set to 0, and the UDP Length field. When sending a UDP message, UDP is aware of all of these values. When receiving a UDP message, IP indicates all of these values to UDP. Figure 10-3 shows the UDP pseudo header.

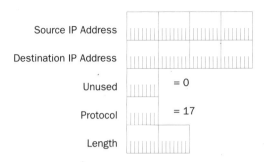

Figure 10-3. *The structure of the UDP pseudo header.*

The UDP Checksum field is calculated over the combination of the UDP pseudo header, the UDP message, and a 0x00 padding byte. The checksum calculation relies on summing 16-bit words. Therefore, the checksum quantity must be an even number of bytes. The padding byte is used only if the length of the message is an odd number of bytes. The padding byte isn't included in the UDP length and isn't sent as part of the UDP message. Figure 10-4 shows the resulting quantity for the calculation of the UDP Checksum field.

Figure 10-4. *The resulting quantity used for the UDP checksum calculation.*

Note   The UDP pseudo header and Checksum field don't provide data integrity. IP header fields can be modified as long as the UDP Checksum field is updated. This is how a network address translator (NAT) works. An NAT is a router that translates public and private addresses during the forwarding process. For example, when translating a source IP address from a private address to a public address, the NAT also recalculates the UDP checksum.

UDP Ports

A UDP port defines a location or message queue for the delivery of messages for Application Layer protocols using UDP services. Included in each UDP message is the source port (the message queue from which the message was sent) and a destination port (the message queue to which the message was sent). The Internet Assigned Numbers Authority (IANA) assigns port numbers, known as well-known port numbers, to specific Application Layer protocols. Table 10-1 shows well-known UDP port numbers used by Windows 2000 components.

Table 10-1. Well-Known UDP Port Numbers

Port Number	Application Layer Protocol
53	Domain Name System (DNS)
67	BOOTP client (Dynamic Host Configuration Protocol [DHCP])
68	BOOTP server (DHCP)
69	Trivial File Transfer Protocol (TFTP)
137	NetBIOS Name Service
138	NetBIOS Datagram Service
161	Simple Network Management Protocol (SNMP)
520	Routing Information Protocol (RIP)
445	Direct hosting of Server Message Block (SMB) datagrams over TCP/IP
1812, 1813	Remote Authentication Dial-In User Service (RADIUS)

See *http://www.isi.edu/in-notes/iana/assignments/port-numbers* for the most current list of IANA-assigned UDP port numbers.

Typically, the server side of an Application Layer protocol listens on the well-known port number. The client side of Application Layer protocols uses either the well-known port number or, more commonly, a dynamically allocated port number. These dynamically allocated port numbers are used for the duration of the process and are also known as ephemeral or short-lived ports. The following registry setting determines the range of TCP and UDP port numbers that TCP/IP uses for Windows 2000:

MaxUserPort

```
Location: HKEY_LOCAL_MACHINE\SYSTEM\CurrentControlSet\Services\
Tcpip\Parameters
Data type: REG_DWORD
Valid range: 5000-65534
Default: 5000
Present by default: No
```

By default, the maximum port number is 5000. Dynamically allocated port numbers are within the range of 1024 through 5000 (0 through 1023 are reserved for well-known ports controlled by the IANA).

A UDP port number can be referenced by name by a Microsoft Windows Sockets application using the *GetServByName()* function. The name is resolved to a UDP port number through the SERVICES file stored in the *SystemRoot*\system32\drivers\etc folder.

A sending node determines the destination port (using either a specified value or the *GetServByName()* function) and the source port (either specified or by obtaining a dynamically allocated port through Windows Sockets). The sending node then indicates the source IP address, destination IP address, source port, destination port, and the message to TCP/IP to be sent. The UDP module calculates the length and the checksum, and indicates the UDP message with the appropriate source IP address and destination IP address to the IP module.

When receiving a UDP message at the destination, IP verifies the IP header and, based on the value of 17 (0x11) in the Protocol field, passes the UDP message, the source IP address, and the destination IP address to the UDP module. After verifying the UDP checksum, the UDP module verifies the destination port. If a process is listening on the port, the UDP message is passed to the application. If no process is listening on the port, UDP informs the ICMP module and an ICMP Destination Unreachable-Port Unreachable message is sent to the sender of the UDP message.

Figure 10-5 shows the process of demultiplexing an incoming UDP message.

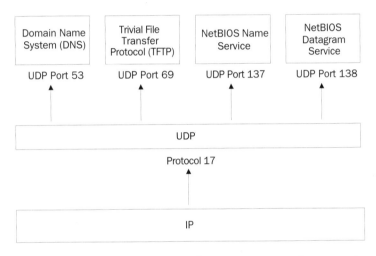

Figure 10-5. *The demultiplexing of a UDP message to the appropriate Application Layer protocol using the IP Protocol field and the UDP Destination Port field.*

Best Practices   UDP ports are separate from TCP ports even for the same port number. A UDP port represents a UDP message queue for an Application Layer protocol. A TCP port represents one side of a TCP connection for an Application Layer protocol. The Application Layer protocol using the UDP port isn't necessarily the same Application Layer protocol using the TCP port. A good example of the differentiation between TCP and UDP Application Layer protocols is the Extended Filename Server (EFS) protocol, which uses TCP port 520, and the Routing Information Protocol (RIP), which uses UDP port 520. Clearly these are separate Application Layer protocols. Therefore, it is good practice to never refer to a port by just its port number. The port number alone is ambiguous. Always refer to either a TCP port number or a UDP port number.

Summary

UDP provides a connectionless and unreliable delivery service for applications that do not require the guaranteed delivery service of TCP. Application Layer protocols use UDP for lightweight interaction, for broadcast or multicast traffic, or when the Application Layer protocol provides its own reliable delivery service. The UDP header provides a checksum and the identification of source and destination port numbers to multiplex UDP message data to the proper Application Layer protocol.

Chapter 11
Transmission Control Protocol (TCP) Basics

At the Transport Layer there are two protocols that Application Layer protocols typically use for transporting data: TCP and User Datagram Protocol (UDP). TCP is the Transport Layer protocol that provides end-to-end reliable delivery service.

Introduction to TCP

TCP is a fully formed Transport Layer protocol that provides a reliable data-transfer service and a method to pass TCP-encapsulated data to an Application Layer protocol. TCP has the following characteristics:

- **Connection-oriented** Before data can be transferred, two Application Layer processes must formally negotiate a TCP connection using the TCP connection establishment process. TCP connections are formally closed using the TCP connection termination process. For more information on TCP connection processes, see Chapter 12, "Transmission Control Protocol (TCP) Connections."

- **Full duplex** For each TCP peer, the TCP connection consists of two logical pipes: an outgoing pipe and an incoming pipe. With the appropriate Network Interface Layer technology, data can be flowing out of the outgoing pipe and into the incoming pipe simultaneously. The TCP header contains both the sequence number of the outgoing data and an acknowledgment of the incoming data.

- **Reliable** Data sent on a TCP connection is sequenced and a positive acknowledgment is expected from the receiver. If no acknowledgment is received, the segment is retransmitted. At the receiver, duplicate segments are discarded and segments arriving out of sequence are placed back in the proper sequence. A TCP checksum is always used to verify the bit-level integrity of the TCP segment.

- **Byte stream** TCP views the data sent over the incoming and outgoing logical pipes as a continuous stream of bytes. The sequence number and acknowledgment number in each TCP header are defined along byte boundaries. TCP isn't aware of record or message boundaries within the byte stream. The Application Layer protocol must provide the proper parsing of the incoming byte stream.

- **Sender- and receiver-side flow control** To avoid sending too much data at one time and congesting the routers of the IP internetwork, TCP implements sender-side flow control that gradually scales the amount of data sent at one time. To avoid having the sender send data that the receiver can't buffer, TCP implements receiver-side flow control that indicates the amount of space left in the receiver's buffer. For more information on how TCP implements sender and receiver-side flow control, see Chapter 13, "Transmission Control Protocol (TCP) Data Flow."

- **Segmentation of Application Layer data** TCP will segment data obtained from the Application Layer process so that it will fit within an IP datagram sent on the Network Interface Layer link. TCP peers exchange the maximum-sized segment that each can receive and adjust the TCP maximum segment size using Path Maximum Transmission Unit (PMTU) discovery.

- **One-to-one delivery** TCP connections are a logical point-to-point circuit between two Application Layer protocols. TCP doesn't provide a one-to-many delivery service.

TCP typically is used when the Application Layer protocol requires a reliable data transfer service and such service isn't provided by the Application Layer protocol itself.

The TCP Segment

TCP segments are sent as IP datagrams. A TCP segment, consisting of a TCP header and a segment, is encapsulated with an IP header using IP Protocol number 6. The segment can be a maximum size of 65,495 bytes: 65,535 less the minimum-size IP header (20 bytes) and the minimum-size TCP header (20 bytes). The resulting IP datagram is then encapsulated with the appropriate Network Interface Layer header and trailer. Figure 11-1 displays the resulting frame.

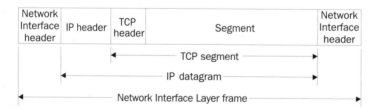

Figure 11-1. *TCP segment encapsulation showing the IP header and Network Interface Layer header and trailer.*

In the IP header of TCP segments, the Source IP Address field is set to the unicast address of the host interface that sent the TCP segment. The Destination IP Address field is set to the unicast address of a specific host.

The TCP Header

The TCP header is of variable-length size consisting of the fields as shown in Figure 11-2. When TCP options aren't present, the TCP header is 20 bytes long.

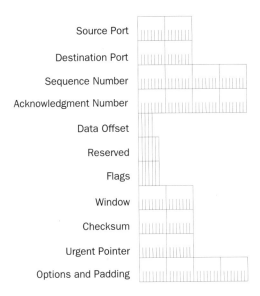

Figure 11-2. *The structure of the TCP header.*

The fields in the TCP header are defined as follows:

- **Source Port** A 2-byte field that indicates the source Application Layer protocol sending the TCP segment. The combination of the source IP address in the IP header and the source port in the TCP header provides a *socket*—a unique, globally significant address from which the segment was sent.

- **Destination Port** A 2-byte field that indicates the destination Application Layer protocol. The combination of the destination IP address in the IP header and the destination port in the TCP header provides a *socket*—a unique, globally significant address to which the segment is sent.

- **Sequence Number** A 4-byte field that indicates the outgoing byte-stream-based sequence number of the segment's first octet. The Sequence Number field is always set, even when there's no data in the segment. In this case, the Sequence Number field is set to the number of the outgoing byte stream's next octet. When establishing a TCP connection, TCP segments sent with the SYN (Synchronization) flag set the Sequence Number field to the Initial Sequence Number (ISN). This indicates that the first octet in the outgoing byte stream sent on the connection is ISN + 1.

- **Acknowledgment Number** A 4-byte field that indicates the sequence number of the next octet in the incoming byte stream that the receiver expects to receive. The acknowledgment number provides a positive acknowledgment of all octets in the incoming byte stream up to, but not including, the acknowledgment number. The acknowledgment number is significant in all TCP segments with the ACK (Acknowledgment) flag set.

- **Data Offset** A 4-bit field that indicates where the TCP segment data begins. The Data Offset field is also the TCP header's size. As in the IP header's Header Length field, the Data Offset field is the number of 32-bit words (4-byte blocks) in the TCP header. For the smallest TCP header (no options), the Data Offset field is set to 5 (0x5), indicating that the segment data begins in the twentieth octet offset starting from the beginning of the TCP segment (the offset starts its count at 0). With a Data Offset field set to its maximum value of 15 (0xF), the largest TCP header can be 60 bytes long including TCP options.

- **Reserved** A 6-bit field that's reserved for future use. The sender sets these bits to 0.

- **Flags** A 6-bit field that indicates six TCP flags. The six TCP flags, known as URG (Urgent), ACK (Acknowledgment), PSH (Push), RST (Reset), SYN (Synchronize), and FIN (Finish), are discussed in greater detail in the "TCP Flags" section of this chapter.

- **Window** A 2-byte field that indicates the number of bytes of available space in the receive buffer of the sender of this segment. The receive buffer is used to store the incoming byte stream. By advertising the window size with each segment, a TCP receiver is telling the sender how much data can be sent and successfully buffered. The sender shouldn't be sending more data than can fit in the receiver's buffer. If there's no more space in the receiver's buffer, a window size of 0 bytes is advertised. With a window size of 0, the sender can't send any more data until the window size is a non-zero value. The advertisement of the window size is an implementation of receiver-side flow control.

- **Checksum** A 2-byte field that provides a bit-level integrity check for the TCP segment (TCP header and segment). The Checksum field's value is calculated in the same way as the IP header checksum, over all the 16-bit words in a TCP pseudo header, the TCP header, the segment, and, if needed, a padding byte of 0x00. The padding byte is used only if the segment length is an odd number of octets. The value of the Checksum field is set to 0x00-00 during the checksum calculation.

- **Urgent Pointer** A 2-byte field that indicates the location of urgent data in the segment. The Urgent Pointer field and urgent data are discussed in the "TCP Urgent Data" section of this chapter.

- **Options**   One or more TCP options can be added to the TCP header but must be done so in 4-byte increments so that the TCP header size can be indicated with the Data Offset field. TCP options are discussed in the "TCP Options" section of this chapter.

The following Network Monitor trace (Capture 11-01 in the \Captures folder on the companion CD-ROM) shows the TCP header structure for File Transfer Protocol (FTP) traffic:

```
+ Frame: Base frame properties
+ ETHERNET: ETYPE = 0x0800 : Protocol = IP:  DOD Internet Protocol
+ IP: ID = 0xDFC8; Proto = TCP; Len: 1500
   TCP: .A...., len: 1460, seq:1038577021-1038578481, ack:3930983524,
win:17520, src:   20  dst: 1163
      TCP: Source Port = FTP [default data]
      TCP: Destination Port = 0x048B
      TCP: Sequence Number = 1038577021 (0x3DE76D7D)
      TCP: Acknowledgement Number = 3930983524 (0xEA4E0C64)
      TCP: Data Offset = 20 (0x14)
      TCP: Reserved = 0 (0x0000)
    + TCP: Flags = 0x10 : .A....
      TCP:..0.....=No urgent data
      TCP:...1....=Acknowledgment field significant
      TCP:....0...=No Push function
      TCP:.....0..=No Reset
      TCP:......0.=No Synchronize
      TCP:.......0=No Fin
      TCP: Window = 17520 (0x4470)
      TCP: Checksum = 0xB489
      TCP: Urgent Pointer = 0 (0x0)
      TCP: Data: Number of data bytes remaining = 1460 (0x05B4)
+ FTP: Data Transfer To Client, Port = 1163, size 1460
```

TCP Ports

A TCP port defines a location for the delivery of TCP connection data. Included in each TCP segment is the source port that indicates the Application Layer process from which the segment was sent, and a destination port that indicates the Application Layer process to which the segment was sent. There are port numbers that are assigned by the Internet Assigned Numbers Authority (IANA) to specific Application Layer protocols. Table 11-1 shows assigned TCP port numbers used by Microsoft Windows 2000 components.

Table 11-1. Well-Known TCP Port Numbers

Port Number	Application Layer Protocol
19	Network News Transfer Protocol (NNTP)
20	FTP Server (data channel)
21	FTP Server (control channel)
23	Telnet Server
25	Simple Mail Transfer Protocol (SMTP)
69	Trivial File Transfer Protocol (TFTP)
80	Hypertext Transfer Protocol (HTTP) (Web Server)
139	NetBIOS Session Service
339	Lightweight Directory Access Protocol (LDAP)
445	Direct-Hosted Server Message Block (SMB)

See *http://www.isi.edu/in-notes/iana/assignments/port-numbers* for the most current list of IANA-assigned TCP port numbers.

Typically, the server side of an Application Layer protocol listens on the well-known port number. The client side of an Application Layer protocol uses either the well-known port number or, more commonly, a dynamically allocated port number. These dynamically allocated port numbers are used for the duration of the process and are known also as ephemeral or short-lived ports. The following registry setting determines the range of port numbers that TCP/IP for Windows 2000 uses:

MaxUserPort

```
Location: HKEY_LOCAL_MACHINE\SYSTEM\CurrentControlSet\Services\Tcpip\Parameters
Data type: REG_DWORD
Valid range: 5000-65534
Default: 5000
Present by default: No
```

By default, the maximum port number is 5000. Dynamically allocated port numbers are within the range of 1024 through 5000 (0 to 1023 are reserved for well-known ports controlled by the IANA).

A TCP port number can be referenced, by name, by a Windows Sockets application using the *GetServByName()* function. The name is resolved to a TCP port number through the SERVICES file stored in the *SystemRoot*\system32\drivers\etc folder.

A sending node determines the destination port (using either a specified value or the *GetServByName()* function) and the source port (using either a specified value, or by obtaining a dynamically allocated port through Windows Sockets). The sending node then passes the source IP address, destination IP address, source port, destination port, and the segment to TCP/IP to be sent. The TCP module calculates the Checksum field and indicates the TCP segment with the appropriate source IP address and destination IP address to the IP module.

When receiving a TCP segment at the destination, IP verifies the IP header. Then, based on the value of 6 in the Protocol field, IP passes the TCP segment, the source IP address, and the destination IP address to the TCP module. After verifying the TCP Checksum field, the TCP module verifies the destination port. If a process is listening on the port, the TCP segment is passed to the application. If no process is listening on the port, TCP sends a TCP Connection Reset segment to the sender. See Chapter 12, "Transmission Control Protocol (TCP) Connections," for a detailed discussion of the TCP Connection Reset segment.

Figure 11-3 shows the demultiplexing of received TCP connection data based on the TCP destination port.

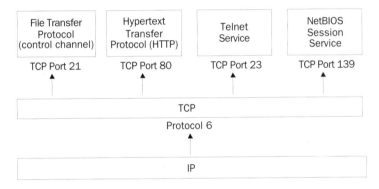

Figure 11-3. *The demultiplexing of a TCP segment to the appropriate Application Layer protocol using the IP Protocol field and the TCP Destination Port field.*

Best Practices   TCP ports are separate from UDP ports, even for the same port number. A TCP port represents one side of a TCP connection for an Application Layer protocol. A UDP port represents a UDP message queue for an Application Layer protocol. The Application Layer protocol using the TCP port isn't necessarily the same Application Layer protocol using the UDP port. For example, the Extended Filename Server (EFS) protocol uses TCP port 520, and the Routing Information Protocol (RIP) uses UDP port 520. Clearly these are separate Application Layer protocols. Therefore, it's good practice to never refer to a port by just its port number. The port number alone is ambiguous. Always refer to either a "TCP port number" or a "UDP port number."

TCP Flags

Figure 11-4 shows the six TCP flags in the Flags field of the TCP header.

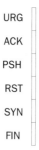

URG

ACK

PSH

RST

SYN

FIN

Figure 11-4. *The six TCP flags in the Flag field of the TCP header.*

The TCP flags are defined as follows:

- **URG (Urgent Pointer field is significant)**   Indicates that the segment portion of the TCP segment contains urgent data and to use the Urgent Pointer field to determine the location of the urgent data in the segment. Urgent data is discussed in more detail in the "TCP Urgent Data" section of this chapter.

- **ACK (Acknowledgment field is significant)**   Indicates that the Acknowledgment field contains the next octet that the receiver expects to receive. The ACK flag is always set, except during the first phase of a TCP connection establishment.

- **PSH (the Push function)**   Indicates that the contents of the TCP receive buffer should be passed to the Application Layer protocol. The data in the receive buffer must consist of a contiguous block of data from the left edge of the buffer. In other words, there can't be any missing segments of the byte stream up to the segment containing the PSH flag; the data can't be passed to the Application Layer protocol until missing segments arrive. Normally, the TCP receive buffer is flushed (the contents are passed to the Application Layer protocol) when the receive buffer fills with contiguous data or during normal TCP connection maintenance processes. The PSH flag overrides this default behavior and immediately flushes the TCP receive buffer. The PSH flag is used also for interactive Application Layer protocols such as Telnet, where each keystroke in the virtual terminal session is sent with the PSH flag set. Another example of using the PSH flag is the setting of the PSH flag on the last segment of a file transferred with FTP. Data sent with the PSH flag doesn't have to be immediately acknowledged.

- **RST (reset the connection)**   Indicates that the connection is being aborted. For active connections, a TCP segment with the RST flag set is sent in response to a TCP segment received on the connection that's incorrect, causing the connection to fail. The sending of an RST segment for an active connection forcibly and ungracefully terminates the connection, causing data stored in send and receive buffers or in transit to be lost. For TCP connections being established, a RST segment is sent in response to a connection establishment request to deny the connection attempt.

- **SYN (synchronize sequence number)**   Indicates that the segment contains an ISN. During the TCP connection establishment process, TCP sends a TCP segment with the SYN flag set. Each TCP peer acknowledges the receipt of the SYN flag by treating the SYN flag as if it were a single byte of data. The Acknowledgment Number field for the acknowledgment of the SYN segment is set to ISN + 1.

- **FIN (finish sending data)**   Indicates that the TCP segment sender is finished sending data on the connection. When a TCP connection is gracefully terminated, each TCP peer sends a TCP segment with the FIN flag set. A TCP peer doesn't send a TCP segment with the FIN flag set until all outstanding data to the other TCP peer has been sent and acknowledged. Each peer acknowledges the receipt of the FIN flag by treating the FIN flag as if it were a single byte of data. When both TCP peers have sent segments with the FIN flag set and received acknowledgment of their receipt, the TCP connection is terminated.

The TCP Pseudo Header

The TCP pseudo header is used to associate the TCP segment with the IP header. The TCP pseudo header is added to the beginning of the TCP segment only during the checksum calculation and isn't sent as part of the TCP segment. The use of the TCP pseudo header assures the receiver that a routing or fragmentation process didn't improperly modify key fields in the IP header.

The TCP pseudo header consists of the Source IP Address field, the Destination IP Address field, an Unused field set to 0x00, the Protocol field for TCP (6), and the length of the TCP segment. When sending a TCP segment, TCP knows all of these values. When receiving a TCP segment, IP indicates all of these values to TCP. Figure 11-5 illustrates the TCP pseudo header.

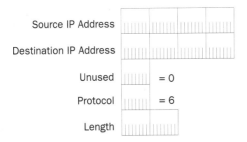

Figure 11-5. *The structure of the TCP pseudo header.*

The TCP checksum is calculated over the combination of the TCP pseudo header, the TCP segment, and a 0x00 padding byte. The checksum calculation relies on summing 16-bit words. Therefore, the quantity over which the checksum being calculated must be an even number of octets. The padding byte is used only if the segment length is an odd number of octets. The padding byte isn't included in the IP length and isn't sent as part of the TCP segment. Figure 11-6 shows the resulting quantity for the TCP checksum.

Figure 11-6. *The resulting quantity used for the TCP checksum calculation.*

Note   The TCP pseudo header and Checksum field aren't providing data authentication and integrity as the IP Security (IPSec) Authentication header does. Key fields in the IP header can be modified as long as the TCP checksum is updated. This is how a network address translator (NAT) works. An NAT is a router that translates public and private addresses during the forwarding process. For example, when translating a source IP address from a private address to a public address, the NAT also recalculates the TCP Checksum field.

TCP Urgent Data

Normal data sent on a TCP connection is data corresponding to the incoming- and outgoing-byte stream data. For some data-transfer situations, there must be a method of sending control data to interrupt a process or inform the Application Layer protocol of asynchronous events. This control data is known as *out of band data*—data that isn't part of the TCP byte stream but is needed to control the data flow. Out of band data for TCP connections can be implemented in the following ways:

- **Use a separate TCP connection for the out of band data.**   The separate TCP connection sends control commands and status information without being combined on the data stream of the data connection. This is the method used by FTP. FTP uses a TCP connection on port 21 for control commands such as login, gets (downloading a file to the FTP client), and puts (uploading a file to the FTP server), and a separate TCP connection on port 20 for the sending or receiving of file data.

- **Use TCP urgent data.**   TCP urgent data is sent on the same TCP connection as the data. When TCP urgent data is used, the urgent data is indicated as being present by setting the URG flag, and the urgent data is distinguished from the non-urgent data using the Urgent Pointer field. Urgent data within the TCP segment must be processed before the non-urgent data. Urgent data is used by the Telnet protocol to send control commands, even though the advertised receive window of the Telnet server is 0.

The interpretation of the Urgent Pointer value depends on the TCP implementation's adherence to either RFC 793, the original TCP RFC, or RFC 1122, which defines requirements for Internet hosts.

- RFC 793 defines the value of the Urgent Pointer field as the positive offset from the beginning of the TCP segment to the first byte of non-urgent data.
- RFC 1122 defines the value of the Urgent Pointer field as the positive offset from the beginning of the TCP segment to the last byte of urgent data.

These two definitions of the Urgent Pointer field differ by one byte. Both hosts on a TCP connection must use the same interpretation, otherwise data corruption could occur. There's no interoperability of these two interpretations, nor is there a mechanism to negotiate the interpretation during the TCP connection establishment process.

The definition of the Urgent Pointer field in RFC 793 was made in error (the correct interpretation is actually given later in the RFC during the discussion of event processing, section 3.9). The correct use of the Urgent Pointer field is the RFC 1122 version. However, numerous implementations of TCP use the RFC 793 definition of the Urgent Pointer field.

More Info   The use of the TCP Urgent Pointer field is documented in RFCs 793 and 1122. These RFCs can be found in the \RFC folder on the companion CD-ROM.

Figure 11-7 shows the placement of urgent data within the TCP segment, and the RFC 793 and RFC 1122 interpretation of the Urgent Pointer field.

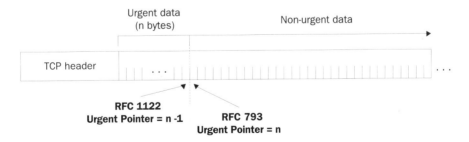

Figure 11-7. *The location of TCP urgent data within a TCP segment.*

The following Windows 2000 registry setting allows you to configure the interpretation of the TCP Urgent Pointer field:

TcpUseRFC1122UrgentPointer
Key: HKEY_LOCAL_MACHINE\SYSTEM\CurrentControlSet\Services\Tcpip\Parameters
Value type: REG_DWORD
Valid range: 0-1
Default: 0
Present by default: No

Set this value to 1 to use the RFC 1122 interpretation of the Urgent Pointer field, or set to 0 to use the RFC 793 interpretation. The default is the RFC 793 interpretation.

TCP Options

As in IP, TCP options are used to extend TCP functionality. There are a variety of defined TCP options used for negotiating maximum segment sizes, scaling window sizes, performing selective acknowledgments, recording timestamps, and providing padding for 4-byte boundaries. A node isn't required to support all TCP options; however, the support for processing TCP options is required. The presence of TCP options is indicated by a Data Offset field with a value greater than 5 (0x5). A TCP header with a size greater than 20 bytes contains TCP options.

A TCP option is either a single octet or multiple octets. For multiple octet options, the TCP option is in type-length-value format, as shown in Figure 11-8, where the length is the length in octets of the entire option. A TCP option type is known as an *option kind*.

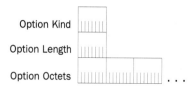

Figure 11-8. *The format for a multiple-octet TCP option.*

End Of Option List and No Operation

To implement 4-byte boundary support for TCP options, the following single-octet TCP options are defined:

- The End Of Option List TCP option is a single octet with the option kind set to 0 (0x00), which indicates that no other options follow. The End Of Option List option isn't used to delimit TCP options. If the set of TCP options falls along a 4-byte boundary, the End Of Option List option isn't needed.

- The No-Operation TCP option is a single octet with the option kind set to 1 (0x01), which is used between TCP options for a 4-byte alignment. The No-Operation option isn't required, so TCP implementation must be able to correctly interpret TCP options that aren't on 4-byte boundaries.

Maximum Segment Size Option

The TCP maximum segment size (MSS) is the maximum-sized segment that can be sent on the connection. The value for the MSS can be obtained by taking the IP Maximum Transmission Unit (MTU) and subtracting the IP header size and the TCP header size. For a typical IP header (without options) and a typical TCP header (without options), the MSS is 40 octets less than the IP MTU, as shown in Figure 11-9.

Figure 11-9. *The TCP maximum segment size defined in terms of the IP MTU and the TCP and IP header sizes.*

The MSS TCP option is used to communicate a receiver's MSS. The MSS TCP option is included only in TCP segments with the SYN flag set during the TCP connection establishment process. Figure 11-10 shows the MSS TCP option structure.

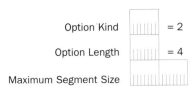

Figure 11-10. *The structure of the TCP Maximum Segment Size option.*

The fields in the TCP MSS option are defined as follows:

- **Option Kind** Set to 2 (0x02) to indicate the MSS option kind.
- **Option Length** Set to 4 (0x04) to indicate that the size of the entire TCP option is 4 bytes.
- **Maximum Segment Size** Two bytes that indicate the maximum receive-segment size of the sender of this TCP segment. For IP datagrams sent on an Ethernet network segment using Ethernet II encapsulation, the MSS is 1460 (an IP MTU of 1500 less 40 bytes for minimum-sized IP and TCP headers).

The following Network Monitor trace (Capture 11-02 in the \Captures folder on the companion CD-ROM) shows the MSS TCP option at the end of the TCP header for a SYN segment on an Ethernet network:

```
+ Frame: Base frame properties
+ ETHERNET: ETYPE = 0x0800 : Protocol = IP:  DOD Internet Protocol
+ IP: ID = 0x28EA; Proto = TCP; Len: 48
```

```
    TCP: ....S., len: 0, seq:3928116524-3928116524, ack: 0, win:16384, src: 1162
dst: 21 (FTP)
        TCP: Source Port = 0x048A
        TCP: Destination Port = FTP [control]
        TCP: Sequence Number = 3928116524 (0xEA224D2C)
        TCP: Acknowledgement Number = 0 (0x0)
        TCP: Data Offset = 28 (0x1C)
        TCP: Reserved = 0 (0x0000)
    +   TCP: Flags = 0x02 : ....S.
        TCP: Window = 16384 (0x4000)
        TCP: Checksum = 0x854E
        TCP: Urgent Pointer = 0 (0x0)
        TCP: Options
            TCP: Maximum Segment Size Option
                TCP: Option Type = Maximum Segment Size
                TCP: Option Length = 4 (0x4)
                TCP: Maximum Segment Size = 1460 (0x5B4)
            TCP: Option Nop = 1 (0x1)
            TCP: Option Nop = 1 (0x1)
        +   TCP: SACK Permitted Option
```

When two TCP peers exchange their MSS during the connection establishment process, both peers will adjust their initial MSS to the minimum value reported by both. For example, when an Ethernet node sends an MSS of 1460 and an FDDI node sends an MSS of 4312 (the FDDI IP MTU of 4352, less 40 octets), both nodes agree to send maximum-sized TCP segments of 1460 octets. The initial MSS is adjusted on an ongoing basis through Path MTU discovery. For example, two FDDI nodes on two separate FDDI rings—connected by routers over Ethernet network segments—exchange a TCP MSS of 4312. However, once TCP segments of 4312 octets are sent, Path Maximum Transmission Unit (PMTU) discovery messages will adjust the MSS for the connection to 1460. For more information on PMTU, see Chapter 7, "Internet Control Message Protocol (ICMP)."

The MSS TCP option won't prevent problems that could occur between two hosts on the same network segment that are separated by a Network Interface Layer technology with a lower IP MTU size. For example, consider hosts A and B in Figure 11-11. Hosts A and B are on separate FDDI rings connected by a Fast Ethernet backbone.

Both FDDI rings and the Ethernet backbone are on the same network segment as the router. Therefore, when hosts A and B exchange MSS, both agree to send maximum-sized TCP segments with the size of 4312 octets. However, when they begin to send bulk data with maximum-sized segments, the translating bridges implemented by the Layer 2 switches have no facilities for translating 4352-octet FDDI payloads to 1500-octet Ethernet payloads. Therefore, the Layer 2 switch silently drops the maximum-sized TCP segments. Because the switch isn't an IP router, no Path MTU discovery messages are sent to the TCP peers to lower the MSS. The connection fails after one peer retransmits a maximum-sized TCP segment for the maximum allowable times.

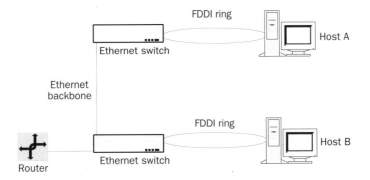

Figure 11-11. *Hosts on two FDDI rings, connected by an Ethernet backbone.*

If Host A were an FTP server and Host B were an FTP client, the user at Host B would be able to connect and log in to the FTP server. However, when the user issued a get or put instruction to send a file, the connection would hang and eventually terminate.

The only solution to this problem is to adjust the IP MTU on the FDDI nodes to the lowest value supported by all the Network Interface Layer technologies on the network segment. In this case, you would use the MTU Windows 2000 registry setting described in Chapter 4, "Internet Protocol (IP) Basics," to lower the IP MTU of the two FDDI adapters to 1500.

TCP Window Scale Option

The TCP window size defined in RFC 793 is a 16-bit field for a maximum receive-window size of 65,535 bytes. This means that a sender can have only 65,535 bytes of data in transit before having to wait for an acknowledgment. While this isn't an issue on typical LAN and WAN links, it's possible on newer LAN and WAN technologies operating at gigabit-per-second speeds with a sizeable transit delay to have more than 65,535 bytes in transit. If TCP can't fill the pipe and keep it filled, it's operating at less efficiency.

The TCP Window Scale option described in RFC 1323 allows the receiver to advertise a larger window size than 65,535 bytes. The Window Scale option includes a window scaling factor which, when combined with the 16-bit window size in the TCP header, increases the receive window size to a maximum of 1,073,725,440 bytes (1 gigabyte). The Window Size option is sent only in an SYN segment during the connection establishment process. Both TCP peers selectively indicate different window scaling factors used for their receive window sizes. The receiver of the TCP connection establishment request (the SYN segment) can't send a Window Scale option unless the initial SYN segment contains it.

Figure 11-12 illustrates the Window Scale TCP option structure.

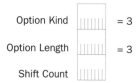

Option Kind = 3

Option Length = 3

Shift Count

Figure 11-12. *The structure of the TCP Window Scale option.*

The fields in the TCP Window Scale option are defined as follows:

- **Option Kind** Set to 3 (0x03) to indicate the Window Scale option kind.

- **Option Length** Set to 3 (0x03) to indicate that the size of the entire TCP option is 3 octets.

- **Shift Count** One byte that indicates the scaling factor as the exponent of 2. For example, for a Shift Count of 5, the scaling factor is 2^5, or 32. The exponent is used rather than a whole number so that implementations can take advantage of binary shift programming techniques to quickly calculate the actual window size. For example, for a Shift Count of 5, the actual window size is the value of the Window field with five 0s added (the Window field is left-shifted by 5). The maximum value of the Shift Count is 14 for a window scaling factor of 2^{14}, or 16,384.

The following Network Monitor trace (Capture 11-03 in the \Captures folder on the companion CD-ROM) shows the Window Scale TCP option at the end of the TCP header for a SYN segment:

```
+ Frame: Base frame properties
+ ETHERNET: ETYPE = 0x0800 : Protocol = IP:  DOD Internet Protocol
+ IP: ID = 0x2A1A; Proto = TCP; Len: 64
  TCP: ....S., len:    0, seq:   6727680-6727680, ack:        0, win:65528,
src: 1049  dst:    21 (FTP)
        TCP: Source Port = 0x0419
        TCP: Destination Port = FTP [control]
        TCP: Sequence Number = 6727680 (0x66A800)
        TCP: Acknowledgement Number = 0 (0x0)
        TCP: Data Offset = 44 (0x2C)
        TCP: Reserved = 0 (0x0000)
      + TCP: Flags = 0x02 : ....S.
        TCP: Window = 65528 (0xFFF8)
        TCP: Checksum = 0xBDC5
        TCP: Urgent Pointer = 0 (0x0)
        TCP: Options
          + TCP: Maximum Segment Size Option
            TCP: Option Nop = 1 (0x1)
            TCP: Window Scale Option
                TCP: Option Type = Window Scale
```

```
             TCP: Option Length = 3 (0x3)
             TCP: Window Scale = 3 (0x3)
        TCP: Option Nop = 1 (0x1)
        TCP: Option Nop = 1 (0x1)
      + TCP: Timestamps Option
        TCP: Option Nop = 1 (0x1)
        TCP: Option Nop = 1 (0x1)
      + TCP: SACK Permitted Option
```

Notice the use of the No-Operation TCP option (Nop) preceding the Window Scale option to align the Window Scale option on 4-byte boundaries.

When the Window Scale option is used, the window size advertised in each TCP segment for the connection is scaled by the factor indicated in the peer's SYN segment. Therefore, the TCP header's Window field is no longer a byte counter of the amount of space left in the receive buffer. Rather, the Window field is a block counter where the block size in bytes is the scaling factor. For example, for a TCP peer using a Shift Count of 3, the Window field in outgoing TCP segments is actually indicating the number of 8-byte blocks remaining in the receive buffer.

The use of scaling windows is controlled through the following Windows 2000 registry setting:

Tcp1323Opts

```
Key:HKEY_LOCAL_MACHINE\SYSTEM\CurrentControlSet\Services\Tcpip\Parameters
Value type: REG_DWORD
Valid range: 0-3
Default: 3
Present by default: No
```

Set this value to 0 to disable both window scaling and timestamps. Set this value to 1 to enable only window scaling. Set this value to 2 to only enable timestamps. Set this value to 3 to enable both window scaling and timestamps. The default value is 3.

Note   When tracing TCP connection data, make sure that you also look at the connection establishment process to determine whether window scaling is being used. Otherwise, you might misinterpret the Window field value during the connection.

Selective Acknowledgment Option

The acknowledgment scheme for TCP was originally designed as a positive cumulative acknowledgment scheme where the receiver sends a segment with the ACK flag set and the Acknowledgment field set to the next octet the receiver expects to receive. This use of the Acknowledgment field provides an acknowledgment of all bytes up to, but not including, the sequence number in the Acknowledgment field. This scheme provides reliable byte-stream data transfer, but can result in lower TCP throughput in environments with high-packet losses.

If a segment at the beginning of the current send window isn't received and all other segments are, the data received can't be acknowledged until the missing segment arrives. The sender will begin to retransmit the segments of the current send window until the acknowledgment for all the segments received has arrived. The sender will needlessly retransmit some segments, consequently wasting network bandwidth. This problem is exacerbated in environments such as satellite links, with high bandwidth and high delay, when TCP has a large window size. The more segments in the send window, the more segments can be retransmitted unnecessarily when segments are lost.

RFC 2018 describes a method of selective acknowledgment (SACK) using TCP options that selectively acknowledges the non-contiguous data blocks that have been received. When the sender receives a selective acknowledgment, it can retransmit just the missing blocks, preventing the sender from waiting for the retransmission time-out for the unacknowledged segments and retransmitting segments that have successfully arrived.

The selective acknowledgment scheme defines the following two different TCP options:

- The SACK-Permitted option to negotiate the use of selective acknowledgments during the connection establishment process.
- The SACK option to indicate the non-contiguous data blocks that have been received.

More Info Selective acknowledgment (SACK) is described in RFC 2018, which can be found in the \RFC folder on the companion CD-ROM.

The SACK-Permitted Option

The SACK-Permitted option is sent in segments with the SYN flag set and indicates that the TCP peer can receive and interpret the SACK option once data is flowing on the connection. The SACK-Permitted option is 2 bytes consisting of an Option Kind set to 4 (0x04) and an Option Length set to 2 (0x02), as shown in Figure 11-13.

Option Kind = 4

Option Length = 2

Figure 11-13. *The structure of the TCP SACK-Permitted option.*

The following Network Monitor trace (Capture 11-04 in the \Captures folder on the companion CD-ROM) shows the TCP SACK-Permitted option at the end of the TCP header for a SYN segment:

```
+ Frame: Base frame properties
+ ETHERNET: ETYPE = 0x0800 : Protocol = IP:  DOD Internet Protocol
+ IP: ID = 0x28EA; Proto = TCP; Len: 48
```

```
   TCP: ....S., len: 0, seq:3928116524-3928116524, ack: 0, win:16384, src: 1162
dst: 21 (FTP)
      TCP: Source Port = 0x048A
      TCP: Destination Port = FTP [control]
      TCP: Sequence Number = 3928116524 (0xEA224D2C)
      TCP: Acknowledgement Number = 0 (0x0)
      TCP: Data Offset = 28 (0x1C)
      TCP: Reserved = 0 (0x0000)
    + TCP: Flags = 0x02 : ....S.
      TCP: Window = 16384 (0x4000)
      TCP: Checksum = 0x854E
      TCP: Urgent Pointer = 0 (0x0)
      TCP: Options
        + TCP: Maximum Segment Size Option
          TCP: Option Nop = 1 (0x1)
          TCP: Option Nop = 1 (0x1)
          TCP: SACK Permitted Option
              TCP: Option Type = Sack Permitted
              TCP: Option Length = 2 (0x2)
```

Notice the use of the two No-Operation TCP option (Nop) fields preceding the SACK-Permitted option to align the SACK-Permitted option on 4-byte boundaries.

The SACK Option

The SACK option is sent as needed in segments of the open connection with the ACK flag set. As Figure 11-14 illustrates, the SACK option is a variable-size option, depending on how many contiguous blocks are being acknowledged.

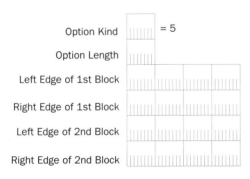

Figure 11-14. *The structure of the TCP SACK option.*

The fields in the TCP SACK option are defined as follows:

- **Option Kind**   Set to 5 (0x05) to indicate the SACK option kind.

- **Option Length**   Set to 10 (a single non-contiguous block), 18 (two non-contiguous blocks), 26 (three non-contiguous blocks), or 34 (four non-contiguous blocks) octets to indicate the size of the entire TCP option.
- **Left Edge of Nth Block**   A 4-byte field that indicates the sequence number of this block's first octet.
- **Right Edge of Nth Block**   A 4-byte field that indicates the next sequence number expected to be received immediately following this block.

The following Network Monitor trace (Capture 11-05 in the \Captures folder on the companion CD-ROM) shows the SACK TCP option at the end of the TCP header for data being acknowledged:

```
+ Frame: Base frame properties
+ ETHERNET: ETYPE = 0x0800 : Protocol = IP:  DOD Internet Protocol
+ IP: ID = 0xFA0D; Proto = TCP; Len: 64
  TCP: .A...., len:    0, seq:    925293-925293, ack:  55053434, win:32767,
src: 1242  dst:  139 (NBT Session)
        TCP: Source Port = 0x04DA
        TCP: Destination Port = NETBIOS Session Service
        TCP: Sequence Number = 925293 (0xE1E6D)
        TCP: Acknowledgement Number = 55053434 (0x3480C7A)
        TCP: Data Offset = 44 (0x2C)
        TCP: Reserved = 0 (0x0000)
      + TCP: Flags = 0x10 : .A....
        TCP: Window = 32767 (0x7FFF)
        TCP: Checksum = 0x436E
        TCP: Urgent Pointer = 0 (0x0)
        TCP: Options
            TCP: Option Nop = 1 (0x1)
            TCP: Option Nop = 1 (0x1)
          + TCP: Timestamps Option
            TCP: Option Nop = 1 (0x1)
            TCP: Option Nop = 1 (0x1)
            TCP: SACK Option
                TCP: Option Type = SACK
                TCP: Option Length = 10 (0xA)
                TCP: Left Edge of Block  = 55054882 (0x3481222)
                TCP: Right Edge of Block = 55059226 (0x348231A)
```

In the trace, the sender of this segment is acknowledging the receipt of all contiguous octets in the byte stream up to, but not including, octet 55053434, and the receipt of the block of contiguous data from octets 55054882 through 55059225. There's a missing segment consisting of the octets 55053434 through 55054881. Notice the use of the Nop to align the SACK option on 4-byte boundaries.

The use of SACK is controlled through the following Windows 2000 registry setting:

SackOpts
```
Key:HKEY_LOCAL_MACHINE\SYSTEM\CurrentControlSet\Services\Tcpip\Parameters
Value type: REG_DWORD
Valid range: 0-1
Default: 1
Present by default: No
```

SackOpts either enables (=1) or disables (=0) the use of SACK. SackOpts is enabled by default.

For more information on the use of selective acknowledgments to retransmit data, see Chapter 14, "Transmission Control Protocol (TCP) Retransmission and Time-Out."

TCP Timestamps Option

To set the retransmission time-out (RTO) on TCP segments sent, TCP monitors the round-trip time (RTT) on an ongoing basis. Normally, TCP calculates the RTT of a TCP segment and its acknowledgment once for every full send window of data. While this works well in many environments, for high-bandwidth and high-delay environments such as satellite links with large window sizes, the sampling rate of one segment for each window size can't monitor the RTT to determine the current RTO and prevent unnecessary retransmissions.

To calculate the RTT on any TCP segment, the segment is sent with the TCP Timestamps option described in RFC 1323. The TCP Timestamps option places a timestamp value based on a local clock on an outgoing TCP segment. The acknowledgment for the data in the TCP segment echoes back the timestamp, and the RTT can be calculated from the segment's echoed timestamp and the time (relative to the local clock) that the segment acknowledgment arrived.

More Info The TCP Timestamps option is described in RFC 1323, which can be found in the \RFC folder on the companion CD-ROM.

Including the Timestamps option in the SYN segment during the connection establishment process indicates its use for the connection. Both sides of the TCP connection can selectively use timestamps. Once indicated during connection establishment, the timestamp can be included in TCP segments at the discretion of the sending TCP peer.

Figure 11-15 shows the TCP Timestamps option structure.

The fields in the TCP Timestamps option are defined as follows:

- **Option Kind** Set to 8 (0x08) to indicate the Timestamps option kind.
- **Option Length** Set to 10 (0x0A) to indicate that the size of the entire TCP option is 10 octets.
- **TS Value** A 4-byte field that indicates the timestamp value of this TCP segment. The TS Value is calculated from an internal clock that's based on real time. The TS Value increases over time and wraps around when needed.

- **TS Echo Reply** A 4-byte field set on a TCP segment that acknowledges data received (with the ACK flag set) that's set to the same value as the TS Value for the received segment being acknowledged. In other words, the TS Echo Reply is an echo of the TS Value of the acknowledged segment.

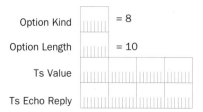

Figure 11-15. *The structure of the TCP Timestamps option.*

Figure 11-16 illustrates an example of the values of the TS Value and TS Echo Reply for an exchange of data between two hosts.

Host A

1 Block 1, TS Value = 100, TS Echo Reply = 9000

2 Ack on Block 1, TS Value = 9020, TS Echo Reply = 100

3 Block 2, TS Value = 158, TS Echo Reply = 9020

4 Ack on Block 2, TS Value = 9053, TS Echo Reply = 158

5 Block 3, TS Value = 9098, TS Echo Reply = 158

6 Ack on Block 3, TS Value = 210, TS Echo Reply = 9098

Host B

Figure 11-16. *An example of the use of the TCP Timestamps option.*

Host A's internal clock starts its TS Value at 100. Host B's internal clock starts its TS Value at 9000. Segments 1 through 4 are for two data blocks sent by Host A. Segments 5 and 6 are for a data block sent by Host B. Notice how the TS Echo Reply value for the acknowledgments are set to the TS Value of the segments they're acknowledging. To prevent gaps in the sending of data from increasing the RTT, the TS Echo Reply is used for RTT measurement only if the segment is an acknowledgment of new data sent.

The following Network Monitor trace (Capture 11-06 in the \Captures folder on the companion CD-ROM) shows two frames—a frame of data containing the Timestamps TCP option and its corresponding acknowledgment:

```
+ Frame: Base frame properties
+ ETHERNET: ETYPE = 0x0800 : Protocol = IP:  DOD Internet Protocol
+ IP: ID = 0x1A15; Proto = TCP; Len: 1500
  TCP: .A....., len: 1448, seq:  55050538-55051986, ack: 925293, win:16564,
src:  139 (NBT Session) dst: 1242
```

```
      TCP: Source Port = NETBIOS Session Service
      TCP: Destination Port = 0x04DA
      TCP: Sequence Number = 55050538 (0x348012A)
      TCP: Acknowledgement Number = 925293 (0xE1E6D)
      TCP: Data Offset = 32 (0x20)
      TCP: Reserved = 0 (0x0000)
  +   TCP: Flags = 0x10 : .A....
      TCP: Window = 16564 (0x40B4)
      TCP: Checksum = 0xBD81
      TCP: Urgent Pointer = 0 (0x0)
      TCP: Options
          TCP: Option Nop = 1 (0x1)
          TCP: Option Nop = 1 (0x1)
          TCP: Timestamps Option
              TCP: Option Type = Timestamps
              TCP: Option Length = 10 (0xA)
              TCP: Timestamp = 4677 (0x1245)
              TCP: Reply Timestamp = 7114 (0x1BCA)
      TCP: Data: Number of data bytes remaining = 1448 (0x05A8)
+ NBT: SS: Session Message Cont., 1448 Bytes
```

```
+ Frame: Base frame properties
+ ETHERNET: ETYPE = 0x0800 : Protocol = IP:  DOD Internet Protocol
+ IP: ID = 0xF60D; Proto = TCP; Len: 52
  TCP: .A...., len:    0, seq:    925293-925293, ack:  55051986, win:32722,
src: 1242  dst:  139 (NBT Session)
      TCP: Source Port = 0x04DA
      TCP: Destination Port = NETBIOS Session Service
      TCP: Sequence Number = 925293 (0xE1E6D)
      TCP: Acknowledgement Number = 55051986 (0x34806D2)
      TCP: Data Offset = 32 (0x20)
      TCP: Reserved = 0 (0x0000)
  +   TCP: Flags = 0x10 : .A....
      TCP: Window = 32722 (0x7FD2)
      TCP: Checksum = 0x84D1
      TCP: Urgent Pointer = 0 (0x0)
      TCP: Options
          TCP: Option Nop = 1 (0x1)
          TCP: Option Nop = 1 (0x1)
          TCP: Timestamps Option
              TCP: Option Type = Timestamps
              TCP: Option Length = 10 (0xA)
              TCP: Timestamp = 7126 (0x1BD6)
              TCP: Reply Timestamp = 4677 (0x1245)
```

Notice that in the second frame the Reply Timestamp (TS Echo Reply) field is set to 4677, echoing the Timestamp (TS Value) field.

The use of TCP timestamps for Windows 2000 is controlled through the Tcp1323Opts registry setting discussed in the "TCP Window Scale Option" section of this chapter.

For more information on RTT, RTO, and retransmission behavior, see Chapter 14, " Transmission Control Protocol (TCP) Retransmission and Time-Out."

Summary

TCP provides connection-oriented and reliable data transfer for applications that require end-to-end guaranteed delivery service. Application Layer protocols use TCP for one-to-one traffic. The TCP header provides sequencing, acknowledgment, a checksum, and the identification of source and destination port numbers to multiplex TCP segment data to the proper Application Layer protocol. TCP options are used to indicate maximum segment sizes and window scaling and provide selective acknowledgments and timestamping.

Chapter 12
Transmission Control Protocol (TCP) Connections

TCP is a connection-oriented protocol. Before data can flow on a TCP connection, the connection must be formally established through a handshaking process. To stop the flow of data on a TCP connection and release the resources of the connection, the connection must be terminated through a similar handshake process.

The TCP Connection

A TCP connection is a bi-directional, full-duplex logical circuit between two processes (Application Layer protocols) in an Internet Protocol (IP) internetwork. The TCP connection's endpoints are identified by an [IP address, TCP port] pair. The connection is uniquely identified by both endpoints: [IP address 1, TCP port 1, IP address 2, TCP port 2]. TCP uses those four numbers to demultiplex the data portion of the TCP segment to the proper Application Layer process.

A TCP connection can be visualized as a bi-directional data pipe containing two logical pipes between the two TCP peers, as Figure 12-1 illustrates. One logical pipe is used for outbound data and the other logical pipe is used for inbound data (relative to the TCP peer). The outbound data pipe for one TCP peer is the inbound data pipe for the other TCP peer.

Figure 12-1. *A TCP connection showing both inbound and outbound logical pipes.*

TCP connections must be:

- Established through a handshake process where both TCP peers agree to create a TCP connection
- Maintained through a periodic keep-alive process that ensures that both TCP peers are active on the connection
- Terminated through a handshake process where both TCP peers agree to close the TCP connection

TCP Connection Establishment

To create a TCP connection over which full-duplex data can begin to flow, each TCP peer must learn the following information from the other TCP peer:

- The starting sequence number for data sent on the inbound pipe
- The size of the buffer to receive data sent on the outbound pipe (the receive window size of the other TCP peer)
- The maximum segment size that can be received
- The TCP options that are supported

Learning this information is done through an exchange of three TCP segments called the TCP connection establishment process, or the TCP three-way handshake.

To create a TCP connection, a server system must allow a TCP connection, and a client system must initiate a TCP connection. The server system issues a passive OPEN function call to permit incoming connection requests on a specific port number. The passive OPEN function call does not create any TCP traffic. The client system issues an active OPEN function call. An active OPEN function call creates and sends the first segment of the TCP three-way handshake.

Figure 12-2 displays the TCP connection establishment process. The diagram shows the three TCP segments that are exchanged and the information in the TCP header that is vital to the connection establishment. Prior to segment 1, TCP Peer 2 issued a passive OPEN to receive TCP connection requests. TCP Peer 1 issues an active OPEN and creates segment 1. Segments 2 and 3 complete the connection establishment process. The vertical arrows show the passage of time during the connection establishment process.

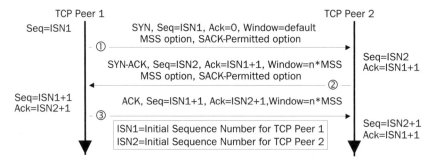

Figure 12-2. *The TCP connection establishment process showing the exchange of three TCP segments.*

Segment 1: The Synchronize (SYN) Segment

TCP Peer 1 sends the first TCP segment, known as the SYN segment, to TCP Peer 2. The SYN segment then establishes TCP connection parameters, such as the Initial Sequence

Number (ISN) that TCP Peer 1 uses. The SYN segment as sent by a Microsoft Windows 2000 computer contains the following fields in the TCP header:

- **Destination Port**   Set to the TCP port number of the passive OPEN on TCP Peer 2. For typical TCP connections, the destination port in the SYN segment is a well-known TCP port in the range of 1 to 1023.

- **Source Port**   Set to the local TCP port number of the active OPEN on TCP Peer 1. For typical TCP connections, the source port is a dynamically allocated port in the range of 1024 to 5000.

- **Sequence Number**   Set to the ISN for data to be sent by TCP Peer 1 for the outbound data pipe (ISN1 in Figure 12-2). A Windows 2000 TCP peer chooses the ISN based on a startup-derived, 2048-bit random key and an RC4-based random number to reduce the predictability of the next TCP connection's ISN.

- **Acknowledgment Number**   Set to 0. Because the ACK flag is not set, the Acknowledgment Number field is insignificant. Only after a TCP peer learns the sequence number for inbound data on the connection can the ACK flag be set and the Acknowledgment Number field set to the appropriate value.

- **SYN Flag**   Indicates that the segment contains the ISN for data sent by TCP Peer 1.

- **Window**   Set to a default value, indicating an initial value for the size of TCP Peer 1's receive buffer.

- **MSS in the MSS TCP Option**   Set to the maximum-sized TCP segment that TCP Peer 1 can receive.

- **Selective Acknowledgment (SACK)-Permitted TCP Option**   Included to indicate that TCP Peer 1 can receive and interpret the SACK option included in TCP segments that TCP Peer 2 sends.

The following Network Monitor trace (Capture 12-01, included in the \Captures folder on the companion CD-ROM) shows a SYN segment for a File Transfer Protocol (FTP) session:

```
+ ETHERNET: ETYPE = 0x0800 : Protocol = IP:  DOD Internet Protocol
+ IP: ID = 0x28EA; Proto = TCP; Len: 48
  TCP: ....S., len: 0, seq:3928116524-3928116524, ack: 0, win:16384, src: 1162
dst: 21 (FTP)
      TCP: Source Port = 0x048A
      TCP: Destination Port = FTP [control]
      TCP: Sequence Number = 3928116524 (0xEA224D2C)
      TCP: Acknowledgement Number = 0 (0x0)
      TCP: Data Offset = 28 (0x1C)
      TCP: Reserved = 0 (0x0000)
      TCP: Flags = 0x02 : ....S.
          TCP: ..0..... = No urgent data
          TCP: ...0.... = Acknowledgement field not significant
          TCP: ....0... = No Push function
          TCP: .....0.. = No Reset
```

```
        TCP: ......1. = Synchronize sequence numbers
        TCP: .......0 = No Fin
TCP: Window = 16384 (0x4000)
TCP: Checksum = 0x854E
TCP: Urgent Pointer = 0 (0x0)
TCP: Options
    TCP: Maximum Segment Size Option
        TCP: Option Type = Maximum Segment Size
        TCP: Option Length = 4 (0x4)
        TCP: Maximum Segment Size = 1460 (0x5B4)
    TCP: Option Nop = 1 (0x1)
    TCP: Option Nop = 1 (0x1)
    TCP: SACK Permitted Option
        TCP: Option Type = Sack Permitted
        TCP: Option Length = 2 (0x2)
```

Segment 2: The SYN-ACK Segment

Upon receipt of the SYN segment, TCP Peer 2 sends the second TCP segment known as the SYN-ACK segment to TCP Peer 1. The SYN-ACK segment establishes TCP connection parameters such as the ISN used by TCP Peer 2 and acknowledges TCP connection parameters used by TCP Peer 1. The SYN-ACK segment as sent by a Windows 2000 computer contains the following fields in the TCP header:

- **Destination Port**   Set to the Source Port of the SYN segment.

- **Source Port**   Set to the local TCP port number of the passive OPEN on TCP Peer 2 as indicated by the Destination Port number of the SYN segment.

- **Sequence Number**   Set to the ISN for data to be sent by TCP Peer 2 for the outbound data pipe (ISN2 in Figure 12-2).

- **Acknowledgment Number**   Set to the value of the TCP Peer 1's ISN plus 1 (ISN1 + 1). The SYN flag occupies a single octet of the sequence space of Peer 1. The acknowledgment number is the next octet in the byte stream that TCP Peer 2 expects to receive. If the SYN flag acts as a single octet of non-data, the next octet that TCP Peer 2 expects to receive is actual data, and must therefore begin with ISN1 + 1.

- **SYN Flag**   Indicates that the segment contains the ISN for data sent by TCP Peer 2.

- **ACK Flag**   Indicates that the Acknowledgment Number field is significant.

- **Window**   Set to an application-specified value or the value of an integral number of MSS-sized segments according to an operating system default value. This value indicates an initial value for the size of TCP Peer 2's receive buffer (n*MSS in Figure 12-2). For Windows 2000 TCP/IP hosts using Ethernet, the default receive-window size is 17,520 octets, or 12 MSS segments (at 1460 octets).

- **MSS in the MSS TCP Option**   Set to the maximum-sized TCP segment that TCP Peer 2 can receive.
- **SACK-Permitted TCP Option**   Indicates that TCP Peer 2 can receive and interpret the SACK option included in TCP segments that TCP Peer 1 sends.

The following Network Monitor trace (Capture 12-01, included in the \Captures folder on the companion CD-ROM) shows a SYN-ACK segment for an FTP session (continued from the previous ACK segment):

```
+ ETHERNET: ETYPE = 0x0800 : Protocol = IP:  DOD Internet Protocol
+ IP: ID = 0xDFAB; Proto = TCP; Len: 48
  TCP: .A..S., len:    0, seq:1035688768-1035688768, ack:3928116525,
win:17520, src:   21 (FTP) dst: 1162
        TCP: Source Port = FTP [control]
        TCP: Destination Port = 0x048A
        TCP: Sequence Number = 1035688768 (0x3DBB5B40)
        TCP: Acknowledgement Number = 3928116525 (0xEA224D2D)
        TCP: Data Offset = 28 (0x1C)
        TCP: Reserved = 0 (0x0000)
        TCP: Flags = 0x12 : .A..S.
            TCP: ..0..... = No urgent data
            TCP: ...1.... = Acknowledgement field significant
            TCP: ....0... = No Push function
            TCP: .....0.. = No Reset
            TCP: ......1. = Synchronize sequence numbers
            TCP: .......0 = No Fin
        TCP: Window = 17520 (0x4470)
        TCP: Checksum = 0xE7D1
        TCP: Urgent Pointer = 0 (0x0)
        TCP: Options
            TCP: Maximum Segment Size Option
                TCP: Option Type = Maximum Segment Size
                TCP: Option Length = 4 (0x4)
                TCP: Maximum Segment Size = 1460 (0x5B4)
            TCP: Option Nop = 1 (0x1)
            TCP: Option Nop = 1 (0x1)
            TCP: SACK Permitted Option
                TCP: Option Type = Sack Permitted
                TCP: Option Length = 2 (0x2)
```

Segment 3: The ACK Segment

Upon receipt of the SYN-ACK segment, TCP Peer 1 sends the third TCP segment, known as the ACK segment, to TCP Peer 2. The ACK segment establishes final TCP connection parameters used by TCP Peer 1 and acknowledges TCP connection parameters that TCP

Peer 2 uses. The ACK segment, as sent by a Windows 2000 computer, contains the following fields in the TCP header:

- **Destination Port**   Set to the Source Port of the SYN-ACK segment.
- **Source Port**   Set to the local TCP port number of the active OPEN on TCP Peer 1 as indicated by the Destination Port number of the SYN-ACK segment.
- **Sequence Number**   Set to ISN1 + 1.
- **Acknowledgment Number**   Set to the value of the TCP Peer 2's ISN plus 1 (ISN2 +1). The SYN flag occupies a single octet of the sequence space of TCP Peer 2. The acknowledgment number is the next octet in the byte stream that TCP Peer 1 expects to receive. If the SYN flag is acting as a single octet of non-data, the next octet that TCP Peer 1 expects to receive is actual data, and must therefore begin with ISN2 + 1.
- **ACK Flag**   Indicates that the Acknowledgment Number field is significant.
- **Window**   Set to an application-specified value, or the value of an integral number of MSS-sized segments, according to an operating system default value. This value indicates an initial value for the size of TCP Peer 1's receive buffer (n*MSS in Figure 12-2). For Windows 2000 TCP/IP hosts using Ethernet, the default receive-window size is 17,520 octets, or 12 MSS segments (at 1460 octets).

The following Network Monitor trace (Capture 12-01, included in the \Captures folder on the companion CD-ROM) shows an ACK segment for an FTP session (continued from the previous SYN-ACK segment):

```
+ ETHERNET: ETYPE = 0x0800 : Protocol = IP:  DOD Internet Protocol
+ IP: ID = 0x28EB; Proto = TCP; Len: 40
  TCP: .A...., len:    0, seq:3928116525-3928116525, ack:1035688769,
win:17520, src: 1162  dst:   21 (FTP)
        TCP: Source Port = 0x048A
        TCP: Destination Port = FTP [control]
        TCP: Sequence Number = 3928116525 (0xEA224D2D)
        TCP: Acknowledgement Number = 1035688769 (0x3DBB5B41)
        TCP: Data Offset = 20 (0x14)
        TCP: Reserved = 0 (0x0000)
        TCP: Flags = 0x10 : .A....
            TCP: ..0..... = No urgent data
            TCP: ...1.... = Acknowledgement field significant
            TCP: ....0... = No Push function
            TCP: .....0.. = No Reset
            TCP: ......0. = No Synchronize
            TCP: .......0 = No Fin
        TCP: Window = 17520 (0x4470)
        TCP: Checksum = 0x1496
        TCP: Urgent Pointer = 0 (0x0)
```

Result of TCP Connection Establishment Process

The results of the TCP connection establishment process are that:

- Each TCP peer knows the sequence number of the first octet of data to be sent on the connection (TCP Peer 1's Acknowledgment Number field is set to TCP Peer 2's Sequence Number field; TCP Peer 2's Acknowledgment Number field is set to TCP Peer 1's Sequence Number field).

- Each TCP peer knows the MSS that can be sent on the connection. The connection's MSS is the minimum of the two MSSs advertised by TCP Peer 1 and TCP Peer 2. Path Maximum Transmission Unit (PMTU) discovery adjusts the initial MSS for the duration of connection. For more information on PMTU discovery, see Chapter 7, "Internet Control Message Protocol (ICMP)."

- Each TCP peer knows the size of the other peer's receive buffer (the window size) indicating the maximum amount of data that can be sent without waiting for an ACK and updated window size. Although a large amount of data can be sent, TCP peers use the slow start and congestion avoidance algorithms to slowly scale the amount of data sent to avoid congesting the internetwork.

- Each TCP peer is aware that the other peer is capable of receiving SACKs using the SACK TCP option. For more information on SACK, see Chapter 13, "Transmission Control Protocol (TCP) Data Flow."

Microsoft Windows 2000 Registry Settings for TCP Connections

The TCP connection establishment process is controlled by the following Windows 2000 registry settings:

TcpMaxConnectRetransmissions

```
Location: HKEY_LOCAL_MACHINE\SYSTEM\CurrentControlSet\Services\Tcpip\Parameters
Data type: REG_DWORD
Valid range: 0-255
Default value: 2
Present by default: No
```

TcpMaxConnectRetransmissions sets how many SYN segment retransmissions are sent when attempting to establish a TCP connection. The retransmission time-out is doubled between each retransmission. With the initial retransmission time-out of 3 seconds and the default value of TcpMaxConnectRetransmissions of 2, it takes 21 seconds to time out a TCP connection attempt (initial SYN, wait 3 seconds, first retransmitted SYN, wait 6 seconds, second transmitted SYN, wait 12 seconds).

The following summary of a Network Monitor trace (Capture 12-02, included in the \Captures folder on the companion CD-ROM) shows this behavior:

```
1 0.000  TCP_Peer_1  Intel 123456  TCP  ....S., len:  0, seq: 748701-748704, ack: 0
2 2.923  TCP_Peer_1  Intel 123456  TCP  ....S., len:  0, seq: 748701-748704, ack:0
3 6.009  TCP_Peer_1  Intel 123456  TCP  ....S., len:  0, seq: 748701-748704, ack:0
```

This summary trace displays the elapsed time between successive frames.

TcpNumConnections

```
Location: HKEY_LOCAL_MACHINE\SYSTEM\CurrentControlSet\Services\Tcpip\Parameters
Data type: REG_DWORD
Valid range: 0-0xFFFFFE
Default value: 0xFFFFFE
Present by default: No
```

TcpNumConnections sets the maximum number of TCP connections that can be open. By default, 16,777,214 (0xFFFFFE) connections can be open.

TCP Half-Open Connections

A TCP half-open connection is a TCP connection that has not completed the connection establishment process. A SYN segment has been received and an SYN-ACK has been sent, but the final ACK has not been received. Until the final ACK is received, data cannot be sent on the connection. Figure 12-3 illustrates the TCP half-open connection.

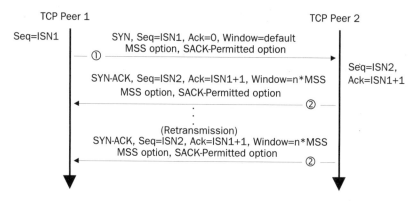

Figure 12-3. *A TCP half-open connection showing the SYN segment and retransmissions of the SYN-ACK segment.*

While the SYN-ACK segment contains no data, the SYN flag occupies a single byte of the sequence space and is treated as data. Therefore, TCP retransmission and time-out behaviors used for recovering from lost data are used to recover from a lost SYN-ACK segment. In the case of retransmitting an SYN-ACK segment, the default time-out is 3 seconds and the SYN-ACK is retransmitted twice by default. Therefore, the first SYN-ACK is sent; 3 seconds later the first retransmission is sent; and 6 seconds later the second retransmission is sent. After waiting 12 seconds for a response to the final retransmission, the connection is abandoned and the memory and the connection's internal table entries are released. A total of 21 seconds elapse from the time the first SYN-ACK is sent to when the connection is abandoned.

The SYN Attack

The SYN attack is a denial-of-service attack that exploits the retransmission and time-out behavior of the SYN-ACK to create a large number of half-open connections. Depending on the TCP/IP protocol implementation, a large number of half-open connections could do any of the following:

- Use all available memory.
- Use all possible entries in the TCP Transmission Control Block (TCB), an internal table used to track TCP connections. Once the half-open connections use all the entries, further connection attempts are responded to with a TCP connection reset. TCP connection resets are discussed in the "TCP Connection Reset" section of this chapter.
- Use all available half-open connections. Once all the half-open connections are used, further connection attempts are responded to with a TCP connection reset.

To create a large number of TCP half-open connections, malicious users send a large number of SYN segments from a spoofed IP address and TCP port number. The spoofed IP address and TCP port number are for a process that will not respond to the SYN-ACKs being sent by the attacked host. SYN attacks typically are used to render Internet servers inoperative.

To see a SYN attack in progress on a Windows 2000 host, use the NETSTAT command to display the active TCP connections. For example:

```
c:\>netstat -n -p tcp
  Active Connections
     Proto  Local Address      Foreign Address      State
     TCP    127.0.0.1:1030     127.0.0.1:1032       ESTABLISHED
     TCP    127.0.0.1:1032     127.0.0.1:1030       ESTABLISHED
     TCP    10.1.1.5:21        192.168.0.1:1025     SYN_RECEIVED
     TCP    10.1.1.5:21        192.168.0.1:1026     SYN_RECEIVED
     TCP    10.1.1.5:21        192.168.0.1:1027     SYN_RECEIVED
     TCP    10.1.1.5:21        192.168.0.1:1028     SYN_RECEIVED
     TCP    10.1.1.5:21        192.168.0.1:1029     SYN_RECEIVED
     TCP    10.1.1.5:21        192.168.0.1:1030     SYN_RECEIVED
     TCP    10.1.1.5:21        192.168.0.1:1031     SYN_RECEIVED
     TCP    10.1.1.5:21        192.168.0.1:1032     SYN_RECEIVED
     TCP    10.1.1.5:21        192.168.0.1:1033     SYN_RECEIVED
     TCP    10.1.1.5:21        192.168.0.1:1034     SYN_RECEIVED
     TCP    10.1.1.5:21        192.168.0.1:1035     SYN_RECEIVED
```

This is an example of a SYN attack. There are a number of TCP connections in the SYN_RECEIVED state, and the foreign address is a spoofed private address with incrementally increasing TCP port numbers. The SYN_RECEIVED is the state of a TCP connection that has received a SYN, sent a SYN-ACK, and is waiting for the final ACK. TCP connection states are discussed in greater detail later in the "TCP Connection States" section of this chapter.

Windows 2000 TCP/IP has been modified from previous versions to detect and defend against a SYN attack in progress by using the following registry settings:

TcpMaxConnectResponseRetransmissions

```
Location: HKEY_LOCAL_MACHINE\SYSTEM\CurrentControlSet\Services\Tcpip\Parameters
Data type: REG_DWORD
Valid range: 0-255
Default value: 2
Present by default: No
```

TcpMaxConnectResponseRetransmissions sets the number of retransmissions of a SYN-ACK for half-open connections. For values greater than 1, TCP/IP uses SYN attack protection.

SynAttackProtect

```
Location: HKEY_LOCAL_MACHINE\SYSTEM\CurrentControlSet\Services\
Tcpip\Parameters
Data type: REG_DWORD
Valid range: 0-1
Default value: 0
Present by default: No
```

SynAttackProtect either enables (=1) or disables (=0) SYN attack protection. When enabled, half-open connections time out more quickly if a SYN attack is detected.

TcpMaxHalfOpen

```
Location: HKEY_LOCAL_MACHINE\SYSTEM\CurrentControlSet\Services\Tcpip\Parameters
Data type: REG_DWORD
Valid range: 100-65535
Default value: 100 for Windows 2000 Server, 500 for Windows 2000 Professional
Present by default: No
```

TcpMaxHalfOpen sets the maximum number of TCP connections in the SYN_RECEIVED state before SYN attack protection takes effect.

TcpMaxHalfOpenRetried

```
Location: HKEY_LOCAL_MACHINE\SYSTEM\CurrentControlSet\Services\Tcpip\Parameters
Data type: REG_DWORD
Valid range: 80-65535
Default value: 80 for Windows 2000 Server, 400 for Windows 2000 Professional
Present by default: No
```

TcpMaxHalfOpenRetried sets the maximum number of TCP connections in the SYN_RECEIVED state for which at least one retransmission has been sent before SYN attack protection takes effect.

TcpMaxPortsExhausted
Location: HKEY_LOCAL_MACHINE\SYSTEM\CurrentControlSet\Services\Tcpip\Parameters
Data type: REG_DWORD
Valid range: 0-65535
Default value: 5
Present by default: No

TcpMaxPortsExhausted sets the maximum number of TCP connection requests that have been refused before SYN attack protection takes effect.

TCP Connection Maintenance

A TCP connection can be maintained through the periodic exchange of a TCP keepalive segment. A TCP keepalive segment is an ACK segment containing no data. The Sequence Number field in the TCP header of the keepalive segment is set to 1 less than the current sequence number for the outbound data stream. For example, if a TCP peer's next octet of data is 18745323, the TCP keepalive sent by the TCP peer has the Sequence Number field set to 18745322.

Upon receiving this ACK segment, the other TCP peer sends back an ACK segment with the Acknowledgment Number field set to the next octet that it expects to receive. In this example, the TCP peer sends an ACK segment with the Acknowledgment Number field set to 18745323. This simple exchange confirms that both TCP peers are still participating in the TCP connection.

Figure 12-4 shows the TCP keepalive.

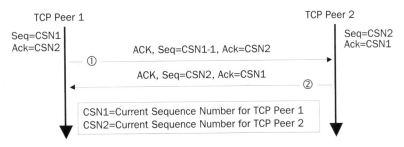

Figure 12-4. *A TCP keepalive showing the sending of an exchange of ACK segments to confirm both ends of the connection are still present.*

Windows 2000 TCP keepalives are disabled by default. If enabled through the use of the *setsockopt()* Windows Sockets function, a keepalive segment is sent every 2 hours by default, as controlled by the KeepAliveTime registry setting. Even if enabled, other upper layer protocols such as NetBIOS send their own keepalive. If the keepalive interval that the upper layer protocol uses is less than the TCP keepalive interval, TCP keepalives are never sent. For example, NetBIOS sessions over TCP/IP send a NetBIOS keepalive every 60 minutes. Therefore, TCP keepalives enabled for a NetBIOS session are never used.

The following Windows 2000 registry settings control TCP keepalive behavior:

KeepAliveTime

```
Location: HKEY_LOCAL_MACHINE\SYSTEM\CurrentControlSet\Services\Tcpip\Parameters
Data type: REG_DWORD
Valid range: 0-0xFFFFFFFF
Default value: 0x6DDD00 (7,200,000)
Present by default: No
```

KeepAliveTime sets the number of milliseconds between each TCP keepalive segment if no data has been sent on the connection and if keepalives have been enabled on the connection. The default value of 7,200,000 milliseconds corresponds to 2 hours.

KeepAliveInterval

```
Location: HKEY_LOCAL_MACHINE\SYSTEM\CurrentControlSet\Services\Tcpip\Parameters
Data type: REG_DWORD
Valid range: 0-0xFFFFFFFF
Default value: 0x3E8 (1000)
Present by default: No
```

KeepAliveInterval sets the number of milliseconds between successive retransmissions of the keepalive segment when a response to the initial keepalive is not received. The number of TCP keepalive retransmissions is controlled by the TcpMaxDataRetransmissions registry setting, which has a default value of 5. After sending five TCP keepalive retransmissions, the connection is abandoned.

Therefore, with the default values of KeepAliveTime, KeepAliveInterval, and TcpMaxData-Retransmissions, a TCP connection on which keepalives have been enabled by the application is abandoned after 2 hours and 6 seconds.

Notice that for keepalives, the exponential backoff behavior between successive retransmissions is not done. For more information on the retransmission behavior of TCP, see Chapter 14, "Transmission Control Protocol (TCP) Retransmission and Time-Out."

TCP Connection Termination

Just as the TCP connection establishment process requires the sending of a SYN segment and its acknowledgment, the TCP connection termination process requires the sending of a FIN segment, a TCP segment where the FIN (Finish) flag is set, and its acknowledgment. The FIN segment indicates that the FIN segment sender will send no more data on the connection. Because a TCP connection is made up of two logical pipes (an outbound and inbound pipe for each TCP peer), both pipes must be closed and the closure must be acknowledged.

Figure 12-5 shows a TCP connection termination.

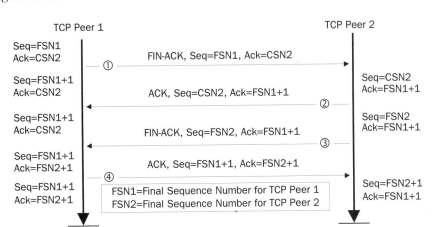

Figure 12-5. *A TCP connection termination showing the exchange of four TCP segments.*

Typical TCP connection termination processes are the exchange of four TCP segments.

Segment 1

A TCP peer (TCP Peer 1) that wants to terminate outbound data flow sends a TCP segment that contains no data with the following:

- The Sequence Number field set to the current sequence number for outbound data. When closing the connection, the current sequence number is the final sequence number for outbound data (FSN1 in Figure 12-5).
- The Acknowledgment Number field set to the next byte of inbound data that the TCP peer expects to receive. This number also corresponds to the current sequence number of TCP Peer 2 (CSN2 in Figure 12-5).
- The ACK flag is set, indicating that the Acknowledgment Number field is significant.
- The FIN flag is set, indicating that no more data will be sent from this TCP peer on the connection.

The following Network Monitor trace (Capture 12-03, included in the \Captures folder on the companion CD-ROM) shows an FIN-ACK segment for an FTP session being closed by an FTP server:

```
+ ETHERNET: ETYPE = 0x0800 : Protocol = IP:  DOD Internet Protocol
+ IP: ID = 0xDFF9; Proto = TCP; Len: 40
  TCP: .A...F, len:    0, seq:1035689055-1035689055, ack:3928116597,
win:17448, src:   21 (FTP)  dst: 1162
      TCP: Source Port = FTP [control]
      TCP: Destination Port = 0x048A
      TCP: Sequence Number = 1035689055 (0x3DBB5C5F)
```

```
    TCP: Acknowledgement Number = 3928116597 (0xEA224D75)
    TCP: Data Offset = 20 (0x14)
    TCP: Reserved = 0 (0x0000)
    TCP: Flags = 0x11 : .A...F
        TCP: ..0..... = No urgent data
        TCP: ...1.... = Acknowledgement field significant
        TCP: ....0... = No Push function
        TCP: .....0.. = No Reset
        TCP: ......0. = No Synchronize
        TCP: .......1 = No more data from sender
    TCP: Window = 17448 (0x4428)
    TCP: Checksum = 0x1377
    TCP: Urgent Pointer = 0 (0x0)
```

Segment 2

Similar to the SYN flag, the FIN flag occupies a byte of the TCP sequence space and therefore must be acknowledged as if it were a byte of data. Therefore, the TCP peer receiving the FIN-ACK segment (TCP Peer 2) sends an ACK with the following:

- The Sequence Number field set to the current sequence number for outbound data (CSN2 in Figure 12-5).

- The Acknowledgment Number field set to 1 more than the final sequence number for inbound data on the connection (FSN1 + 1).

- The ACK flag is set, indicating that the Acknowledgment Number field is significant.

The following Network Monitor trace (Capture 12-03, included in the \Captures folder on the companion CD-ROM) shows an ACK segment sent from the FTP client in response to a FIN-ACK sent by the FTP server:

```
+ ETHERNET: ETYPE = 0x0800 : Protocol = IP:  DOD Internet Protocol
+ IP: ID = 0x291E; Proto = TCP; Len: 40
    TCP: .A...., len:    0, seq:3928116597-3928116597, ack:1035689056,
win:17234, src: 1162  dst:   21 (FTP)
        TCP: Source Port = 0x048A
        TCP: Destination Port = FTP [control]
        TCP: Sequence Number = 3928116597 (0xEA224D75)
        TCP: Acknowledgement Number = 1035689056 (0x3DBB5C60)
        TCP: Data Offset = 20 (0x14)
        TCP: Reserved = 0 (0x0000)
        TCP: Flags = 0x10 : .A....
            TCP: ..0..... = No urgent data
            TCP: ...1.... = Acknowledgement field significant
            TCP: ....0... = No Push function
            TCP: .....0.. = No Reset
            TCP: ......0. = No Synchronize
```

```
          TCP: .......0 = No Fin
     TCP: Window = 17234 (0x4352)
     TCP: Checksum = 0x144D
     TCP: Urgent Pointer = 0 (0x0)
```

Notice how the acknowledgment number is 1 more (1035689056) than the sequence number of the previous FIN-ACK (1035689055), explicitly acknowledging the receipt of the FIN-ACK segment.

Once the FIN is acknowledged, the TCP peer that sent the initial FIN-ACK segment cannot send data (TCP Peer 1). However, only one logical pipe has been terminated. The inbound data pipe for TCP Peer 1 is still open and data can still flow and be acknowledged with ACK segments that contain no data.

Segment 3

If the TCP peer with the open outbound data pipe (TCP Peer 2) still has data to send, data can be sent and acknowledged by TCP Peer 1. This is known as a TCP half-close. An example of a TCP half-close is when a client application sends the FIN-ACK segment and the server application still has data to send to the client before it can terminate its side of the connection.

Once all outstanding data from TCP Peer 2 is sent and acknowledged, TCP Peer 2 can close its outbound logical pipe to TCP Peer 1. TCP Peer 2 sends a segment with the following:

- The Sequence Number field set to the current sequence number for outbound data. When closing the connection, the current sequence number is the final sequence number for outbound data (FSN2 in Figure 12-5).

- The Acknowledgment Number field set to the next byte of inbound data that the TCP peer expects to receive. In this case, the acknowledgment number is the same as that acknowledged in Segment 2 (FSN1 + 1).

- The ACK flag is set, indicating that the Acknowledgment Number field is significant.

- The FIN flag is set, indicating that no more data will be sent from this TCP peer on the connection.

The following Network Monitor trace (Capture 12-03, included in the \Captures folder on the companion CD-ROM) shows a FIN-ACK segment for the FTP client closing its outbound pipe:

```
+ Frame: Base frame properties
+ ETHERNET: ETYPE = 0x0800 : Protocol = IP:  DOD Internet Protocol
+ IP: ID = 0x291F; Proto = TCP; Len: 40
   TCP: .A...F, len:    0, seq:3928116597-3928116597, ack:1035689056,
win:17234, src: 1162  dst:   21 (FTP)
       TCP: Source Port = 0x048A
       TCP: Destination Port = FTP [control]
       TCP: Sequence Number = 3928116597 (0xEA224D75)
```

```
TCP: Acknowledgement Number = 1035689056 (0x3DBB5C60)
TCP: Data Offset = 20 (0x14)
TCP: Reserved = 0 (0x0000)
TCP: Flags = 0x11 : .A...F
    TCP: ..0..... = No urgent data
    TCP: ...1.... = Acknowledgement field significant
    TCP: ....0... = No Push function
    TCP: .....0.. = No Reset
    TCP: ......0. = No Synchronize
    TCP: .......1 = No more data from sender
TCP: Window = 17234 (0x4352)
TCP: Checksum = 0x144C
TCP: Urgent Pointer = 0 (0x0)
```

Segment 4

As in Segment 2, the FIN flag occupies a byte of the TCP sequence space and therefore must be acknowledged as a byte of data is acknowledged. Therefore, the TCP peer receiving the FIN-ACK segment (TCP Peer 1) sends an ACK with the following:

- The Sequence Number field set to the current sequence number for outbound data (FSN1 + 1).

- The Acknowledgment Number field set to 1 more than the final sequence number for inbound data on the connection (FSN2 + 1).

- The ACK flag is set, indicating that the Acknowledgment Number field is significant.

The following Network Monitor trace (Capture 12-03, included in the \Captures folder on the companion CD-ROM) shows an ACK segment that the FTP server sent in response to a FIN-ACK sent by the FTP client:

```
+ Frame: Base frame properties
+ ETHERNET: ETYPE = 0x0800 : Protocol = IP:  DOD Internet Protocol
+ IP: ID = 0xDFFA; Proto = TCP; Len: 40
   TCP: .A...., len:     0, seq:1035689056-1035689056, ack:3928116598,
win:17448, src:  21 (FTP)  dst: 1162
        TCP: Source Port = FTP [control]
        TCP: Destination Port = 0x048A
        TCP: Sequence Number = 1035689056 (0x3DBB5C60)
        TCP: Acknowledgement Number = 3928116598 (0xEA224D76)
        TCP: Data Offset = 20 (0x14)
        TCP: Reserved = 0 (0x0000)
        TCP: Flags = 0x10 : .A....
            TCP: ..0..... = No urgent data
            TCP: ...1.... = Acknowledgement field significant
            TCP: ....0... = No Push function
            TCP: .....0.. = No Reset
```

```
        TCP: ......0. = No Synchronize
        TCP: .......0 = No Fin
   TCP: Window = 17448 (0x4428)
   TCP: Checksum = 0x1376
   TCP: Urgent Pointer = 0 (0x0)
```

Notice how the acknowledgment number is 1 more (3928116598) than the sequence number of the previous FIN-ACK (3928116597), explicitly acknowledging the receipt of the FIN-ACK segment.

TCP Peer 2's outbound pipe is terminated when the ACK segment is received. The TCP connection, with both logical pipes gracefully terminated, is closed.

Note   TCP connection terminations do not have to use four segments. In some cases, segments 2 and 3 are combined. The result is a FIN-ACK/FIN-ACK/ACK sequence.

TCP Connection Reset

The TCP connection termination process is for the graceful, mutually agreed closure of both pipes of a TCP connection. Both TCP peers exchange FIN segments that are acknowledged explicitly, indicating that all data on the outbound pipe has been sent and acknowledged. Another way to terminate a TCP connection is through a TCP connection reset—a TCP segment with the RST (Reset) flag set.

A TCP connection reset is sent when a parameter problem exists in the TCP header of an inbound TCP segment that cannot be reconciled. For example, an improper source or destination IP address or TCP port number could cause an established connection to be aborted.

Aborting an established TCP connection through a TCP reset also can be intentionally done through Windows Sockets. However, aborting a TCP connection will cause all TCP data that is in transit, or in buffers waiting to be sent, to be discarded.

A TCP connection reset is used also to reject a TCP connection attempt in response to the receipt of a SYN segment. The most common reason a TCP peer denies a connection attempt with a connection reset is that the destination port in the SYN segment does not correspond to an Application Layer process running at the recipient of the SYN segment. Connection attempts also can be denied when the maximum allowed TCP connections is reached. Figure 12-6 shows a TCP connection reset.

Note   When a User Datagram Protocol (UDP) message arrives to a destination port that does not correspond to an Application Layer process, an Internet Control Message Protocol (ICMP) Destination Unreachable-Port Unreachable message is sent to the sender of the UDP message.

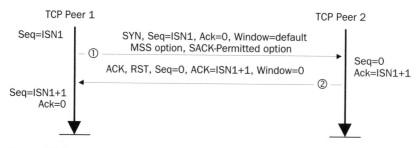

Figure 12-6. *A TCP connection reset showing the SYN and RST segments.*

The following Network Monitor trace (Capture 12-04, included in the \Captures folder on the companion CD-ROM) shows the sequence of packets sent between a host running an FTP client and a host that is not an FTP server. Frame 1 is an SYN segment to the FTP control port; Frame 2 is the connection reset.

```
Frame 1
+ ETHERNET: ETYPE = 0x0800 : Protocol = IP:  DOD Internet Protocol
+ IP: ID = 0x2927; Proto = TCP; Len: 48
  TCP: ....S., len: 0, seq:4065871748-4065871748, ack: 0, win:16384, src: 1164
dst:   21 (FTP)
      TCP: Source Port = 0x048C
      TCP: Destination Port = FTP [control]
      TCP: Sequence Number = 4065871748 (0xF2584784)
      TCP: Acknowledgement Number = 0 (0x0)
      TCP: Data Offset = 28 (0x1C)
      TCP: Reserved = 0 (0x0000)
      TCP: Flags = 0x02 : ....S.
          TCP: ..0..... = No urgent data
          TCP: ...0.... = Acknowledgement field not significant
          TCP: ....0... = No Push function
          TCP: .....0.. = No Reset
          TCP: ......1. = Synchronize sequence numbers
          TCP: .......0 = No Fin
      TCP: Window = 16384 (0x4000)
      TCP: Checksum = 0x82BE
      TCP: Urgent Pointer = 0 (0x0)
    + TCP: Options

Frame 2
+ ETHERNET: ETYPE = 0x0800 : Protocol = IP:  DOD Internet Protocol
+ IP: ID = 0xE18A; Proto = TCP; Len: 40
  TCP: .A.R.., len: 0, seq: 0-0, ack:4065871749, win: 0, src: 21 (FTP) dst: 1164
      TCP: Source Port = FTP [control]
      TCP: Destination Port = 0x048C
      TCP: Sequence Number = 0 (0x0)
```

```
TCP: Acknowledgement Number = 4065871749 (0xF2584785)
TCP: Data Offset = 20 (0x14)
TCP: Reserved = 0 (0x0000)
TCP: Flags = 0x14 : .A.R..
     TCP: ..0..... = No urgent data
     TCP: ...1.... = Acknowledgement field significant
     TCP: ....0... = No Push function
     TCP: .....1.. = Reset the connection
     TCP: ......0. = No Synchronize
     TCP: .......0 = No Fin
TCP: Window = 0 (0x0)
TCP: Checksum = 0xEF6E
TCP: Urgent Pointer = 0 (0x0)
```

In the connection reset segment:

- The RST and ACK flags are set.
- The sequence number is 0.
- The acknowledgment number is 1 more than the sequence number of the SYN segment (ISN1 + 1). As in the SYN-ACK segment of a connection establishment process, the SYN flag occupies a byte of sequence space and is explicitly acknowledged as if it were a byte of data.
- The window size is 0.

Upon receipt of a connection reset, the initiating peer can either try again (in practice, three attempts are made) or abandon the connection attempt. For the Windows 2000 FTP utility, the error message "Connection Was Refused" is displayed.

TCP Connection States

A TCP connection exists in one of the following states, as listed in Table 12-1.

Table 12-1. TCP Connection States

State	Description
CLOSED	No TCP connection exists.
LISTEN	An Application Layer protocol has issued a passive open and is willing to accept TCP connection attempts.
SYN SENT	An Application Layer protocol has issued an active open and a SYN segment is sent.
SYN RCVD	A SYN segment is received and a SYN-ACK is sent.
ESTABLISHED	The final ACK for the TCP connection establishment process is sent and received. Data can now be transferred in both directions.

(continued)

Table 12-1. *(continued)*

State	Description
FIN WAIT-1	The initial FIN-ACK segment to close one side of the connection is sent.
FIN WAIT-2	The ACK in response to the initial FIN-ACK is received.
CLOSING	A FIN-ACK is received but the ACK is not for the FIN-ACK sent. This is known as a simultaneous close, when both TCP peers send FIN-ACKs at the same time.
TIME WAIT	FIN-ACKs have been sent and acknowledged by both TCP peers and the TCP connection termination process is completed. Once the TIME WAIT state is reached, TCP must wait twice the maximum segment lifetime (MSL) before the connection's TCP port number can be reused. The MSL is the maximum amount of time a TCP segment can exist in an internetwork, and its recommended value is 240 seconds. This delay prevents a new connection's TCP segments using the same port numbers from being confused with duplicated TCP segments of the old connection.
CLOSE WAIT	A FIN-ACK has been received and a FIN-ACK has been sent.
LAST ACK	The ACK in response to the FIN-ACK has been received.

Figure 12-7 shows the states of a TCP connection.

The connection states that a TCP peer goes through depend on whether the TCP peer is the initiator of the TCP connection establishment or the initiator of the TCP connection termination.

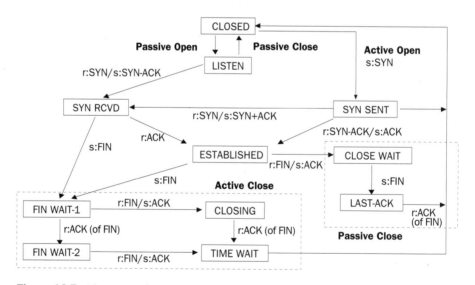

Figure 12-7. *The states of a TCP connection.*

Figure 12-8 shows the connection states of two TCP peers during the connection establishment process.

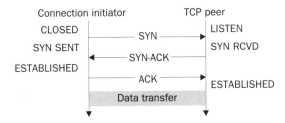

Figure 12-8. *The states of a TCP connection during TCP connection establishment.*

Figure 12-9 shows the connection states of two TCP peers during the connection termination process.

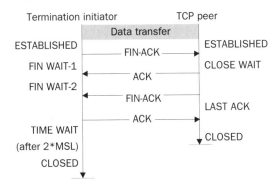

Figure 12-9. *The states of a TCP connection during TCP connection termination.*

Controlling TCP Connection Terminations in Microsoft Windows 2000

The TIME WAIT state is used to delay the re-use of the same parameters for a TCP connection, ensuring that duplicates of the old connection's TCP segments in transit are not confused with a new connection's TCP segments. The RFC 793 recommended value for the MSL is 2 minutes. Therefore, the time that the TCP connection is in the TIME WAIT state is 4 minutes (2*MSL).

TCP connections in the TIME WAIT state are controlled by the following Windows 2000 registry settings:

TcpTimedWaitDelay

```
Location: HKEY_LOCAL_MACHINE\SYSTEM\CurrentControlSet\Services\Tcpip\Parameters
Data type: REG_DWORD
Valid range: 30-300
Default value: 0xF0 (240)
Present by default: No
```

The value of TcpTimedWaitDelay is the number of seconds that a TCP connection remains in the TIME WAIT state. The default is the RFC 793 recommended value of 240 seconds (4 minutes).

MaxFreeTWTcbs

Location: HKEY_LOCAL_MACHINE\SYSTEM\CurrentControlSet\Services\Tcpip\Parameters
Data type: REG_DWORD
Valid range: 1-0xFFFFFFFF
Default value: 0x3E8 (1000)
Present by default: No

The value of the MaxFreeTWTcbs is the number of TCP connections allowed in the TIME WAIT state. If the number of TCP connections in the TIME WAIT state exceeds this value, the oldest TCP connection is immediately released.

The default values for TcpTimedWaitDelay and MaxFreeTWTcbs work well for many situations. However, for some that require the opening and closing of many outbound connections in a short amount of time, the large delay before a TCP port number can be re-used can result in the use of all possible TCP ports. Once this state of full capacity is reached, new TCP connections cannot be made until existing TCP connections go from the TIME WAIT state to the CLOSED state.

There are three methods that can prevent this problem from occurring:

1. Set the value of TcpTimedWaitDelay to a lower value to free TCP port numbers more quickly. The TcpTimedWaitDelay can be set as low as 30 seconds.

2. Set the value of MaxFreeTWTcbs to a lower value to force the freeing of TCP connections in the TIME WAIT state more quickly.

3. Set the value of MaxUserPort to a higher value. MaxUserPort specifies the maximum port number that can be used when an application requests an available port using Windows Sockets. The default value of MaxUserPort is 5000. Dynamically allocated ports start at 1024. Therefore, with the default setting of 5000, only 3977 dynamic TCP ports are available. In a high-traffic, high-use environment such as a proxy server on the Internet, it is possible to have 3977 TCP ports in either an established or TIME WAIT state. Setting this value higher allows more TCP ports to be in use simultaneously.

Summary

TCP connections are created through the TCP connection establishment process, where two TCP peers exchange SYN segments and determine starting sequence numbers, window sizes, maximum segment sizes, and other TCP options. TCP connections can be maintained through the exchange of periodic keepalive segments, although this is not commonly done. To terminate a TCP connection, each TCP peer must send a FIN segment and have it acknowledged. A TCP connection reset segment is used to either abort a current connection or refuse a connection attempt.

Chapter 13
Transmission Control Protocol (TCP) Data Flow

TCP data flow provides reliable data transfer through the sequencing of outbound data and the acknowledgment of inbound data. Along with reliability, TCP data transfer includes behaviors to prevent inefficient use of the network and provide sender and receiver-side flow control.

Basic TCP Data Flow Behavior

The following mechanisms govern TCP data flow, whether for interactive traffic, such as Telnet sessions, or for bulk data transfer, such as the downloading of a large file with the File Transfer Protocol (FTP):

- **Acknowledgments**   TCP acknowledgments are delayed and cumulative for contiguous data, and selective for non-contiguous data.
- **Sliding send and receive windows**   A send window for the sender and a receive window for the receiver control the amount of data that can be sent. Send and receive windows provide receiver-side flow control. As data is sent and acknowledged, the send and receive windows slide along the sequence space of the sender's byte stream.
- **Avoidance of small segments**   Small segments—TCP segments that aren't at the TCP maximum segment size (MSS)—are allowed, but are governed to avoid inefficient internetwork use.
- **Sender-side flow control**   While TCP sliding windows provide a way for the receiver to determine flow control, the sender also uses flow control algorithms to avoid sending too much data and congesting the internetwork.

TCP Acknowledgments

A TCP acknowledgment (ACK) is a TCP segment with the ACK flag set. In an ACK, the Acknowledgment Number field indicates the next byte in the contiguous byte stream that the ACK's sender expects to receive. Additionally, if the TCP Selective ACK (SACK) option is present, the ACK indicates up to four blocks of non-contiguous data received.

Delayed Acknowledgments

When a TCP peer receives a segment, the acknowledgment for the segment (either cumulative or selective) isn't sent immediately. The TCP peer delays the sending of the ACK segment for the following reasons:

- If, during the delay, additional TCP segments are received, a single ACK segment can acknowledge the receipt of multiple TCP segments.

- For full-duplex data flow, delaying the ACK makes it possible for the ACK segment to contain data. This is known as piggybacking the data on the ACK, or piggyback ACKs. If the incoming TCP segment contains data that requires a response from the receiver, the response can be sent along with the ACK. This is common for Telnet traffic where each keystroke of the Telnet client is sent to the Telnet server process. The received Telnet keystroke must be echoed back to the Telnet client. Rather than sending an ACK for the keystroke received and then sending the echoed keystroke, a single TCP segment containing the ACK and the echoed keystroke is sent.

- TCP has the time to perform general connection maintenance. The Application Layer protocol has additional time to retrieve data from the TCP receive buffer and an updated window size can be sent with ACK.

RFC 1122 states that the acknowledgment delay shouldn't be any longer than 0.5 seconds. By default, TCP/IP for Windows 2000 uses an acknowledgment delay of 200 milliseconds (0.2 seconds), which can be configured per interface by the TcpDelAckTicks registry setting.

TcpDelAckTicks

```
Location: HKEY_LOCAL_MACHINE\SYSTEM\CurrentControlSet\Services\Tcpip\Parameters\
Interfaces\InterfaceName
Data type: REG_DWORD
Valid range: 0-6
Default value: 2
Present by default: No
```

TcpDelAckTicks sets the delayed acknowledgment timer (in 100-millisecond intervals) of an interface. The default value of 2 is for a 200-millisecond delayed acknowledgment timer. A value of 0 disables delayed acknowledgments; an ACK is sent immediately for each segment received that contains data.

Cumulative for Contiguous Data

As originally defined in RFC 793, the TCP acknowledgment scheme is a cumulative acknowledgment scheme. The presence of the ACK flag and the value of the Acknowledgment Number field explicitly acknowledge all bytes in the received byte stream from the Initial Sequence Number (ISN) + 1 (the first byte of data sent on the connection), up to but not including the number in the Acknowledgment Number field (Acknowledgment Number − 1). Figure 13-1 illustrates the cumulative acknowledgment scheme of TCP.

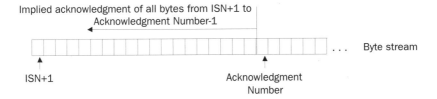

Figure 13-1. *The cumulative acknowledgment scheme of TCP.*

An ACK with a new Acknowledgment Number field is sent when a TCP segment is received containing data that's contiguous with previous data received. TCP segments received that aren't contiguous with the previous segments received aren't acknowledged. Only when the missing segments are retransmitted and received, creating a contiguous block of one or more TCP segments, is an ACK segment sent with the new Acknowledgment Number field.

While the original cumulative acknowledgment scheme for TCP works well and provides reliable data transfer, in high-loss environments this relatively simple acknowledgment scheme can slow throughput and use additional network bandwidth.

For example, a TCP peer sends six TCP segments. If the first of the six segments is dropped and the last five segments arrive, no ACK for the five received segments is sent. With normal TCP retransmission behavior, after the retransmission time-out, the sending TCP peer begins to retransmit all six segments. When the retransmission of the first TCP segment arrives, the receiving TCP peer sends an ACK segment confirming receipt of all six segments. While the dropped first segment has been successfully recovered, TCP has needlessly sent duplicates of segments that have successfully arrived.

Selective for Non-Contiguous Data

With SACK, the Acknowledgment Number field still indicates the last contiguous byte received, but the TCP SACK option can acknowledge non-contiguous received segments. With the SACK option, the left and right edges of the blocks of non-contiguous data received are explicitly acknowledged, preventing their needless retransmission. Figure 13-2 illustrates TCP's SACK scheme.

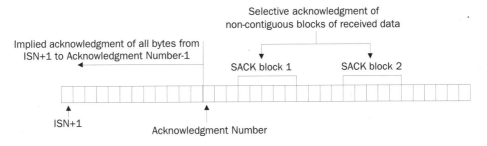

Figure 13-2. *The selective acknowledgment (SACK) scheme of TCP.*

Using the previous example, if six TCP segments are sent and the first TCP segment is dropped, the receiving TCP peer sends an ACK segment with the following settings: the Acknowledgment Number field set to the first byte of the missing TCP segment, and the SACK option set with the left and right edge of the block consisting of the second to the sixth received TCP segments. Upon receipt of the ACK with the SACK option, the sender marks the selectively acknowledged TCP segments and doesn't retransmit them. The sending TCP peer retransmits the first TCP segment after its retransmission time-out. Upon receipt, the receiving TCP peer sends an ACK segment with the Acknowledgment Number field set to the first octet past the sixth TCP segment.

SACK is especially important for the recovery of data on a TCP connection with a large window size. The previous example has a window size of six segments. Imagine a high-bandwidth, high-delay link such as a satellite channel with a window size of 200 segments. The sender will transmit 200 segments at a time. If cumulative acknowledgments are used, and the first segment is dropped, the sender will needlessly retransmit many of the successfully received segments before the dropped segment is recovered. With SACK, no needless retransmissions of successfully received segments occur.

TCP Sliding Windows

To govern the amount of data that can be sent at any one time and to provide receiver-side flow control, data transfer between TCP peers is performed using a window. The window is the span of data on the byte stream that the receiver permits the sender to send. The sender can send only the bytes of the byte stream that lie within the window. New data can be sent only with the receiver's permission. The window slides along the sender's outbound byte stream and the receiver's inbound byte stream.

The Acknowledgment Number and Window fields' values in ACKs that the receiver sends determine the actual bytes within the window. The Acknowledgment Number field indicates the next byte of data that the receiver expects to receive. The Window field indicates the amount of space left in a receive buffer to store incoming TCP data on this connection. The span of data within the window is from Acknowledgment Number through the value of (Acknowledgment Number + Window − 1).

For a given logical pipe—one direction of the full duplex TCP connection—the sender maintains a send window and the receiver maintains a receive window. When there's no data or ACK segments in transit, a logical pipe's send window and receive window are matched. In other words, the span of data that the sender is permitted to send is matched to the span of data that the receiver is able to receive.

Send Window

To maintain the send window, the sender must account for the bytes in the outbound byte stream that have been:

- Sent and acknowledged (Sent/ACKed)

- Sent but not acknowledged (Sent/UnACKed)
- Unsent but fit within the current send window (Unsent/Inside)
- Unsent but lie beyond the current send window (Unsent/Outside)

Figure 13-3 illustrates the types of data that exist for the send window.

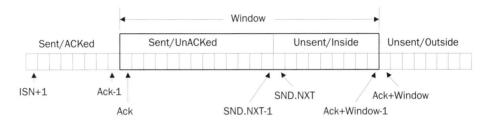

Figure 13-3. *The types of data for the TCP send window.*

The span of data that lies within the send window is the Sent/UnACKed and Unsent/Inside data.

Sent/ACKed Data

Sent/ACKed data is data that's been sent and acknowledged as received. The first byte of Sent/ACKed data is the value of (ISN + 1). Recall from the TCP connection establishment process that the TCP peer chooses an ISN that's explicitly acknowledged as if it were a data byte. Therefore, the first byte of user data sent on the connection is ISN + 1. Recall also that the acknowledgment number is the next byte of data the receiver expects to receive, explicitly acknowledging all bytes received up to but not including the acknowledgment number. Therefore, the last byte of ACKed data is the value of (Acknowledgment Number − 1).

Sent/UnACKed Data

Sent/UnACKed data is data that's been sent but for which no acknowledgments have been received. The Sent/UnACKed data is either in transit, dropped from the internetwork, has arrived at the receiver but no acknowledgment has been sent (because of delayed acknowledgments), or the ACK for the Sent/UnACKed data's in transit.

To distinguish Sent/UnACKed data from Unsent/Inside data, TCP maintains a variable known as SND.NXT, which is the value of the next byte to be sent. The value of SND.NXT becomes the Sequence Number field of the next TCP segment sent.

The first byte of Sent/UnACKed data is the Acknowledgment Number field's value of the last ACK segment received from the receiver. The last byte of Sent/UnACKed data is the value of (SND.NXT − 1).

Unsent/Inside Data

Unsent/Inside data is data that's not yet been sent but is within the current send window. Unsent/Inside data can be sent because the receiver has permitted it. It's natural to assume that if the data has been permitted, the sender will send all data within the send window before waiting for an acknowledgment and an updated window size from the receiver. In other words, there's no Unsent/Inside data when waiting for an acknowledgment.

However, as will be discussed later in this chapter, when starting the initial data flow and when encountering congestion, the sender-side flow control mechanisms of slow start and congestion avoidance prevent the sender from sending all the data that falls within the receiver's send window. In such cases, these mechanisms govern the amount of data sent before waiting for an acknowledgment.

The first byte of Unsent/Inside data is the value of the SND.NXT variable. The last byte of Unsent/Inside data is the last byte of data within the send window, the value of (Acknowledgment Number + Window − 1).

Unsent/Outside

Unsent/Outside data is data that's unsent and outside the current send window and represents future data that will be sent. Unsent/Outside data relative to the current send window should never be sent because it falls outside the receive window. The receiver's receive window is a direct reflection of buffer space remaining to store incoming data. The receiver discards data that can't be stored in the receive buffer for the connection, and sends an ACK segment with the current acknowledgment number. The first byte of Unsent/Outside data is the value of (Acknowledgment Number + Window).

Sliding the Send Window

The send window has a left edge (defined by the boundary between Sent/ACKed and Sent/UnACKed data) and a right edge (defined by the boundary between Unsent/Inside and Unsent/Outside data). When an ACK is received with a higher acknowledgment number, the send window closes and the left edge advances to the right. When an ACK is received where the sum of the (Acknowledgment Number + Window) is a greater value than the previous sum of the (Acknowledgment Number + Window), the send window opens and the right edge advances to the right. The sum of the (Acknowledgment Number + Window) fields in an ACK is the acknowledgment number of the ACK for the last TCP segment that will fit within the current send window. Figure 13-4 illustrates the sliding of the send window.

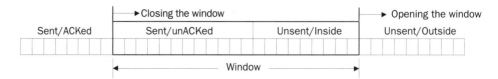

Figure 13-4. *The sliding of the send window showing window closing and opening.*

It's possible for the send window to close but not open—for the left edge of the send window to advance while the right edge doesn't. For example, the sender receives an ACK with an increased acknowledgment number but a decreased window, such that the sum of the (Acknowledgment Number + Window) doesn't change. This can happen when the receiver receives the data, which is acknowledged, but the received data hasn't been passed to the Application Layer protocol on the receiver. Therefore, the value of the Acknowledgment Number field in the ACK increases because of the contiguous data arriving, but the window decreases by the same amount, keeping the sum of the (Acknowledgment Number + Window) the same.

Zero Send Window

When the receiver advertises a window size of zero, the left and right edges of the send window are at the same boundary—the boundary between Sent/ACKed data and Unsent/Outside data. A zero window size can occur when the receiver's receive buffer fills with acknowledged data but the data hasn't yet been retrieved by the Application Layer protocol. This can happen when TCP hasn't yet indicated the data to the Application Layer protocol or when the Application Layer protocol hasn't explicitly informed TCP that it's ready to receive the next block of data from the TCP receive buffer.

With a zero send window, no new data can be sent until an ACK with a non-zero window size is received. However, because no new data is sent, the receiver isn't sending any new ACKs. This can produce a deadlock situation where the sender waits to receive a new window size and the receiver doesn't send a new window size because there are no new ACKs to send. Consequently, receiver and sender behaviors are defined to prevent the deadlock.

When the data in the TCP receive buffer is passed to the Application Layer protocol, the receiver sends an ACK segment with the current acknowledgment number and new non-zero window size. However, this segment is an ACK containing no data. ACK segments without data aren't sent reliably; the receiver doesn't acknowledge them, nor does the sender retransmit the ACK segments when it doesn't receive acknowledgment of those segments' receipt. Therefore, if an ACK sent by the sender to update the window size is lost, the sender would have no notification that new data can be sent. The TCP connection is indefinitely deadlocked; the receiver has informed the sender that new data can be sent, but the sender still considers the window size to be zero.

To prevent the deadlock of the dropped ACK that the receiver sent, the sender periodically sends a TCP segment containing 1 byte of new data for the connection. Because the data byte is Unsent/Outside data, the receiver discards the data and sends an ACK with the current acknowledgment number and window size. This sender-side mechanism is known as *probing the window*. The first window probe is sent after the current retransmission time-out, and the interval for successive probes is determined by doubling the timeout for the previous probe.

Receive Window

To maintain the receive window, the receiver must account for the bytes in the inbound byte stream that have been:

- Received, acknowledged, and retrieved by the Application Layer protocol (Rcvd/ACKed/Retr)
- Received, acknowledged, and not retrieved by the Application Layer protocol (Rcvd/ACKed/NotRetr)
- Received, but not acknowledged (Rcvd/UnACKed)
- Not received, but inside the current receive window (NotRcvd/Inside)
- Not received, but outside the current receive window (NotRcvd/Outside)

Figure 13-5 illustrates the types of data that exist for the receive window.

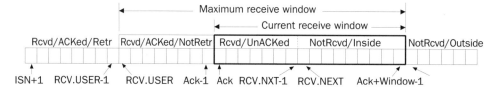

Figure 13-5. *The types of data for the TCP receive window.*

The span of data that lies within the maximum receive window is Rcvd/ACKed/NotRetr, Rcvd/UnACKed, and NotRcvd/Inside. The span of data that lies within the current receive window is Rcvd/UnACKed and NotRcvd/Inside.

Notice the difference between the maximum receive window and the current receive window. The maximum receive window is a fixed size and corresponds to a receive buffer used to store inbound TCP segments. The current receive window is of variable size and is the amount of space that's left in the receive buffer to store inbound TCP segments. The current receive window's size is the value of the Window field advertised in ACKs sent back to the sender, and is the difference between maximum-receive window size and the amount of data that's been received and acknowledged but not passed to the Application Layer protocol.

Rcvd/ACKed/Retr Data

Rcvd/ACKed/Retr data is data that's been received, acknowledged, and retrieved by the Application Layer protocol. The first byte of Rcvd/ACKed/Retr data is the value of (ISN + 1). To track the next byte to be passed to the Application Layer protocol, TCP maintains a variable called RCV.USER. Therefore, the last byte of Rcvd/ACKed/Retr data is the value of (RCV.USER − 1).

Rcvd/ACKed/NotRetr Data

Rcvd/ACKed/NotRetr data is data that's been received and acknowledged but hasn't been passed up to the Application Layer protocol. This category of data is the difference between the fixed-size maximum receive window and the variable-size current receive window. The first byte of Rcvd/ACKed/NotRetr data is the value of RCV.USER. The last byte of Rcvd/ACKed/NotRetr data is the current (Acknowledgment Number − 1).

Rcvd/UnACKed Data

Rcvd/UnACKed data is data that's been received but not acknowledged. To keep track of the next contiguous byte to be received, TCP maintains a variable called RCV.NEXT. When an ACK segment is sent, the ACK segment's Acknowledgment Number field is set to the value of RCV.NEXT. The first byte of Rcvd/UnACKed data is the current acknowledgment number. The last byte of Rcvd/UnACKed data is the value of (RCV.NEXT − 1).

If there are no TCP segments in transit and the receiver hasn't yet sent the ACK for TCP segments received, the send window's Sent/UnACKed data is the same data as the receive window's Rcvd/UnACKed data. In this situation, the value of RCV.NEXT kept by the receiver is equal to the value of SND.NEXT kept by the sender.

NotRcvd/Inside Data

NotRcvd/Inside data is data that can be received and will fit within the current receive window. The first byte of NotRcvd/Inside data is the value of RCV.NEXT. The last byte of NotRcvd/Inside data within the receive window is the value of (Acknowledgment Number + Window − 1).

NotRcvd/Outside Data

NotRcvd/Outside data is data that's not been received and is outside the current receive window, and represents future data that will be received. NotRcvd/Outside data relative to the current receive window should never be received because it falls outside the current receive window. The receiver discards data that can't be stored in the current receive window and sends an ACK with the current acknowledgement number. The first byte of NotRcvd/Outside data is the value of (Acknowledgment Number + Window).

Sliding the Receive Window

The current receive window has a left edge (defined by the boundary between Rcvd/ACKed/NotRetr and Rcvd/UnACKed data) and a right edge (defined by the boundary between NotRcvd/Inside and NotRcvd/Outside data). When an ACK segment is sent with an acknowledgment number set to RCV.NEXT, the current receive window closes and the left edge advances to the right. When the Rcvd/ACKed/NotRetr data is passed up to the Application Layer protocol, the maximum receive window opens and the right edge advances to the right. When this occurs, space is made available in the fixed-size receive buffer and new data can be received. The maximum receive window slides to the right by the number of bytes passed to the Application Layer protocol. When the maximum receive window slides as a result of data being passed to the Application Layer protocol, the current receive window slides also, since the right edge of the maximum receive window and the current receive window are the same. The next ACK that the receiver sends will contain an updated window size. The increase in the sum of the acknowledgment number and the window size indicates to the sender that more data can be sent.

Figure 13-6 illustrates the sliding of the receive window.

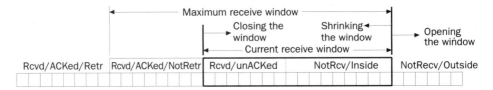

Figure 13-6. *Sliding the receive window showing window closing, opening, and shrinking.*

If the Application Layer protocol doesn't receive the data in a timely fashion, the receive window closes instead of sliding. This is indicated to the sender by increasing the acknowledgment number for new data received and decreasing the value of the Window field by the same amount, thereby keeping the sum of (Acknowledgment Number + Window) the same. In an extreme situation, the maximum receive window is filled with Rcvd/ACKed/NotRetr data and the left and right edges are the same (a zero receive window).

Shrinking the Window

Shrinking the window is the movement of the right edge of the receive window to the left. To shrink the receive window, an ACK segment is sent where the (Acknowledgement Number + Window) sum decreases. Normally, the (Acknowledgement Number + Window) sum either increases or remains the same. RFC 1122 discourages shrinking the window. However, a sending TCP peer must be prepared to adjust its send window accordingly. The receiver discards any data sent that's suddenly outside the shrunken receive window.

Microsoft Windows 2000 Maximum Receive Window Size

The TCP/IP for Windows 2000 maximum receive window size is set to 16,384 bytes by default (the Microsoft Windows NT 4.0 default maximum receive window size is 8192 bytes). The default maximum receive window size and the maximum segment size (MSS) of the connection negotiated during the TCP connection establishment process determine the maximum receive window size. For maximum efficiency in bulk data transfers, the maximum receive window size is adjusted to be an integral multiple of the MSS for the connection.

The maximum receive window size is calculated using the following algorithm (based on the default maximum window size of 16,384 bytes):

1. Assume a maximum receive window size of 16,384 bytes (16 KB). In the synchronize (SYN) segment sent to establish a TCP connection, include the TCP MSS option and set the window size to 16,384.

2. When the SYN-ACK is returned, examine the TCP MSS option to determine the MSS for the connection (the minimum MSS of the two TCP peers).

3. Based on the connection's MSS, divide 16,384 by the connection's MSS and round up to the next integer value.

4. If the result of rounding up isn't at least four times the connection's MSS, set the window size to four times the MSS (up to a maximum of 65,535). Window scaling must be in effect to use window sizes greater than 65,535.

Ethernet Example

For the maximum receive window size for an Ethernet-based TCP connection, the algorithm produces the following:

1. Assume a maximum receive window size of 16,384 bytes (16 KB). In the SYN segment sent to establish a TCP connection, set the window size to 16,384.

2. When the SYN-ACK is returned, examine the TCP MSS option to determine the connection's MSS (the minimum of the MSS of the two TCP peers). The MSS for two Ethernet-based TCP peers is 1460.

3. Based on the connection's MSS, divide 16,384 by the connection's MSS and round up to the next integer value. 16,384/1460 = 11.22, which, when rounded up to the next integer value, is 12. Therefore, the maximum receive window size for two Ethernet TCP peers is 17,520 (12*1460).

The default of 17,520 for Ethernet assumes that additional TCP options, such as SACK and TCP timestamps, aren't being used. If used, the maximum receive window size will be adjusted accordingly.

Token Ring (4-Mbps Ring with an IP MTU of 4168)

For the maximum receive window size for a 4-Mbps Token Ring-based TCP connection, the algorithm produces the following:

1. Assume a maximum receive window size of 16,384 bytes (16 KB). In the SYN segment sent to establish a TCP connection, set the window size to 16,384.

2. When the SYN-ACK is returned, examine the TCP MSS option to determine the connection's MSS (the minimum of the MSS of the two TCP peers). The MSS for two 4-Mbps Token Ring TCP peers is 4128.

3. Based on the connection's MSS, divide 16,384 by the connection's MSS and round up to the next integer value. 16,384/4128 = 3.97, which, when rounded up to the next integer value, is 4. Therefore, the maximum receive window size for two 4-Mbps Token Ring TCP peers is 16,512 (4*4128).

Token Ring (16-Mbps Ring with an IP MTU of 17,928)

For the maximum receive window size for a 16-Mbps Token Ring-based TCP connection, the algorithm produces the following:

1. Assume a maximum receive window size of 16,384 bytes (16 KB). In the SYN segment sent to establish a TCP connection, set the window size to 16,384.

2. When the SYN-ACK is returned, examine the TCP MSS option to determine the connection's MSS (the minimum of the MSS of the two TCP peers). The MSS for two 16-Mbps Token Ring TCP peers is 17,888.

3. Based on the connection's MSS, divide 16,384 by the connection's MSS and round up to the next integer value. 16,384/17,888 = 0.9, which, when rounded up to the next integer value, is 1.

4. The result of rounding up isn't at least 4 times the connection's MSS. Therefore, the window size is set to 4 times the MSS, or 71,552 (17,888*4). However, without window scaling, this window size can't be accommodated. Therefore, the maximum window size is set to a single MSS, or 17,888.

Changing the Default Maximum Receive Window Size

The default maximum receive window size can be set through the *setsockopt()* Windows Sockets function on a per socket basis or through the following registry settings:

GlobalMaxTcpWindowSize

```
Location: HKEY_LOCAL_MACHINE\SYSTEM\CurrentControlSet\Services\Tcpip\Parameters
Data type: REG_DWORD
Valid range: 0-0x3FFFFFFF
Default value: 0x4000 (16,384)
Present by default: No
```

GlobalMaxTcpWindowSize sets the number of bytes in the default maximum receive window for all interfaces (unless overridden per interface using TcpWindowSize registry setting). Values greater that 65,535 can be used only in conjunction with enabling window scaling with the Tcp1323Opts registry setting and with TCP peers that support window scaling. The maximum value, 0x3FFFFFFF, or 1,073,741,823, reflects the largest window size possible using window scaling.

TcpWindowSize

```
Location: HKEY_LOCAL_MACHINE\SYSTEM\CurrentControlSet\Services\Tcpip\Parameters
and
Location: HKEY_LOCAL_MACHINE\SYSTEM\CurrentControlSet\Services\Tcpip\Parameters\Interfaces\
        InterfaceName
Data type: REG_DWORD
Valid range: 0-0x3FFFFFFF
Present by default: No
```

TcpWindowSize sets the number of bytes in the default maximum receive window for all interfaces unless overridden using the GlobalMaxTcpWindowSize registry setting or the interface-based TcpWindowSize registry setting. The default value is the smallest of the following values:

- 0xFFFF (65,535)
- GlobalMaxTcpWindowSize

- The larger of 4 times the connection MSS
- 16,384 rounded up to an even multiple of the connection MSS

Values greater than 65,535 can be used only in conjunction with enabling window scaling with the Tcp1323Opts registry setting and with TCP peers that support window scaling. The maximum value, 0x3FFFFFFF, or 1,073,741,823, reflects the largest window size possible using window scaling.

Small Segments

A small segment is a TCP segment that's smaller than the MSS. To increase the efficiency of sending data, TCP avoids the sending and receiving of small segments through the Nagle algorithm and by avoiding silly window syndrome (SWS).

The Nagle Algorithm

For interactive data, such as the data of a Telnet or Rlogin session, much of the traffic is made up of individual keystrokes sent by the client and echoed by the server. For each keystroke, a single byte of data is sent. This is a network efficiency of 2 percent (the number of bytes of data [1 byte] divided by the number of bytes of overhead needed to send the data [40 bytes]). For interactive sessions, such as Telnet, each typed character must be sent and echoed back to the Telnet client application in order to be displayed on the user's screen. Therefore, sending small segments can't be avoided for interactive sessions. Preventing the sending of a small segment would mean that the user wouldn't see the keystroke as entered on the keyboard.

In the case of Telnet and Rlogin, a single keystroke echoed back to the user generates the following three TCP segments:

1. The client application sends the keystroke byte as a small TCP segment with the Push (PSH) flag set.
2. The keystroke TCP segment is passed to the server application, which sends an echo of the keystroke back to the client application (along with an ACK of the keystroke byte) as a small TCP segment with the PSH flag set.
3. The echoed keystroke TCP segment is passed to the client application, which sends an ACK of the echoed keystroke segment.

Typical interactive sessions consist of multiple keystrokes in rapid succession.

To minimize the low efficiency of sending small TCP segments, TCP is required to use the Nagle algorithm, named after John Nagle, the author of RFC 896, which describes the algorithm. The Nagle algorithm's premise is that a TCP connection can send only a single unacknowledged small segment. If a small segment is sent and not acknowledged, no other small segments can be sent.

> **More Info** The Nagle algorithm is described in RFC 896, which can be found in the \RFC folder on the companion CD-ROM.

In the case of interactive session traffic, such as Telnet and Rlogin, a keystroke segment is sent. Additional keystrokes entered by the user are accumulated in the TCP send buffer until the ACK for the outstanding small segment arrives. The next segment sent could contain multiple keystrokes. Depending on the average time to receive acknowledgments and the user's typing speed, this simple rule can decrease the number of TCP segments sent in the session by a factor of 3 or more.

The Nagle algorithm adapts itself to the environment on which the TCP segments are being sent. In a high-bandwidth, low-delay environment, such as a local area network (LAN), ACKs return more quickly and less accumulation occurs. However, in a high-bandwidth, low-delay environment, lower efficiency can be tolerated because of the higher capacity of the LAN. In a low-bandwidth, high-delay environment, such as a wide area network (WAN), ACKs return less quickly, producing more accumulation. This results in more efficient data transfer for environments with less capacity.

TCP/IP for Windows 2000 uses the Nagle algorithm by default. The Nagle algorithm is disabled through the TCP_NODELAY Windows Sockets option. Developers should disable the Nagle algorithm only when the immediate sending of multiple small segments is required. To improve performance of file locking and manipulation, Windows 2000 disables the Nagle algorithm for NetBIOS over TCP/IP (NetBT) and non-NetBIOS-based redirector and server communication.

Silly Window Syndrome

Whenever data is passed to the receiver's Application Layer protocol, the receive window opens and a new window size is advertised. Depending on how much data is retrieved from the receive buffer, this mechanism can cause the following behavior:

1. The sender and receiver are in a zero window state. The sender has sent all the data it can. The receiver has acknowledged all the data in the receive buffer and is waiting for the Application Layer protocol to retrieve the data before it's free to advertise a non-zero window size.

2. The Application Layer protocol retrieves a single byte of data from the receive buffer. The receive window advances by 1 byte.

3. The receiver sends an ACK with the window size set to 1.

4. The sender, realizing that the value of (Acknowledgement Number + Window) has increased, advances its send window by 1 byte. Because the receiver has permitted the sending of a single byte, the sender sends a single byte.

Each time the Application Layer protocol fetches a single byte of data from the buffer, the sender sends a single-byte TCP segment. The data sent on the TCP connection consists of a steady pattern of small segments. The behavior is known as the silly window syndrome (SWS). Both the sender and the receiver avoid SWS.

Receiver-Side SWS Avoidance

The receiver avoids SWS by not advertising a new window size unless the new window size is at least either an MSS or half of the maximum receive window size. Figure 13-7 illustrates receiver-side SWS avoidance.

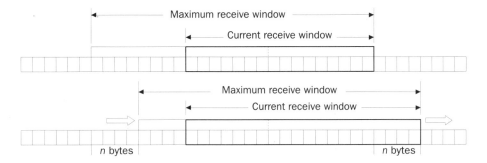

Figure 13-7. *SWS avoidance as implemented by the receiver.*

As data is passed to the application, the receive window advances. If the receive window advances n bytes, receiver-side SWS dictates that a new window size can't be advertised unless n is at least MSS bytes or half the maximum receive window.

Sender-Side SWS Avoidance

The sender avoids SWS by not sending a TCP segment containing data unless the advertised receive window size is at least MSS bytes. However, as previously discussed, small segments must be allowed for interactive data. Therefore, small segments are allowed if:

- The data is being pushed and adheres to the Nagle algorithm. Interactive data typically sets the TCP header's PSH flag. A single small segment can be sent according to the Nagle algorithm.

- The data is at least half the size of the maximum receive window and adheres to the Nagle algorithm.

Sender-Side Flow Control

Receiver-side flow control is implemented through the send and receive windows. The receiver can inform the sender to stop sending data by reducing the advertised receive window to 0. However, once a non-zero receive window size is advertised, there's nothing in the TCP sliding window mechanism that prevents the sender from sending all possible segments in the send window.

For example, during the TCP connection process, the maximum receive window size is determined. If the TCP peers are Ethernet-based, the maximum receive window and the advertised receive window at the end of the TCP connection establishment process for two Windows 2000-based hosts is 17,520 bytes, or 12 MSS-sized TCP segments (assuming no TCP options are present). According to the TCP sliding window mechanism, the sender can immediately send all 12 segments that fit within the receive window without waiting for an acknowledgment. While this behavior is permitted, it also can lead to network congestion, especially when sending TCP segments across multiple routers.

To prevent the flooding of segments that fit within the advertised receive window, TCP implementations, including Windows 2000, use the following algorithms:

- **The slow start algorithm**   Provides an exponential scaling of the number of segments within the send window that a sender can send before waiting for an acknowledgment.

- **The congestion avoidance algorithm**   Provides a linear scaling of the number of segments that a sender can send within the send window before waiting for an acknowledgment.

While slow start and congestion avoidance algorithms were developed to solve separate problems, they're used together to provide sender-side flow control.

Both the slow start and congestion avoidance algorithms maintain an additional variable called the congestion window *(cwind)* to help define how much data can be sent. For both algorithms, the size of the actual send window is the minimum of the advertised receive window and the congestion window (the value of *cwind)*.

Slow Start Algorithm

The premise of the slow start algorithm is that TCP increases the congestion window *(cwind)* by the MSS (or one segment size) for every ACK received that acknowledges new data. Every time *cwind* is updated, it's compared to the current advertised receive window size, and the minimum of both values is used to update the actual send window size.

When TCP data begins to flow on a connection after the connection establishment process or after a prolonged idle time, the following slow start process is used to increase the actual send window size (assuming two Ethernet-based TCP peers):

1. Set *cwind's* initial value to 2MSS (two MSS-sized segments). Compare *cwind's* value and the currently advertised receive window size (17,520 or 12 MSS). Set the actual send window size to the minimum of *cwind* and the currently advertised receive window size. Result: *cwind* = 2MSS, advertised receive window size = 12MSS, actual send window = 2MSS.

2. Two TCP segments are sent. The sender waits for acknowledgments.

3. When the sender receives an acknowledgment, *cwind* is set to 3MSS. Compare *cwind's* value and the currently advertised receive window size. Set the actual send window size to the minimum of *cwind* and the currently advertised receive window size. Result: *cwind* = 3MSS, advertised receive window size = 12MSS, actual send window = 3MSS.

4. Three TCP segments are sent. The sender waits for acknowledgments.

5. When the sender receives an acknowledgment, *cwind* is set to 4MSS. Compare *cwind's* value and the currently advertised receive window size. Set the actual send window size to the minimum of *cwind* and the currently advertised receive window size. Result: *cwind* = 4MSS, advertised receive window size = 12MSS, actual send window = 4MSS.

6. Four TCP segments are sent. The sender waits for acknowledgments.

This process continues until *cwind* becomes greater than the currently advertised receive window (12 MSS), at which point the currently advertised receive window governs how much data can be sent at a time, and slow start is finished. There's no more sender-side flow control unless a TCP segment needs to be retransmitted.

The following Network Monitor trace (Capture 13-01, included in the \Captures folder on the companion CD-ROM) illustrates the slow-start behavior for the downloading of a file using FTP up to 6MSS.

```
17  FTP Server  FTP Client  ....S., len:    0, seq:  10482005-10482005, ack:    0
18  FTP Client  FTP Server  .A..S., len:    0, seq:    376829-376829, ack:10482006
19  FTP Server  FTP Client  .A...., len:    0, seq:  10482006-10482006, ack: 376830
20  FTP Server  FTP Client  .A...., len: 1460, seq:  10482006-10483465, ack: 376830
21  FTP Server  FTP Client  .A...., len: 1460, seq:  10483466-10484925, ack: 376830
22  FTP Client  FTP Server  .A...., len:    0,  seq:   376830-376830, ack: 10484926
23  FTP Server  FTP Client  .A...., len: 1460, seq:  10484926-10486385, ack:376830
24  FTP Server  FTP Client  .A...., len: 1460, seq:  10486386-10487845, ack: 376830
25  FTP Server  FTP Client  .A...., len: 1460, seq:  10487846-10489305, ack:376830
26  FTP Client  FTP Server  .A...., len:    0,  seq:   376830-376830, ack: 10489306
27  FTP Server  FTP Client  .A...., len: 1460, seq:  10489306-10490765, ack: 376830
28  FTP Server  FTP Client  .A...., len: 1460, seq:  10490766-10492225, ack:376830
29  FTP Server  FTP Client  .A...., len: 1460, seq:  10492226-10493685, ack:376830
30  FTP Server  FTP Client  .A...., len: 1460, seq:  10493686-10495145, ack:376830
31  FTP Client  FTP Server  .A...., len:    0, seq:    376830-376830, ack: 10495146
32  FTP Server  FTP Client  .A...., len: 1460, seq:  10495146-10496605, ack: 376830
33  FTP Server  FTP Client  .A...., len: 1460,  seq:  10496606-10498065, ack: 376830
34  FTP Server  FTP Client  .A...., len: 1460, seq:  10498066-10499525, ack: 376830
35  FTP Server  FTP Client  .A...., len: 1460, seq:  10499526-10500985, ack: 376830
36  FTP Server  FTP Client  .A...., len: 1460, seq:  10500986-10502445, ack: 376830
37  FTP Client  FTP Server  .A...., len: 0,     seq:   376830-376830, ack: 10500986
38  FTP Server  FTP Client  .A...., len: 1460, seq:  10502446-10503905, ack: 376830
39  FTP Server  FTP Client  .A...., len:  1460, seq:  10503906-10505365, ack: 376830
40  FTP Server  FTP Client  .A...., len: 1460, seq:  10505366-10506825, ack: 376830
41  FTP Server  FTP Client  .A...., len: 1460, seq:  10506826-10508285, ack: 376830
42  FTP Server  FTP Client  .A...., len: 1460, seq:  10508286-10509745, ack: 376830
43  FTP Server  FTP Client  .A...., len: 1460, seq:  10509746-10511205, ack: 376830
```

The slow start algorithm for this data transfer is as follows:

1. The TCP connection establishment process is done in frames 17-19. *cwind* is set to 2MSS.

2. Frames 20 and 21 are the two segments corresponding to the current actual send window size of 2MSS.

3. Frame 22 is an ACK for frames 20 and 21. *cwind* is set to 3MSS.

4. Frames 23-25 are the three segments corresponding to the current send actual window size of 3MSS.

5. Frame 26 is an ACK for frames 23-25. *cwind* is set to 4MSS.

6. Frames 27-30 are the four segments corresponding to the current actual send window size of 4MSS.

7. Frame 31 is an ACK for frames 27-30. *cwind* is set to 5MSS.

8. Frames 32-36 are the five segments corresponding to the current actual send window size of 5MSS.

9. Frame 37 is an ACK for frames 21-35. *cwind* is set to 6MSS.

10. Frames 38-43 are the six segments corresponding to the current actual send window size of 6MSS.

The rate at which the size of the actual send window increases depends on how quickly ACK segments are returned. In a high-bandwidth, low-delay environment such as a LAN, the actual send window opens quickly. In a low-bandwidth, high-delay environment such as a WAN, the actual send window opens more slowly.

Although called the slow start algorithm, the actual send window size can increase at an exponential rate based on the receipt of multiple ACKs for multiple segments sent. For example, when starting the actual send window at 2MSS, two segments are sent. If an ACK is sent for each segment sent, the actual send window increases to 4MSS; four segments are sent. If an ACK is sent for each segment sent, the actual send window increases to 8MSS. The actual send window has quickly grown from 2MSS to 4MSS, and then to 8MSS. The actual window growth depends on how many ACK segments are received.

Congestion Avoidance Algorithm

Once data is flowing on the TCP connection, the actual send window is governed by the currently advertised receive window and receiver-side flow control is in effect. When a TCP segment must be retransmitted, the assumption is that the packet loss is a result of congestion at a router, rather than damage to the packet causing a checksum calculation to fail. If the packet loss is a result of congestion at a router, the sender's transmission rate must be immediately lowered and then gradually scaled back up to the rate at which data was being sent before the congestion occurred. For TCP connections, the transmission rate is the amount of data that the sender can send before having to wait for an acknowledgment.

When the congestion occurs, the slow start algorithm is used to scale the actual window size to half of the value of the advertised receive window size when the congestion occurred. Then, the congestion avoidance algorithm takes over. To keep track of when to use slow start and when to use congestion avoidance, an additional variable called the slow start threshold *(ssthresh)* is used. When a connection is established, *ssthresh* is set to 65,535. As with slow start, during congestion avoidance, the actual send window is the minimum of *cwind* and the currently advertised receive window.

The premise of the congestion avoidance algorithm is to increase *cwind* by 1MSS for each round-trip time. The round-trip time is the time it takes for a TCP segment to be sent and acknowledged. The congestion avoidance algorithm provides a smooth, linear increase in *cwind,* thereby increasing the actual send window. There are different ways of implementing the change in *cwind* for congestion avoidance.

- One method is to increase *cwind* by MSS*MSS/*cwind* (integer division) for each segment that's acknowledged. For example, if *cwind* is set to 7MSS, for each segment that's acknowledged, *cwind* is incremented by MSS*MSS/7*MSS, or MSS/7. Therefore, after 7 acknowledged segments, *cwind* increases by 1MSS. When *cwind* is incremented by a quantity that's not a full MSS, sender-side SWS prevents a small segment from being sent. Only after *cwind* is incremented to another MSS can another full segment be sent.

- Another method is to track the current actual send window size in increments of the MSS. When the number of segments that correspond to the size of the current actual send window size are ACKed, increment *cwind* by an MSS. Thus, the actual send window grows by 1MSS for each full window of data that's been acknowledged.

With slow start, the actual send window increases by 1MSS for each ACK received in a round-trip time. With congestion avoidance, the actual send window increases by a single MSS for multiple ACKs received in a round-trip time.

When congestion occurs (when a TCP segment must be retransmitted), the combination of slow start and congestion avoidance works as follows:

1. The slow start threshold *(ssthresh)* is set to half the value of the current send window with a minimum value of 2MSS. The congestion window *(cwind)* is set to 2MSS.

2. Set the actual send window to the minimum of the currently advertised receive window and *cwind*.

3. Send the appropriate number of TCP segments.

4. As ACKs are received, increment *cwind*. If *cwind* < *ssthresh,* increment *cwind* using slow start. If *cwind* > *ssthresh,* increment *cwind* using congestion avoidance. If *cwind* = *ssthresh,* then the TCP implementation is free to choose slow start or congestion avoidance.

5. Return to step 2.

The result of using the combination of slow start and congestion avoidance is that when congestion occurs, the sender uses slow start to quickly (exponentially) scale the actual send window size to half the size of the actual send window when the congestion occurred. Then, congestion avoidance is used to more slowly (arithmetically) scale the actual send window size up to the currently advertised receive window size. This gradual increase in the amount of data being sent allows the internetwork to clear its routing buffers and recover from the congestion.

Summary

TCP achieves reliable data transfer through the cumulative or selective acknowledgment of TCP segments received. Selective acknowledgments improve TCP performance in high-loss environments or for TCP connections with large window sizes. To provide receiver-side flow control, TCP uses sliding send and receive windows. With each ACK segment, the receiver indicates how much more data can be sent and successfully buffered. To avoid sending small segments, TCP uses the Nagle algorithm and SWS avoidance. To provide sender-side flow control, TCP uses the slow start and congestion avoidance algorithms. Slow start is used to increase the size of the actual send window by 1MSS for each ACK segment received. Congestion avoidance is used to increase the size of the actual send window by one MSS for each round-trip time. Slow start and congestion avoidance are used to avoid congesting an IP internetwork when sending and retransmitting data.

Chapter 14
Transmission Control Protocol (TCP) Retransmission and Time-Out

The reliable service of TCP requires that all segments containing data be acknowledged by the receiver. When an acknowledgment (ACK) for a segment is not received within a determined amount of time, the sender retransmits the segment. The sender might retransmit the segment multiple times before abandoning the connection. The retransmission and time-out behaviors of TCP directly affect TCP performance and can help prevent congestion on the internetwork.

Retransmission Time-Out and Round-Trip Time

For each connection, TCP maintains a variable called the retransmission time-out (RTO), whose value is the amount of time within which an ACK for the segment is expected. If TCP doesn't receive an ACK before the RTO expires, the segment is retransmitted.

The RTO must allow enough time for the following:

1. The initially sent TCP segment to traverse the internetwork (the transit time from source to destination).

2. The initially sent TCP segment to be received and processed by the destination node (the destination's inbound packet-processing time).

3. The generation of an ACK for the segment (the ACK generation time). A component of the ACK generation time is the delayed acknowledgment time of the destination node. Rather than sending an ACK segment for each TCP data segment received, TCP delays ACKs. Delayed ACKs can contain data, include updated window sizes, and acknowledge multiple segments received.

4. The generated ACK to traverse the internetwork (the transit time from destination to source).

5. The generated ACK to be received and processed by the sending node (the source's inbound packet-processing time).

The sum of all these times is known as the round-trip time (RTT). The RTT varies over time and must be constantly measured throughout the TCP connection's life. The RTO is based on the currently known RTT and should always be greater than the currently known RTT to prevent unnecessary retransmissions.

To prevent the following behaviors, the RTO should be neither too large nor too small:

- When the RTO is too large, the sending TCP peer must wait too long before retransmitting a lost segment. This lowers throughput for connections with some degree of packet loss.
- When the RTO is too small, segments will be retransmitted unnecessarily. Retransmitted segments increase the load on the internetwork and waste internetwork capacity.

If the ACK for the initially sent segment doesn't arrive within the RTO, the ACK is either arriving late or not at all. The main causes of ACK segments arriving late are either an increase in the transit time from the source to the destination, or an increase in the transit time from the destination to the source.

The following are reasons why the ACK isn't received at all:

1. The initially sent TCP segment is dropped at a router because of congestion.
2. The initially sent TCP segment is dropped at a router or the destination because of damage to the packet. Damage to the packet occurs when electronic or optical errors impact the encoded signal, causing bits within the packet to change values. Damaged packets are silently discarded after failing checksum calculations.
3. The ACK for the TCP segment is dropped at a router because of congestion.
4. The ACK for the TCP segment is dropped at a router or the destination because of damage to the packet.

It's much more probable that the TCP segment or its ACK was discarded by a congested router rather than the TCP segment or its ACK was damaged and silently discarded.

Note   Unlike TCP segments containing data, ACKs that contain no data aren't sent reliably. The ACK sender doesn't set an RTO for the ACK and doesn't retransmit the ACK segment. Therefore, a lost ACK is recovered by the sender retransmitting the segment(s) that the lost ACK is acknowledging, and not by the sender of the lost ACK retransmitting the ACK.

Congestion Collapse

The proper measurement of the RTT and determination of the RTO for sent TCP segments are important to prevent a phenomenon of routed internetworks known as congestion collapse. Congestion collapse occurs when the buffers of the internetwork routers fill to capacity and the routers begin to discard packets.

Congestion collapse begins with a steady increase in the load on the internetwork. As hosts send more data, more data is queued in the buffers of the internetwork routers. As this occurs, the transit time from the source to the destination and from the destination to the source increases. Therefore, the actual RTT grows larger than the currently known RTT of sending hosts.

The current RTO for sent segments is based on the currently known RTT. When the actual RTT increases so that it's greater than the current RTO, sent TCP segments will have ACKs that arrive late. When the ACKs don't arrive in the time based on the current RTO, the segments are retransmitted. Now there are two copies of each retransmitted segment, effectively doubling the load on the internetwork at a time when the load needs to be decreased. As more TCP segments are retransmitted, eventually the buffers on the internetwork routers fill and the routers begin to discard packets.

Congestion collapse can be avoided through the ongoing determination of the current RTT, which is monitored on a per window basis or per segment basis. Changes in the current RTT are used to update the RTO.

The recurrence of congestion collapse is avoided through the combination of the slow start and congestion avoidance algorithms of the sending host, as discussed in Chapter 13, "Transmission Control Protocol (TCP) Data Flow." When the retransmission timer for a segment expires, TCP assumes that retransmission timer expiration is a result of the segment being discarded by a router experiencing congestion. Slow start and congestion avoidance are used to slowly scale the number of segments sent before waiting for an acknowledgment up to the number of segments that will fit in the receiver's advertised receive window.

Slow start and congestion avoidance are used together to prevent the congestion collapse from recurring. Without slow start and congestion avoidance, once an internetwork becomes congested, it becomes congested again as the sending hosts begin transmitting new data and the internetwork oscillates between congested and uncongested states.

Retransmission Behavior

TCP uses the following exponential backoff behavior to determine the RTO of successive retransmissions of the same segment:

1. When the TCP segment is initially sent, the RTO for the segment is set to the currently known RTO for the connection.

2. After RTO number of seconds, when the retransmission timer expires, the segment RTO is set to twice the RTO for the segment's previous transmission and is retransmitted.

Step 2 is repeated for the maximum number of retransmissions before the TCP connection is abandoned. In Windows 2000, the TcpMaxDataRetransmissions registry setting controls the maximum number of retransmissions.

TcpMaxDataRetransmissions

    Location: HKEY_LOCAL_MACHINE\SYSTEM\CurrentControlSet\Services\Tcpip\Parameters
    Data type: REG_DWORD
    Valid range: 0-0xFFFFFFFF
    Default value: 5
    Present by default: No

TcpMaxDataRetransmissions sets the maximum number of retransmissions of a TCP segment containing data before the connection is abandoned.

The following Network Monitor trace (Capture 14-01, included in the \Captures folder on the companion CD-ROM) shows the maximum number of retransmissions and the doubling of the RTO between successive retransmissions:

```
1        0.000000    LOCAL            0060083E4607    TCP         .A...., len:
0, seq:   1311725-1311725, ack:23 FTP Server           FTP Client
2        0.000000    0060083E4607     LOCAL           FTP         Data
Transfer To Server, Port = 1296, size 1460   FTP Client      FTP Server
3        0.000000    0060083E4607     LOCAL           FTP         Data
Transfer To Server, Port = 1296, size 1460   FTP Client      FTP Server
4        0.000000    0060083E4607     LOCAL           FTP         Data
Transfer To Server, Port = 1296, size 1460   FTP Client      FTP Server
5        0.000000    0060083E4607     LOCAL           FTP         Data
Transfer To Server, Port = 1296, size 1460   FTP Client      FTP Server
6        0.000000    0060083E4607     LOCAL           FTP         Data
Transfer To Server, Port = 1296, size 1460   FTP Client      FTP Server
7        0.000000    0060083E4607     LOCAL           FTP         Data
Transfer To Server, Port = 1296, size 1460   FTP Client      FTP Server
8        0.500720    0060083E4607     LOCAL           FTP         Data
Transfer To Server, Port = 1296, size 1460   FTP Client      FTP Server
9        1.001440    0060083E4607     LOCAL           FTP         Data
Transfer To Server, Port = 1296, size 1460   FTP Client      FTP Server
10       2.002880    0060083E4607     LOCAL           FTP         Data
Transfer To Server, Port = 1296, size 1460   FTP Client      FTP Server
11       4.005760    0060083E4607     LOCAL           FTP         Data
Transfer To Server, Port = 1296, size 1460   FTP Client      FTP Server
12       8.011520    0060083E4607     LOCAL           FTP         Data
Transfer To Server, Port = 1296, size 1460   FTP Client      FTP Server
```

This Network Monitor trace was captured from a File Transfer Protocol (FTP) client where the uploading of a file was in progress and the cable connecting the network adapter of the FTP server was pulled. Frames 8-12 show the retransmission behavior of TCP/IP for Windows 2000. Notice how the initial RTO is 0.5 seconds and successive retransmissions have RTOs that are approximately doubled. After the last retransmission, the FTP server waits 16 seconds before abandoning the connection and recovering the connection's resources. It takes a total of 31.5 seconds to abandon the connection. The connection abandonment time is 63 times the RTO for the connection (the sum of RTO for the initial segment sent, 2*RTO for the first retransmission, 4*RTO for the second retransmission, 8*RTO for the third retransmission, 16*RTO for the fourth retransmission, and 32*RTO for the fifth retransmission).

Note The retransmission time-outs are doubled, but the elapsed time for sending the retransmitted segment isn't exactly doubled in the Network Monitor trace because of delays in processing, queuing, and the physical transmission of network frames.

Retransmission Behavior for New Connections

For new connections initiated by a Windows 2000 host, the TcpMaxConnectRetransmissions registry setting determines the maximum number of retransmissions of the synchronize (SYN) segment.

TcpMaxConnectRetransmissions

```
Location: HKEY_LOCAL_MACHINE\SYSTEM\CurrentControlSet\Services\Tcpip\Parameters
Data type: REG_DWORD
Valid range: 0-255
Default value: 2
Present by default: No
```

TcpMaxConnectRetransmissions sets the maximum number of retransmissions of a SYN segment before the connection attempt is abandoned. Exponential backoff is used between successive retransmissions of the SYN segment. With an initial RTO value of 3 seconds, it takes 21 seconds to abandon a connection attempt (the sum of 3 seconds for the initial SYN, 6 seconds for the first retransmission, and 12 seconds for the second retransmission). The initial RTO's value is controlled using the TcpInitialRTT registry setting described in the "Calculating the RTO" section of this chapter.

For new connections initiated by a TCP peer for a Windows 2000 host, the TcpMaxConnectResponseRetransmissions registry setting determines the SYN-ACK segment's maximum number of retransmissions.

TcpMaxConnectResponseRetransmissions

```
Location: HKEY_LOCAL_MACHINE\SYSTEM\CurrentControlSet\Services\Tcpip\Parameters
Data type: REG_DWORD
Valid range: 0-255
Default value: 2
Present by default: No
```

TcpMaxConnectResponseRetransmissions sets the maximum number of retransmissions of a SYN-ACK segment sent in response to an SYN segment before the connection attempt is abandoned. Exponential backoff is used between successive retransmissions of the SYN-ACK segment. With an initial RTO value of 3 seconds, it takes 21 seconds to abandon the connection (the sum of 3 seconds for the first SYN, 6 seconds for the first retransmission, and 12 seconds for the second retransmission). If TcpMaxConnectResponseRetransmissions is greater than 1, SYN attack protection is used. See Chapter 12, "Transmission Control Protocol (TCP) Connections," for more information on the SYN attack.

Dead Gateway Detection

Dead gateway detection is an algorithm that detects the failure of the currently configured default gateway. If it detects a failure, dead gateway detection automatically switches to a new default gateway, providing there are multiple default gateways configured. Dead gateway detection uses TCP retransmission behavior to detect and recover from a downed router configured as the default gateway.

When an individual TCP connection retransmits a segment multiple times (half of TcpMaxDataRetransmissions), its forwarding IP address is changed to the next default gateway. When 25 percent of all TCP connections using the failed default gateway have been moved to the next default gateway, the default route in the IP routing table is updated with the next default gateway as the forwarding IP address.

If the new default gateway isn't available, dead gateway detection is used to switch to the next default gateway in the configured list. When the last default gateway in the list is reached and becomes unavailable, the next default gateway is the first default gateway in the list. When the computer is restarted, the first default gateway in the list is used.

For a detailed example of how dead gateway detection works, consider a host with the following configuration:

- The IP address of 10.0.0.99/24.
- Two default gateways are configured: 10.0.0.1 and 10.0.0.2.
- The default route 0.0.0.0/0 has 10.0.0.1 as its forwarding IP address.
- There are currently 10 TCP connections for locations off the 10.0.0.0/24 subnet using 10.0.0.1 as their forwarding IP address.
- TcpMaxDataRetransmissions is set at its default value of 5.

When the router at 10.0.0.1 fails, dead gateway detection uses the following process to change the default route to use the forwarding IP address of 10.0.0.2:

1. A TCP connection (one of the 10 TCP connections at the host) sends a data segment. Because no acknowledgment is received, the segment is retransmitted. After the third retransmission, the forwarding IP address for this specific TCP connection is changed to 10.0.0.2. At this point, 10 percent of the TCP connections using the forwarding IP address of 10.0.0.1 have been switched to 10.0.0.2.

2. Another TCP connection sends a data segment. Because no acknowledgment is received, the segment is retransmitted. After the third retransmission, the forwarding IP address for this specific TCP connection is changed to 10.0.0.2. At this point, 20 percent of the TCP connections using the forwarding IP address of 10.0.0.1 have been switched to 10.0.0.2.

3. Another TCP connection sends a data segment. Because no acknowledgment is received, the segment is retransmitted. After the third retransmission, the forwarding IP address for this specific TCP connection is changed to 10.0.0.2. At this point, 30 percent of the TCP connections using the forwarding IP address of 10.0.0.1 have been switched to 10.0.0.2.

4. Because more than 25 percent of the TCP connections using 10.0.0.1 as their forwarding IP address have had their forwarding IP addresses changed, the default route in the IP routing table is updated to use 10.0.0.2 as the forwarding IP address.

The EnableDeadGWDetect registry setting controls dead gateway detection in Windows 2000.

EnableDeadGWDetect

```
Location: HKEY_LOCAL_MACHINE\SYSTEM\CurrentControlSet\Services\Tcpip\Parameters
Data type: REG_DWORD
Valid range: 0-1
Default value: 1
Present by default: No
```

EnableDeadGWDetect enables (=1) or disables (=0) dead gateway detection. Dead gateway detection is enabled by default.

Using the Selective Acknowledgment (SACK) TCP Option

The SACK TCP option allows the receiver to selectively acknowledge non-contiguous blocks of data received. However, the sender shouldn't discard selectively acknowledged segments from its transmission queue until the segments are included in a cumulative acknowledgment.

RFC 2018 allows the data receiver to discard non-contiguous segments even though those segments have been selectively acknowledged. This is known as reneging on a selective acknowledgment, and its practice is discouraged. To keep reneged data from being lost on a connection, the sender must retransmit selectively acknowledged data until it's acknowledged by the Acknowledgment Number field in an ACK from the receiver.

More Info   TCP selective acknowledgments are described in RFC 2018, which can be found in the \RFC folder on the companion CD-ROM.

The retransmission behavior of selectively acknowledged segments is as follows:

1. For each segment, maintain a SACK flag that's enabled when the segment is selectively acknowledged.

2. When initial RTO timers begin to expire, only retransmit the segments that haven't been selectively acknowledged (segments for which the SACK flag is disabled).

3. If an ACK is received that cumulatively acknowledges the retransmitted segment, the send window closes and opens depending on the new (Acknowledgment Number + Window) sum and new segments can be sent. The SACK flags on non-cumulatively acknowledged segments are maintained.

4. If a retransmitted segment times out, indicating that the receiver might have reneged on the selectively acknowledged segments, disable the SACK flags of all segments in the current window and retransmit them normally.

This mechanism recovers from the possibility that the receiver discarded the non-contiguous received segments. If necessary, the entire window of data is resent.

Calculating the RTO

The determination of the RTO is an important function of TCP. The RTO must be adjusted to the internetwork's changing conditions. If the determined RTO is less than the RTT, segments are unnecessarily retransmitted.

In RFC 793, the suggested method of computing the RTO—known as the Smoothed Round-Trip Time (SRTT)—is based on the following formulas:

$$SRTT = (\alpha * SRTT) + ((1-\alpha) * RTT)$$

$$RTO = min[UpperBound, max[LowerBound, (\beta * SRTT)]]$$

Thus, the new RTO is based on the determination of the current RTT, the previous SRTT, a smoothing factor (α), and a variance factor (β). RFC 793 cited this formula as an example method of computing the RTO. In practice, this formula was found to be inadequate in determining the RTO in an environment where the RTT changed suddenly. Instead, RFC 1122 states that TCP must use the following formulas as documented in "Congestion Avoidance and Control," a paper written by Van Jacobson and Michael J. Karels:

$$SRTT = RTT + 8 * (New\_RTT - RTT)$$

$$Dev = Dev + (|New\_RTT - RTT| - Dev)/4$$

$$RTO = SRTT + Dev/4$$

With this new way of calculating the RTO, the RTO is based on the average and variance (Dev) of the RTT. The RTO is self-tuning for different environments (the low-delay Local Area Network [LAN] and the high-delay Wide Area Network [WAN]) and is sensitive to sudden changes in the RTT for environments such as the Internet.

 More Info RTO calculation is described in RFCs 793 and 1122, which can be found in the \RFC folder on the companion CD-ROM.

In Windows 2000, the TcpIntialRTT registry setting controls the RTO's initial value for establishing connections or sending data on new connections.

TcpInitialRTT

Location: HKEY_LOCAL_MACHINE\SYSTEM\CurrentControlSet\Services\Tcpip\Parameters\
    Interfaces*InterfaceName*
Data type: REG_DWORD
Valid range: 0-0xffff
Default value: 3
Present by default: No

TcpInitialRTT sets the number of seconds for the initial RTO for SYN segments, SYN-ACK segments, and for initial data segments sent on a new connection for each interface. Increasing this value from its default will have a multiplicative effect on the amount of time it takes to time-out from a connection establishment or when sending data on a new connection.

For new connections being established by a host, the connection abandonment time is 7*TcpInitialRTT (assuming the default value of TcpMaxConnectRetransmissions). For arbitrary values of TcpIntialRTT and TcpMaxConnectRetransmissions, the connection abandonment time is:

$$\text{TcpIntialRTT}*[2^{(\text{TcpMaxConnectRetransmissions}+1)} - 1]$$

For new connections being requested from a host, the connection abandonment time is 7*TcpInitialRTT (assuming the default value of TcpMaxConnectResponseRetransmissions). For arbitrary values of TcpIntialRTT and TcpMaxConnectResponseRetransmissions, the connection abandonment time is:

$$\text{TcpIntialRTT}*[2^{(\text{TcpMaxConnectResponseRetransmissions}+1)} - 1]$$

As data segments are sent, the RTO is adjusted from the TcpInitialRTT to a value closer to the connection's RTT. By default, the connection's RTT isn't sampled for each segment sent. Rather, the RTT is sampled once for every full send window of data sent. If the send window is 12*MSS, the RTT is sampled once every 12 segments. For each sample of the RTT, the time that the sampled segment is sent is recorded based on the current value of an internal clock. When the ACK for the segment is received, the RTT is determined from the difference between the recorded value of when the segment was sent and the current value of the internal clock.

The RTT sampling rate is 1/(window size). For small window sizes, this sampling rate is adequate. However, for large windows, the sampling rate is inadequate and can't keep up with rapid changes in the RTT. The result is increased network bandwidth utilization from unneeded retransmissions when the currently known RTO is less than the current RTT. In these situations, the TCP Timestamps option is used to provide a sampling rate that's equal to the sending rate.

Using the TCP Timestamps Option

As described in Chapter 11, "Transmission Control Protocol (TCP) Basics," the TCP Timestamps option allows TCP peers to place a timestamp value on each segment. The

TCP Timestamps option contains two 32-bit fields to track timestamps: TS Value and TS Echo Reply. The TS Value field stores the current timestamp value. The TS Echo Reply field stores the timestamp echo, the value of the TS Value field of the segment being acknowledged.

The use of TCP timestamps allows an RTT to be calculated by subtracting the timestamp echo in the acknowledgment from the current time value of the timestamp clock.

As an example, TCP Peer A sends a data segment to TCP Peer B, which sends an ACK back. The data segment's TS Value has the value 1285458 when it's sent and is echoed in the ACK segment's TS Echo Reply field. When the ACK is received and processed, the current value of TCP Peer A's timestamp clock is 1286506. Therefore, the RTT for this segment is based on the TCP timestamp value of 1048, or (1286506 − 1285458).

This basic method of RTT determination is complicated by the following factors:

- There might be pauses in sending data.
- ACKs are delayed and can acknowledge multiple TCP segments.
- Segments can arrive out of sequence.
- Segments can be dropped and must be retransmitted.

Figure 14-1 illustrates the problem with pauses in sending data. TCP Peer A sends TCP Peer B a series of segments and then pauses. Then TCP Peer A sends more segments. The new segment after the pause has the TS Echo Reply field set to the TS Value field of the last ACK received. If TCP Peer B now calculates the RTT for the last ACK sent, the RTT is inflated by the time of the pause in sending data.

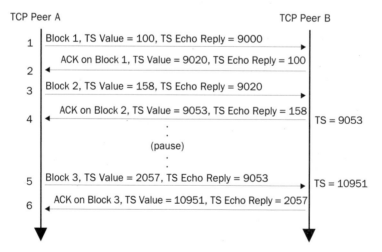

Figure 14-1. *The behavior of TCP timestamps with pauses in data.*

From Figure 14-1, the TCP timestamp interval calculated from TCP segment 5 is calculated as 1898 (10951 − 9053), clearly the wrong value, as it includes the pause in sending data. With an RTO adjusted to this higher value of the RTT, throughput for data sent by TCP Peer 2 isn't optimal because the RTO is too high. To prevent this behavior, the RTT is calculated only for TCP segments that acknowledge new data sent. Therefore, in the example shown in Figure 14-1, the RTT is calculated only by TCP Peer A. TCP Peer B doesn't calculate RTT because the segments received by TCP Peer B don't acknowledge data sent by TCP Peer B.

For delayed ACKs, segments that arrive out of order, and retransmitted segments, the value of TS Echo Reply for ACKs is based on the following algorithm:

1. For correct TCP timestamp behavior, TCP keeps track of two variables for each connection: *tsrecent* is the value of the TS Echo Reply that will be sent in the next ACK, and *lastack* is the value of the Acknowledgment Number field from the last ACK sent.

2. Upon receipt of a new segment, if the segment contains the byte numbered *lastack*, which means that a contiguous segment has arrived, update *tsrecent* with the value of the TS Value field from the arriving segment. If the segment doesn't contain *lastack*, ignore the value of the TS Value field of the arriving segment.

3. When sending a segment with the TCP Timestamp option, set the value of TS Echo Reply to the value of *tsrecent*.

4. When sending an ACK, set the value of *lastack* to the value of the Acknowledgment Number field in the ACK.

For delayed acknowledgments, the RTT determination must include the acknowledgment delay. Therefore, when sending a delayed acknowledgment, the TS Echo Reply of the delayed ACK is set to the TS Value of the first segment being acknowledged. Figure 14-2 illustrates this behavior.

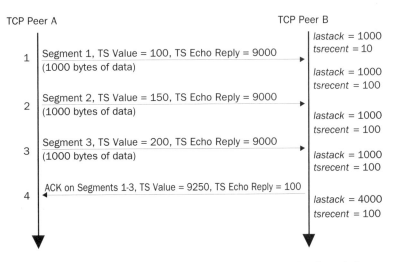

Figure 14-2. *The behavior of TCP timestamps for delayed acknowledgments.*

Prior to receiving any TCP segments, the value of *tsrecent* is 10 and the value of *lastack* is 1000. When TCP segment 1 arrives, it contains the *lastack* byte and therefore *tsrecent* is updated with the TS Value of 100. When TCP segment 2 arrives, it doesn't contain the *lastack* byte and *tsrecent* remains at the value of 100. When TCP segment 3 arrives, it doesn't contain the *lastack* byte and *tsrecent* remains at the value of 100. When the delayed ACK is sent, the value of TS Echo Reply is set to *tsrecent* and *lastack* is set to the value of the Acknowledgment Number field.

When segments arrive out of sequence, the value of *tsrecent*, and therefore the value of TS Echo Reply, isn't updated. TS Echo Reply and *tsrecent* are updated only when the missing segment(s) arrives. Figure 14-3 illustrates this behavior.

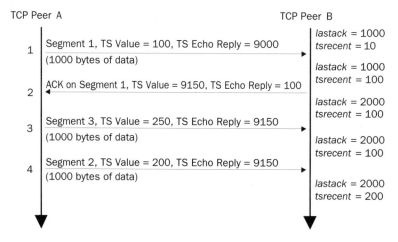

Figure 14-3. *The behavior of TCP timestamps for out-of-order segments.*

Prior to receiving any TCP segments, the value of *tsrecent* is 10 and the value of *lastack* is 1000. When TCP segment 1 arrives, it contains the *lastack* byte and therefore *tsrecent* is updated with the TS Value field value of 100. When the ACK on segment 1 is sent, the value of TS Echo Reply field is set to *tsrecent* and *lastack* is set to the Acknowledgment Number field's value.

When TCP segment 3 arrives, it doesn't contain the *lastack* byte, and *tsrecent* remains at the value of 100. When TCP segment 2 arrives, it does contain the *lastack* byte and the value of *tsrecent* is updated.

When a segment is dropped and must be retransmitted, the segments arrive out of sequence, the value of *tsrecent*, and therefore the value of the TS Echo Reply field, isn't updated. Because the RTT doesn't include the retransmission time-out for the retransmitted segment, *tsrecent* and TS Echo Reply are updated only when the missing, retransmitted segment arrives. Figure 14-4 illustrates this behavior.

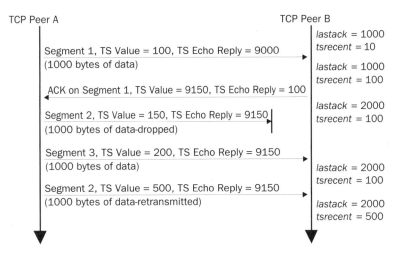

Figure 14-4. *The behavior of TCP timestamps for retransmitted segments.*

Prior to receiving any TCP segments, the value of *tsrecent* is 10 and the value of *lastack* is 1000. When TCP segment 1 arrives, it contains the *lastack* byte and therefore *tsrecent* is updated with the TS Value of 100. When the ACK on segment 1 is sent, the value of TS Echo Reply is set to *tsrecent* and *lastack* is set to the value of the Acknowledgment Number field.

When TCP segment 3 arrives, it doesn't contain the *lastack* byte and *tsrecent* remains at the value of 100. When the retransmitted TCP segment 2 arrives, it does contain the *lastack* byte and the value of *tsrecent* is updated.

Karn's Algorithm

When a TCP segment whose RTT is being calculated is sent, the time that the segment is sent is recorded. If the RTO expires, an exact duplicate is sent and its time is recorded. When the ACK is received, how is the RTT computed? When the TCP Timestamps option isn't being used, the ACK doesn't distinguish between the original TCP segment and its retransmitted copy. TCP has the problem of acknowledgment ambiguity. When multiple copies of a TCP segment are sent, the ACK doesn't identify a specific instance of the TCP segment being acknowledged.

If we choose to calculate the RTT based on the first instance of the segment and the first instance is lost, the measured RTT is larger than the actual RTT for the connection because it includes the RTO for retransmitting the segment. The measured RTT is the difference between the time the first segment was sent and the time the ACK for the retransmitted instance was received. The new RTO grows larger than it should, resulting in lowered throughput for retransmitted segments. As more TCP segments are lost, the RTO based on this method of RTT calculation grows larger.

If we choose to calculate the RTT based on the retransmitted instance of the segment, and the reason the RTO expired is a result of a sudden increase in the RTT, the ACK for the first instance arrives soon after the retransmitted segment is sent. The measured RTT (the difference between the time the retransmitted segment was sent and the time the ACK for the first instance was received) is now smaller than the connection's actual RTT. The updated RTO gets smaller when it should get larger, eventually resulting in unnecessary retransmissions for subsequent segments.

To prevent these conditions from incorrectly changing the RTO, RTT measurements for TCP segments that have been retransmitted are ignored. Only the RTT for ACKs that are acknowledging a single instance of a TCP segment are considered. However, ignoring the RTT for retransmitted segments introduces a new problem. When the actual RTT increases suddenly, the RTO for a TCP segment is too small and results in a retransmission. Because the RTT isn't calculated for the retransmitted segment, the RTO remains at its inadequate value. Subsequent TCP segments sent would also be retransmitted.

To keep subsequent TCP segments from being sent with an inadequate RTO when the actual RTT increases suddenly, TCP/IP implementations, including Windows 2000, use Karn's algorithm. Karn's algorithm is named after its creator, Phil Karn, in the paper "Improving Routing-Trip Time Estimates in Reliable Transport Protocols," by Phil Karn and Craig Partridge. Karn's algorithm states that when an ACK for a retransmitted segment arrives, it shouldn't be used to update the RTO. However, use the RTO of the retransmitted segment (that has been exponentially backed off) as a temporary RTO for subsequent TCP segments. When an ACK for a non-retransmitted TCP segment arrives, use its RTT to update the RTO. Then, use the updated RTO for subsequent TCP segments.

For example, if the RTO for a TCP connection is 300 ms and the actual RTT for the connection suddenly rises to 400 ms, Karn's algorithm will cause the following behavior:

1. Segment A is sent and its RTO is set to 300 ms.
2. Because the RTO for Segment A is lower than the connection's actual RTT, the retransmission timer for Segment A expires. Segment A's RTO is set to 600 ms and retransmitted (using exponential backoff and a factor of 2).
3. The ACK for Segment A arrives (400 ms after the first instance of Segment A was sent).
4. Because the ACK is for a retransmitted segment, it isn't used to update the RTO.
5. TCP temporarily sets the RTO for subsequent segments to 600 ms (the RTO of the retransmitted Segment A).
6. Segment B is transmitted and Segment B's RTO is set to 600 ms.
7. The ACK for Segment B arrives in 400 ms.
8. Because the ACK is for a segment that hasn't been retransmitted, its RTT is calculated and used to update the RTO.
9. Subsequent segments are sent using the updated RTO.

Karn's Algorithm and the Timestamps Option

Karn's algorithm applies when the ACKs are ambiguous—when TCP can't distinguish the original TCP segment from a retransmitted instance. However, with the TCP Timestamps option, each TCP segment has a steadily increasing value of the timestamp clock (the TS Value field in the TCP Timestamps option header) and is therefore unique within the time that segments are being retransmitted. The ACK for different instances of a TCP segment can be distinguished from another because the ACK contains the echo of the timestamp value of the segment being acknowledged. Therefore, Karn's algorithm doesn't apply when TCP timestamps are being used.

If a segment is retransmitted because of a segment loss, the ACK for the retransmitted segment contains the timestamp value for the retransmitted segment, and not the original segment. Therefore, the RTT is accurately calculated as the difference in the current TCP time clock and the ACK's timestamp echo.

If a segment is retransmitted because of a sudden increase in RTT, the ACK contains the timestamp value of the first instance. Therefore, the RTT is accurately calculated as the difference in the current TCP time clock and the timestamp echo in the ACK for the first segment.

Fast Retransmit

When a TCP segment arrives and the sequence number isn't the next sequence number the receiver was expecting (a non-contiguous, out-of-order segment), an immediate ACK is sent with the Acknowledgment Number field set to the next sequence number the receiver was expecting. This ACK is a duplicate of an ACK that was previously sent and isn't subject to the delayed acknowledgment behavior for new contiguous data received.

Upon receipt of this duplicate ACK, the sender can't determine whether the duplicate ACK was sent by the receiver because of a TCP segment that arrived out of order or because a segment was lost.

- If a TCP segment arrived out of order, the TCP segment that contains the next byte the receiver expects to receive should arrive at the receiver shortly thereafter and a cumulative ACK will be sent. Therefore, for out-of-order segments, only one or two duplicate ACKs most likely will be sent.

- If a TCP segment is lost, all of the segments sent beyond the contiguous segment arriving at the receiver generate an immediate duplicate ACK. Therefore, if three or more duplicate ACKs arrive at the sender, the TCP segment containing the next byte the receiver expects is most likely lost and must be retransmitted.

Fast retransmit is the retransmission of a TCP segment before the retransmission timer for the segment expires, based on the receipt of three duplicate ACKs where the ACK's acknowledgment number is the retransmitted segment's sequence number. The retransmitted segment is the missing segment.

More Info Fast retransmit and fast recovery are described in RFC 2581, which can be found in the \RFC folder on the companion CD-ROM.

As Figure 14-5 illustrates, TCP Peer A sends five TCP segments and the first segment is lost. As the non-contiguous segments arrive, TCP Peer B sends an immediate ACK with the ACK number it expects to receive. After the third duplicate ACK for sequence number 1000, TCP Peer A retransmits the first segment.

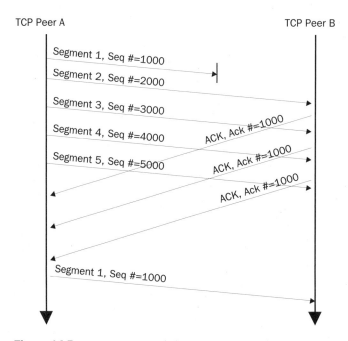

Figure 14-5. *Fast retransmit behavior, when the first of five segments is dropped.*

In Windows 2000, the TcpMaxDupAcks registry value controls fast retransmit behavior.

TcpMaxDupAcks

```
Location: HKEY_LOCAL_MACHINE\SYSTEM\CurrentControlSet\Services\Tcpip\Parameters
Data type: REG_DWORD
Valid range: 1-3
Default value: 2
Present by default: No
```

TcpMaxDupAcks sets the maximum number of duplicate ACKs (ACKs that are duplicates of the original ACK received) that must be received before fast retransmit is used to retransmit the missing segment. The default value of TcpMaxDupAcks is 2, rather than the RFC 2581-discussed value of 3.

Fast Recovery

Fast retransmit causes the sender to retransmit the missing TCP segment before its retransmission timer expires. If the retransmission timer expires, slow start and congestion avoidance algorithms are used to gradually increase the actual send window up to the advertised receive window. Because the retransmission timer didn't expire, congestion avoidance is performed, but not slow start. This behavior is known as fast recovery and is described in RFC 2581. For more information on slow start and congestion avoidance, see Chapter 13, "Transmission Control Protocol (TCP) Data Flow."

Fast recovery assumes that the arrival of duplicate ACKs indicates that segments sent before the missing TCP segment have already been received, and aren't adding to the internetwork congestion. Therefore, Windows 2000 can scale the congestion window faster than when using slow start.

The fast recovery algorithm is as follows:

1. Upon receipt of the third duplicate ACK, the value of the slow start threshold (*ssthresh*) is set to one half the value of the congestion window (*cwind*), with a minimum value of 2*MSS.

2. The missing segment is retransmitted and *cwind* is set to (*ssthresh* + 3*MSS). This increases *cwind* to a value that reflects the receipt of three TCP segments at the receiver (based on the receipt of three duplicate ACKs).

3. For each additional duplicate ACK, *cwind* is increased by MSS. Once again, *cwind* is being increased because of an additional segment that has arrived at the receiver.

4. If allowed by the values of *cwind* and the advertised receive window size, the next TCP segment(s) is transmitted.

5. When the ACK arrives that acknowledges the receipt of the missing new segment and all other contiguous segments, *cwind* is set to the value of *ssthresh*. At this value of *cwind*, slow start is avoided and congestion avoidance is performed.

Summary

To recover from lost TCP segments, TCP connections maintain an RTO for each segment. If the RTO expires, the segment is retransmitted and the RTO is doubled for the retransmitted segment. After a maximum number of retransmissions, the TCP connection is abandoned. The RTO is based on calculations from samples of the RTT, using either a single sample per window of data or TCP timestamps. When TCP segments are sent without timestamps, Karn's algorithm is used to update the RTO when an ACK for a retransmitted segment is received. Fast retransmit and fast recovery are used to re-send a missing segment before its RTO expires, and to more quickly scale the send window.

Part IV
Application Layer Protocols and Services

Chapter 15
Dynamic Host Configuration Protocol (DHCP) Service

To communicate successfully with each other, all TCP/IP hosts must be properly configured. These hosts require a valid and unique IP address, a subnet mask, and a default gateway address, although the default gateway can be omitted if the host is to communicate only on the local subnet. For larger networks, additional configuration items are required, such as DNS server IP addresses, WINS server IP addresses, and NetBIOS node types.

In small networks, carrying out this configuration requires a degree of TCP/IP skill, which might not be readily available. On large networks, ensuring that all hosts are properly configured can be a considerable management and administrative task, especially in a dynamic network with roaming users and their laptops. Manual configuration or reconfiguration of a large number of computers can be time-consuming, and errors in configuring an IP host can result in the host being unable to communicate with the rest of the network.

DHCP is a client server protocol that simplifies the management of client IP configuration and the assignment of IP configuration data. With DHCP, administrators define all necessary configuration parameters on a central server, which then provides hosts with all necessary IP configuration information.

DHCP provides three key benefits to those planning, designing, and maintaining an IP network:

- **Centralized administration of IP configuration**   The DHCP administrator can centrally manage all IP configuration information. This eliminates the need to manually configure individual hosts when TCP/IP is first deployed, or when IP infrastructure changes are required.

- **Seamless IP host configuration**   The use of DHCP ensures that DHCP clients get accurate and timely IP configuration parameters without user intervention. Because the configuration is automatic, troubleshooting is largely eliminated.

- **Flexibility**   By using DHCP, the administrator has increased flexibility over changes in IP configuration information, allowing the administrator to change IP configuration more simply as infrastructure changes are needed.

Chapter Contents

This chapter describes the Microsoft Windows 2000 DHCP protocol implementation in detail. Additionally, the companion CD-ROM contains several Network Monitor traces that demonstrate the DHCP protocol in operation. This chapter contains the following sections:

- **Overview to DHCP in Windows 2000** A description of the DHCP protocol as implemented in Windows 2000
- **DHCP Messages** A description of the format of the messages sent between DHCP clients and DHCP servers
- **DHCP Options** A description of the options that a DHCP host can request from a DHCP server

Overview to DHCP in Windows 2000

This section presents an overview of DHCP and defines key DHCP terms.

What Is DHCP?

DHCP is a client server protocol that automatically provides an IP host with its IP address and other related configuration information such as the subnet mask and default gateway. RFCs 2131 and 2132 define DHCP as an Internet Engineering Task Force (IETF) standard based on the Bootstrap Protocol (BOOTP) protocol, with which it shares many implementation details. DHCP allows hosts to obtain all necessary TCP/IP configuration information from a DHCP server.

> **More Info** DHCP is an IETF standard based on the BOOTP protocol and is defined in RFCs 2131 and 2132, which can be found in the \RFC folder on the companion CD-ROM.

All Windows 2000 Servers (including Server, Advanced Server, and Data Center Server) include a DHCP Server service, which is an optional installation. All Microsoft Windows clients automatically install the DHCP client service as part of TCP/IP, including Windows 2000, Windows NT 4.0, Windows 98, and Windows 95.

DHCP Overview and Key Terms

Before examining DHCP in detail, it's necessary to provide you with a basic DHCP overview and to review definitions of key terms.

DHCP Clients and Servers

A computer that gets its configuration information from DHCP is known as a *DHCP client*. DHCP clients communicate with a *DHCP server* to obtain IP addresses and related TCP/IP configuration information. DHCP servers hold information about available IP addresses and related configuration information as defined by the DHCP administrator.

DHCP Scopes and Options

A set of IP addresses and associated configuration information that can be supplied to a DHCP client is known as a *scope*. A scope is a set of IP addresses that the server can issue to DHCP clients, along with one or more *options*. An option is a specific configuration item such as a subnet mask and a default gateway IP address, which the DHCP administrator wants the DHCP server to provide to the DHCP client.

A DHCP administrator can create one or more scopes on one or more Windows 2000 servers running the DHCP service. However, since DHCP servers don't communicate scope information with each other, the administrator must be careful to ensure that the scopes are defined carefully so that multiple DHCP servers are not handing out the same IP address to different clients, or handing out addresses that are taken by existing, manually configured IP hosts.

The IP addresses defined in a DHCP scope are continuous and are associated with a subnet mask. To allow for the possibility that some IP addresses in the scope might have been already assigned and in use, the DHCP administrator can specify an *exclusion*—one or more IP addresses in the scope that won't be handed out to DHCP clients.

> **Note**   In networks with multiple subnets and multiple networks, it is useful to have standards for separating the dynamic IP addresses given out by DHCP from the addresses used by manually configured hosts.

DHCP options are defined in detail in RFC 2132, and key Windows DHCP options are described later in this chapter. In the DHCP protocol packet, each option begins with a single tag octet, which defines the option. An option can be fixed length, such as the NetBIOS Node Type (Option 46); variable length, such as the Domain Name Server (DNS) Domain Name (Option 15); or an array of items, such as the list of DNS Servers (Option 6).

With the Windows 2000 DHCP service, the DHCP administrator can manage options at the following five different levels:

- **Pre-Defined Options**   Allow the DHCP administrator to specify default option values for all options supported on the DHCP server and to create new option types for use on this server.
- **Server Options**   Values assigned to all clients and scopes defined on the DHCP server (unless they're overridden by scope, class, or client-assigned options).
- **Scope Options**   Values applied only to clients of a specific scope (unless they're overridden by class or client-assigned options).
- **Class Options**   Allow the administrator to set user- or vendor-defined option classes, providing option data to a specified class of DHCP clients (that is, all Windows 2000 clients). Options set at this level are overridden only by options assigned at the client level.
- **Reserved Client Options**   Set for an individual DHCP client. Only properties manually configured at the client computer can override options assigned at this level.

Option Classes

A DHCP *options class* is an additional set of options that can be provided to a DHCP client based on the computer being a member of a class of computers. The administrator can use these to sub-manage option values provided to DHCP clients. There are two types of options classes supported by the Windows 2000 DHCP server: vendor classes and user classes.

When an administrator configures options classes on a DHCP server, a client belonging to that class, for example, all Windows 2000 computers, can be provided with class-specific option types for its configuration. To support earlier DHCP clients that are unable to support sending of the class ID, the administrator can configure default classes to provide option values. This allows the administrator to leverage options specifically provided in a particular client class, simultaneously allowing the administrator to provide all necessary options for other clients.

A DHCP client can indicate in the DHCP protocol messages it sends to a server that the client is a member of a particular user or vendor class. The administrator can use DHCP to define option values that are returned only for this client class. For example, the administrator can configure options specific to Windows 2000 computers, which can be sent option values (for example, whether or not to release a DHCP lease when shutting down). Other clients, such as Windows 95, which cannot support this feature, wouldn't receive these values.

For a DHCP client to receive option values for these extended options, the client must specify a user class string option, containing a string identifying the client type. The DHCP server can then use this to identify extra options to be sent to the client. The user class option is set using the IPCONFIG command.

DHCP Messages

DHCP clients communicate with DHCP servers by sending application layer *messages* to, and receiving messages from, a DHCP server. There are eight DHCP message types, which are sent using User Data Protocol (UDP). DHCP clients with a bound IP address and a valid lease communicate with the DHCP server using unicast IP datagrams, while clients in the process of obtaining an IP address communicate using broadcast packets, sent to the limited broadcast IP address 255.255.255.255. The DHCP client binds to UDP port 68, while the DHCP server binds to UDP port 67.

While the general message format and individual message details are defined in the "DHCP Messages" section of this chapter, we'll define the eight DHCP messages here:

- **DHCPDISCOVER**   Broadcast by a DHCP client broadcast to locate a DHCP server.
- **DHCPOFFER**   Sent by a DHCP server to a DHCP client, in response to DHCPDISCOVER, along with offered configuration parameters.
- **DHCPREQUEST**   Sent by the DHCP client to DHCP servers to request parameters from one server while implicitly declining offers from other servers, and to confirm the validity of previously allocated addresses (for example, after a reboot or to extend an existing DHCP lease).

- **DHCPACK**   Sent by a DHCP server to a DHCP client to confirm an IP address and to provide the client with those configuration parameters that the client has requested and the server is configured to provide.
- **DHCPNAK**   Sent by a DHCP server to a DHCP client denying the client's DHCPREQUEST. This might occur if the requested address is incorrect because of the client having moved to a new subnet or because the DHCP client's lease has expired and can't be renewed.
- **DHCPDECLINE**   Sent by a DHCP client to a DHCP server, informing the server that the offered IP address is in use.
- **DHCPRELEASE**   Sent by a DHCP client to a DHCP server, relinquishing an IP address and canceling the remaining lease. This is sent to the server that provided the lease.
- **DHCPINFORM**   Sent from a DCHP client to a DHCP server, asking only for additional local configuration parameters; the client already has an externally configured IP address. This message type is also used for Rogue server detection.

DHCP Leases and Reservations

The IP addresses acquired by DHCP generally aren't permanent. When a DHCP client is configured using DHCP, it acquires a *lease* on the assigned address. The lease duration is defined by the DHCP administrator. In Windows 2000, the administrator can specify either a lease time, between 1 minute and 999 days, or an unlimited lease time.

While most IP addresses will be dynamically allocated, Windows 2000 allows a DHCP administrator to create a reservation. A *reservation* is a permanent address lease that the DHCP administrator creates in order to assign a specific IP address (and DHCP options) to a specific DHCP client. The administrator creates the reservation by specifying the IP address to be allocated and the host's MAC address. The reservation ensures that the DHCP client with a Network Interface Card (NIC) having that MAC address will always obtain the same IP address and options.

DHCP Relay Agents

When a Windows 2000 DHCP client is initially booted, it broadcasts DHCP messages to obtain or renew a lease from a DHCP server. The DHCP administrator uses a *DHCP Relay Agent* to centralize DHCP servers, and avoid needing a DHCP server on each subnet. Also referred to as a BOOTP relay agent, a DHCP relay agent is a host, or an IP router, that listens for DHCP client messages being broadcast on a subnet and then transfers the messages to a configured DHCP server. The DHCP server will send DHCP messages to the relay agent that then broadcasts them onto the subnet for the DHCP client.

The Windows 2000 server's Routing and Remote Access Service includes a DHCP relay agent. A DHCP administrator needs to enable the Routing and Remote Access Service, add the DHCP relay agent, and configure the DHCP server's IP address. Additionally, most modern hardware routers can be configured to provide relay facilities. On many routers, this is referred to as BOOTP Forwarding.

Unauthorized DHCP Server Detection

Properly configured DHCP servers provide IP configuration information for IP networks. However, when an incorrectly configured DHCP server is introduced into a network, or any DHCP server is introduced into the wrong network, problems might arise. For example, if a client obtains a lease from an incorrectly configured DHCP server, the client might receive an invalid IP address, which will prevent it from communicating on the network. This can prevent users from logging on. With Windows 2000, an *unauthorized DHCP server* is simply a DHCP server that hasn't explicitly been authorized. Unauthorized DHCP servers are also referred to as Rogue DHCP servers.

In a Windows 2000 domain environment, the DHCP service on an unauthorized server will fail to initialize. The administrator must explicitly authorize all Windows 2000 DHCP servers that operate in an Active Directory domain environment. At initialization time, the DHCP service in Windows 2000 will check for authorization and won't start if the server detects it's in a domain environment and the server hasn't been explicitly authorized.

Automatic Private IP Addressing (APIPA)

DHCP clients need to find a DHCP server to get an initial lease. In most cases, the DHCP client will find a server either on a local subnet or via a relay agent. To allow for the possibility that the DHCP server is unavailable, Windows 2000 and Windows 98 provide APIPA. APIPA is a facility of the Windows 2000 TCP/IP implementation that allows a computer to obtain IP configuration information without a DHCP server or manual configuration.

APIPA avoids the problem of IP hosts being unable to communicate if, for some reason, the DHCP server is unavailable. APIPA is also useful for small workgroup networks where no DHCP server is implemented. Because auto-configuration does not support a default gateway, it works only with a single subnet and it's inappropriate for larger networks.

If the DHCP client is unable to locate a DHCP, the computer will auto-configure itself with an IP address randomly chosen from the IANA-reserved class B network 169.254.0.0, and with the subnet mask 255.255.0.0. The auto-configured computer will then test to verify that the IP address it has chosen isn't already in use, using a gratuitous Address Resolution Protocol (ARP) broadcast. If the chosen IP address is in use, the computer will randomly select another address. The computer will make up to 10 attempts to find an available IP address.

Once the selected address has been verified as available, the client will be configured to use that address. The DHCP client will continue to check for a DHCP server in the background every 5 minutes, and if a DHCP server is found, the configuration offered by the DHCP server will be used.

DNS Integration

The DNS service, which Chapter 16, "Domain Name Service (DNS)," describes in more detail, provides name resolution for DNS clients. Windows 2000 clients support dynamic DNS update, which allows DHCP clients to automatically update their configured DNS servers with forward- and reverse-lookup information.

Routing and Remote Access Service Integration

The Windows 2000 Routing and Remote Access Service includes a Remote Access Service server facility, which allows Dial-Up Networking or Virtual Private Network (VPN) clients to access a Routing and Remote Access Service server and join a local network. To other computers on the local network, these clients appear to be peer clients. In this case, the remote access server acts as a gateway between the remote client and the local network. Remote access service clients will need IP addresses for the local network in order to operate. While the Remote Access Service client can be manually configured with an appropriate IP address, this is an administrative overhead. Alternatively, the Windows 2000 Routing and Remote Access Service can be configured to obtain any required IP addresses from a DHCP server.

When a Windows 2000 remote access server is configured to use DHCP to obtain IP addresses, the remote access server obtains 10 IP addresses from a DHCP server. The remote access server uses the first IP address obtained from DHCP for itself and allocates subsequent addresses to TCP/IP-based remote access clients as they connect. IP addresses that are freed when remote access clients disconnect are reused. When all 10 IP addresses are used, the remote access server obtains 10 more addresses. When the Routing and Remote Access Service is stopped, all IP addresses obtained through DHCP are released.

If a DHCP server is not available when the Routing and Remote Access Service is started, then APIPA addresses in the range from 169.254.0.1 through 169.254.255.254 are used.

Multicast Scopes

In addition to providing leases to unicast IP addresses, the Windows 2000 DHCP service supports multicast scopes. A *multicast scope* is a set of addresses in the Class D range, for use by multicast applications. This feature allows the DHCP administrator to control the specific multicast addresses in use by multicast applications. Applications must be specifically written to DHCP to obtain leases for multicast IP addresses.

BOOTP Support

DHCP is based on BOOTP, an older protocol with similar funtionality. BOOTP is an established protocol standard used for configuring IP hosts. BOOTP was designed originally to enable boot configuration for diskless workstations. Modern DHCP servers respond to both BOOTP requests and DHCP requests.

BOOTP clients initialize themselves in two distinct steps, as follows:

1. The BOOTP client requests an IP address and other configuration information, such as a default gateway address, a DNS server IP address, and the like, from a BOOTP server. This information includes the boot image file name and the server name where an IP address should be obtained.

2. The BOOTP client then contacts the server and downloads the boot image file using Trivial File Transfer Protocol (TFTP).

Although DHCP has superceded BOOTP, Windows 2000's DHCP server provides support for BOOTP clients. The administrator can define a scope for use only by BOOTP clients. Alternatively, the administrator can define a scope to be used for both BOOTP and DHCP clients.

How DHCP Works

Hosts use the DHCP protocol to obtain an initial lease, to renew an existing lease, and to detect unauthorized DHCP servers.

Obtaining an Initial Lease

Initial lease acquisition occurs the first time a DHCP client boots up, as Figure 15-1 illustrates.

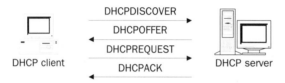

Figure 15-1. *DHCP messages exchanged during initial lease acquisition.*

The following Network Monitor Trace (Capture 15-01, included in the \Captures folder on the companion CD-ROM) illustrates this process:

```
1 4.426365  KAPOHO10  *BROADCAST DHCP  Discover  (xid=43474883)  0.0.0.0
255.255.255.255    IP
2 4.426365  LOCAL     *BROADCAST DHCP  Offer     (xid=43474883)  TALLGUY
255.255.255.255    IP
3 4.426365  KAPOHO10  *BROADCAST DHCP  Request   (xid=43474883)  0.0.0.0
255.255.255.255    IP
4 4.436379  LOCAL     *BROADCAST DHCP  ACK       (xid=43474883)  TALLGUY
255.255.255.255    IP
```

In this trace, the DHCP client first broadcasts a DHCPDISCOVER message to find a DHCP server. Because the host doesn't have an IP address, it communicates with the DHCP server by means of a local area broadcast. If there's more than one DHCP server able to provide the DHCP client with a valid IP address, it's possible for the DHCP client to receive one or more DHCPOFFER responses. If this occurs, the client will choose the "best" offer, which for Windows 2000 DHCP clients will be the first offer received. To help the client decide which is the best offer, the DHCPOFFER message will also contain values for options that the client has requested and that are configured on the offering DHCP server.

Any DHCP server that receives a DHCPREQUEST message and that can assign the DHCP client a lease will issue a DHCPOFFER message, which contains an offered IP address (and option values). If the client can accept this lease, it will issue a DHCPREQUEST to the DHCP server, requesting the offered IP address. This request also will contain all the configuration options that the DHCP client wishes to obtain.

The final message, a DHCPACK, is sent from the DHCP server to the DHCP client to confirm that the DHCP client has the IP address. The DHCPACK also provides values for the requested options that were specified by the DHCP administrator on the server issuing the DHCPACK.

Renewing a Lease

As Figure 15-2 illustrates, DHCP clients will attempt to renew the lease either at each reboot or at regular intervals after the DHCP client has initialized.

Figure 15-2. *DHCP messages exchanged during lease renewal.*

The following Network Monitor trace (Capture 15-02, included in the \Captures folder on the companion CD-ROM) illustrates this process:

```
1 81.757561    KAPOH010    *BROADCAST   DHCP    Request (xid=492D15B9) 0.0.0.0
255.255.255.255    IP
2 81.767576    LOCAL       *BROADCAST   DHCP    ACK     (xid=492D15B9) TALLGUY
255.255.255.255    IP
```

As shown in the Network Monitor trace, a lease renewal involves just two DHCP messages—DHCPREQUEST and DHCPACK. If the DHCP client renews a lease while booting up, broadcast IP packets are used to send these messages as shown in trace 15-2. If the lease renewal is made while the DHCP client is running, the DHCP client and the DHCP server communicate via unicast.

When a client obtains a lease, DHCP provides values for all configuration options requested by the client. By reducing the lease time, the DHCP administrator can force clients to regularly renew leases and obtain updated configuration details. This can be useful when the administrator wishes to change a subnet's IP configuration.

A DHCP client will first attempt to reacquire its lease at half the lease time, also known as T1. If this fails, the client will attempt a further lease renewal at 87.5 percent of the lease time, known as T2. If the lease isn't reacquired before it expires (for example, if the DHCP server is unreachable), as soon as the lease expires, the client immediately unbinds the IP address and attempts to acquire a new lease.

Changing Subnets and Servers

If the DHCP client requests a lease via a DHCPREQUEST message, that the DHCP server cannot fulfill (for example, when a laptop is moved to a different subnet), the DHCP server sends a DHCPNAK message to the client. The client will then acquire a new lease using the lease acquisition process described earlier. Figure 15-3 illustrates this sequence of DHCP messages.

Figure 15-3. *DHCP messages exchanged when DHCP client boots in a new subnet.*

The following Network Monitor trace (Capture 15-03, included in the \Captures folder on the companion CD-ROM) illustrates this process:

```
1  68.198064    KAPOHO10    *BROADCAST   DHCP   Request  (xid=2DBB2B8B)
0.0.0.0              255.255.255.255  IP
2  68.198064    LOCAL       *BROADCAST   DHCP   NACK     (xid=2DBB2B8B)
TALLGUY              255.255.255.255  IP
3  69.419821    KAPOHO10    *BROADCAST   DHCP   Discover (xid=749C146A)
0.0.0.0              255.255.255.255  IP
4  69.419821    LOCAL       *BROADCAST   DHCP   Offer    (xid=749C146A)
TALLGUY              255.255.255.255  IP
5  69.429836    KAPOHO10    *BROADCAST   DHCP   Request  (xid=749C146A)
0.0.0.0              255.255.255.255  IP
6  69.429836    LOCAL       *BROADCAST   DHCP   ACK      (xid=749C146A)
TALLGUY              255.255.255.255  IP
```

When a DHCP client boots up, it broadcasts a DHCPREQUEST message to renew its lease. This ensures that the DHCP renewal request is sent to the DHCP server that provides DHCP addresses for the subnet the client is now on, which might be different from the server that provided the initial lease. When the DHCP server receives the broadcast, it compares the address the DHCP client is requesting with the scopes configured on the server. If it's impossible to satisfy the client request, the DHCP server issues a DHCPNAK, and the DHCP client then acquires a new lease.

If the DHCP client is unable to locate any DHCP server when rebooting, to renew its lease, it issues an ARP broadcast for the default gateway that was previously obtained, if one was provided. If the IP address of the gateway is successfully resolved, the DHCP client assumes that it's still located on the same network where it obtained its current lease, and continues to use this lease.

If the ARP broadcast that the client sent for the default gateway receives no response, the client assumes that it's been moved to a network that has no DHCP services currently available (such as a home network), and it auto-configures itself using APIPA. Once it auto-configures itself, the DHCP client will try, every 5 minutes, to locate a DHCP server.

Using the DHCP Relay Agent

DHCP relay agents listen for DHCPDISCOVER and DHCPREQUEST (and DHCPINFORM) messages that are broadcast. The DHCP relay agent then waits a configured amount of time and, if no response is detected, sends the message to the configured DHCP server via unicast. The server then acts on the message, and sends the reply back to the DHCP relay agent. The relay agent then broadcasts the message on the local subnet allowing the DHCP client to receive it.

Detecting Unauthorized DHCP Servers

As part of the initialization of the DHCP service, all DHCP servers perform Rogue Server Detection. As Figure 15-4 illustrates, if the server isn't authorized in the Active Directory, it shuts down. This process can be seen in Network Monitor trace 15-4 (Capture 15-04, included in the \Captures folder on the companion CD-ROM), which contains a trace of an unauthorized server performing Rogue Server Detection, and succeeding.

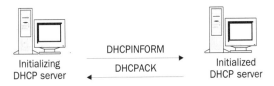

Figure 15-4. *A DHCP server performing Rogue Server Detection.*

Rogue server detection begins with the initializing DHCP server issuing DHCPINFORM queries to determine if there are other initialized DHCP servers on any attached network. If so, these servers respond with a DHCPACK message that contains the name of the domain in which they have been authorized. If other DHCP servers are found, as can be seen in the Network Monitor trace 15-4, a Windows 2000 DHCP service that's starting will bind to the Active Directory and issue a series of LDAP calls to discover whether or not it is authorized. If the server isn't authorized, the service terminates. This detection is carried out once per hour by the DHCP server, in order to detect newly de-authorized servers.

If DHCP event logging is enabled, a message is written to the DHCP event log. The event log message to accompany trace 15-4 is as follows:

```
00,05/17/99,18:34:08,Started,,,
61,05/17/99,18:34:08,Server found that belongs to DS
domain,10.10.1.200,kapoho.com,
01,05/17/99,18:34:08,Stopped,,,
```

In this example, the DHCP service started up and performed the Unauthorized DHCP Server detection. This authorization failed and the DHCP service, therefore, was stopped. Any attempts to restart the DHCP service would be unsuccessful until the DHCP server was authorized.

Updating DNS Entries

When a DHCP lease is granted to an IP host, it's important for the host name and IP address mapping to be provided to the DNS. Traditionally, this was a manual task, which involved creating the DNS forward- and reverse-lookup entries.

More Info   Windows 2000 implements Dynamic DNS update protocol described in RFC 2136. This protocol enables Windows 2000 clients to automatically send DNS entries to a DNS server. This RFC can be found in the \RFC folder on the companion CD-ROM.

Each time a DHCP client receives a new lease or renews an existing lease, the client sends its fully qualified name to the DHCP server as part of the DHCPREQUEST message. The DHCPREQUEST message requests the DHCP server to register a reverse-lookup address mapping in the DNS server on behalf of the client. The DHCP client usually handles the forward-lookup registration on its own, if it's capable.

The DHCP administrator can configure the DHCP server to send DNS updates for both the forward- and reverse-lookup address mappings to the DNS server. This is useful for down-level DHCP clients that don't support dynamic DNS updates.

Network Monitor trace 15-5 (Capture 15-05, included in the \Captures folder on the companion CD-ROM) illustrates a DHCP server registering both the forward- and reverse-lookup mappings for a new address lease. In the trace, the DHCP server queries for the DNS Start of Authority (SOA) record for the forward-lookup zone, then updates the forward-lookup entry for the DHCP client. The DHCP server then queries the DNS server for the reverse-lookup zone, and performs the update of the DHCP client's reverse lookup entry.

For the dynamic updates to be successful, the DNS server must support dynamic DNS updates and have the forward- and reverse-lookup zones configured to allow dynamic updates. The Windows 2000 DNS service supports dynamic DNS updates, but the default for new zones doesn't allow dynamic updates. If, for some reason, the dynamic updating of a zone isn't configured when the DHCP server attempts to update the DNS entry, the server will receive an error from the DNS server. This can be seen in Network Monitor trace 15-6 (Capture 15-06, included in the \Captures folder on the companion CD-ROM), where the reverse-lookup zone is configured to not allow dynamic updates. In this case, the DHCP server sends the update, but receives an error in return.

DHCP Messages

The format of DHCP messages is based on the message format used with the BOOTP protocol, as described in this section. The descriptions of the DHCP messages will refer to DHCP options, which are described in more detail in the "DHCP Options" section of this chapter.

General Message Format

RFC 2131 defines the format of the messages sent between a DHCP client and a DHCP server. The basic message format is illustrated in Figure 15-5.

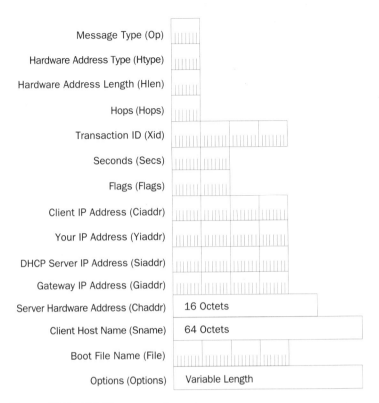

Figure 15-5. *DHCP message format.*

Table 15-1 displays the individual fields in the DHCP message, and a short description for each.

Table 15-1. DHCP Message Fields and Descriptions

Fields	Description
Message Type (Op)	Message type.
Hardware Address Type (Htype)	Hardware address type, as defined in ARP section of RFC 1700 (for example, "0x1" means 10 MB Ethernet).
Hardware Address Length (Hlen)	Hardware address length, in octets (for example, "0x6'" for 10 MB Ethernet).
Hops (Hops)	DHCP client sets this to 0. Relay agent can use this optionally when the DHCP client is booting via a relay agent.
Transaction ID (Xid)	A random number used to denote a conversation between a DHCP client and a DHCP server (for example, a lease acquisition).
Seconds (Secs)	Filled in by DHCP client. Number of seconds elapsed since DHCP client commenced address acquisition process.

(continued)

Table 15-1. *(continued)*

Fields	Description
Flags (Flags)	Flags set by client. In RFC 2131, the Broadcast flag is the only flag defined. A DHCP client that can't receive unicast IP datagrams until it has been configured with an IP address sets this Broadcast flag.
Client IP Address (Ciaddr)	Filled in only if client has an IP address and can respond to ARP requests to defend this IP address.
Your IP Address (Yiaddr)	The address given by the DHCP server to the DHCP client.
DHCP Server IP Address (Siaddr)	IP address of the DHCP server that's offering a lease (returned by DHCPOFFER).
Gateway IP Address (Giaddr)	DHCP Relay Agent IP Address, used when booting via a DHCP relay agent.
Client Hardware Address (Chaddr)	Client hardware address.
Server Host name (Sname)	Windows 2000 doesn't use this field.
Boot File Name (File)	The name of the file containing a boot image for a BOOTP client.
Options (Options)	A variable-length set of fields containing DHCP options.

As Figure 15-5 illustrates, DHCP messages consist of a fixed part—236 octets in length—plus a variable-length section, used to hold options. As DHCP messages are transmitted using UDP, all DHCP messages must fit fully into a UDP Datagram, which limits the variable-length section to MTU 264 bytes (allowing for the IP header of 20 bytes, and the UDP header of 8 bytes). Thus, for Ethernet, this limit is 1236 bytes.

DHCPDISCOVER

A DHCP client that wishes to find a DHCP server to provide a lease sends the DHCPDISCOVER message. Using DHCP, this is the first step in obtaining an IP address. Because the DHCP client has a valid IP address, the DHCPDISCOVER message is transmitted using the limited-broadcast IP address 255.255.255.255 and a source IP address of 0.0.0.0.

Before transmitting the DHCPDISCOVER message, the DHCP client fills in the fields (described earlier) in the fixed-length portion of the DHCP message as follows:

- **Op**   Set to 1, BOOTREQUEST
- **Htype, Hlen**   Set based on the type of network in use
- **Hops, Secs, Glags**   Set to 0
- **Xid**   Client selects a random 32-bit value
- **Ciaddr, Yiaddr, Siaddr, Giaddr**   All set to 0
- **Chaddr**   Set to the client MAC address of the interface acquiring a DHCP lease, and is the address used in all subsequent DHCP messages to refer to this interface on this client
- **Cname, File**   Set to 0

The Windows 2000 DHCP client also sets a series of options in the DHCPDISCOVER message. The options are set as follows:

- **Magic Cookie**   Always set to 99.130.83.99 to indicate that vendor extensions follow.
- **Client Identifier**   Set to the DHCP client's hardware address.
- **Host Name**   Set to the client's host name.
- **Client Class**   Set to "MSFT 5.0" to indicate that this is a Windows 2000 system.
- **Parameter Request List**   Set to indicate the parameters the client wants to obtain from the server. For Windows 2000, these are 0x01 (subnet mask), 0x0F (DNS domain name), 0x03 (default gateway), 0x06 (DNS servers), 0x2C (WINS server address), 0x2E (NetBIOS node type), 0x2F (NetBIOS Scope ID), 0x2B (vendor class information).

Note   The Windows 98 DHCPDISCOVER message doesn't send client class information and doesn't request vendor class information. Additionally, the Windows 98 DHCPDISCOVER message sends an Option Request message for Option 57, a maximum DHCP message size that isn't acted on by the Windows 2000 DHCP server.

The following Network Monitor trace (part of Capture 15-01, included in the \Captures folder on the companion CD-ROM) shows a DHCPDISCOVER message sent from a Windows 2000 client discovering available DHCP servers:

```
+ Frame: Base frame properties
+ ETHERNET: ETYPE = 0x0800 : Protocol = IP:  DOD Internet Protocol
+ IP: ID = 0x120; Proto = UDP; Len: 328
+ UDP: IP Multicast: Src Port: BOOTP Client, (68); Dst Port: BOOTP Server
(67); Length = 308 (0x134)
  DHCP: Discover           (xid=43474883)
      DHCP: Op Code          (op)     = 1 (0x1)
      DHCP: Hardware Type     (htype)  = 1 (0x1) 10Mb Ethernet
      DHCP: Hardware Address Length (hlen) = 6 (0x6)
      DHCP: Hops             (hops)   = 0 (0x0)
      DHCP: Transaction ID    (xid)    = 1128745091 (0x43474883)
      DHCP: Seconds          (secs)   = 0 (0x0)
    + DHCP: Flags            (flags)  = 0 (0x0)
      DHCP: Client IP Address (ciaddr) = 0.0.0.0
      DHCP: Your   IP Address (yiaddr) = 0.0.0.0
      DHCP: Server IP Address (siaddr) = 0.0.0.0
      DHCP: Relay  IP Address (giaddr) = 0.0.0.0
      DHCP: Client Ethernet Address (chaddr) = 00600801D303
      DHCP: Server Host Name  (sname)  = <Blank>
      DHCP: Boot File Name    (file)   = <Blank>
      DHCP: Magic Cookie = 99.130.83.99
```

```
DHCP: Option Field       (options)
    DHCP: DHCP Message Type     = DHCP Discover
    DHCP: Unrecognized Option   = 251 (0xFB)
    DHCP: Client-identifier     = (Type: 1) 00 60 08 01 d3 03
    DHCP: Requested Address     = 12.12.12.12
    DHCP: Host Name             = KAPOHO10
    DHCP: Client Class information = (Length: 8) 4d 53 46 54 20 35 2e 30
    DHCP: Parameter Request List = (Length: 10) 01 0f 03 06 2c 2e 2f 1f 21 2b
    DHCP: End of this option field
```

DHCPOFFER

When a DHCP server receives a DHCPREQUEST, the server uses the Chaddr field to identify the client requesting the DHCP lease. The server first checks its database to see if the DHCP client requesting the lease has an existing lease or a reservation for a lease. If it doesn't, the DHCP server then checks to see if it has a configured scope from which to allocate an IP address lease.

To determine which scope to use for address assignment, the DHCP server examines the Giaddr field in the DHCPDISCOVER message. If giaddr is 0, the DHCP server uses the interface that the message was received on to determine the scope. Conversely, if the Giaddr field is not 0, the server uses the scope that corresponds to the subnet the DHCP relay agent resides in. The Giaddr field is set by a DHCP relay agent, and is based on the subnet that the originating DHCP client is in.

If there's no existing lease for the client, the DHCP server examines the chosen scope to find an IP address for the DHCP client. If the client had a previously assigned lease, but the lease expired, and the address is available, the DHCP server offers this address. Otherwise, the server picks an available address from the scope being used for the allocation.

If the DHCP server can offer a lease, it will construct a DHCPOFFER message with the following fields set in the fixed-length portion of the DHCP message:

- **Op** Set to 2
- **Htype** Set according to the network hardware in use
- **Xid** Set to the Xid in the received DHCPDISCOVER
- **Yiaddr** Set to the IP address being offered to the DHCP client
- **Siaddr** Set to the IP address of the DHCP server offering the lease
- **Chaddr** Set to the client's hardware address as received in the DHCPDISCOVER message

The DHCP server also sets a series of options as follows:

- **Magic Cookie** Set to 99.130.83.99
- **DHCP Message Type** Set to 2 (DHCPOFFER)
- **Subnet Mask** Obtained from the scope definition

- **Renewal Time (T1)** Set to 50 percent of the lease time, in seconds
- **Rebinding Time (T2)** Set to 87.5 percent of the lease time, in seconds
- **IP Address Lease Time** The duration of the lease, in seconds
- **Server Identifier** The IP address of the server offering the lease
- **Domain Name** If requested in the DHCPDISCOVER message (and configured for the scope), the DNS domain name specified in the scope definition
- **Domain Name Server** If requested in the DHCPDISCOVER message (and configured for the scope), the list of DNS servers specified in the scope definition
- **NetBIOS Name Server** If requested in the DHCPDISCOVER message (and configured for the scope), the list of WINS servers specified in the scope
- **NetBIOS Node Type** If requested in the DHCPDISCOVER message (and configured for the scope), the NetBIOS node type specified in the scope definition

The DHCP client, having issued a DHCPDISCOVER, might receive zero, one, or more DHCPOFFER messages. If no DHCPOFFER message is received, the DHCP client retransmits the DHCPOFFER message. If the DHCP client receives no offer after three attempts, the client initiates auto-configuration using APIPA.

A DHCPOFFER message is shown in the following Network Monitor trace (part of Capture 15-01, included in the \Captures folder on the companion CD-ROM), which details a Windows 2000 client being offered a lease on the IP address 10.10.1.51:

```
+ Frame: Base frame properties
+ ETHERNET: ETYPE = 0x0800 : Protocol = IP:  DOD Internet Protocol
+ IP: ID = 0xD8B; Proto = UDP; Len: 337
+ UDP: IP Multicast: Src Port: BOOTP Server, (67); Dst Port: BOOTP Client
(68); Length = 317 (0x13D)
  DHCP: Offer              (xid=43474883)
      DHCP: Op Code          (op)     = 2 (0x2)
      DHCP: Hardware Type    (htype)  = 1 (0x1) 10Mb Ethernet
      DHCP: Hardware Address Length (hlen) = 6 (0x6)
      DHCP: Hops             (hops)   = 0 (0x0)
      DHCP: Transaction ID   (xid)    = 1128745091 (0x43474883)
      DHCP: Seconds          (secs)   = 0 (0x0)
    + DHCP: Flags            (flags)  = 0 (0x0)
      DHCP: Client IP Address (ciaddr) = 0.0.0.0
      DHCP: Your   IP Address (yiaddr) = 10.10.1.51
      DHCP: Server IP Address (siaddr) = 10.10.1.100
      DHCP: Relay  IP Address (giaddr) = 0.0.0.0
      DHCP: Client Ethernet Address (chaddr) = 00600801D303
      DHCP: Server Host Name  (sname)  = <Blank>
      DHCP: Boot File Name    (file)   = <Blank>
      DHCP: Magic Cookie = 99.130.83.99
      DHCP: Option Field      (options)
```

```
DHCP: DHCP Message Type      = DHCP Offer
DHCP: Subnet Mask            = 255.255.255.0
DHCP: Renewal Time Value (T1) = 4 Days,  0:00:00
DHCP: Rebinding Time Value (T2) = 7 Days,  0:00:00
DHCP: IP Address Lease Time  = 8 Days,  0:00:00
DHCP: Server Identifier      = 10.10.1.100
DHCP: Domain Name            = kapoho.com
DHCP: Router                 = 10.10.1.100
DHCP: Domain Name Server     = 10.10.1.200 10.10.2.200
```

DHCPREQUEST

A DHCP client sends the DHCPREQUEST to a DHCP server, usually as part of an initial lease acquisition (that is, responding to a DHCPOFFER), or as part of a subsequent lease renewal. A DHCP host can use it to confirm its previously allocated IP address and associated configuration parameters as well.

Based either on the information in a DHCPOFFER message, or on the currently configured DHCP properties, the Windows 2000 client constructs a DHCPREQUEST message with the following fields set in the fixed-length portion of the DHCP message:

- **Op** Set to 1.
- **Htype, Hlen** Set according to the network hardware in use.
- **Xid** Set to either the xid in the original DHCPDISCOVER (for new leases) or a new transaction ID (for lease renewals and IP address confirmations).
- **Chaddr** Set to the client's hardware address as specified in the original DHCPDISCOVER message.
- **Ciaddr** For new leases, this field is set to 0; for lease renewals, this is set to the IP address being renewed (or if the lease has expired, the IP address last leased by the DHCP client).

The Windows 2000 DHCP client also sets a series of options in the DHCPREQUEST message. The options are set as follows:

- **Magic Cookie** Always set to 99.130.83.99.
- **DHCP Message Type** Set to 0x03 (DHCPREQUEST).
- **Client Identifier** Set to the DHCP client's hardware address.
- **Requested Address** This is the address, offered in the DHCPOFFER message. (If multiple offers were received, this is the address the client chose from the set of addresses that were offered, and which the client is now requesting.)
- **Server ID** The client is addressing the DHCP request to this server.
- **Host Name** This is the DHCP client's host name.
- **Dynamic DNS Updates** This option, not defined in RFC 2131, contains the Host Name that the DHCP server will use to format DNS forward- and reverse-lookup updates.

- **Client Class Information**   Specifies the DHCP client's vendor class. For Windows 2000 computers, the class-identifier string is "MSFT 5.0." The DHCP server uses this to identify the client-class type and to identify any vendor-specific information to be returned.

- **Parameter Request List**   The list of configuration parameters that the client wishes to obtain. For Windows 2000 clients this request list contains options 0x01 (subnet mask), 0x03 (router), 0x06 (DNS server list), 0x0F (domain name), 0x2B (vendor-specific information), 0x2C (WINS server list), 0x2E (NetBIOS node type), and 0x2F (NetBIOS scope).

Note   Windows 98 DHCPREQUEST messages are similar to those sent by Windows 2000 clients. The Windows 98 client sends Option 57 (maximum DHCP message size), although the Windows 2000 DHCP server doesn't acknowledge this. The Windows 98 client, however, doesn't send the Dynamic DNS updates option or vendor class information in the Parameter Request list.

The following Network Monitor trace (part of Capture 15-01, included in the \Captures folder on the companion CD-ROM) shows a DHCPREQUEST message with a Windows 2000 client requesting a lease on the IP address 10.10.1.51:

```
+ Frame: Base frame properties
+ ETHERNET: ETYPE = 0x0800 : Protocol = IP:  DOD Internet Protocol
+ IP: ID = 0x121; Proto = UDP; Len: 365
+ UDP: IP Multicast: Src Port: BOOTP Client, (68); Dst Port: BOOTP Server
(67); Length = 345 (0x159)
  DHCP: Request              (xid=43474883)
      DHCP: Op Code          (op)    = 1 (0x1)
      DHCP: Hardware Type     (htype) = 1 (0x1) 10Mb Ethernet
      DHCP: Hardware Address Length (hlen) = 6 (0x6)
      DHCP: Hops             (hops)  = 0 (0x0)
      DHCP: Transaction ID    (xid)   = 1128745091 (0x43474883)
      DHCP: Seconds          (secs)  = 0 (0x0)
    + DHCP: Flags            (flags) = 0 (0x0)
      DHCP: Client IP Address (ciaddr) = 0.0.0.0
      DHCP: Your   IP Address (yiaddr) = 0.0.0.0
      DHCP: Server IP Address (siaddr) = 0.0.0.0
      DHCP: Relay  IP Address (giaddr) = 0.0.0.0
      DHCP: Client Ethernet Address (chaddr) = 00600801D303
      DHCP: Server Host Name  (sname)  = <Blank>
      DHCP: Boot File Name    (file)   = <Blank>
      DHCP: Magic Cookie = 99.130.83.99
      DHCP: Option Field     (options)
          DHCP: DHCP Message Type     = DHCP Request
          DHCP: Client-identifier     = (Type: 1) 00 60 08 01 d3 03
          DHCP: Requested Address     = 10.10.1.51
```

```
          DHCP: Server Identifier       = 10.10.1.100
          DHCP: Host Name               = KAPOHO10
          DHCP: Dynamic DNS updates     = (Length: 38) 00 00 00 4b 41 50 4f 48
4f 31 30 2e 72 65 64 6d ...
          DHCP: Client Class information = (Length: 8) 4d 53 46 54 20 35 2e 30
          DHCP: Parameter Request List = (Length: 10) 01 0f 03 06 2c 2e 2f 1f 21 2b
          DHCP: End of this option field
```

DHCPACK

The DHCP server sends the DHCPACK message to the DHCP client in response to the DHCPREQUEST or DHCPINFORM message. The DHCPACK message is a confirmation by the DHCP server that it has issued the DHCP client with a lease on an IP address and provides values for any required options (as specified in the Parameter Request list of the DHCPREQUEST message).

The Windows 2000 DHCP server constructs a DHCPACK message with the following fields set in the fixed-length portion of the DHCP message:

- **Op** Set to 2.
- **Htype, Hlen** Set according to the network hardware in use.
- **Xid** Set to either the xid in the original DHCPDISCOVER (for new leases) or a new transaction ID (for lease renewals and IP address confirmations).
- **Yiaddr** Set to the client's IP address. The DHCP server issues this address to the client.
- **Chaddr** Set to the client's hardware address as specified in the original DHCPDISCOVER message.

The Windows 2000 DHCP server also sets a series of options in the DHCPREQUEST message. The options are set as follows:

- **Magic Cookie** Always set to 99.130.83.99
- **DHCP Message Type** Set to 0x05 (DHCPACK)
- **Renewal Time (T1)** Set to 50 percent of the lease time, in seconds
- **Rebinding Time (T2)** Set of 87.5 percent of the lease time, in seconds
- **IP Address Lease Time** The duration of the lease, in seconds
- **Server ID** The client is addressing the DHCP request to this server
- **Subnet Mask** The client's subnet mask
- **Dynamic DNS Updates** Sent in response to the Dynamic DNS updates in the DHCPREQUEST message

Additionally, the DHCP server will send all option values for any of the options requested in the DHCPREQUEST message. The following Network Monitor trace (part of Capture

15-01, included in the \Captures folder on the companion CD-ROM) shows a Windows 2000 DHCP server confirming a lease on IP address 10.10.1.51 to a Windows 2000 client:

```
+  Frame: Base frame properties
+ ETHERNET: ETYPE = 0x0800 : Protocol = IP:  DOD Internet Protocol
+ IP: ID = 0xD90; Proto = UDP; Len: 342
+ UDP: IP Multicast: Src Port: BOOTP Server, (67); Dst Port: BOOTP Client
(68); Length = 322 (0x142)
   DHCP: ACK                   (xid=43474883)
       DHCP: Op Code           (op)     = 2 (0x2)
       DHCP: Hardware Type      (htype)  = 1 (0x1) 10Mb Ethernet
       DHCP: Hardware Address Length (hlen) = 6 (0x6)
       DHCP: Hops              (hops)   = 0 (0x0)
       DHCP: Transaction ID     (xid)    = 1128745091 (0x43474883)
       DHCP: Seconds           (secs)   = 0 (0x0)
     + DHCP: Flags             (flags)  = 0 (0x0)
       DHCP: Client IP Address (ciaddr) = 0.0.0.0
       DHCP: Your   IP Address (yiaddr) = 10.10.1.51
       DHCP: Server IP Address (siaddr) = 0.0.0.0
       DHCP: Relay  IP Address (giaddr) = 0.0.0.0
       DHCP: Client Ethernet Address (chaddr) = 00600801D303
       DHCP: Server Host Name   (sname)  = <Blank>
       DHCP: Boot File Name    (file)   = <Blank>
       DHCP: Magic Cookie = 99.130.83.99
       DHCP: Option Field      (options)
           DHCP: DHCP Message Type     = DHCP ACK
           DHCP: Renewal Time Value (T1) = 4 Days,  0:00:00
           DHCP: Rebinding Time Value (T2) = 7 Days,  0:00:00
           DHCP: IP Address Lease Time  = 8 Days,  0:00:00
           DHCP: Server Identifier      = 10.10.1.100
           DHCP: Subnet Mask            = 255.255.255.0
           DHCP: Dynamic DNS updates    = (Length: 3) 03 ff ff
           DHCP: Domain Name            = kapoho.com
           DHCP: Router                 = 10.10.1.100
           DHCP: Domain Name Server     = 10.10.1.200 10.10.2.200
```

DHCPDECLINE

When a DHCP client receives an IP address from a DHCP server, the client must determine whether the IP address is in use. In fact, the Windows 2000 DHCP server can be configured to check that the address is in use before even issuing the address. However, both Windows 2000 and Windows 98 clients perform this check after receiving a DHCPACK. The client performs the check by issuing an ARP broadcast for the address.

If the DHCP client receives an ARP reply, indicating that the address is in use, the client broadcasts a DHCPDECLINE to the DHCP server and unbinds the address. The Windows 2000 DHCP server marks the address as "bad" in the DHCP database. The client is then free to acquire a lease for another IP address.

Network Monitor trace 15-7 (Capture 15-07, included in the \Captures folder on the companion CD-ROM) contains a trace of a Windows 2000 system acquiring a lease. In the trace, the DHCP server offers and acknowledges an IP address against which the DHCP client performs a gratuitous ARP. Because the address is in use, the ARP finds a host using the address, and the DHCP client broadcasts the DHCPDECLINE. This allows the DHCP server to mark the address as "bad_address" in the DHCP database. The DHCP client also writes an Event Log Warning message to the DHCP client's event log, as well as to the event log of the client currently holding the disputed IP address (if that system is a Windows 2000 computer).

The Windows 2000 client constructs a DHCPDECLINE message with the following fields set in the fixed-length portion of the DHCP message:

- **Op** Set to 1
- **Htype, Hlen** Set according to the network hardware in use
- **Xid** Set to xid in the original DHCPDISCOVER or DHCPREQUEST
- **Ciaddr** Set to the IP address that's in dispute (that is, the one the client was issued but has determined is already in use)
- **Chaddr** Set to the client's hardware address as specified in the original in the DHCPDISCOVER message

The Windows 2000 DHCP client also sets a series of options in the DHCPDECLINE message as follows:

- **Magic Cookie** Always set to 99.130.83.99
- **DHCP Message Type** Set to 0x04 (DHCPDECLINE)
- **Client Identifier** The MAC address of the client issuing the DHCPDECLINE message
- **Requested Address** The disputed IP address
- **Server ID** The IP address of the server that issued the client with the disputed address

The following trace (part of Capture 15-07, included in the \Captures folder on the companion CD-ROM) shows the DHCPDECLINE message in detail:

```
+ Frame: Base frame properties
+ ETHERNET: ETYPE = 0x0800 : Protocol = IP:  DOD Internet Protocol
+ IP: ID = 0xC58; Proto = UDP; Len: 328
+ UDP: IP Multicast: Src Port: BOOTP Client, (68); Dst Port: BOOTP Server
(67); Length = 308 (0x134)
```

```
DHCP: Decline              (xid=3D136017)
   DHCP: Op Code            (op)     = 1 (0x1)
   DHCP: Hardware Type      (htype)  = 1 (0x1) 10Mb Ethernet
   DHCP: Hardware Address Length (hlen) = 6 (0x6)
   DHCP: Hops               (hops)   = 0 (0x0)
   DHCP: Transaction ID     (xid)    = 1024679959 (0x3D136017)
   DHCP: Seconds            (secs)   = 0 (0x0)
 + DHCP: Flags              (flags)  = 0 (0x0)
   DHCP: Client IP Address (ciaddr) = 10.10.1.50
   DHCP: Your   IP Address (yiaddr) = 0.0.0.0
   DHCP: Server IP Address (siaddr) = 0.0.0.0
   DHCP: Relay  IP Address (giaddr) = 0.0.0.0
   DHCP: Client Ethernet Address (chaddr) = 00600801D303
   DHCP: Server Host Name  (sname)  = <Blank>
   DHCP: Boot File Name     (file)   = <Blank>
   DHCP: Magic Cookie = 99.130.83.99
   DHCP: Option Field       (options)
     DHCP: DHCP Message Type     = DHCP Decline
     DHCP: Client-identifier     = (Type: 1) 00 60 08 01 d3 03
     DHCP: Requested Address     = 10.10.1.50
       DHCP: Option MUST NOT be Present
     DHCP: Server Identifier     = 10.10.1.100
     DHCP: End of this option field
```

DHCPNAK

The DHCP server uses DHCPNAK messages to tell a DHCP client that an address it's requesting can't be provided. This can occur when a client that has a lease is off-line or, for administrative reasons, the DHCP administrator cancels the lease. In that case, the DHCP server could re-allocate the address to another client. It can also occur on clients that move between different subnets.

If the requested address comes from a scope that does not match the scope of the value in the Giaddr field or the scope of the interface on which it was received (if the Giaddr field is 0), the DHCP server determines that the DHCP client has moved to a different subnet.

Upon receiving a DHCPNAK message, Windows DHCP clients immediately release the IP address and attempt to acquire a new IP address.

The following Network Monitor trace (part of Capture 15-03, included in the \Captures folder on the companion CD-ROM) illustrates the DHCPNAK. The trace shows a DHCPREQUEST for an address, followed by a DHCPNAK indicating that it's not available:

```
+ Frame: Base frame properties
+ ETHERNET: ETYPE = 0x0800 : Protocol = IP:  DOD Internet Protocol
```

```
+ IP: ID = 0xAE; Proto = UDP; Len: 353
+ UDP: Src Port: BOOTP Client, (68); Dst Port: BOOTP Server (67); Length = 333
(0x14D)
   DHCP: Request            (xid=199F7780)
      DHCP: Op Code          (op)     = 1 (0x1)
      DHCP: Hardware Type    (htype)  = 1 (0x1) 10Mb Ethernet
      DHCP: Hardware Address Length (hlen) = 6 (0x6)
      DHCP: Hops             (hops)   = 0 (0x0)
      DHCP: Transaction ID   (xid)    = 429881216 (0x199F7780)
      DHCP: Seconds          (secs)   = 0 (0x0)
    + DHCP: Flags            (flags)  = 0 (0x0)
      DHCP: Client IP Address (ciaddr) = 10.10.1.50
      DHCP: Your   IP Address (yiaddr) = 0.0.0.0
      DHCP: Server IP Address (siaddr) = 0.0.0.0
      DHCP: Relay  IP Address (giaddr) = 0.0.0.0
      DHCP: Client Ethernet Address (chaddr) = 00600801D303
      DHCP: Server Host Name  (sname)  = <Blank>
      DHCP: Boot File Name    (file)   = <Blank>
      DHCP: Magic Cookie = 99.130.83.99
      DHCP: Option Field      (options)
         DHCP: DHCP Message Type     = DHCP Request
         DHCP: Client-identifier     = (Type: 1) 00 60 08 01 d3 03
         DHCP: Host Name             = KAPOHO10
         DHCP: Dynamic DNS updates   = (Length: 38) 00 00 00 4b 41 50 4f 48
         4f 31 30 2e 72 65 64 6d ...
         DHCP: Client Class information = (Length: 8) 4d 53 46 54 20 35 2e 30
         DHCP: Parameter Request List = (Length: 10) 01 0f 03 06 2c 2e 2f 1f 21 2b
         DHCP: End of this option field
+ Frame: Base frame properties
+ ETHERNET: ETYPE = 0x0800 : Protocol = IP:  DOD Internet Protocol
+ IP: ID = 0xCBEA; Proto = UDP; Len: 328
+ UDP: Src Port: BOOTP Server, (67); Dst Port: BOOTP Client (68); Length = 308
(0x134)
   DHCP: NACK              (xid=199F7780)
      DHCP: Op Code          (op)     = 2 (0x2)
      DHCP: Hardware Type    (htype)  = 1 (0x1) 10Mb Ethernet
      DHCP: Hardware Address Length (hlen) = 6 (0x6)
      DHCP: Hops             (hops)   = 0 (0x0)
      DHCP: Transaction ID   (xid)    = 429881216 (0x199F7780)
      DHCP: Seconds          (secs)   = 0 (0x0)
    + DHCP: Flags            (flags)  = 128 (0x80)
      DHCP: Client IP Address (ciaddr) = 0.0.0.0
      DHCP: Your   IP Address (yiaddr) = 0.0.0.0
      DHCP: Server IP Address (siaddr) = 0.0.0.0
```

```
DHCP: Relay  IP Address (giaddr) = 0.0.0.0
DHCP: Client Ethernet Address (chaddr) = 00600801D303
DHCP: Server Host Name  (sname)  = <Blank>
DHCP: Boot File Name    (file)   = <Blank>
DHCP: Magic Cookie = 99.130.83.99
DHCP: Option Field      (options)
    DHCP: DHCP Message Type     = DHCP NACK
    DHCP: Server Identifier     = 10.10.1.100
```

DHCPRELEASE

The DHCP client sends this message to the DHCP server releasing the IP address and canceling the lease. The released IP address can then be reused for other DHCP clients. The Windows 2000 DHCP server doesn't acknowledge the DHCPRELEASE. The DHCPRELEASE message is unicast from the DHCP client to the DHCP server that originally issued the lease that the client is releasing.

The Windows 2000 DHCP client constructs a DHCPRELEASE message with the following fields set in the fixed-length portion of the DHCP message:

- **Op**   Set to 1
- **Htype, Hlen**   Set according to the network hardware in use
- **Xid**   Set to a new transaction ID
- **Ciaddr**   Set to the client's IP address that's being released
- **Chaddr**   Set to the client's hardware address as specified in the original DHCPDISCOVER message

The Windows 2000 client also sets a series of options in the DHCPRELEASE message. The options are set as follows:

- **Magic Cookie**   Always set to 99.130.83.99
- **DHCP Message Type**   Set to 0x07 (DHCPRELEASE)
- **Server Identifier**   The server that originally issued the lease
- **Client Identifier**   The DHCP client's MAC address

The following Network Monitor trace (Capture 15-08, included in the \Captures folder on the companion CD-ROM), shows a DHCPRELEASE message sent from a Windows 2000 computer, releasing the IP address 10.10.1.61:

```
+ Frame: Base frame properties
+ ETHERNET: ETYPE = 0x0800 : Protocol = IP:  DOD Internet Protocol
+ IP: ID = 0xFA; Proto = UDP; Len: 328
+ UDP: Src Port: BOOTP Client, (68); Dst Port: BOOTP Server (67); Length = 308
(0x134)
  DHCP: Release           (xid=771D3A02)
    DHCP: Op Code         (op)     = 1 (0x1)
```

```
      DHCP: Hardware Type      (htype)  = 1 (0x1) 10Mb Ethernet
      DHCP: Hardware Address Length (hlen) = 6 (0x6)
      DHCP: Hops               (hops)   = 0 (0x0)
      DHCP: Transaction ID     (xid)    = 1998404098 (0x771D3A02)
      DHCP: Seconds            (secs)   = 0 (0x0)
    + DHCP: Flags              (flags)  = 128 (0x80)
      DHCP: Client IP Address (ciaddr) = 10.10.1.61
      DHCP: Your   IP Address (yiaddr) = 0.0.0.0
      DHCP: Server IP Address (siaddr) = 0.0.0.0
      DHCP: Relay  IP Address (giaddr) = 0.0.0.0
      DHCP: Client Ethernet Address (chaddr) = 00600801D303
      DHCP: Server Host Name   (sname)  = <Blank>
      DHCP: Boot File Name     (file)   = <Blank>
      DHCP: Magic Cookie = 99.130.83.99
      DHCP: Option Field       (options)
          DHCP: DHCP Message Type    = DHCP Release
          DHCP: Server Identifier    = 10.10.1.100
          DHCP: Client-identifier    = (Type: 1) 00 60 08 01 d3 03
          DHCP: End of this option field
```

DHCPINFORM

RFC 2131 defines a new DHCP message type, DHCPINFORM. DHCP clients could use the DHCPINFORM message to request additional configuration information, regardless of how the DHCP clients were originally configured. Thus, a DHCP client, configured with a static IP address, could use the DHCPINFORM messages to request additional local configuration parameters from a DHCP server. DHCPINFORM is also used by Windows 2000 remote access clients to automatically obtain a DNS domain name, after the Point-to-Point Protocol (PPP) connection is configured.

More Info DHCPINFORM is described in RFC 2131, which can be found in the \RFC folder on the companion CD-ROM.

In Windows 2000, the key use of the DHCPINFORM message is to enable a Windows 2000 DHCP server to discover the name of the Directory Services (DS) enterprise root on which each server is installed as part of rogue DHCP server detection. This information is requested within the DHCPINFORM message by including information in the message's vendor-specific options area. When other DHCP servers running the Windows 2000 DHCP Server service receive the DHCPINFORM message, the DHCP servers process, acknowledge, and respond with the requested information about the DS enterprise root.

The Windows 2000 server constructs a DHCPINFORM message with the following fields set in the fixed-length portion of the DHCP message:

- **Op** Set to 1
- **Htype, Hlen** Set according to the network hardware in use

- **Xid**   The DHCP server generates a new transaction ID
- **Ciaddr**   Set to the DHCP server's IP address

The Windows 2000 DHCP server also sets a series of options in the DHCPINFORM message as follows:

- **Magic Cookie**   Always set to 99.130.83.99
- **DHCP Message Type**   Set to 0x08 (DHCPINFORM)
- **Vendor-Specific Information**   For unauthorized server detection, this field is set to 0x5E

DHCP Options

The Windows 2000 server provides DHCP leases, which include IP addresses, subnet masks, and values for specific options as requested by the DHCP client. This section defines the options that Windows 2000 DHCP servers support and those that Windows 2000 clients can request.

What Are DHCP Options?

A DHCP option is a configuration parameter that a DHCP server can send to a DHCP client. These can be standard options, used in all DHCP messages (or all messages of a particular type such as DHCPDISCOVER), such as the Magic Cookie option, or DHCP message types. Additionally, DHCP options can contain configuration parameters that are explicitly requested by DHCP clients, such as the default gateway IP address.

The Windows 2000 DHCP server supports the standard option types, defined in RFC 2132. Moreover, Windows 2000 defines extra vendor-specific options that the administrator can use to provide Windows 2000 DHCP clients with additional information.

More Info   Standard option types are defined in RFC 2131, which can be found in the \RFC folder on the companion CD-ROM.

Option Formats

As defined by RFCs 2131 and 2132, options can be of either fixed length or variable length, and might or might not have associated data. All options begin with an octet holding the option code to identify it. Fixed-length options without data consist of only a tag octet. The only fixed-length options without data are Option 0 (Pad) and Option 255 (End). All other options are of variable length and have a length octet following the tag octet. The length octet value excludes the two octets that specify the tag and length. The length value indicates the number of octets that the option will contain. Some variable-length options have a fixed-length field but a length option will still be specified.

The vendor option class is formatted slightly differently in that there's a single option (vendor-specific information) that consists of a list of sub-options.

Options Supported by Windows 2000

The Windows 2000 DHCP service supports all options specified in RFC 2132. However, most of the defined options are no longer in use, or aren't used by Windows or MS-DOS DHCP clients. For the full list of options that Windows 2000 DHCP service supports, refer to Windows 2000 Server Help. The options that the Windows 2000 DHCP server supports fall into the following three groups:

- Options that are present in all messages (or all occurrences of a specific message type)
- Standard options that clients can request and that the DHCP server will provide, if the administrator at the DHCP server has defined the option value
- Vendor options that are returned based on the client class

Options Present in All DHCP Messages

Table 15-2 displays the DHCP options that appear in all DHCP messages (or in all occurrences of a particular DHCP message):

Table 15-2. DHCP Options Appearing in All DHCP Messages

Option Name	Option Code	Option Length	Option Description
Pad	0	1 octet	Used to cause subsequent fields to align. Can be used in any DHCP message.
Subnet Mask	1	4 octets	Used in conjunction with an offered IP address. Used in DHCPOFFER and DHCPACK messages.
Host Name	12	Variable length; minimum length is 1 octet	Specifies the name of the client. Used in DHCPDISCOVER, DHCPREQUEST, and DHCPNAK messages.
Vendor-Specific Information	43	Variable length	Used by clients and servers to exchange vendor-specific information. The definition of this information is vendor-specific and isn't defined in RFC 2132. Used in DHCPINFORM messages.
Requested Address	50	4 octets	The DHCP client is requesting (or declining) this address. Used in DHCPREQUEST and DHCPDELCINE messages.
Lease Time	51	4 octets	The length of the lease in seconds. Present in only DHCPOFFER and DHCPACK messages.
DHCP Message Type	53	1 octet	Used to define the DHCP Message type. The values are as follows: 1 – DHCPDISCOVER 2 – DHCPOFFER 3 – DHCPREQUEST 4 – DHCPDECLINE 5 – DHCPACK 6 – DHCPNAK 7 – DHCPRELEASE 8 – DHCPINFORM Used in all DHCP messages.

(continued)

Table 15-2. *(continued)*

Option Name	Option Code	Option Length	Option Description
Server Identifier and	54	4 octets	The DHCP server's IP address. Used in DHCPREQUEST, DHCPACK, DHCPDECLINE, DHCPRELEASE messages.
Parameter Request List	55	Variable length; but for Windows 2000 Clients, this will be 8 octets in length	Used by a DHCP client to request values for specific configuration parameters. Each octet is a valid DHCP option code (defined in RFC 2132) for options that the DHCP client is requesting values for from the DHCP server. Occurs in DHCPDISCOVER, DHCPREQUEST, and DHCPINFORM messages.
Renewal Time (T1)	58	4 octets	Length of time until client enters renewal state, in seconds. Used in DHCPOFFER and DHCPACK messages.
Rebinding Time (T2)	59	4 octets	Length of time until the client enters rebinding state, in seconds. Used in DHCPOFFER and DHCPACK messages.
Client Identifier	61	Variable length; minimum length is 2 octets; for Ethernet, the length is 6 octets	A value to identify the client uniquely. For Windows 2000 clients, this is the client MAC address. Used in DHCPDISCOVER, DHCPREQUEST, DHCPDECLINE, DHCPNAK, and DHCPRELEASE messages.
Dynamic DNS Update	81	Variable length	This is the fully qualified domain name of the host and the DHCP server uses it to send dynamic DNS updates to a DNS server. Used in DHCPREQUEST messages.
End	255	1 octet	Marks the end of the Options field in a DHCP message. Used in all DHCP messages.

Options Requested by DHCP Clients

The options that clients can request and receive values for (assuming the administrator has specified values for them on the DHCP server) are shown in Table 15-3.

Table 15-3.   Options for Which Clients Can Request and Receive Values

Option Name	Option Code	Option Length	Option Description
Router	3	Variable; but always a multiple of 4	A list of IP addresses for routers on the client's subnet, which should be listed in order of preference. Generally, there will be only one router—the default gateway—but multiple gateways can be specified.
Domain Name Servers	6	Variable; but always a multiple of 4	A list of IP addresses for Domain Name System servers (per RFC 1035) available to the client.

(continued)

Table 15-3. *(continued)*

Option Name	Option Code	Option Length	Option Description
DNS Domain Name	15	Variable length set of ASCII characters	The DNS domain name that the DHCP client should use when resolving host names using DNS.
WINS Server Names	44	Variable; but always a multiple of 4	A list of WINS Server IP Addresses for client use. This will typically be a primary and secondary server.
NetBIOS Over TCP/IP Node Type	46	1 octet	Used to tell a TCP/IP client how NetBIOS names should be resolved, as follows: 0x1 B-node (broadcast) 0x2 P-node (point-to-point) 0x4 M-node (mixed) 0x8 H-node (hybrid) See Chapter 17 for more detail on the NetBIOS Node Type.
NetBIOS Scope ID	47	Variable; minimum length is 1	Specifies the NetBIOS over TCP/IP scope for the client, as specified in RFCs 1001 and 1002.

Vendor-Specific Options

In addition to the standard options noted above, the administrator can set specific options to be returned to clients of a particular class (such as Windows 2000, Windows 98, and so forth).

Table 15-4 shows the options that can be returned to a client running Microsoft Windows 2000.

Table 15-4. Options that Can Be Returned to a Client Running Windows 2000

Option Name	Option Code	Option Length	Option Description
Microsoft Disable NetBIOS Option	1	4	Informs the Windows 2000 client whether or not to disable NetBIOS
Microsoft Release On Shutdown	2	4	Informs the Windows 2000 client whether or not to release the DHCP lease on shutdown
Microsoft Default Router Metric Base	2	4	Specifies the default router metric base

Summary

DHCP is a simple client server protocol that makes TCP/IP network configuration much simpler for the Administrator. DHCP is based on the BOOTP protocol, which explains some of the message formats. Windows 2000 implements the latest RFCs that define both the DHCPINFORM message type, plus the new Vendor and User class options. The DHCP Server in Windows 2000 will support all down-level Microsoft networking clients that support DHCP.

Chapter 16
Domain Name Service (DNS)

Every host that runs TCP/IP must have a unique IP address that's used when communicating with other computers in a network. Computers operate easily with IP addresses, but people don't; users would rather identify systems by a name. To facilitate effective and efficient communication, users need to be able to refer to computers by name, and still have their computer use IP addresses transparently.

In the early days of the ARPANET, the forerunner to today's Internet, there were only a small number of computers attached to the network. The Network Information Center (NIC), located at Stanford Research Institute (SRI), was responsible for compiling a single file, HOSTS.TXT, which contained the names and addresses of every computer. Administrators would email SRI, which would then update the HOSTS.TXT file. Next, ARPANET users would download the new version of HOSTS.TXT using File Transfer Protocol (FTP).

As the ARPANET grew, it became obvious that this approach wouldn't scale, for the following three key reasons:

- The bandwidth consumed in transmitting updated versions of an ARPANET-wide host file was proportional to the square of the number of hosts in the ARPANET. With the number of hosts growing at an exponential rate, the long-term impact was likely to be a load that no one host was going to be able to sustain.

- The static flat host file also meant that no two computers on the ARPANET could have the same name. As the number of hosts grew, the risk of adding a duplicate name grew, as did the difficulty of trying to control this centrally.

- The nature of the underlying network was changing—the large, timesharing computers that had once made up the ARPANET were being superseded by networks of workstations—each of which needed to have a unique host name. This would be difficult, if not impossible, to control centrally.

As the ARPANET continued to grow, it became clear that ARPANET needed a better solution. Several proposals were generated based on the concept of a distributed naming service, which was based on a hierarchical name space. RFCs 882 and 883 emerged, which described the design for a domain name system, based on a distributed database containing generalized resource information. This design evolved, and RFCs 1034 and 1035 were issued to describe the Domain Name System (DNS) service used in today's Internet. This design continues to evolve, and a number of proposed updates and refinements are being discussed as this chapter is being written.

Chapter Contents

This chapter describes Microsoft Windows 2000's implementation of the DNS protocol. Additionally, there are Network Monitor traces on the companion CD-ROM that demonstrate the DNS protocol in operation.

This chapter contains the following sections:

- **Overview to DNS in Windows 2000**   A description of the DNS protocol as implemented in Windows 2000
- **How DNS Works**   A description of how DNS works, illustrated by various Network Monitor traces
- **DNS Messages**   Describes the format of the messages sent between DNS clients and DNS servers, and the functions provided
- **Server-Server DNS Messages**   Describes the format of messages sent between DNS servers

This chapter doesn't discuss the administration of a DNS system, however. The care and feeding of a DNS service could, and does, fill complete books, and we won't duplicate that effort here. See the bibliography for details of recommended books covering DNS administration considerations.

Overview to DNS in Microsoft Windows 2000

To facilitate communications between computers, computers can be given names within a name space. The specific name space defines the rules for naming a computer, and for how names are resolved into IP addresses. When one computer communicates with other computers, it must resolve, or convert, a computer name into an IP address based on the rules of the name space being used. This resolution will be done by a name-resolution service.

There are two main name spaces, and name-resolution methods, used within Windows 2000: NetBIOS, implemented by Windows Internet Naming Service (WINS) (described in Chapter 17), and the DNS, described in this chapter. Windows 2000 also provides support for other name spaces, such as Novell Netware and Banyan Vines, although discussion of these is outside the scope of this book.

In this section, we'll describe DNS and the protocol used to provide name resolution.

What Is DNS?

The DNS is an IETF-standard name service. The DNS service enables client computers on your network to register and resolve DNS domain names. These names are used to find and access resources offered by other computers on your network or other networks, such as the Internet. The following are the three main components of DNS:

- **Domain name space and associated resource records (RRs)**   A distributed database of name-related information.

- **DNS Name Servers**   Servers that hold the domain name space and RRs, and that answer queries from DNS clients.
- **DNS Resolvers**   The facility within a DNS client that contacts DNS name servers and issues name queries to obtain resource record information.

Key DNS Terms

This section describes the key components of the DNS and defines key DNS terms.

Domain Name Space

The *domain name space* is a hierarchical, tree-structured name space, starting at an unnamed root used for all DNS operations. In the DNS name space, each node and leaf in the domain name space tree represents a named domain. Each domain can have additional child domains. Figure 16-1 illustrates the structure of Internet domain name space.

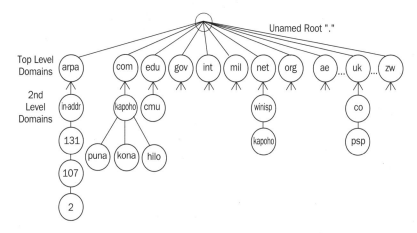

Figure 16-1. *Domain name space for the Internet.*

Domain Names

Each node in the DNS tree, as Figure 16-1 illustrates, has a separate name, referred to in RFC 1034 as a label. Each DNS label can be from 1 through 63 characters in length, with the root domain having a length of zero characters.

A specific node's *domain name* is the list of the labels in the path from the node being named to the DNS Tree root. DNS convention is that the labels that compose a domain name are read left to right—from the most specific to the root (for example, *www.kapoho.com*). This full name is also known as the *fully qualified domain name (FQDN)*.

Domain names can be stored as upper case or lower case, but all domain comparisons and domain functions are defined, by RFC 1034, to be case insensitive. Thus, *www.kapoho.com* is identical to *WWW.KAPOHO.COM* for domain naming operations.

Top-Level Domains

A *top-level domain* is a DNS domain directly below the root. As Figure 16-1 illustrates, a number of top-level domains have been defined. Additional names (at least for the Internet) are difficult to create. The following are the three categories of top-level domains:

- **"ARPA"** This is a special domain—used today for reverse-name lookups.
- **3-letter domains** There are six 3-character, top-level domains noted below.
- **2-letter country-based domain names** These country code domains are based on the International Organization for Standardization (ISO) country name, and are used principally by companies and organizations outside the US. The exception is the UK, which uses .uk as the top-level domain, even though the ISO country code is GB.

Table 16-1 shows the six top-level domains in use today, as defined by RFC 1591.

Table 16-1. 3-Character Top-Level Domains in Use in the Internet

3-Character Domain Name	Use
com	Commercial organizations, such as microsoft.com for the Microsoft Corporation
edu	Educational institutions, now mainly four-year colleges and universities, such as cmu.edu for Carnegie Mellon University
gov	Agencies of the US Federal Government, such as fbi.gov for the US Federal Bureau of Investigation
int	Organizations established by international treaties, such as nato.int for NATO
mil	US military, such as af.mil for the US Air Force
net	Computers of network providers, organizations dedicated to the Internet, Internet Service Providers (ISPs), and so forth, such as internic.net for the Internet Network Information Center (InterNIC)
org	A top-level domain for groups that don't fit anywhere else, such as non-government or non-profit organizations (for example, reiki.org for information about Reiki)

Note While these are the only 3-letter domains available today, there is pressure to expand this number; we may well end up with more in the future.

Resource Records (RR)

A *resource record* is a record containing information relating to a domain that the DNS database can hold and that a DNS client can retrieve and use. For example, the host RR for a specific domain holds the IP address of that domain (host); a DNS client will use this RR to obtain the IP address for the domain.

Each DNS server contains the RRs relating to those portions of the DNS namespace for which it's authoritative (or for which it can answer queries sent by a host). When a DNS server is authoritative for a portion of the DNS name space, those systems' administrators are responsible for ensuring that the information about that DNS name space portion is correct. To increase efficiency, a given DNS server can cache the RRs relating to a domain in any part of the domain tree.

There are numerous RR types defined in RFCs 1035 and 1036, and in later RFCs. Most of the RR types are no longer needed or used, although all are fully supported by Windows 2000. Table 16-2 lists the key RRs that might be used in a Windows 2000 network. (For more detail on the contents of specific RRs, see the "DNS Resource Records" section later in this chapter.)

Table 16-2. Key Resource Records as Used by a Windows 2000 Network

Resource Record Type	Contents	Use
A	Host Address	Used to hold a specific host's IP address.
CNAME	Canonical Name (alias)	Used to make an alias name for a host.
MX	Mail Exchanger	Provides message routing to a mail server, plus backup server(s) in case the target server isn't active.
NS	Name Server	Provides a list of authoritative servers for a domain or indicates authoritative DNS servers for any delegated sub-domains.
PTR	Pointer	Used for reverse lookup—resolving an IP address into a domain name using the IN-ADDR.ARPA domain.
SOA	Start of Authority	Used to determine the DNS server that's the primary server for a DNS zone and to store other zone property information.
SRV	Service Locator	Provides the ability to find the server providing a specific service. Active Directory uses SRV records to locate domain controllers, global catalog servers, and Lightweight Directory Access Protocol (LDAP) servers.

RRs can be attached to any node in the DNS tree, although RRs won't be provided in some domains (for example, Pointer (PTR) RRs are found only in domains below the in-addr.arpa domain). Thus, higher-level domains, such as microsoft.com, can have individual RRs (for example, Mail Exchange (MX) record for mail to be sent to the Microsoft Corporation) as well as having sub-domains that also might have individual RRs (for instance, eu.microsoft.com, which has a host record www.eu.microsoft.com).

Canonical Names

The Canonical Name (CNAME) RR enables the administrator to create an alias to another domain name. The use of CNAME RRs are recommended for use in the following scenarios:

- When a host specified in an (A) RR in the same zone needs to be renamed. For example, if you need to rename kona.kapoho.com to hilo.kapoho.com, you could create a CNAME entry for kona.kapoho.com to point to hilo.kapoho.com.

- When a generic name for a well-known service, such as ftp or www, needs to resolve to a group of individual computers (each with an individual (A) RR). For example, you might want *www.kapoho.com* to be an alias for kona.kapoho.com and hilo.kapoho.com. A user will access *www.kapoho.com* and generally won't be aware of which computer is actually servicing this request.

DNS Query Operation

A DNS client issues a *query operation* against a DNS server to obtain some or all of the RR information relating to a specific domain, for instance, to determine which host (A) record or records are held for the domain named kapoho.com. If the domain exists and the requested RRs exist, the DNS server will return the requested information in a *query reply message*. The query reply message will return both the initial query and a reply containing the relevant records, assuming the DNS server can obtain the required RRs.

A DNS query, referred to in RFC 1034 as a standard query, contains a target domain name, a query type, and a query class. The query will contain a request for the specific RR(s) that the resolver wished to obtain (or a request to return all RRs relating to the domain).

DNS Update Operation

A DNS *update operation* is issued by a DNS client against a DNS server to update, add, or delete some or all of the RR information relating to a specific domain, for instance, to update the host record for the computer named kona.kapoho.com to point to 10.10.1.100. The update operation is also referred to as a dynamic update.

DNS Zones

A DNS server that has complete information for part of the DNS name space is said to be the *authority* for that part of the name space. This authoritative information is organized into units called *zones*, which are the main units of replication in DNS. A zone contains one or more RRs for one or more related DNS domains.

The following are the three DNS zone types implemented in Windows 2000:

- **Standard Primary**   Holds the master copy of a zone and can replicate it to secondary zones. All changes to a zone are made on the standard primary.
- **Standard Secondary**   Contains a read-only copy of zone information that can provide increased performance and resilience. Information in a primary zone is replicated to the secondary by use of the zone transfer mechanism.
- **Active Directory-integrated**   A Microsoft proprietary zone type, where the zone information is held in the Windows 2000 Active Directory (AD) and replicated using AD replication.

Traditionally, the master copy of each zone is held in a primary zone on a single DNS server. On that server, the zone has a Start Of Authority (SOA) record that specifies it to be the primary zone. To improve performance and redundancy, a primary zone can be automatically distributed to one or more secondary zones held on other DNS servers. When changes are made to the zone, for instance, to add an (A) record, the changes are made to the primary zone and are transferred to the secondary zone. The transfer of zone information is handled by the zone replication process, which is described later in the "Zone Transfer" section.

When a zone is first created in Windows 2000, the zone will only hold information about a single DNS domain name, for example, kapoho.com. After the zone is created, the administrator can then add RRs to the zone, or can set the domain to be dynamically updated. For example, the administrator could add (A) records (host records) for hosts in the domain, such as kona.kapoho.com. If dynamic updates are enabled for the zone, a Windows 2000 computer can then directly update the A and PTR records on the DNS server (if the DNS client is also a DHCP client, the administrator can configure a DHCP server to send the updates).

Once the administrator has created the zone, he can add additional sub-domains to the zone (for example, jh.kapoho.com). These might be added to provide DNS services to a new building that is managed separately from the parent domain. This sub-domain, which might reside in a separate zone, would have RRs added (for example, a host record for jasmine.jh.kapoho.com).

As Figure 16-2 illustrates, if other domains are added below the domain used initially to create the zone, these domains can either be part of the same zone or belong to another. For example, the sub-domain jh.kapoho.com, which is subordinate to kapoho.com, could be held in the same zone as kapoho.com, or in a separate zone. This allows the sub-domain to be managed and included as part of the original zone records, or to be delegated away to another zone created to support that sub-domain.

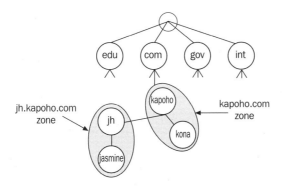

Figure 16-2. *Zones versus domains.*

In this example, the domain kapoho.com has a sub-domain of jh.kapoho.com. Additionally, both domains contain a single host record. In this example, the domains jh.kapoho.com and kapoho.com are held in separate zones on different DNS servers. The kapoho.com zone holds one host record for kona.kapoho.com. The jh.kapoho.com domain holds the host record for the host jasmine.jh.kapoho.com.

Active Directory-Integrated Zones

A major new feature in the Windows 2000 DNS service is the ability to store DNS zones within the AD. An *Active Directory-integrated zone* is a primary DNS zone that's held within the AD and replicated to other AD primary zones, using AD replication (and not traditional zone transfer). Although this method of holding zones is a Microsoft proprietary approach, it can provide some useful benefits.

The main advantage of AD-integrated zones is that the zones become, in effect, multi-master, with the capability of updates being made to any DNS server. This can increase the fault tolerance of the DNS service. In addition, replication of zone information occurs using AD replication, which can be more efficient across slow links, because of the way that AD compresses replication data between sites.

Reverse-Lookup Zones

Most queries sent to a DNS server involve a search based on the DNS name of another computer as stored in an address (A) RR. This type of query expects an IP address as the resource data for the answered response. This type of query is generally referred to as a forward query. DNS also provides a reverse-lookup process, which enables a host to determine another host's name based on its IP address. For example, "What is the DNS domain name of the host at IP address 10.10.1.100?"

To allow for reverse queries, a special domain, in-addr.arpa, was defined and reserved in the Internet DNS name space. Sub-domains within the in-addr.arpa domain are named using the reverse ordering of the numbers in the dotted-decimal notation of IP addresses. The reverse ordering of the domain name is needed because, unlike DNS names, IP addresses are read from left to right, but are interpreted in the opposite manner (that is, the left-most part is more generalized than the right-most part). For this reason, the order of IP address octets is reversed when building the in-addr.arpa domain tree; for example, the reverse-lookup zone for the subnet 192.168.100.0 is 100.168.192.in-addr.arpa.

This approach enables the administration of lower limbs of the DNS in-addr.arpa tree to be delegated to an organization when it obtains a set of IP addresses from an IP registry.

The in-addr.arpa domain tree makes use of the PTR RR. The PTR RR is used to associate the IP address to the owning domain name. This lookup should correspond to an Address RR for the host in a forward-lookup zone. The success of a PTR RR used in reverse query depends on the validity of its pointer data, the (A) RR, which must exist.

Note The in-addr.arpa domain is used only for Internet Protocol version 4 (IPv4)-based networks. In the Windows 2000 DNS Microsoft Management Console (MMC) snap-in, the DNS server's New Zone wizard will use this domain when it creates a new reverse-lookup zone. Internet Protocol version 6 (IPv6)-based reverse-lookup zones are based on the domain ip6.int.

Reverse Queries

A reverse query is one in which the DNS server is requested to return the DNS domain name for a host at a particular IP address. Reverse-Lookup Query messages are, in effect, standard queries, but relating to the reverse-lookup zone. The reverse-lookup zone is based on the in-addr.arpa domain name and mainly holds PTR RRs.

Note   The creation of reverse-lookup zones and the use of PTR RRs for identifying hosts are optional parts of the DNS standard. Reverse-lookup zones aren't required in order to use Windows 2000, although some networked applications can be configured to use the reverse-lookup zones as a form of additional security.

Inverse Queries

Inverse queries originally were described in RFC 1032, but now are outdated. Inverse queries were meant to look up a host name based on its IP address and use a nonstandard DNS query operation. The use of inverse queries is limited to some of the earlier versions of NSLOOKUP.EXE, a utility used to test and troubleshoot a DNS service. The Windows 2000 DNS server recognizes and accepts inverse query messages and answers them with a "fake" inverse query response.

DNS Query Classes

DNS queries fall into one of two classes: recursive queries and iterative queries.

A *recursive query* is a DNS query sent to a DNS server in which the querying host asks the DNS server to provide a complete answer to the query, even if that means contacting other servers to provide the answer. When sent a recursive query, the DNS server will use separate iterative queries to other DNS servers on behalf of the querying host to obtain an answer for the query.

An *iterative query* is a DNS query sent to a DNS server in which the querying host requests it to return the best answer the DNS server can provide without seeking further assistance from other DNS servers.

In general, host computers issue recursive queries against DNS servers. The host assumes that the DNS server either knows the answer to the query, or can find the answer. On the other hand, a DNS server will generally issue iterative queries against other DNS servers if it is unable to answer a recursive query from cached information.

DNS Resolver

In Windows 2000, the DNS *resolver* is a system component that performs DNS queries against a DNS server (or servers). The Windows 2000 TCP/IP stack is usually configured with the IP address of at least one DNS server to which the resolver sends one or more queries for DNS information.

In Windows 2000, the resolver is part of the DNS Client service. This service is installed automatically when TCP/IP is installed, and runs as part of the Services.Exe process. Like most Windows 2000 services, the DNS Client service will log on using the Windows 2000 System account.

DNS Resolver Cache

An IP host might need to contact some other host on a regular basis, and therefore would need to resolve a particular DNS name many times (such as the name of the mail server). To avoid having to send queries to a DNS server each time the host wants to resolve the name, Windows 2000 hosts implement a special cache of DNS information.

The DNS Client service caches RRs from query responses that the DNS Client service receives. The information is held for a set Time-To-Live (TTL) and can be used to answer subsequent queries. By default, the cache TTL is based on the TTL value received in the DNS query response. When a query is resolved, the authoritative DNS server for the resolved domain defines the TTL for a given RR.

You can use the IPCONFIG command with the /DISPLAYDNS option to display the current resolver cache contents. The output looks like the following:

```
D:\2031AS>ipconfig /displaydns
Windows 2000 IP Configuration
    localhost.
    ----------------------------------------------------------
        Record Name . . . . . : localhost
        Record Type . . . . . : 1
        Time To Live  . . . . : 31523374
        Data Length . . . . . : 4
        Section . . . . . . . : Answer
        A (Host) Record . . . : 127.0.0.1
    kona.kapoho.com.
    ----------------------------------------------------------
        Record Name . . . . . : KONA.kapoho.com
        Record Type . . . . . : 1
        Time To Live  . . . . : 2407
        Data Length . . . . . : 4
        Section . . . . . . . : Answer
        A (Host) Record . . . : 195.152.236.200
    1.0.0.127.in-addr.arpa.
    ----------------------------------------------------------
        Record Name . . . . . : 1.0.0.127.in-addr.arpa
        Record Type . . . . . : 12
        Time To Live  . . . . : 31523373
        Data Length . . . . . : 4
        Section . . . . . . . : Answer
        PTR Record  . . . . . : localhost
```

Negative Caching

The DNS Client service further provides negative caching support. Negative caching occurs when an RR for a queried domain name doesn't exist or when the domain name itself doesn't exist, in which case, the lack of resolution is stored. Negative caching prevents the repetition of additional queries for RRs or domains that don't exist.

If a query is made to a DNS server and the response is negative, subsequent queries for the same domain name are answered negatively for a default time of 300 seconds. To avoid the continued negative caching of stale information, any query information negatively cached is held for a shorter period than is used for positive query responses. However, this negative caching time-out value can be changed in the registry using the following NegativeCacheTime registry value:

NegativeCacheTime

```
Location: HKEY_LOCAL_MACHINE \System\CurrentControlSet\Services\Dnscache\Parameters
Data type: REG_DWORD--Time, in seconds
Default value: 0x12c (300 decimal, or 5 minutes)
Valid range: 0-0xFFFFFFFF (the suggested value is less one day, to prevent
very stale records)
Present by default: Yes
```

Negative caching reduces the load on DNS servers, but should the relevant RRs become available, later queries can be issued to obtain the information.

If all DNS servers are queried and none is available, for a default of 30 seconds, succeeding name queries will fail instantly, instead of timing out. This can save time for services that query the DNS during the boot process, especially when the client is booted from the network.

Zone Transfer

To improve the resilience and performance of the DNS service, it's normal to have at least one standard secondary zone for each standard primary zone, where the secondary zone is held on another DNS server. Depending on the exact nature of the organization, multiple standard secondary zones might be appropriate. When changes are made to the primary zone, it's important that the zone information is promptly replicated to all secondary zones. The process of transferring zone information from a primary to a secondary zone is called a *zone transfer*.

Zone transfers usually occur automatically, in intervals difined in the zone's SOA record. Zone transfers can also be performed manually by using the DNS MMC Snap-in, which might be done if the administrator suspects the secondary zone hasn't been properly updated.

When a standard secondary zone is created on a Windows 2000 DNS server, the DNS server will transfer all RRs from the standard primary zone to the new standard secondary. The DNS server does this to obtain and replicate a full copy of all RRs for the zone. In many of the early DNS server implementations, this same method of full transfer for a zone is used also when the secondary zone requires updating to align it with the primary zone, after changes are made to the primary zone. For large zones, this can be very time-consuming and wasteful of network resources. This can be an issue because a zone transfer will be needed each time the primary zone is updated, such as when a new host is added to the domain or if the IP address for a host is changed.

After the RRs have been replicated, the server on which the new standard secondary zone resides will check with the server on which the primary zone resides at regular intervals to determine if there are any changes to the primary zone. This is determined by polling the primary zone on a regular basis, the time period being defined by the Administrator in the Zone SOA record in the standard primary zone, and checking if the zone's version number has changed. If the version number has been incremented, a zone transfer is necessary. This process is shown in the following Network Monitor trace (Capture 16-01, included in the \Captures folder on the companion CD ROM):

```
1 563.890835 Router Mahimahi DNS 0x6000:Std Qry for kapoho.com. of type SOA on
class INET addr. 10.10.2.200 10.10.1.200
2 563.890835 Mahimahi Router DNS 0x6000:Std Qry Resp. for kapoho.com. of type
SOA on class INET addr. 10.10.1.200 10.10.2.200
3 563.890835 Router Mahimahi DNS 0x4000:Std Qry for kapoho.com. of type Req
for incrmntl zn Xfer on class INET 10.10.2.200 10.10.1.200
4 563.890835 MahiMahi Router DNS 0x4000:Std Qry Resp. for kapoho.com. of type
SOA on class INET addr. 10.10.1.200 10.10.2.200
```

In this trace, the DNS server holding the secondary zone queries the primary zone. The SOA is then returned. The secondary zone discovers a higher version number on the primary DNS server and requests a zone transfer.

For manually maintained DNS servers, this traditionally has been a key troubleshooting issue—changes are made to a primary zone, but the version number is unchanged, and thus the changes are not replicated to the secondary. With Windows 2000, changes made to the zone, either via manual update using the DNS MMC Snap-in or via dynamic registration, trigger an update to the version number, thus enabling the secondary to carry out the zone transfer at the next poll interval.

Incremental Zone Transfers

For large zones, zone transfers can consume a significant amount of bandwidth, especially when a zone transfer is carried across slow WAN links. To improve the efficiency of zone transfers, Windows 2000 implements a new method of replicating DNS zones, *incremental zone transfer,* which involves transferring only the changes to the zone, rather than the entire zone. This can significantly reduce the traffic needed to keep a secondary zone current. Incremental zone transfer is defined in RFC 1995.

With incremental zone transfers, the differences between the source and replicated versions of the zone are first determined. If the zones are identified as the same version—as indicated by the serial number field in the SOA RR of each zone—no transfer is made.

If the serial number for the zone at the source is greater than at the requesting secondary server, a transfer is made of only those changes to RRs for each incremental zone version. For an incremental zone-transfer query to succeed and changes to be sent, the zone's source DNS server must keep a history of incremental zone changes to use when answering these queries. Windows 2000 holds the incremental zone transfer information for each zone in a text file \Winnt\system32\dns folder whose name is based on the name of the file holding the the zone data (which was specified when the zone was defined). Thus, if the zone information for the kapoho.com zone is held in the file kapoho.com.dns, the incremental update log is held in kapoho.com.dns.log.

Directory-Integrated Zone Replication

Standard zones use the traditional zone replication mechanisms to transfer zone information. Active Directory-integrated zones, however, use AD replication to replicate updates. This provides the following three key benefits:

- DNS servers become multi-master. With standard DNS zones, all updates need to be made to a single DNS server—in other words, to the server containing the primary zone. With AD integration, any DNS server can accept the updates, which provide both improved performance and scaling, as well as better fault tolerance.

- AD replication is both more efficient and quicker. AD replication transfers updated-only properties, and not the entire zone, which means only the changes are transmitted across the network. Additionally, replication between sites, typically involving slower links, is highly compressed.

- The administrator only needs to plan and implement a single replication topology for AD. This will also replicate DNS changes.

For organizations using AD, Active Directory-integrated zones are generally recommended. If the organization is, however, using third-party DNS servers, these servers probably won't support AD-integrated zones.

Zone Delegation

DNS is a distributed database of information designed specifically to overcome the limitations of the earlier HOSTS.TXT approach to name resolution. The key to scaling DNS to handle large name spaces/networks, such as the Internet, is the ability to delegate the administration of domains. A *zone delegation* occurs when the responsibility of the RRs of a sub-domain is passed from the owner of the parent domain to the owner of the sub-domain.

At the heart of the Internet are 13 root servers, named A.ROOT-SERVERS.NET through M.ROOT-SERVERS.NET. The root servers are widely distributed. The root servers hold data for all the top-level domains, such as .com, .org, and .net, as well as for geographical domains, such as .uk, and .jp. These root-name servers enable Internet hosts to have access to the complete DNS database. Below the root and top-level domains are the domains and sub-domains belonging to individual organizations. In some top-level domains, additional hierarchy levels are provided. For example, in the .uk domain, there are sub-domains co.uk for UK-based companies (for instance, psp.co.uk) and ac.uk for academic institutions (for instance, ic.ac.uk for Imperial College), and so forth.

As illustrated in Figure 16-2, delegation occurs as a cut in the DNS with responsibility for the domain below the cut to be delegated from the domain above the cut. Within the kapoho.com domain is a sub-domain jh.kapoho.com. Responsibility for the subordinate domain has been delegated to a different server.

To implement a delegation, the parent zone must have both an A RR and a Name Service (NS) record—both pointing to the new delegated domain's root. In the kapoho.com zone, illustrated in Figure 16-2, there must be an A and an NS record that point to jh.kapoho.com. The Windows 2000 server has a delegation wizard to simplify the task of implementing a delegation.

Forwarder and Slave DNS Servers

If a resolver contacts a DNS server to resolve a domain name and return relevant RRs, the contacted DNS server will first attempt to perform the lookup using its own cache. If this fails, by default the DNS server will then start to issue iterative queries to resolve the domain. This will start at the root. If the DNS server is one of several at a site connected to the outside world by slow links, this default behavior might not be desirable.

As illustrated by Figure 16-3, a *forwarder* is a DNS server that other DNS servers contact before attempting to perform the necessary name resolution.

In this example, when any of the DNS clients send recursive queries to DNS servers A, B, and C, they'll attempt to answer the query from locally held zones or from their local cache. If this isn't successful, instead of these servers issuing iterative queries to external DNS servers, they'll send a recursive query to DNS server D, which has a better chance of answering the query from its own cache. This arrangement will reduce the external traffic needed to resolve host queries.

If the forwarder (server D in the example) is unable to answer the queries sent by DNS Servers A, B, or C, these servers will attempt to resolve the queries themselves by issuing iterative queries, which, again, might not be desirable. A Slave server is a forwarder that will only forward queries. This forces the DNS server to use only its configured forwarders for all name-resolution activities.

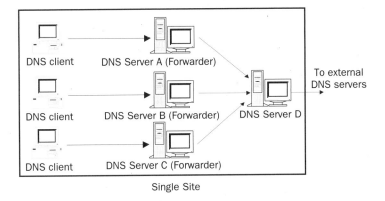

Figure 16-3. *DNS forwarder.*

Round Robin Load Balancing

Round robin is an approach for performing load balancing. It's used to share and distribute the network resource load. With round robin, the answers contained in a query, for which multiple RRs exist, are rotated each time the query is answered. Round robin is a very simple method for load balancing a client's use of Web servers and other frequently queried multi-homed computers.

For round robin to work, multiple address (A) RRs for the queried name must exist in the zone being queried. For example, suppose there were three physical Web servers servicing *www.kapoho.com*, with the IP addresses of 10.1.1.151, 10.1.152, and 10.1.1.153. To invoke round robin, the administrator would need to define three (A) records for *www.kapoho.com* (pointing to the different servers). The first query for this domain would be returned in the order 10.1.1.151, 10.1.1.152, and 10.1.1.153. The following query would return 10.1.1.152, 10.1.1.153, and 10.1.1.151, and so on. Because the client usually will take the first IP address, the first query would use the IP address 10.1.1.151, while the second would use 10.1.1.152.

Dynamic Update DNS Client

For large networks, getting all the necessary RR information into the DNS and keeping it current can be a significant task. Maintenance of host records can be a full-time job for one or more people, in some environments. To simplify the task, Windows 2000 includes support for dynamic updates to DNS, as described in RFC 2136.

With Dynamic DNS, the client sends a DNS registration message to the DNS server, instructing the server to update the (A) record for the dynamic update host. Additionally, if the client is also a DHCP client, every time there's an address event (for instance, a new address or address renewal), as part of the DHCP lease-management process, the DHCP client sends DHCP Option 81 to the DHCP server along with its fully qualified name. Option 81 instructs the DHCP server to register a PTR RR on its behalf. Windows 2000 computers that are statically configured will register both the (A) RR and the PTR RR with the DNS server themselves.

If a Windows 2000 DHCP client talks to a lower-level DHCP server that doesn't handle Option 81, the client registers a PTR RR on its own. The Windows 2000 DNS server is capable of handling dynamic updates.

This approach (client updating the (A) record, DHCP server updating the PTR record) is taken because only the client knows which IP addresses on the host map to a given host name. The DHCP server might not be able to properly do the (A) RR registration because it has incomplete knowledge. If appropriate, the DHCP server also can be configured to register both records with the DNS.

IPv6 Support

IP version 6 (IPv6) is a new version of the Internet Protocol. Although Windows 2000 won't ship with a native IPv6 TCP/IP stack, the Windows 2000 DNS server does provide support for IPv6 by implementing several additional pieces of functionality, including the following:

- **AAAA RR** This new record type is defined to store a host's IPv6 address. A multi-homed IPv6 host, for example, a host that has more than one IPv6 address, must have more than one AAAA record. The AAAA RR is similar to the (A) resource, using the larger IP address size. The 128-bit IPv6 address is encoded in the data portion of an AAAA RR in network byte order (high-order byte first).

- **AAAA query** An AAAA query for a specified domain name in the Internet class returns all associated AAAA RRs in the answer section of a response. A type AAAA query doesn't perform additional section processing.

- **IP6.INT domain** This domain is used to provide reverse-lookup faculties for IPv6 hosts (as the in-addr.arpa domain does for IPv4 addresses).

Similar to in-addr.arpa domain for IPv4, an IPv6 address is represented as a name in the IP6.INT domain by a sequence of nibbles separated by dots with the suffix ".IP6.INT." The sequence of nibbles is encoded in reverse order; for instance, the low-order nibble is encoded first, with the highest-order nibble last. Each nibble is represented by a hexadecimal digit. For example, the inverse-lookup domain name corresponding to the address 4321:0:1:2:3:4:567:89a:b would be b.a.9.8.7.6.5.0.4.0.0.0.3.0.0.0.2.0.0.0.1.0.0.0.0.-0.0.1.2.3.4.IP6.INT.

Finally, to support IPv6, all existing DNS query types that perform type A additional section processing, such as NS or mail exchange (MX) query types, must support both A and

AAAA records and must do any processing associated with both of these record types. This means the DNS server will add any relevant IPv4 addresses and any relevant IPv6 addresses available locally to the additional section of a response when processing any one of these queries.

How DNS Works

Configuring DNS Client Functions

With Windows 2000, there's generally very little configuration to do for a client, with respect to DNS. Generally, it's only necessary to configure the host with the IP address of a primary (and a secondary) DNS server. This can be simplified by using DHCP to assign the IP address of the DNS server(s).

Usually, DNS default client behavior is adequate. However, in certain cases, some change to the default behavior might be appropriate. The registry keys described below can be used to change how the Windows 2000 DNS client works.

Specifying a Default TTL

By default, the TTL for the (A) and PTR RR updates sent by a DNS client is 20 minutes. To increase it, you can configure the following registry value:

DefaultRegistrationTTL
```
Key: HKEY_LOCAL_MACHINE\SYSTEM\CurrentControlSet\Services\Tcpip\Parameters
Value type: REG_DWORD--seconds
Default: 0x4B0 (1200 decimal, or 20 minutes)
Valid range: 0-0xffffffff
Present by default: No
```

Disabling Dynamic Updates

While the automatic updating of DNS zones by a host can be useful, in some environments this might not be desirable. The following registry key can disable dynamic DNS updates either for a Windows 2000 computer as a whole, or for just one interface on that computer.

DisableDynamicUpdate
```
Key: KEY_LOCAL_MACHINE\SYSTEM\CurrentControlSet\Services Tcpip\Parameters
Or
HKEY_LOCAL_MACHINE\SYSTEM\CurrentControlSet\Services Tcpip\Parameters\Interfaces\<interface>
Value type: REG_DWORD--Boolean
Valid range: 0, 1 (False, True)
Default: 0 (False; dynamic DNS enabled)
Present by default: No
```

Resolving Names

DNS name resolution occurs when a resolver, operating at a host, sends a DNS server a query message containing a domain name. The query message instructs the DNS to find the name and return certain RRs. The query message contains the domain name to search for, plus a code indicating the records that should be returned.

The following Network Monitor Trace (Capture 16-01, included in the \Captures folder on the companion CD-ROM) shows the process of issuing and resolving a name query.

```
1 4.866998 LOCAL 3COM  884403 DNS 0x1587:Std Qry for kona.kapoho.com. of type
Host  TALLGUY 10.10.2.200
+ Frame: Base frame properties
+ ETHERNET: ETYPE = 0x0800 : Protocol = IP:  DOD Internet Protocol
+ IP: ID = 0xEEA8; Proto = UDP; Len: 61
+ UDP: Src Port: Unknown, (4715); Dst Port: DNS (53); Length = 41 (0x29)
  DNS: 0x1587:Std Qry for kona.kapoho.com. of type Host Addr on class INET addr.
      DNS: Query Identifier = 5511 (0x1587)
    + DNS: DNS Flags = Query, OpCode - Std Qry, RD Bits Set, RCode - No error
      DNS: Question Entry Count = 1 (0x1)
      DNS: Answer Entry Count = 0 (0x0)
      DNS: Name Server Count = 0 (0x0)
      DNS: Additional Records Count = 0 (0x0)
      DNS: Question Section: kona.kapoho.com. of type Host Addr on class INET addr.
          DNS: Question Name: kona.kapoho.com.
          DNS: Question Type = Host Address
          DNS: Question Class = Internet address class

2 4.866998 3COM  884403 LOCAL DNS 0x1587:Std Qry Resp. for kona.kapoho.com. of
type 10.10.2.200 TALLGUY IP
+ Frame: Base frame properties
+ ETHERNET: ETYPE = 0x0800 : Protocol = IP:  DOD Internet Protocol
+ IP: ID = 0x7BAA; Proto = UDP; Len: 77
+ UDP: Src Port: DNS, (53); Dst Port: Unknown (4715); Length = 57 (0x39)
  DNS: 0x1587:Std Qry Resp. for kona.kapoho.com. of type Host Addr on class
INET addr.
      DNS: Query Identifier = 5511 (0x1587)
    + DNS: DNS Flags = Response, OpCode - Std Qry, AA RD RA Bits Set, RCode -
No error
      DNS: Question Entry Count = 1 (0x1)
      DNS: Answer Entry Count = 1 (0x1)
      DNS: Name Server Count = 0 (0x0)
      DNS: Additional Records Count = 0 (0x0)
      DNS: Question Section: kona.kapoho.com. of type Host Addr on class INET addr.
          DNS: Question Name: kona.kapoho.com.
          DNS: Question Type = Host Address
          DNS: Question Class = Internet address class
      DNS: Answer section: kona.kapoho.com. of type Host Addr on class INET addr.
```

```
DNS: Resource Name: kona.kapoho.com.
DNS: Resource Type = Host Address
DNS: Resource Class = Internet address class
DNS: Time To Live = 1200 (0x4B0)
DNS: Resource Data Length = 4 (0x4)
DNS: IP address = 10.10.2.200
```

In the trace shown above, a client sends a DNS query to request the DNS server to return all A records for kona.kapoho.com. The query response contains the question entry and the answer RR(s). In this case, there's only one A record to return pointing to 10.10.2.200.

Network Monitor trace 16-2 (Capture 16-02, included in the \Captures folder on the companion CD-ROM) shows a Reverse-Lookup Query message. In this trace, the querying host tries to discover the host name for the host at 10.10.1.52. To determine this, the resolver queries for 52.1.10.10.in-addr.arpa and requests any PTR records. The DNS has the relevant PTR record, which shows the host to be kapoholt.kapoho.com.

Resolving Aliases

If the resolver is attempting to perform name resolution on a name that a user provided, it won't know in advance whether the name relates to a Host (A) RR or to a CNAME. If it relates to the CNAME, the server can return the CNAME. However, in this instance, the CNAME must still be resolved. To avoid extra DNS traffic, when a DNS server returns a CNAME in response to a Host record lookup, the DNS server will also return the A record relating to the CNAME.

The following Network Monitor Trace (Capture 16-03, included in the \Captures folder on the companion CD-ROM) shows the process of issuing and resolving a canonical name.

```
1       6.559432    DNS Server    DNS Client    DNS         0x1590:Std
Qry for ns1.kapoho.com. of type Host A TALLGUY        10.10.2.200
+ Frame: Base frame properties
+ ETHERNET: ETYPE = 0x0800 : Protocol = IP:  DOD Internet Protocol
+ IP: ID = 0xEFCD; Proto = UDP; Len: 60
+ UDP: Src Port: Unknown, (4761); Dst Port: DNS (53); Length = 40 (0x28)
  DNS: 0x1590:Std Qry for ns1.kapoho.com. of type Host Addr on class INET addr.
     DNS: Query Identifier = 5520 (0x1590)
   + DNS: DNS Flags = Query, OpCode - Std Qry, RD Bits Set, RCode - No error
     DNS: Question Entry Count = 1 (0x1)
     DNS: Answer Entry Count = 0 (0x0)
     DNS: Name Server Count = 0 (0x0)
     DNS: Additional Records Count = 0 (0x0)
     DNS: Question Section: ns1.kapoho.com. of type Host Addr on class INET addr.
        DNS: Question Name: ns1.kapoho.com.
        DNS: Question Type = Host Address
        DNS: Question Class = Internet address class
2       6.569446    DNS Client    DNS Server    DNS         0x1590:Std
```

```
Qry Resp. for ns1.kapoho.com. of type  10.10.2.200     TALLGUY        IP
+ Frame: Base frame properties
+ ETHERNET: ETYPE = 0x0800 : Protocol = IP:  DOD Internet Protocol
+ IP: ID = 0x807B; Proto = UDP; Len: 95
+ UDP: Src Port: DNS, (53); Dst Port: Unknown (4761); Length = 75 (0x4B)
  DNS: 0x1590:Std Qry Resp. for ns1.kapoho.com. of type Canonical name on
class INET addr.
        DNS: Query Identifier = 5520 (0x1590)
    + DNS: DNS Flags = Response, OpCode - Std Qry, AA RD RA Bits Set, RCode -
No error
        DNS: Question Entry Count = 1 (0x1)
        DNS: Answer Entry Count = 2 (0x2)
        DNS: Name Server Count = 0 (0x0)
        DNS: Additional Records Count = 0 (0x0)
        DNS: Question Section: ns1.kapoho.com. of type Host Addr on class INET addr.
            DNS: Question Name: ns1.kapoho.com.
            DNS: Question Type = Host Address
            DNS: Question Class = Internet address class
        DNS: Answer section: ns1.kapoho.com. of type Canonical name on class
INET addr.(2 records present)
            + DNS: Resource Record: ns1.kapoho.com. of type Canonical name on
class INET addr.
            + DNS: Resource Record: kona.kapoho.com. of type Host Addr on class
INET addr.
```

In this trace, the DNS client sends a DNS query to the DNS server requesting the Host record for ns1.kapoho.com, which is actually an alias for kona.kapoho.com. In the DNS reply, there are two answer RRs. The first is the CNAME RR for ns1.kapoho.com, and contains the canonical name. The second answer RR is the Host record for kona.kapoho.com, which will contain the IP address of this computer.

Dynamically Updating DNS

Dynamic updating of DNS zones, described in RFC 2136, is a mechanism that enables DNS clients to add or delete RRs or sets of RRs (RRSets) to a zone. In addition, update requests can state prerequisites (specified separately from update operations), which can be tested before an update can occur. Such updates are said to be atomic, that is, all prerequisites must be satisfied for the update operation to be carried out. The Windows 2000 TCP/IP client and the DHCP server issue dynamic update requests to update the DNS with host A and PTR records.

More Info Dynamic updating of DNS zones is described in RFC 2136, which can be found in the \RFC folder on the companion CD-ROM.

The following Network Monitor Trace (Capture 16-04, included in the \Captures folder on the companion CD-ROM) shows the process of dynamically registering an (A) RR.

```
1        6.270000    DNS Client    DNS Server    DNS         0x61:Dyn Upd
PRE/UPD records to KAPOHOLT.kapoho.c 10.10.1.52      195.152.236.200
+ Frame: Base frame properties
+ ETHERNET: ETYPE = 0x0800 : Protocol = IP:  DOD Internet Protocol
+ IP: ID = 0x1082; Proto = UDP; Len: 115
+ UDP: Src Port: Unknown, (3276); Dst Port: DNS (53); Length = 95 (0x5F)
  DNS: 0x61:Dyn Upd PRE/UPD records to KAPOHOLT.kapoho.com. of type Canonical
name
      DNS: Query Identifier = 97 (0x61)
    + DNS: DNS Flags = Query, OpCode - Dyn Upd, RCode - No error
      DNS: Zone Count = 1 (0x1)
      DNS: Prerequisite Section Entry Count = 2 (0x2)
      DNS: Update Section Entry Count = 1 (0x1)
      DNS: Additional Records Count = 0 (0x0)
    + DNS: Update Zone: kapoho.com. of type SOA on class INET addr.
    + DNS: Prerequisite: KAPOHOLT.kapoho.com. of type Canonical name on class
Unknown Class(2 records present)
      DNS: Update: KAPOHOLT.kapoho.com. of type Host Addr on class INET addr.
         DNS: Resource Name: KAPOHOLT.kapoho.com.
         DNS: Resource Type = Host Address
         DNS: Resource Class = Internet address class
         DNS: Time To Live = 1200 (0x4B0)
         DNS: Resource Data Length = 4 (0x4)
         DNS: IP address = 10.10.1.52
2        6.270000    DNS Server    DNS Client    DNS         0x61:Dyn Upd
Resp. PRE/UPD records to KAPOHOLT.ka 195.152.236.200    10.10.1.52
+ Frame: Base frame properties
+ ETHERNET: ETYPE = 0x0800 : Protocol = IP:  DOD Internet Protocol
+ IP: ID = 0x86BD; Proto = UDP; Len: 115
+ UDP: Src Port: DNS, (53); Dst Port: Unknown (3276); Length = 95 (0x5F)
  DNS: 0x61:Dyn Upd Resp. PRE/UPD records to KAPOHOLT.kapoho.com. of type
Canonical name
      DNS: Query Identifier = 97 (0x61)
    + DNS: DNS Flags = Response, OpCode - Dyn Upd, RCode - No error
      DNS: Zone Count = 1 (0x1)
      DNS: Prerequisite Section Entry Count = 2 (0x2)
      DNS: Update Section Entry Count = 1 (0x1)
      DNS: Additional Records Count = 0 (0x0)
    + DNS: Update Zone: kapoho.com. of type SOA on class INET addr.
    + DNS: Prerequisite: KAPOHOLT.kapoho.com. of type Canonical name on class
Unknown Class(2 records present)
      DNS: Update: KAPOHOLT.kapoho.com. of type Host Addr on class INET addr.
         DNS: Resource Name: KAPOHOLT.kapoho.com.
         DNS: Resource Type = Host Address
         DNS: Resource Class = Internet address class
         DNS: Time To Live = 1200 (0x4B0)
```

```
        DNS: Resource Data Length = 4 (0x4)
        DNS: IP address = 10.10.1.52
```

In this trace, the dynamic update message is sent from the DNS client to the DNS server to update the (A) RR for the host kapoholt.kapoho.com, which is now at IP address 10.10.1.52.

Transferring Zone Information

There are three methods of performing zone transfer:

- **Traditional Zone Transfer**   This approach involves the secondary requesting a full copy of the zone from the primary.

- **Incremental Zone Transfer**   This approach, as defined in RFC 1995, requires the DNS server hosting the primary zone to keep a record of the changes that are made between each increment of the zone's sequence number. The secondary can thus request only the changes that occurred since the last time the secondary was updated.

- **AD Zone Transfer**   AD zones are replicated to all domain controllers in the Windows 2000 domain using AD replication.

> **More Info**   The Incremental Zone Transfer approach is defined in RFC 1995, and the traditional zone-transfer mechanism is defined in RFC 1034. These RFCs can be found in the \RFC folder on the companion CD-ROM.

The traditional zone-transfer mechanism, which RFC 1034 defines, can be wasteful of network resources if the change in the transferred RRs is small in relation to the overall zone. The following Network Monitor Trace (Capture 16-05, included in the \Captures folder on the companion CD-ROM) shows a zone transfer.

```
1 60.1765 Secondary Primary TCP ....S., len: 0, seq:3436924871-3436924871, ack
2 60.1765 Primary Secondary TCP .A..S., len: 0, seq:2396712099-2396712099, ack
3 60.1765 Secondary Primary TCP .A....., len: 0, seq:3436924872-3436924872, ack
4 60.1765 Secondary Primary DNS 0x0:Std Qry for kapoho.com. of type Req for zn
Xfer on class INET addr.
5 60.1865 Primary   Secondary DNS 0x0:Std Qry Resp. for kapoho.com. of type
SOA on class INET addr.
6 60.1865 Primary Secondary DNS 0x636F:Rsrvd for _ of type Unknown Type on class
7 60.1865 Secondary Primary TCP .A....., len: 0, seq:3436924904-3436924904, ack
8 60.2366 Secondary Primary TCP .A...F, len: 0, seq:3436924904-3436924904, ack
9 60.2366 Primary Secondary TCP .A....., len: 0, seq:2396714217-2396714217, ack
10 60.2366 Primary Secondary TCP .A...F, len: 0, seq:2396714217-2396714217, ack
```

This Network Monitor trace 16-5 shows a zone transfer of the zone kapoho.com from the primary to a secondary server. In this trace, the secondary DNS server first initiates a TCP connection with the primary server and issues a zone-transfer message. The primary zone's

DNS server then transfers the zone RRs. In a zone-transfer, the first and last record transferred is the SOA record. After all the records are transferred, the TCP connection is terminated.

Incremental zone transfers, described in RFC 1995, can be more efficient than traditional zone transfers for both large and dynamic zones. However, they place additional processing requirements on the DNS server, which needs to keep track of the zone differences and sends only the changed records. By default, standard zones will use incremental transfers where possible.

The following Network Monitor trace 16-6 (Capture 16-06, included in the \Captures folder on the companion CD-ROM) shows an incremental zone transfer.

```
1      563.890835   LOCAL      3COM 6B15C7    DNS       0x6000:Std Qry for
kapoho.com. of type SOA on class INET addr.
2      563.890835   3COM 6B15C7    LOCAL      DNS       0x6000:Std Qry Resp.
for kapoho.com. of type SOA on class INET addr.
3      563.890835   LOCAL      3COM 6B15C7    DNS       0x4000:Std Qry for
kapoho.com. of type Req for incrmntl zn Xfer on class INET addr.
4      563.890835   3COM 6B15C7    LOCAL      DNS       0x4000:Std Qry Resp.
for kapoho.com. of type SOA on class INET addr.
```

In this trace, the DNS server initiating the zone transfer first queries for the SOA record, then requests an incremental zone transfer. In this example, the reply, contained in the fourth packet, fully fits inside a single UDP datagram. Had this not been the case, the reply message would have indicated that the reply was truncated, and the requesting server would have created a TCP session to the other DNS server and requested the zone transfer via TCP.

Active Directory replication is a proprietary solution, which can be used only with Windows 2000 domain controllers. Standard and incremental zone transfers rely on the servers holding secondary zones to pull changes from the primary zone. AD replication, on the other hand, is push in nature. For zones that change little, AD replication will ensure that all DNS servers holding the zone are updated quickly, while for more dynamic zones, will tend to smooth the replication traffic. Active Directory replication is beyond the scope of this book.

DNS Resource Records

What Are Resource Records?

An RR is information related to a DNS domain; for example, the host record defining a host IP address. Each RR will contain a common set of information, as follows:

- **Owner**   Indicates the DNS domain in which the resource record is found.

- **TTL**   The length of time used by other DNS servers to determine how long to cache information for a record before discarding it. For most RRs, this field is optional. The TTL value is measured in seconds, with a TTL value of 0 indicating that the RR contains volatile data that's not to be cached. As an example, SOA records have a default TTL of 1 hour. This prevents these records from being cached by other DNS servers for a longer period, which would delay the propagation of changes.

- **Class**   For most RRs, this field is optional. Where it's used, it contains standard mnemonic text indicating the class of an RR. For example, a class setting of IN indicates the record belongs to the Internet (IN) class. At one time there were multiple classes (such as CH for Chaos Net), but today, only the IN class is used.

- **Type**   This required field holds a standard mnemonic text indicating the type for an RR. For example, a mnemonic of A indicates that the RR stores host address information.

- **Record-Specific Data**   This is a variable-length field containing information describing the resource. This information's format varies according to the type and class of the RR.

Note   With Windows 2000, nearly all of the DNS information is either automatically added to the server or can be left to a default value. For most organizations running Windows 2000, DNS will be self-maintaining once the DNS servers are installed and the relevant zones created. However, the details on RR types can be useful for those integrating Windows 2000 with a non-Windows 2000 DNS server, or for troubleshooting.

Standard DNS zone files contain the set of RRs for that zone as a text file. In this text file, each RR is on a separate line and contains all the above data items, as a set of text fields, separated by white space. In the zone file, each RR consists of the above data items, although different records will contain slightly differently formatted record-specific data.

Sample Zone Data

The zone data for the kapoho.com zone noted earlier in this chapter is as follows:

```
;  Database file kapoho.com.dns for kapoho.com zone.
;  Zone version:  22508
;
@  IN  SOA kona.kapoho.com. administrator.kapoho.com. (
   22508          ; serial number
   900            ; refresh
   600            ; retry
   86400          ; expire
   3600         ) ; minimum TTL
;
;  Zone NS records
;  There are two DNS servers holding this domain
@   NS  kona.kapoho.com.
@   NS  kapoholt.kapoho.com.
;
;  Zone records for Kapoho.com
;
```

```
@        600    A    10.10.1.52
@        600    A    10.10.2.200
@        600    A    10.10.2.211
hilo     900    A    10.10.2.211
kapoholt        A    10.10.1.52
kona            A    10.10.2.200
tallguy  1200   A    10.10.1.100
         1200   A    10.10.2.100
;
;  Delegated sub-zone:  jh.kapoho.com.
;
jh                     NS    kapoholt.kapoho.com.
;  End delegation
```

Zone data for AD-integrated zones are held as a series of AD objects representing this data. For more detail on how the AD holds DNS-integrated zones, see the Windows 2000 Server Help.

Where Are RRs Located?

RRs for standard zones are stored in the folder *systemroot*\system32\dns. The RRs for each zone are held in a separate text file, which is named after the zone with an extension of .dns; for example, kapoho.com.dns.

Active Directory-Integrated Zone RRs

RRs for AD-integrated DNS zones are stored within the AD itself. The AD uses the following two main object classes to hold this DNS information:

- **dnsZone**   Represents an AD-integrated zone that contains dnsNode objects. This object class is the AD equivalent of a Standard zone held as a text file. The dnsZone objects have a dnsProperty attribute that defines key details about the zone, such as whether this zone can be dynamically updated.

- **dnsNode**   Corresponds to the individual RRs in the zone. Each dnsNode object will have a dnsRecord attribute containing the resource information.

Resource Records Supported by Windows 2000

Windows 2000 supports all RFC-compliant RRs. Many of these aren't commonly, or ever, used. The following sections list the most commonly used RRs and contain tables that include the RR type, the syntax, and an example.

Host Address (A)

This RR contains a host address RR that maps a DNS domain name to an IPv4 32-bit address.

Type	**A**
Syntax	Owner A IPv4_address
Example	kona A 10.10.2.200

IPv6 Host Record (AAAA)

This RR contains a host address RR that maps a DNS domain name to an IPv6 128-bit address.

Type	**AAAA**
Syntax	Owner Class IPv6_address
Example	ipv6host AAAA 4321:0:1:2:3:4:567:89a:b

Canonical Name (CNAME)

This RR maps an alias or alternate DNS domain name in the Owner field to a canonical or actual DNS domain name. There must also be an (A) RR for the canonical DNS domain name, which must resolve to a valid DNS domain name in the name space. The fully qualified canonical name should end with a full stop (".").

Type	**CNAME**
Syntax	Alias_name CNAME Canonical_name
Example	ns1 CNAME kona.kapoho.com

Mail Exchanger (MX)

The MX record provides message routing to a mail-exchanger host for any mail that's to be sent to the target domain. This RR also contains a 2-digit preference value to indicate the preferred ordering of hosts, if multiple exchanger hosts are specified. Each exchanger host specified in an MX record must have a corresponding host A address RR in the current zone.

Type	**MX**
Syntax	Owner MX preference mail_exchanger_host_name
Example	kapoho MX 10 mail.kapoho.com

Pointer (PTR)

This RR, used for Reverse Name Lookup message, points from the IP address in the Owner field to another location in the DNS name space as specified by the target_domain_name. Usually, this is used only in the in-addr.arpa domain tree to provide reverse lookups of address-to-name mappings. In most cases, each record provides information that points to another DNS domain-name location, such as a corresponding host (A) address RR in a forward-lookup zone:

Type	**PTR**
Syntax	Owner PTR target_domain_name
Example	200 PTR kona.kapoho.com

Service Locator (SRV)

The SRV RR enables a computer to locate a host providing specific service, such as a Windows 2000 Active Directory Domain Controller. This enables the administrator to have multiple servers, each providing a similar TCP/IP-based service to be located using a single DNS query operation. This record is mainly used to support the Windows 2000 AD, where all relevant DNS RRs can be automatically populated into the DNS.

Type	SRV
Syntax	service.protocol.name SRV preference-weight port target
Example	_ldap._tcp.dc._msdcs 600 SRV 0 100 389 kona.kapoho.com
	600 SRV 0 100 389 kapoholt.kapoho.com
	600 SRV 0 100 389 hilo.kapoho.com

DNS Messages

DNS messages are sent between a DNS client and a DNS server or between two DNS servers. These messages are usually transmitted using User Data Protocol (UDP) with the DNS server binding to UDP port 53. In some cases, the message length, particularly for responses, might exceed the maximum size of a UDP datagram. In such cases, an initial response is sent with as much data as will fit into the UDP datagram. The DNS server will turn on a flag to indicate a truncated response. The client can then contact the server using TCP (port 53), and reissue the request—taking advantage of TCP's capability to reliably handle longer streams of data. This approach uses UDP's performance for most queries while providing a simple mechanism to handle longer queries.

DNS Messages

DNS originally provided dynamic lookup for essentially static, manually updated data, such as host records manually added to a zone. The original DNS messages involved sending a query to a DNS server and getting a response. RFC 2165 defines the dynamic update facility, which makes use of update messages, whose format is similar to and derived from query messages. Both message types are described below.

DNS Query Message Format

All DNS query messages share a common basic format, as Figure 16-4 illustrates.

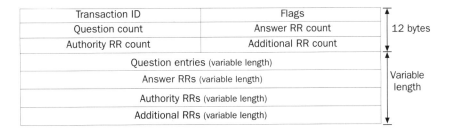

Figure 16-4. *Generic DNS query message format.*

As can be seen from Figure 16-4, the DNS query message consists of a fixed-length 12-byte header, plus a variable portion holding questions and DNS RRs.

DNS Query Message Header

The DNS Message header consists of the following fields:

- **Transaction ID**   A 16-bit field used to identify a specific DNS transaction. The originator creates the transaction ID and the responder copies the transaction ID into a reply message. This enables the client to match responses received from a DNS server to the requests that were sent to the server.
- **Flags**   A 16-bit field containing various service flags, described in more detail below.
- **Question Count**   A 16-bit field indicating the number of entries in the question section of a name service packet.
- **Answer RR Count**   A 16-bit field indicating the number of entries in the answer RRs section of a DNS message.
- **Authority RR Count**   A 16-bit field indicating the number of authority RRs in the DNS message.
- **Additional RR Count**   A 16-bit field indicating the number of additional RRs in the DNS message.

The Flags field contains a number of status fields that are communicated between client and server. Figure 16-5 below displays the format of the Flags field.

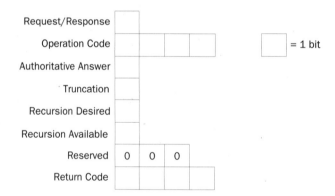

Figure 16-5. *DNS message Flags field.*

The individual fields in the flags field are as follows:

- **Request/Response**   This 1-bit field is set to 0x0 to indicate a name-service request, and 0x1 to indicate a name-service response.
- **Operation Code**   This 4-bit field indicates the specific name-service operation of the name-service packet, as the following table shows:

Operation Code	Operation
0x0	Query
0x1	Inverse Query
0x2	Server Status Request

- **Authoritative Answer**   Returned in a reply to indicate whether the responder is authoritative for the domain name in the question sections.
- **Truncation**   Set to 0x1 if the total number of responses couldn't fit into the UDP datagram (for instance, if the total number exceeds 512 bytes). In this case, only the first 512 bytes of the reply are returned.
- **Recursion Desired**   Set to 0x1 to indicate a recursive query. For queries, if this bit is not set and the name server contacted isn't authoritative for the query, the DNS server will return a list of other name servers that can be contacted for the answer. This is how delegations are handled during name resolution.
- **Recursion Available**   DNS servers set this field to 0x1 to indicate that they can handle recursive queries.
- **Reserved**   These 3 bits are reserved, and set to zero.
- **Return Code**   A 4-bit field holding the return code. A value of 0x0 indicates a successful response (for instance, for name queries, this means the answer is in the reply message). A value of 0x3 indicates a name error, which is returned from an authoritative DNS server to indicate that the domain name being queried for doesn't exist.

DNS Query Question Entries

In a DNS query, the question entry contains the domain name being queried. Figure 16-6 displays the Question field layout.

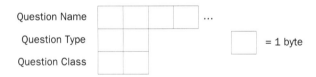

Figure 16-6. *Question field layout.*

The question entry is made up of the following three fields:

- **Question Name**   The domain name being queried. The format of this field is discussed later.
- **Question Type**   Indicates the records that should be returned, expressed as a 16-bit integer, as shown in the following table.

Type Value	Record(s) Returned
0x01	Host record
0x02	Name server (A) record
0x05	Alias (CNAME) record
0x0C (12)	Reverse-lookup (PTR) record

0x0F (15)	Mail exchanger (MX) record
0x21 (33)	Service (SRV) record
0xFB (251)	Incremental zone transfer (IXFR) record
0xFC (252)	Standard zone transfer (AXFR) record
0xFF (255)	All records

- **Question Class**   Normally set to 0x00-01. This represents the IN question class.

The Question Name field holds the name of the domain being queried. In DNS, these domain names are expressed as a sequence of labels. The domain kapoho.com, for example, consists of two labels (*kapoho* and *com*). In the Question Name field, the domain name has a sequence for each label, as 1-byte length fields followed by the label. The domain kapoho.com, therefore, would be expressed as 0x6kapoho0x3com0x0, where the hex digits represent the length of each label, the ASCII characters represent the individual labels, and the final hex 0 indicates the end of the name.

Resource Records (RRs)

When a DNS server sends a query reply back to a DNS host, the answer, authority, and additional information sections of the DNS message can contain RRs, which answer the question in the question section. Figure 16-7 illustrates the format of these RRs.

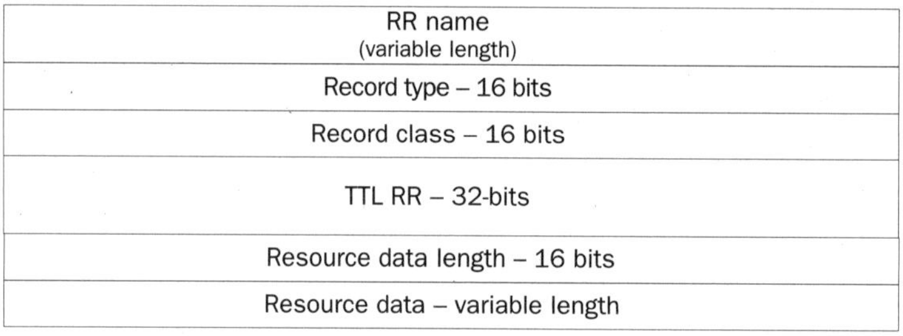

RR name (variable length)
Record type – 16 bits
Record class – 16 bits
TTL RR – 32-bits
Resource data length – 16 bits
Resource data – variable length

Figure 16-7. *DNS RR format.*

The fields in an RR are as follows:

- **RR Name**   The DNS domain name held as a variable-length field. The format of this field is the same as the format of the Question Name field, described in the "DNS Query Question Entries" section of this chapter.
- **Record Type**   The RR type value, as noted above.
- **Record Class**   The RR class code; there's only one record class used currently: 0x00-01, Internet Class.
- **TTL RR**   Time to live, expressed in seconds held in a 32-bit unsigned field.
- **Resource Data Length**   A 2-byte field holding the length of the resource data.
- **Resource Data**   Variable-length data corresponding to the RR type.

In DNS, domain names are expressed as a sequence of labels. The DNS name kapoho.-com, for example, would consist of two labels (kapoho and com). When DNS domain names are contained in an RR, they are formatted using a length-value format. With this format, each label in a DNS message is formatted with a 1-byte-length field followed by the label. The domain kapoho.com, therefore, would be expressed as 0x06kapoho0x03-com0x00, where the hex digits represent the length of each label, the ASCII characters hold the individual labels, and the final hex zero indicates the end of the name.

DNS Update Message Format

The format of a DNS Update message is very similar to DNS query messages, and many of the fields are the same. The DNS Update message contains a header defining the update operation to be performed and a set of RRs, which contain the update. Figure 16-8 displays the general format of the DNS Update message.

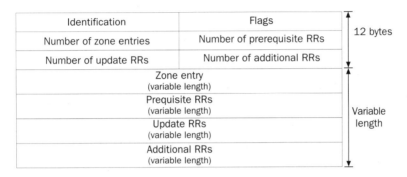

Figure 16-8. *General Update message flags*

DNS Update Message Flags

The DNS Update message has a flag section, similar to query messages but with a slightly different format. Figure 16-9 shows the format of the Flag field section for DNS Update messages.

Figure 16-9. *DNS Update message flags.*

The DNS Update message flags are used as follows:

- **Request/Response** A 1-bit field, set to 0x0 to indicate an update request, and 0x1 to indicate an update response.
- **Operation Code** Set to 0x5 for DNS updates.
- **Return Code** For update responses, indicates the result of the query. The defined result codes are shown in Table 16-3.

Table 16-3. Defined Result Return Code Flags for Update Responses

Result Code Value	Meaning
0x0	No error–update successful.
0x1	Format error–the DNS server was unable to understand the update request.
0x2	The name server encountered an internal failure while processing this request.
0x3	Some name that ought to exist doesn't exist.
0x4	The operation code isn't supported.
0x5	The name server refuses to perform the operation for policy for security reasons.
0x6	Some name that ought not to exist does exist.
0x7	Some RR set that ought not to exist does exist.
0x8	Some RR set that ought to exist doesn't exist.
0x9	The server isn't authoritative for the zone named in the Zone section.
0xA	A name used in the Prerequisite or Update section is not within the zone denoted by the Zone section.

Name-Query Message

A Name Lookup message uses the DNS message format defined in RFC 1034 and described earlier in the "DNS Query Message Format" section of this chapter. Network Monitor trace 16-1 (Capture 16-01, included in the \Captures folder on the companion CD-ROM) shows an example name query. In this trace, the following fields are set:

- **Query Identifier** Set to a unique number so that the resolver can match the response to the query
- **Flags** Set to indicate a standard query, with recursion if necessary
- **Question Count** Set to 1
- **Question Entry** Set to the domain name to resolve (kona.kapoho.com) and the RR to return (the host A record)

Name-Query Response Message

A Name-Query Response message is sent in response to a Name Query and is sent using the same query message format as the query response. Network Monitor trace 16-1 (Capture 16-01, included in the \Captures folder on the companion CD-ROM) displays an example query response in which the following fields are set:

- **Query Identifier**   Set to the unique number set in the query, to allow the resolver to match the response to the original query
- **Flags**   Set to indicate a response and a successful lookup
- **Question Count**   Set to 1
- **Answer Count**   Set to 1
- **Question Entry**   Set to the question contained in the query message
- **Answer Entry**   The RR requested in the query (the host record, containing the IP address of the queried domain)

Network Monitor trace 16-3 (Capture 16-03, included in the \Captures folder on the companion CD-ROM) shows a slightly different response message. In this trace, a resolver is attempting to resolve the (A) RR for ns1.kapoho.com. There's no Host (A) RR for this name, but there's an alias (CNAME). In the response, the replying DNS server returns two RRs: the CNAME RR, as well as the A Record for the canonical name (kona.kapoho.com).

Reverse-Name Query Message

Reverse-Name Query messages use the same message format as normal queries. The only differences in the contents are as follows:

- The domain name being queried is different. For a reverse lookup, the resolver will construct a domain name in the in-addr.arpa domain based on the IP address that's being queried.
- The queried record will be a PTR record, rather than an (A) record.

The Reverse-Name Query Reply message is also the same as a Query Reply message, except that a PTR record, rather than a host record, is returned. A reverse lookup can be seen in Network Monitor trace 16-2 above. In the trace, the resolver is looking for the host name of the host at 10.10.1.52, and thus queries for the domain 52.1.10.10.in-addr.arpa. The Reverse-Name Query Reply returns the requested PTR record, which shows the host name at this IP address to be kapoholt.kapoho.com.

Name Update Message

Name Update messages use the Name Update message format defined in RFC 2136 and described earlier in the "DNS Update Message Format" section of this chapter. Network Monitor trace 16-4 shows an example Name Update message. In this update, the key update message fields are set as follows:

- **Query Identifier**   Like query messages, update messages contain an identifier to enable the sender to match the response to the original update.
- **Flags**   Set to indicate a request and a dynamic update.
- **Update Zone**   Set to 1, and the zone section contains the zone to be updated.
- **Prerequisites Zone**   Set to 2, with two prerequisite records specified.
- **Update Zone**   Contains the RR that's to be updated.

Name Update Response Message

A Name Update Response message is issued in response to a Name Update Request. Network Monitor trace 16-4 contains an example of this in which the response can be seen to be identical to the request, except that the DNS flags in the message header are set to indicate this is a successful response. If the response had been unsuccessful, the response message would have contained an error code.

Summary

DNS was once an option for most Windows NT networks that used WINS (NetBIOS) for most domain operations, and as the basis of file and print sharing. DNS is now a key component in Windows 2000 networks and is required in those networks that deploy Windows 2000 Active Directory. In this chapter we have examined what DNS is and how it works, including DNS message formats and how the message appears on the wire. The chapter also has shown a number of Network Monitor captures, which are also contained on the companion CD-ROM for deeper study.

Chapter 17
Windows Internet Name Service (WINS)

In the early days of personal computing, both IBM and Microsoft used NetBIOS to provide programmers and applications with access to networking functions and features. NetBIOS was originally developed for IBM by Sytek Corporation as an extension to the BIOS, which an application could access by making BIOS calls.

In Microsoft Windows 2000, NetBIOS is both a transport-independent network interface, and a session management and data transport protocol. NetBIOS can work over any of the Windows 2000 network transport protocols, including NetBEUI, NWLink (IPX), and TCP/IP. Applications using NetBIOS can run over any of the configured transport protocols. Windows networking clients traditionally have used NetBIOS for a variety of functions, including file and printer sharing and browsing.

RFCs 1001 and 1002 define the functions and features of a NetBIOS service on a TCP/UDP transport, also known as NetBIOS over TCP/IP (NBT). These RFCs, which were published in 1987, document the following three principal services for NetBIOS applications running over TCP/IP:

- **Name service**   provides computers with the ability to acquire and defend NetBIOS names, and to locate the holders of those names.
- **Session service**   provides reliable message exchange, conducted between a pair of NetBIOS applications.
- **Datagram service**   provides an unreliable, non-sequenced, connectionless message-passing service for NetBIOS applications.

The NetBIOS session and datagram services, which enable NetBIOS applications to send messages to each other, are based on individual computers having NetBIOS names. The NetBIOS name service provides these applications with the ability to acquire/register a name, locate computers holding a specific name, and resolve a given NetBIOS name into an IP address. The datagram and session functions are outside the scope of this chapter.

The WINS is a NetBIOS Name server that clients can use to register, defend, and look up NetBIOS names. WINS provides several benefits to an organization:

- Name-registration and name-resolution facilities for down-level NetBIOS-based computers

- Dynamic database maintenance to support computer-name registration and resolution

- Centralized management of a scalable NetBIOS name database

WINS implements the name service features of a NetBIOS Name server defined in RFCs 1001 and 1002. However, to scale for larger networks, WINS also provides replication facilities.

In earlier versions of Microsoft Windows NT, WINS played a critical role in locating services, particularly the Windows NT directory services. Clients use NetBIOS to locate Windows NT 4.0 Domain Controllers. NetBIOS session and datagram services are used as the basis for directory operations. File and print sharing also make use of NetBIOS.

An organization that uses all Windows 2000 computers or a mixture of Windows 2000 computers and third-party operating systems such as UNIX, and whose applications fully support the use of Domain Name System (DNS), can eliminate NetBIOS, having no need for WINS. However, doing so would mean any application reliant on NetBIOS, such as the computer browser service, would not function.

Most organizations, however, need to support older computers—down-level clients—that require NetBIOS network names. This includes computers that run Microsoft Windows for Workgroups, Microsoft Windows 95, Microsoft Windows 98, and all versions of Windows NT. Organizations supporting computers running these operating systems will continue to find WINS an important service during the deployment of Windows 2000.

Chapter Contents

This chapter describes the NetBIOS name service protocol, as implemented by WINS, in detail. Additionally, there are Network Monitor traces on the companion CD-ROM that demonstrate the NetBIOS name service protocol in operation.

This chapter contains the following sections:

- **Overview to WINS in Windows 2000**   Describes the NetBIOS name service protocol as implemented in Windows 2000

- **How WINS Works**   Describes in detail how WINS clients and servers communicate, illustrated by Network Monitor traces

- **NetBIOS Name Service Messages**   Describes the format of the messages sent between WINS clients and WINS servers, and the functions provided

Overview of WINS in Windows 2000

What Is WINS?

In Windows 2000, WINS consists of two components: Windows Internet Name Service (WINS) and a WINS client service. WINS is a NetBIOS name server, which enables a client to register NetBIOS names in a central database and to resolve NetBIOS names into IP addresses. The WINS client uses the WINS server to register names and to provide name-resolution facilities (converting NetBIOS names into IP addresses). In functional terms, WINS is much like DNS, with clients registering names and performing name lookup, and servers handling the registration and resolution. The key difference is that WINS is based on NetBIOS names, rather than on DNS host names.

RFCs 1001 and 1002 define the functions of a NetBIOS Name server in some detail. In this respect, the WINS server is an RFC-compliant NetBIOS Name server providing name-registration and name-resolution facilities. The WINS server is scalable—able to function well in networks of all sizes.

> **More Info**   Read about the functions of a NetBIOS Name server in RFCs 1001 and 1002, which can be found in the \RFC folder on the companion CD-ROM.

All Windows 2000 servers (including Server, Advanced Server, and Datacenter Server) include a WINS service, although this service is not installed by default. All Windows clients include a WINS client, including Windows 2000, Windows NT 4.0, Windows 98, and Windows 95. For Windows 2000 clients, the WINS client function is automatically installed.

Key WINS Terms

In Windows 2000, NetBIOS is both a network interface, allowing applications and key system components to communicate across a network, and a protocol for allowing that communication. System processes that make use of NetBIOS include the Windows file sharing service, and the computer browser service. The following is an explanation of key terms relating to WINS and an overview of WINS operations.

Network Resources and End-Nodes

For applications to inter-operate and for users to access key resources, every network resource needs a name. A *network resource* is a process running on a specific computer. This could be the Server service running on the Exchange Server computer, or Server service running on a file server. The specific computer that runs the network resource process is referred to as an *end-node*.

NetBIOS Names

Each network resource in Windows 2000 is identified by a *NetBIOS name*. In Windows 2000, each NetBIOS name can be up to 15 characters in length. The final, sixteenth character allowed in RFCs 1001 and 1002 is reserved for the NetBIOS name suffix. The NetBIOS name can't start with an "*", and the NetBIOS name isn't case-sensitive.

The NetBIOS name space is flat, unlike DNS, which is hierarchical. This means that a NetBIOS name can be used only once within a network. Two computers with a Server service running can't have the same name. This can pose problems for very large organizations, and the NetBIOS scope parameter provides one solution to this issue.

NetBIOS Name Types

A NetBIOS name can be a *unique name,* owned by just one end-node, or it can be part of an *Internet group,* which can include multiple end-nodes. Each computer running Windows 2000 has a Server service and a Workstation service for the purposes of sharing files. These services would each have a unique NetBIOS name. When resolving a NetBIOS address to an IP address, unique names resolve to a single IP address, whereas Internet group addresses typically resolve to multiple addresses.

NetBIOS Name Suffix

Although RFCs 1001 and 1002 allow NetBIOS names to be 16 characters, as noted earlier, the sixteenth character in the Windows NetBIOS name is reserved for a special suffix. The *NetBIOS name suffix* is used by all Windows Networking software to identify functionality installed on the registered device. This enables an end-node to register multiple names, based on the computer, domain, or user name, and a suffix to indicate the services available on that machine. WINS clients can then construct a NetBIOS name based on computer, user, or domain name, and the appropriate suffix to locate those relevant network resources.

For example, the Messenger service has the suffix 0x03. To send a message to COMPUTER42, the client would send a message to the Workstation service on Computer42, or COMPUTER42[03]. Note that in the full 16-character NetBIOS name notation, the first 9 characters of the NetBIOS name would be COMPUTER42, the next 6 characters would be " " (blank), and the final character would be 0x03.

Table 17-1 lists common NetBIOS suffixes used with Windows 2000. The suffixes are listed in hexadecimal format because many of them are unprintable otherwise.

Table 17-1. Common NetBIOS Suffixes Used with Windows Networking

Name	NetBIOS Suffix (hex)	Type	Usage
<computername>	00	U	Workstation Service
<computername>	01	U	Messenger Service
<computername>	03	U	Messenger Service
<computername>	20	U	Server Service

(continued)

Table 17-1. *(continued)*

Name	NetBIOS Suffix (hex)	Type	Usage
<username>	03	U	Messenger Service
<domain>	00	G	Domain Name
<domain>	1B	U	Domain Master Browser
<domain>	1C	G	Domain Controllers
<domain>	1E	G	Browser Service Elections
<..—__MSBROWSE__>	01	G	Master Browser

In addition to these common names used by Windows 2000, other applications such as Microsoft Exchange, Lotus Notes, and others also register NetBIOS names. See knowledge base articles *Q119495*, *Q163409*, and *Q194338* for more details on these names.

> **Note**   Microsoft produces a series of knowledge base articles describing features and functions of the various Windows operating systems. Some of these knowledge base articles can be found on Technet, while the full Microsoft Knowledge Base is available on the Web at *http://support.microsoft.com/search/*. At the Web site, you can search for an article by its Q ID number.

NetBIOS Name Service Operations

NetBIOS name service operations involve registering, defending, querying, and releasing NetBIOS names. Additionally, NetBIOS session and datagram services use these name service operations to locate resources. For example, if a Windows 2000 computer user wants to access a file share on a remote system, that user enters the remote computer name and share name using Microsoft Explorer. Explorer uses NetBIOS name services to determine the remote server's IP address, and can then issue NetBIOS session-level commands to access the shared resource.

NetBIOS name service operations are carried out on the wire, using either IP broadcasts or a NetBIOS name server. The use of broadcasts might be acceptable for small local area networks (LANs). However, in larger networks, the use of broadcasts, which could result in broadcast storms, is undesirable. Such networks should implement WINS.

NetBIOS Scope

The NetBIOS name space is flat, meaning that all names must be unique on an internetwork. If you have a computer called KAPOHO and it's properly defending its computer name, no other network computer can call itself KAPOHO. This limitation can cause difficulties for larger organizations.

As RFC 1001 describes, an approach to resolving this flat name space is the use of an additional qualifier for the NetBIOS name. RFC 1001 defines the *NetBIOS scope* as *"the population of computers across which a registered NetBIOS name is known."* To identify the NetBIOS scope, the NetBIOS scope identifier is used. The *NetBIOS scope identifier* is a character string, similar in format and function to the DNS domain name.

The use of the NetBIOS scope, however, is limited in that a user can't specify the scope directly. The NetBIOS scope of a Windows 2000 computer is defined as part of the computer's IP parameters received from a DHCP server or in the computer's registry. Thereafter, the NetBIOS scope is automatically appended to all NetBIOS names. The effect is that an end node with a given NetBIOS scope can communicate only with other end-nodes configured with the same NetBIOS scope.

You can set the NetBIOS scope either by specifying a scope as part of a DHCP scope, or by editing the registry. The registry key used to manually change node type is as follows:

```
Key: HKEY_LOCAL_MACHINE\SYSTEM\CurrentControlSet\Services\NetBT\Parameters or
Key: HKEY_LOCAL_MACHINE\SYSTEM\CurrentControlSet\Services\NetBT\
Adapters\Interface\<interface>
Value name: ScopeId
Value type: REG_SZ-Character string
Valid range: Any valid DNS domain name consisting of two dot-separated parts,
or an
asterisk (*)
Default: None
Present by default: No
```

Caution   While the use of the NetBIOS scope identifier might offer some benefits, it also might make communication with other systems more difficult. Additionally, the inadvertent use of a NetBIOS scope identifier can make troubleshooting problems that arise from its inadvertent use more difficult to resolve. In general, you should probably avoid all use of this feature.

NetBIOS Node Types

To allow for the various sizes of NetBIOS networks, RFCs 1001 and 1002 use the concept of *node type* to determine how a particular computer should handle name service functions. The node type defines how name service operations are to be performed.

An end-node can be one of four node types, defined in RFCs 1001 and 1002:

- **B-Node (Broadcast Node)**   Name-registration and name-resolution operations are performed using broadcasts only. This is usually the best option for very small, single subnet networks.

- **P-Node (Point to Point Node)**   Name-registration and name-resolution operations are done using a NetBIOS name server (WINS) only. This node type can be used to eliminate local subnet broadcasts, but may cause network resources on the local subnet to not be resolved.

- **M-Node (Mixed Node)**   A combination of B-Node and P-Node, where name registration and resolution are done via broadcast. But if name resolution isn't successful using broadcasts, the NetBIOS name server is used. This is useful in cases where the WINS server is on a remote network, as it will first attempt to resolve the name locally before using WAN resources for the resolution.

- **H-Node (Hybrid Node)**   A combination of P-node and B-node, where name registration and resolution are done using a WINS server. But if the name resolution isn't successful using the WINS server, broadcasts are used. This is the default node type when using WINS servers.

By default, computers running Windows 2000 are B-Node. If you configure your Windows 2000 computer to use a WINS server, by default it becomes H-Node. You can configure your computer to be P-Node or M-Node by manually editing the registry. Additionally, the administrator can set Dynamic Host Configuration Protocol (DHCP) parameters to set the node type for a DHCP client.

The registry key used to manually change node type is as follows:

```
Key: HKEY_LOCAL_MACHINE\SYSTEM\CurrentControlSet\Services\Netbt\Parameters or
Key: HKEY_LOCAL_MACHINE\SYSTEM\CurrentControlSet\Services\Netbt\
Adapters\Interfaces\<interface>
Value name: NodeType
Value type: REG_DWORD - Number
Valid range: 1,2,4,8 (B-Node, P-node, M-node, H-node)
Default: 1 or 8 based on the WINS server configuration
Present by default: No
```

Microsoft-Modified B-Node

As defined in RFCs 1001 and 1002, B-Node behavior doesn't generally scale beyond a single subnet. This can be overcome partly by configuring routers to forward broadcasts, but as this also doesn't scale, it's rarely done. To overcome these inherent limitations, Microsoft has extended the B-Node for name service operations. Known as modified B-Node, these extensions add the following name-lookup facilities to B-Node:

- **The NetBIOS name cache**   An in-memory cache of recently resolved names that can be searched before other name-resolution methods are attempted
- **The LMHOSTS file**   A flat-file, contained in *systemroot*\system32\drivers*etc* that contains a static list of NetBIOS names and their IP addresses

If using LMHOSTS is, for some reason, undesirable, you can disable this by reconfiguring your computer's TCP/IP parameters.

Name Registration

Whenever a network resource becomes available for use—for example, when a file server starts up—the network resource must *register* its relevant NetBIOS name. The registration procedure ensures that the name being registered isn't already in use by another comptuer. For P-Node, M-Node, and H-Node clients, the client also informs the WINS server of the name and IP address.

Time To Live (TTL)

In general, NetBIOS names aren't held or owned permanently. With WINS, each name registered successfully has a limited *time to live* (TTL). When the TTL for a NetBIOS name expires, it's up to the network resource to re-register that name. If a network resource registers a name with a WINS server and the TTL expires, the name can be removed from the WINS server. Windows 2000 clients attempt to re-register their NetBIOS names at one-half of the TTL, or when the computer is rebooted.

Name Defense

Once registered, all unique NetBIOS names need to be defended to ensure that two different network resources don't claim the same NetBIOS name. If a computer attempts to register a NetBIOS name that's already being used by another computer, the name's owner needs to defend the name. If a network resource finds that the name it's attempting to resister is already in use—for example, a computer booting up is configured with a computer name of one that's already running—the network resource should fail gracefully. Windows 2000 processes, such as the Server service, also will write an error event to the event log for later analysis and troubleshooting.

If the name's owner is a B-Node client, the owner must accept responsibility for *defending* the name by listening for a Name Registration Request and broadcasting a negative Name Registration Response.

For P-Node clients, name defense is more complicated. If a P-Node client attempts to register a name with a WINS server that the WINS server believes to be in use, the WINS server will first attempt to contact the computer that has previously registered the NetBIOS name. If the WINS server successfully contacts the registered owner, the WINS server sends a negative Name Registration message to the client attempting to register the name. If, on the other hand, the WINS server can't reach the previously registered owner of the name, it will send a positive Name Registration Response.

NetBIOS Name Resolution

When a computer wishes to communicate with another, using NetBIOS, it must determine the remote computer's IP address before communications can be established. *Name resolution* is the process of determining a computer's IP address based on a NetBIOS name. The general approach a WINS client takes to resolving names is as follows:

- Check whether the name really can be resolved using NetBIOS. If the name entered by the user or specified by the application is longer than 15 characters, or contains a ".", DNS name resolution will be performed.

- Next, the client will check to see if the name is in the local NetBIOS name cache. See below for more information on the NetBIOS name cache.

- If the computer is configured to use LMHOSTS, this file will be consulted for the name's IP address.

If the name can't be resolved either alternatively (for example, by DNS) or locally, Windows 2000 WINS clients will go through further name-resolution steps. These specific steps will vary depending on the NetBIOS node type and whether a WINS proxy has been configured as follows:

- B-Node clients will broadcast NetBIOS Name Request messages to the local subnet. If a computer holding the name is on that local subnet, the computer will issue a positive Name Query response, containing the required IP address. If there's a WINS proxy agent on the subnet when a NetBIOS Name Request message is broadcast, and there's no reply, the WINS proxy agent will attempt to resolve the name on behalf of the client (see below for more detail about the WINS proxy agent). This is a good approach for very small networks (possibly with no WINS servers) and is the default for a computer with no WINS server configured.

- P-Node clients will unicast NetBIOS Name Request messages to the configured WINS server. If the WINS server has the required name, it will send a positive Name Query Response, containing the required IP address; otherwise, the computer will send a negative Name Query Response. If the WINS client gets no response from its WINS server, and is configured with the IP addresses of additional WINS servers, the client will try these additional WINS servers. This approach minimizes broadcasts on the local network but can cause wide area network (WAN) resolution traffic, even if the network resource is local to the WINS client.

- M-Node clients will first attempt to use B-Node behavior to resolve the name, and if this isn't successful, M-Node clients will attempt P-Node behavior. This is particularly useful when the client is on the other side of a WAN link to the network resource, but will cause additional broadcast traffic on the local subnet.

- H-Node clients will first attempt to use P-Node behavior to resolve the name, and if this isn't successful, H-Node clients will attempt to use B-Node behavior. As with P-Node, this approach reduces local broadcast traffic for names held by the WINS server, but will use the local broadcast to attempt to resolve the name.

Note   Early WINS clients handled only a maximum of two WINS servers (a primary and a secondary). To provide additional fault tolerance for clients' computers, Windows 2000 or Windows 98 allows you to specify up to 12 WINS servers per interface. These extra WINS server addresses are used only if the primary and secondary WINS servers fail to respond.

If none of these steps is successful in resolving the NetBIOS name, the Windows 2000 computer will attempt to use host name resolution, first checking the local HOSTS file, and then contacting configured DNS servers. If, after all these steps, the name still can't be resolved, the Windows 2000 computer sends an Error message to the caller.

This series of steps is intended both to provide the maximum amount of fault tolerance to the client, and to accommodate incorrectly configured systems. It's all too easy, for example, for a new administrator to add NetBIOS names to the HOSTS file instead of the LMHOSTS file.

If a computer uses broadcasting to resolve a NetBIOS name, it can't be sure that a lack of response is significant. Because UDP is used as the transport for NetBIOS name operations, the packet could have been dropped. To compensate for the unreliability, the client resolving a name, by default, broadcasts the name resolution request three times, with a 750-millisecond interval between each attempt. Use the following registry entry to change the number of broadcasts attempted:

```
Key: HKEY_LOCAL_MACHINE\SYSTEM\CurrentControlSet\Services\Netbt\Parameters
Or
Key: HKEY_LOCAL_MACHINE\SYSTEM\CurrentControlSet\Services\Netbt\Parameters\
     Adapters\Interfaces\<interface>
Value name: BcastNameQueryCount
Value type: REG_DWORD-Number
Valid range: 1-0xFFFF
Default: 3
Present by default: No
```

Use the following registry entry to change the interval between broadcasts:

```
Key: HKEY_LOCAL_MACHINE\SYSTEM\CurrentControlSet\Services\Netbt\Parameters\
     Adapters\Interfaces\<interface>
Value name: BcastQueryTimeout
Value type: REG_DWORD-Time in milliseconds
Valid range: 100-0xFFFFFFFF
Default: 0x2ee (750 decimal)
Present by default: No
```

Note   While it might seem like a good idea to reduce the number of broadcasts, if you reduce the number to one, or make the time interval too small, you might increase the possibility that a busy WINS server won't be able to respond quickly enough. In that case, the client would fail to resolve a name for a system that otherwise might have been able to respond (using the default values). Test any changes to these parameters carefully.

NetBIOS Name Cache

To minimize the use of WINS Name Resolution Queries, WINS clients use a NetBIOS name cache that holds recently resolved NetBIOS names. If a client needs to resolve a NetBIOS name, it will examine this cache before transmitting a Name Resolution Query.

By default, the NetBIOS Name cache holds 16 name resolutions, which is probably adequate for most client computers. Cache entries are held by default for 10 minutes, although you can modify this time-out value. If a client resolves more NetBIOS names than the cache can hold, the oldest entries are discarded, and the new name (and IP address) is added to the name cache. You can configure the name cache to be one of the following three sizes:

- **Small**   Holds 16 entries (this is the default)
- **Medium**   Holds 128 entries
- **Large**   Holds 256 entries

Use the following registry entry to modify the NetBIOS name cache size:

```
Key: HKEY_LOCAL_MACHINE\SYSTEM\CurrentControlSet\Services\Netbt\Parameters
Value name: Size/Small/Medium/Large
Value type: REG_DWORD
Valid range: 1, 2, 3 (Small, Medium, Large)
Default: 1 (Small)
Present by default: No
```

By default, entries in the NetBIOS name cache time out and are deleted after 10 minutes. To adjust this time-out period, use the following registry entry:

```
Key: HKEY_LOCAL_MACHINE\SYSTEM\CurrentControlSet\Services\Netbt\Parameters
Value name: CacheTimeout
Value type: REG_DWORD
Valid range: 60000-0xFFFFFFFF
Default: 0x927c0 (600000 milliseconds = 10 minutes)
Present by default: No
```

The value holds the length of time, in milliseconds, for which a NetBIOS lookup is cached. You can use the NBTSTAT -c command from the Windows 2000 command prompt to view the entries in the local NetBIOS name cache.

Note   By increasing the size of the NetBIOS name cache, and increasing the cache time-out value, you can reduce the number of lookups performed against a busy server. For many environments with largely static IP addresses for all key servers, this change might be appropriate. However, by making this change, you also increase the probability that an entry in the cache is no longer accurate (which could occur in a highly dynamic TCP/IP network). This tradeoff between accuracy and amount of lookup traffic should be considered carefully and tested thoroughly.

Name Release

If the network resource terminates gracefully, it can no longer defend the name, and the resource performs *name release*. For B-Node clients, this is done simply by stopping the name defense of the name being released. For P-Node clients, name release is accomplished by sending a Name Release message to the WINS server.

WINS Proxy

Older, or third-party, NetBIOS clients might not be able to be configured to use WINS. Instead, they would rely on B-Node behavior. To provide these clients with use of a WINS server's resources, use a *WINS proxy*, which is a WINS client that you can configure to act on behalf of other computers that are unable to use WINS. A WINS proxy can also be used during the migration from a broadcast environment to a WINS environment. You can set up a WINS server and a WINS proxy, then migrate systems over one by one without affecting name resolution for the systems that have not yet been converted.

The WINS proxy functions as follows:

- When a B-Node WINS client registers a NetBIOS name, the WINS proxy performs a name lookup, first using its local NetBIOS name cache and, if necessary, sending a Name Resolution Query to the WINS server. If the name is found, the proxy sends a negative Name Registration Response back to the B-Node client attempting to register the name.

- When a B-Node client releases its name, the proxy simply deletes the client's name from its name cache, and sends a name release to the WINS server.

- When a B-Node client broadcasts a name resolution, the proxy attempts to resolve the name, first by using information locally contained in its cache of remote names or by sending a Name Resolution Query to the WINS server. If the name lookup is successful, the proxy sends a Name Query Response. If it's not successful, the proxy sends a negative Name Query Response.

You can configure a system to act as a WINS proxy for B-Node clients on the local subnet by editing the following registry key:

```
Key: HKEY_LOCAL_MACHINE\SYSTEM\CurrentControlSet\Services\Netbt\Parameters Or
Key: HKEY_LOCAL_MACHINE\SYSTEM\CurrentControlSet\Services\Netbt\Parameters\
     Adapters\Interfaces\<interface>
Value name: EnableProxy
Value type: REG_DWORD-Boolean
Valid range: 0, 1 (False, True)
Default: 0 (False)
Present by default: No
```

Setting this value entry to 0x1 enables the system to act as a proxy name server for the networks to which NetBIOS over TCP/IP is bound (or to the chosen interface). A WINS proxy name server listens for broadcast Name Resolution Queries, resolves them using WINS (or the proxy's NetBIOS name cache), and broadcasts the result back to the client. The WINS proxy provides B-Node WINS clients with the ability to inter-operate with WINS servers.

Note Windows 2000 servers that run the Routing and Remote Access Service's Connection Sharing (NAT) feature can also be configured to act as a WINS proxy for clients on the private network. See the Windows Server Help for more information about Connection Sharing.

WINS Database Entries

When a name is registered, or released, the WINS server updates its internal database. A *WINS database entry* holds the name of the network resource, its associated IP address, TTL, and version number. The version number is the basis for WINS server replication.

WINS Server Replication

In large enterprise networks, having a single WINS server isn't advisable. A single server providing a service to a large number of clients would represent a single point of failure. Also, IT would potentially require clients to use WAN links to resolve names of network resources that might turn out to be local.

To provide redundancy, load balancing, and scalability, and to reduce the WAN traffic involved with Name Registration and Name Query options, WINS servers can be configured for *replication*, which replicates WINS database entries from one server to another. WINS server replication enables a WINS client computer to register NetBIOS names on one WINS server, and to have that WINS server replicate the name so that it's available to all WINS servers, and to all WINS clients, in an organization. This can expedite client name resolution because the use of WAN links for WINS queries is avoided.

For a WINS server to replicate its information, the server must be configured with at least one other WINS server as a *replication partner*. WINS replication partners replicate names known on one server to the other partner servers. There are two replication roles for a WINS server: pull partner and push partner. A *pull partner* is a WINS server that pulls WINS entries from its configured partner(s). A *push partner* is a WINS server that pushes updated WINS entries to its configured partner(s).

All replication traffic is pulled, with one partner requesting updates from a configured partner. The main difference between push and pull partners is who and what triggers the replication event. Pull partners pull name-to-IP address mapping updates from their replication partners, either when the WINS service starts or at intervals configured by the administrator. On the other hand, push partners inform configured partners that updates exist, either when the WINS service starts or after a certain number of updates have accumulated. After the partner has received the notification that updates exist, the partner can pull these changes down to update its local WINS database.

Note   The WINS replication topology for an organization is determined by an administrator based on the business needs for NetBIOS name resolution. Replication involves pairs of servers replicating from one to the other, which can involve WAN traffic. Microsoft recommends making all replication push/pull, which is a good default, especially for LAN-connected WINS servers. When replicating across WAN links, pull replication (where each partner pulls at a predefined interval) might be a better alternative.

Adapter Status

NetBIOS end-nodes can query the status of another system. This status is known as the *adapter status*. The Windows 2000 NBTSTAT.EXE command can be used to issue a node status query against another computer, although this will return only the NetBIOS names owned by the remote computer. RFC 1002 defines a number of statistics that are returned in an Adapter Status message, but these are not displayed by NBTSTAT.EXE.

How WINS Works

To understand how WINS itself works, you also must understand how WINS clients operate and how NBT, in general, works. This section describes key functions and features of both NetBIOS name services and WINS clients and servers.

Registering NetBIOS Names

The process of registering and renewing NetBIOS names by an end-node varies depending on the NetBIOS node type configured for the end-node. In general, an end-node that wants to register the NetBIOS name issues a NetBIOS Name Registration Request to register the name. Once the name is registered, other computers can then resolve that name and use the resulting IP address to communicate with the end-node. When the network resource terminates, it generally releases the name.

Name Registration Request

When a network resource starts up, it attempts to register the related NetBIOS names. The network resource issues a NetBIOS Name Registration Request, depending on the node type as follows:

- **B-Node**   When a B-Node client registers a name, it broadcasts a name-registration packet to the local network. If the name is currently in use by another node, the name's owner sends a negative Name Registration Reply. A B-Node client that doesn't receive a negative Name Registration Reply then considers itself the owner of the name, and carries out name defense against that name.

- **P-Node**   When a P-Node client registers a name, it sends the name to the configured WINS server as a unicast packet. If the name being registered has previously been registered, the WINS server attempts to contact the registered owner to check whether the name is actively being used. If the name is still in use, the WINS server sends a negative Name Registration Reply to the client; if the name isn't in use, the WINS server sends a positive Name Registration Reply. The WINS server might also send a Wait Acknowledgment message to the client attempting to register the name. This message indicates that the WINS server is still attempting to determine whether the name can, in fact, be registered.

- **M-Node**   An M-Node client attempts to register the name via broadcast, as for a B-Node client. In the absence of an objection, the client attempts to register the name using P-Node behavior, and a WINS server. While the broadcast approach might yield an owner of the name, and therefore would terminate the name-registration process, it's insufficient to confirm name ownership.
- **H-Node**   A Windows 2000 H-Node client registers the name via WINS. If this is successful, the registering client assumes ownership of the name.

Network Monitor trace 17-1 (Capture 17-01, included in the \Captures folder on the companion CD-ROM) shows a name registration by an H-Node client for the name KAPOHO10[00]. Network Monitor trace 17-2 (Capture 17-02 in the \Captures folder on the companion CD-ROM) shows a name registration by a B-Node client for the name KAPOHO10[00].

Positive Name Registration Reply

Positive Name Registration Replies are sent from a WINS server to a WINS client upon successfully registering a NetBIOS name. If a WINS client sends a WINS server a request to register a unique NetBIOS name, and that name isn't presently registered, the WINS server will register the name and send a positive Name Registration message to the computer that registered the name. Computers that send NetBIOS Name Registration Requests via broadcast, such as a B-Node client, won't receive a positive Name Registration Reply.

If a WINS client sends a WINS server a request to register a group name, the WINS server will always send a positive Name Registration Reply. B-node clients send NetBIOS Name Registration. A B-Node client broadcasts multiple Name Registration messages, and if no negative Name Registration Replies are received, it assumes ownership of the NetBIOS name. Network Monitor trace 17-1 shows a successful name registration by an H-Node client, including a positive Name Registration message.

Negative Name Registration Reply

A WINS server that receives a request to register a unique NetBIOS name that's already registered should reject the request by issuing a negative Name Registration Reply message, provided that the end-node owning that name is able to defend the name. Before sending the negative Name Registration Response, the WINS server checks with the current owner of the NetBIOS name to determine whether that computer's still active. This situation could occur, for example, if a laptop is moved to a different subnet, or for some reason is reconfigured to have a new IP address.

A computer sending NetBIOS Name Registration Requests via broadcast, for example a B-Node client, also receives a negative Name Registration Reply if another computer is active on that subnet and currently owns the name. A computer registering NetBIOS names using WINS sends its Registration Request messages using unicast; the WINS server sends a negative Name Response message if the name being registered has previously been registered by some other end-node, and if that other end-node can defend the name.

Network Monitor trace 17-3 (Capture 17-03, included in the \Captures folder on the companion CD-ROM) shows a computer attempting to register the NetBIOS name KAPOHO10 with a WINS server. This name is in use on another computer and the second packet in this trace shows the negative Name Response message.

Wait Acknowledgment

If a WINS server receives a request to register a unique NetBIOS name that's already registered, it checks with the registered owner of that name. In this case, it might issue a Wait Acknowledgment message to the computer attempting to register the name. The purpose of this is to inform the client that the WINS server might not yet be able to provide a name reply. To enable the client to be aware that the server hasn't failed (and isn't performing name service operations), a WINS server sends a Wait Acknowledgment message if it can't answer the query within a certain time.

Network Monitor trace 17-4 (Capture 17-04, included in the \Captures folder on the companion CD-ROM) shows a Wait Acknowledgement message. The WINS server has to contact another system, and issues the Wait Acknowledgement while that contact is accomplished. This message is part of a name resolution failure, which is discussed later in the section "Resolving NetBIOS Name Registration Conflicts."

Name Renewal Request

NetBIOS names registered with a WINS server have a limited life and must be refreshed before that life expires. The default TTL for NetBIOS name entries held in WINS is 6 days, but the administrator can change this to any time between 1 minute and 365 days. When an end-node registers a NetBIOS name with a WINS server, the end-node receives a positive Name Reply, which contains a TTL for the name.

Much like DHCP clients, a WINS client attempts to renew any NetBIOS names it holds at half the TTL, for instance, every 3 days. Additionally, each time the computer is restarted, or the Windows service that registers a NetBIOS name restarts, a new Name Registration message is sent to the WINS server, renewing the name (assuming, of course, that the WINS server successfully registers the name).

Network Monitor trace 17-5 (Capture 17-05, included in the \Captures folder on the companion CD-ROM) shows a name refresh for the name KAPOHO10[00].

Resolving NetBIOS Name Registration Conflicts

A name conflict occurs when two (or more) end-nodes want to register the same unique NetBIOS name. In most cases, this is caused by configuration errors, such as giving two computers the same name or by improperly configuring a service. When two computers attempt to register a unique NetBIOS name, the second end-node attempting to register the NetBIOS name will fail, causing an error to be logged.

Network Monitor trace 17-4 (Capture 17-04, included in the \Captures folder on the companion CD-ROM) shows a computer (IP address 10.10.1.52) attempting to register the name JASMINE[00]. However, the WINS server already has a registration for that name. The WINS server first issues a wait acknowledgment to the computer at 10.10.1.52, and then queries the registered owner of the NetBIOS name JASMINE[00]. The query is a simple Name Query Request sent to the registered owner at IP address 10.10.1.102. This computer is active and responds to the request with a Name Query Response. Because WINS has ascertained that the registered owner still owns the name, WINS sends a registration response back to 10.10.1.52 with an error code set, indicating that the name is active.

Releasing NetBIOS Names

A name can be released one of two ways: actively or silently. A Windows 2000 computer configured to use WINS can release any held NetBIOS names by sending the WINS server a Name Release message containing the NetBIOS name to release. Alternatively, if an end-node fails to renew the name, after the name's TTL has expired, the name will become available for use by another end-node.

With Windows 2000, the NBTSTAT.EXE command, used with the -RR switch, releases all currently registered NetBIOS names, and then re-registers them. This can be useful for diagnostic purposes.

Name Release Request and Name Release Response

When an end-node wants to release a registered NetBIOS name, the end-node sends a Name Release Request message to the WINS server. The WINS server then sends back a Name Release Response. Usually, the release response has a result code of 0, indicating that the name was successfully released. In theory, a negative Name Release message could be sent, although it would be ignored by the end-node sending the Name Release.

Network Monitor trace 17-6 (Capture 17-06, included in the \Captures folder on the companion CD-ROM) shows the computer at IP address 10.10.1.52 releasing the NetBIOS names it owns. It does this by sending the WINS server, at 10.10.1.200, a Name Release message. For each name released, the WINS server sends a Release Response.

Resolving NetBIOS Names

When a Windows 2000 computer needs to resolve a NetBIOS name, it issues a NetBIOS Name Query Request, either using a broadcast or sending the request directly to a WINS server, depending on node type. If the Name Query Request is sent to a WINS server and is one that can be resolved, the WINS server sends a Name Query Response to the computer issuing the query. If the WINS server can't resolve the name, it will issue a negative Name Query Request. If the computer performing the name resolution is using B-Node behavior, it will issue a Name Query Request; and if the end-system owning the name is on the local subnet, it will respond. However, if there's no end-node owning that name on the net, the host that's querying the name will time out, although this can take longer than getting a negative Name Query Response from a WINS server.

Name Query Request

A Name Query message contains the NetBIOS name to be resolved and is sent either to the local network or to the WINS server, or both, depending on the NetBIOS node type. If the end-node uses broadcast to find the name, it issues three broadcasts, by default, before failing.

When a user performs some operation using names on a Windows 2000 computer—such as typing NET VIEW \\XXX at the Windows 2000 command prompt, or typing \\XXX in Explorer's Address box—it isn't always clear what type of name is being resolved: host name or NetBIOS name. Nor is it obvious which name-resolution method will give the fastest results. In Windows NT 4.0, the operating system first attempts one name resolution (such as NetBIOS resolution or Host Name resolution), and if that doesn't succeed, the operating system tries the other method. This results in delays, if the wrong method is chosen. To reduce the delay, Windows 2000 attempts to resolve the names using both methods simultaneously.

Network Monitor trace 17-7 (Capture 17-07, included in the \Captures folder on the companion CD-ROM) shows an M-Node client attempting to resolve the name XXX. Network Monitor trace 17-8 (Capture 17-08, included in the \Captures folder on the companion CD-ROM) shows the same attempted resolution by an H-node client. The same computer generated both traces through the user by typing NET VIEW \\XXX at the Windows 2000 command prompt.

Notice that, in both of these traces, a DNS Query is attempted before any NetBIOS name resolution is performed. Also note that in trace 17-7, the M-Node client first attempts to resolve the name by broadcasting on the local network. When this fails, the client contacts the WINS server. In trace 17-8, the H-Node client first attempts to contact WINS. When this fails to resolve the name, the H-Node client then broadcasts the Name Query Request message.

Positive Name Query Response

When a NetBIOS host or a WINS server receives a Name Query Request for a NetBIOS name that can be resolved, the receiving system returns a Name Query Response. The Name Query Response will have the return code set to 0x0 (indicating successful resolution) and will include an RR giving the IP address of the system owning the name. If the name being queried is a unique name, only one IP address will be returned. If the name being queried is a group name, one or more IP addresses can be returned.

Network Monitor trace 17-9 (Capture 17-09, included in the \Captures folder on the companion CD-ROM) shows WINS successfully resolving the NetBIOS name KONA[00]. The response contains an RR, with the IP address of the end-node holding the NetBIOS name 10.10.2.200.

Negative Name Query Response

When a WINS server receives a Name Query Request for a NetBIOS name that can't be resolved, the WINS server returns a negative Name Query Response. The negative Name Query Response will have the return code set to indicate that the requested name doesn't exist.

Network Monitor traces 17-6 and 17-7 both show negative Name Query Responses.

Refreshing NetBIOS Names

Each registered NetBIOS name has a TTL. If the owning end-node wants to continue using the NetBIOS name, it must refresh the name before the TTL expires. For names registered with WINS, the TTL value is configured by the administrator. Windows 2000 computers will attempt to re-register each NetBIOS name at half the TTL.

Network Monitor trace 17-4 (Capture 17-04, included in the \Captures folder on the companion CD-ROM) shows an end-node re-registering the NetBIOS name TALLGUY[03] using a Name Refresh message. In this trace, the refresh is successful, therefore the WINS server responds with a Registration Response message.

Determining Adapter Status

RFCs 1001 and 1002 provide for a mechanism so that an end-node can determine the status of a local or remote adapter of another end-node. The adapter status information includes the NetBIOS names registered at that end-node and counts of various statistics.

In Windows 2000, you can use the NBTSTAT.EXE command, with the –A or –a switch to obtain a remote computer's NetBIOS adapter status. If the remote host has NBT disabled, however, this command will fail.

Network Monitor trace 17-11 (Capture 17-11, included in the \Captures folder on the companion CD-ROM) shows a trace of an adapter status Request and Response message. The command used to generate this trace, along with its output, is as follows:

```
D:\2031AS>nbtstat -a 10.10.1.52
\Device\NetBT_Tcpip_{6D137606-FEEF-11D2-8389-0020AF4B1775}:
Node IpAddress: [10.10.1.51] Scope Id: []

            NetBIOS Remote Machine Name Table

        Name               Type         Status
    ---------------------------------------------------
      KAPOHOLT         <00>  UNIQUE      Registered
      KAPOHO           <00>  GROUP       Registered
      KAPOHO           <1E>  GROUP       Registered
      KAPOHOLT         <20>  UNIQUE      Registered
      KAPOHOLT         <03>  UNIQUE      Registered
      ADMINISTRATOR    <03>  UNIQUE      Registered

    MAC Address = 00-60-08-01-D3-03
```

NetBIOS Name Service Messages

Most interactions between a WINS client and a WINS server consist of a request (such as a Name Registration Request) sent from a client to a server, and a subsequent response sent in the opposite direction. For example, when a WINS client needs to resolve a NetBIOS name, it sends a Name Request message to the WINS server and receives either a negative Name Reply or a positive Name Reply message in return.

NetBIOS Name Service messages are sent using UDP, with UDP port 137 on both the client and the server. Because all Name Service messages use UDP, which is an inherently unreliable transport protocol, there might not be a strict one-to-one relationship between requests and responses. However, there's never more than one response generated for any given request. This means, for example, that a WINS client might send more than one Name Resolution Request before it receives a request. If the WINS server can't answer the question promptly, it might send one or more Wait Acknowledgment messages back to the client.

As Figure 17-1 illustrates, the general format of a Name Service message is similar to DNS messages, described in Chapter 16.

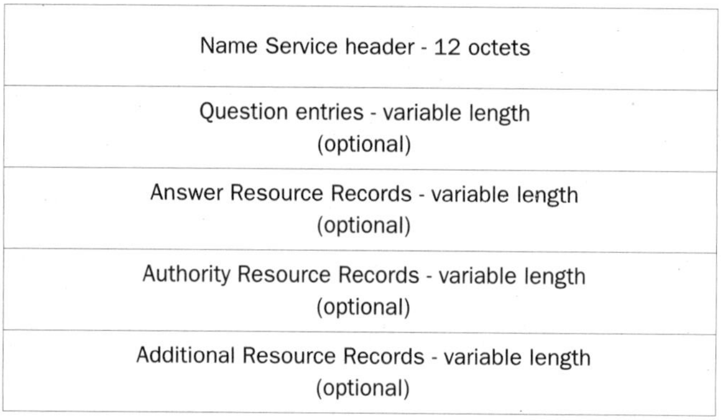

Name Service header - 12 octets
Question entries - variable length (optional)
Answer Resource Records - variable length (optional)
Authority Resource Records - variable length (optional)
Additional Resource Records - variable length (optional)

Figure 17-1. *NetBIOS Name Service message format.*

A NetBIOS Name Service messages consists of five sections:

- **Name Service header**   Fixed length (12 octets long), holding information about the type of NetBIOS Name Service message, plus counts of the other records in the message.

- **Question entries**   Variable length (length defined in Name Service header) for NetBIOS Name Registration, Refresh, or Release messages; this field holds the NetBIOS name being acted on by the message.

- **Answer Resource Records**   Variable length (length defined in Name Service header) holding RRs returned in response to a question.

- **Authority Resource Records**   Variable length (length defined in Name Service header) holding RRs used to indicate the authority for the question being asked. These aren't used in Windows 2000.
- **Additional Resource Records**   Variable length (length defined in Name Service header) holding other RRs, not provided in direct answer to a question.

NetBIOS Name Service messages contain a header and one or more additional entries, depending on the Name Service messages. The specific entries that are included in each NetBIOS Name Service record are given in the description of each NetBIOS Name Service message.

Name Service Header

Figure 17-2 displays the format of the Name Service header.

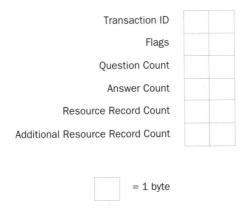

= 1 byte

Figure 17-2. *NetBIOS Name Service message header layout.*

The Name Service header is a fixed-length set of fields, which identifies the type of name-service packet, and the number of question entries, answer records, authority RRs, and additional records existing in the message. The other sections of a Name Query message carry either the NetBIOS names to be used in the name operation or RRs (such as the IP address) returned by a Name Service Query.

The Name Service header section consists of the following fields:

- **Transaction ID**   A 16-bit field used to identify a specific name-service transaction. The originator creates the transaction ID when it sends the request to the responder, and the responder copies the transaction ID into the reply message. If a WINS client is, for example, registering multiple names, each Name Registration Request will have a different transaction ID.
- **Flags**   A 16-bit field containing various Name Service flags, described in more detail below.

- **Question Count**   A 16-bit field indicating the number of entries in the question section of a name-service packet. The sender of a NetBIOS Name Service Request (for example, a WINS client attempting to register a name) will always set this value to 0x00-01or more, although typically it's set at 0x00-01). The responder for a Name Service Request will always set this field to 0.

- **Answer Count**   A 16-bit field indicating the number of entries in the answer RRs section of a name-service packet. The sender of a Name Service Request will set this count to 0. The responder for a Name Service Request will set this to indicate the number of answers returned. This will generally be 0x01 for unique NetBIOS name lookups, and a larger number for Internet group name lookups.

- **RR Count**   A 16-bit field indicating the number of entries in the authority RR section of a name-service packet. This number is used for recursive NetBIOS name queries, which aren't implemented in Windows 2000. This field is set to 0 in NetBIOS Name Service messages to indicate that there are no authority records present.

- **Additional RR Count**   A 16-bit field indicating the number of entries in the additional RRs section of a name-service packet. These records are used when an RR needs to be included in any name-service operation that isn't a response to a Name Query Request, such as a name release (the additional RR will include the name being released).

Name Service Header Flags Field

The Flags field, contained in the NetBIOS Name Service header, contains details on the purpose of each Name Service message. Figure 17-3 displays this field's format.

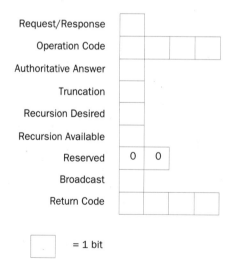

Figure 17-3. *NetBIOS Name Service Flags field layout.*

The Flags field holds the following fields:

- **Request/Response**   A 1-bit field set to 0x0 to indicate a Name-Service Request, and set to 1 to indicate a Name Service Response.
- **Operation Code**   A 4-bit field that indicates the specific name-service operation of the name-service packet, as shown in Table 17-2.

Table 17-2. Name Service Operation Codes and Meanings

Operation Code	Operation
0x0	Name Query Request
0x5	Name Registration Request
0x6	Name Release
0x7	Wait Acknowledgment
0x8	Name Refresh

- **Authoritative Answer**   Indicates whether the responder is authoritative. For Name Service requests, this is always set to 0x0. For responses, the computer responding to the request sets it to 0x1 if it's authoritative for a NetBIOS name.
- **Truncation**   Set to 0x1 if the total number of responses can't fit into the UDP datagram (for instance, the total number exceeds 576 bytes). RFC 1001 offers the possibility of using TCP to obtain the full answers, but Windows 2000 doesn't support this.
- **Recursion Desired**   Set to 0x1 by the sender of a Name Query, Name Registration, or Name Release if the sender wishes the receiver to iterate on the query. Windows 2000 WINS clients set this flag to 0x1 for all name queries. If the flag was set in a Name Service message sent to a Windows 2000 WINS server, the WINS server will set it in the corresponding reply. However, Windows 2000 doesn't support recursion.
- **Recursion Available**   Set to 0x0 on all Name Request messages. The Windows 2000 WINS server will set to 0x1 in Name Service Replies to indicate that it can perform recursive Name Query, Name Registration, and Name Release messages. If set to 0x0 in a Name Service Response, the client must iterate for Name Service Queries and perform challenges for any name registrations.
- **Reserved**   Two reserved bits set to 0x0.
- **Broadcast**   Set to 0x0 if the Name Service message is being sent via a unicast packet (for instance, to a WINS server), or 0x1 if it's being broadcast.
- **Return Code**   A 4-bit field holding the return code. All Name Service Requests set the value to 0x0, which indicates a successful response. For Name Query Requests, this means the answer is in the Reply message; for name registrations, it means the registration was successful.

NetBIOS Name Representation

NetBIOS names represented in name-service packets are encoded. The encoding scheme was originally designed to make NetBIOS names, contained in Name Service message packets, similar to DNS names. This was considered important since the DNS specifications, at the time that RFCs 1001 and 1002 were written, were more restrictive in terms of the range of characters that can be used in the name. The full name of the network resource is the concatenation of the encoded 16-character NetBIOS name, the "." character, and the NetBIOS scope identifier.

Creating the full NetBIOS resource name involves the following three steps:

1. The 16-character NetBIOS name is converted into a 32-bit unicode representation.

2. The "." character and the NetBIOS scope identifier are appended to the encoded 16-character NetBIOS name.

3. The resulting name is then encoded according to the rules for DNS Name Query.

The first step involves converting the original 16-byte NetBIOS name into a 32-byte string. This is done by mapping each 4-bit (half-byte) nibble to an ASCII character, as shown in Table 17-3.

Table 17-3. Converting an Original 16-Byte NetBIOS Name into a 32-Byte String

Nibble Value (in Hex)	Encoded ASCII Character
0	A
1	B
2	C
3	D
4	E
5	F
6	G
7	H
8	I
9	J
A	K
B	L
C	M
D	N
E	O
F	P

This conversion results in a name string that contains only the characters A-F, thus providing compatibility with DNS names, which were more restrictive about the content of names than NetBIOS.

As an example, consider the name of the Workstation service on the server KAPOHO (KAPOHO[03]). The full 16-character name would be "KAPOHO   [03]", that is, the name "KAPAHO" followed by nine blanks (or 0x20), and terminated by the hex value 0x03. Expressed in hex, this name becomes:

```
4B-41-50-4F-48-4F-20-20-20-20-20-20-20-20-20-03
```

Converting this name into nibbles, the string would then become:

```
4-B-4-1-5-0-4-F-4-8-4-F-2-0-2-0-2-0-2-0-2-0-2-0-2-0-2-0-2-0-0-3
```

Using Table 17-3, this nibble string is then encoded into a 32-byte ASCII string, which is:

```
ELEBFAEPEIEPCACACACACACACACACAAA
```

The third step involves converting the name into the DNS name format. In DNS, domain names are expressed as a sequence of labels. If the DNS name is kapoho.com, for example, this DNS name would consist of two labels (kapoho and com). Each label in a DNS message is formatted with a 1-byte length field followed by the label. The domain kapoho.com, therefore, would be expressed as 0x06kapoho0x03com0x00, where the hex digits represent the length of each label, the ASCII characters represent the individual labels, and the final hex 0 indicates the end of the name.

To complete the NetBIOS name encoding, the first label will be the encoded 16-character NetBIOS name, with additional labels for the NetBIOS scope identifier, if this is used. In the example, if there is no NetBIOS scope identifier, the name would be:

```
0x20ELEBFAEPEIEPCACACACACACACACACAAA
```

If a NetBIOS scope identifier, for example KAPOHO.COM, were to be used, the name would become:

```
0x20ELEBFAEPEIEPCACACACACACACACACAAA0x06kapoho0x03com0x00
```

> **Note**   This encoding scheme seems quite complicated at first sight. It was originally designed to be compatible with the emerging DNS standards and to make it easier for computers to parse. Fortunately, the Microsoft Network Monitor decodes the NetBIOS name, thus simplifying viewing NetBIOS names in Network Monitor traces.

Question Entries

In a NetBIOS name packet, a question entry represents the NetBIOS name being registered, refreshed, released, or queried. The format of a NetBIOS Name Service Question entry is based on DNS question entries. Figure 17-4 displays the Question field layout.

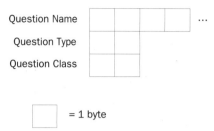

Figure 17-4. *Name Service Question Entry field layout.*

The question entry is made up of the following three fields:

- **Question Name**   The NetBIOS name being registered, refreshed, and so forth. The name is encoded using the NetBIOS name representation scheme described earlier in the NetBIOS Name Representation section.
- **Question Type**   The type of question. Set to either 0x00-20, indicating that the question name is a NetBIOS name, or 0x00-21.
- **Question Class**   The question class. Set to 0x00-01. This represents the IN (Internet) question class.

Resource Records (RRs)

RRs are used to send resource information between a client and server. Figure 17-5 displays the layout of an RR.

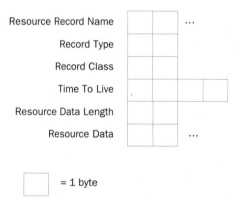

Figure 17-5. *Name Service RR field layout.*

The fields in an RR are as follows:

- **Resource Record Name**   The NetBIOS name, represented in the compressed name format
- **Record Type**   The RR type code—see below for details

- **Record Class**   The RR class code—there's only one record class, 0x00-01, the Internet Class.
- **Time To Live**   The RR's TTL, expressed in seconds.
- **Resource Data Length**   A 2-byte field holding the resource data's length.
- **Resource Data**   Variable-length data corresponding to the RR type. RFC 1002 defines values for Record Type fields as follows:

Value	Description
0x00-00	IP Address RR
0x00-02	Name Server RR
0x00-0A	Null RR
0x00-20	NetBIOS General Name Service RR
0x00-21	NetBIOS Node Status RR

Most Name Service records are either NetBIOS General Name Service RRs (record type 0x00-20) or NetBIOS Node Status RRs (record type 0x00-21).

Figure 17-6 displays the layout for the RR data used in General Name Service RRs (record type 0x00-20).

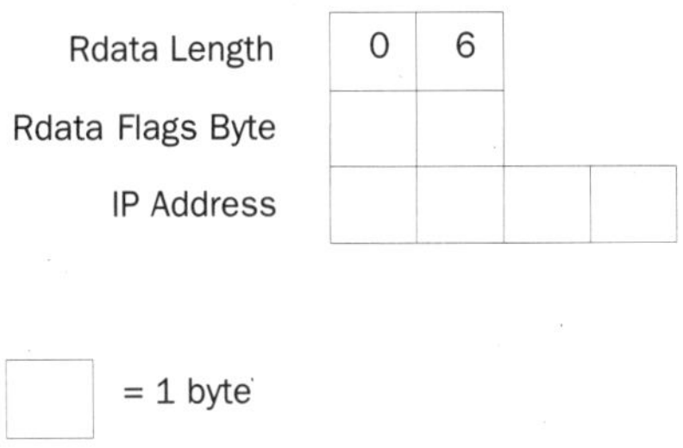

Figure 17-6. *RR data layout for record type 0x00-20.*

As Figure 17-6 shows, the RR contains a length of 6 bytes, an RDATA flag byte, and the IP address relating to this name. For instance, in a Name Registration message, this is the IP address of the owner registering the name.

Figure 17-7 displays the layout of the RDATA flag byte.

The RDATA contains the following three fields:

- **Group Flag**   Set to 0x1 if the name is a group name; otherwise set to 0x0.
- **Owner Node Type**   A 2-bit field, formatted as follows:
  0x0 – B-Node
  0x1 – P-Node
  0x2 – M-Node
  0x3 – H-Node
- **Reserved**   13 bits set to binary 0.

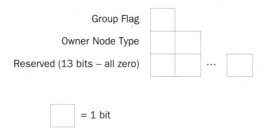

Figure 17-7. *RDATA flag byte layout.*

With respect to the owner node type, RFC 1002 defines the value of 11 as "Reserved for future use." In Windows 2000, this indicates H-Node.

Figure 17-8 displays the RDATA field for node status response RRs (Name Service record type 0x21).

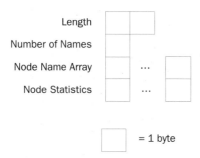

Figure 17-8. *RDATA layout for node status response.*

As Figure 17-8 shows, the RDATA field for node status responses contains the following fields:

- **Length**   16 bits holding the total length of the RDATA section
- **Number Of Names**   8 bits holding the number of names in the node name array
- **Node Name Array**   A variable-length array of the NetBIOS names owned by the node responding to the node status request
- **Node Statistics**   A set of statistics about the node's NetBIOS service

The Network Monitor trace 17-11 (Capture 17-11, included in the \Captures folder on the companion CD-ROM) illustrates the Statistics field. The values for this field, however, are not displayed by the NBTSTAT command.

Resource Record Name Compression

To ensure that Name Service Request and Response messages fit into a single UDP packet, NBT uses a compression mechanism for NetBIOS Name Service messages in which a given

NetBIOS name appears more than once. For example, in Name Registration Request messages, the NetBIOS name being registered is held both in the Question fields (the Question Name field) and in the Additional RR field (which contains both the NetBIOS name and IP address of the end-node that's registering the NetBIOS name).

In these cases, the name registration information contained in the Additional Resource Name field of the NetBIOS Name Service records uses the compressed label pointer technique that DNS uses, as defined in RFC 883.

Name Registration Message

A Name Registration message contains a header, a question record, and an additional RR holding the IP address of the node registering the name.

The fields are set as follows:

- **Transaction ID**   Set to a random number.
- **Response Flag**   Set to 0x0 (indicating a request).
- **Op Code**   Set to 0x5 (indicating registration).
- **Recursion Desired**   Set to 0x1.
- **Broadcast Flag**   Set if name-registration packet is being broadcast.
- **Question Count**   Set to 0x01.
- **Answer Resource**   Record Count set to 0x00.
- **Name Service Resource Record Count**   Set to 0x00.
- **Additional Resource Record Count**   Set to 0x01.
- **Question Record Section**   Contains the NetBIOS name being registered.
- **Additional Resource Record**   The format is described in the following bullet list.

The additional RR field in a Name Registration Request message contains details regarding this RR, and includes the following fields:

- **Resource Record**   Name in pointer format
- **Resource Record Type**   Set to 0x00-20
- **Requested TTL**   Set to 300,000 milliseconds
- **RDATA Flags**   Indicates the name type (group, unique) and the node type of the node registering the name
- **IP Address**   Belongs to the end-node registering this name

A Name Registration message can be seen in Network Monitor trace 17-1 (Capture 17-01, included in the \Captures folder on the companion CD-ROM).

Positive Name Registration Response

A positive Name Registration Response contains a header and an answer record. In a positive Name Registration Response message returned by a Windows 2000 WINS server, the header fields are set as follows:

- **Transaction ID**   Set to a random number corresponding to the Name Registration Request registering the name
- **Response Flag**   Set to 0x1 to indicate a response
- **Op Code**   Set to 0x5 (registration)
- **Authoritative Answer Flag**   Set to 0x1
- **Recursion Desired**   Set to 0x1
- **Recursion Available**   Set to 0x1
- **Broadcast Flag**   Set to 0x0
- **Question Count**   Set to 0x00
- **Return Code**   Set to 0x0 to indicate the name was successfully registered
- **Question Count**   Set to 0x00
- **Answer Resource Record Count**   Set to 0x01
- **Name Service Resource Record Count**   Set to 0x00
- **Additional Resource Record Count**   Set to 0x00
- **Answer Resource Record**

The answer RR confirms the details of the NetBIOS name that were registered with the WINS server, and contains the following fields:

- **Resource Record Name**   Such as the registered NetBIOS name (in coded format)
- **Resource Record Type**   Set to 0x00-20
- **Actual TTL For The Record Registered**   Set based on the TTL configured at the WINS server
- **IP Address**   Set to the IP address that belongs to the end-node that registered this name

A Positive Name Registration Response message can be seen in Network Monitor trace 17-1 (Capture 17-01, included in the \Captures folder on the companion CD-ROM).

Negative Name Registration Response

A negative Name Registration Response is returned when the WINS server is unable to register the requested NetBIOS name. This usually occurs when an end-node attempts to register a unique NetBIOS name that's owned by another end-node.

The negative Name Registration record is formatted as follows:

- **Transaction ID**   Set to a random number corresponding to the Name Registration Request registering the name
- **Response**   Set to 0x1 to indicate a response
- **Op Code**   Set to 0x5
- **Authoritative Answer Flag**   Set to 0x1
- **Recursion Desired**   Set to 0x1
- **Recursion Available**   Set to 0x1
- **Result Code**   Indicates why the NetBIOS name couldn't be registered
- **Broadcast Flag**   Set to 0x0
- **Question Count**   Set to 0x0
- **Answer Resource Record Count**   Set to 0x1
- **Name Service Resource Record Count**   Set to 0x0
- **Additional Resource Record Records**   Set to 0x0
- **Answer Resource Record**   Confirms the details of the name that failed to be registered

RFC 1001 defines the following values for the return code field, as Table 17-4 displays:

Table 17-4. Values for the Return Code Field

Return Code Value	Reason for the Error
0x1	Format error–the request was improperly formatted
0x2	Server failure–there's a problem with the name server, such that it can't process the Name Registration Request
0x4	Unsupported–the request isn't supported by the NetBIOS name server (not used by WINS)
0x5	Registration Request refused–for policy reasons, the NBNS won't register this name from this host (not used by WINS)
0x6	Name active–another node owns the name
0x7	Name conflict–more than one end-node owns a unique NetBIOS name

The most common return code will be 0x6—name active. This occurs whenever the name that the end-node is requesting WINS to register has already been registered by another end-node. This can be seen in Network Monitor trace 17-3 (Capture 17-03, included in the \Captures folder on the companion CD-ROM).

Name Refresh Message

As noted earlier, the end-node owning a NetBIOS name will attempt to refresh the name (essentially re-leasing the NetBIOS name) at half the TTL by issuing a Name Refresh message to the WINS server. The Name Refresh message is similar to a Name Registration Request message and is formatted as follows:

- **Transaction ID**   Set to a random number.
- **Response**   Set to 0x0 to indicate a request.
- **Op Code**   Set to 0x4, indicating a name refresh. RFC 1002 defines the name refresh op code as 0x09, but Windows 2000 clients set this to 0x04.
- **Authoritative Answer Flag**   Set to 0x0.
- **Recursion Desired**   Set to 0x1.
- **Recursion Available**   Set to 0x0.
- **Result Code**   Set to 0x0.
- **Broadcast Flag**   Set to 0x0.
- **Question Record Count**   Set to 0x1.
- **Answer Resource Record Count**   Set to 0x0.
- **Name Service Resource Record Count**   Set to 0x0.
- **Additional Resource Records**   Set to 0x1.
- **Question Record**   Contains the NetBIOS name being refreshed. The format is the same as for the question record in a Name Registration Request.
- **Additional Resource Record**   Confirms the details of the name to be re-freshed. The format is the same as for the additional RR in a Name Registration Request.

WINS usually responds to a Name Refresh message with a positive Name Registration Response record, as seen in Network Monitor trace 17-5 (Capture 17-05, included in the \Captures folder on the companion CD-ROM).

Name Release Request Message

A Name Release Request message is sent when an end-node releases a NetBIOS name. This usually happens when a Windows 2000 service is stopped or is being shut down. A Name Release Request message is formatted as follows:

- **Transaction ID**   Set to a random number.
- **Response**   Set to 0x0 to indicate a request.
- **Op Code**   Set to 0x6, meaning name release.
- **Authoritative Answer Flag**   Set to 0x0.
- **Recursion Desired**   Set to 0x0.
- **Recursion Available**   Set to 0x0.

- **Broadcast Flag**   Set to 0x0.
- **Result Code**   Set to 0x0.
- **Question Record Count**   Set to 0x1.
- **Answer Resource Record Count**   Set to 0x0.
- **Name Service Resource Record Count**   Set to 0x0.
- **Additional Resource Records**   Set to 0x1.
- **Question Record**   Contains the NetBIOS name being released. The format is the same as for the Question record in a Name Registration Request.
- **Additional Resource Record**   Confirms the details of the name that's to be released. The format is the same (such as the DNS pointer format) as for the additional RR in a Name Registration Request.

Network Monitor trace 17-6 (Capture 17-6, included in the \Captures folder on the companion CD-ROM) illustrates the Name Release Request message. When an end-node sends a Name Release Request message to a WINS server, the WINS server usually responds with a positive Name Release Response message, although an error can occur at the WINS server and result in the WINS server sending a negative Name Release Response message. The end-node sending the original name release message doesn't take any action on a negative Name Release Response message.

Name Release Response Message

A WINS server sends a Name Release Response message in response to a Name Release Request message. A positive Name Release Response is indicated by the result code 0x0. A negative Name Release Response has the same format as a positive Name Release, except that the result code contains details of the error.

A Name Release Response message is formatted as follows:

- **Transaction ID**   Set to the same transaction ID contained in the Name Release Request message.
- **Response**   Set to 0x1 to indicate a response.
- **Op Code**   Set to 0x6, meaning name release.
- **Authoritative Answer Flag**   Set to 0x0.
- **Recursion Desired**   Set to 0x0.
- **Recursion Available**   Set to 0x0.
- **Broadcast Flag**   Set to 0x0.
- **Result Code**   Set to 0x0 (success) or to indicate reason for the failure.
- **Question Record Count**   Set to 0x0.
- **Answer Resource Record Count**   Set to 0x1.
- **Name Service Resource Record Count**   Set to 0x0.

- **Additional Resource Records** Set to 0x0.
- **Answer Resource Record** Contains the NetBIOS name that has been released. The format is the same as for the Question record in a Name Registration Request.

If the WINS server successfully releases the NetBIOS name, the return code is 0x0. Table 17-5 indicates what the return codes will be if the WINS server can't release the name.

Table 17-5. Explanation of Return Code Value and Error

Return Code Value	Reason for the Error
0x1	Format error—the request was improperly formatted
0x2	Server failure—there's a problem with the Name server, such that it can't process the Name Release Request
0x5	Registration Request refused—for policy reasons, the NBNS won't release this name from this host (not used by WINS)
0x6	Name active—another node owns the name; only the node owning the name can release it

A Name Release Response message can be seen in Network Monitor trace 17-6 (Capture 17-06, included in the \Captures folder on the companion CD-ROM).

Name Query Request Message

A computer that wants to resolve a NetBIOS name sends a Name Query Request message. This message, which can be sent via broadcast or direct to a WINS server, is formatted as follows:

- **Transaction ID** Set to a random 16-bit value.
- **Response** Set to 0x0 to indicate a request.
- **Op Code** Set to 0x0, meaning Name Query.
- **Authoritative Answer Flag** Set to 0x0.
- **Recursion Desired** Set to 0x1.
- **Recursion Available** Set to 0x0.
- **Broadcast Flag** Set to 0x1 if broadcast, and 0x0 if sent to a WINS server.
- **Result Code** Set to 0x0.
- **Question Record Count** Set to 0x1.
- **Answer Resource Record Count** Set to 0x0.
- **Name-Service Resource Record Count** Set to 0x0.
- **Additional Resource Records** Set to 0x0.
- **Question Record** Contains the NetBIOS name that the sender wishes to resolve.

The Network Monitor trace 17-9 (Capture 17-09, included in the \Captures folder on the companion CD-ROM) illustrates a Name Query Request, and shows a query being sent to a WINS server.

Positive Name Query Response Message

If the node that has received a Name Query can resolve the name, it formats and sends a positive Name Query Response to the node that issued the original Name Query message. The positive Name Query message contains the IP address of the system owning the NetBIOS node and is formatted as follows:

- **Transaction ID**   Set to the transaction ID specified in the Name Query message.
- **Response**   Set to 0x1 to indicate a response.
- **Op Code**   Set to 0x0, meaning Name Query.
- **Authoritative Answer Flag**   Set to 0x1.
- **Recursion Desired**   Set to 0x1.
- **Recursion Available**   Set to 0x1.
- **Broadcast Flag**   Set to 0x1 if broadcast, and to 0x0 if sent from a WINS server.
- **Result Code**   Set to 0x0.
- **Question Record Count**   Set to 0x0.
- **Answer Resource Record Count**   Set to 0x1.
- **Name Service Resource Record Count**   Set to 0x0.
- **Additional Resource Records**   Set to 0x0.
- **Answer Resource Record**   Contains details of the name including the name type (unique, group) and the name TTL; also contains details of the node that owns the name (the IP address and the node type).

A Positive Name Query Response message can be seen in Network Monitor trace 17-9 (Capture 17-09, included in the \Captures folder on the companion CD-ROM).

Negative Name Response Message

When a WINS server gets a Name Query Response that it can't resolve, it sends a negative Name Response message to the node that sent the original Name Query message. The negative Name Response message is formatted as follows:

- **Transaction ID**   Set to the transaction ID specified in the Name Query message.
- **Response**   Set to 0x1 to indicate a response.
- **Op Code**   Set to 0x0, meaning Name Query.

- **Authoritative Answer Flag**   Set to 0x1.
- **Recursion Desired**   Set to 0x1.
- **Recursion Available**   Set to 0x1.
- **Broadcast Flag**   Set to 0x1 if broadcast, and to 0x0 if sent from a WINS server.
- **Result Code**   Set to 0x0.
- **Question Record Count**   Set to 0x0.
- **Answer Resource Record Count**   Set to 0x1.
- **Name Service Resource Record Count**   Set to 0x0.
- **Additional Resource Records**   Set to 0x0.
- **Answer Resource Record**   Contains details of the name including the name type (unique, group) and the name TTL; also contains details of the node that owns the name (the IP address and the node type).

Wait Acknowledgment Message

A WINS server sends a Wait Acknowledgment message to a client asking it to wait for the completion of a name-service operation. Network Monitor trace 17-4 (Capture 17-04, included in the \Captures folder on the companion CD-ROM) illustrates a Wait Acknowledgment message. The format of a Wait Acknowledgment message is as follows:

- **Transaction ID**   Set to the transaction ID specified in the name message previously sent to the WINS server.
- **Response**   Set to 0x1 to indicate a response.
- **Op Code**   Set to 0x7, meaning Wait Acknowledgment message.
- **Authoritative Answer Flag**   Set to 0x1.
- **Recursion Desired**   Set to 0x0.
- **Recursion Available**   Set to 0x0.
- **Broadcast Flag**   Set to 0x0.
- **Result Code**   Set to 0x0.
- **Question Record Count**   Set to 0x0.
- **Answer Resource Record Count**   Set to 0x1.
- **Name Service Resource Record Count**   Set to 0x0.
- **Additional Resource Records**   Set to 0x0.
- **Answer Resource Record**   Contains details of the name-service operation that the WINS server is asking the receiver of this message to wait for.

A Negative Name Query Response message can be seen in Network Monitor trace 17-10 (Capture 17-10, included in the \Captures folder on the companion CD-ROM).

Summary

WINS provides NetBIOS name resolution for networks of any size, although it will most likely be used in networks that span multiple subnets. While Windows 2000 makes heavier use of DNS than Windows NT 4.0, the need for WINS will continue until all down-level clients or NetBIOS applications that rely on NetBIOS are replaced by either Windows 2000 or by updated applications.

Chapter 18
File and Printer Sharing

Overview

Microsoft Windows 2000 introduces improved methods for sharing and accessing printers and files over internetworks via Internet Printing Protocol (IPP) and the latest generation of the Common Internet File System (CIFS). IPP in Windows 2000 allows clients to install printer drivers over their intranet or the Internet, as well as to send print jobs via IPP encapsulated in HTTP/1.1. HTTP/1.1 is a standard Internet protocol fully supported in Internet Information Service (IIS) 5.0, and is discussed in Chapter 19 of this book. CIFS is an operating-system-independent protocol that evolved from the NetBIOS file-sharing mechanisms of earlier versions of Windows. It allows clients to access files and printers over the Internet as if they were directly connected to their corporate local area network (LAN). Microsoft and several other vendors are jointly developing CIFS specifications, and a specification draft has been submitted to the Internet Engineering Task Force (IETF) in expectation that it might be adopted as an informational RFC.

Chapter Contents

This chapter focuses on the mechanisms that allow efficient, secure sharing of files and printers over an intranet or the Internet in Windows 2000. Specifically, this focuses on the following two application-level protocols:

- **Internet Printing in Windows 2000** An analysis of Internet Printing Protocol/1.0, and its functionality in Windows 2000.
- **CIFS** CIFS allows printer sharing and read/write file access over the Internet, independent of an operating system.

Introduction to Internet Printing

Internet printing in Windows 2000 allows a user to install, use, and monitor a printer over an internet. Using IPP, a user can install a printer using a Web browser or the Add Printer wizard, but can specify a URL or IP address instead of a Universal Naming Convention (UNC) path to the printer. When submitting a print request, the user can then use the installed printer interface to print directly to the URL. The print server must, however, be running IIS to accept these print requests. Because the print server uses the HTTP functionality of IIS, it can return information regarding the print job in browser-ready format. The underlying protocol that allows Internet printing to function is the IPP, which is sent encapsulated in an HTTP/1.1 request to the print server.

IPP Operation

IPP is defined in RFCs 2565 through 2569, as well as RFC 2639. It functions within Active Directory (AD) in Windows 2000, as IPP recommends that printer objects be represented in a directory service. A *printer object* is the server-side component of the IPP protocol, which, in Windows 2000, is a computer running IIS and acting as the print server for one or more output devices. Because it's an object represented in the directory service, a printer object's attributes can be queried to determine its capabilities. However, the printer object isn't to be confused with the output device. The *output device* is the physical device, whether it's a printer, fax printer, or even software, such as desktop publishing or document archive software. The physical output device doesn't need to be IPP-aware or -compliant because the printer object (the IPP server) handles the IPP.

A user can query AD to locate a printer object by attributes, such as its location or capabilities. When a user sends a document for printing via IPP, the client computer submits the document as a print job, which contains a listing of the document's print attributes. The print submission is sent to the printer object, which validates the submission's attributes and creates a new job object. The newly created job object is a queryable object, which facilitates reporting on print status and errors, and is sent to the physical output device by the printer object. Printing properties and access control mechanisms are made very flexible for administrators because the printer object and the output device are separate entities. For example, an administrator can restrict access to a printer object, which would limit printing to a subset of people. Additionally, the administrator can use a single printer object to represent more than one physical output device. Although AD isn't the focus of this book, it's important to understand the relationship between directory services objects and the entities that they represent.

> **Note** Unless otherwise specified, the terms "printer" and "printer object" will be used interchangeably throughout this chapter.

An IPP client is a computer running an HTTP/1.1-compatible browser, such as Microsoft Internet Explorer or Netscape Navigator (versions 4 or later), and an installed printer software interface representing the print object. The user at the client computer installs the printer by entering its URL or IP address in either a Web browser or the Add Printer wizard. After the printer has been added on the client computer, the user can submit print jobs from any application as if the printer were a network printer. The client IPP software processes the print job in the appropriate format for the printer object, then submits the job as an encapsulated HTTP/1.1 request to the printer object, which might be a print server or the actual output device. RFC 2566 specifies three different scenarios for setup of the printer object(s) and output device(s). Figures 18-1, 18-2, and 18-3 diagram each of these scenarios.

Hosted Printing

In hosted printing, the IPP client sends a print job to the printer object, which can be represented in AD. The client can locate the printer object by querying AD for printers that are capable of specific functionality. However, queries for dynamic information, such as job status and queue length, are submitted to the printer object itself. The printer object in this scenario is a print server running the IPP service (IIS, for example), and the output device is a physical print device or software application that can be installed directly on the print server network. The output device doesn't need to support any IPP functionality, because the printer object, in this case the IIS server, performs all processing related to IPP and sends the job to the output device as it would any locally submitted print job. The printer object is also responsible for providing status monitoring and notification functionality to the requesting client via HTTP/1.1, which is why the server must be running IIS to serve as an IPP printer object.

IPP Client
HTTP/1.1 browser,
IPP protocol, spooler
and print driver

Directory Service Represented
Printer Object
(Printer published in a directory
service such as Active Directory)

Output Device
(not IPP-enabled)

Printer Object
(Running IPP service and
functioning as a print server)

Figure 18-1. *IPP hosted printing.*

Fan Out Printing

Fan out printing is very similar to hosted printing, except that the print object can transparently direct the print job to any of a number of output devices. These devices can be physical print devices, fax printers, or software on the local computer or another computer on the network. As with hosted printing, the output device doesn't need to use IPP, because the IPP server/printer object handles that functionality. Client queries relating to job status are submitted to the printer object, and not to the output devices.

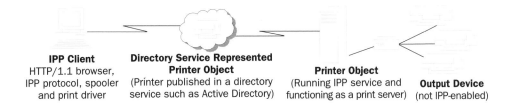

IPP Client
HTTP/1.1 browser,
IPP protocol, spooler
and print driver

Directory Service Represented
Printer Object
(Printer published in a directory
service such as Active Directory)

Printer Object
(Running IPP service and
functioning as a print server)

Output Device
(not IPP-enabled)

Figure 18-2. *IPP fan out printing.*

Embedded Printing

In embedded printing, the printer object and the output device are the same entity, and might or might not be represented in AD. Unlike hosted and fan out printing, there's no intermediary server acting as the print object and print server for the output device. Embedded printing requires that the output device be capable of receiving and processing IPP client requests, as well as returning information to the client via HTTP. Therefore, this implementation requires additional functionality on the part of the output device. Some printer vendors have already provided this functionality.

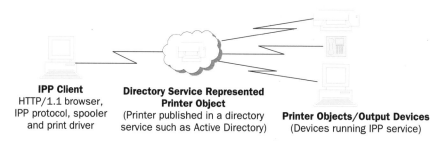

IPP Client
HTTP/1.1 browser,
IPP protocol, spooler
and print driver

**Directory Service Represented
Printer Object**
(Printer published in a directory
service such as Active Directory)

Printer Objects/Output Devices
(Devices running IPP service)

Figure 18-3. *IPP embedded printing.*

IPP Specifications

IPP structure and semantics are defined in RFCs 2565 and 2566. IPP specifications define two layers: transport and operation. The transport layer of the protocol consists of HTTP/1.1 requests and responses, defined in Chapter 19, "Internet Information Server (IIS) and the Internet Protocols." The operation layer is a message body embedded in the HTTP/1.1 requests and responses. Each request or response message contains a sequence of attributes that describe the capabilities and characteristics of every object involved in the print transaction. These object attributes can be described as:

- **Printer attributes** Printer object attributes fall into two categories: printer description attributes and printer job-template attributes. Printer description attributes are those that define properties, such as the printer object's location and state. Printer job-template attributes describe the printer object's capabilities, such as the types of jobs it can handle and its default settings.

- **Job attributes** Job attributes are properties of a print job that's been processed by the printer object and assigned to a job object. Job attributes can be job-template attributes, which are attributes submitted by the client requesting override of the default printer job-template attributes. For example, a printer object can, by default, assign a specific priority to print jobs that the client wishes to override. Job attributes can also be job-description attributes, which provide parameters, such as the job's size, state, and identification. Some job-description attributes are provided by the client when requesting the print job, and others are provided by the print object as it processes the print request.

For example, a requesting client can provide information regarding the number of pages in a print request (client-side job-description attributes), and the printer object can assign a job a Uniform Resource Identifier (URI) when it accepts the job for printing (server-side job-description attributes).

- **Operation attributes** Unlike printer-object and job-object attributes, which provide characteristics relating to the objects involved in a print transaction, operation attributes describe the transaction itself. These attributes identify properties, such as where the job is being sent and what localization parameters might need to be defined in the transaction.

- **Unsupported attributes** Because IPP attributes are extensible, a client can issue a request containing attributes that aren't supported by the print object. If this is the case, the IPP server returns a message to the client listing which attributes it can't support, so that the client can issue only requests that the print object can fulfill. This process allows client and server to "negotiate" job parameters during the request/response sequences.

More Info   IPP structure and semantics are defined primarily in RFCs 2565 and 2566, which can be found in the \RFC folder on the companion CD-ROM.

IPP Request/Response Mechanisms

IPP operations are passed between client and server as a series of HTTP/1.1 request and response messages. When a client wants to submit a print request to a print object (IPP server), the client issues a request message to the printer-object URI containing operation attributes, object attributes, and the document data itself. Each request message must be followed by a response message from the other party. The response message contains a code indicating success or failure of the requested operation, as well as operation attributes, object attributes, and status messages that the server generated. After the server has accepted the print request and created a job object with its own URI, the client can request the addition of further documents to the same job object. While a printer isn't required to support job objects that contain more than one document, allowing the submission of multiple documents to a single job object increases printing efficiency and allows print requests to be "batched." Because each job object is queryable, the client can use a single job URI to obtain status reports on multiple documents, if the server supports this mechanism.

Each operation request that the client issues must contain a Version-Number, an Operation-ID, a Request-ID, and any attributes required by the request type. Each server response message must contain a Version-Number, a Status-Code, the Request-ID that the client issued, and any attributes that are specific to that request type. Figure 18-4 illustrates the encoding for these requests and responses.

As Figure 18-4 demonstrates, the Version-Number is the version identifier for the request/response sequence. The Operation-ID is used in a request message to specify what operation the client wants to request of the print object, and the Status-ID is sent in the server's response message to indicate whether that operation was successfully received and processed. The Request-ID is used to assign a number to the request for tracking purposes. The 1-byte Attributes tag identifies the type of attributes being sent in this request or response message (printer, job, operation, or unsupported), and the variable-length Attributes sequence lists the attributes particular to that type. The end of the attributes is indicated by a 1-byte End-Of-Attributes tag, and the remaining bytes might or might not consist of the actual print data being sent.

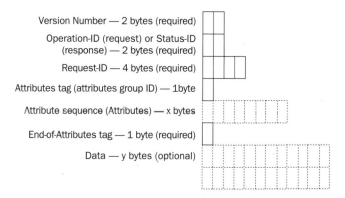

Version Number — 2 bytes (required)
Operation-ID (request) or Status-ID (response) — 2 bytes (required)
Request-ID — 4 bytes (required)
Attributes tag (attributes group ID) — 1byte
Attribute sequence (Attributes) — x bytes
End-of-Attributes tag — 1 byte (required)
Data — y bytes (optional)

Figure 18-4. *Request/response encoding.*

Operations

An IPP client requests submission of a print job by sending an HTTP Request message containing an operation request and attributes to the printer's URI. The printer uses the information provided by the client to construct a new job object, whose URI is then passed back to the client so that the client can use this URI for purposes of querying or adding to the job. IPP/1.0 defines certain operations that can be requested of a printer or a job. These operations are defined in Table 18-1.

Table 18-1. IPP Operations

Operation	Type (Printer or Job)	Description
Print-Job	Printer	Required. Allows a client to submit a print job and supply the document data, which isn't considered a separate rate object and therefore has no attributes of its own. Includes operation attributes character set and natural language attributes, and printer-URI.
Print-URI	Printer	Identical to a Print-Job operation except that the client supplies a job-URI reference to the print data as opposed to submitting the data itself. The printer then validates the job-URI before responding to the client.
Validate-Job	Printer	Similar to a Print-Job operation except that no data is supplied in the request/response process. The client

(continued)

Table 18-1. *(continued)*

Operation	Type (Printer or Job)	Description
		uses it to verify that a print job submitted to this printer would be accepted and processed.
Create-Job	Printer	Similar to Print-Job, except that the client sends no document data in the operation, but issues attributes for multiple print requests to submit them to a single job object.
Get-Printer-Attributes	Printer	Required. Allows the client to request printer attributes to determine the capabilities of the printer.
Get-Jobs	Printer	Allows the client to request a list of job objects owned by the printer object.
Send-Document	Job	Allows the client to send a multi-document job-object request, so that multiple requests can be submitted under a single job.
Send-URI	Job	Identical to the Send-Document operation, except that the client supplies a document-URI operation attribute rather than the document data itself.
Cancel-Job	Job	Required. Allows a client to request cancellation of a print job.
Get-Job	Job	Required. Allows a client to request the attributes of the Attributes job object identified in the message.

Each of these operations can be sent as part of either a request or response message between client and printer, and each operation includes attributes that identify the details of the request or response. Printer attributes cam be sent as part of a printer operation message, and job-object attributes can be sent as part of a job operation.

Attributes

Attributes are extensible characteristics or properties of any object in IPP, such as printer objects, job objects, and operations. Attribute specifications include the name of the attribute, followed by its syntax in parentheses. Tables 18-2, 18-3, 18-4, and 18-5 describe these attributes.

Table 18-2. IPP Operation Attributes

Attribute	Description
Attributes-charset	Required. Must be supplied as the first attribute in any request or response so as to define the character set that the client or the IPP server uses.
Attributes-natural-language	Required. Must be supplied as the second attribute in any request or response message so as to define the natural language that the client or IPP server uses.

Table 18-3. IPP Job-Template Attributes

Attribute	Description
Job-priority (integer (1:100))	Priority for job scheduling; 1 is the lowest priority and 100 is the highest.
Job-hold-until (type3 keyword | name (MAX))	Named time frame during which the job must become eligible for printing; values include the following: no-hold (immediately); daytime (during the day); evening (evening); night (night); weekend (weekend); second-shift (after close of business); and third-shift (after midnight).
Job-sheets (type3 keyword | name (MAX))	Which job start/end sheets must be printed with the job (if any). Key-word values: none (no job sheet printed); standard (site-specific standard sheets are printed, administrator-defined values).
Multiple-document handling (type2 keyword)	If a job consists of more than one document, this controls the placement of pages onto media sheets (such as large sheets of paper used in commercial printing). Keywords: single-document (multiple documents must be treated as a single media sheet); separate-documents-uncollated-copies (each document is treated as a single, non-collated media sheet); separate-documents-collated-copies (each document is treated as a single media sheet and the media sheets are collated); single-document-new-sheet (each document instance in the job must be forced onto a new sheet).
Copies (integer (1:MAX))	Number of copies to be printed, ranging from 1 through the maximum number supported by the output device (such as number of collation trays for collated copies, or the maximum number of non-collated copies allowed by the output device).
Finishings (1setOf rangeOfInteger (1:MAX))	Identifies the finishing operations used for each copy of each document in the job. Enum values: 3-no finishing; 4-staple; 5-punch; 6-cover (used to specify a cover sheet); 7-bind (specifies site-defined binding operations).
Page-ranges (1setOf rangeOfInteger (1:MAX))	Range of pages to be printed for a document. A page range of "1:5, 24:24" would specify pages 1-5 and page 24 should be printed.
Page-ranges-supported (Boolean)	Indicates whether the printer supports printing of ranges. 0 = No, 1 = Yes.
Sides (type2 keyword)	Specifies whether printing is one-sided or two-sided. Keyword values: one-sided; two-sided-long-edge; duplex or head-to-head; two-sided-short-edge.
Number-up (integer (1:MAX))	Number of pages to place on a single side of the selected medium.
Orientation-requested (type2 enum)	Page orientation, such as portrait, landscape, reverse landscape, reverse-portrait (used in commercial printing).
Media (type3 keyword | name (MAX))	Media type used by the printer, such as paper type, paper size, paper tray, electronic form.
Printer-resolution (resolution)	The resolution used by the printer for the job.
Print-quality (type2 enum)	Print quality used by the printer for the job. Enum values: 3-draft; 4-normal; 5-high.

Table 18-4. IPP Job-Description Attributes

Attribute	Description
Job-uri (URI)	Required. The URI for this print job.
Job-id (integer (1:MAX))	Required. Job ID that's generated by the print object upon receipt of a new job and returned to the requesting client for identification purposes.
Job-printer-uri (URI)	Required. Identifies the printer object that created the job object.
Job-more-info (URI)	Contains the URI referencing a resource that has more information about the job object (such as, an HTML page listing job status information).
Job-name (name (MAX))	Required. User-friendly name assigned to the print job. Generated by the print object and returned to the client.
Job-originating-user-name (name (MAX))	Required. Name of the user who submitted the print job. Can be used for authentication purposes in access-controlled print environments.
Job-state (type1 enum)	Required. Identifies the current job state. Values: 3-pending; 4-pending-held; 5-processing; 6-processing-stopped; 7-canceled; 8-aborted; 9-completed.
Job-state-reasons (1setOf type2 keyword)	Provides additional information about the job-state attribute, such as "none," "job-incoming," "submission-interrupted," "job-outgoing," and so forth.
Job-state-message (text (MAX))	Job-state and job-state-reasons information provided in friendly message format.
Number-of-documents (integer (0:MAX))	Indicates the number of documents in the job.
Output-device-assigned (name (127))	Identifies the output device to which the printer object assigned the print job. If this is an embedded printer object, the attribute is unnecessary.
Time-at-creation (integer (0:MAX))	Time at which the job object was created.
Time-at-processing (integer (0:MAX))	Time at which the job object began processing.
Time-at-completed (integer (0:MAX))	Time at which the job object was completed, canceled, or aborted.
Number-of-intervening-jobs (integer (0:MAX))	The number of jobs "ahead" of this job in the queue.
Job-message-from-operator (text (127))	Message sent to the client from an operator or administrator of the printer.
Job-k-octets (integer (0:MAX))	Total size in k octets (units of 1024 octets, or kilobytes) of the document.
Job-impressions (integer (0:MAX))	Total size of the document in number of impressions (pages as chosen by the client, such as "letter," "legal," and so forth).
Job-media-sheets (integer (0:MAX))	Total number of media sheets to be produced for the job.

(continued)

Table 18-4. *(continued)*

Attribute	Description
Job-k-octets-processed (integer (0:MAX))	The total number of k octets processed so far.
Job-impressions-completed (integer (0:MAX))	Number of impressions completed, which includes interpreting, marking, and stacking the output, and both sides of the impression.
Job-media-sheets-completed (integer (0:MAX))	The media sheets completed for the job, whether both sides of the sheet have been processed or not.
Attributes-charset (charset)	Required. Identifies the character set used in the job.
Attributes-natural-language (naturalLanguage)	Required. Identifies the natural language of the job (English, French, and so forth).

Table 18-5. IPP Printer-Description Attributes

Attribute	Description
Printer-uri-supported (1setOf uri)	Required. Contains one or more URIs used to submit print jobs to this print object. Multiple URIs allow the print object to be represented as multiple objects in a directory service, but represent a single IPP server.
Uri-security-supported (1setOf type2 keyword)	Required. Identifies the security mechanisms for each of the URIs that identify a printer object (such as "none" or "SSL3").
Printer-name (name (127))	Required. Friendly name of the printer object.
Printer-location (text (127))	Friendly text identifying the location of the printer.
Printer-info (text (127))	Friendly description of the printer.
Printer-more-info (URI)	Specifies a URI where more information about the printer can be obtained, such as an HTML page listing the printer's capabilities.
Printer-driver-installer (URI)	URI used to locate the driver installer for the printer object.
Printer-make-and-model (text (127))	The make and model of the printer object.
Printer-more-info-manufacturer (URI)	Manufacturer's information about this printer.
Printer-state (type1 enum)	Required. Identifies whether the printer is idle, pending, processing, or stopped.
Printer-state-reasons (1setOf type2 keyword)	Provides more information about the reported state of the printer, such as "paused," "shutdown," and so forth.
Printer-state-message (text (MAX))	Friendly message that represents the printer state to the user.
Operations-supported (1setOf type2 enum)	Required. Operations that are supported by the printer for its job objects.
Charset-configured (charset)	Required. The configured character set of the printer.
Charset-supported (1setOf charset)	Required. A list of character sets supported by the printer.

(continued)

Table 18-5. *(continued)*

Attribute	Description
Natural-language-configured (naturalLanguage)	Required. The configured natural language of the printer.
Generated-natural-language-supported (1setOf naturalLanguage108)	Required. A list of natural languages supported by the printer.
Document-format-default (mimeMediaType)	Required. The default document format that the printer assumes if the client doesn't specify a particular format.
Document-format-supported (1setOf mimeMediaType)	Required. Multipurpose Internet Mail Extensions (MIME) media types supported by the printer.
Printer-is-accepting-jobs (Boolean)	Required. Indicates whether the printer is currently accepting job requests.
Queued-job-count (integer (0:MAX))	Recommended. The number of jobs in the print queue for this printer object.
Printer-message-from-operator (text (127))	Text sent from an administrator or operator to the client.
Color-supported (Boolean)	Indicates whether the printer is capable of color printing.
Reference-uri-schemes-supported (1setOf uriScheme)	List of URI schemes that the printer can accept jobs from, such as FTP, HTTP, and so forth.
Pdl-override-supported (type2 keyword)	Required. Specifies whether the printer object is capable of overriding document defaults as supplied by the application that requested the print job with IPP settings.
Printer-up-time (integer (1:MAX))	Required. Amount of time, in seconds, that the printer has been up and running.
Printer-current-time (dateTime)	The current date and time where the printer is located.
Multiple-operation-time-out (integer (1:MAX))	Maximum time, in seconds, that the printer waits for additional instructions on a multi-document job before taking recovery action.
Compression-supported (1setOf type3 keyword)	Printer-supported HTTP compression types, such as "none," "gzip," "deflate," "compress."
Job-k-octets-supported (rangeOfInteger (0:MAX))	Upper and lower boundaries of k octets that the printer can accept in a single job.
Job-impressions-supported (rangeOfInteger (0:MAX))	Upper and lower bounds for the number of impressions per job.
Job-media-sheets-supported (rangeOfInteger (0:MAX))	Upper and lower bounds of the number of media sheets supported per job.

Internet Printing Security

Because a printer object can be represented by more than one URI, an administrator is provided very flexible control options. For example, a printer can be represented by one URI that accepts unsecured HTTP connections, and another URI that only accepts SSL3 (Secure Socket Layer) connections. The printer administrator can grant specific permissions to each of the URIs, thereby permitting some clients to print over an unsecured connection while forcing others to print only over a secured connection. Additionally, because the printer object can be published in AD, all Windows 2000 security mechanisms can be applied to the printer. While IPP provides mechanisms for printing via HTTP, it doesn't provide full file-sharing functionality; CIFS provides that functionality.

Introduction to CIFS

Common Internet File System (CIFS) is a cross-platform mechanism allowing clients to request file and print services from a network server based on the widely used NetBIOS file-sharing/SMB (Server Message Block) protocol. CIFS was quietly introduced as part of Service Pack 3 for Microsoft Windows NT 4.0. The version of CIFS included with Windows 2000 contains many new features, but remains backwards-compatible with previous versions of Windows. CIFS is an open protocol, which means that all aspects of communication are publicly documented. This allows software vendors to easily create client and server software.

The chief advantage that CIFS provides over protocols such as HTTP and FTP, is that it allows simultaneous read-write access to a file, as opposed to file read or transfer capabilities only. CIFS supports distributed, replicated virtual volumes (such as Distributed File System (DFS)), file and record locking, file change notification, read-ahead and write-behind operations, and most of the functionality typically associated only with direct connections to a corporate network. CIFS functions over any IP-based network, including the Internet.

CIFS Operation

Name Resolution and Connection Establishment

CIFS communication is established via standard SMB session and NetBIOS name resolution mechanisms. A CIFS server must register its name with a name resolution service, such as Windows Internet Naming Service (WINS) or Domain Name System (DNS). A client wishing to establish a connection to the CIFS server first queries its WINS or DNS server to obtain the IP address of the CIFS server. After resolving the IP address of the CIFS server, the client establishes a connection to the CIFS server via a connection-oriented protocol, such as TCP. The client can parse the name reference to the CIFS server into a server-name portion and a relative-name portion. For example, if the URL that led the client to the CIFS server was *http://cifsserver.company.com,* the client would parse the URL and consider the server name to be "cifsserver.microsoft.com," and would use "/documents/CIFS/whitepapers" to indicate the relative file structure that it wished to navigate on that CIFS server.

To establish a session with the CIFS server, the client issues an SMB session-request packet to the CIFS server's registered name over TCP port 139 (the NetBIOS session service). The client begins the session negotiation by issuing a list of dialects (SMB languages) that it understands to the CIFS server. The dialects are numbered 0 through n (the last dialect the client understands). The server responds to the client with a NEGOTIATE packet identifying the highest dialect that both machines understand, as well as parameters specific to that dialect. In the case of Windows 2000 clients and servers, the negotiated dialect will most likely be NT LM 0.12, which allows the server to issue parameters that specify things such as encryption key lengths, maximum-message sizes, and whether the server is DFS-aware. Table 18-6 lists the components of a CIFS server NEGOTIATE response.

Table 18-6. Components of a CIFS Server NEGOTIATE Response

Server Response	Description
WordCount	A count of the parameter words in the packet (17 in the case of NT LM 0.12 dialect).
DialectIndex	The index of the selected dialect. For example, if the client offered eight dialects, numbered 0–7, with 7 representing NT LM 0.12, the index would equal 7).
SecurityMode	Security Mode of the selected dialect consists of 2 bits. If bit 0=0, this indicates share level security; if bit 0=1, this indicates user level security. If bit 1=1, this indicates that passwords must be encrypted.
MaxMpxCount	Maximum number of pending multiplexed requests.
MaxNumberVcs	Maximum number of virtual connections between client and server.
MaxBufferSize	Maximum transmit buffer size (>=1024). This is the size of the largest message that the client can transmit to the server.
MaxRawSize	Maximum raw-buffer size. This is the maximum-message size that the server can send or receive for SMB_COM_WRITE_RAW or SMB_COM_READ_RAW operations.
SessionKey	The unique key identifying this session.
Capabilities	Server capabilities. These parameters are listed in Table 18-7.
SystemTimeLow	System (Universal Time Coordinate [UTC]) time of the server (low).
SystemTimeLow	System (UTC) time of the server (high).
ServerTimeZone	Time zone of the server (min from UTC).
EncryptionKeyLength	Length of the encryption key.
ByteCount	Count of the data bytes.
EncryptionKey[]	The challenge encryption key.
OemDomainName	The name of the domain in original equipment manufacture (OEM) characters.

By returning a list of its capabilities, the server informs the client as to which operations might or might not be performed at the client's request. Table 18-7 lists the bit definitions of the server's capabilities.

Table 18-7. Bit Definitions of Server Capabilities

Capability	Encoding	Description
CAP_RAW_MODE	0x0001	The server supports SMB_COM_READ_RAW and SMB_COM_WRITE_RAW.
CAP_MPX_MODE	0x0002	The server supports SMB_COM_READ_MPX and SMB_COM_WRITE_MPX.
CAP_UNICODE	0x0004	The server supports unicode strings.

(continued)

Table 18-7. *(continued)*

Capability	Encoding	Description
CAP_LARGE_FILES	0x0008	The server supports large files with 64-bit offsets.
CAP_NT_SMBS	0x0010	The server supports the SMBs particular to the NT LM 0.12 dialect.
CAP_RPC_REMOTE_APIS	0x0020	The sever supports remote Application Programming Interface (API) requests via Remote Procedure Call (RPC).
CAP_STATUS32	0x0040	The server can respond with 32-bit status codes.
CAP_LEVEL_II_OPLOCKS	0x0080	The server supports level 2 oplocks.
CAP_LOCK_AND_READ	0x0100	The server supports the SMB_COM_LOCK_AND_READ SMB.
CAP_NT_FIND	0x0200	The server supports NT Find.
CAP_DFS	0x1000	The server is DFS-aware.
CAP_LARGE_READX	0x4000	The server supports SMB_COM_READ_ANDX requests that exceed the negotiated buffer size.

As part of the setup process, the CIFS server can request client authentication by issuing a request for the credentials that will be used for the session establishment. After the client has been validated, the server assigns a UID (user ID) to the client session, and additional sessions can be set up over the same connection without the user being re-prompted for a password. CIFS can use any authentication supported by client and server, including Windows 2000 Kerberos authentication mechanisms.

The connection between client and server in an SMB session is called a virtual circuit, or VC, which is formed over the transport services, such as TCP. Within a VC, the server assigns a Tree ID (TID) to each transaction. The TID provides a unique identifier for each file session, as well as defining the types of access allowed over that connection. A Process ID (PID) identifies the process environment for that session, and a File ID (FID) is assigned to each file opened during the session. If a VC is closed, all environments within the VC (TID, PID, FID) also will be closed. However, the closing of a single FID might not result in the closing of the VC, as multiple operations can be requested over a single VC.

Session Disconnection

When a client wishes to disconnect its session to a CIFS server, it follows a teardown process that's essentially the reverse of the session-establishment process. Any open files are closed and their associated FID and PIDs then can be disconnected. The TID is disconnected and the user logs off, which results in the server discarding that client's UID. If the client should reconnect, the user will be prompted again for credentials because the UID assigned during the last session no longer exists. Figure 18-5 illustrates the steps in SMB connection and disconnection. The diagram illustrates a simplified session in which only a single read or write operation is requested by the client, but covers all of the steps in session establishment and teardown.

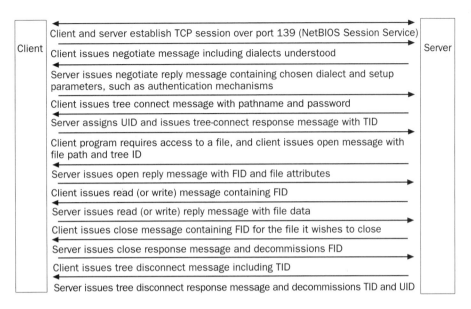

Figure 18-5. *SMB session setup and teardown.*

Connection Management

CIFS provides mechanisms that allow for efficient disconnections when a client and server have completed all session traffic, or when a connection is lost or malfunctioning. A client can issue a connection request only once to a CIFS server in any given session. If the CIFS server receives another connection request from a client with whom it already has an established session, the server disconnects the original session with the client. This is to help ensure that a client that was unexpectedly disconnected from its session can effectively establish another session with the server. If a client is generating malformed or illegal requests to the CIFS server, the server can issue an error to the client and then disconnect the session, again potentially allowing the client to correct the problem and reconnect. A server can also disconnect a session with a client in the case of hard transport errors or if the client has been inactive for a long period of time and the server needs the connection.

File and Printer Access

After a client has established an SMB session with a CIFS server, the client can begin requesting files by issuing "open" messages to the server for the file(s) it wishes to access. A file can be opened for read access, write access, or both. For example, accessing a printer is accomplished via a read request to the printer, and printing is accomplished via a write request to the printer.

Distributed File System Operations

Any client and CIFS server supporting dialects NT LM 0.12 or later support DFS operations. Using DFS, the CIFS server can represent multiple shares on multiple servers in a single namespace that appears to the client to be located on a single server. The CIFS server and can redirect the client software to another location on the network to access a resource, but the client will believe the resource is local to the server with which (he or she) originally negotiated a connection.

Read-Ahead and Write-Behind

CIFS supports read-ahead and write-behind operations. Read-ahead allows a client to cache read data locally so that it doesn't have to incur traffic over its connection to the server in order to obtain the next block of data it wants to read. Write-behind allows a client to perform and cache write operations on a file that then can be uploaded to the server, rather than having to submit each read/write operation separately. Files on the server also can be called locked or unlocked. An unlocked file is a file to which no computer has been granted exclusive access for either read or write purposes. CIFS supports caching, read-ahead, and write-behind, even for unlocked files, because the files are said to be "safe" as long as no client is actively writing to the file. If a client wants to write to a file, it must either submit the write data to the server for the server to write, or it can request an operation lock from the server.

Opportunistic Locks

When a client is actively writing to a file on the server, it's more efficient for the client to locally buffer its data and submit it as a batched request. However, this increases the possibility that the same file might be opened by another client and data might also be written by that client. To help a client increase the efficiency of its data buffering, CIFS allows for opportunistic locks (oplocks), which allow the client to "lock" the file so that it can't be written to simultaneously by another client. The following are three types of oplocks used in CIFS:

- **Exclusive oplocks** In an exclusive oplock, a client (Client A) requests exclusive access to a file, where Client A is the only computer permitted to write data to the file. When Client A opens the file, it requests an exclusive oplock from the server. If another client (Client B) has already opened the file, the server refuses to issue the oplock to the requesting client. When this occurs, Client A is neither permitted to buffer any data nor to perform any read-ahead unless it knows that it has the read-ahead range locked. If there's no other client currently accessing the file, the exclusive oplock will be granted to Client A and it can both read-ahead and buffer data that's to be written to the file. If Client C opens the file while Client A has an exclusive oplock, the server will instruct Client A to break its lock. Breaking the lock requires Client A to submit any buffered lock or write data it's currently holding, acknowledge receipt of the notification, and purge its read-ahead buffer so that the file can be released for access by Client C.

- **Level II oplocks**   Level II oplocks allow multiple clients to open the same file, provided that no client is writing to that file. In a level II oplock, Client A can open a file and request an exclusive oplock to it. If it's the only client accessing the file, the server grants the oplock. When Client B requests access to the same file, the server contacts Client A and requests that it break its lock to a level II oplock if Client A hasn't been writing to the file. This is a result of the fact that some down-level client applications request read/write access to files even when they don't intend to perform write operations. After the server has synchronized with Client A to ensure that Client A has no lock buffer data, access to the file is granted to Client B at a level II oplock status. This informs Client B that it can't buffer any locks to the file, although it's been granted access. Either client can eventually write to the file; should this occur, the server notifies all level II oplock clients to break their locks, thus allowing the data to be written by a single client and ensuring that the server doesn't have to synchronize with all connected clients in order to allow this to occur.

- **Batch oplocks**   Batch oplocks are commonly used by applications that run command batches requiring them to repeatedly open and close multiple files in order to read and execute their command sequences. When Client A wants to obtain a batch oplock to server files, it requests the oplock from the server. If the files aren't opened by other clients, the batch oplock is granted. Client A can now open the files, leave them open while executing its command sequences, and buffer data as needed. If Client B requests access to one of the files while Client A has a batch oplock, the server notifies Client A to clean up its data and synchronize with the server. In most cases, this results in Client A finishing its current batch operation and closing the file(s) in question, and Client B being able to open the file.

Summary

Internet Printing Protocol significantly extends the functionality and ease of printing in Windows 2000. Using IPP, installing and using a printer can be as simple as typing a URL into a Web browser. Detailed queries and status reports can also be generated from the browser interface, and users can now print directly to devices such as fax machines and document software. Common Internet File System allows platform-independent sessions to be established between a client and a server over any Internet or intranet. Via this connection, clients may access file and print resources, and can also use DFS to seamlessly access multiple servers that are represented as a single name space. These mechanisms provide remote clients with the same functionality they have when directly connected to a network, while maintaining secure communications paths.

Chapter 19
Internet Information Server (IIS) and the Internet Protocols

IIS 5.0 is an integrated service available in Microsoft Windows 2000. IIS 5.0 provides Web publishing, file transfer, and mail services via HypterText Transfer Protocol (HTTP), File Transfer Protocol (FTP), and Simple Mail Transfer Protocol (SMTP). In this chapter, we will look at each protocol and the functionality it provides. IIS 5.0 also provides services for Network News Transfer Protocol (NNTP), although this chapter won't discuss these services.

Chapter Contents

This chapter contains the following three sections:

- **HTTP** An analysis of the specifications and functionality of HTTP/1.1; HTTP/1.1 is the most recent HTTP specification and is implemented in IIS 5.0
- **FTP** A description of the FTP mechanisms as implemented in IIS 5.0, including enhancements to recoverability of lost connections
- **SMTP** A look at SMTP and its usage in IIS 5.0

This chapter isn't intended to serve as a "how-to" manual for the use of these protocols, but is instead a technical reference of their functionality

HTTP

Introduction and Terminology

HTTP was first defined in RFC 1945 (HTTP/1.0), although it existed in a looser fashion, now referred to as HTTP/0.9, beginning in 1990. From 1990 to 1996, HTTP continued to grow in a rather uncontrolled manner, with different vendors customizing the protocol to suit their own needs. The publishing of RFC 1945 in 1996 was an attempt to summarize and unify these implementation details and, as a result, the industry expected it to be replaced rather quickly. HTTP/1.0 lacked sufficient definition for caching, hierarchical proxies, virtual hosts, and persistent connections. A more stringent version, HTTP/1.1, was defined in RFC 2068, which is now obsolete, and later in RFC 2616. IIS 5.0 is HTTP/1.1 compliant, and thus that version will be the focus of this section.

HTTP is an application-level protocol used for communication between client computers and HTTP servers to transfer data. Client requests are frequently submitted, from browser software such as Microsoft Internet Explorer and Netscape Navigator, to HTTP servers such as IIS. Before analyzing HTTP in depth, we must understand certain basic terms as they relate to the protocol:

- **Message**   The basic unit of communication between a client and a server.
- **Resource**   An object or service available on the server that's identified in a message.
- **Request**   A message from the client to the server that requests a resource.
- **Response**   A message from the server to the client that returns information initiated by a request message.
- **Request method**   A descriptor of the action to be performed on the requested resource.
- **Client**   Any program that establishes a connection to an HTTP server to issue requests.
- **Server**   A process that accepts HTTP requests for connections from client programs, and provides response data. A single program can utilize both client and server components.
- **Cache**   A client proxy or server's store of response messages, used to retain resources that are designated as cacheable. By caching responses, retrieval of data that's been recently requested doesn't require additional network traffic, as the request can be fulfilled locally.
- **Cacheable**   A response message that's permitted to be stored by the requestor, as determined by a set of rules governing cacheability.
- **Tunnel**   A Transport Layer intermediary between client and server programs that doesn't take part in the request/response process, except to relay information between the programs. A tunnel is closed when both endpoint parties to the communication have closed their connections.
- **Gateway**   An HTTP server that receives requests on behalf of another server, often appearing to the client to be the server that was queried.
- **Proxy**   A program that acts as both client and server in HTTP communication, receiving request messages from a client program, repackaging the requests as if the proxy were the client, and returning the responses to the original requestor.
- **Uniform Resource Identifier (URI)**   A standard format used to describe a resource requested from a server.
- **Uniform Resource Locator (URL)**   A standard naming method used to define the location of any resource on the Internet. URLs take the format *protocol://hostname:port/filename*, for example, *http://backoffice.microsoft.com:80/hello.asp*.
- **Range**   HTTP messages are represented in sequences, or ranges, of bytes. When a client wishes to retrieve a resource from an HTTP server, it might need

to specify a range of the total bytes that make up the resource, as the entire resource might be too large to transfer in a single transaction. Servers might also specify the range measurement that they're capable of accepting, such as bytes.

- **Entity**   A resource, or portion of a resource, that's being referred to in a request/response exchange between clients, proxies, and servers.

- **Variant**   Resources can be represented by more than one name; additional names for a single resource are called variants.

HTTP Operation

HTTP is a request/response protocol. A client wishing to retrieve a resource from an HTTP server issues a request message containing a request method, URI, protocol version ID, and resource-specific information. This request can be issued to the server, a tunneling agent, a proxy, or a gateway, and each participant in the transaction can simultaneously process multiple HTTP connections. HTTP requests are typically issued over TCP port 80, although the participant applications can specify other ports. Most implementations of HTTP/1.0 required that a separate connection be established for each request; in HTTP/1.1, multiple transactions can now be processed over a single connection, called a *keep-alive*, which greatly improves protocol performance. HTTP itself doesn't provide mechanisms for guaranteed delivery of datagrams, but relies on underlying protocols, such as TCP, for this functionality.

Upon receiving a request message, an HTTP server responds with a message indicating success or error, as well as protocol-version information and possible resource-specific data, including the data itself. The protocol version must be sent in the format "HTTP/$x.y$," where x is the "major" version identifier and y is the "minor" version identifier. By sending version numbers as part of the HTTP message, clients and servers negotiate communication format, with both client and server sending the highest protocol version they both understand. With the exception of tunnels, which don't maintain any awareness of the contents of HTTP data, each party in the process can potentially cache message content to facilitate faster retrieval for future requests.

A proxy isn't permitted to send a request message in a protocol version higher than the proxy itself supports. Additionally, it's required to either downgrade any incoming request message with a higher version than its own, respond to the client with an error message, or switch to tunnel mode. Proxies are also required to upgrade any lower protocol version requests to match their own, but return the response to the client in the same major version as the original request.

URIs

A URI is simply a standard format for defining a retrievable resource. A familiar term, the URL, is actually a subset of URI, as is the less familiar Uniform Resource Name (URN). A retrievable item can be requested by referencing the item's location, as in the case of a URL, or by referencing the item's distinguished name, as in the case of a URN. The HTTP protocol doesn't limit the length of URIs, and servers are required to be capable of receiving a URI whose length is at least as long as that of any resource they serve.

URI Syntax

URIs can be absolute or relative to a base URI. Although RFC 2396 defines generic syntax, several RFCs define URI's syntax. An absolute URI lists the entire scheme (this is usually the name of the protocol used in this request) and path that will be used to request the resource, while relative URIs build on a previously established base location and scheme. Typical URI construction is:

```
"scheme:""//""hostname"":""port""/absolute_path""?""query"
```

It might appear as:

```
http://search.microsoft.com:443/us/SearchMS.asp?so=RECCNT&qu=dogbiscuits&boolean=
PHRASE&intCat=0&intCat=1&intCat=2&intCat=3&intCat=4&intCat=5&intCat=
6&intCat=7&intCat=8&intCat=9&p=1&nq=NEW
```

In this example, the scheme is "http:", indicating that the request will be passed over the HTTP protocol. The slashes are reserved characters that serve as separators between scheme and scheme-specific details. The host name given here is "search.microsoft.com", and the ":443" issues the request over TCP port 443. If no port is specified, the request will be issued over the default TCP port 80, and if the target server is not listening for requests over this port number, an error will result. The absolute path given here is the published directory "us," containing the SearchMS.asp active server page. The presence of a question mark following this path indicates that a query is being performed, and the remainder of the URI is query parameter information.

HTTP Messages

HTTP messages are the basic form of communication between a client and a server in HTTP communication, and follow a well-defined syntax.

Message Types

RFC 822 defines HTTP request and response messages as being used to transfer data and resources, called entities, from client to server, and vice versa. These messages are comprised of a start line that might or might not be followed by header fields, which are often simply referred to as headers. An end-of-line marker (carriage return line feed [CRLF]) indicates the end of the headers, and message body data might follow. HTTP/1.1 dictates that no more than one CRLF be used sequentially in any HTTP message to eliminate unnecessary parsing on the part of either the server or client, although flawed implementations of HTTP often issue multiple CRLFs in succession. If a CRLF is received where none is expected, it's ignored. Syntax of a typical HTTP message is:

```
Request-Line|Response-Line  *((general-header|request-header|response-
header|entity-header)CRLF)CRLF [message-body]
```

More Info   HTTP request and response messages are defined in RFC 822, which can be found in the \RFC folder on the companion CD-ROM.

Message Headers

HTTP header fields are used to define parameters regarding the message being transmitted, whether the message is general, request, response, or entity information. Header fields can be preceded by any amount of linear white space (LWS), and consist simply of the header name followed by a colon (:) and the header value. General header fields apply to both request and response messages, but don't relate to the entity being transferred. Request and response header fields are specific to their respective message types, and entity header fields provide additional information about the resource being passed in the message.

Request Messages

Client programs issue request messages both to establish communication parameters and to initiate resource transfer and manipulation. The following example shows a portion of the message generated by a client requesting a resource from a server:

```
HTTP: GET Request (from client using port 1036)
    HTTP: Request Method = GET
    HTTP: Uniform Resource Identifier = /images/logo.gif
    HTTP: Protocol Version = HTTP/1.1
```

The lines above are actually a single line, with spaces separating the individual elements, and are finished with a CRLF sequence. This line identifies four criteria: the general type of request being made (a GET, in this case); the method token, or action to perform on the requested resource (again a GET); the URI of the requested resource (/images/logo.gif); and the protocol version number (HTTP/1.1). The client HTTP port number listed in this request isn't to be confused with the server TCP port. While the client made its HTTP request over port 1036, the request was issued to TCP port 80, as can be seen below:

```
TCP: .AP..., len: 247, seq: 815985-816232, ack:3911620698, win: 8760, src: 1036 dst: 80
    TCP: Source Port = 0x040C
    TCP: Destination Port = Hypertext Transfer Protocol
```

Request Message Methods

Methods are actions that a request message can ask to be performed at the server or applied to a resource entity. Table 19-1 lists common HTTP/1.1 methods and the actions that they request.

Table 19-1. Common HTTP/1.1 Method Codes

Method	Description
OPTIONS	Requests information regarding the server capabilities or what actions can be performed on a specified resource. No action is actually performed on the resource, as this is an information-gathering method. Results of this method can't be cached. If the request-URI is an asterisk (*), the client is testing the capabilities of the server to facilitate further action. If the request-URI is anything other than an asterisk, the client can retrieve information only about the capabilities of the resource specified.

(continued)

Table 19-1. *(continued)*

Method	Description
GET	Requests retrieval of the specified information. GET methods can also be conditional GETs, where the retrieval is performed only if specified conditions are met, or partial GETs, where the client can specify that it's already received and cached some portion of the requested data, and needs to retrieve the portions that it doesn't yet have.
HEAD	The HEAD method is identical to the GET method, except that the server isn't permitted to return the actual resource in its response, but merely information about the resource. This method is often used to test validity of hypertext links so as not to request a resource that might not actually be available.
POST	A client uses POST to send a large block of data to the server. The POST command is often used to supply a server with information that a user has input into an HTML form. POST methods name a specific file on the server as part of the URI—the file named is generally a server-side script or executable that's capable of processing the data the client is sending.
PUT	The PUT method is used to create an entity under the requested URI. Generally, PUT is used as a simple method of uploading a file to the server. PUT might create new files, or might replace files that already exist and have the same name as the entity named in the PUT request.
DELETE	The DELETE method requests that a specific resource be deleted from the server. Even though the server might respond with a message indicating success, the client won't know if the deletion actually occurred, as the deletion might be halted by human intervention.
TRACE	The TRACE method is used to request a loopback of the request message. This is used primarily as a troubleshooting tool to determine what data is actually being received at the other end of the request. No entities are passed in a TRACE method.
CONNECT	CONNECT is used for proxies that can dynamically become tunnels, as is required by secure socket layer (SSL) tunneling.

Safe Methods

Methods can be said to be safe, meaning that if they're properly implemented, they should cause no ill effects on the server. For example, the GET and HEAD methods are considered safe methods because they retrieve only data from the server and don't actually manipulate that data while it resides on the server.

Response Messages

After a server receives a client request message, it returns an HTTP response message, similar in construct to the client request, in the following format:

```
Status line *(( general header | response header | entity header ) CRLF) CRLF
[message body]
```

Each of these components will be analyzed in further detail in this section.

Response Message Status Lines

When a server receives a request message from a client, it evaluates the request method and might or might not perform an action on the requested resource as a result. Regardless of whether or not the action is performed, the server must respond to the requesting client. The response is sent in the form of a status line, with the following syntax:

```
Status Line <space> HTTP version <space> Status code <space> Reason phrase <CRLF>
```

Status codes are organized into classes, which identify the generic response type. Table 19-2 lists the classes and meanings of status codes defined in HTTP/1.1.

Table 19-2. HTTP/1.1 Status Code Classes and Meanings

Number	Class	Indication
1xx	Informational	This indicates a provisional response and returns only a status line indicating status and optional headers. Essentially, this is the server's method of responding with an acknowledgment message.
2xx	Successful	The server understands and accepts the client's request.
3xx	Redirection	The requestor needs to take further action to retrieve the requested resource. If the method used in the subsequent request message is GET or HEAD, the redirect can occur without any user intervention.
4xx	Client Error	The server believes that the client has performed an error. The server should provide an explanation of the error, and indicate whether this is a permanent or temporary error. Additionally, the server should wait for TCP acknowledgment of client receipt of the error message so it doesn't close the connection prematurely.
5xx	Server Error	The server is incapable of performing the request, the client isn't allowed access to the resource, or a server error has occurred. The server should include an explanation of the error and indicate whether the error is temporary or permanent.

Each class of status response has codes that the server returns to the client indicating specific information. Table 19-3 summarizes the individual codes that a server can return to a requesting client as defined in RFC 2616. The messages listed are merely recommendations and can be customized without affecting the protocol.

Table 19-3. HTTP/1.1 Status Codes

Code	Message	Meaning
100	Continue	The client should continue sending the remainder of the request; if the entire request has already been sent, the message is ignored by the client upon receipt.
101	Switching Protocols	The client has requested to switch to another application protocol by issuing an Upgrade message header; the server will switch to that protocol immediately following this status line.

(continued)

Table 19-3. *(continued)*

Code	Message	Meaning
200	OK	The client's request has been successfully processed; remaining information returned will vary according to the type of client request.
201	Created	A new resource has been successfully created at the client's request.
202	Accepted	The client's request has been accepted, but not yet processed. The server should indicate to the client when the request might be fulfilled or provide a pointer to a status monitor for the request.
203	Non-Authoritative Information	The server would normally issue a 200 (OK) response, but the server isn't authoritative for the information returned in the message. This indicates that the information was gathered from another source, and therefore this server can't verify it.
204	No Content	The server has fulfilled the client request, but doesn't need to return a new object. The server can, however, return information that causes the user interface to be updated.
205	Reset Content	The server has fulfilled the client request and is instructing the user agent (client software) to reset the current document view. This is commonly used to allow a user to input form data, then clear the form so that more data can be entered.
206	Partial Content	The client has issued a partial GET request, and the server has fulfilled that request. The server must indicate what portion of the requested data it has fulfilled for this particular GET.
300	Multiple Choices	The requested resource exists in multiple locations, and the server is providing a list of these locations to the client. The server can indicate preference for a specific location, but the client chooses what it deems the appropriate location.
301	Moved Permanently	The requested resource has been moved permanently and future requests for the resource should be directed to the location the server returns.
302	Found	The requested resource exists elsewhere, but its location might change and the client should therefore continue to use the same request URI. Most browsers don't implement this correctly, and treat a 302 response in the same manner as a 301.
303	See Other	The response to the request exists under a different URI and should be retrieved via a GET method. The 303 response shouldn't be cached, although the response received from the redirection location can potentially be cached.
304	Not Modified	The client has performed a conditional GET, but the document hasn't been modified.
305	Use Proxy	This response must be issued only by the server, and indicates that the requested resource must be accessed via the proxy provided in the response.
306	Unused	This status code was used in previous implementations of HTTP, has no function in HTTP/1.1, and is reserved.

(continued)

Table 19-3. *(continued)*

Code	Message	Meaning
307	Temporary Redirect	The requested resource temporarily exists under a different URI, which should be provided to the client as a hyperlink to the new URI (for pre-HTTP/1.1 clients that don't understand the 307 code). Automatic redirection without user input should occur only if the client issued a GET or HEAD request that triggered this message.
400	Bad Request	The client issued a malformed request that the server couldn't interpret and one that shouldn't be issued again without modification.
401	Unauthorized	The requested resource requires authentication; the server must issue a WWW-Authenticate challenge. If the client has already responded to a challenge response, this message indicates that the credentials presented don't have permission to access the resource.
402	Payment Required	Reserved for future use.
403	Forbidden	The server refuses to fulfill the request made by the client. The server can indicate why the refusal has been generated with this message, or can disguise the reason by issuing a 404 message instead.
404	Not Found	The requested URI wasn't found on the server; the server isn't required to give an indication as to whether this condition is temporary or permanent. This message is typically used when the server doesn't wish to reveal or doesn't know why the resource is unavailable.
405	Method Not Allowed	The request method isn't permitted on this URI. A list of valid methods for the URI must be returned as part of the response.
406	Not Acceptable	The resource identified in the request is capable of generating responses only to the accept headers that it returns to the client, and not to the accept header that the client originally sent.
407	Proxy Authentication Required	Similar to a 401, but indicates that the client must authenticate with the proxy that forwarded the request.
408	Request Timeout	The server didn't receive a request from the client within the time that the server was prepared to wait. The client can reissue the request later.
409	Conflict	The request made by the client couldn't be fulfilled because it conflicts with the current state of the resource. Information can be returned that allows the user to correct the condition causing the conflict and resubmit the request. This message is seen most often in response to PUT requests that can cause version conflicts in a resource.
410	Gone	The requested resource is no longer available and its new location is unknown.
411	Length Required	The server will not accept the request unless the client reissues the request with the addition of a valid Content-Length header field.
412	Precondition Failed	The client issued a request containing precondition header fields and one or more of the fields evaluated to false. This allows the client to perform conditional requests.

(continued)

Table 19-3. *(continued)*

Code	Message	Meaning
413	Request Entity Too Large	The request is larger than the server is capable of processing, and is being refused. The server is permitted to close the connection with the client so that the request can't be resubmitted.
414	Request URI Too Long	The request URI is longer than the server is capable of accepting. This typically occurs when the user has input too much data into a form that's sent using a GET request.
415	Unsupported Media Type	The client issued a request method that isn't supported for the resource in question.
416	Requested Range Not Satisfiable	The request included a Range Request header field that doesn't overlap with any of the values for the requested resource.
417	Expectation Failed	The request included an Expect Request header that the server can't fulfill.
500	Internal Server Error	The server can't fulfill the request because of an unexpected error.
501	Not Implemented	The server doesn't recognize the request method and is incapable of fulfilling it.
502	Bad Gateway	The server is acting as a gateway and received an invalid response from the requested server.
503	Service Unavailable	The server is experiencing a temporary condition that causes it to be unable to fulfill the request, such as overloading or maintenance being performed.
504	Gateway Timeout	The server is acting as a gateway or proxy and didn't receive a response from the upstream server in time to process the request. Some proxies return this as a result of Domain Name System (DNS) time-out errors.
505	HTTP Version Not Supported	This server doesn't support the HTTP version specified in the request message.

 More Info HTTP/1.1 status codes are defined in RFC 2616, which can be found in the \RFC folder on the companion CD-ROM.

A typical server response line might appear as follows:

```
HTTP: Response (to client using port 1036)
    HTTP: Protocol Version = HTTP/1.1
    HTTP: Status Code = OK
    HTTP: Reason = OK
```

Note that this data doesn't appear to list the actual code number returned by the server to the client. However, analysis of the raw data sent shows that the following information was actually sent:

```
HTTP/1.1 200 OK
```

Status codes are extensible, meaning that server implementations can issue codes not listed in the preceding tables. Because the client might nor might not understand the meaning of a particular extended status code, the code must be issued as an extension of an existing class. If the specific code number is unrecognized, the client responds as if it received a generic code from that class. For example, if the server issues error code 509 and the client doesn't recognize this code, it treats the error as a 500 error. A table of IIS 5.0 error codes and descriptions can be found in the \Appendix folder on the companion CD-ROM.

Header Fields

A client can generate request headers to query parameters regarding a resource, or to negotiate content with the server. A server can issue response headers to provide information that can't be included in the status line. Both request and response headers can indicate the presence of an entity to be transferred by including entity header fields and possible entity data. While these field names can't be universally extended without an accompanying change in the protocol version, extension headers can be used, provided both the client and the server understand them to be header fields. Any header that's not recognized by the recipient is ignored.

Headers are also said to be end-to-end headers or hop-by-hop headers. End-to-end headers are transmitted to the final message recipient, and must be stored as part of a cached entry. Proxies are forbidden to modify many end-to-end headers, cautioned against modifying others, and might or might not be permitted to add headers to a message. Hop-by-hop headers are useful only to the next recipient on a path, and proxies neither cache nor forward these headers.

RFC 2616-defined headers are summarized in Tables 19-4, 19-5, 19-6, and 19-7. Sender and recipient can refer to either the client or the server in these tables, as both can send messages containing header fields during the transaction.

Table 19-4. Request Header Fields

Header Name	Type	Interpretation	Example
Accept	End-to-end	Used to specify which media types are considered acceptable for the response. These might be limited to specific types of media, or might list groups of acceptable media. If no Accept header is present, it's assumed that all media types are acceptable. If the client issues an Accept header that the server isn't capable of fulfilling, the server issues a 406 (Not Acceptable) response.	Accept: image/gif; image/x-xbitmap; image/jpeg; image/pjpeg; */*. Gifs, bitmaps, and jpegs are acceptable media types; "*/*" indicates that all media are acceptable. "Image/*" would indicate that all image types are acceptable.

(continued)

Table 19-4. *(continued)*

Header Name	Type	Interpretation	Example
Accept-Charset	End-to-end	Indicates acceptable-response character sets. If no Accept-Charset header is present, it's assumed that all character sets are acceptable. Character sets can be given an associated quality value, representing user preference for a given character set.	Accept-Charset: iso-8859-5, Unicode-1-1;q=0.8. Indicates that this client accepts both character sets listed, with a preference as indicated by codes assigned to the q value.
Accept-Encoding	End-to-end	Used to designate acceptable content codings, such as compress or gzip. Content coding is discussed later in this chapter.	Accept-Encoding: gzip, compress. Indicates that both gzip and compress codings are acceptable.
Accept-Language	End-to-end	Defines acceptable languages, such as English, German, and Japanese.	Accept-Language: en-us U.S. English will be accepted.
Authorization	End-to-end	Clients attempting to authenticate with a server will issue their credentials in the Authorization header. Results can be cached.	Authorization: Basic bWNO0Tg6bWN0ND-MyPQ==.
Expect	End-to-end	The client expects specific behavior from the server; if the server doesn't understand the Expect header, it must return a 417 (Expectation Failed) error.	Expect: 100-continue. Indicates that the client expects the server to continue the message exchange.
From	End-to-end	Used to identify the user that initiated this sequence of messages. Typically, this is utilized by robots that gather information on behalf of a human being; by providing the e-mail address of the robot's *owner*, the user can be contacted if the robot causes server problems.	From: owner@microsoft.com.
Host	End-to-end	Identifies the host name and port number of the owner of the requested resource. If no port number is specified, port 80 is assumed. This header is used to allow the server to distinguish between multiple sites responding to the same IP and TCP port.	Host: technet.microsoft.com.

(continued)

Table 19-4. *(continued)*

Header Name	Type	Interpretation	Example
If-Match	End-to-end	Used to make the request message conditional; generally, this is used to verify that the client's resource is current.	If-Match: *. Indicates that this allows a match with any current version of the resource, rather than a specific entity tag.
If-Modified-Since	End-to-end	Used to make a method conditional upon whether the specified resource has been modified since a particular date. Used by the browser to determine if a specific resource has been updated since it was last cached.	If-Modified-Since: Sat, 11 Sept 1999 12:26:31 GMT.
If-None-Match	End-to-end	Used to facilitate efficient caching by verifying that there's no match on the server for the specified resource; also used by clients to ensure that a PUT method doesn't inadvertently replace a resource.	If-None-Match: "a0cde3e0c444be1:18e2." Indicates this value could be followed with a PUT method to place the resource on the server.
If-Range	End-to-end	A client can use this tag to determine whether a resource it has a partial copy of has changed. If the resource hasn't changed, the client might then be able to request the remainder of the entity range to obtain the complete resource.	If-Range: "a0cde3e0c444be1:18e2."
If-Unmodified-Since	End-to-end	Used to make a method conditional; the converse of the If-Modified-Since header field.	If-Unmodified-Since: Sat, 11 Sept 1999 12:26:31 GMT.
Max-Forwards	End-to-end	Used in conjunction with the Trace and Options headers to limit the number of proxies that can forward the request message. This is generally used to troubleshoot paths that are suspected to be looping back upon themselves.	Max Forwards: 3.
Proxy-Authorization	Hop-by-hop	Used by a client to identify itself to a proxy that requires authentication, which has usually been indicated by the return of a 407 (Proxy Authentication Required) message to the client.	Proxy Authorization: Basic bQR0OTg6b-WN0NDMyNP==.
Range	End-to-end	Used to specify the portion of a resource that the client wants to retrieve. In some cases, this header can be used in conjunction with the If-Range header.	Range: "a0cde3e0c444be1:18e2."

(continued)

Table 19-4. *(continued)*

Header Name	Type	Interpretation	Example
Referer [sic]	End-to-end	A client uses the Referer header (misspelled throughout the HTTP RFCs as well as in actual implementation) to inform a server as to where the client received the reference that directed it to the server for the Request URI message.	Referer: http:// partnering.microsoft.com/ exchange/pf/root.asp.
TE	Hop-by-hop	Indicates the extension transfer codings that the client is willing to accept in a response message. If accompanied by a *trailers* keyword, the client will accept the resource in chunked transfer coding, which means means that it will accept the response as a series of *pieces* of the requested entity. This header applies only to the current connection and must be reissued as necessary.	TE: trailers, deflate. Indicates the client's willingness to accept resources in chunks that are deflate-encoded.
User-Agent	End-to-end	Used to pass information regarding the software that the client is using to send its requests. Servers can then tailor their responses to the limitations or capabilities of this software.	User-Agent: Mozilla/4.0 (compatible; MSIE 5.0; Microsoft Windows NT; DigExt). Indicates that the browser software being used is Internet Explorer 5, and lists its capabilities.
Vary	End-to-end	Used to specify header fields that dictate whether a future response to a request for this resource can be issued from cache, rather than being re-retrieved from a server.	Vary: *. Can be issued by a server to dictate that a proxy can't issue a response from its cache, as the server wishes to negotiate all content itself.

Table 19-5. Response Header Fields

Header	Type	Interpretation	Example
Accept-Ranges	End-to-end	Allows the server to specify whether it will accept range requests from a client, and in what format.	Accept-Ranges: bytes. Indicates that the server will accept range requests that are specified in bytes.
Age	End-to-end	The sender's estimate of the amount of time elapsed since it cached the named resource received from an origin server. Essentially, how *old* a cached entity is.	Age: 86,400. Indicates that the resource was cached 86,400 seconds previously.

(continued)

Table 19-5. *(continued)*

Header Name	Type	Interpretation	Example
Etag	End-to-end	The entity tag identifier; might be used to compare against other entities received from this source.	ETag: "077d777c8f1be1:189e."
Location	End-to-end	Used to redirect a client to another location for a requested resource, or, if it is part of a 201 (Created) response, to indicate where the new resource is located.	Location: /exchange/pf/root.asp.
Proxy-Authenticate	Hop-by-hop	Must be included as part of a 407 (Proxy Authentication Required) response, and includes the authentication scheme for the requested URI. This header isn't passed farther down the path, as the authentication is to occur between the client and the proxy.	Proxy-Authenticate: Basic realm="Enterprise Server." RFC 2617, "HTTP Authentication: Basic and Digest Access Authentication," extensively describes authentication mechanisms.
Retry-After	End-to-end	Used by a server to inform a client as to how long a service is expected to be unavailable. Usually part of a 503 (Service Unavailable) response message or a 3xx (Redirection) response in order to direct the client to wait a specified amount of time before attempting to retrieve the requested entity.	Retry-After: Fri, 31 Dec 1999 23:59:59 GMT. Tells the client to wait until a specified date before attempting to retrieve the resource, while the following example specifies a wait time in seconds: Retry-After: 240.
Server	End-to-end	Used by the server to indicate what software it uses to service HTTP requests.	Server: Microsoft-IIS/5.0.
WWW-Authenticate	End-to-end	Issued always as part of a 401 (Unauthorized) message to indicate the authorization scheme that the server requires the client to pass.	WWW-Authenticate: Basic realm="partnering.microsoft.com."

Table 19-6. Entity Header Fields

Header Name	Type	Interpretation	Example
Allow	End-to-end	List of methods allowed for the resource identified by the Request-URI message. This doesn't prevent a client from requesting a disallowed method. If a client requests a method that's not allowed for a resource, the server will issue a 405 (Method Not Allowed) error and must include an Allow header in the response so that the client can adjust its request.	Allow: GET, HEAD, PUT, POST. Specifies that the GET, HEAD, PUT, and POST methods are acceptable for the identified resource.

(continued)

Table 19-6. *(continued)*

Header Name	Type	Interpretation	Example
Content-Encoding	End-to-end	Specifies encoding methods applied to the resource specified in the Request-URI message so that the message recipient knows which decoding mechanisms to apply.	Content-Encoding: gzip. Specifies the type of encoding used to compress the requested resource.
Content-Language	End-to-end	Defines the natural language of the entity being transferred.	Content-Language: en-us. Language content is U.S. English.
Content-Length	End-to-end	Specifies the length of the entity body in a decimal number of octets.	Content-Length: 4110. Indicates a length of 4110 octets.
Content-Location	End-to-end	A server can use this to specify resource location that the client requested, particularly if the resource is accessible from a separate location than was originally requested in the client message. This value is also used to set the base-URI.	Content-Location: http://192.168.0.1/Default.htm. Specifies Default.htm at the listed IP address as the base-URI for the requested resource.
Content-Range	End-to-end	When a server returns a partial entity-body in its response, it uses content-range to specify the range of the full entity that's covered by this partial entity. Essentially, this is a *marker* to identify the portion of the resource being sent. Servers returning status codes 206 (Partial Content) or 416 (Requested Range Not Satisfiable) will utilize the Content-Range header field.	Content-Range: bytes 500-999/1500. Informs the client that the range encompasses bytes 500–999 of a 1500-byte resource.
Content-Type	End-to-end	Identifies the media type of the entity being sent.	Content-Type: text/html. Indicates the message being sent consists of HTML text.
Expires	End-to-end	The resource specified is considered *stale* at its expiration date and shouldn't be returned from cache at that point; rather, the resource should again be retrieved from the server.	Expires: Mon, Nov 16 1999 17:38:01 GMT.
Last-Modified	End-to-end	Indicates the date that the server believes to be the last modification date for the resource in question.	Last-Modified: Sun, 29 Aug 1999 02:44:51 GMT.

Table 19-7. General Header Fields

Header Name	Type	Interpretation	Example
Cache-Control	End-to-end	Issues directives regarding cache-ability of this information that must be obeyed by all points along the request chain. HTTP/1.0 caches that don't implement cache-control can simply assume the entity isn't cacheable.	Cache-Control: private. Indicates that the server is issuing a message that can't be cached by any intermediary points, as the content is privately cacheable only by the client that requested it.
Connection	Hop-by-hop	Used to specify options for a single connection along the path; mustn't be propagated farther along the path. Any headers included in the connection header mustn't include end-to-end headers.	Connection: keepalive. Indicates that the connection between these two points is to be kept open after this message is forwarded. An HTTP/1.0 recipient might not be capable of interpreting a keepalive, and therefore might remove and ignore the header fields pertaining to the keepalive.
Date	End-to-end	Indicates the date and time that this message originated.	Date: Fri, 03 Sep 1999 00:58:28 GMT.
Pragma	End-to-end	Used to provide instructions to each recipient of the message along the path. These directives are implementation-specific, and therefore might be ignored by proxies that don't understand their meaning. However, the proxy is required to forward the header whether or not it understands its directives.	Pragma: no-cache. Specifies that a proxy is expected to pass the request message on to a server even though the proxy might already have the requested item in its own cache.
Trailer	Hop-by-hop	Used to inform a client that there are header fields in this message pertaining to chunked transfer-encoding, so that the client can know that it needs to use these for decoding and reassembly.	Trailer: Range. Indicates the presence of a Range header in this message.
Transfer-Encoding	Hop-by-gop	Used to indicate what type of encoding has been applied to the body of the message, so that the recipient can determine how to decode it.	Transfer-Encoding: Chunked, deflate. Indicates the encoding applied to this message, in the order it was applied.

(continued)

Table 19-7. *(continued)*

Header Name	Type	Interpretation	Example
Upgrade	Hop-by-hop	Frequently issued by a server as part of a 101 (Switching Protocols) message to indicate additional communication protocols that it supports. The client can also use this header for negotiating the protocols to be used. Because this header applies only to the current connection, it must be supplied as part of a Connection header.	Upgrade: HTTP/1.2, SHTTP/1.3, IRC/7.0.
Via	End-to-end	Must be used by proxies and gateways to indicate the protocols and intermediate recipients between the requesting client and the issuing server. This is used for purposes of tracking the path of a request/response transaction.	Via: 1.0 microsoft.com, 1.1 technet.microsoft.com (Microsoft-IIS/5.0). Specifies the order of the hops made and the HTTP server program running at those hops, in this case, IIS 5.0.
Warning	End-to-end	Used to issue warnings regarding message content. These warnings are issued in human-readable language.	Warning: 110 Response is stale. Indicates that the message has exceeded its *freshness lifetime*, or the indicator of how long the entity can be considered accurate.

HTTP Codings

Content Codings

HTTP uses content codings to specify data-transformation mechanisms, such as compression, that have been applied to an entity. By specifying the coding method in header fields, client and server applications can determine how to decode the entity to make it legible. Content-codings are registered with the Internet Assigned Numbers Authority (IANA), and include the following:

- **GNU's Not Unix (GNU) Zip (Gzip)**   A file compression format defined in RFC 1952
- **Compress**   A UNIX compression-encoding format
- **Deflate**   A combination of the zlib and deflate encoding and compression mechanisms defined in RFCs 1950 and 1951
- **Identity**   The default encoding mechanism, which indicates that there's no encoding performed on the entity

Transfer Codings

Transfer codings are used to ensure safe passage of an entity through the request/response path. Transfer coding isn't an entity property, as is content coding. Rather, transfer coding is applied to the entire entity message body. Transfer-coding values indicate whether encoding has been or can be applied to the message. If transfer coding is applied to a message, the values must indicate whether the data has been chunked, or broken into more manageable pieces. This coding mustn't be applied more than once to the message body so that a client can accurately determine message-transfer length. Any server that receives transfer-coding values it doesn't understand should return a 501 (Not Implemented) response so that the client can request or apply a different encoding mechanism. The encoding formats used for transfer encoding are the same as those listed for content coding, with the addition of the chunked value.

Chunked Transfer Coding

Chunked transfer coding is used to modify the body of a message so that it can be sent as a series of smaller pieces. Each chunk is sent with its own size information and, possibly, entity headers, so that the recipient can accurately determine whether it has received all the chunks that comprise the message. HTTP/1.1-compliant applications are required to be capable of receipt and decoding of chunked transfer coding, and must ignore any extensions to transfer-coding values that they don't understand.

HTTP Content Negotiation

Content negotiation is the process by which communicating parties in HTTP transactions determine the preferred representation for a response. Client software might be able to interpret only specific entity media types, as might also be the case at the server. Additionally, user preferences for parameters, such as language and file format, affect the negotiation process. Content negotiation can be said to be agent-driven, wherein the client chooses the best media representation after receiving a response from a server; server-driven, meaning that the server will specify preferred representations; or transparent, which is a combination of both agent-driven and server-driven negotiation.

Agent-Driven Content Negotiation

In agent-driven negotiation, the client software, called a user agent, issues a request message to a server that indicates its own capabilities by means of header fields, such as Accept, Accept-Charset, and Accept-Language. When the server receives this request, it responds with a message indicating its own capabilities, and the user agent then responds with its own choice of representation from the list provided by the server.

Agent-driven negotiation is advantageous in situations when the user wants to dictate certain content parameters, such as the language used to display a Web page, or when the server can't ascertain the client's capabilities by analyzing its request message. Additionally, load-balancing for heavily trafficked servers can be provided via public caches (additional servers or proxies that maintain cached copies of the information on the origin server), and agent-driven negotiation can be used to determine message parameters with the computers providing these caches. However, agent-driven negotiation has the disadvantage of requiring additional message transfer between client and server, because the client must first request a listing of the server's capabilities before choosing a message format.

Server-Driven Content Negotiation

In server-driven content negotiation, the server uses an algorithm to select what it considers to be the best format for messages between itself and the client. The server can base its determination on parameters it receives in the client's request message, as well as on its own capabilities, and even parameters, such as the requesting client's network address. Server-driven negotiation allows the server to send the requested entity in its initial response package, as determined by its best guess as to which media type the client prefers (based on header fields such as Accept, Accept-Charset, and Accept-Language), rather than waiting for another request after the client has received a response and chosen from the list of available formats.

Server-driven negotiation provides advantages in reducing the number of messages that need to be transferred to determine acceptable media types, but also has several disadvantages. First, this type of negotiation requires the server to guess as to what is the preferred format on the client's end, which might or might not match what the user prefers. Second, because this negotiation type requires the user agent to describe its capabilities in each request it makes to the server, it might be inefficient and might also violate the user's privacy. Third, the server must perform additional processing for each response to determine the optimal format for that response. Last, servers that are providing public caches to facilitate load balancing for another server might not be able to service requests for different users from their caches, because each user agent might provide different parameters.

Transparent Content Negotiation

Transparent content negotiation provides a combination of both agent-driven and server-driven negotiation mechanisms. When a cache receives a client request containing parameters that it's capable of fulfilling, it can negotiate the content format itself, rather than forwarding the request parameters to the origin server. In this case, the cache is acting as the server would in server-driven negotiation, thus saving work at the server that originally provides a resource. HTTP/1.1 doesn't provide any guidelines for transparent negotiation, although many implementations provide their own mechanisms as extensions of HTTP/1.1.

HTTP Caching

To make HTTP as efficient as possible, clients, servers, proxies, and gateways can cache content retrieved as part of the request/response process. Caching in HTTP/1.1 is server-specified, meaning that the originating server for any resource decides whether or not a message can be cached by other machines along the path. Servers might specify that a message can't be cached by any computer, must be cached by these computers, or can be cached based on variables, such as the age of the message. Originating servers don't, however, always assign dictates as to whether or not, or for how long a message can be cached, so caches also use a mechanism called *heuristic expiration*. In heuristic expiration, a cache uses information contained in message headers to estimate the point at which the message can be considered stale, and thus would need to be re-retrieved, should it be requested. Because this is inherently unreliable in providing accurate gauges as to message freshness, HTTP/1.1 strongly encourages servers to provide explicit expiration on any responses they send. RFC 2616 outlines implementation details for caching and content expiration.

FTP

Introduction and Terminology

While HTTP is perhaps the most well-known protocol in use on the Internet today, it isn't the only available mechanism for data transfer. IIS 5.0 also utilizes FTP, as defined, primarily, in RFC 959. While additions to FTP have been proposed in several RFCs and drafts, its core functionality remains much the same. This chapter doesn't provide instruction in how to use FTP, but instead defines the protocol itself.

> **More Info**   User documentation and instructions for using FTP may be found in RFCs 412, 959, and 1635, which can be found in the \RFC folder on the companion CD-ROM.

FTP is used to share and transfer files between computers, as well as use other computers for remote storage purposes. As is the case in HTTP, FTP is an Application Layer protocol that relies on TCP to ensure guaranteed delivery of datagrams. While the RFC definition of FTP doesn't provide any true method for recovering a lost connection and picking up file transfer where it left off, IIS 5.0 implements a process called FTP restart to add this functionality. FTP is an inherently non-secure protocol because it transmits passwords used in transactions as clear text. To help provide secure mechanisms to be used in FTP transmissions, security extensions to the FTP protocol are defined in RFC 2228.

As with HTTP, FTP has its own unique terminology, some of which is defined below:

- **FTP commands**   Commands issued between two computers in an FTP session to control the flow of information from one computer to the other.
- **Control connection**   A connection established between client and server components for the exchange of FTP commands and replies.
- **Reply**   An acknowledgment sent by the server over the control connection in response to client commands.
- **Data connection**   A full-duplex connection established for the purpose of transferring data between two computers, whether they're made up of a client and a server or two servers.
- **Data Transfer Process (DTP)**   The entity that establishes data connections, as well as managing connections once they've been opened. A DTP can be

active, meaning that it is listening for connections between client and server, or passive, meaning that data is currently being passed and the DTP is idle.

- **Protocol Interpreter (PI)**   On the client side of an FTP session, the user-PI initiates a control connection from the client port to the server FTP process, as well as issuing commands from client to server. On the server side of an FTP session, the server-PI listens for a user-PI connection and commands, and governs the issuing of responses and the server DTP. The server-PI and server-DTP comprise the server FTP process.

- **Logical byte size**   The defined byte size of data that's internally stored on a computer. One operating system can store its on-disk data in a different byte size than another.

- **Transfer byte size**   The byte size used in transferring data from one computer to another, which might or might not be the same byte size used to store the data on-disk. In FTP transfers, all data, regardless of logical byte size, is sent in 8-bit increments.

FTP Operation

FTP connections can be established between either a client and a server, or between two servers. Unless otherwise specified, this chapter focuses on client-server FTP sessions. An FTP session between client and server can be initiated either by a user, through an FTP client interface, or programmatically. In any case, the actual connection is initiated by the user-PI. The user-PI is responsible for sending a command to the server-PI requesting that a connection be opened between them. The server-PI listens for connection requests over port 21 by default, and upon receiving a connection request from a user-PI, begins the process of establishing a control connection.

Every FTP session actually consists of two separate connections—a control connection and a data connection. The control connection follows telnet specifications, and is used to negotiate communication parameters, issue commands and responses, and monitor the status of any data connection that's opened between the two computers. The task of opening and monitoring the data connection is handled by components on both client and server called DTPs. The data connection is the actual mechanism over which data transfer occurs. While a data connection can be dynamically opened and closed in a single session between the two computers, the control connection always remains open.

A user can initiate an FTP session between a client and server, or between two servers. In a client-server session, the user can use FTP software, consisting of an interface to the user-PI and user-DTP, to initiate a control connection between the client and the server FTP process (comprised of the server-PI and server-DTP). In Microsoft Windows 2000, client software can be a browser, such as Internet Explorer, or the connection can be initiated from the command prompt simply by typing **FTP <*hostname or IP address of an FTP server*>.** After the control connection has been established between client and server, the user can issue commands to the server that cause the server to open a data connection between the two computers. Data is then passed bi-directionally (fullduplexed) over this connection. When the data transfer is complete, the data connection can be closed, although the control connection remains open until the user initiates its disconnection and the server performs the actual process of closing the connection. Figure 19-1 diagrams this process.

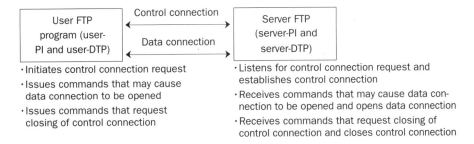

Figure 19-1. *A client-server FTP session.*

Because the control and data connections are separate entities, a user can also initiate data transfer between two servers by establishing control connections with each of the servers, and issuing commands that cause the servers to open a data connection between them. The control connections must remain open while the data transfer is in progress because these connections are used to define the parameters of the data transfer, but the data connection does not need to be established with the client computer at all. If the control connection between either of the servers and the client is closed while the data transfer between the two servers is still in progress, the server whose control connection was lost will close the data connection between itself and the other server. Figure 19-2 illustrates this process.

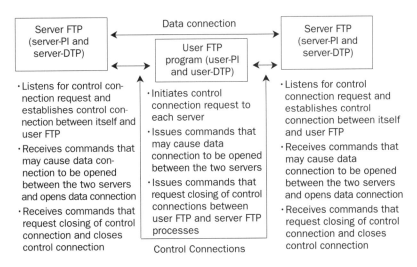

Figure 19-2. *A user-initiated server-to-server FTP session.*

FTP Data

Data Transfer

FTP data transfer always occurs over the data connection between the two computers; the control connection is reserved for passing and receiving FTP commands that control the session, as well as the data-transfer parameters. Sender and receiver in any FTP session must negotiate data-transfer format to ensure that the receiving end can correctly reconstruct the data that is sent. Because each computer can store its data in its own specific logical byte sizes (the number of bits that comprise a data byte on the disk), mechanisms must be in place to ensure that the data sent to the receiving computer is transmitted in an agreed-upon format. The FTP specification provides for specific data structures and data-type representations.

Data Structures

FTP classifies three different data structures, or characteristics, of a file stored on the computer. Some systems store data as a series of fixed-length records, while other computers store data as a series of characters and separators. Because of the disparity in storage formats, transfers of data must be made in a format that the sending and receiving computers can reconstruct and write appropriately to their own disks. In FTP, these structures are defined as file structure, record structure, and page structure, as listed below:

- **File structure**   This data is stored as a continuous series of bytes that have no internal structure, such as record markers. File structure is the default data structure used in FTP transfers, and is assumed by both parties unless a command is issued specifying one of the other structures.

- **Record structure**   This data is stored on-disk as a series of sequential records. All FTP implementations are required to accept record structures for text files, whether the text is in ASCII or EBCDIC format.

- **Page structure**   These files can be discontinuous data, containing sections of file data interspersed with descriptors of that data. FTP refers to these file sections as pages.

When page-structure data is sent between two hosts via FTP, each page must be sent with a page header comprised of 1-byte fields that provide informational parameters. Each header begins with a Header Length field that defines the number of bytes comprising the header. Following this is a page index, or number, that identifies this page's place in the overall file, and a Data Length field that specifies the length of the page data itself. The next field in the header identifies the page type, which can be a normal data page; a descriptor page that defines properties for the file; an access-controlled page, which provides information about access control to the file; or the last page in the file. There might also be optional header fields that define properties, such as access control to the individual page.

Data Types

Within each of the data structures defined in FTP, data can be stored as different data types. These data types define the on-disk byte size of the file data. Some data types provide explicit definition of data byte size, while others provide implicit definition by using logical byte size. Acceptable data types in IIS FTP transfers are defined below:

- **ASCII type**   Default data type used in FTP transfers, which must be accepted by all compliant implementations of FTP. ASCII is most often used for the transmission of text files. In an ASCII transfer, the sending computer retrieves the requested file from its own disk in whatever format was used to store it. The file is then converted to ASCII, which dictates 8-bit character bytes, and transmitted in 8-bit increments (transfer byte size is always 8 bits, regardless of data type). The receiving computer reassembles the 8-bit ASCII text and stores it to disk in its own native format.

- **Image type**   Sent as a continuous stream of bits that the receiving computer must store as a series of contiguous bits. The recipient might need to pad the end of each file or record (depending on its own internal storage mechanisms) with 0s that are stripped off when the file is retrieved. This data type is most efficient for files that need to be stored in binary format, as opposed to ASCII text (executable files versus text documents, for example).

Connections and Transmission Modes

In order to transmit data between a client and server using FTP, both a control connection and a data connection must be established. The control connection is used both to set parameters for the data connection and to monitor the passage of data over the data connection. While the control connection remains open during the entire client-server FTP session, the data connection may be dynamically opened and closed.

Data Connection Establishment and Management

FTP connections between client and server are initiated by the user-PI. FTP server-PIs listen on port 21 (by default) for connection requests. When the server-PI hears a connection request from a user-PI, it opens a control connection. The use of non-default ports for connections can only be initiated by the user-PI, and not the server-PI. When the client issues a command that initiates data transfer, the server DTP opens a data connection and data transfer begins. Both user-DTP and server-DTP monitor the connection to determine which computer might be sending or receiving at any given time. When an active transfer is occurring, the DTP on the receiving computer is passive and the DTP on the sending computer is actively controlling data transfer. Because the data connection is automatically closed upon completion of a data transfer, a data connection can be kept open either by negotiating a non-default port before beginning transfer, or by switching to a different transfer mode for the file(s) in question. FTP defines the following three transfer modes.

Stream Mode

In stream mode data transfer, the data is sent as a series of bytes, with little to no processing performed on the data before it is sent. Data that's sent in stream mode can be of any representation type (file, record, or image). If file structure data is sent, the end of the file is indicated by the sending computer closing the data connection. If the data being sent is record structure, each record is followed by a two-character control code that indicates the end of the record; the end of the file itself is indicated by a similar control code.

Block Mode

Block-mode data is sent as a series of data blocks with no filler bits, preceded by header bytes that contain a Count field and possible descriptor code. The Count field indicates each block's length in bytes. The descriptor code indicates whether this is the last block in either the record or the file, whether the data is suspected to contain errors (possibly because of bad media), or to identify a restart marker, which will be described later in this section. Any data-representation type can be used in block mode, and record structures are permitted.

Compressed Mode

Compressed-mode data is sent as three types of information: regular data, compressed data, and control information. Regular data is sent as a simple byte string. Compressed data uses an algorithm to compress filler bytes and represent them with a single filler byte, thus decreasing the actual number of bytes that need to be sent. Control information is sent as a 2-byte escape sequence and descriptor code, which are the same codes used in block-mode data transfer, including a possible restart marker.

FTP Restart

FTP restart is implemented in Windows 2000, and provides a mechanism for resuming file transfers that were interrupted before completion. FTP itself provides little in terms of recovery mechanisms, but does provide for the insertion of restart markers in both block and compressed data modes. When an FTP server implements FTP restart, it periodically sends a restart marker (essentially a place marker) in the data being transferred to the receiving computer.

The receiver collects these restart markers, and if the data connection is lost, it can use them to resume the file transfer where it was left off. Upon resuming the connection between itself and the server, the client will first query the server to determine if the file has changed since the interruption of the transfer. If the file hasn't changed, the client issues the last restart marker value to the server and requests that the transfer be resumed at that point. If the file has changed since the data transfer interruption, the client requests that the entire file be transmitted from the beginning.

While the server inserts restart markers only in transmission of block or compressed data, stream data can also be recovered if the connection is lost. Because stream data is sent simply as a series of bytes, the client need only calculate the byte offset of the last data it received, and request the server to resume the file transfer at that offset point.

FTP restart commands aren't used only when a connection has been broken; many FTP clients send the command REST 0 before downloading a new file from a server. This command is used to ensure that the data transfer will begin with the first byte of the requested file.

FTP Commands and Responses

FTP communication between a client and server is transmitted as a series of commands that the client needs fulfilled, and responses from the server in response to those commands. This process is similar to the HTTP request/response functionality in HTTP communication.

FTP Commands

The user-PI issues commands over the control connection to initiate file transfer. FTP commands can be commands that verify the user's identity with the FTP server, such as USER, ACCT, and PASS; commands that navigate the file system on the remote host, such as CDUP, XCUP, and CWD; session origination and termination commands, such as QUIT, BYE, and REIN; or commands that control the parameters of file transfer as well as the transfer itself, such as PORT, TYPE, MODE, GET, PUT, RETR, and STOR. Client commands and Windows 2000 FTP server-recognized commands can be found in the \Appendix folder of the companion CD-ROM.

FTP Replies

FTP servers issue reply codes in response to client commands. These reply codes are sent in the form of a three-digit number, with the value of the first and second digits indicating the type of response. These codes are extensible, and a listing of specific codes and their meanings may be found in the \Appendix folder of the companion CD-ROM.

The first digit in an FTP response code indicates the general type of response the server wants to pass to the client. The second digit is used to provide a more specific indication as to the meaning of the response. Values for the third digit in a response code are extensible, meaning that they can be customized for specific implementations. Tables 19-8 and 19-9 below describe the representations of the first and second digits in response codes. As an example of response-code meanings, a server issuing code 250 would indicate that the requested file-system action was successfully completed; the "2" indicates success, and the "5" indicates a file-system operation.

Table 19-8. FTP Response Codes—First Digit

First Digit Value	Indicator	Description
1yz	Positive Preliminary Reply	The requested action is being processed; another command can't be sent until another reply is received from the server.
2yz	Positive Completion Reply	The requested action has been completed and a new command can now be sent.
3yz	Positive Intermediate Reply	The requested action is accepted, and will continue, processing pending further information from the client, which should now be issued.
4yz	Transient Negative Completion Reply	A temporary error has occurred that prevented processing of the command, and the command (or command sequence) should now be issued by the user.
5yz	Permanent Negative Completion Reply	An error has occurred that prevented processing of the command; the command shouldn't be reissued without modification. This modification might be as simple as correcting a misspelling, or this error might indicate a non-transient server error.

Table 19-9. FTP Response Codes—Second Digit

Second Digit Value	Indicator	Description
x0z	Syntax	There is a syntax error, the issued command is unimplemented by the server, or the server doesn't recognize the command category.
x1z	Information	Replies to information requests, such as help.
x2z	Connections	Refers to control and data connections.
x3z	Authentication and Accounting	Replies to user login or accounting procedures.
x4z	Unspecified	Unspecified.
x5z	File System	File system status as it relates to the requested transfer or command.

SMTP

Introduction and Terminology

SMTP is designed to do exactly what its name implies—provide reliable, efficient mechanisms for the transfer of electronic mail. SMTP transfers messages from the client to a server and between servers, but it isn't responsible for managing mailboxes or for allowing a client to download incoming mail. RFC 821 defines SMTP, although features and refinements have been added in numerous subsequent RFCs. While SMTP uses familiar terminology, a few terms might be unknown and are defined below:

- **Sender-SMTP Process**   The process that initiates an SMTP connection to a receiver-SMTP process to send mail. The sender-SMTP process controls the transfer of mail between itself and the receiver-SMTP, issues commands, and receives replies from the receiver-SMTP.

- **Receiver-SMTP Process**   The process that waits for a sender-SMTP process to establish a connection, then receives commands from the sender-SMTP and carries out the operations specified in those commands.

- **Transmission Channel**   The full-duplex channel opened between sender- and receiver-SMTP processes for the purposes of command/reply sequences and mail transfer.

- **Reverse-Path**   Specifies the mail's sender. The reverse-path can be simply the name of the user who is sending the mail, or can include a list of hosts that relayed this mail from its original sender-SMTP. The first host listed is the most recent relay, and the last host listed is the first relay.

- **Forward-Path**   Specifies the mail's recipient(s). Optionally, the forward-path can specify a list of relays to be used to route the mail to its intended recipient(s), with the current receiving-SMTP being the first relay in the list and the final destination being the last.

- **Reverse-Path Buffer**   Used to hold the list of reverse-path parameters for a transaction, possibly including a list of hosts who relayed the mail. This can be cleared as a result of various commands being issued.

- **Forward-Path Buffer**   Used to hold the list of forward-path parameters for a transaction, possibly including a list of relay hosts to whom the mail is to be routed. This can also be cleared as a result of various commands.

More Info   SMTP is defined in RFC 821, which can be found in the \RFC folder on the companion CD-ROM.

SMTP Operation

While numerous enhancements have been added to SMTP since RFC 821, it remains a fairly simple protocol. SMTP, like HTTP and FTP, is an Application Layer protocol that relies on underlying protocols to ensure data delivery. Although SMTP can utilize other protocols, TCP can be assumed to be the underlying protocol throughout this section.

SMTP communication is initiated by a user's mail system, referred to herein as the client or the sender-SMTP. The client establishes a full-duplex transmission channel to a SMTP server, or receiver-SMTP, by issuing either an HELO or EHLO command to begin a session. Extended implementations of SMTP, such as that included with IIS 5.0, might require the client to provide authentication credentials that verify the client is permitted to use the SMTP server. Most often, these are simply a username and password that are recognized by the receiving system.

After the transmission channel has been established, the client issues a MAIL command that informs the receiver-SMTP that it wants to send mail. If the server is capable of receiving mail at that time, it responds with an OK reply. The sender-SMTP (client) then issues one or more RCPT commands that identify the recipient(s) of the messages it wants to send; each RCPT command represents a single mail recipient. The recipients can be other users in the same mail system or users in external domains.

If the SMTP server is capable of receiving mail addressed to the recipient named in the RCPT command, it issues an OK reply to the client and the client is free to issue another RCPT command. If the receiver-SMTP isn't capable of delivering mail to the designated recipient, it returns an error reply to the sender-SMTP, and the client can then move on to the next command. The command/reply sequence is strictly ordered; the client must receive a single reply before the server can issue another command, and a server isn't permitted to issue more than one reply to any command.

Because not all recipients can be using the same SMTP system, the client must provide the name of the ultimate destination host as well as the mailbox name in that mail system. The syntax of SMTP mail addresses is the familiar

`username@domain`

format, where information to the right of the "@" symbol identifies the destination host, and the username identifies the name of the mailbox to which the mail should be delivered. SMTP differentiates between sending and mailing; if mail is *sent*, the client is designating that the mail should be delivered immediately to the recipient's mail interface, provided the recipient is online and using a mail system that uses this functionality. More often, however, mail is *mailed*, which designates that it be delivered to the recipient's mailbox on a receiving server. Additionally, the send functionality isn't a required SMTP implementation, and it can be assumed that this chapter refers to the mail functionality unless specified otherwise.

SMTP mail has both a forward-path and a reverse-path. The forward-path is the path that the mail must take to reach its final destination, whether it uses a direct path or a series of relays. It's important not to confuse SMTP relays with routers; SMTP relays are SMTP servers that can receive mail from one SMTP host and forward that mail to another SMTP host, independent of underlying routing mechanisms. The reverse-path in an SMTP mail is the name of the sender-SMTP, which can be as simple as

`username@somedomain`

or can consist of a list of relay hosts between the original sender and the current receiver-SMTP. The MAIL command uses the reverse-path as its argument, and the RCPT command uses the forward-path. If multiple recipients' mailboxes reside on the same SMTP host, SMTP encourages the sending of a single copy of the mail to the destination SMTP host.

Once the receiver-SMTP has accepted the recipient addresses and provided the appropriate reply, the client is free to begin issuing the DATA command, which informs the server of its intent to begin transferring the mail message. The server replies with a code accepting the sender-SMTP's intent, and the client then issues the data. The mail data includes not only the body of the mail, but also the memo header information, such as the To:, cc:, bcc:, and subject lines. If the transfer of the mail data is successful, the server replies with a message indicating receipt and processing, and the client can now issue commands to terminate the transmission connection.

If the sender specifies invalid destination information in the forward-path of the mail, but the server knows the correct destination, the server can reply to the sender-SMTP with a message allowing the client to correct the error. When the client wishes to terminate the SMTP session, it indicates this by issuing the QUIT command, and the server then closes the transmission connection.

A typical SMTP session might look similar to the one below:

```
SMTP: 00:36:17 [rx] 220-server.somenet.net; Sun, 5 Sep 1999 21:36:29 -0700 (PDT)
SMTP: 00:36:17 [tx] HELO LRW2KPRO
SMTP: 00:36:17 [rx] 250 server.somenet.net Hello ser.ver.name.here.any.net
[10.26.53.60], pleased to meet you
SMTP: 00:36:17 [tx] MAIL FROM: <laurarobinson@somenet.net>
SMTP: 00:36:17 [rx] 250 <laurarobinson@somenet.net>... Sender ok
SMTP: 00:36:17 [tx] RCPT TO: <laurarobinson@someothernet.net>
SMTP: 00:36:18 [rx] 250 <laurarobinson@someothernet.net>... Recipient ok
SMTP: 00:36:18 [tx] RCPT TO: <lrobinson@somecompany.com>
SMTP: 00:36:18 [rx] 250 <lrobinson@somecompany.com>... Recipient ok
SMTP: 00:36:18 [tx] RCPT TO: <lrobinson@someothercompany.com>
SMTP: 00:36:18 [rx] 250 <lrobinson@someothercompany.com>... Recipient ok
SMTP: 00:36:18 [tx] DATA
SMTP: 00:36:19 [rx] 354 Enter mail, end with "." on a line by itself
SMTP: 00:36:19 [tx]
.
SMTP: 00:36:19 [rx] 250 VAA07817 Message accepted for delivery
SMTP: 00:36:19 [tx] QUIT
SMTP: 00:36:20 [rx] 221 server.somenet.net closing connection
```

SMTP Commands

The sender-SMTP issues the SMTP commands, which follow a straightforward syntax, as shown below (brackets indicate optional command parameters):

```
<SMTP-COMMAND> [<SP> <COMMAND-ARGUMENTS>] <CRLF>
```

The sender-SMTP process issues commands to perform functions, such as opening a transmission channel or initiating a mail transfer, and the receiver-SMTP process returns the responses. Commands can be issued individually, or as part of a series of commands, but each command must be followed by a reply from the receiver-SMTP. Table 19-10 lists common SMTP commands, their descriptions, and their syntax.

Table 19-10. Common SMTP Commands, Descriptions, and Syntax

Command	Description	Syntax
ATRN	Authenticated TURN—If the session between sender-SMTP and receiver-SMTP has been authenticated (the user has provided valid identification credentials), this specifies that the receiver-SMTP must either return an OK reply and assume the role of sender for the mail, or return a refusal (Bad Gateway, 502) and retain the role of receiver-SMTP.	ATRN [<SP> domain name [","domain name]] <CRLF>
AUTH	AUTHENTICATE—Used to begin an authenticated mail-transfer session (where a user can provide a username and password to the receiver-SMTP to continue the session).	AUTH LOGIN <CRLF>
DATA	DATA—The lines following this command are specified as mail data from the sender to the receiver.	DATA <CRLF>
EHLO	EXTENDED HELLO—A client that supports SMTP extensions issues this command rather than the HELO command when initiating a session. If the SMTP server receiving this command supports SMTP extensions, it'll return a 250 (Requested Mail Action Okay, Completed) response. If the SMTP server receiving the message doesn't support SMTP extensions, it will return a 500 (Syntax Error, Command Unrecognized) message, which will indicate to the sender-SMTP that it can't use extended SMTP commands.	EHLO <SP> <domain> <CRLF>
ETRN	ETRN—An extended SMTP command that requests the SMTP server to begin processing its mail queues for messages waiting at the server to be delivered to the client.	ETRN <SP> [<option character>] <node-name> <CRLF>
EXPN	EXPAND—Asks the receiver-SMTP to verify that the argument passed is a mailing list. If the argument does represent a mailing list, the membership of the list is returned to the sender-SMTP, in the form of users' full names and mailboxes.	EXPN <SP> <mailing list name> <CRLF>
HELO	HELLO—Used to identify the sender-SMTP to the receiver-SMTP and begin a new transaction.	HELO <SP> <host name of sender-SMTP> <CRLF>
HELP	HELP—Causes the receiver-SMTP to return help information to the sender; might or might not contain arguments.	HELP [<SP> <arguments>] <CRLF>
MAIL	MAIL—Used to initiate a mail transaction between sender- and receiver-SMTPs; clears the reverse-path buffer, forward-path buffer, and mail buffer, and inserts the reverse-path argument from this command into the reverse-path buffer.	MAIL <SP> <reverse-path> <CRLF>

(continued)

Table 19-10. *(continued)*

Command	Description	Syntax
NOOP	NO OP—Has no effect on any buffers and specifies no action other than that the receiver- SMTP return an OK reply.	NOOP <CRLF>
QUIT	QUIT—Specifies that the receiver return an OK reply and close the transmission channel.	QUIT <CRLF>
RCPT	RECIPIENT—Identifies the recipient of the mail being sent; multiple recipients are specified by repeated issuing of the command.	RCPT <SP> TO:<reverse-path> <CRLF>
RSET	RESET—Specifies that the current mail transaction be aborted and all buffers be cleared. The receiver-SMTP responds with an OK message.	RSET <CRLF>
SAML	SEND AND MAIL—Initiates a transaction specifying mail data be delivered to any recipient named who is actively connected and capable of receiving mail, as well as delivering to the mailbox(es) of the specified recipient(s). Clears the reverse-path buffer, the forward-path buffer, and the mail buffer, and inserts the reverse-path information provided with the command into the reverse-path buffer.	SAML <SP> FROM:<reverse-path> <CRLF>
SEND	SEND—Initiates a transaction specifying that mail data be immediately delivered to any recipient named who is actively connected and capable of receiving mail. If a recipient isn't connected or capable of receiving mail, a 450 (Mailbox Unavailable) response is returned. Clears the reverse-path buffer, the forward-path buffer, and the mail buffer, and inserts the reverse-path information provided with the command into the reverse-path buffer.	SEND <SP> FROM:<reverse-path> <CRLF>
SIZE	SIZE—Allows the sender-SMTP to specify the mail size that it wants to send, which the server can refuse if the size is too large. Only valid in SMTP implementations that support service extensions.	SIZE <SP> 1000000 <CRLF> or MAIL <SP> FROM: <reverse-path> <SP> SIZE = 100000 <CRLF>
SOML	SEND OR MAIL—Initiates a transaction specifying that mail data be immediately delivered to any recipient named who is actively connected and capable of receiving mail. If a recipient isn't connected or capable of receiving mail, specifies delivery to the recipient's mailbox. Clears the reverse-path buffer, the forward-path buffer, and the mail buffer, and inserts the reverse-path information provided with the command into the reverse-path buffer.	SOML <SP> FROM:<reverse-path> <CRLF>
TURN	TURN—Specifies that the receiver-SMTP must either return an OK reply and assume the role of sender for the mail, or return a refusal (502) and retain the role of receiver-SMTP.	TURN <CRLF>

(continued)

Table 19-10. *(continued)*

Command	Description	Syntax
VRFY	VERIFY—Requests that the receiver-SMTP verify the username specified in the argument. If the username is valid, the full name and mailbox of the user are returned. Has no effect on reverse-path buffer, forward-path buffer, or mail buffer.	VRFY <SP> <username> <CRLF>

SMTP Replies

SMTP replies are issued by the receiver-SMTP in response to sender-SMTP commands. Every command must generate one (and only one) reply. Similar to the response codes issued by FTP servers, SMTP-receivers issue a three-digit code number followed by descriptive text. As in FTP, the first digit of the response code indicates the general type of response, and the second digit provides additional information within that response category. Tables 19-11 and 19-12 list the values and meanings of both first- and second-digit values. A table of specific SMTP replies may be found in the \Appendix folder of the companion CD-ROM.

Table 19-11. SMTP Response Codes—First Digit

First Digit Value	Indicator	Description
1yz	Positive Preliminary Reply	The command has been accepted and is waiting confirmation of this reply and further instruction as to whether the receiver-SMTP should continue or abort processing. However, there are no SMTP commands that allow this type of reply, so there are no continue or abort commands.
2yz	Positive Completion Reply	The requested action has been completed and another command can now be issued.
3yz	Positive Intermediate Reply	The command has been accepted and is being held, pending receipt of further information from the sender-SMTP.
4yz	Transient Negative Completion Reply	A transient error has occurred that prevented processing of the command, and the command (or command sequence) should be reissued by the sender-SMTP.
5yz	Permanent Negative Completion Reply	An error has occurred that prevented processing of the command; the command (or command sequence) shouldn't be reissued without modification. This modification can be as simple as correcting a misspelling, or this error might indicate a non-transient server error.

Table 19-12. SMTP Response Codes—Second Digit

Second Digit Value	Indicator	Description
x0z	Syntax	There is a syntax error, the command issued is unimplemented by the server, or the server doesn't recognize the command category.
x1z	Information	Replies to information requests, such as "Help."
x2z	Connections	Replies, referring to the transmission channel.
x5z	Mail System	Mail system status as it relates to the requested transfer or command.

Since RFC 821 was published, extensions to the protocol have been introduced that allow for mechanisms, such as authentication; message size declaration, which allows a server to limit the size of mail that it'll accept; *turning* of the transmission connection, so that sender and receiver switch roles; and delivery status notifications. These specifications have been included on the CD that accompanies this book.

Summary

Internet Information Services 5.0 provides enhanced support for web-based services via its implementations of the HTTP/1.1, SMTP, and FTP protocols. HTTP/1.1 improves upon earlier implementations of HTTP in its support for multiple requests over a single connection, header compression, authentication mechanisms, and enhanced caching and proxy definitions. SMTP allows an IIS server to send and receive electronic messages on behalf of the clients it serves, facilitating e-mail communication for companies that may not require a full-fledged messaging system. In IIS 5.0, SMTP is implemented as a secure protocol, allowing for authentication and verification mechanisms. IIS 5.0's implementation of FTP has also been improved, providing FTP Restart, which allows a lost download connection to be resumed at the point at which it left off. By complying to the most recent standards for each of these protocols, IIS 5.0 ensures that web services can be provided in the most quick and efficient manner possible.

Chapter 20
Securing IP Communications with IP Security (IPSec)

The TCP/IP protocol suite was designed in the early 1980s as a replacement for the initial ARPANet protocols. Although the original protocols had enabled the ARPANet to get started, they weren't felt to be an effective long-term solution. Something better was needed—and this became the TCP/IP protocol suite, which today is the de facto networking standard and the basis of the Internet.

In the TCP/IP protocol suite, as originally developed, an application is responsible for providing any security that might be needed to protect itself or its users. Microsoft Windows 2000 file sharing, for example, employs the user's access token, created at login, and Access Control Lists, to ensure that only authorized users perform the actions they've been authorized to perform. While the protocols, such as IP, TCP, and UDP, do provide some protection against physical data corruption by using checksums, the value of checksums is limited and provides no protection against sophisticated hackers.

Requiring the application to implement security was entirely appropriate for the early days of the ARPANET, when users were mainly academics and research staff; this approach continues to be adequate for many users today. As the use of TCP/IP has grown, however, so has the need to provide security at a lower level in the TCP/IP stack. This security is required both for the Internet, which is becoming increasingly commercial, and for private IP networks, to protect against insider attacks.

IP Security (IPSec) is a suite of protocols and cryptographic algorithms that extend the IP protocol to provide authentication and privacy. IPSec provides strong security to all applications that use IP and allows the network administrator to provide in-depth security.

Essentially, IPSec extends the IP datagram structure to provide both strong authentication and privacy. IPSec does this by adding additional headers to each secured IP datagram sent between two hosts. This provides good end-to-end protection of the IP datagrams, transparently to higher level protocols.

Much of the development of IPSec took place as part of the development of IP version 6 (IPv6), described in Chapter 9, "Internet Protocol Version 6 (IPv6)." However, because of the slow adoption of IPv6, the need for a solution based on IP version 4 (IPv4) became apparent. As a result, IPSec has been modified to work with IPv4, enabling you to implement IPSec on existing IPv4 networks, and reducing the urgency to upgrade to IPv6.

Chapter Contents

This chapter describes the IPSec protocols, as implemented in Windows 2000. Additionally, there are Network Monitor traces on the companion CD-ROM that demonstrate IPSec in operation. This chapter contains the following sections:

- **Overview to IPSec**   A description of what IPSec is and its key components
- **How IPSec Works**   A description of how IPSec works
- **Authentication Header (AH)**   A description of the AH header and its fields
- **Encapsulating Security Payload (ESP) Header**   A description of the ESP header and its constituent fields

The subject of IPSec, like many of the topics in this book, could easily fill an entire book in its own right. Here, however, we will omit details of the cryptographic algorithms in use of key management, and the administration and management aspects of IPSec. The bibliography contains books you might want to consult for further research. For more information about configuring IPSec policy on a Windows 2000 computer, see the Windows 2000 Server Help.

IPSec Overview

IPSec is a suite of related protocols and services that extends the IP datagram structure (described in Chapter 5, "Internet Protocol (IP) Addressing") to provide additional security at the IP datagram level. In this section, we will review IPSec's key building blocks.

What Is IPSec?

IPSec is designed to provide additional security to IP datagrams in transit across a network, over and beyond that provided by an application. It does this by first creating a Security Association (SA) between two computers, and then using this SA to transform IP datagrams to add the security into the IP packets. IPSec supports two specific transforms: the AH and the ESP.

The specific services provided by IPSec, which are based on standardized cryptographic technologies, are as follows:

- **Authentication**   IPSec verifies the origin and the integrity of each IP datagram by assuring the genuine identity of the sending computer. IPSec in

Windows 2000 provides authentication based on pre-shared keys, public keys (such as X.509 certificates), or via Kerberos and the Windows 2000 Active Directory (AD).

- **Integrity**   IPSec protects the data in an IP datagram from unauthorized modification during transit, ensuring that the information that's received is the same as the information that was sent. IPSec uses cryptographic hash functions to uniquely sign each packet. The receiving computer can check the signature before passing the IP datagram up the stack, and if the signature is not valid, the packet is discarded.

- **Confidentiality**   IPSec ensures that data is disclosed only to the intended recipient by encrypting the data contained in an IP datagram.

- **Nonrepudiation**   IPSec ensures that the sender of an IP datagram is the only person who could have sent the datagram, thus ensuring that the sender can't later deny having sent it. Nonrepudiation is achieved by a combination of authentication and integrity checking.

- **Anti-replay**   IPSec ensures the uniqueness of each IP packet to avoid a packet sequence being captured and replayed (such as an inter-bank transfer). Anti-replay is enabled by the use of sequence numbers added into the IP datagram's header.

- **Key management**   IPSec enables keys to be determined, exchanged, and updated in a secure fashion.

IPSec Architecture

Figure 20-1 illustrates the overall IPSec architecture within Windows 2000.

This figure shows the key components of IPSec, which are described later in more detail. The diagram shows an application on Computer 1 communicating with an application on Computer 2. The traffic between them is sent using normal WINSOCK or NetBIOS Application Programming Interface (API) calls, which will result in IP datagrams being transferred over a physical network. The IPSec Policy Agent obtains the IPSec Policy from the AD. The Policy Agent will use the Internet Key Exchange (IKE) protocol to negotiate the specific details of how the data is to be protected. The IPSec driver is then responsible for implementing the IP datagram transformations, based on the IPSec policy.

IPSec Policy

An IPSec policy describes how IPSec will operate on a computer. For example, the policy could require all communications with certain computers to be encrypted and to not communicate if suitable encryption couldn't be negotiated. Alternatively, the policy could state that the computer should always try to use IPSec but fall back to normal clear text communication if the other computer isn't IPSec-enabled. You can define various named policies, but at any given time, only one policy can be active on a single computer.

Figure 20-1. *A diagram showing the IPSec architecture.*

The IPSec policy contains a series of rules that describe the policy in details. Each rule includes the following:

- **Filter List** Specifies which network traffic will be secured by the rule
- **Filter Action** Specifies how traffic matching the filter will be handled (dropped, encrypted, etc.)
- **Authentication Methods** Specifies how two computers will authenticate themselves to the other (Keberos, pre-shared key, or X509 Certificates)
- **Connection Type** Allows the rule to be applied to local area network (LAN) traffic, wide area network (WAN) traffic, or both
- **Tunnel Settings** Allows you to specify a tunnel endpoint for IPSec tunnels

IPSec Policy Agent

The IPSec Policy Agent is a Windows 2000 service that runs within the context of the LSASS.EXE process, and can be seen in the list of services in the Windows 2000 Services MMC Snap-in. The Policy Agent is responsible for retrieving IPSec policy information (from either the AD or the local registry) and passing it to the other IPSec components that need IPSec policies.

The IPSec Policy Agent is loaded and started at system start time and obtains system policy at that point. The Agent continues to poll the AD (or the registry) at regular intervals for any updates to IPSec policy.

IPSec Security Associations

After the computer's IPSec policy has been obtained, it will be applied to all IP traffic sent or received by that computer. However, before two computers can use IPSec features to transform IP packets, they must first negotiate an SA. The SA defines the specific details of how the two computers will use IPSec, the specific keys to be used, key lifetimes, and which authentication and encryption protocols should be applied. The IPSec policy defines the specific options that two computers can negotiate, such as any encryption algorithms. After an SA has been negotiated, communication between the two computers can proceed. IP datagrams will be transformed as mandated by the active IPSec policy.

With IPSec, two SAs are formed. The first SA is known as the Internet Security Association and Key Management Protocol (ISAKMP) SA. Creating this SA involves negotiation of IPSec policy (encryption algorithms, integrity algorithms, and so forth), covering the creation of the ISAKMP SA, initial key exchange, and machine authentication. This SA ensures that both computers have verified securely the identity of the other computer, and have the keys necessary to negotiate additional SAs.

The ISAKMP SA is then used to negotiate a second SA, known as the IPSec SA. The IPSec SA is used for the actual transformation of data that will be transferred between the computers. The creation of the IPSec SA involves agreement by the two computers over IPSec policy, the creation of keys to be used for the required transformations, and the integrity and encryption algorithms to be used. After these have been negotiated, they're passed to the IPSec driver.

Internet Key Exchange (IKE)

Setting up an SA between two computers is performed by the IKE. IKE is an Application Layer protocol, that combines the ISAKMP with the Oakley key determination algorithms. This protocol was formerly known as ISAKMP/Oakley. ISAKMP centralizes security association management, while Oakley generates and manages the authenticated keys.

> **Note**   IKE is a relatively new term, and much of the IPSec literature still refers to this as ISAKMP/Oakley.

ISAKMP

IPSec uses the ISAKMP protocol to negotiate SAs. ISAKMP defines procedures for authenticating a peer, creation and management of SAs, key generation techniques, and threat mitigation (such as denial of service and replay attacks). ISAKMP defines a framework for key management, and is independent of the key exchange protocols, encryption/integrity algorithms, and authentication methods in use.

> **More Info** The details of ISAKMP are outside the scope of this book, but RFC 2408 defines the protocol in detail. This RFC can be found in the \RFC folder on the companion CD-ROM.

Oakley Key Determination Protocol

The establishment of keys is an essential part of cryptographic-based packet protection. Oakley is a scalable, secure key distribution mechanism used within ISAKMP to establish the keys used in IPSec packet transforms. Oakley is based on, and is a refinement of, the Diffie-Hellman key exchange algorithm. This algorithm enables two computers to agree on a shared key without requiring encryption. This shared key can then be used for authentication or encryption.

> **More Info** The details of the Diffie-Hellman algorithm and the Oakley protocol are outside the scope of this book, but RFC 2412 defines them in more detail. This RFC can be found in the \RFC folder on the companion CD-ROM.

IPSec Driver

The IPSec driver is a kernel-mode device driver that's responsible for enforcing IPSec policies on packets received from, or sent to, other computers. The IPSec driver watches for outbound IP packets that the IPSec policy requires to be transformed, as well as for inbound IP packets that need to be verified and/or decrypted. The IPSec policy driver then will carry out the required transform before passing the datagram on to the Network Driver Interface Specification (NDIS) driver (for packets to be sent), or to the TCP/IP driver (for received packets).

Security Parameters Index (SPI)

Before there can be multiple SAs at any one time between two computers, it's vital that both sender and receiver know the particular SA that relates to each IP datagram. The SPI is used for this purpose. It's a 32-bit pseudo-random number transferred in each IP datagram (in the AH or ESP headers), and is used to indicate the inbound or outbound packet to which it relates.

During the ISAKMP negotiation, the receiver's IPSec driver creates an SPI. The SPI is transferred to the sender's ISAKMP, which delivers it to the sending IPSec driver. The sending IPSec driver includes the SPI in every AH or ESP header.

IPSec Modes

IPSec has two main modes of operation: transport mode and tunnel mode. Transport mode is mainly for a computer in an end-to-end scenario. Transport mode provides protection for upper layer protocols by adding an extra header between the original IP datagram and the IP datagram's payload. IPSec tunnel mode is designed for use by network routers, and enables them to protect IP datagrams passed between two IPSec-enabled routers over an insecure transit network. With tunnel mode, the original IP datagram is wrapped (tunneled) inside a new IP datagram, meaning that the entire original IP datagram is now fully encrypted.

IPSec transport mode provides good end-to-end security and authentication within a corporate network, as well as across a less secure network. Tunnel mode provides additional security, and is more appropriate when used as part of a Virtual Private Network using the Internet as a backbone.

Sample Network Monitor Traces

Network Monitor traces 20-1 and 20-2 (Captures 20-01 and 20-02, included in the \Captures folder on the companion CD-ROM) show the creation of an SA followed by a PING command. Network Monitor trace 20-1 shows the creation of an SA to support use of the AH between the two computers, while 20-2 shows the use of the ESP header. In both cases, the first six packets are the main mode negotiation, and the following four packets are the quick mode negotiation. This is followed by the actual PING command. Both traces show IPSec being used in transport mode.

How IPSec Works

In this section, we will look at the details of how IPSec works on Windows 2000 computers.

Note   IPSec currently is not available for Microsoft Windows 95, Windows 98, or Windows NT. It is unlikely that IPSec would ever be provided for Windows 95 and Windows 98, and currently there are no plans for providing IPSec for Windows NT.

Obtaining IPSec Policy

IPSec policy can be configured manually to apply to individual computers whether or not they participate in a Windows 2000 AD domain. For computers participating in an AD domain, however, site, domain, and Organizational Unit (OU) policies override any local IPSec policies. The preferred scenario for IPSec deployment is for IPSec policy information to be stored in the AD and applied using Group policy Objects (GPOs).

A GPO, which holds IPSec polices, can be applied to an AD site, an AD domain, or an AD OU. In an enterprise environment, a hierarchy of GPOs can be created and applied at each of these levels. The AD inheritance rules and the order of GPO objects defined for each level determine the effective IPSec policy for a given computer.

GPO objects reside in the AD. They are stored in the Policies container within the domain-naming context's System container. In the domain kapoho.com, for example, this System container has the distinguished name CN=Policies,CN=System,DC=kapoho,DC=com. Individual IPSec polices are contained within the AD in the Security container. In the domain kapoho.com, this System container has the distinguished name CN=IPSecurity,CN=System,DC=kapoho,DC=com. This container holds an IPSec policy object for each defined IPSec policy.

> **Note** The use of GPOs for controlling a computer's policy is a complex subject, and is outside the scope of this book. The creation of GPO objects and IPSec policies and their application to computers in an enterprise should be planned with great care. If the effective IPSec policy is incorrectly set, it can result in a computer not communicating with other computers.

When a Windows 2000 computer is first initialized, the IPSec Policy Agent will issue Lightweight Directory Access Protocol (LDAP) queries against the AD and obtain the relevant IPSec policy. For computers in a domain, the IPSec policy is applied using Group policy.

Although not the preferred deployment scenario, the administrator can define local computer IPSec policies that are stored in the registry. This is most useful for computers that aren't members of a Windows 2000 domain. The local policy database, which is similar to AD-held IPSec policies, is held in the registry key HKLM\SYSTEM\CurrentControlSet\Services\PolicyAgent\Policy\Local.

Applying IPSec Policy

It's the responsibility of the IPSec driver to apply IPSec policy. When the IPSec driver receives a packet for transmission to another computer, it first checks to see if that packet matches the IP filter list specified in any of the rules in the active IPSec policy. If so, and if no SA has been set up, the IPSec driver notifies IKE, which will negotiate an IPSec SA with the other computer. If necessary, an ISAKMP SA will be established first. After the SA is established, the IPSec driver will apply the relevant IPSec transform to the IP datagram, and then will send it to the NDIS driver for onward transmission.

Processing of inbound datagrams is similar to, although the reverse of, outbound processing. When the NDIS driver sends an IP datagram to the IPSec driver, the IP driver will examine the filter list to determine if there's a match. If so, the IPSec will use the SA (identified by the SPI in the IPSec header) to determine the transform to be applied to the packet. Based on this transform, the IPSec driver then verifies the packet's integrity, and decrypts the packet if appropriate. If errors occur, such as if the packet was changed in flight, the packet is silently discarded. After the packet transform has been applied, the SA's IPSec driver routes the datagram to the TCP/IP driver that routes the packets to the appropriate application.

Creating Security Associations (SAs)

The process of establishing an SA for use by an application involves two distinct phases, involving two specific SA s. In the first phase, also known as main mode, the two computers establish the ISAKMP SA. This provides the security environment in which other SAs can be established. Although there are two phases here, we'll only discuss the main mode, which is the more complex of the two.

To establish the ISAKMP SA, the sending computer sends a list of potential security levels to the responder. The responder then negotiates with the sender on a mutually agreeable level by use of the ISAKMP protocol.

After the ISAKMP SA is established, the two computers can communicate with each other to negotiate an SA used for the transfer of application data. This second SA is known as the IPSec SA. The ISAKMP SA provides the secure connection in which IPSec SAs can be negotiated. Quick mode is somewhat simpler and requires fewer exchanges.

On Windows 2000, negotiation of an ISAKMP SA and an IPsec SA requires 10 datagrams to be passed between sender and receiver. These can be seen in the Network Monitor traces noted earlier in this chapter.

Generating New Keys

To further secure the transfer of application data, IPSec can create new keying material either after a certain amount of time (for instance, after 30 minutes) or after a certain amount of data has been transferred. This adds overhead, but provides additional security. This is done by renegotiating either the ISAKMP SA or the IPSec SA. The quick mode noted above can perform this update.

Authentication Header (AH) Details

The AH header is designed to provide authentication of data contained in an IP datagram, and is an extension to the original IP header. As specified in RFC 2402, AH provides data integrity through keyed hashing. Windows 2000 supports two hash algorithms: HMAC MD5 and HMAC SHA. The specific hashing algorithm is negotiated during the SA setup.

More Info   Read about how the Authentication header provides data integrity through keyed hashing in RFC 2402, which can be found in the \RFC folder on the companion CD-ROM.

The AH header provides data and address integrity by hashing the IP header and payload, except for those portions of the IP header that could change during the transmission of an IP datagram across a network such as Time-To-Live (TTL) or the IP header checksum. This hash value is then included in the AH. The IP addresses in the IP header and the port numbers in the Transport Protocol header are part of the hash, thus addressing can be verified as unmodified. Because the IP data payload is also hashed, the data can be verified as being unmodified.

AH also provides anti-replay protection by providing sequence numbers for anti-replay protection. The sequence number is a part of the data that's hashed, and thus can be verified as having not been changed. Additionally, the sequence number on each incoming Sequence Number field is compared to the current sequence number. If the number is too far out of sequence or if it matches a recent sequence number, the packet is rejected as a replay.

AH Header Layout

Figure 20-2 displays the layout of the AH header.

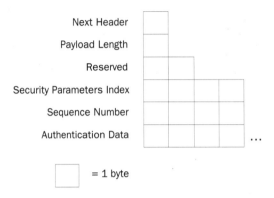

Figure 20-2. *AH header.*

As Figure 20-2 illustrates, the AH header consists of the following fields:

- **Next Header**   This 1-byte field is used to identify the next part of the IP datagram, usually 0x11 (to indicate UDP) or 0x06 (indicating TCP).

- **Payload Length**   This 1-byte field specifies the length of AH in 32-bit words, minus 2.

- **Reserved**   This 2-byte field is reserved and must be set to 0. The value is included in the Authentication Data field calculation, but is otherwise ignored.

- **SPI**   This 4-byte field, in combination with the Destination IP Address field and Security Protocol (AH), is used to identify the SA for this datagram.

- **Sequence Number**   This unsigned 4-byte field holds a monotonically increasing counter value. Even if the receiving computer chooses not to use it, it's a mandatory field. The first packet sent using a particular SA would always have a sequence number of 1. If anti-replay (the default) is enabled, the transmitted sequence number must never be allowed to cycle. To allow for additional large numbers of packets to be transferred between two hosts, a new SA, and therefore a new set of keys and a new sequence number, must be negotiated prior to the transmission of the 2^{32}nd packet on a given SA.

- **Authentication Data**   This variable-length field holds the integrity check (hash), for the IP datagram.

AH Packet Transform

Figure 20-3 illustrates the effect of the AH on the original datagram.

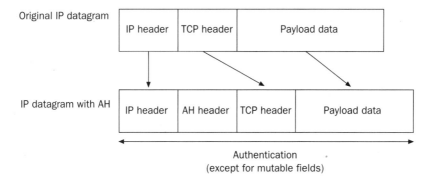

Figure 20-3. *Effect of AH header on IP datagram.*

As can be seen in Figure 20-3 and in Network Monitor trace 20-1 (Capture 20-01, included in the \Captures folder on the companion CD-ROM), the AH header is added to the IP datagram just after the IP header. IP treats the AH header as a protocol header, identified as protocol 51 (0x33). Using the AH header therefore increases the amount of overhead per packet. Its use also requires extra central processing unit (CPU) power to compute the authentication data, although with Windows 2000 hardware offload, much of this computing power can reside on the network card. Notice that the original IP header isn't modified; this allows intermediate routers to forward the packets regardless of whether or not they support IPSec.

Computing the Authentication Data

The AH Authentication field value is computed including:

- The IP header fields that are either not changed in transit (immutable fields), or that are predictable in value upon arrival at the endpoint for the SA.
- The AH header (Next Header, Payload Len, Reserved, SPI, Sequence Number, and the Authentication Data [which is set to 0 for this computation], and explicit padding bytes, if any).
- The upper level protocol data, which is assumed to be immutable in transit.

Each field within an IP datagram header that can change during transit (for example, TLL) is set to a value of 0 for purposes of calculating the authentication data. This includes the Authentication Data field's value itself.

Encapsulating Security Payload (ESP) Details

The ESP header is used to provide data confidentiality (encryption) as well as data authentication. Similar to the AH header, the ESP header is an extension of the original IP header and is specified in RFC 2406. The purpose of the ESP header is to provide confidentiality via the encryption of the IP datagram. The encryption algorithms that Windows 2000 supports are DES-CBC and Triple DES (a.k.a. 3DES). ESP also provides hashing and uses either MD5 or SHA, as in AH.

More Info   Read about the Encapsulating Security Payload (ESP) header in RFC 2406, which can be found in the \RFC folder on the companion CD-ROM.

When the IPSec policy on a computer is set to require encryption via the ESP header, the negotiation of the SA will determine which encryption algorithm is used.

Note   If you are using an export version of Windows 2000 or communicate with computers outside the United States, be sure to include DES in the IPSec policy. Also, if you plan to deploy ESP outside of the U.S. or Canada, some additional planning should be done to avoid inadvertent violation of U.S., or other, laws.

When applying the ESP transform, the IPSec driver encrypts and then hashes the entire IP datagram, except for the IP and ESP headers. This means that information in the IP header (for example, the source and destination IP addresses) isn't protected. Obviously, encrypting the IP header would mean that no device could read the addressing. You can also use AH and ESP together. Using both security methods provides data encryption and verification as well as address verification. When used together, ESP is always applied first, then AH.

ESP Header Layout

Figure 20-4 illustrates the layout of the ESP header.

As Figure 20-4 displays, the ESP header consists of the following fields:

- **Security Parameters Index**   This 4-byte field, in combination with the Destination IP Address field, is used to identify the SA for this datagram.
- **Sequence Number**   This unsigned 4-byte field holds a monotonically increasing counter value. Even if the receiving computer chooses not to use it, it's a mandatory field. The first packet sent using a particular SA would always have a sequence number of 1. If anti-replay (the default) is enabled, the transmitted sequence number must never be allowed to cycle. If the Sequence Number field increments to its limit, a new set of keys and a new sequence number must be negotiated prior to the transmission of the 2^{32}nd packet on a given SA.

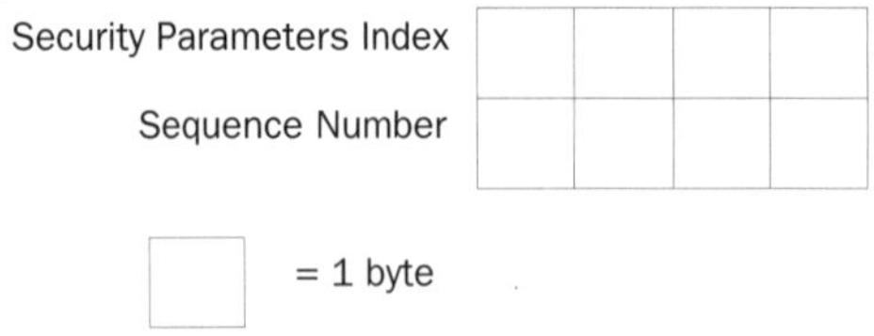

Security Parameters Index

Sequence Number

☐ = 1 byte

Figure 20-4. *ESP header.*

IPSec ESP Packet Layout and Packet Transform

When using the ESP header, the original packet is transformed, in a fashion similar to the AH header. Figure 20-5 displays the IPSec packet format.

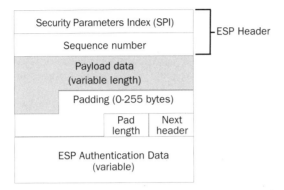

Figure 20-5. *IPSec ESP packet layout.*

As Figure 20-5 and Network Monitor trace 20-2 (Capture 20-02, included in the \Captures folder on the companion CD-ROM) illustrate, the format of an IP datagram when ESP is in use is more complex than with the AH header. Figure 20-6 also shows how the IP datagram is transformed when using the ESP header in transport mode.

As Figure 20-6 illustrates, using ESP adds an ESP header and two trailer fields to the IP datagram. IP views the ESP header as a new protocol type, and identifies it as protocol 50 (0x32). The ESP trailer consists of padding (between 0 through 255 bytes), a Padding Length field, and a Next Header field.

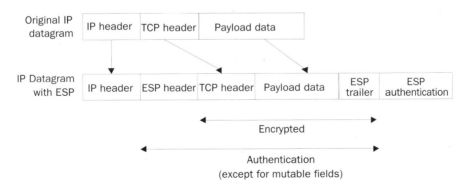

Figure 20-6. *Effect of ESP header on IP datagram.*

The padding in the ESP trailer is used for several reasons:

- The ESP packet format requires that the Padding Length and Next Header fields be right-aligned within a 4-byte word, and the padding is used to achieve this.

- Some encryption algorithms require that the unencrypted plain text is a multiple of some number of bytes and the padding can be used to expand the plain text to the required length.

- Padding can also be used to conceal the payload's actual length, thus providing a measure of additional security.

Summary

IPSec is a complex feature to install and configure, but provides application-transparent, end-to-end security between two Windows 2000 computers, or for all traffic between two IP routers configured to use IPSec tunnel mode when transmitting IP datagrams.

Chapter 21
Virtual Private Networks (VPNs)

For most large and small organizations, computer networks have become a central part of the corporate infrastructure. One specific challenge facing many of these network-centric organizations is how to connect remote sites and remote users.

Traditionally, remote sites have been connected by the use of leased lines or Frame-Relay networks. Remote users have been served by providing dial-in networking facilities, often using inbound free phone numbers. However, these approaches tend to be expensive and inflexible. The basic unit costs of leased lines and inbound free phone facilities have reduced steadily, but as more and more bandwidth is required, the overall costs to the organization have been rising, along with an increasingly complex infrastructure to manage. The lead time required for a leased line can be substantial, depending on the source and destination. This extended lead time can limit flexibility.

VPN technology provides a secure, scalable, and cost-effective solution to this connectivity issue. It allows an organization to connect remote sites to a central site securely over a public internetwork (such as the Internet) and enable remote users to securely connect to the corporate network using the communications infrastructure that the Internet provides. In both scenarios, the connection is made using the Internet as a backbone, while the connections appear to the user or the remote site as a private network.

Chapter Contents

The subject of VPNs is extensive enough to warrant a complete book of its own, and will not be covered wholly in this book. For our purposes, this chapter gives an overview of VPNs and focuses on the two VPN protocols that Microsoft Windows 2000 implements: Point to Point Tunneling Protocol (PPTP) and Layer 2 Tunneling Protocol (L2TP). Because the two VPN protocols leverage the Point to Point Protocol (PPP), the chapter also describes this protocol in relation to VPNs. Additionally, there are Network Monitor traces on the companion CD-ROM that demonstrate the PPTP and L2TP in operation.

This chapter contains the following sections:

- **Overview of VPNs** A description of VPNs and the VPN protocols
- **PPTP** A description of the PPTP VPN protocol
- **L2TP** A description of the L2TP VPN protocol

Overview of Virtual Private Networks

In this section we will discuss what a VPN is and the key protocols involved.

What Is a VPN?

As Figure 21-1 illustrates, a *Virtual Private Network* connects either a network or a single computer to another network across an intermediate network, typically the Internet.

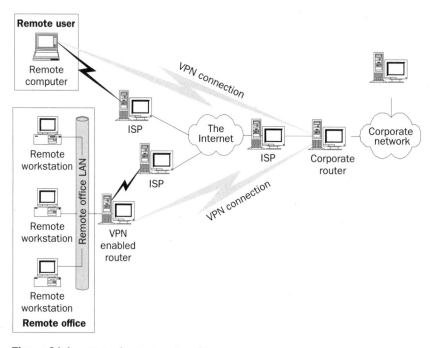

Figure 21-1. *Virtual private networking.*

Figure 21-1 shows the two main VPN usage scenarios: connecting a remote user to the corporate network, and connecting a remote network to the corporate network.

When connecting a remote user using a VPN, the remote user first establishes a normal Dial-Up Networking (DUN) connection to a local Internet Service Provider (ISP). After this connection is established, the remote user can establish a second VPN connection between the remote computer and the corporate VPN-enabled router.

When connecting a remote local area network (LAN) to the corporate network using a VPN, a similar arrangement occurs. In this scenario, the remote office's VPN-enabled router initiates the VPN connection on behalf of clients on the local LAN. The type of connection between the remote router and the ISP isn't important, as long as it can carry IP traffic.

VPN Clients and Servers

In a VPN, the computer initiating the VPN connection is referred to as the *VPN client*. The VPN client then makes a VPN connection to a remote computer, the *VPN server*. In the remote-user scenario, the remote computer is also the VPN client that'll make a connection to the VPN server. This remote computer therefore will have two active DUN connections established (one to the ISP, the other for the VPN). In the remote-office scenario, it's the remote office's router that's the VPN client. In both scenarios, the VPN server is a server in the corporate office that acts as the end point for the VPN connection.

There are, therefore, the following two types of VPNs that can be constructed:

- **The Remote User VPN**   A remote user accesses a corporate intranet and acts as the VPN client.
- **The Remote Network VPN**   The client is a remote router, and the VPN is entirely transparent to the end users.

VPN Protocols

Connections between a VPN client and a VPN server are implemented through the use of one of two VPN protocols: PPTP or L2TP.

PPTP is a Layer 2 protocol that encapsulates PPP frames in IP datagrams for transmission over an IP internetwork. PPTP is an older VPN protocol that Microsoft developed. L2TP, on the other hand, is a newer network protocol based on both Cisco's Layer 2 Forwarding (L2F) protocol and Microsoft's PPTP protocol, which encapsulates PPP frames to be sent over IP, X.25, Frame Relay, or Asynchronous Transfer Mode (ATM). Although L2TP is more flexible than PPTP, it requires more central processing unit (CPU) power than PPTP.

From an end user point of view, these protocols are functionally equivalent. PPTP is described in the "Introduction to Point to Point Tunneling (PPTP)" section of this chapter. L2TP is also described later in the "Introduction to Layer 2 Tunneling Protocol (L2TP)" section of this chapter.

The key technical differences between L2TP and PPTP are as follows:

- PPTP requires that the transit network be based on IP. L2TP requires only that the transit network provide point-to-point connectivity. L2TP can be used over IP or directly over Frame Relay, X.25, or ATM. PPTP can traverse these networks also, but additional protocol overhead is required because it must work within IP.

- PPTP can support only a single tunnel between the VPN client and VPN server. L2TP allows for the use of multiple tunnels between end points. With L2TP, you can create different tunnels for different qualities of service or meet different security requirements.

- L2TP provides header compression. When header compression is enabled, L2TP operates with 4 bytes of overhead, as compared to 6 bytes for PPTP.

For most existing users of Windows operating systems, PPTP will be the preferred protocol today, because it's supported in Microsoft Windows 95, Microsoft Windows 98, Windows NT 4.0, and in Windows 2000. Windows 2000 provides support for L2TP, although third-party L2TP support can be provided by third-party implementations for down-level operating systems.

Tunneling

Both L2TP and PPTP implement VPNs by means of *tunneling*. Tunneling is the encapsulation of an IP datagram inside another datagram. As Figure 21-2 illustrates, the VPN client encapsulates the original IP datagram, sent between two end systems, and sends it to the VPN server, where the datagram is unwrapped and forwarded onto the local network.

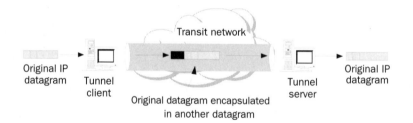

Figure 21-2. *Tunneling in VPNs.*

As Figure 21-2 illustrates, an IP datagram to be sent between the client and a server using a VPN is encapsulated inside a new IP datagram that's sent from both the tunnel client and tunnel server. The new IP datagram has a header that provides the information necessary to enable the packet to be properly forwarded across the transit network.

At the tunnel server, the datagram is unwrapped and the original IP datagram can then be forwarded from the tunnel server. After the original datagram is unwrapped, the tunnel server will act as a router and will make a forwarding decision on the original packet, based on the configuration of the tunnel server and the state of the tunnel server's routing table.

The VPN tunneling is achieved through the use of a Network Driver Interface Specification (NDIS) driver that becomes a client of IP. This is illustrated in Figure 21-3, which shows the architecture of a VPN connection in the remote client scenario.

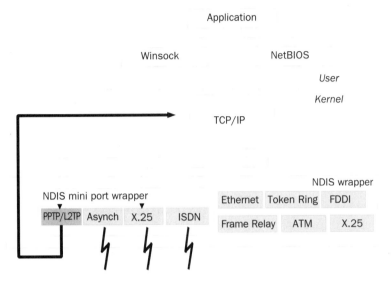

Figure 21-3.   *Tunneling architecture.*

An application on the remote computer will use either NetBIOS or Windows sockets to send a datagram to a remote computer. The payload is sent to the TCP/IP component in Windows 2000, which formats an IP datagram. At this stage in the process, the source IP and destination IP addresses are set as if the two systems were communicating directly.

After the IP datagram has been constructed, it will be sent to the NDIS miniport for the VPN protocol in use. The miniport driver then encapsulates the original IP datagram with the header for the VPN and sends it back to the TCP/IP driver. The TCP/IP driver then constructs a new IP datagram, which is sent to the appropriate NDIS driver for the transit network. While the details of the encapsulation will be different in PPTP and L2TP, this architectural model is used for both VPN protocols.

This encapsulation can be seen in Network Monitor traces 21-1 and 21-2. Network Monitor trace 21-1 (Capture 21-01, included in the \Captures folder on the companion CD-ROM) shows how PPTP encapsulates a datagram, while trace 21-2 (Capture 21-02, included in the \Captures folder on the companion CD-ROM) shows this for a L2TP frame. These traces show a single datagram to demonstrate the encapsulation.

Note Windows 2000 Servers ship with Microsoft Network Monitor 2.0 Lite Version. This version doesn't decode all of these frames completely. You'll need to use the full Network Monitor 2.0 product, supplied with SMS 2.0, to read these frames fully. If you load the SMS version of Network Monitor, be sure to install the Windows 2000 version first.

VPNs and PPP

Both VPN protocols leverage the PPP protocol for most of the underlying mechanisms, such as authentication, compression, and so forth. In effect, the VPN creates a virtual PPP connection between the VPN client and VPN server. This allows the original IP datagram to be transmitted inside a PPP frame, which is then encapsulated in an outer IP datagram for transmission across the transit network. This can be seen in the Network Monitor traces noted above.

PPP has the following three main components:

- A method for encapsulating datagrams over serial links. The VPN protocols leverage this method for encapsulating datagrams between the VPN client and server.

- A Link Control Protocol (LCP) for establishing, configuring, and testing the data-link connection. The LCP is used to establish the VPN link.

- A family of Network Control Protocols (NCPs) for establishing and configuring different network layer protocols. These NCPs are used by VPN protocols as well.

Setting up a PPP link involves the following steps:

1. **Phase 1: PPP link establishment** PPP uses LCP to establish, maintain, and end the connection. During the initial LCP phase, basic communication options are selected. During the link-establishment phase (Phase 1), authentication protocols are selected, but they're not actually implemented until the connection-authentication phase (Phase 2). The actual choice of compression and encryption algorithms and other details occurs during Phase 4.

2. **Phase 2: User authentication** In this phase, the client PC presents the user's credentials to the remote-access server. A secure authentication scheme provides protection against replay attacks and remote-client impersonation.

3. **Phase 3: PPP callback control** The Microsoft implementation of PPP includes an optional callback-control phase. This uses the Callback Control Protocol (CBCP) to initiate callback, if configured.

4. **Phase 4: Invoking network layer protocol(s)** After the previous phases have been completed, PPP invokes the various NCPs that were selected during the link-establishment phase (Phase 1) to configure protocols used by the remote client. For example, during this phase, the IP Control Protocol (IPCP) can assign a dynamic address for the VPN client. In addition, Compression Control Protocol (CCP) is used to negotiate both data compression (using Microsoft

Point-to-Point Compression [MPPC]) and data encryption (using Microsoft Point-to-Point Encryption [MPPE]), for both are implemented in the same routine.

5. **Phase 5: Data-transfer phase**   After the four previous phases of negotiation have been completed, data can begin to flow over the VPN. Each transmitted data packet is wrapped in a PPP header, plus additional VPN headers, which the receiving system removes. If data compression was selected in phase 1 and negotiated in phase 4, data will be compressed before transmission. If data encryption was selected and negotiated during the previous phase, data is encrypted before transmission.

For more details on PPP and PPP encapsulation, see Chapter 2, "Wide Area Network (WAN) Technologies."

VPN Authentication

To set up a VPN tunnel, it's necessary to authenticate the VPN client to the VPN server, and optionally, authenticate the VPN server to the client. This authentication, which PPP carries out as part of the user authentication phase noted above, enables the tunnel client and server to validate the credentials of the other end to ensure that only authorized users can establish a VPN connection.

By default, authentication in PPP isn't mandatory. If authentication of the link is desired, an implementation *must* specify the Authentication-Protocol Configuration Option during the link-establishment phase.

Windows 2000 supports the following primary means of authentication for VPN clients and servers:

- **Password Authentication Protocol (PAP)**   This is a simple authentication method that relies on clear-text password transmission. The remote server requests a username and password, and the client returns these unencrypted. This scheme offers no protection against man in the middle, replay, or client impersonation attacks. Thus, while useful for establishing DUN connections to a dial-up server, it's probably not a good choice for a VPN.

More Info   PAP is described in RFC 1334, which can be found in the \RFC folder on the companion CD-ROM.

- **Shiva Password Authentication Protocol (SPAP)**   This proprietary protocol is a variation of PAP, used when the tunnel server is a Shiva VPN server. SPAP offers additional facilities beyond PAP, but can only be used in conjunction with hardware devices from Shiva (now a division of Intel).

- **Challenge Handshake Authentication Protocol (CHAP)**   This is an industry standard authentication method that provides secure encrypted authentication. CHAP uses challenge-response combined with a one-way MD5 hash of the response (although the username is returned unhashed). This allows the client to prove to the server that it knows the password without actually sending the password over the network.

More Info   CHAP is defined in RFC 1994, which can be found in the \RFC folder on the companion CD-ROM.

- **Microsoft CHAP (MS-CHAP)**   This is a Microsoft adaptation of CHAP designed to authenticate remote Windows workstations. MS-CHAP supports the ability to change passwords during login, a feature not available with CHAP.

More Info   MS-CHAP is defined in RFC 2433, which can be found in the \RFC folder on the companion CD-ROM.

- **Microsoft CHAP V2**   This is an improved version of MS-CHAP that provides mutual authentication, stronger initial encryption keys, and different keys for transmitting and receiving data. To reduce the risk of compromising passwords, MS-CHAP V2 drops the support for password changes at login.

For the end user VPN, it's the end-user credentials—set in the DUN connection object—that are passed and used for authentication at the VPN server. For the remote-network tunnel, the administrator will define the credentials to be passed. PAP, SPAP, CHAP, and MS-CHAP are one-way authentication mechanisms that authenticate the tunnel client to the tunnel server. MS-CHAP V2 also requires the tunnel server to authenticate itself to the tunnel client, which can provide extra security, especially for dial-up connections. If mutual authentication is required, the user credentials for the VPN server must have been provided to the VPN client.

Extensible Authentication Protocol (EAP)

In addition to the basic forms of authentication noted above, Windows 2000 also supports EAP. In Windows 2000, EAP can be configured to provide authentication based on either smart cards or machine certificates. It's also possible for third parties to write custom EAP authentication modules that work with add-on hardware to enable other forms of authentication, such as retinal eye scanning.

The use of a smart card provides an additional level of security, but it's more appropriate for the remote user VPN, because it might not be acceptable to leave the smart card inserted into the remote network's router. For a remote network VPN, machine certificates are more appropriate, but rely on a public key infrastructure to be in place. In both cases, some degree of public key infrastructure will be required to manage and control the certificates, which might limit their attractiveness.

VPN Address Assignment

In a VPN, the VPN client appears to be a part of a central network and will require an IP address based on the central network. This means the VPN client will have at least two

IP addresses: one for the transit network (such as the Internet) and one for the VPN. The Windows 2000 Remote Access Server (RAS) enables the IP addresses to be provided by the user (as part of the DUN connection) or to be dynamically assigned. Dynamically assigned addresses can be based on either a static pool of addresses or obtained by the RAS server from a Dynamic Host Configuration Protocol (DHCP) server.

The dynamic assignment of client addresses is based on the NCP negotiation mechanism, which is part of PPP, described earlier in this chapter in the "VPNs and PPP" section. Although this is generally seamless, it does require the administrator to design and implement a suitable addressing scheme to cater to the VPN users.

VPN Data Compression

The VPN protocols support a PPP-based compression scheme. In Windows 2000, both PPTP and L2TP use MPPC, which is defined in RFC 2118. For Windows 2000 VPN clients, the use of the MPPC software-compression method is controlled by settings in the DUN connection object.

More Info   MPPC is defined in RFC 2118, which can be found in the \RFC folder on the companion CD-ROM.

MPPC can reduce the total amount of data being transferred across the transit network by as much as 50-60 percent for text data, although for binary data, the compression might only amount to 2-3 percent or less. As with all data compression schemes, the percentage by which the original data can be compressed will vary with the nature of the data.

VPN Data Encryption

For the data to be transferred securely across an insecure transit network, some form of data encryption is required. PPTP supports optional use of MPPE, based on the RSA/RC4 encryption algorithm. L2TP protocol uses IP Security (IPSec) encryption to protect the data stream from the client to the tunnel server.

MPPE relies on the initial key generated during user authentication and then refreshes it periodically. IPSec explicitly negotiates a common key during the ISAKMP exchange, and also refreshes it periodically.

Introduction to Point-to-Point Tunneling Protocol (PPTP)

PPTP is a VPN protocol implemented at layer 2 in the Open Systems Interconnection (OSI) model. PPTP encapsulates VPN data inside PPP frames, which are then further encapsulated in IP datagrams for transmission over a transit IP internetwork such as the Internet.

More Info   PPTP is documented in RFC 2637, which can be found in the \RFC folder on the companion CD-ROM.

Creation and maintenance of a PPTP tunnel is carried out using a TCP connection. The VPN client uses an ephemeral port, while the PPTP VPN server responds on TCP port 1723. Subsequent data is encapsulated using Generic Routing Encapsulation (GRE), as described in more detail in the following section.

Installation of PPTP

PPTP is a component of Windows 2000's Routing and Remote Access Service (RRAS), which is installed by default on computers running on Windows 2000 Server Standard Edition, Windows 2000 Advanced Server, or Windows 2000 Datacenter Server. The Windows 2000 RRAS service, however, isn't configured or enabled by default. This task must be performed by the administrator after installation of Windows 2000.

When the RRAS service is first configured and enabled, by default, PPTP is configured for five ports, thus enabling up to five VPN clients to connect simultaneously. The administrator can enable more or fewer PPTP ports by using the Routing and Remote Access Microsoft Management Console (MMC) Snap-in.

PPTP Encapsulation

As noted above, PPTP encapsulates the original IP datagram when it's transmitted between the PPTP client and PPTP server. Figure 21-4 shows the encapsulation of a PPTP packet.

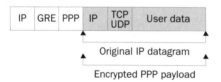

Figure 21-4. *PPTP packet structure.*

Note When viewing Network Monitor captures of PPTP traffic, the IP datagram, as shown in Figure 21-4, would be contained in some Data Link layer protocol such as Ethernet or PPP. The Network Monitor traces included on the companion CD-ROM show the VPN being created across a dial-up link, and use PPP.

In Figure 21-4, the original datagram is first encapsulated in a PPP frame. Using PPP, this part of the datagram can be compressed and encrypted, as discussed below. The PPP frame is then encapsulated inside a GRE frame, which is the payload of a new IP datagram sent between the PPTP client and PPTP server. The source and destination IP addresses of this new datagram will correspond to the IP addresses of the PPTP client and PPTP server. On the wire, this datagram will be further encapsulated in a Data Link Layer frame, with the appropriate header and trailer.

PPTP Encryption

When the original datagram is transmitted through the transit network, it must be encrypted to ensure confidentiality. With PPTP, the PPP is used to provide the encryption. In Windows 2000, the PPP frame is encrypted with MPPE. The encryption keys are generated from the MS-CHAP or EAP-TLS authentication process. To provide for encryption, the PPTP client must be configured to use either the MS-CHAP, MS-CHAP V2, or EAP-TLS authentication protocol.

Introduction to Layer 2 Tunneling Protocol (L2TP)

L2TP is a refinement of PPTP and Cisco's L2F protocol. L2TP was designed to combine the best features of both PPTP and L2F.

L2TP operates, as its name suggests, at Layer 2 in the International Organization for Standardization (ISO) model, and is a network protocol that creates a tunnel between an L2TP client and an L2TP server, and then encapsulates PPP frames to be sent over the tunnel. When using IP as the transport protocol, L2TP can be used as a VPN protocol over the Internet. L2TP has been designed so that it can be used directly over various wide area network (WAN) media (such as Frame Relay) without an IP transport layer, which can extend its usefulness in setting up corporate networks.

> **More Info**   L2TP is documented in RFC 2661, which can be found in the \RFC folder on the companion CD-ROM.

When L2TP is used over IP internetworks, it uses UDP for both tunnel creation and maintenance, and for data transmission. With L2TP, both the tunneled data and the control messages share a single UDP stream, which can simplify the passing of VPN data through corporate firewalls.

L2TP relies on IPSec for encryption services, a combination known as L2TP over IPSec. Both the VPN client and the VPN server must support both L2TP and IPSec. For more information about IPSec, see Chapter 20, "Securing IP Communications with IP Security (IPSec)."

Installation of L2TP

Like PPTP, L2TP is a component of Windows 2000's RRAS, which is installed by default on computers running Windows 2000 Server Standard Edition, Windows 2000 Advanced Server, or Windows 2000 Datacenter Server. Although L2TP is installed by default, an administrator must enable it manually.

When the RRAS service is first configured and enabled, L2TP is configured for five VPN ports (as for PPTP). The administrator can enable more or fewer L2TP ports by using the Routing and Remote Access MMC Snap-In.

LT2P relies on IPSec for encryption. IPSec is installed as part of the default installation of Windows 2000, so the administrator will need to do some additional configuration of IPSec policies to use IPSec with PPTP. See Chapter 20, "Securing IP Communications with IP Security (IPSec)," for more details on IPSec.

L2TP Encapsulation

As with PPTP, L2TP encapsulates the original IP datagram when transferred through the transit network. Since IPSec provides the encryption facilities, however, the L2TP encapsulation takes place in two phases. Figure 21-5 illustrates phase 1, the initial L2TP encapsulation, and phase 2, the IPSec encapsulation.

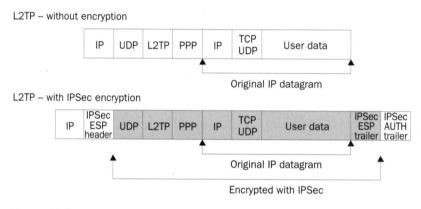

Figure 21-5. *Two phases of encapsulation over L2TP.*

> **Note** When viewing Network Monitor captures of L2TP traffic, the IP datagram, as shown in Figure 21-4, would be contained in some Data Link layer protocol such as Ethernet or PPP. The Network Monitor traces included on the companion CD-ROM show the VPN being created across a dial-up link, and use PPP.

As Figure 21-5 illustrates, the L2TP encapsulation involves the original datagram first being wrapped in a PPP frame, as with PPTP. The PPP frame is then inserted into a new IP datagram with a UDP header and an L2TP header.

The resulting datagram can then have the IPSec transform applied (as noted in Chapter 20). In this case, an IPSec Encapsulating Security Payload (ESP) header and trailer and an IPSec Authentication trailer are applied. These provide message integrity and authentication. The IP header contains the source and destination IP addresses that correspond to the VPN client and VPN server.

L2TP Encryption

As noted above, an L2TP frame is encrypted with the IPSec ESP encryption mechanism. The encryption keys are from the IPSec authentication process. These mechanisms are further described in Chapter 20.

It is possible to have a non-IPSec-based (non-encrypted) L2TP connection where the PPP frame is sent in plain text. However, a non-encrypted L2TP connection isn't recommended for VPN connections over the Internet, because communications of this type aren't secure.

Summary

VPNs provide a good method of linking remote users or remote offices to corporate networks in a secure and scalable way. Windows 2000 provides both PPTP and L2TP, enabling interoperability with RFC-compliant third-party solutions. Implementing VPNs is very straightforward with Windows 2000 both on the client and server.

Glossary

A

Address Resolution Protocol A protocol for resolving IP addresses into physical (MAC) addresses. *See also Inverse ARP and Reverse ARP.*

AH *See Authentication Header.*

APIPA *See Automatic Private IP Addressing.*

ARP *See Address Resolution Protocol.*

ARP Cache A table for each interface of static or dynamically resolved IP addresses and their corresponding media access control (MAC) addresses.

Asynchronous Transfer Mode A very high-speed, connection-oriented networking technology, based on small 53-byte cells.

Authentication Header A part of the IP header provided by IP Security that is used to provide authentication, data integrity, and optional replay-prevention services.

ATM *See Asynchronous Transfer Mode.*

Automatic Private IP Addressing A feature of Windows 2000 (and Windows 98) that enables the system to self-configure an IP address and subnet mask from the range 169.254.0.0/16 in the absence of a static configuration or a DHCP server.

B

Bandwidth Allocation Protocol A protocol that dynamically controls the use of multi-linked lines, adding extra connections when additional bandwidth is required, and dropping lines when not required.

BAP *See Bandwidth Allocation Protocol.*

Berkeley Internet Name Domain A version of the DNS service, written initially for UNIX and ported to a wide variety of operating systems.

BIND *See Berkeley Internet Name Domain.*

C

CIDR See Classless Interdomain Routing.

CIFS *See Common Internet Filing System.*

Classless Interdomain Routing A route aggregation technique to express a range of class C network IDs as a single route.

Common Internet Filing System A platform-independent, RFC-compliant file sharing system. CIFS evolved from Windows' legacy NetBIOS-based file sharing.

Compressed SLIP A simple compression scheme used to compress IP and TCP headers to a 3-5-byte header on a SLIP link.

Congestion Avoidance A TCP algorithm that provides a linear scaling of the actual Send window. The actual Send window is increased by one MSS for each full window of data acknowledged.

C-SLIP *See Compressed SLIP.*

D

DHCP *See Dynamic Host Configuration Protocol.*

DHCP Server A Windows 2000 service that provides DHCP-based IP addresses and IP configuration details to DHCP clients.

Diffie-Hellman Algorithm An algorithm for establishing a shared key over an insecure medium, and a component of the Oakley key determination protocol.

Digital, Intel, and Xerox A consortium which created the original 10 Mbps version of Ethernet (a.k.a. DIX Ethernet).

DIX *See Digital, Intel, and Xerox.*

DNS *See Domain Name System.*

Domain Name System A set of services for holding, updating and resolving computer names and associated IP addresses for computers and other resources on the Internet or on private TCP/IP networks.

Dynamic Host Configuration Protocol A protocol for providing computers with IP host configuration details. Also used to ensure DHCP servers are authorized.

E

Encapsulating Security Payload A part of the IP header provided by IP Security that enables data encryption to provide packet-level privacy.

ESP *See Encapsulating Security Payload.*

F

Fast Recovery A TCP algorithm that more quickly scales the TCP Send window when a segment is retransmitted using Fast Retransmit.

Fast Retransmit A TCP algorithm that retransmits a segment before the retransmission time-out expires when multiple duplicate acknowledgments of the previously received contiguous segment are received.

FCS *See Frame Check Sequence.*

FDDI *See Fiber Distributed Data Interface.*

Fiber Distributed Data Interface A LAN technology based on optical fiber-based token passing ring, with a bit rate of 100 Mbps.

File Transport Protocol A protocol for transferring files between heterogeneous servers and clients. Internet Explorer supports FTP. Additionally, Windows 2000 includes a command-line FTP client and an FTP Server (as part of IIS).

Frame Check Sequence A field in data link protocol (i.e., Ethernet, PPP) used to provide bit-level integrity services for a single frame.

Frame Relay A virtual circuit-based WAN technology designed for the transmission of data. Frame Relay is a streamlined version of X.25.

FTP *See File Transport Protocol.*

G

Gateway A TCP/IP node that has routing capability (also called an IP router).

Gratuitous ARP An ARP Request message sent to a host's own IP address. Gratuitous ARPs are used to check for duplicate IP addresses.

H

Hash A one-way cryptographic algorithm that takes an input message of arbitrary length and produces a fixed-length digest for use with IPSec. If the hash, created by a sender and sent with a message, is the same as what the receiver computes, the message is assumed to have been unaltered. Two hash algorithms used by Windows 2000 are Secure Hash Algorithm (SHA) and Message Digest 5 (MD5).

Host A TCP/IP node that does not have routing capability.

Host Group The set of nodes listening for IP multicast traffic on a specific IP multicast address.

HTTP *See Hyper Text Transfer Protocol.*

Hyper Text Transfer Protocol An application protocol for transferring text, graphics, and other data between an HTTP client and server. Windows 2000 includes an HTTP client, Internet Explorer, and an HTTP Server as part of IIS.

I

ICMP *See Internet Control Message Protocol.*

IETF *See Internet Engineering Task Force.*

IGMP *See Internet Group Management Protocol.*

IIS *See Internet Information Server.*

IKE *See Internet Key Exchange.*

INARP *See Inverse ARP.*

Integrated Systems Digital Network A method of carrying digital transmissions over traditional telephone copper wire to provide higher speed dial-up connections.

Internet Control Message Protocol A protocol that works with IP to report errors and control the flow of data.

Internet Engineering Task Force This is the body that defines the Internet protocol and oversees the development of the Internet and the evolution of the TCP/IP protocol suite. The standards developed by the IETF and IETF working parties are published as RFCs.

Internet Group Management Protocol A protocol for managing multicast group membership.

Internet Information Server A windows 2000 service that provides Web, file transfer, newsgroup, and mail facilities.

Internet Key Exchange A method of exchanging keys used by IP Security, based on ISAMP and Oakley.

Internet Protocol An unreliable, datagram delivery service that operates at the Internet Layer (the Network Layer of the OSI model).

Internet Security Association and Key Management Protocol A framework for managing keys within IP Security.

Inverse ARP Obtains a remote systems' IP address, based on its Network Interface Layer address. Used mainly in Frame Relay. *See also Address Resolution Protocol and Reverse ARP.*

IP *See Internet Protocol.*

IPSec *See IP Security.*

IP Security A suite of protocols and services that provide authentication, integrity, and privacy of IP datagrams.

ISAKMP *See Internet Security Association and Key Management Protocol.*

ISDN *See Integrated Systems Digital Network.*

L

LAN *See Local Area Network.*

LDAP *See Lightweight Directory Access Protocol.*

Lightweight Directory Access Protocol A protocol for communication with a directory. Windows 2000 Active Directory makes heavy use of LDAP.

Link State Advertisement A packet sent by an OSPF router to other OSPF routers to advise the state of a router.

LLC *See Logical Link Control.*

Local Area Network A network of interconnected computers within a relatively small geographic area that can share resources.

Logical Link Control A sub-layer of the OSI Data Link Layer.

LSA *See Link State Advertisement.*

M

MAC *See Media Access Control, MAC Address.*

MAC Address An NIC's hardware address (for Ethernet, this will be the 48-bit Ethernet address).

Maximum Receive Unit The maximum size of a PPP frame.

Maximum Segment Size The maximum size of a TCP segment.

Maximum Transmission Unit The largest frame that can be sent in a packet or frame-based network (e.g., 1526 bytes for Ethernet).

Media Access Control A sub-layer of the ISO Data Link layer, as defined by the IEEE.

MRU *See Maximum Receive Unit.*

MSS *See Maximum Segment Size.*

MTU *See Maximum Transmission Unit.*

N

NBMA *See Non-Broadcast Multiple Access.*

NCP *See Network Control Protocol.*

NetBIOS A network interface for applications and a set of network protocols providing name services, session services, and datagram services for NetBIOS applications.

Network Control Protocol A protocol for negotiating the Data Link characteristics of a point-to-point connection.

Network News Transport Protocol A protocol used by computers for managing the articles posted on network news newsgroups. Windows 2000 includes an NNTP client, Outlook Express, and an NNTP Server (as part of IIS).

NNTP *See Network News Transport Protocol.*

Node A network device running the TCP/IP protocol.

Non-Broadcast Multiple Access A Network Interface Layer technology that supports an IP network segment with more than two nodes, but with no facility to broadcast a single packet to multiple locations (X.25, Frame Relay, and ATM are NBMA network types).

O

Oakley A protocol, used by IP Security, for exchanging keys securely, using the Diffie-Hellman algorithm.

Open Shortest Path First A link state based dynamic routing protocol for use within a single autonomous system.

OSPF *See Open Shortest Path First.*

P

Packet InterNet Groper A troubleshooting utility which uses ICMP Echo Request packets to provide information about reachablity for a destination node.

Path MTU Discovery A method of discovering the highest IP MTU for all links between two hosts.

PDU *See Protocol Data Unit.*

Permanent Virtual Circuit A path through a virtual circuit packet-switching network (e.g., X.25) that is statically programmed into the switches within the network.

PING *See Packet InterNet Groper.*

PMTU *See Path MTU Discovery.*

Point-to-Point Protocol A standardized point-to-point network encapsulation method that provides frame delimitation, protocol identification, and bit-level integrity services.

POP3 *See Post Office Protocol.*

Post Office Protocol A protocol for retrieving email from a mail server. The latest version of this protocol is known as POP3. Outlook Express is a POP3 client.

PPP *See Point-to-Point Protocol*

Protocol Data Unit The payload field for an Ethernet frame.

PVC *See Permanent Virtual Circuit.*

R

Reverse ARP Reverse ARP obtains an IP address of a host from an RARP server, based a MAC address. *See also Address Resolution Protocol and Inverse ARP.*

Request For Comment A formal document or standard, developed by an individual, the IETF, or an IETF working group that defines some part of the Internet Protocol suite. Some RFCs are informational in nature while others are Internet standards. RFCs are never re-issued, but are superceded by new RFCs.

RFC *See Request For Comment.*

RIP *See Routing Information Protocol.*

Router A TCP/IP node that has routing capability (also called a gateway).

Routing Information Protocol A distance vector-based dynamic routing protocol.

S

Serial Line Internet Protocol A simple packet-framing protocol for use on point-to-point links that offers only frame delimitation services. It doesn't provide protocol identification or bit-level integrity services.

Simple Mail Transfer Protocol A protocol for exchanging mail, typically between mail servers. IIS includes a limited function SMTP server.

SLIP *See Serial Line Internet Protocol.*

Slow Start A TCP algorithm that provides a quick scaling of the actual Send window. The actual Send window is increased by one MSS for each acknowledgment segment received.

SMTP *See Simple Mail Transfer Protocol.*

SONET *See Synchronous Optical Network.*

SVC *See Switched Virtual Circuit.*

Switched Virtual Circuit A path through a virtual circuit packet-switching network (e.g., X.25) that is negotiated using a signaling protocol each time a connection is initiated.

Synchronous Optical Network An ANSI standard specification for synchronous data transmission on optical media. SONET provides standards for a number of line rates up to the maximum line rate of 9.953 gigabits per second (Gbps).

T

TCP *See Transport Control Protocol.*

TDI *See Transport Driver Interface.*

Time-To-Live A field in an IP datagram header used to determine how many links on which the datagram can travel before being discarded by an IP router.

Transport Control Protocol A reliable stream-based transport protocol that runs on top of the Internet Protocol.

Transport Driver Interface A layer of the Windows 2000 network architecture.

TTL *See Time-To-Live.*

U

UDP *See User Datagram Protocol.*

User Datagram Protocol An unreliable datagram protocol at the Transport Layer that provides Application Layer process identification and a checksum.

V

Variable Length Subnet Masks A technique of subnetting that produces subnets of different sizes, all derived from an original network ID.

VLSM *See Variable Length Subnet Masks.*

W

WAN *See Wide Area Network.*

Wide Area Network A geographically dispersed network, under private control, but which typically uses network connections from a third party telecommunications vendor. *See also Local Area Network.*

Windows Internet Name Service A NetBIOS Name server, used by clients to register NetBIOS names to IP address mappings and to resolve NetBIOS names into IP addresses.

Windows Sockets This is a series of APIs that an application can call to transfer data using TCP/IP. Winsock is, effectively, a network interface.

WINS *See Windows Internet Name Service.*

WINSOCK *See Windows Sockets.*

World Wide Web The World Wide Web refers to resources available on the Internet and accessed by HTTP.

WWW *See World Wide Web.*

X

X.25 A WAN technology based on virtual circuit-based packet switching. X.25 was designed in the 1970s and provides a reliable, connection-oriented Network Interface Layer.

Bibliography

This bibliography provides a list of additional resources that may be helpful to readers. It is divided into two sections: Books and White Papers. The books are divided up by topic while the white papers are those that are available on Microsoft's web site. Some of the books, particularly those listed under TCP/IP, cover multiple-topic areas. To avoid duplication we have not listed these books twice.

All of these books were available for sale at the time this bibliography was written, however, some books may be out of print, or may have been superceded by new versions.

Books

The books are listed by topic area; within each topic, they are listed alphabetically by author.

DHCP

Droms, Ralph, and Ted Lemon. *DHCP*. Indianapolis: Macmillan Computer Publishing, 1999.

DNS

Albitz, Paul, and Cricket Liu. *DNS and BIND*. 2d ed. Sebastopol, Calif.: O'Reilly & Associates, Inc., 1997.

Masterman, Michael, Herman Kneif, Scott Vinick, et al. *Windows NT DNS*. Indianapolis: New Riders, 1998.

IP Security

Doraswamy, Naganand, and Dan Harkins. *IP Sec: The New Security Standard for the Internet, Intranets and Virtual Private Networks*. Upper Saddle River, N.J.: Prentice Hall, 1999.

Schneier, Bruce. *Applied Cryptography*. New York: John Wiley & Sons, 1995.

Stallings, William. *Cryptography and Network Security*. Upper Saddle River, N.J.: Prentice Hall, 1998.

IP Version 6

Huitema, Christian. *IPV6—The New Internet Protocol*. Upper Saddle River, N.J.: Prentice Hall, 1997.

Thomas, Stephen A. *IPNG and the TCP/IP Protocols*. New York: Wiley Computer Publishing, 1996.

Microsoft Windows NT

Solomon, David. *Inside Windows NT.* Seattle: Microsoft Press, 1998.

Routing

Huitema, Christian. *Routing in the Internet.* Upper Saddle River, N.J.: Prentice Hall, 1999.

Perlman, Radia. *Interconnections: Bridges and Routers.* Reading, Mass.: Addison-Wesley, 1992.

TCP/IP

Bisaillon, Teresa, and Brad Werner. *Hands-On TCP/IP with Windows NT 5.0.* New York: McGraw-Hill Publishing Company, 1998.

Burk, Robin, Martin J Bligh, and Thomas Lee. *TCP/IP Blueprints.* Indianapolis: Sams Publishing, 1997.

Comer, Douglas. *Internetworking with TCP/IP: Principles, Protocols and Architecture.* Vol. 1. New York: Prentice Hall, 1995.

Heywood, Drew. *Networking with Microsoft TCP/IP.* Indianapolis: New Riders Publishing, 1977.

Minasi, Mark, Tod Lammie, and Minica Lammie. *Mastering TCP/IP for NT Server.* Alameda, Calif.: SYBEX, 1997.

Rose, Marshall T. *The Simple Book.* Upper Saddle River, N.J.: Prentice Hall, 1996.

Stevens, W. Richard. *TCP/IP Illustrated. Volume 1: Principles, Protocols, and Architecture.* 3rd ed. New York: Prentice Hall, 1995.

Virtual Private Networks

Kosiur, Dave. *Building and Managing Virtual Private Networks.* New York: John Wiley and Sons, 1998.

Microsoft White Papers and Other Documents

The following are networking-related white papers and other documents that can be found on the Microsoft web site. The title, author, and URL are listed.

All of the following white papers are also available on the companion CD-ROM.

File and Print Sharing

Leach, Paul, and Dan Perry. "CIFS: A Common Internet File System." Seattle: Microsoft Corporation, 1996.

http://www.microsoft.com/Mind/1196/CIFS.htm

IP Security

Microsoft Corporation. "IP Security for Microsoft Windows 2000 Server." Seattle: Microsoft Corporation, 1999.

http://www.microsoft.com/Windows/server/zipdocs/IPSecurity.exe

TCP/IP

MacDonald, Dave. "TCP/IP Implementation Details for Windows 2000 RC 1." Seattle: Microsoft Corporation, 1999.

http://www.microsoft.com/windows/server/Technical/networking/tcpip_implement.asp

Virtual Private Networks

Microsoft Corporation. "Understanding PPTP." Seattle: Microsoft Corporation, 1997.

http://www.microsoft.com/ntserver/zipdocs/understanding_pptp.exe

WINS

Merrick, L. "Windows Internet Naming Service (WINS) Architecture and Capacity Planning." A white paper from Corporate Network Systems and the Business Systems Division. Seattle: Microsoft Corporation, 1999.

http://www.microsoft.com/Windows/server/zipdocs/win2000.exe

Index

Joseph G. Davies is a Microsoft employee and technical writing lead for the *Microsoft Windows 2000 Resource Kit*. He has been a technical writer and instructor of TCP/IP and networking technology topics for six years and has written a large amount of training material for both internal Microsoft training organizations and for a series of courses for a local community college. As a Microsoft instructor and course designer, he has written introductory and advanced courses on TCP/IP and a course on the Windows NT 4.0 Routing and Remote Access Service. More recently, he wrote the Windows 2000 product documentation and Resource Kit content for TCP/IP routing, remote access, and virtual private networks. He has a Bachelor's degree in Engineering Physics and is a Microsoft Certified Systems Engineer (MCSE), Microsoft Certified Trainer (MCT), and Master Certified NetWare Engineer (MCNE).

Thomas Lee is an independent computer consultant who has been working with Windows NT since 1993. After graduating with a BS in Computer Problem Solving from Carnegie Mellon University, he worked on two successful operating system projects (Comshare's Commander II and ICL's VME) before joining Andersen Consulting in 1981 where he was a manager in the London office. He has been an independent consultant since 1987. Most recently, he has worked in Redmond developing Windows 2000 Microsoft Official Curriculum (MOC) training material and is presently engaged in several consulting projects relating to Windows 2000. Thomas is a Fellow of the British Computer Society as well as a Microsoft Certified Systems Engineer (MCSE), Microsoft Certified Trainer (MCT), and Microsoft Valued Professional (MVP). Thomas lives in a cottage in the English countryside with his wife Susan and daughter Rebecca.

The manuscript for this book was prepared and submitted to Microsoft Press in electronic form. Text files were prepared using Microsoft Word 97 for Windows. Pages were composed by nSight, Inc., using Adobe Pagemaker 6.5 for Windows, with text in Garamond Light and display type in ITC Franklin Gothic. Composed pages were delivered to the printer as electronic prepress files.

Cover Designer: Girvin Strategic Branding & Design
Cover Illustrator: Tom Draper Design
Interior Graphic Designer: James D. Kramer
Layout Artist: Tara Lynn Murray
Project Manager: Sarah Kimnach Hains
Tech Editor: Tony Northrup
Copy Editor: Judith Rothberg
Proofreaders: Shimona Katz and Denise Sadler
Indexer: Jack Lewis

There's no *substitute* for *experience.*

Now you can apply the best practices from real-world implementations of Microsoft technologies with NOTES FROM THE FIELD. Based on the extensive field experiences of Microsoft Consulting Services, these valuable technical references outline tried-and-tested solutions you can use in your own company, right now.

Microsoft Press® products are available worldwide wherever quality computer books are sold. For more information, contact your book or computer retailer, software reseller, or local Microsoft Sales Office, or visit our Web site at mspress.microsoft.com. To locate your nearest source for Microsoft Press products, or to order directly, call 1-800-MSPRESS in the U.S. (in Canada, call 1-800-268-2222).

Prices and availability dates are subject to change.

**Deploying Microsoft® Office 2000
(Notes from the Field)**
U.S.A. $39.99
U.K.   £25.99 [V.A.T. included]
Canada $59.99
ISBN 0-7356-0727-3

**Deploying Microsoft SQL Server™ 7.0
(Notes from the Field)**
U.S.A. $39.99
U.K.   £25.99
Canada $59.99
ISBN 0-7356-0726-5

**Optimizing Network Traffic
(Notes from the Field)**
U.S.A. $39.99
U.K.   £25.99 [V.A.T. included]
Canada $59.99
ISBN 0-7356-0648-X

**Managing a Microsoft Windows NT® Network
(Notes from the Field)**
U.S.A. $39.99
U.K.   £25.99
Canada $59.99
ISBN 0-7356-0647-1

**Building an Enterprise Active Directory™
(Notes from the Field)**
U.S.A. $39.99
U.K.   £25.99 [V.A.T. included]
Canada $61.99
ISBN 0-7356-0860-1

Microsoft®
mspress.microsoft.com

Practical, *portable* guides for *troubleshooters*

For hands-on, immediate references that will help you troubleshoot and administer Microsoft Windows NT Server 4.0, Microsoft SQL Server 7.0, or Microsoft Exchange 5.5, get the:

Microsoft® Windows NT® Server 4.0 Administrator's Pocket Consultant
ISBN 0-7356-0574-2 $29.99 ($44.99 Canada)

Microsoft SQL Server™ 7.0 Administrator's Pocket Consultant
ISBN 0-7356-0596-3 $29.99 ($44.99 Canada)

Microsoft Exchange 5.5 Administrator's Pocket Consultant
ISBN 0-7356-0623-4 $29.99 ($44.99 Canada)

Ideal at the desk or on the go, from workstation to workstation, these fast-answers guides focus on what needs to be done in specific scenarios to support and manage these mission-critical IT products. Great software and great learning solutions: Made for each other. Made by Microsoft.

Microsoft Press® products are available worldwide wherever quality computer books are sold. For more information, contact your book or computer retailer, software reseller, or local Microsoft Sales Office, or visit our Web site at mspress.microsoft.com. To locate your nearest source for Microsoft Press products, or to order directly, call 1-800-MSPRESS in the U.S. (in Canada, call 1-800-268-2222).

Prices and availability dates are subject to change.

Microsoft®

mspress.microsoft.com

MICROSOFT LICENSE AGREEMENT

Book Companion CD

IMPORTANT—READ CAREFULLY: This Microsoft End-User License Agreement ("EULA") is a legal agreement between you (either an individual or an entity) and Microsoft Corporation for the Microsoft product identified above, which includes computer software and may include associated media, printed materials, and "online" or electronic documentation ("SOFTWARE PRODUCT"). Any component included within the SOFTWARE PRODUCT that is accompanied by a separate End-User License Agreement shall be governed by such agreement and not the terms set forth below. By installing, copying, or otherwise using the SOFTWARE PRODUCT, you agree to be bound by the terms of this EULA. If you do not agree to the terms of this EULA, you are not authorized to install, copy, or otherwise use the SOFTWARE PRODUCT; you may, however, return the SOFTWARE PRODUCT, along with all printed materials and other items that form a part of the Microsoft product that includes the SOFTWARE PRODUCT, to the place you obtained them for a full refund.

SOFTWARE PRODUCT LICENSE

The SOFTWARE PRODUCT is protected by United States copyright laws and international copyright treaties, as well as other intellectual property laws and treaties. The SOFTWARE PRODUCT is licensed, not sold.

1. GRANT OF LICENSE. This EULA grants you the following rights:

a. Software Product. You may install and use one copy of the SOFTWARE PRODUCT on a single computer. The primary user of the computer on which the SOFTWARE PRODUCT is installed may make a second copy for his or her exclusive use on a portable computer.

b. Storage/Network Use. You may also store or install a copy of the SOFTWARE PRODUCT on a storage device, such as a network server, used only to install or run the SOFTWARE PRODUCT on your other computers over an internal network; however, you must acquire and dedicate a license for each separate computer on which the SOFTWARE PRODUCT is installed or run from the storage device. A license for the SOFTWARE PRODUCT may not be shared or used concurrently on different computers.

c. License Pak. If you have acquired this EULA in a Microsoft License Pak, you may make the number of additional copies of the computer software portion of the SOFTWARE PRODUCT authorized on the printed copy of this EULA, and you may use each copy in the manner specified above. You are also entitled to make a corresponding number of secondary copies for portable computer use as specified above.

d. Sample Code. Solely with respect to portions, if any, of the SOFTWARE PRODUCT that are identified within the SOFTWARE PRODUCT as sample code (the "SAMPLE CODE"):

    i. Use and Modification. Microsoft grants you the right to use and modify the source code version of the SAMPLE CODE, *provided* you comply with subsection (d)(iii) below. You may not distribute the SAMPLE CODE, or any modified version of the SAMPLE CODE, in source code form.

    ii. Redistributable Files. Provided you comply with subsection (d)(iii) below, Microsoft grants you a nonexclusive, royalty-free right to reproduce and distribute the object code version of the SAMPLE CODE and of any modified SAMPLE CODE, other than SAMPLE CODE, or any modified version thereof, designated as not redistributable in the Readme file that forms a part of the SOFTWARE PRODUCT (the "Non-Redistributable Sample Code"). All SAMPLE CODE other than the Non-Redistributable Sample Code is collectively referred to as the "REDISTRIBUTABLES."

    iii. Redistribution Requirements. If you redistribute the REDISTRIBUTABLES, you agree to: (i) distribute the REDISTRIBUTABLES in object code form only in conjunction with and as a part of your software application product; (ii) not use Microsoft's name, logo, or trademarks to market your software application product; (iii) include a valid copyright notice on your software application product; (iv) indemnify, hold harmless, and defend Microsoft from and against any claims or lawsuits, including attorney's fees, that arise or result from the use or distribution of your software application product; and (v) not permit further distribution of the REDISTRIBUTABLES by your end user. Contact Microsoft for the applicable royalties due and other licensing terms for all other uses and/or distribution of the REDISTRIBUTABLES.

2. DESCRIPTION OF OTHER RIGHTS AND LIMITATIONS.

- **Limitations on Reverse Engineering, Decompilation, and Disassembly.** You may not reverse engineer, decompile, or disassemble the SOFTWARE PRODUCT, except and only to the extent that such activity is expressly permitted by applicable law notwithstanding this limitation.

- **Separation of Components.** The SOFTWARE PRODUCT is licensed as a single product. Its component parts may not be separated for use on more than one computer.

- **Rental.** You may not rent, lease, or lend the SOFTWARE PRODUCT.

- **Support Services.** Microsoft may, but is not obligated to, provide you with support services related to the SOFTWARE PRODUCT ("Support Services"). Use of Support Services is governed by the Microsoft policies and programs described in the user manual, in "online" documentation, and/or in other Microsoft-provided materials. Any supplemental software code provided to you as part of the Support Services shall be considered part of the SOFTWARE PRODUCT and subject to the terms and conditions of this EULA. With respect to technical information you provide to Microsoft as part of the Support Services, Microsoft may use such information for its business purposes, including for product support and development. Microsoft will not utilize such technical information in a form that personally identifies you.

- **Software Transfer.** You may permanently transfer all of your rights under this EULA, provided you retain no copies, you transfer all of the SOFTWARE PRODUCT (including all component parts, the media and printed materials, any upgrades, this EULA, and, if applicable, the Certificate of Authenticity), **and** the recipient agrees to the terms of this EULA.

- **Termination.** Without prejudice to any other rights, Microsoft may terminate this EULA if you fail to comply with the terms and conditions of this EULA. In such event, you must destroy all copies of the SOFTWARE PRODUCT and all of its component parts.

3. **COPYRIGHT.** All title and copyrights in and to the SOFTWARE PRODUCT (including but not limited to any images, photographs, animations, video, audio, music, text, SAMPLE CODE, REDISTRIBUTABLES, and "applets" incorporated into the SOFTWARE PRODUCT) and any copies of the SOFTWARE PRODUCT are owned by Microsoft or its suppliers. The SOFTWARE PRODUCT is protected by copyright laws and international treaty provisions. Therefore, you must treat the SOFTWARE PRODUCT like any other copyrighted material **except** that you may install the SOFTWARE PRODUCT on a single computer provided you keep the original solely for backup or archival purposes. You may not copy the printed materials accompanying the SOFTWARE PRODUCT.

4. **U.S. GOVERNMENT RESTRICTED RIGHTS.** The SOFTWARE PRODUCT and documentation are provided with RESTRICTED RIGHTS. Use, duplication, or disclosure by the Government is subject to restrictions as set forth in subparagraph (c)(1)(ii) of the Rights in Technical Data and Computer Software clause at DFARS 252.227-7013 or subparagraphs (c)(1) and (2) of the Commercial Computer Software—Restricted Rights at 48 CFR 52.227-19, as applicable. Manufacturer is Microsoft Corporation/One Microsoft Way/Redmond, WA 98052-6399.

5. **EXPORT RESTRICTIONS.** You agree that you will not export or re-export the SOFTWARE PRODUCT, any part thereof, or any process or service that is the direct product of the SOFTWARE PRODUCT (the foregoing collectively referred to as the "Restricted Components"), to any country, person, entity, or end user subject to U.S. export restrictions. You specifically agree not to export or re-export any of the Restricted Components (i) to any country to which the U.S. has embargoed or restricted the export of goods or services, which currently include, but are not necessarily limited to, Cuba, Iran, Iraq, Libya, North Korea, Sudan, and Syria, or to any national of any such country, wherever located, who intends to transmit or transport the Restricted Components back to such country; (ii) to any end user who you know or have reason to know will utilize the Restricted Components in the design, development, or production of nuclear, chemical, or biological weapons; or (iii) to any end user who has been prohibited from participating in U.S. export transactions by any federal agency of the U.S. government. You warrant and represent that neither the BXA nor any other U.S. federal agency has suspended, revoked, or denied your export privileges.

DISCLAIMER OF WARRANTY

NO WARRANTIES OR CONDITIONS. MICROSOFT EXPRESSLY DISCLAIMS ANY WARRANTY OR CONDITION FOR THE SOFTWARE PRODUCT. THE SOFTWARE PRODUCT AND ANY RELATED DOCUMENTATION ARE PROVIDED "AS IS" WITHOUT WARRANTY OR CONDITION OF ANY KIND, EITHER EXPRESS OR IMPLIED, INCLUDING, WITHOUT LIMITATION, THE IMPLIED WARRANTIES OF MERCHANTABILITY, FITNESS FOR A PARTICULAR PURPOSE, OR NONINFRINGEMENT. THE ENTIRE RISK ARISING OUT OF USE OR PERFORMANCE OF THE SOFTWARE PRODUCT REMAINS WITH YOU.

LIMITATION OF LIABILITY. TO THE MAXIMUM EXTENT PERMITTED BY APPLICABLE LAW, IN NO EVENT SHALL MICROSOFT OR ITS SUPPLIERS BE LIABLE FOR ANY SPECIAL, INCIDENTAL, INDIRECT, OR CONSEQUENTIAL DAMAGES WHATSOEVER (INCLUDING, WITHOUT LIMITATION, DAMAGES FOR LOSS OF BUSINESS PROFITS, BUSINESS INTERRUPTION, LOSS OF BUSINESS INFORMATION, OR ANY OTHER PECUNIARY LOSS) ARISING OUT OF THE USE OF OR INABILITY TO USE THE SOFTWARE PRODUCT OR THE PROVISION OF OR FAILURE TO PROVIDE SUPPORT SERVICES, EVEN IF MICROSOFT HAS BEEN ADVISED OF THE POSSIBILITY OF SUCH DAMAGES. IN ANY CASE, MICROSOFT'S ENTIRE LIABILITY UNDER ANY PROVISION OF THIS EULA SHALL BE LIMITED TO THE GREATER OF THE AMOUNT ACTUALLY PAID BY YOU FOR THE SOFTWARE PRODUCT OR US$5.00; PROVIDED, HOWEVER, IF YOU HAVE ENTERED INTO A MICROSOFT SUPPORT SERVICES AGREEMENT, MICROSOFT'S ENTIRE LIABILITY REGARDING SUPPORT SERVICES SHALL BE GOVERNED BY THE TERMS OF THAT AGREEMENT. BECAUSE SOME STATES AND JURISDICTIONS DO NOT ALLOW THE EXCLUSION OR LIMITATION OF LIABILITY, THE ABOVE LIMITATION MAY NOT APPLY TO YOU.

MISCELLANEOUS

This EULA is governed by the laws of the State of Washington USA, except and only to the extent that applicable law mandates governing law of a different jurisdiction.

Should you have any questions concerning this EULA, or if you desire to contact Microsoft for any reason, please contact the Microsoft subsidiary serving your country, or write: Microsoft Sales Information Center/One Microsoft Way/Redmond, WA 98052-6399.

System Requirements

To use this book's companion CD-ROM, you need a computer equipped with the following minimum configuration:

- Microsoft Windows NT 4.0 with Service Pack 4 (or later) or Windows 2000 Server.

- Microsoft Network Monitor 2.0 (included in Windows 2000 Server).

- A network adapter card that supports promiscuous mode.

- 133-MHz Pentium or higher central processing unit (CPU). A maximum of four CPUs per computer are supported.

- 256 megabytes (MB) of RAM recommended minimum.

- A hard disk partition with approximately 1 GB free disk space. More space might be needed, depending on the following:

  The components being installed: the more components, the more space needed.

  The file system used: FAT requires 100–200 MB more free disk space than other file systems.

  The method used for installation: if installing from across network, allow 100–200 MB more space than if installing from the CD-ROM. (More driver files need to be available during installation across a network.)

- Microsoft Internet Explorer version 4.01, Service Pack 1 (or later).

- VGA or higher-resolution monitor.

- Keyboard.

- Mouse or other pointing device (optional).

- CD-ROM drive.

Also, you must be logged on to your computer as a user with Administrative rights.

Proof of Purchase

0-7356-0556-4

Do not send this card with your registration.
Use this card as proof of purchase if participating in a promotion or
rebate offer on *Microsoft® Windows® 2000 TCP/IP Protocols and Services Technical Reference.*
Card must be used in conjunction with other proof(s) of payment such as your dated sales
receipt—see offer details.

Microsoft® Windows® 2000 TCP/IP Protocols and Services Technical Reference

WHERE DID YOU PURCHASE THIS PRODUCT?

CUSTOMER NAME

mspress.microsoft.com

Microsoft Press, PO Box 97017, Redmond, WA 98073-9830

**For information about Microsoft Press®
products, visit our Web site at
mspress.microsoft.com**

Microsoft®*Press*